# AKIRA

## KATSUHIRO OTOMO

**BOOK
FOUR**

DARK HORSE COMICS®

*translation and english-language adaptation*
**YOKO UMEZAWA, JO DUFFY,**
*and* **DARK HORSE COMICS**

*graphics adaptation and sound effects lettering*
**DAVID SCHMIT** *for* **DIGIBOX**
*and* **ÉDITIONS GLÉNAT**

*digital lettering and additional graphics adaptation*
**DIGITAL CHAMELEON**
*and* **DARK HORSE COMICS**

*publisher*
**MIKE RICHARDSON**

*original series editor*
**KOICHI YURI**

*editor*
**CHRIS WARNER**

*consulting editor*
**TOREN SMITH** *for* **STUDIO PROTEUS**

*collection designer*
**LIA RIBACCHI**

*art director*
**MARK COX**

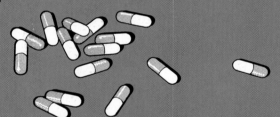

**AKIRA BOOK FOUR**



The artwork of this volume has been produced as a mirror-image of the original Japanese edition to conform to English-language standards.

Published by Dark Horse Comics, Inc., 10956 S.E. Main Street, Milwaukie, OR 97222 • www.darkhorse.com

To find a comics shop in your area, call the Comic Shop Locator Service toll-free at 1-888-266-4226

First edition: September 2001 • ISBN: 1-56971-526-2

Printed in Canada • 10 9 8 7 6 5 4 3 2 1

# THE STORY SO FAR

Thirty-eight years after a cataclysmic explosion levels Tokyo and triggers World War III, Neo-Tokyo prepares for the first postwar Olympic games, a stadium being erected on the original blast site. While making an illegal run into the area, a motorcycle gang led by Kaneda encounters an aged and ailing child with fantastic telekinetic power and the number 26 tattooed on his palm. Kaneda's friend Tetsuo is injured and the child vanishes. The military arrives and takes Tetsuo for medical attention. Later, Kaneda meets the beautiful Kei, part of an underground group opposed to Neo-Tokyo's new order. A second meeting with 26 escalates into mayhem as a team led by the mysterious Colonel arrives to capture the child, named Takashi, by utilizing another child psychic, Masaru. Amidst the ensuing psychic storm, Kei and her associate Ryu fight their way to safety and Kaneda manages to escape, taking a capsule dropped by Takashi. A friend of Kaneda's fails to identify the drug, but it is clearly lethal.

When tests reveal Tetsuo's immense psychic potential, the Colonel takes him to a special facility where yet another child paranormal, Kiyoko, foretells the awakening of Akira, a boy whose godlike psychic abilities destroyed Tokyo. Number 28 of a secret experiment gone wrong, Akira sleeps in frozen stasis in a complex deep beneath the Olympic site.

Growing paranoid and unstable, Tetsuo's dormant powers suddenly switch on and, steeped in growing pain, he escapes the facility, leaving a trail of death. Wandering the streets in agony, Tetsuo murders a rival gang member in a grisly psychic explosion and the terrified gang crown the superhuman madman their new leader, who unleashes them in a violent rampage against the other bike gangs. Kaneda organizes the gangs to fight back, but Tetsuo dispatches them, killing Tetsuo's friend Yamagata. Enraged, Kaneda shoots Tetsuo, who unleashes a tornado of destruction. The Colonel's forces arrive to find the wounded Tetsuo screaming for drugs to ease his pain. Kaneda attacks again, and in the struggle the mystery super-drug drops from his pocket. Tetsuo swallows it and goes into a massive seizure, but miraculously survives, his pain quelled. The Colonel offers to supply Tetsuo with the drug and training to fully utilize his power. Tetsuo, realizing he has few alternatives, becomes Number 41. The Colonel takes Tetsuo, Kaneda, and Kei to the laboratory facility and sequesters Kaneda and Kei.

Meanwhile, Nezu, the resistance leader, meets with Ryu, who reports of suspicious military activity at a site adjacent to the stadium. Nezu is summoned by Lady Miyako, a mystical figure who shares visions of an impending disaster that cannot be averted. Akira's awakening draws closer.

Tetsuo's power grows at an astonishing rate, evidenced by the self-healing of his deadly bullet wound. Tetsuo learns of Akira and the other psychics, and he becomes obsessed with facing them. The children, sensing Tetsuo's potential for freeing Akira, use their abilities to free Kei and Kaneda and lead them to a secret armory where they procure a laser rifle to destroy Tetsuo. Tetsuo finds and confronts the children, who are with the Colonel. Tetsuo recognizes Number 26 and torments the children, whose powers are no longer his match. Tetsuo demands to meet Akira. Kei and Kaneda crash the party and attack Tetsuo with the laser. Teleporting from beneath collapsing rubble, Tetsuo falls from the skyscraper facility and plunges to the ground below, but is completely unharmed.

One of the Colonel's agents secretly helps Kaneda and Kei to freedom, but the Colonel soon forgets about them when he discovers that Tetsuo has discovered Akira's location. Kei leads Kaneda and their benefactor into the sewers, the hidden back door into the secret underground complex. Tetsuo arrives at the facility, but guards and guns are no match for the murderous psychic juggernaut, and Tetsuo breaches the defense perimeter. He boards an elevator and begins the long descent to Akira's sleep chamber. The Colonel arrives in force, and his troops attack Tetsuo, who repels the assault with ease. Scientists discover to their horror that the temperature within Akira's chamber is rising: Akira is responding to Tetsuo's psychic vibrations!

The chamber cracks and releases deadly sub-zero refrigerant, forcing Kei, Kaneda, and the surviving troops to flee the facility. Tetsuo, unharmed by the lethal cold, reaches the chamber. The cell bursts open and Akira emerges, dazed after his decades-long sleep. Tetsuo helps the child to the outside world. A city-wide alert goes into effect as the frantic Colonel employs a last-ditch plan to stop the two by using the laser cannon of the military satellite SOL to gun down Tetsuo and Akira. The weapon opens fire and the terrible blast finds Tetsuo's arm, tearing it to shreds. Kei and Kaneda find Akira and disappear into the city and find sanctuary in the home of Chiyoko, a powerful woman allied with the resistance.

Martial law goes into effect, and panic rules the streets. Everyone wants to find Akira, and for many reasons: to capture him, to destroy him, to use his terrible powers for personal gain. Chiyoko takes Kei, Kaneda, and Akira to Nezu's boat, a temporary safehouse. But Nezu betrays them and Lady Miyako by taking Akira and ordering his men to murder Chiyoko, Kaneda, and Kei. Only Chiyoko's strength and fighting skills — and a little well-placed vomit by the seasick Kaneda — keep the three alive. Knowing that Akira will be taken to Nezu's home, the three go on the offensive and recapture Akira.

But the streets are now crawling with forces trying to find the young superhuman, both sides utilizing child psychics to track Akira down. After harrowing battles and narrow escapes, the Colonel along with Masaru, Kiyoko, and Takashi at last corner Akira. Takashi greets his old friend, but the enraged Nezu, hiding in a nearby building, tries to shoot Akira rather than have him fall into the Colonel's hands. Nezu misses, his errant bullet finding the head of Takashi, who is killed instantly. His death triggers Akira's boundless power, and in an instant, a massive psychic wave surges through Neo-Tokyo, the destruction that obliterated its namesake now revisited upon the glittering metropolis. The citizenry, Kei, Kaneda, and the Colonel among them, struggle desperately to survive the holocaust. As the maelstrom subsides, Akira sits alone at the nexus of the disaster. A lone figure approaches him through the vast field of wreckage. It is Tetsuo, and the two rise together into the air...

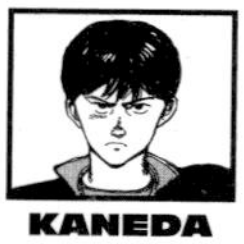
KANEDA

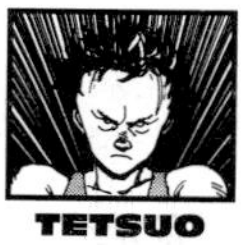
TETSUO

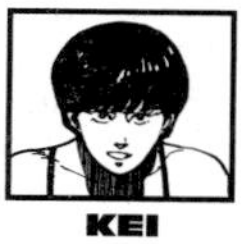
KEI

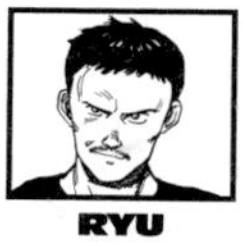
RYU

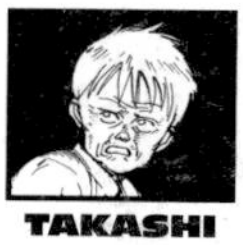
TAKASHI

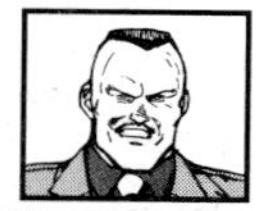
THE COLONEL

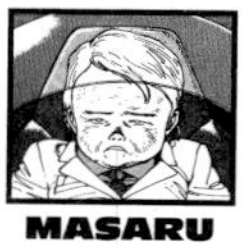
MASARU

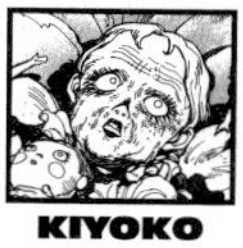
KIYOKO

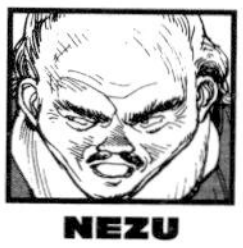
NEZU

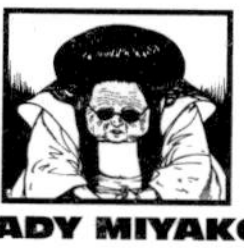
LADY MIYAKO

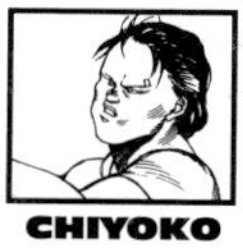
CHIYOKO

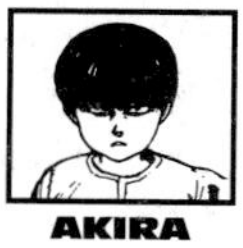
AKIRA

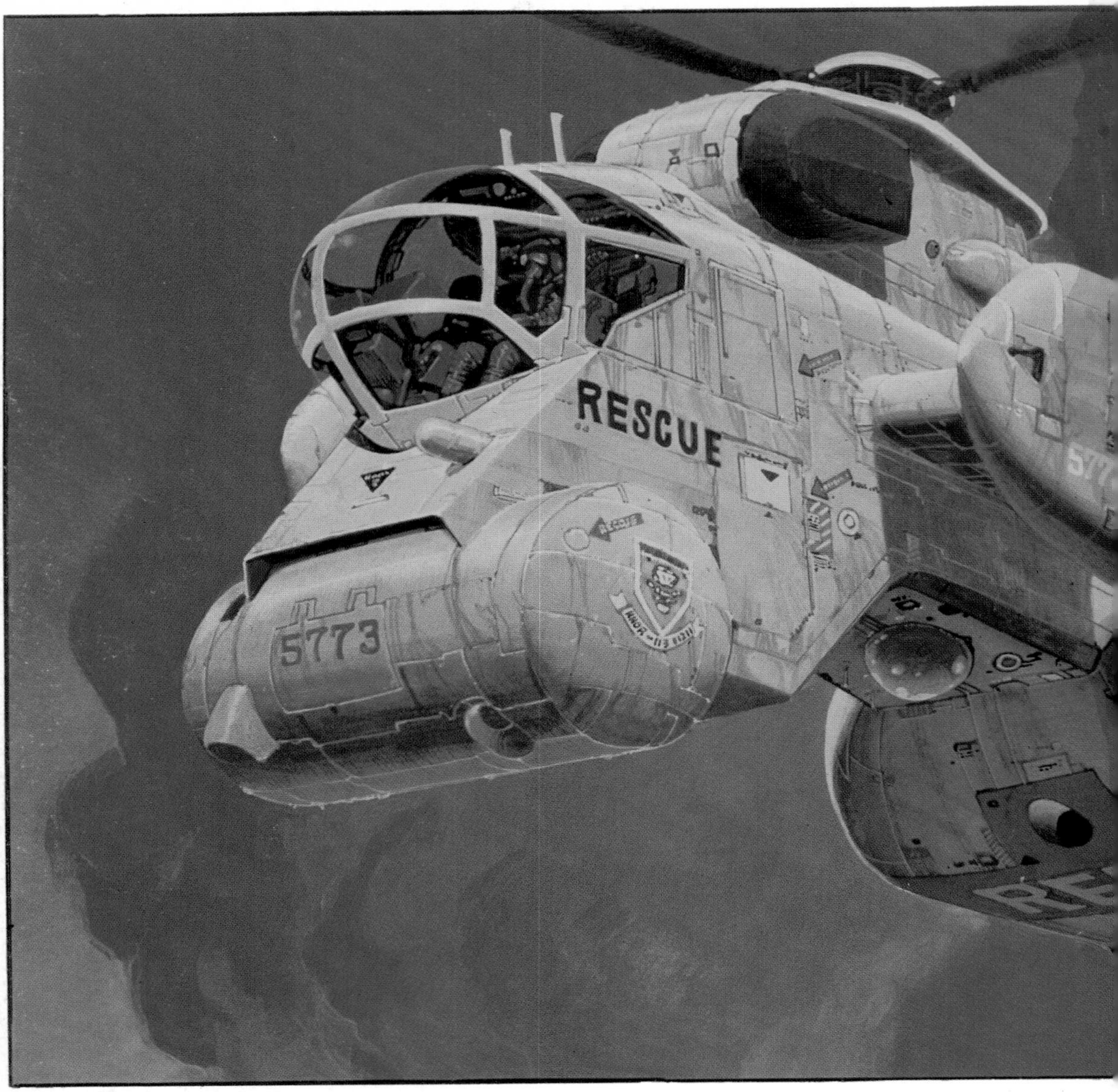
RESCUE
5773

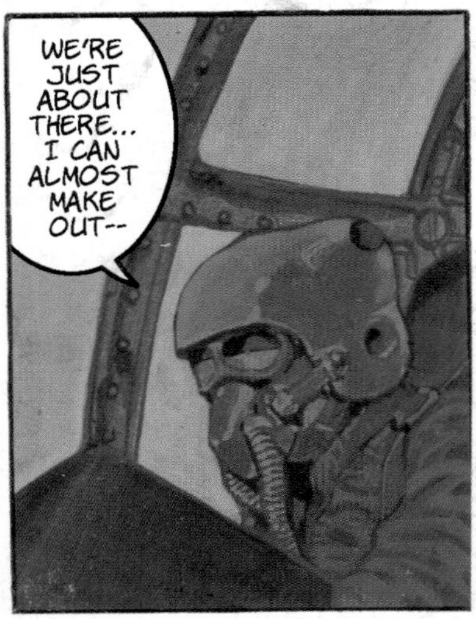
WE'RE JUST ABOUT THERE... I CAN ALMOST MAKE OUT--

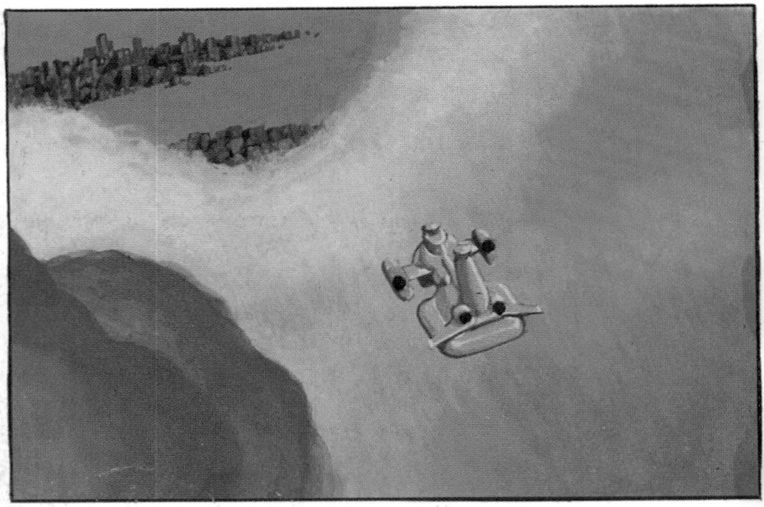

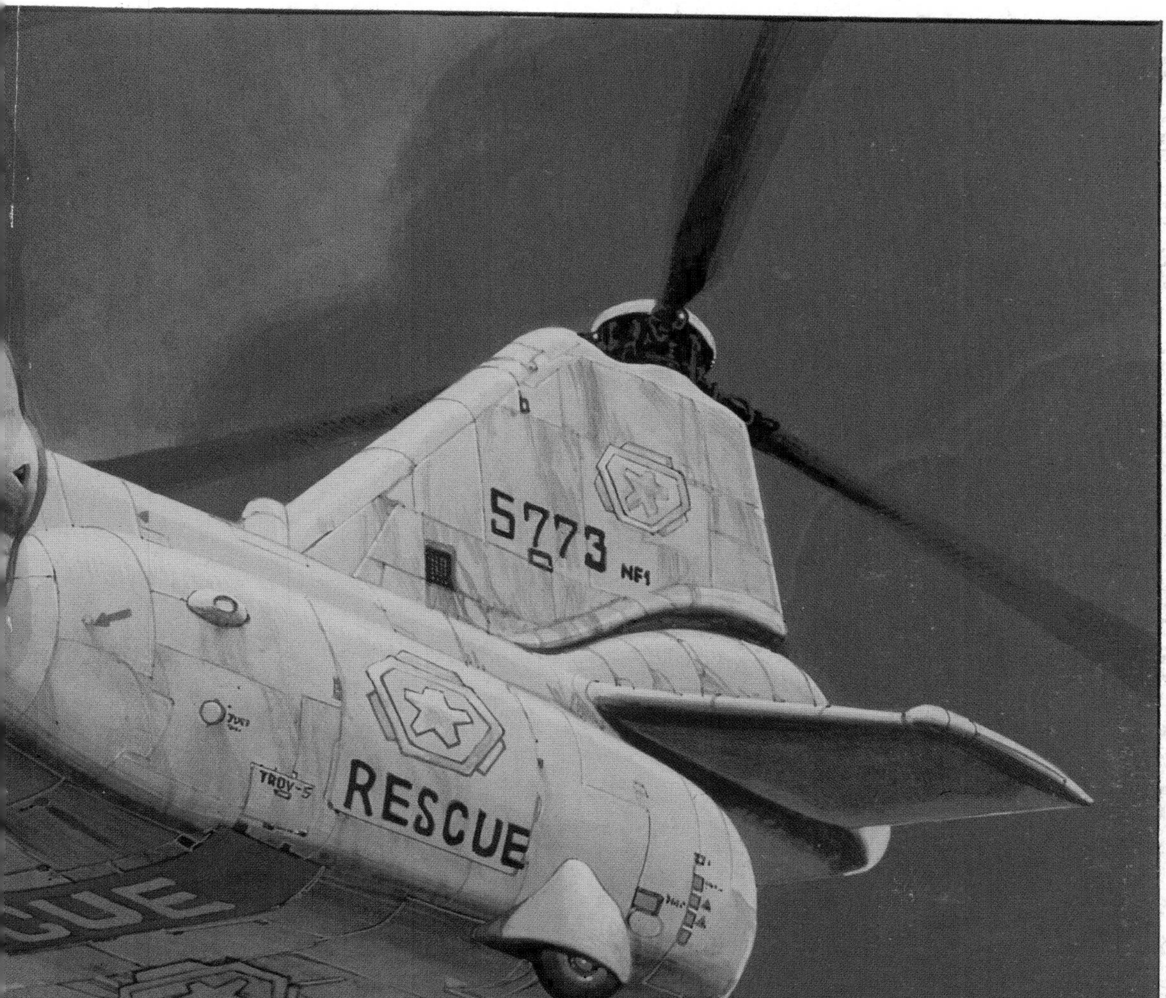
5773
RESCUE
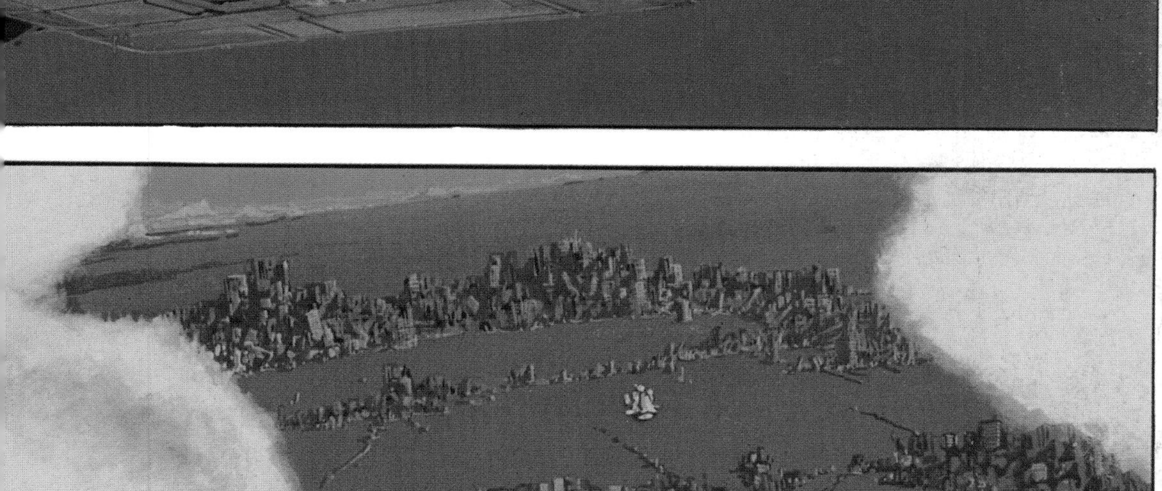

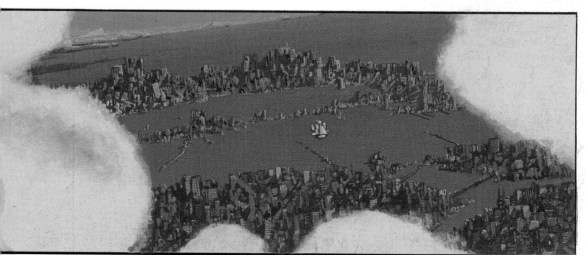

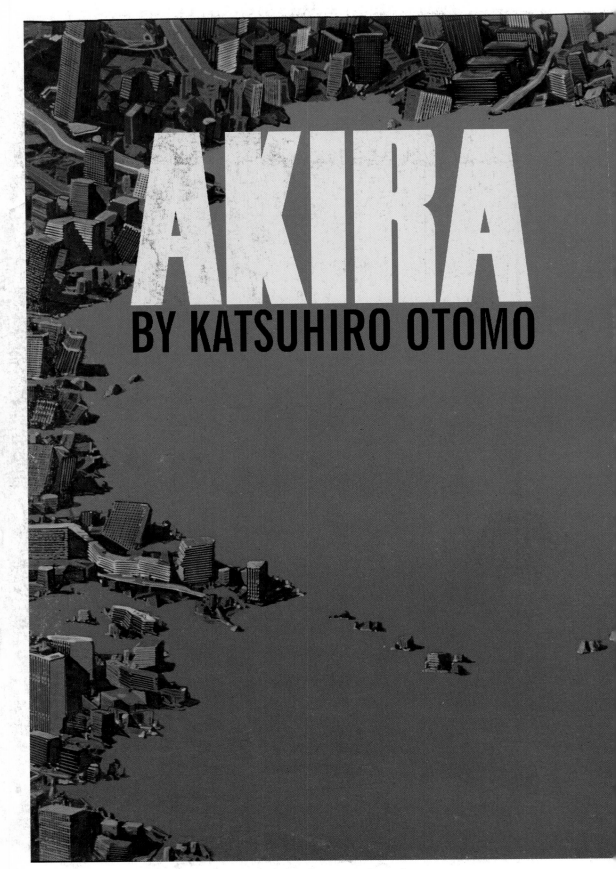

# AKIRA

## BY KATSUHIRO OTOMO

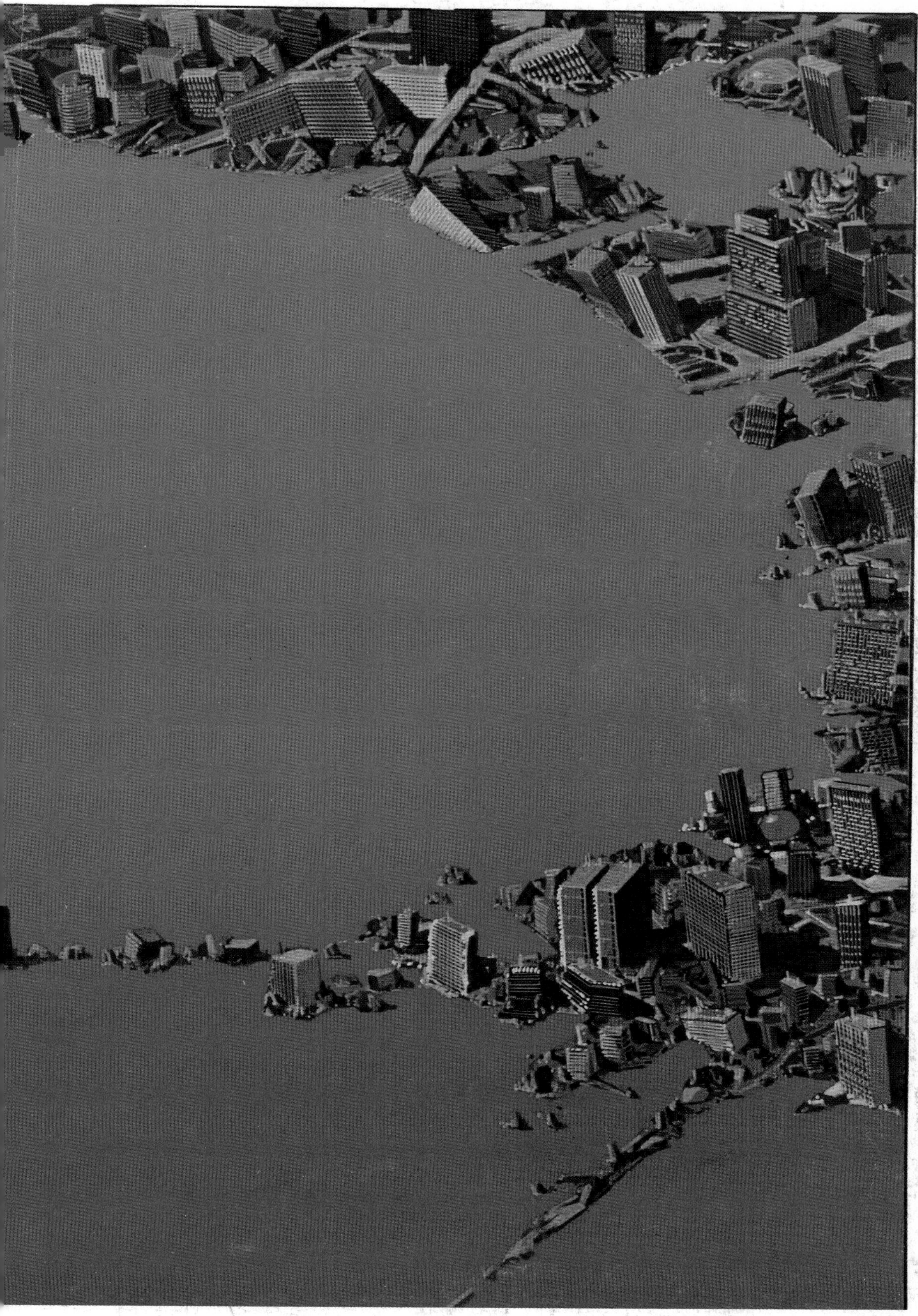

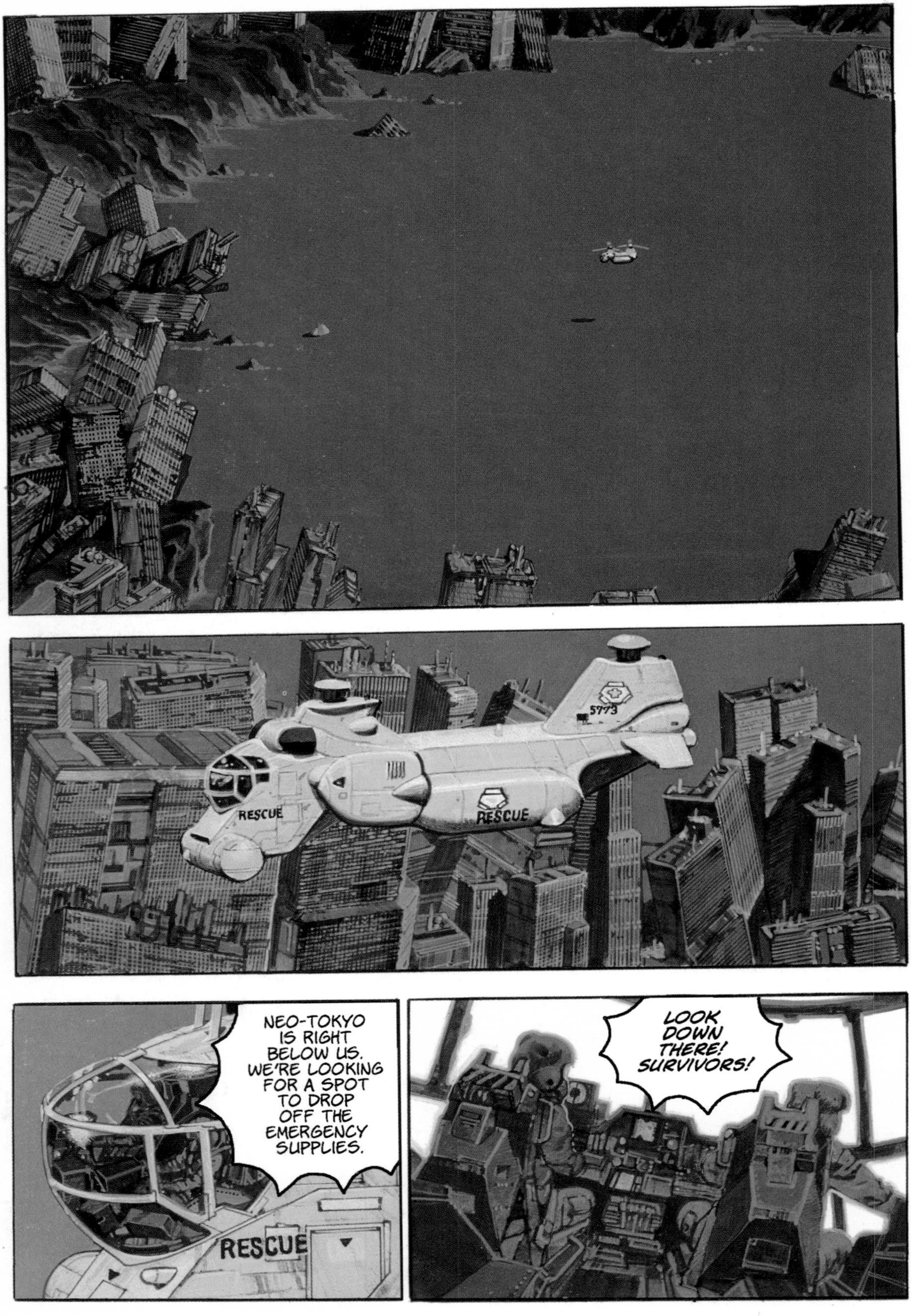
5773
RESCUE
RESCUE
NEO-TOKYO IS RIGHT BELOW US. WE'RE LOOKING FOR A SPOT TO DROP OFF THE EMERGENCY SUPPLIES.
RESCUE
LOOK DOWN THERE! SURVIVORS!

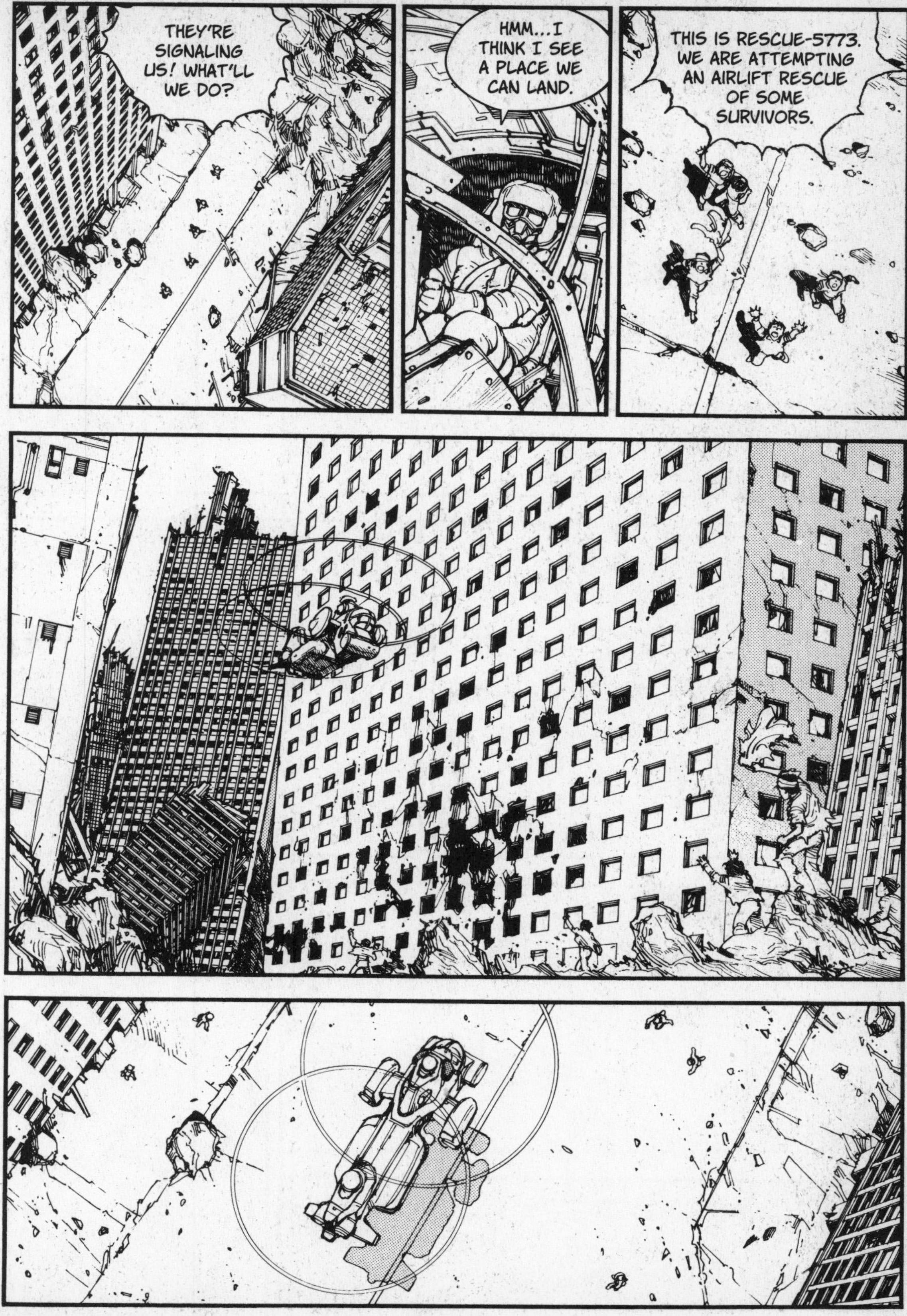
THEY'RE SIGNALING US! WHAT'LL WE DO?
HMM...I THINK I SEE A PLACE WE CAN LAND.
THIS IS RESCUE-5773. WE ARE ATTEMPTING AN AIRLIFT RESCUE OF SOME SURVIVORS.

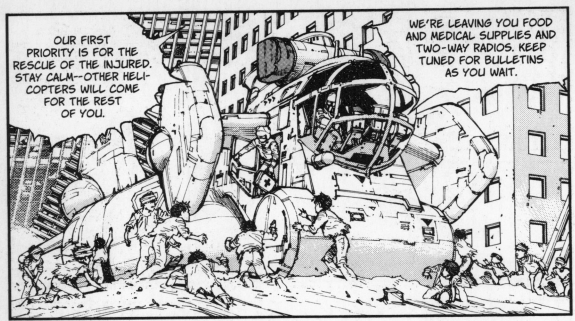

OUR FIRST PRIORITY IS FOR THE RESCUE OF THE INJURED. STAY CALM--OTHER HELICOPTERS WILL COME FOR THE REST OF YOU.

WE'RE LEAVING YOU FOOD AND MEDICAL SUPPLIES AND TWO-WAY RADIOS. KEEP TUNED FOR BULLETINS AS YOU WAIT.

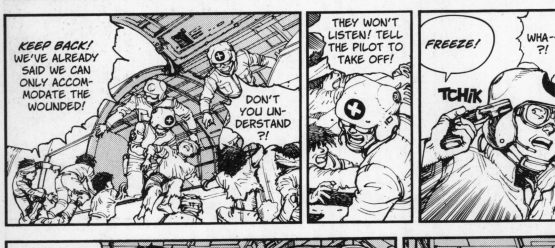

KEEP BACK! WE'VE ALREADY SAID WE CAN ONLY ACCOMMODATE THE WOUNDED!

DON'T YOU UNDERSTAND?!

THEY WON'T LISTEN! TELL THE PILOT TO TAKE OFF!

FREEZE!

WHA--?!

TCHIK

IN THE NAME OF THE EMPIRE, I HEREBY REQUISITION THIS VEHICLE! GIVE IT UP, AND NO FUNNY BUSINESS!

WHO ARE YOU GUYS?!

"REQUISITION"...?

"EMPIRE"...?

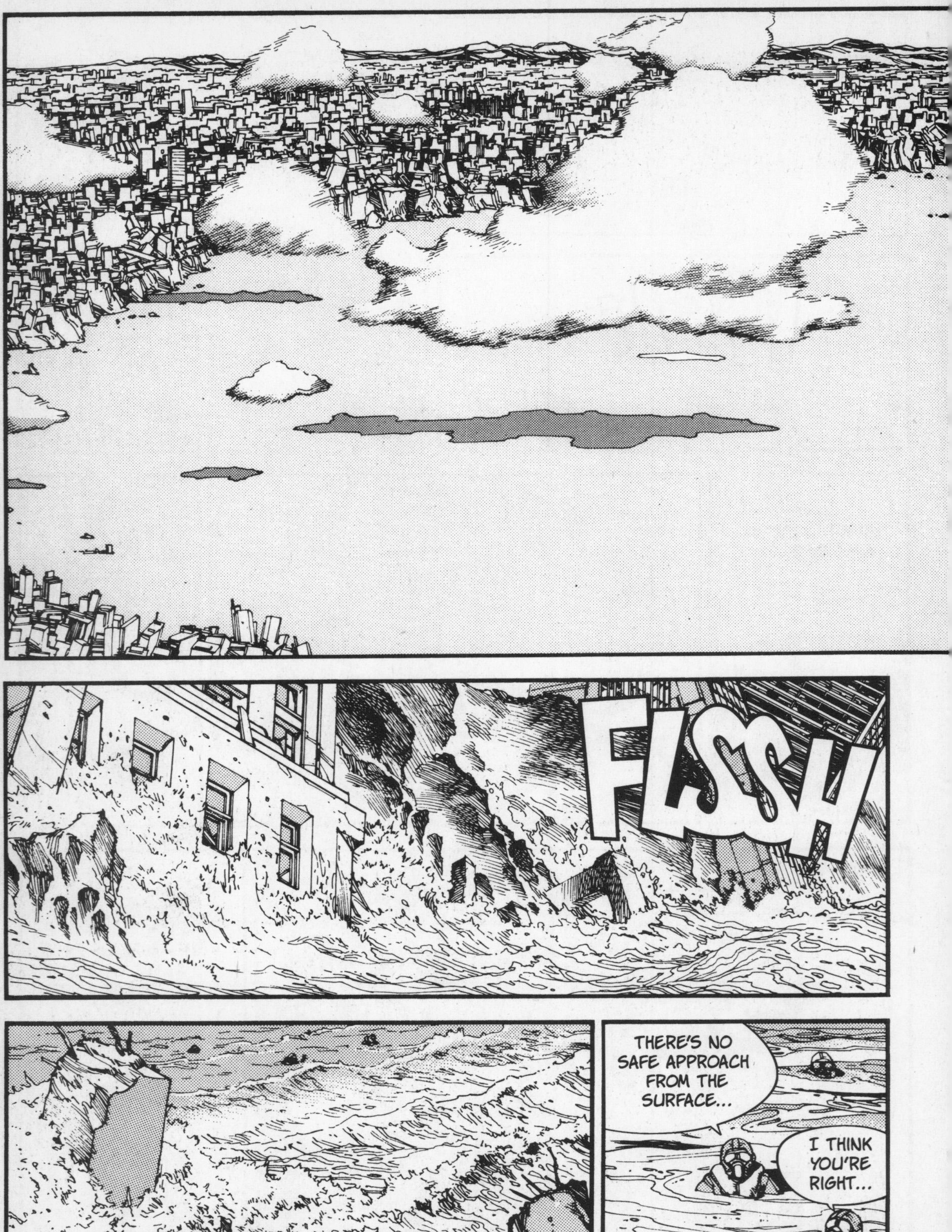
FLSSH
THERE'S NO SAFE APPROACH FROM THE SURFACE...
I THINK YOU'RE RIGHT...

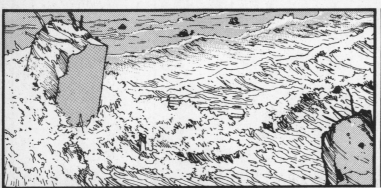

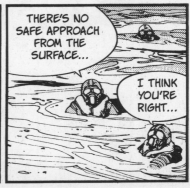

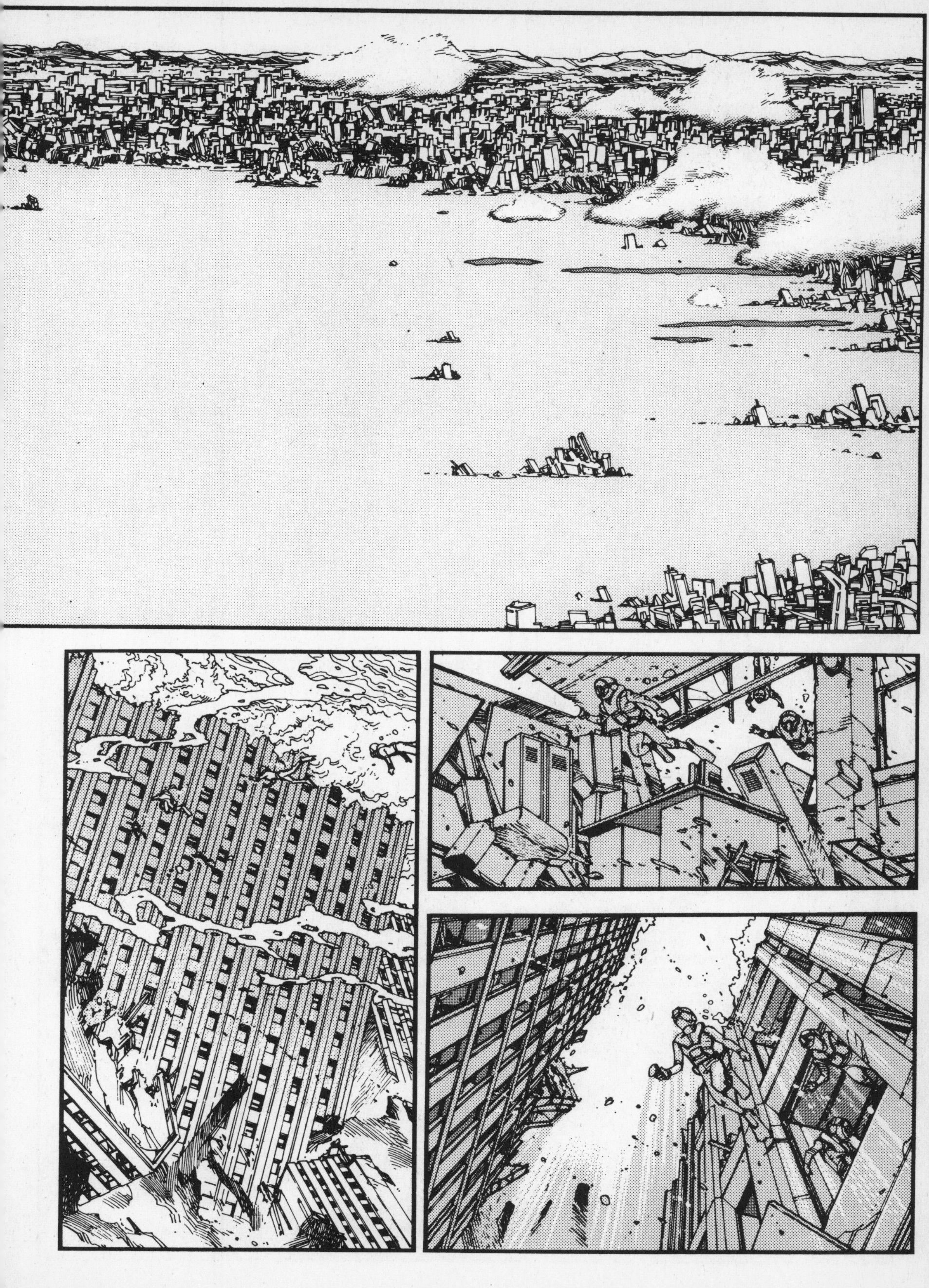

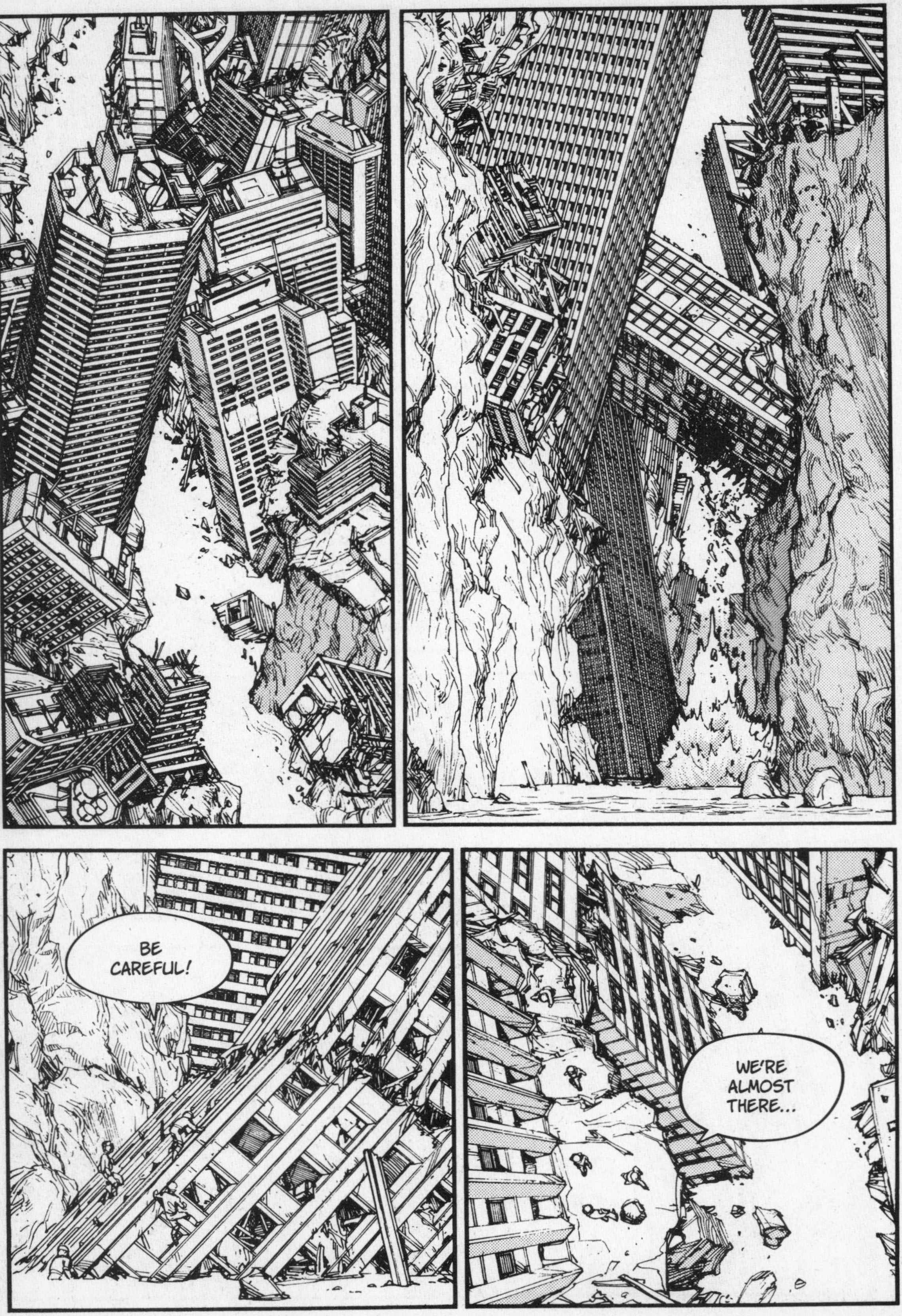
BE CAREFUL!
WE'RE ALMOST THERE...

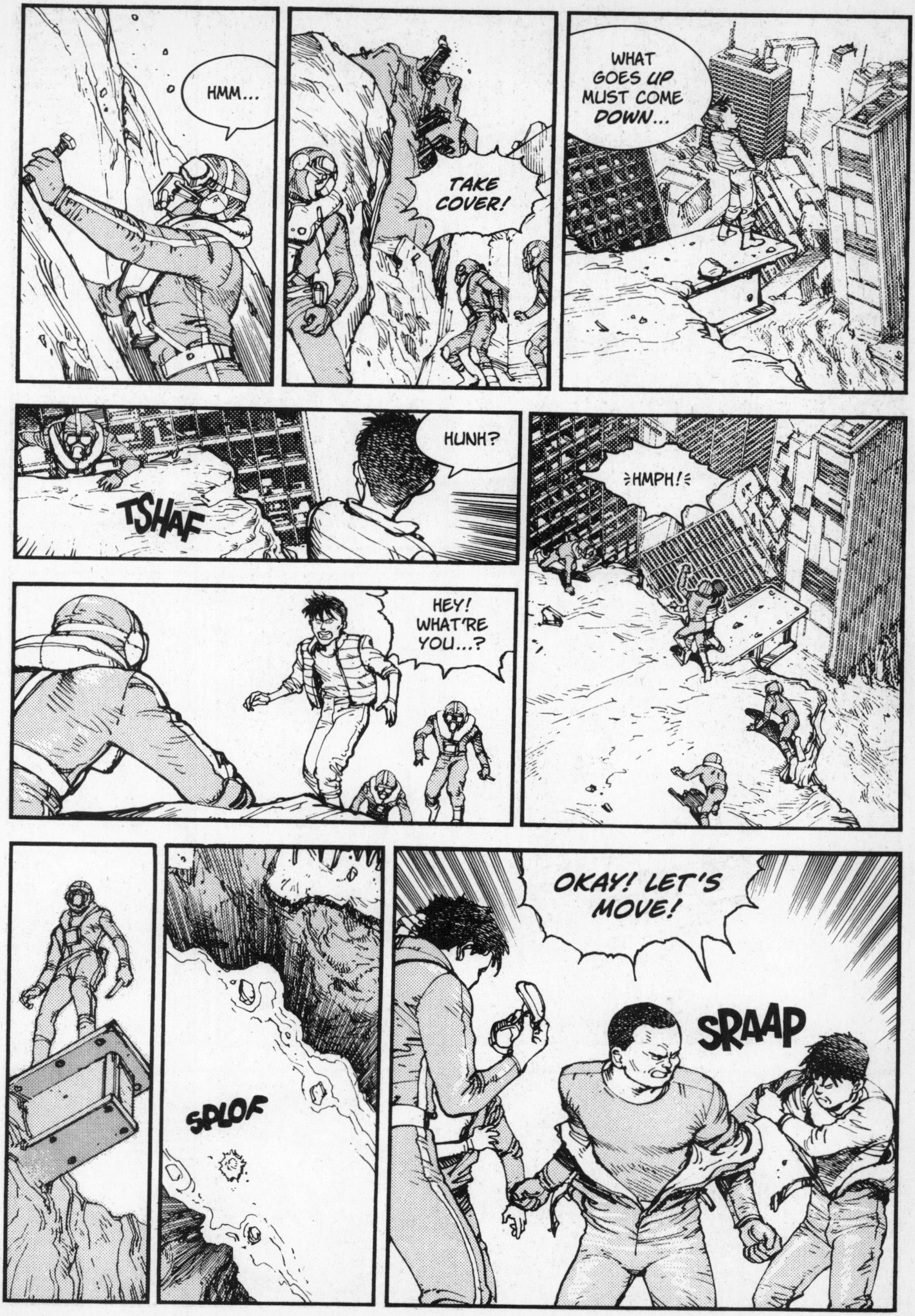
HMM...
TAKE COVER!
WHAT GOES UP MUST COME DOWN...
TSHAF
HUNH?
HMPH!
HEY! WHAT'RE YOU...?
SPLOF
OKAY! LET'S MOVE!
SRAAP

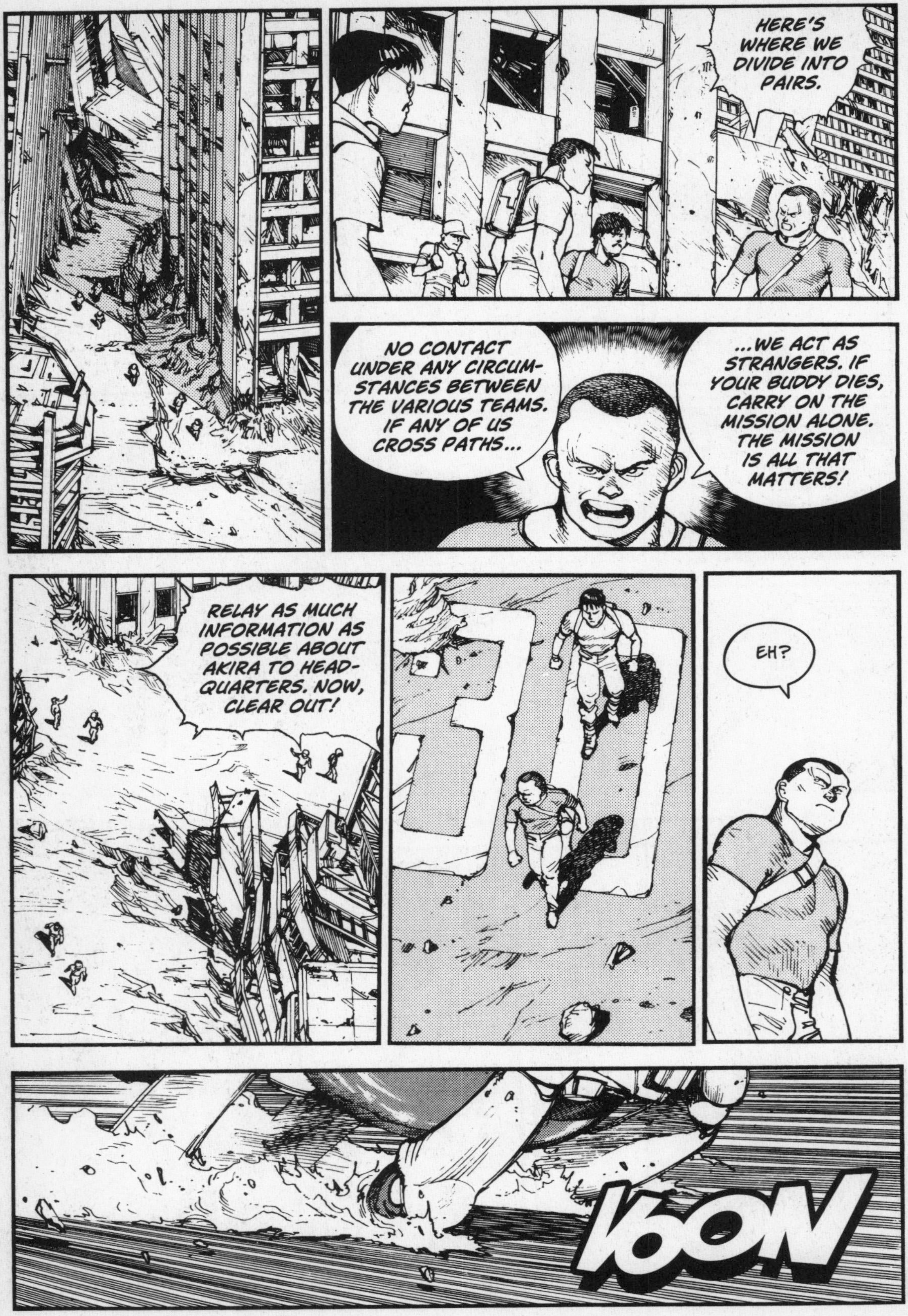
HERE'S WHERE WE DIVIDE INTO PAIRS.
NO CONTACT UNDER ANY CIRCUM-STANCES BETWEEN THE VARIOUS TEAMS. IF ANY OF US CROSS PATHS...
...WE ACT AS STRANGERS. IF YOUR BUDDY DIES, CARRY ON THE MISSION ALONE. THE MISSION IS ALL THAT MATTERS!
RELAY AS MUCH INFORMATION AS POSSIBLE ABOUT AKIRA TO HEAD-QUARTERS. NOW, CLEAR OUT!
EH?
VOON

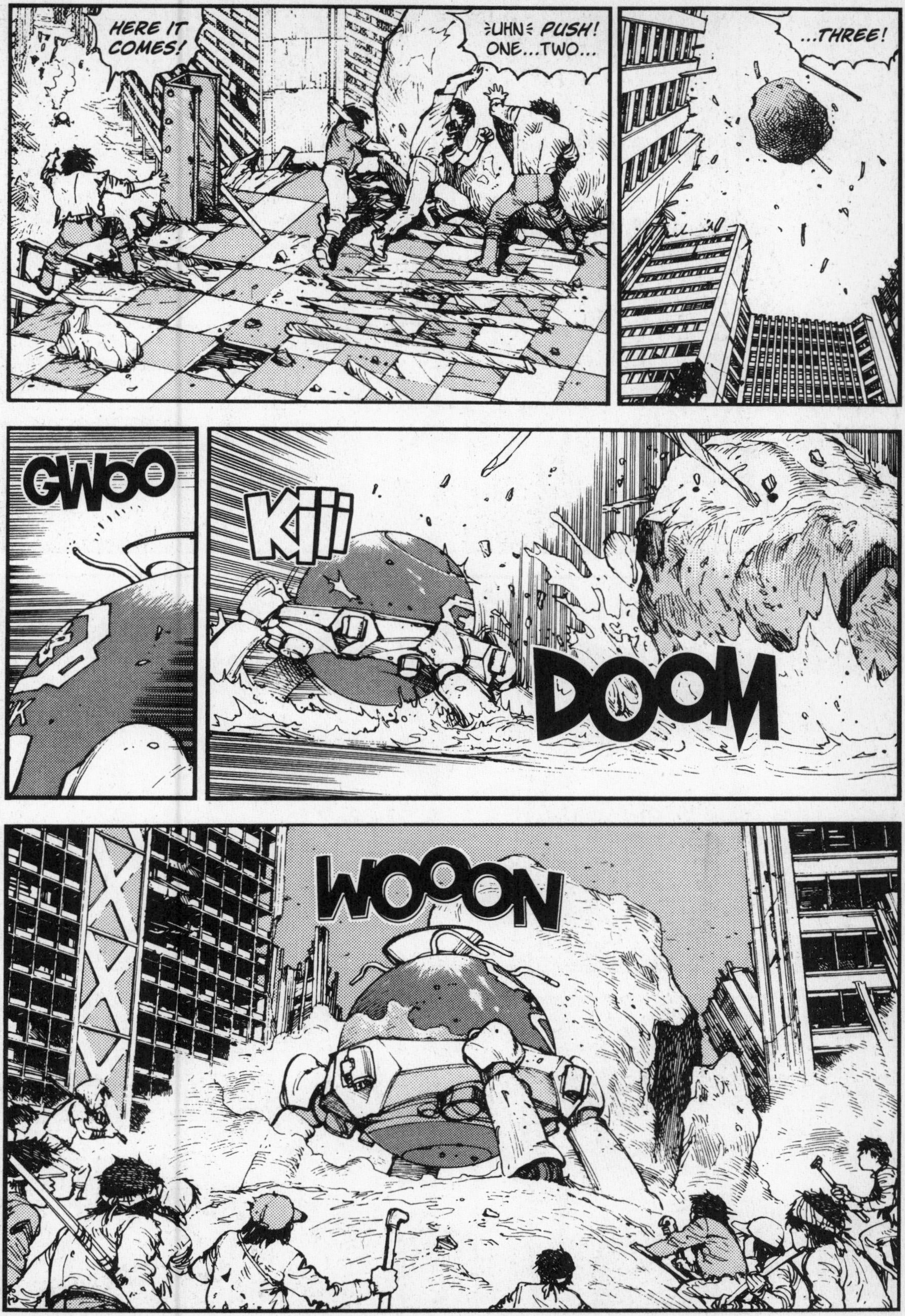
HERE IT COMES!
UHN PUSH! ONE...TWO...
...THREE!
GWOO
KIJI
DOOM
WOOON

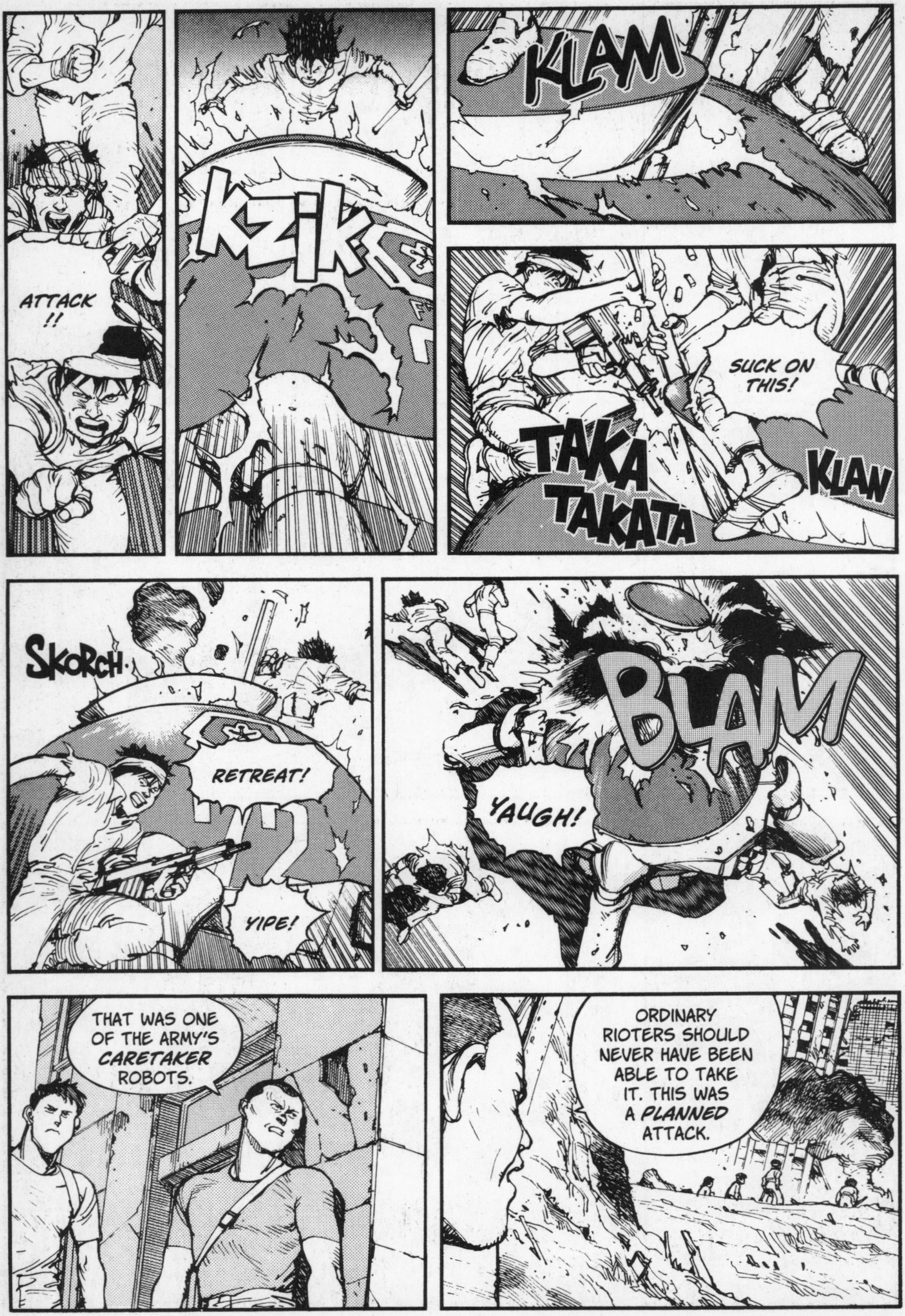
ATTACK !!
KZIK
KLAM
SUCK ON THIS!
TAKA TAKATA
KLAN
SKORCH
RETREAT!
YIPE!
BLAM
YAUGH!
THAT WAS ONE OF THE ARMY'S CARETAKER ROBOTS.
ORDINARY RIOTERS SHOULD NEVER HAVE BEEN ABLE TO TAKE IT. THIS WAS A PLANNED ATTACK.

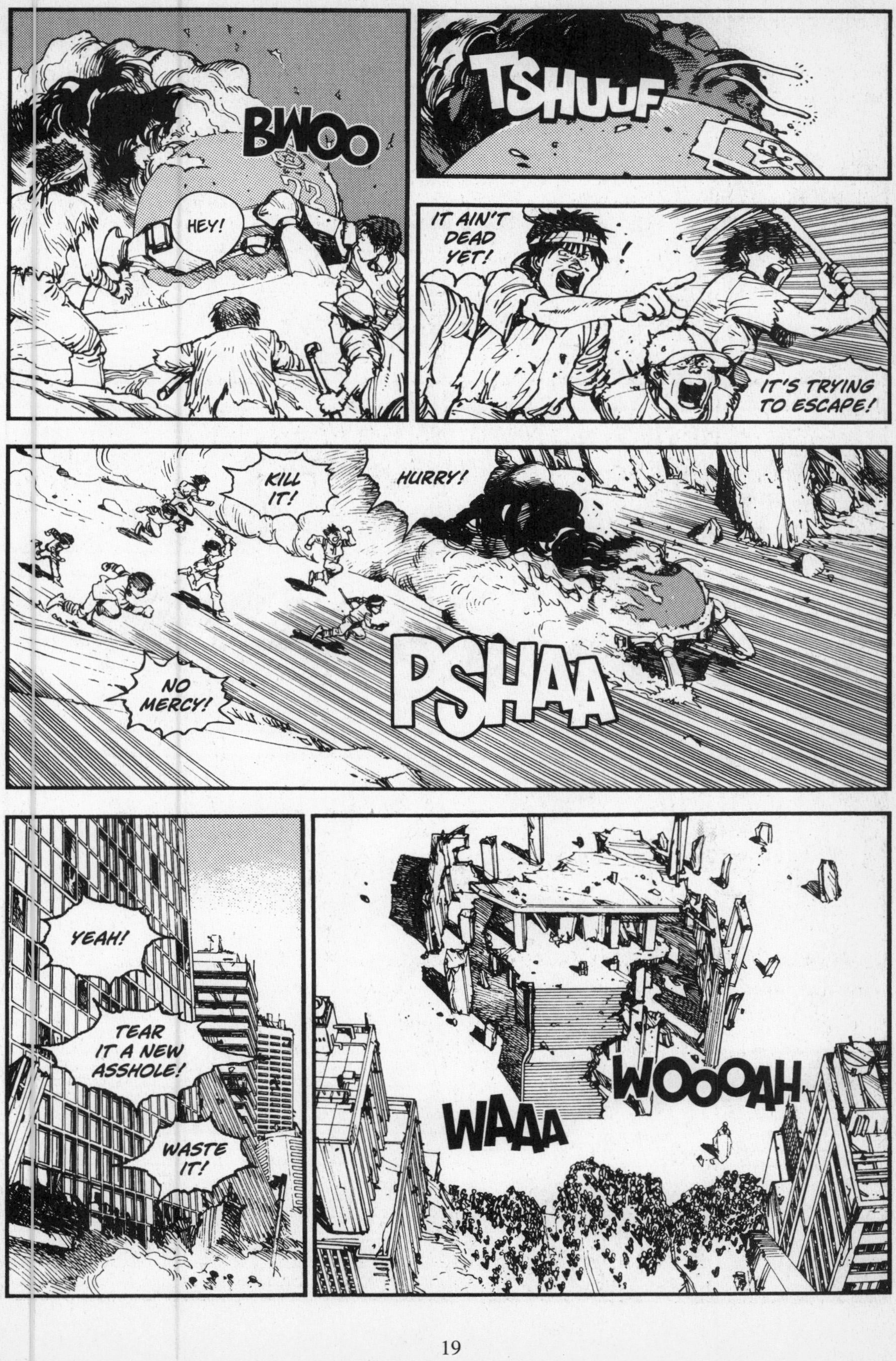
BWOO
HEY!
TSHUUF
IT AIN'T DEAD YET!
IT'S TRYING TO ESCAPE!
KILL IT!
HURRY!
NO MERCY!
PSHAA
YEAH!
TEAR IT A NEW ASSHOLE!
WASTE IT!
WOOOAH
WAAA

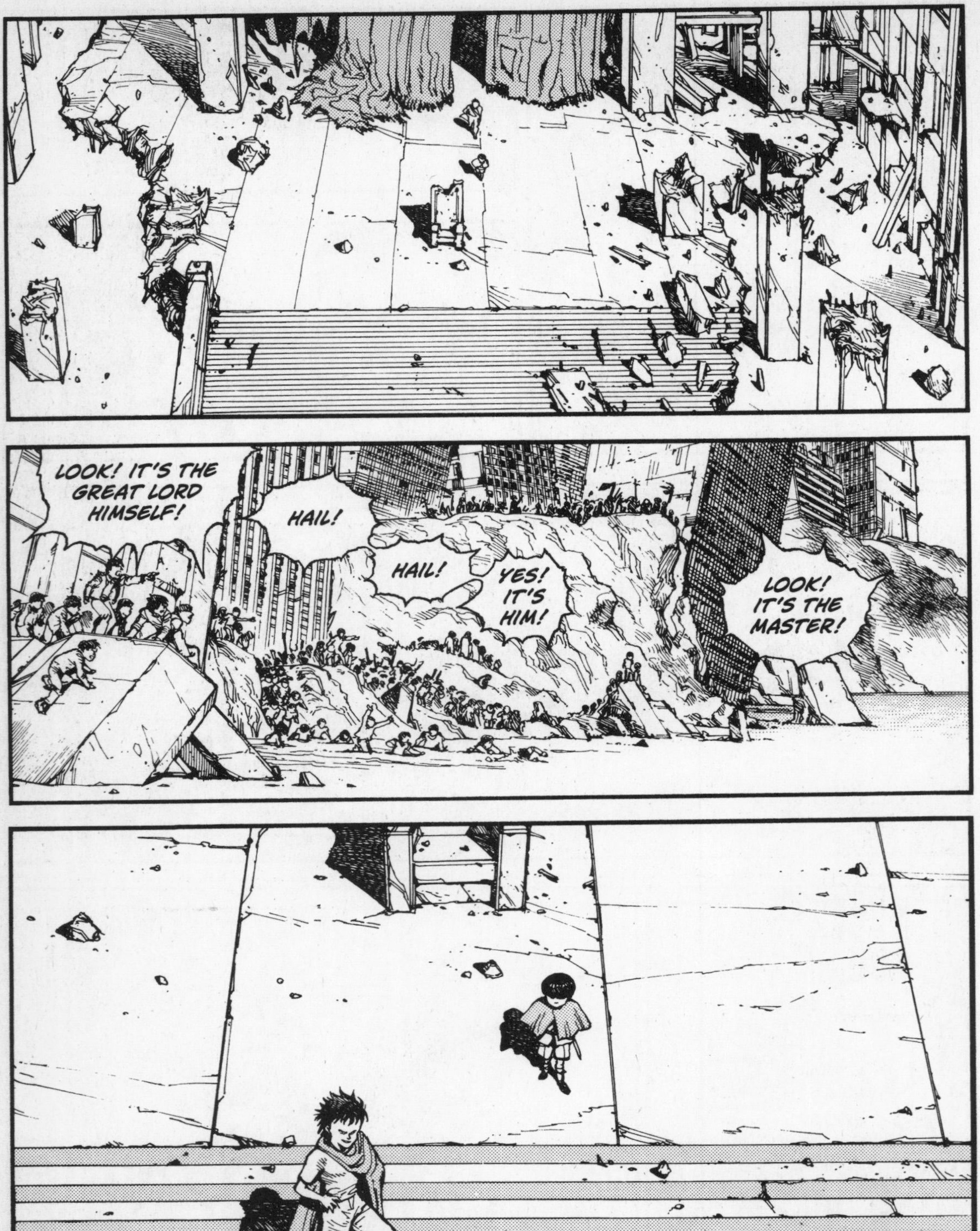
LOOK! IT'S THE GREAT LORD HIMSELF!
HAIL!
HAIL!
YES! IT'S HIM!
LOOK! IT'S THE MASTER!

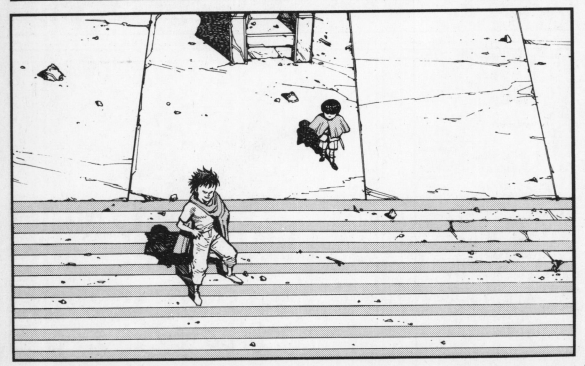

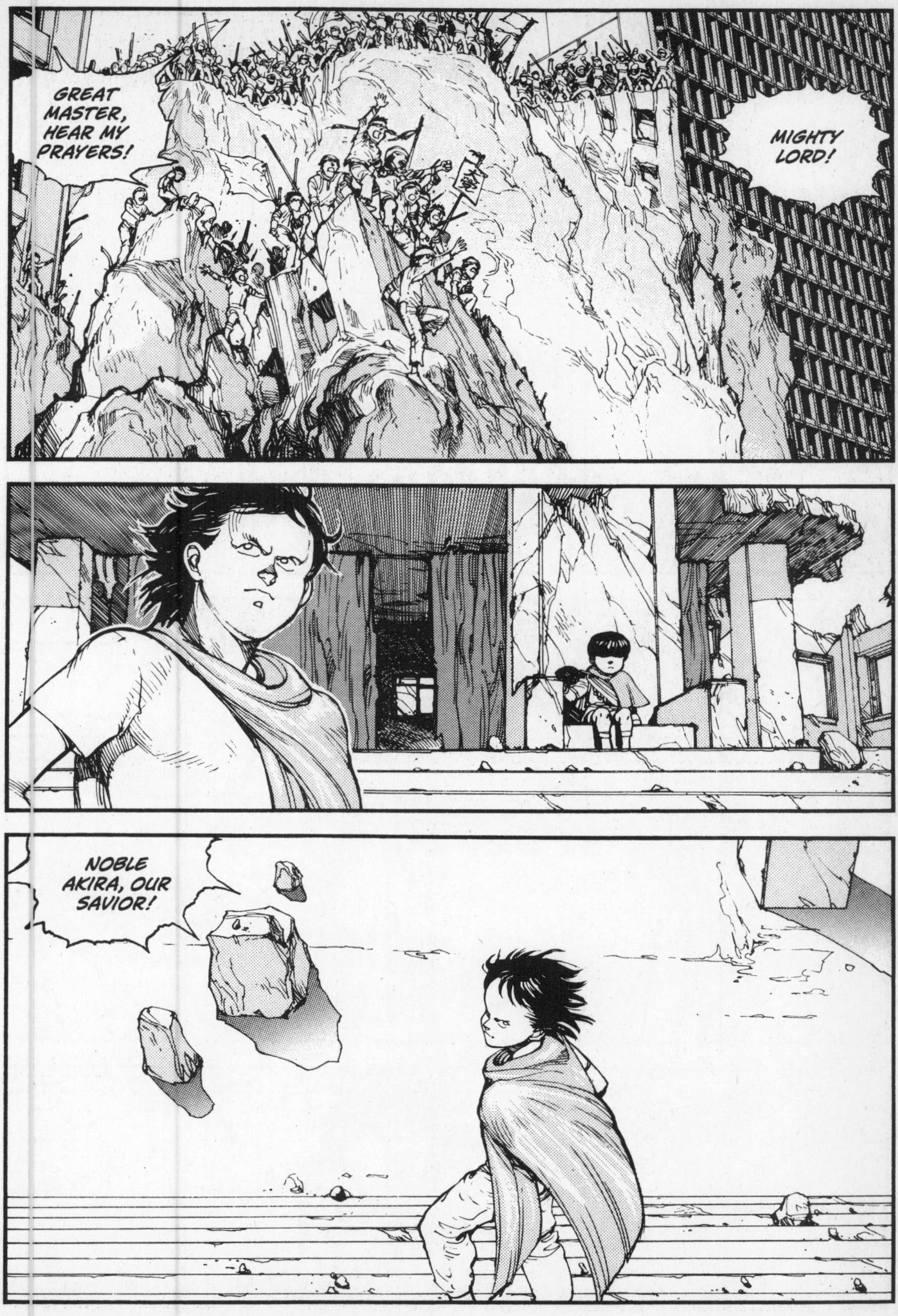
GREAT MASTER, HEAR MY PRAYERS!
MIGHTY LORD!
NOBLE AKIRA, OUR SAVIOR!

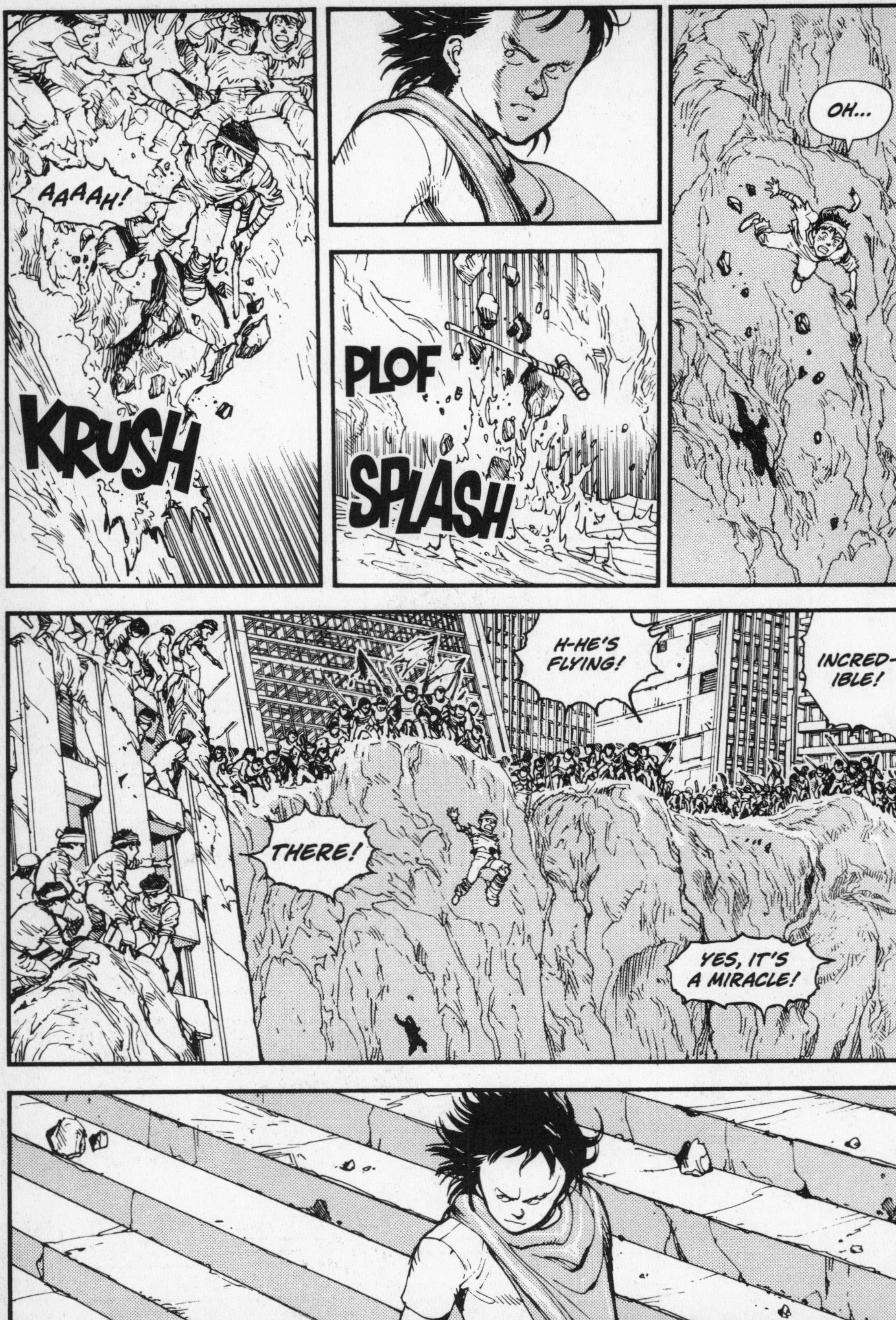
AAAAH!
KRUSH
PLOF
SPLASH
OH...
H-HE'S FLYING!
INCRED-IBLE!
THERE!
YES, IT'S A MIRACLE!

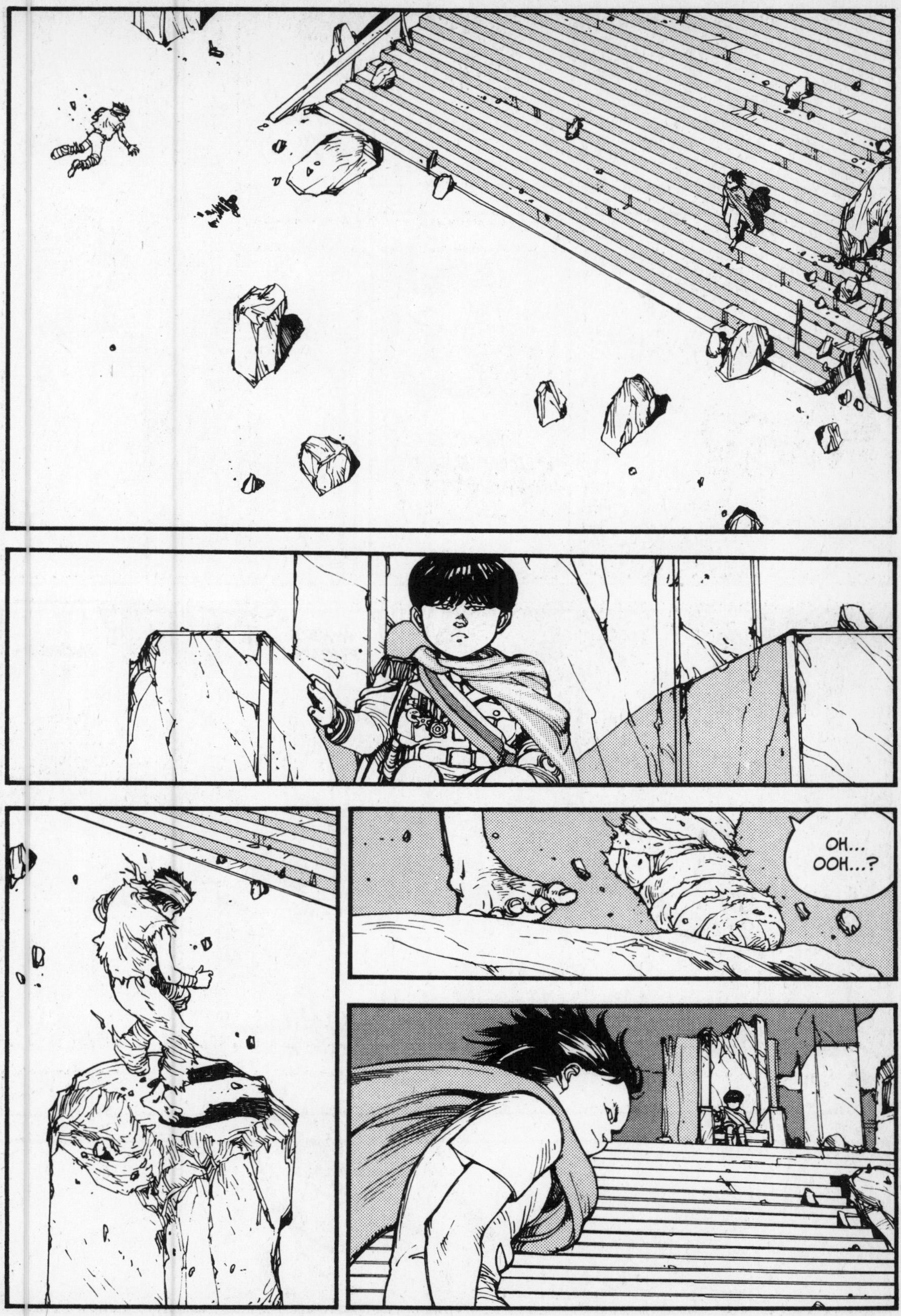
OH...
OOH...?

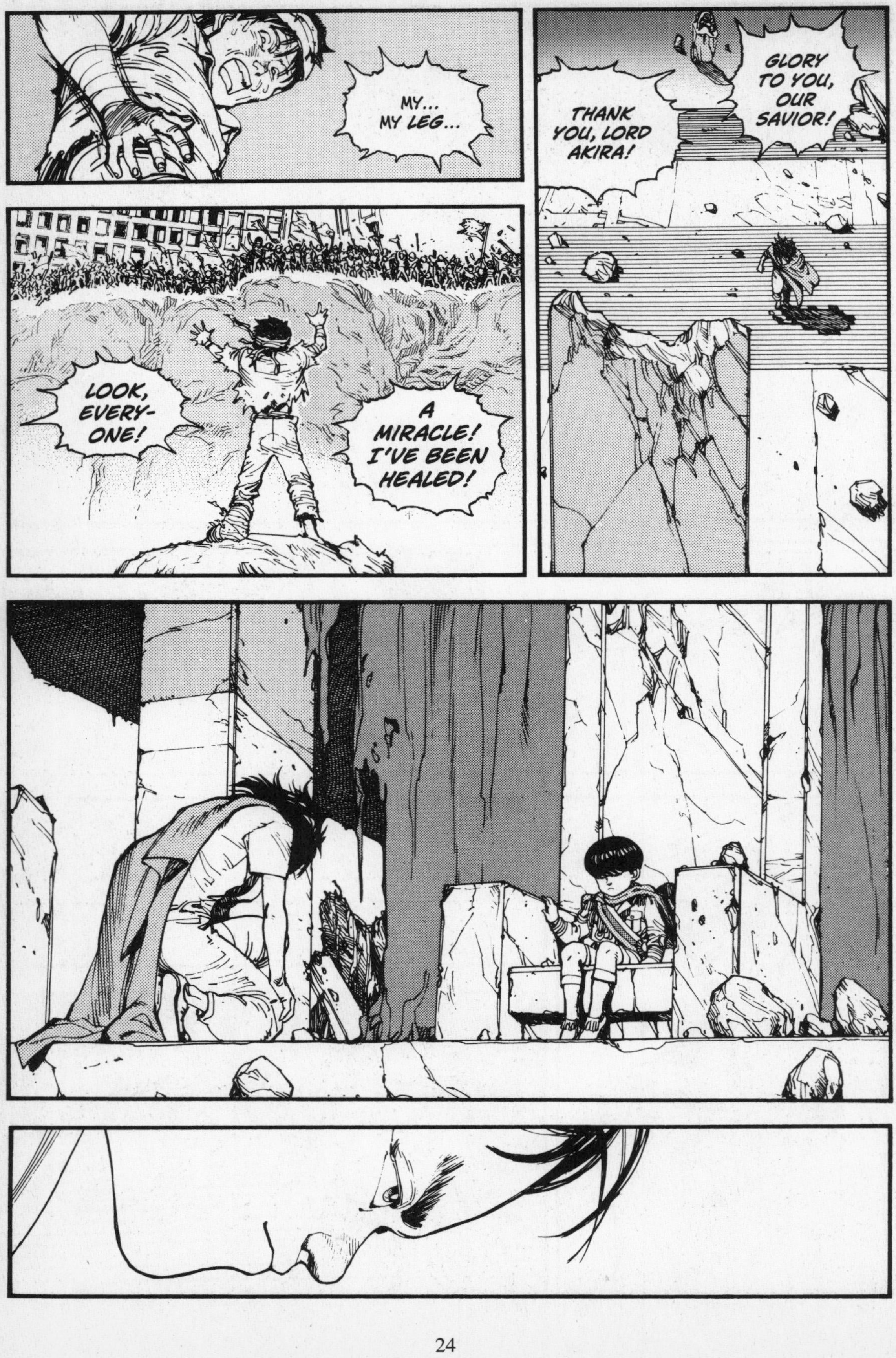
MY... MY LEG...
THANK YOU, LORD AKIRA!
GLORY TO YOU, OUR SAVIOR!
LOOK, EVERY-ONE!
A MIRACLE! I'VE BEEN HEALED!

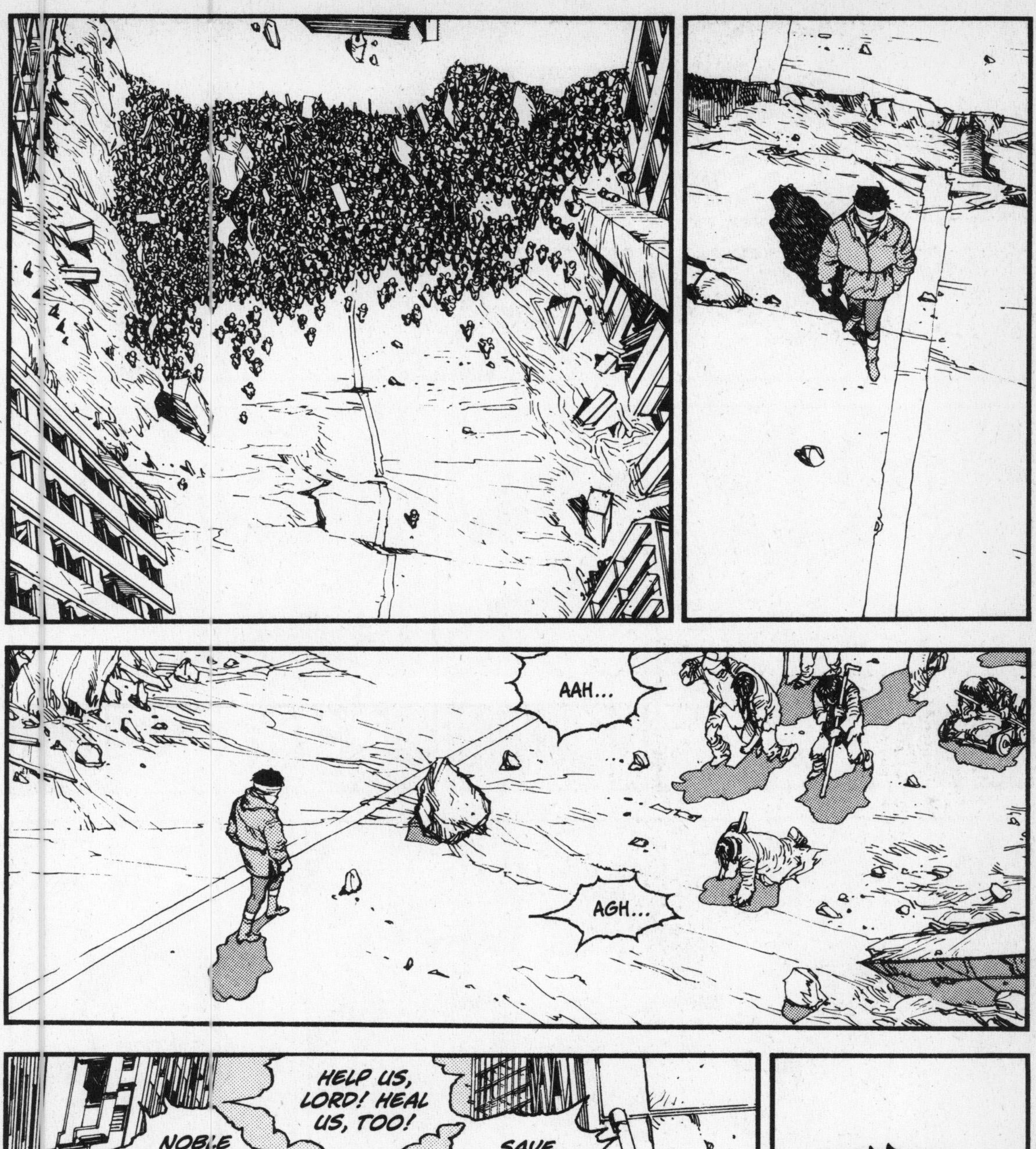
AAH...
AGH...
NOBLE AKIRA!
HELP US, LORD! HEAL US, TOO!
SAVE US!

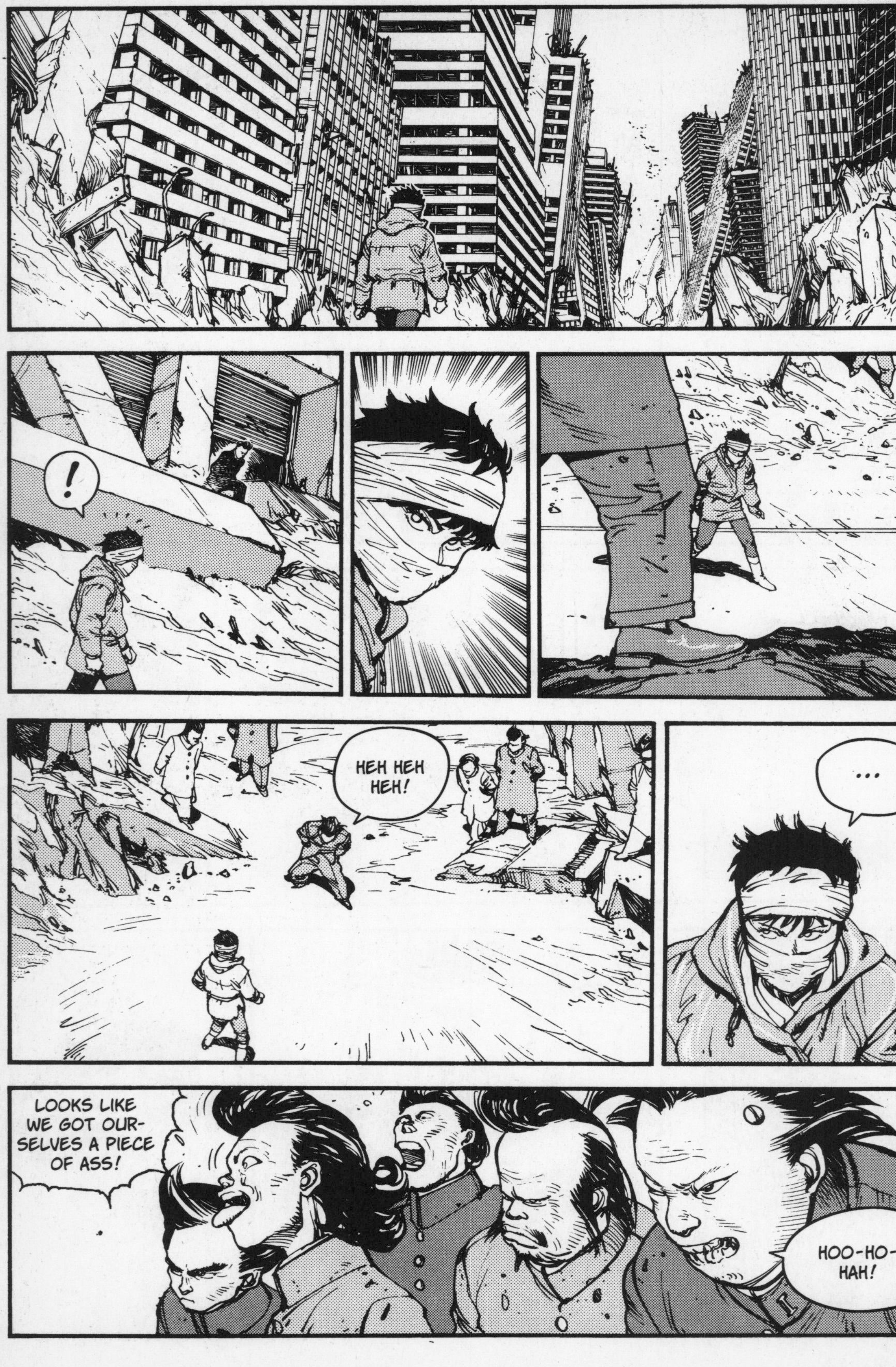
!
HEH HEH HEH!
...
LOOKS LIKE WE GOT OURSELVES A PIECE OF ASS!
HOO-HO-HAH!

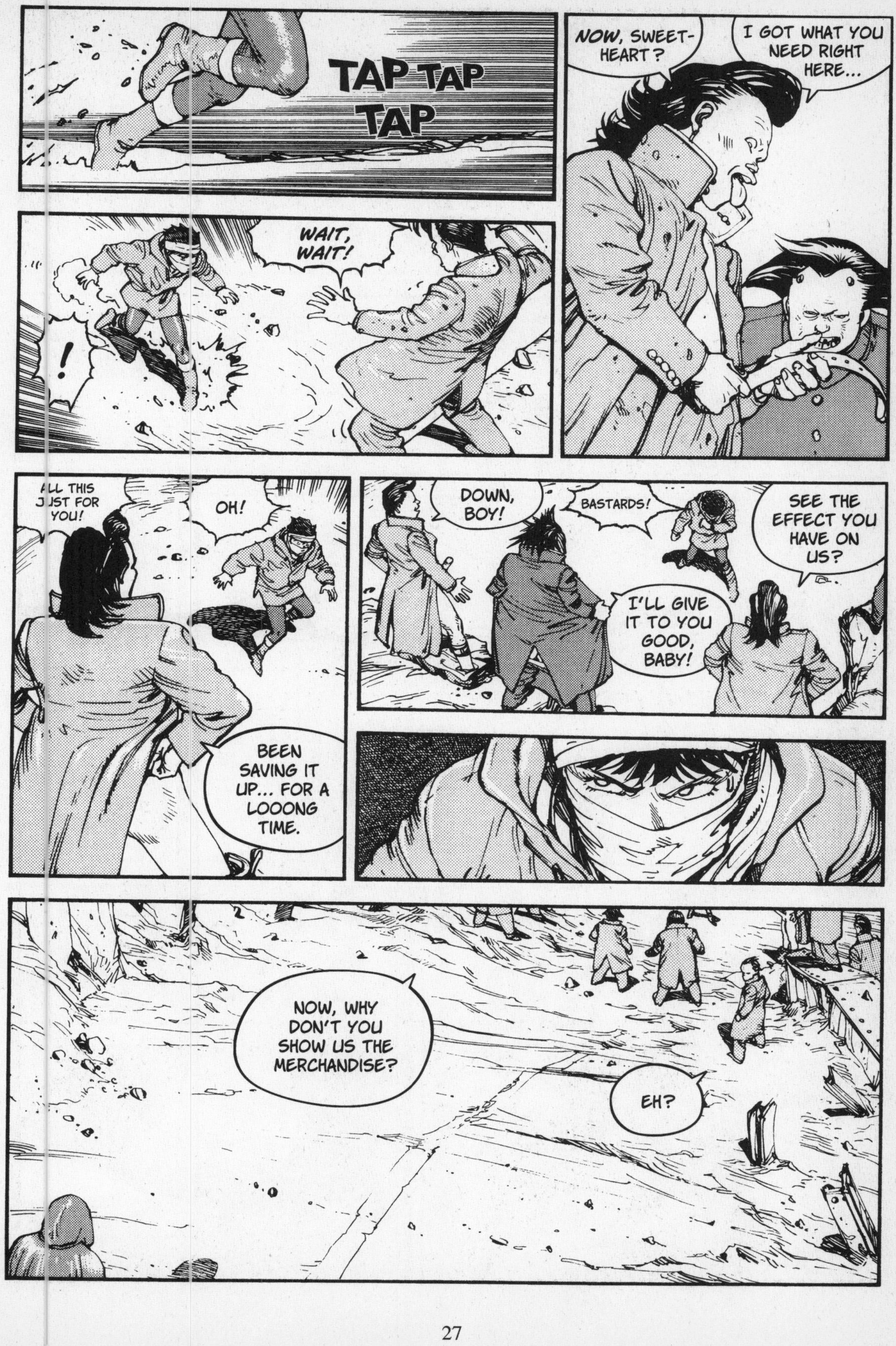
TAP TAP TAP
NOW, SWEET-HEART?
I GOT WHAT YOU NEED RIGHT HERE...
WAIT, WAIT!
!
ALL THIS JUST FOR YOU!
OH!
BEEN SAVING IT UP... FOR A LOOONG TIME.
DOWN, BOY!
BASTARDS!
SEE THE EFFECT YOU HAVE ON US?
I'LL GIVE IT TO YOU GOOD, BABY!
NOW, WHY DON'T YOU SHOW US THE MERCHANDISE?
EH?

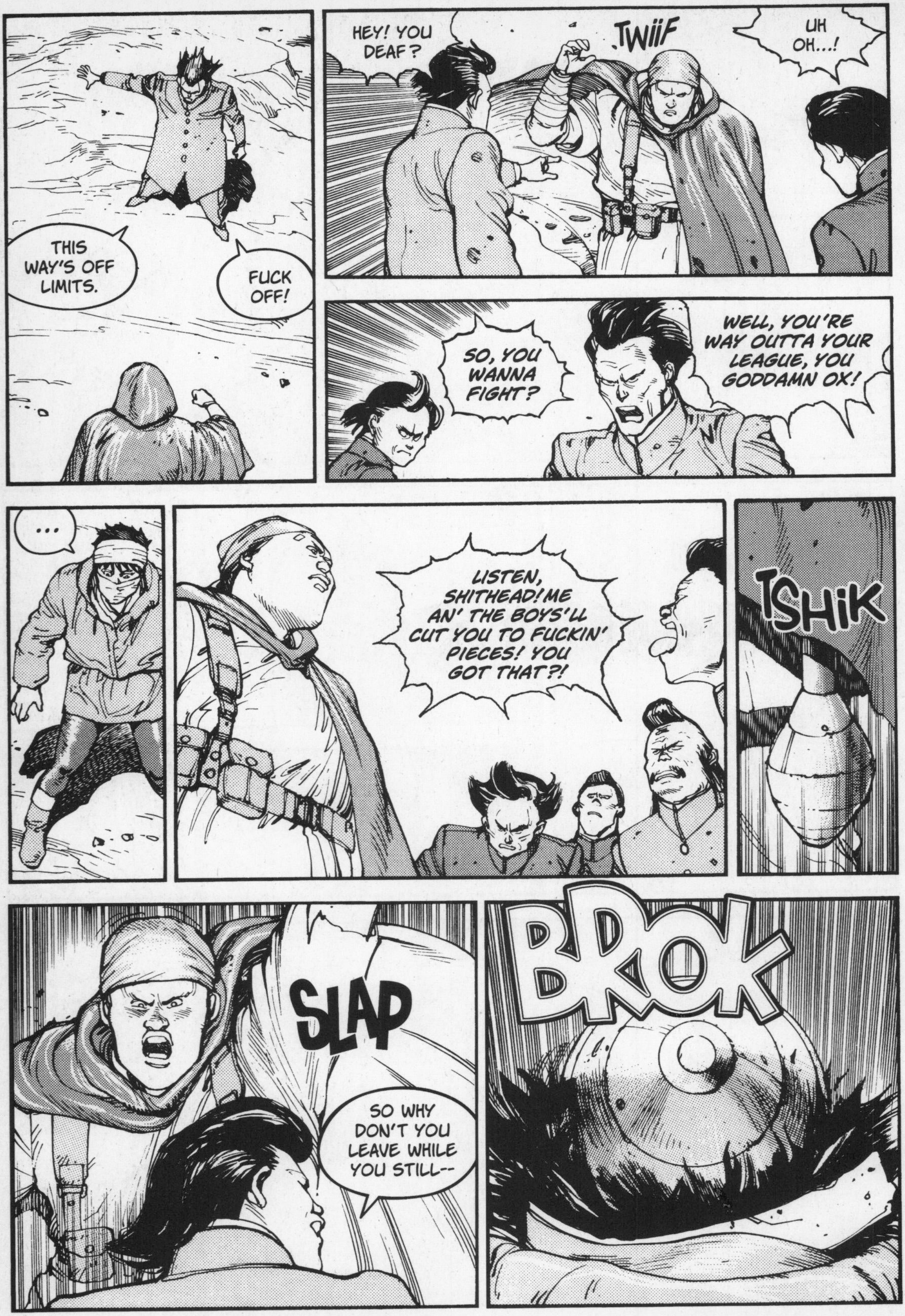
HEY! YOU DEAF?
TWIIF
UH OH...!
THIS WAY'S OFF LIMITS.
FUCK OFF!
SO, YOU WANNA FIGHT?
WELL, YOU'RE WAY OUTTA YOUR LEAGUE, YOU GODDAMN OX!
...
LISTEN, SHITHEAD! ME AN' THE BOYS'LL CUT YOU TO FUCKIN' PIECES! YOU GOT THAT?!
TSHIK
SLAP
SO WHY DON'T YOU LEAVE WHILE YOU STILL--
BROK

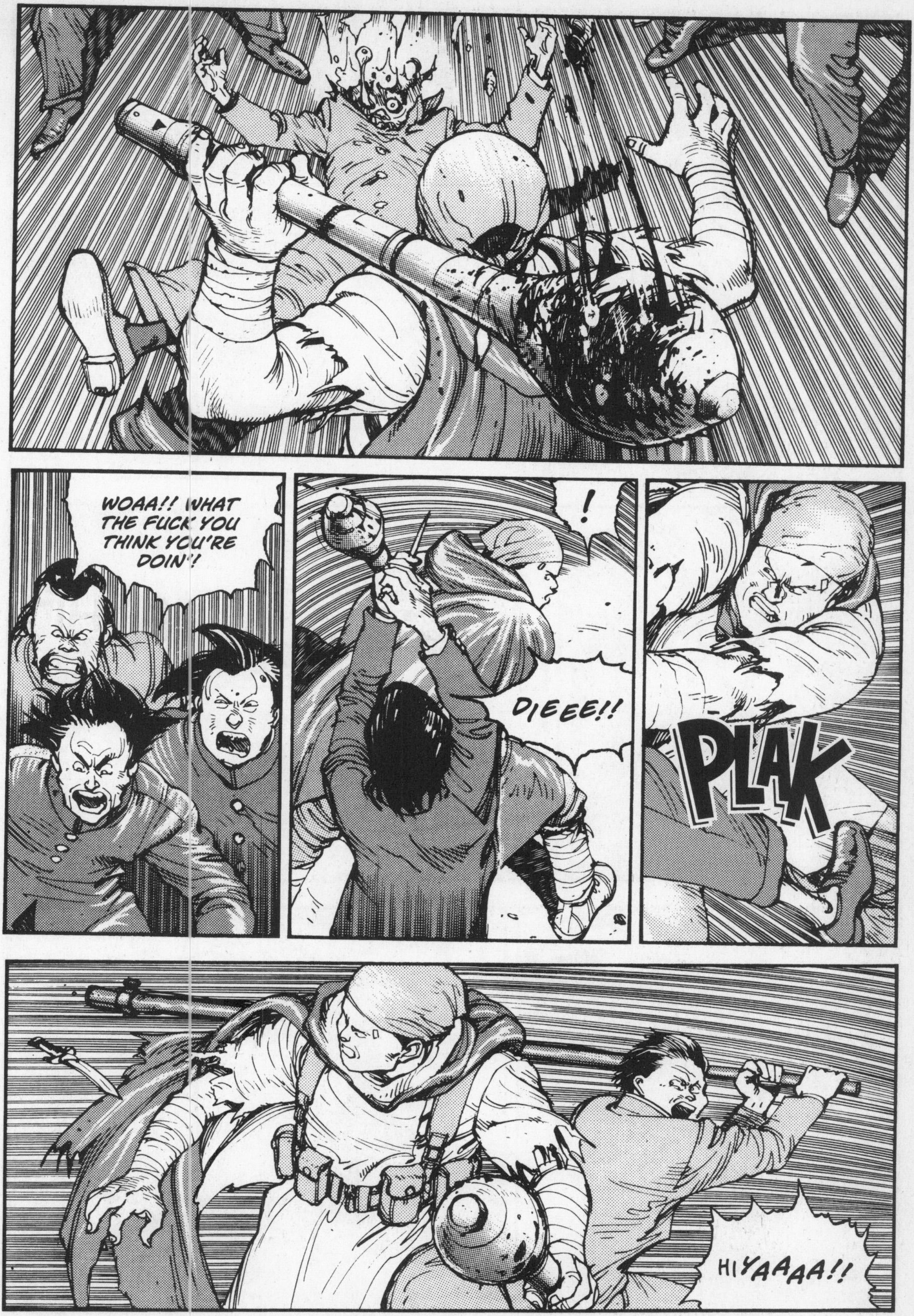
WOAA!! WHAT THE FUCK YOU THINK YOU'RE DOIN'!
!
DIEEE!!
PLAK
HIYAAAA!!

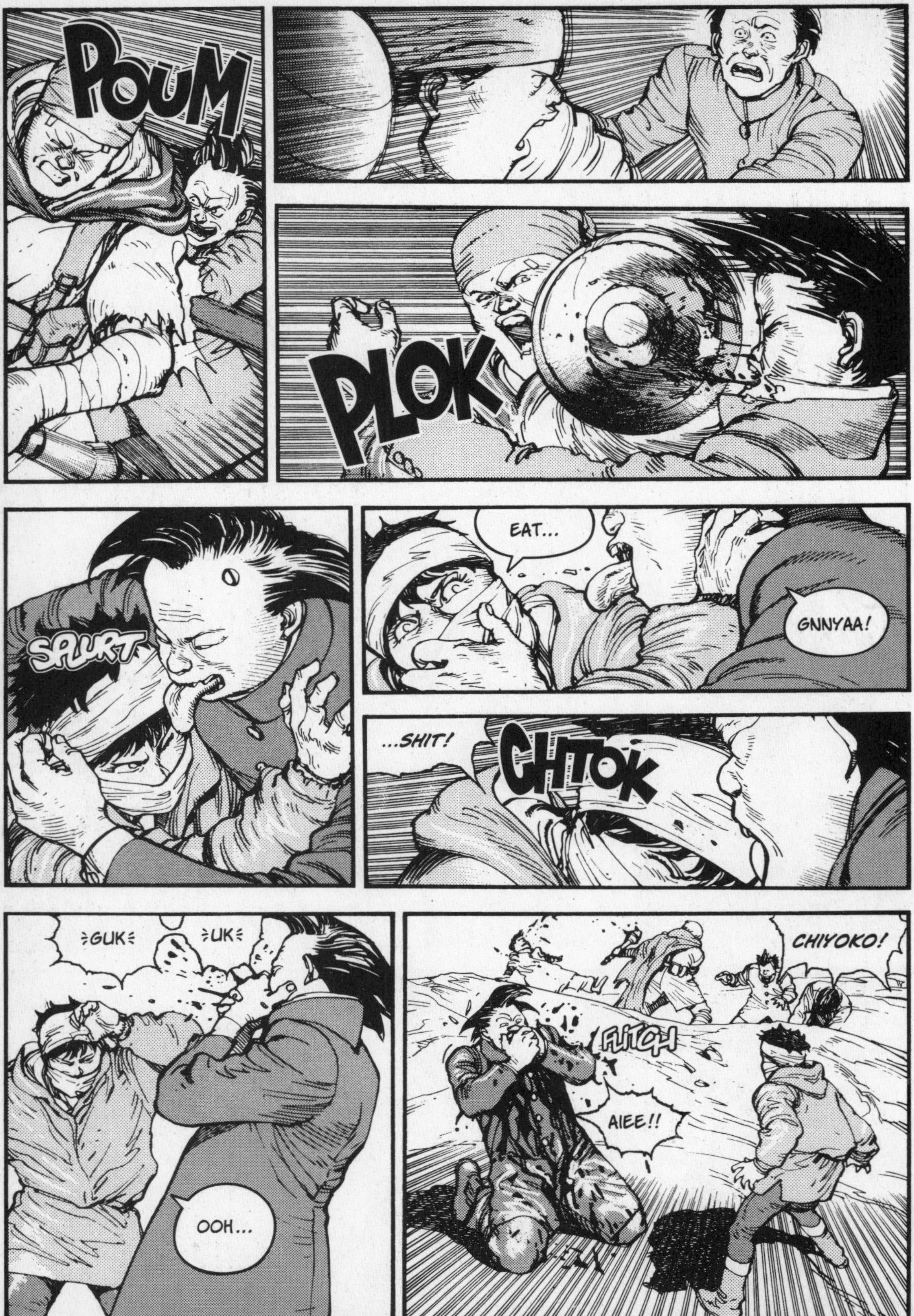
POUM
PLOK
SPLURT
EAT...
GNNYAA!
...SHIT!
CHTOK
GUK
UK
OOH...
CHIYOKO!
FLITCH
AIEE!!

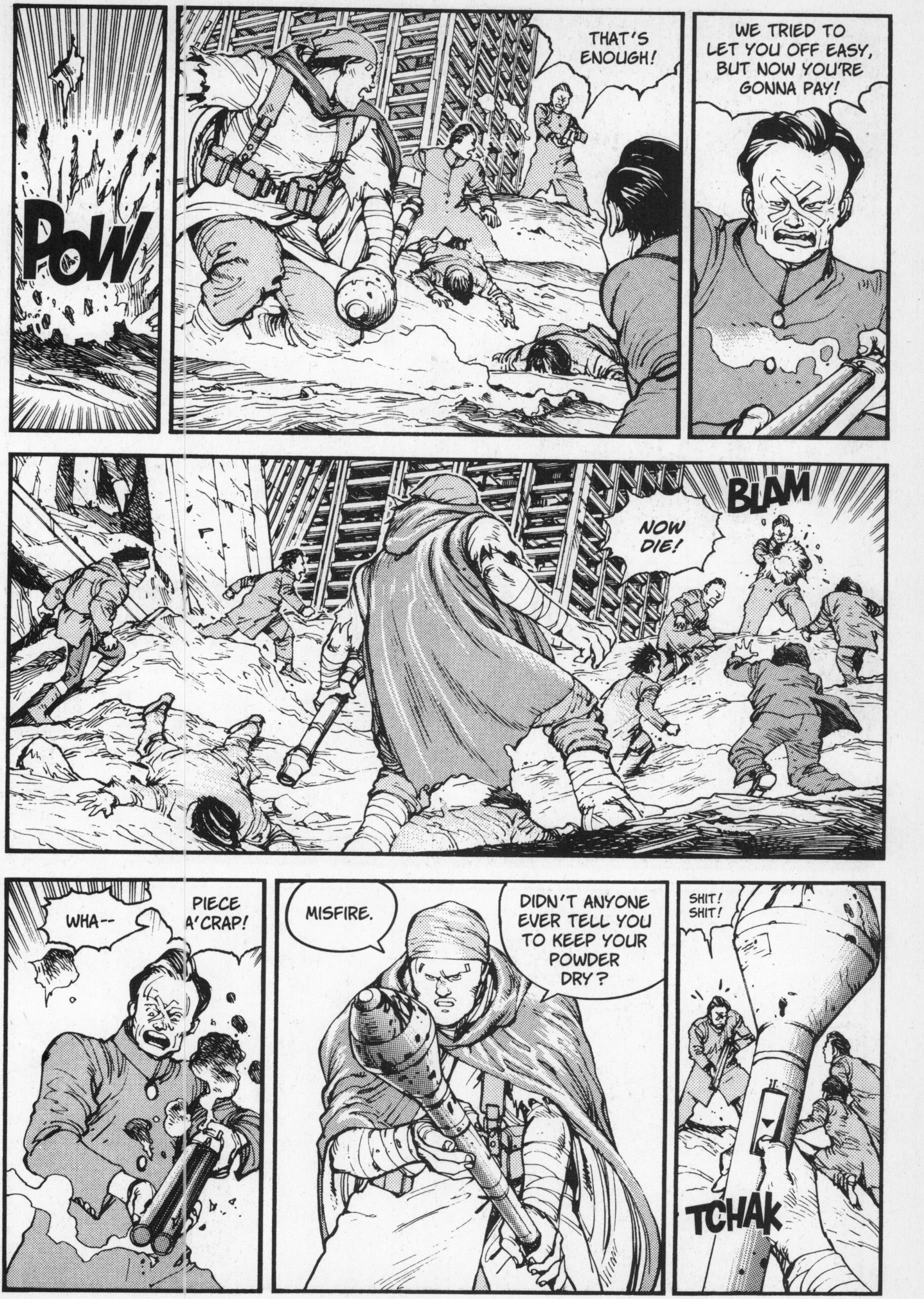
POW
THAT'S ENOUGH!
WE TRIED TO LET YOU OFF EASY, BUT NOW YOU'RE GONNA PAY!
BLAM
NOW DIE!
WHA--
PIECE A'CRAP!
MISFIRE.
DIDN'T ANYONE EVER TELL YOU TO KEEP YOUR POWDER DRY?
SHIT! SHIT!
TCHAK

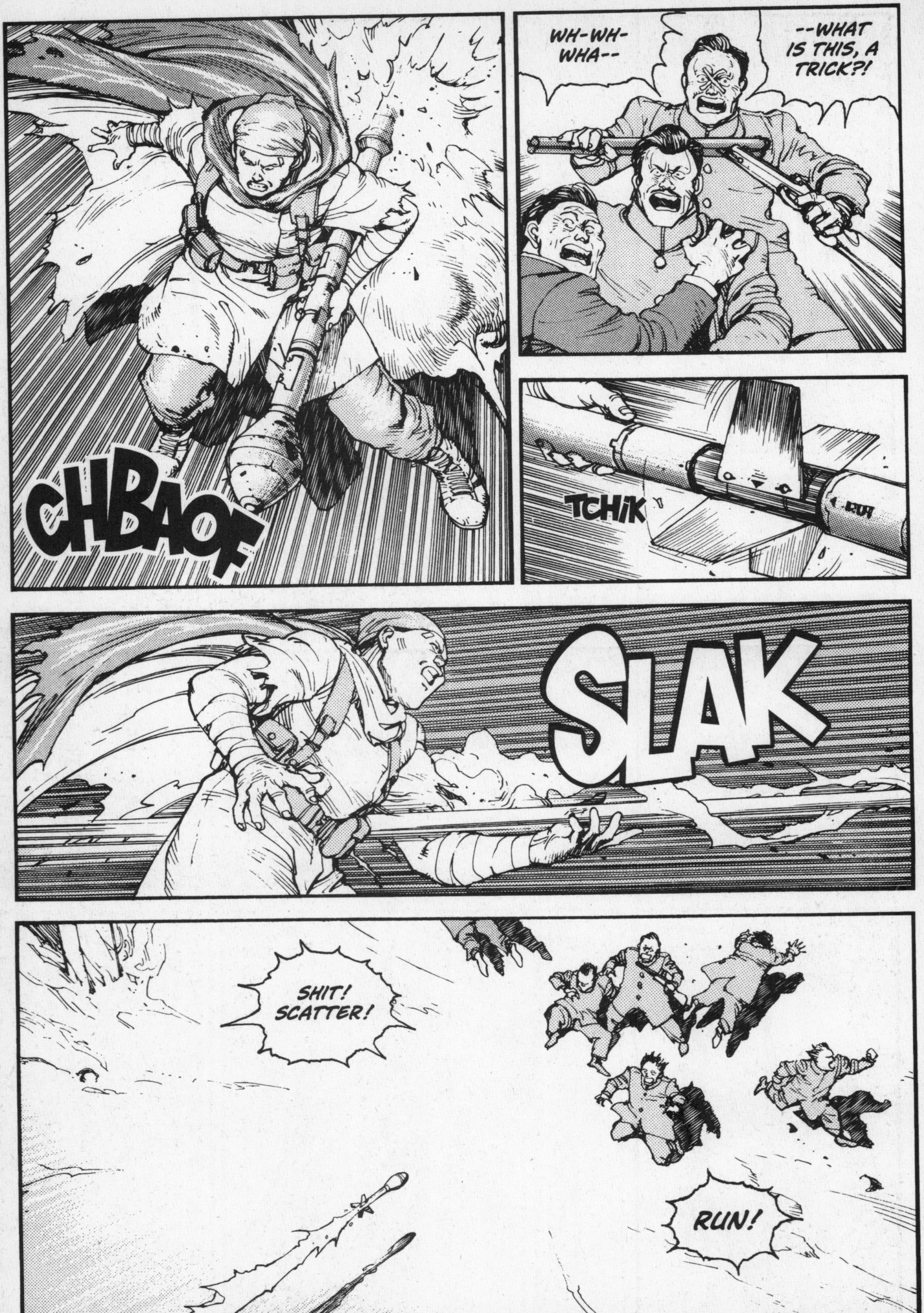
CHBAOF
WH-WH-WHA--
--WHAT IS THIS, A TRICK?!
TCHIK
SLAK
SHIT! SCATTER!
RUN!

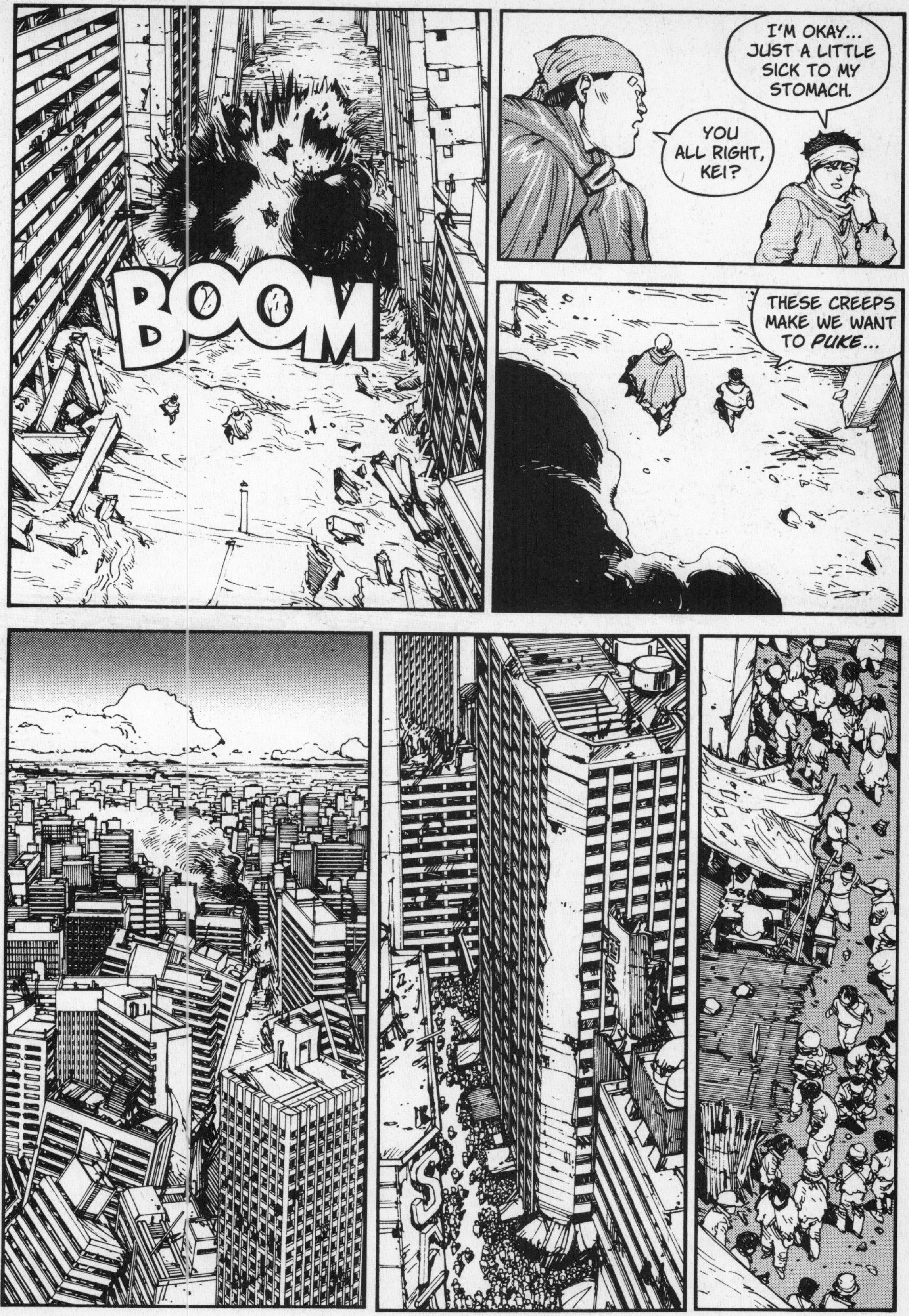
BOOM
YOU ALL RIGHT, KEI?
I'M OKAY... JUST A LITTLE SICK TO MY STOMACH.
THESE CREEPS MAKE WE WANT TO *PUKE*...

WELCOME! COME RIGHT IN! THE BEST BAR IN THE CITY!

SHALL WE TAKE A LITTLE BREAK?

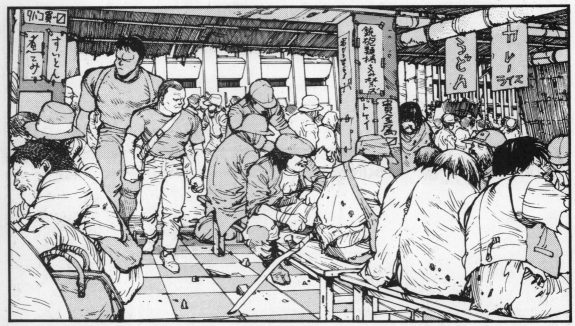

BARKEEP! COUPLE'A BREWS...

TONK

ONLY HOUSE HOOCH. YOU DON'T DRINK 'TIL YOU PAY, GOT IT?

OKAY... HOW MUCH?

THAT *PAPER'S* NO GOOD AROUND HERE!

WHERE HAVE *YOU* BEEN?

BROM

SHOW ME SOMETHING OF *VALUE*...

SOMETHING LIKE *THESE*...

BLINK

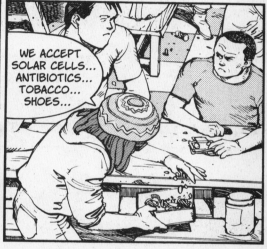

WE ACCEPT SOLAR CELLS... ANTIBIOTICS... TOBACCO... SHOES...

HOW ABOUT...

...THIS?

NOT BAD. YOU'LL EVEN GET SOME *CHANGE*.

KEEP IT. MAYBE YOU CAN TELL ME WHAT'S BEEN GOING ON.

MY FRIEND AND I ARE A LITTLE BEHIND THE TIMES. WE ONLY CAME OUT OF THE SHELTER YESTERDAY.

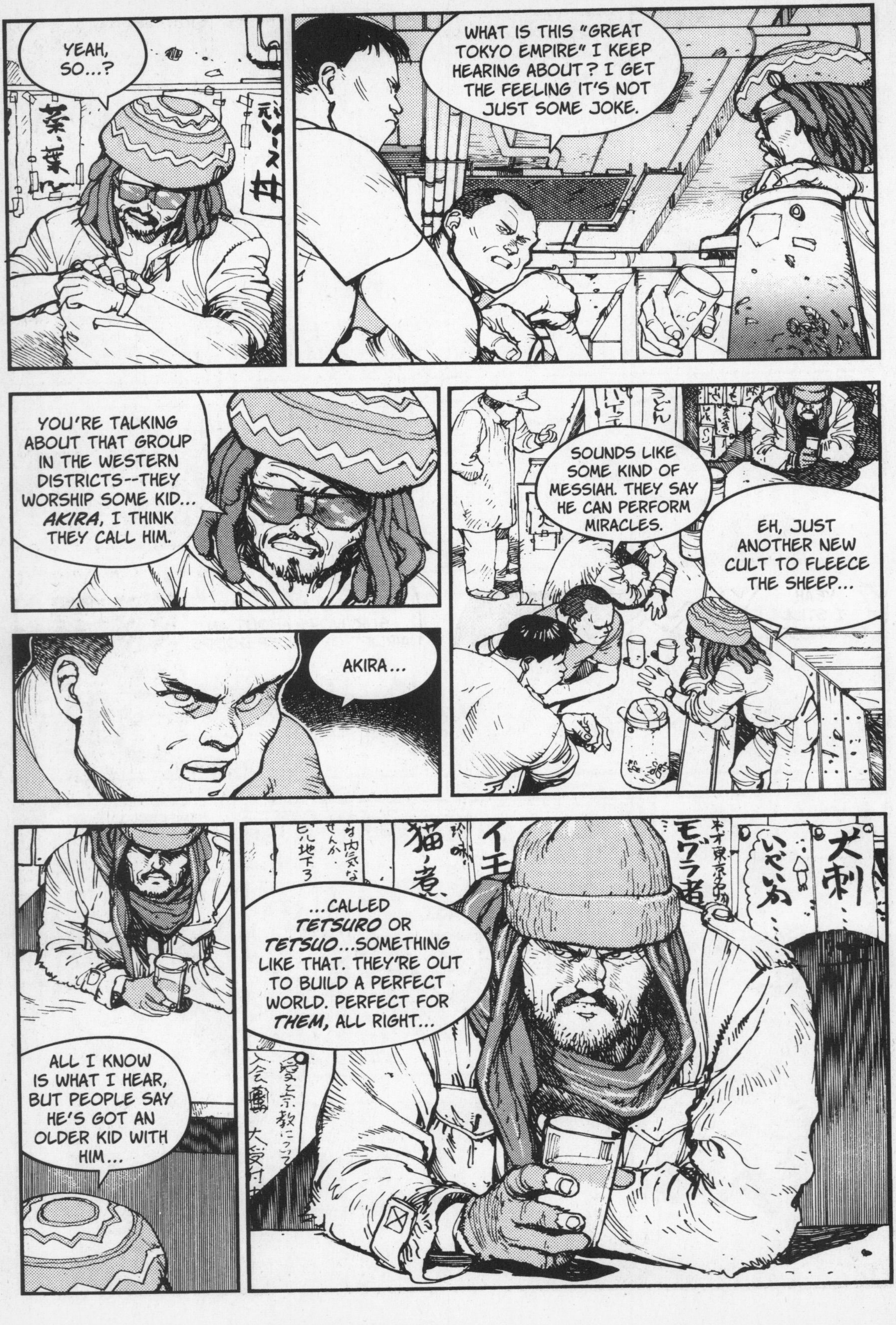
YEAH, SO...?
WHAT IS THIS "GREAT TOKYO EMPIRE" I KEEP HEARING ABOUT? I GET THE FEELING IT'S NOT JUST SOME JOKE.
YOU'RE TALKING ABOUT THAT GROUP IN THE WESTERN DISTRICTS--THEY WORSHIP SOME KID... *AKIRA*, I THINK THEY CALL HIM.
AKIRA...
SOUNDS LIKE SOME KIND OF MESSIAH. THEY SAY HE CAN PERFORM MIRACLES.
EH, JUST ANOTHER NEW CULT TO FLEECE THE SHEEP...
ALL I KNOW IS WHAT I HEAR, BUT PEOPLE SAY HE'S GOT AN OLDER KID WITH HIM...
...CALLED *TETSURO* OR *TETSUO*...SOMETHING LIKE THAT. THEY'RE OUT TO BUILD A PERFECT WORLD. PERFECT FOR *THEM*, ALL RIGHT...

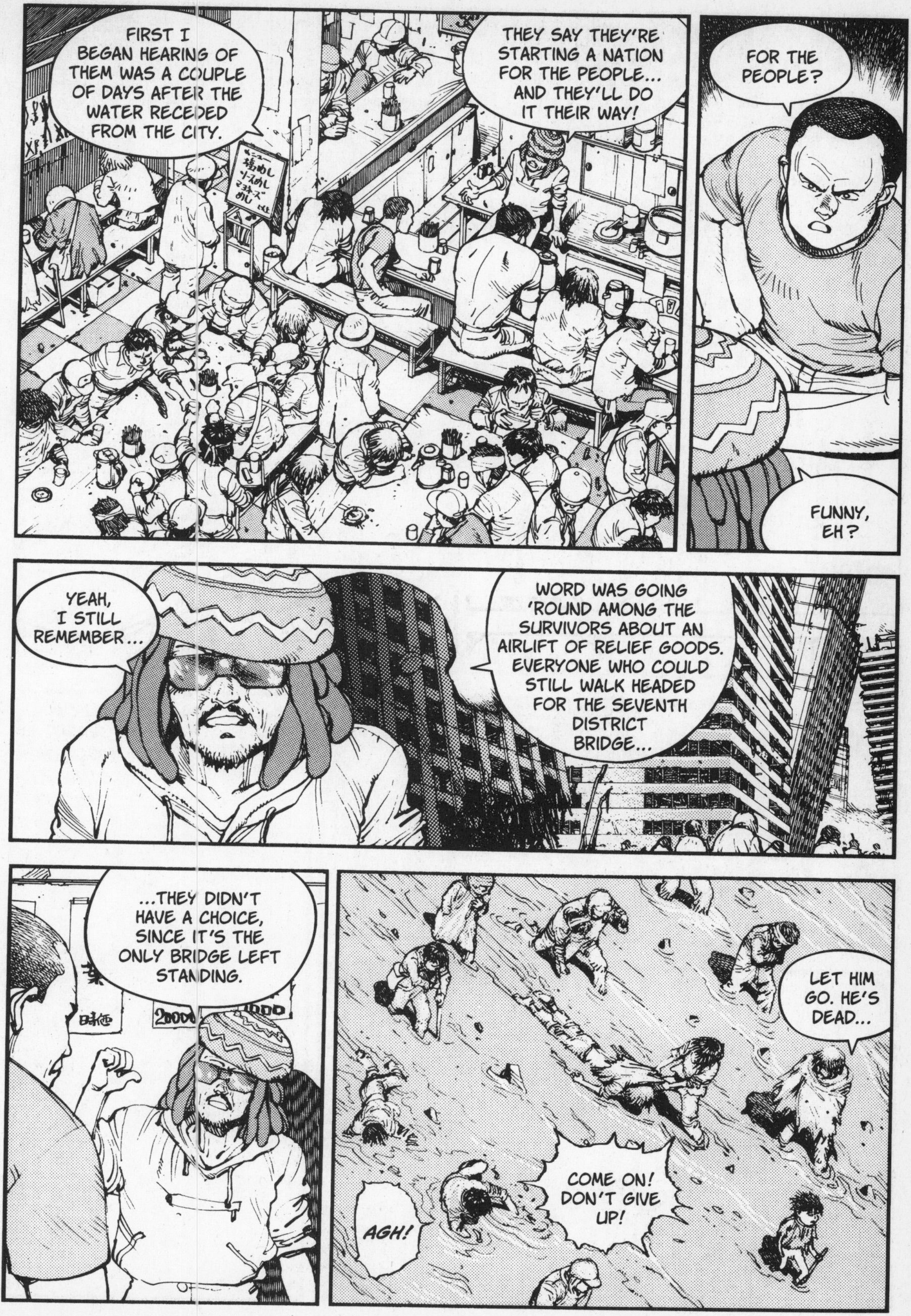
FIRST I BEGAN HEARING OF THEM WAS A COUPLE OF DAYS AFTER THE WATER RECEDED FROM THE CITY.
THEY SAY THEY'RE STARTING A NATION FOR THE PEOPLE... AND THEY'LL DO IT THEIR WAY!
FOR THE PEOPLE?
FUNNY, EH?
YEAH, I STILL REMEMBER...
WORD WAS GOING 'ROUND AMONG THE SURVIVORS ABOUT AN AIRLIFT OF RELIEF GOODS. EVERYONE WHO COULD STILL WALK HEADED FOR THE SEVENTH DISTRICT BRIDGE...
...THEY DIDN'T HAVE A CHOICE, SINCE IT'S THE ONLY BRIDGE LEFT STANDING.
LET HIM GO. HE'S DEAD...
AGH!
COME ON! DON'T GIVE UP!

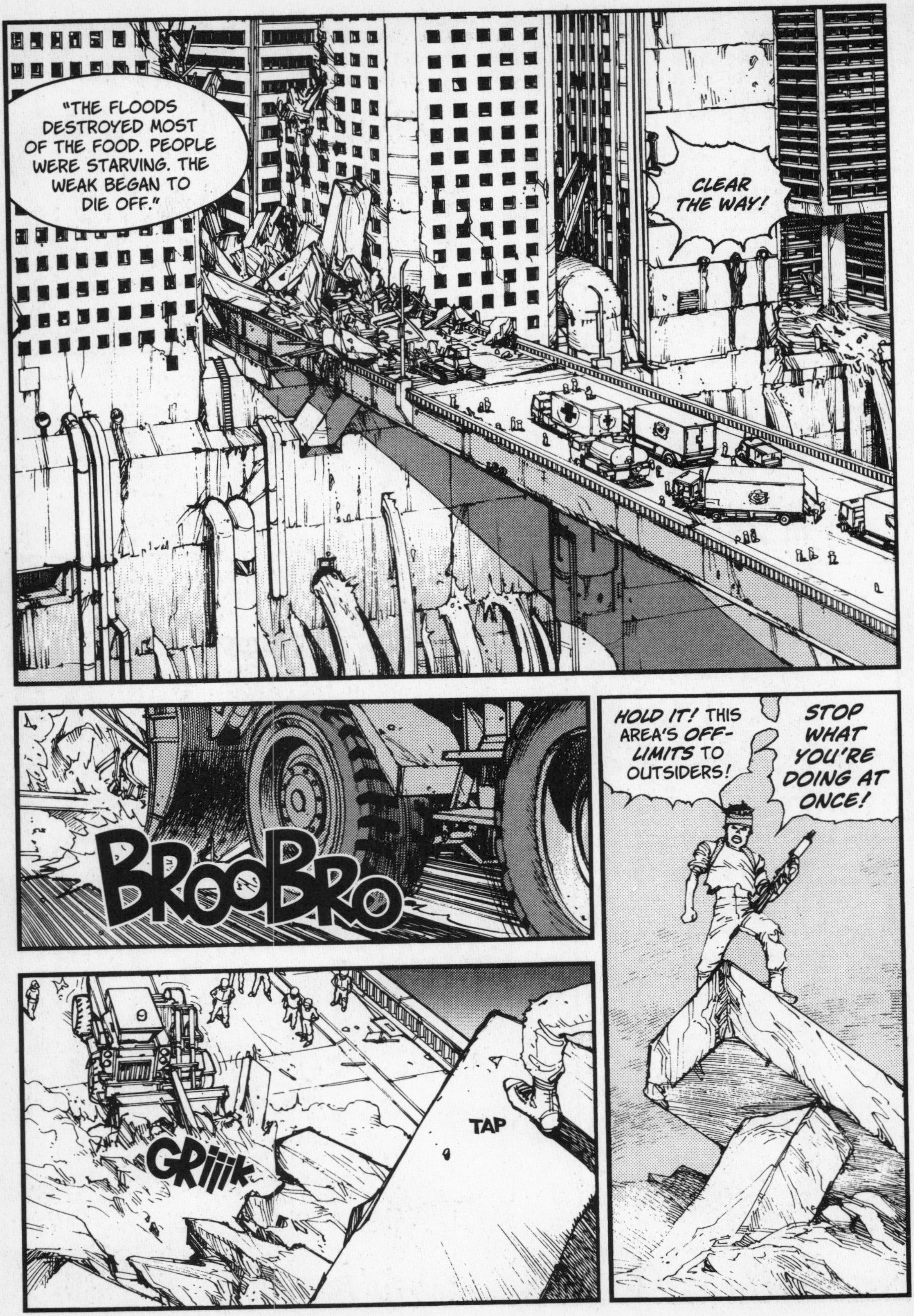
"THE FLOODS DESTROYED MOST OF THE FOOD. PEOPLE WERE STARVING. THE WEAK BEGAN TO DIE OFF."
CLEAR THE WAY!
BROOBRO
HOLD IT! THIS AREA'S OFF-LIMITS TO OUTSIDERS!
STOP WHAT YOU'RE DOING AT ONCE!
GRiiik
TAP

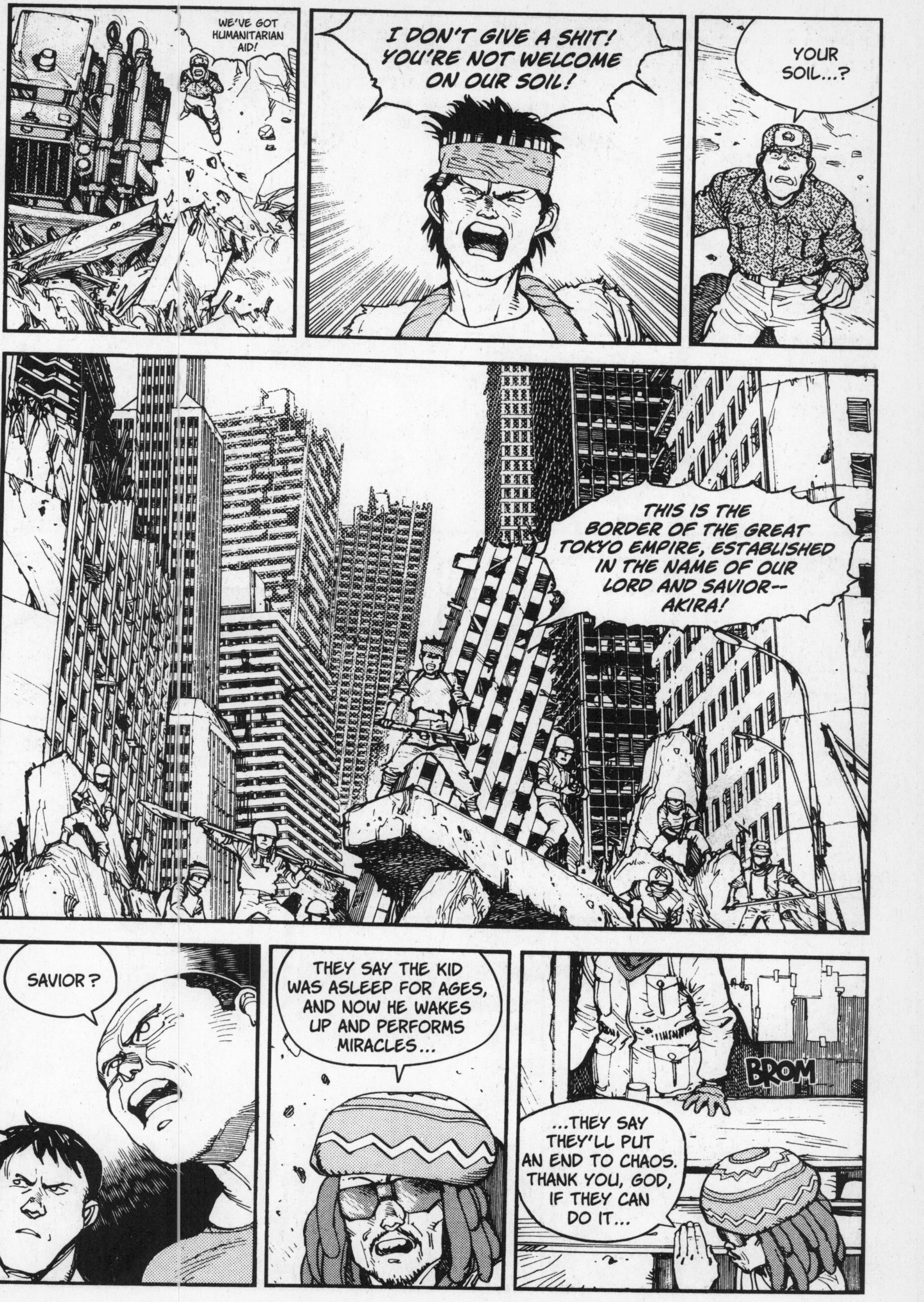

WE'VE GOT HUMANITARIAN AID!
I DON'T GIVE A SHIT! YOU'RE NOT WELCOME ON OUR SOIL!
YOUR SOIL...?
THIS IS THE BORDER OF THE GREAT TOKYO EMPIRE, ESTABLISHED IN THE NAME OF OUR LORD AND SAVIOR-- AKIRA!
SAVIOR?
THEY SAY THE KID WAS ASLEEP FOR AGES, AND NOW HE WAKES UP AND PERFORMS MIRACLES...
BROM
...THEY SAY THEY'LL PUT AN END TO CHAOS. THANK YOU, GOD, IF THEY CAN DO IT...

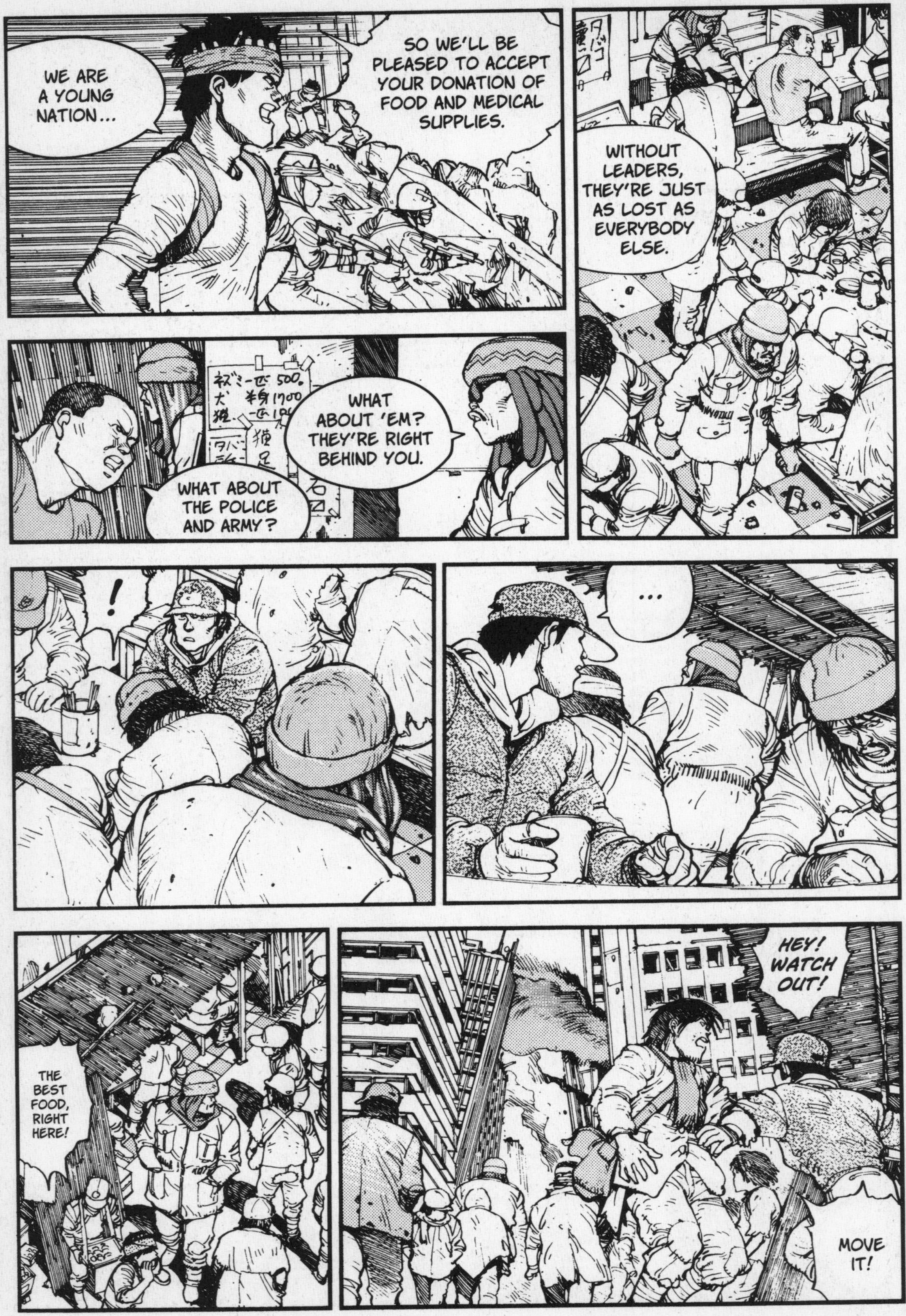
WE ARE A YOUNG NATION...
SO WE'LL BE PLEASED TO ACCEPT YOUR DONATION OF FOOD AND MEDICAL SUPPLIES.
WHAT ABOUT THE POLICE AND ARMY?
WHAT ABOUT 'EM? THEY'RE RIGHT BEHIND YOU.
WITHOUT LEADERS, THEY'RE JUST AS LOST AS EVERYBODY ELSE.
!
...
THE BEST FOOD, RIGHT HERE!
HEY! WATCH OUT!
MOVE IT!

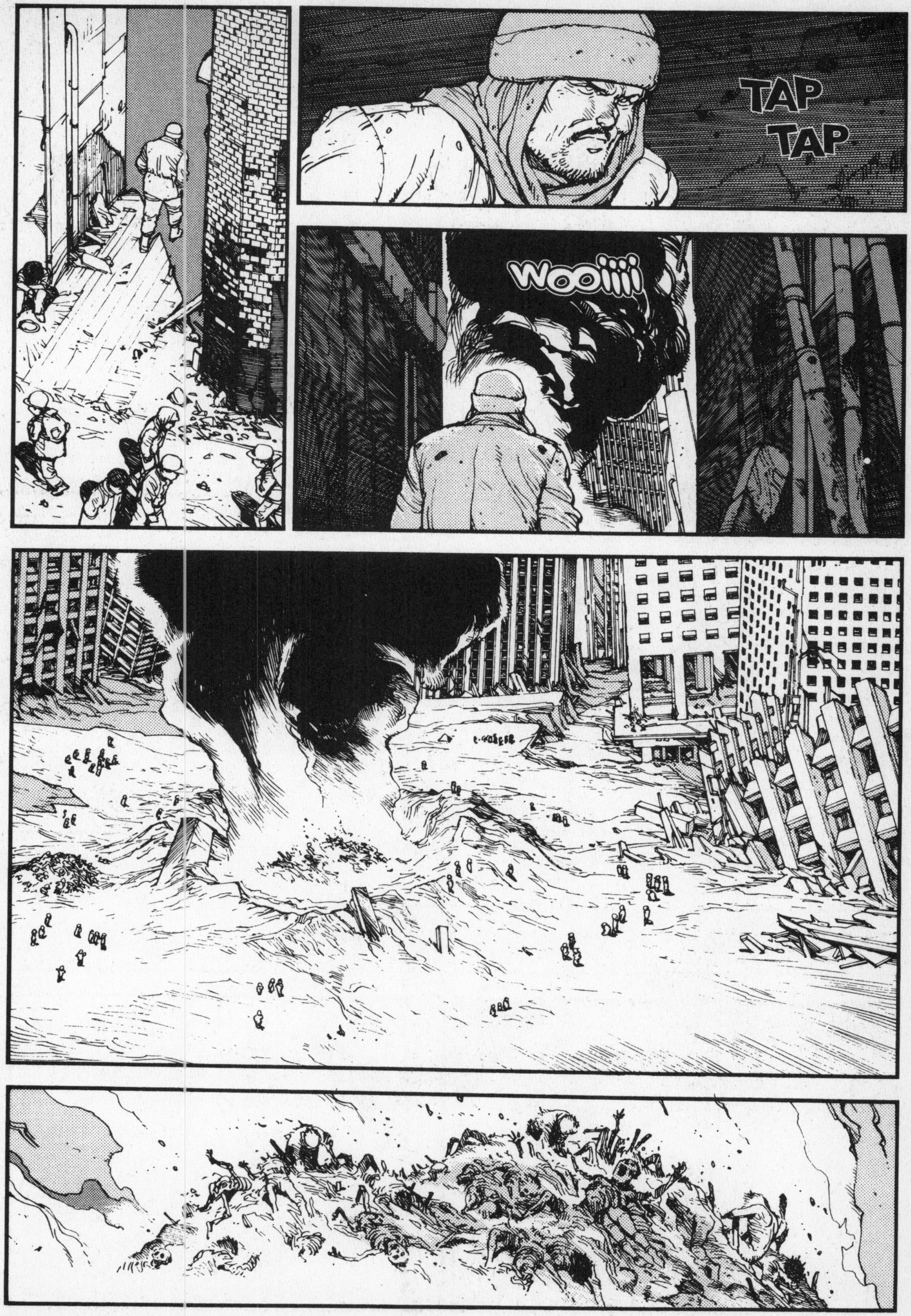
TAP
TAP
Wooiiii

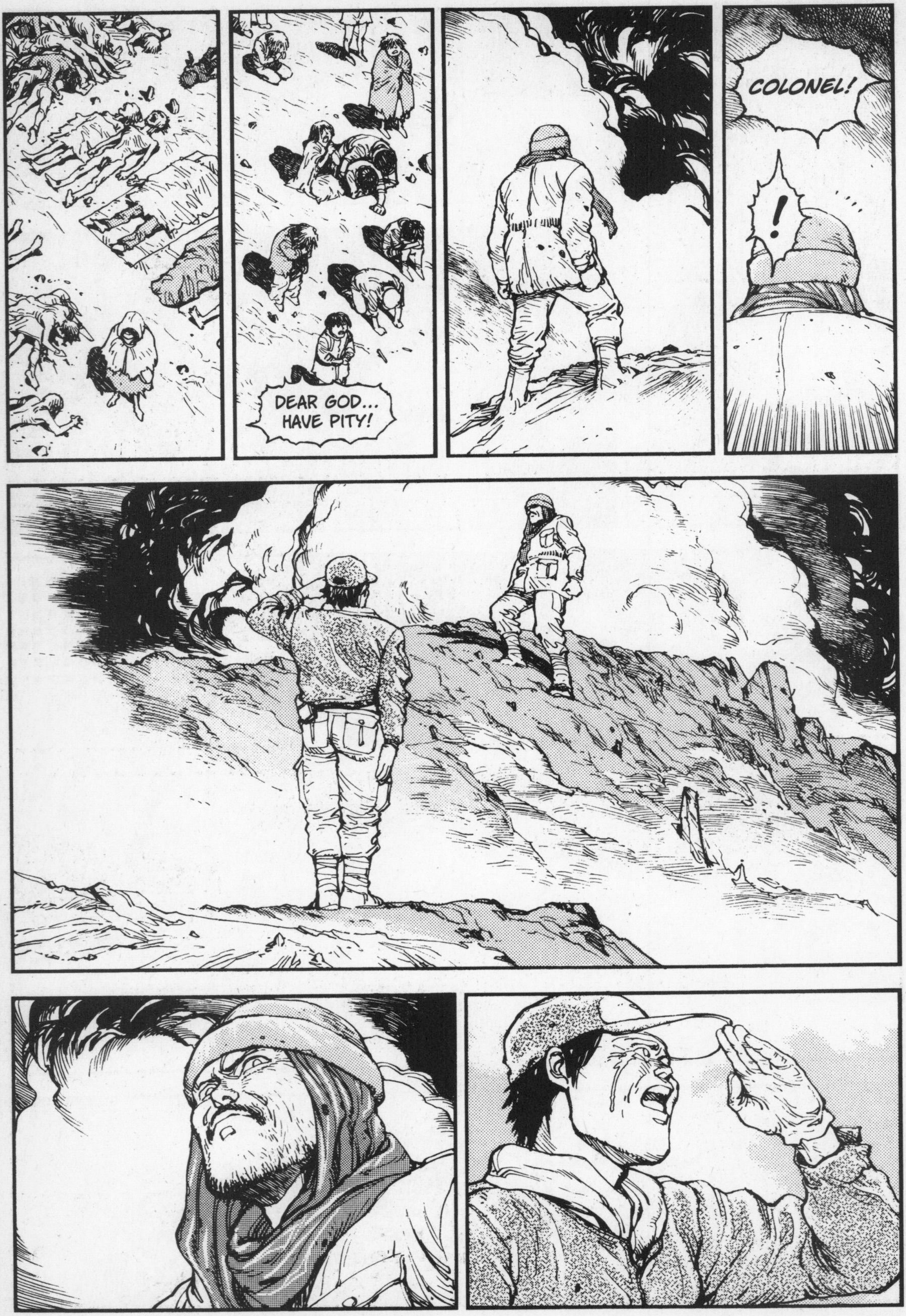
DEAR GOD... HAVE PITY!
COLONEL!
!

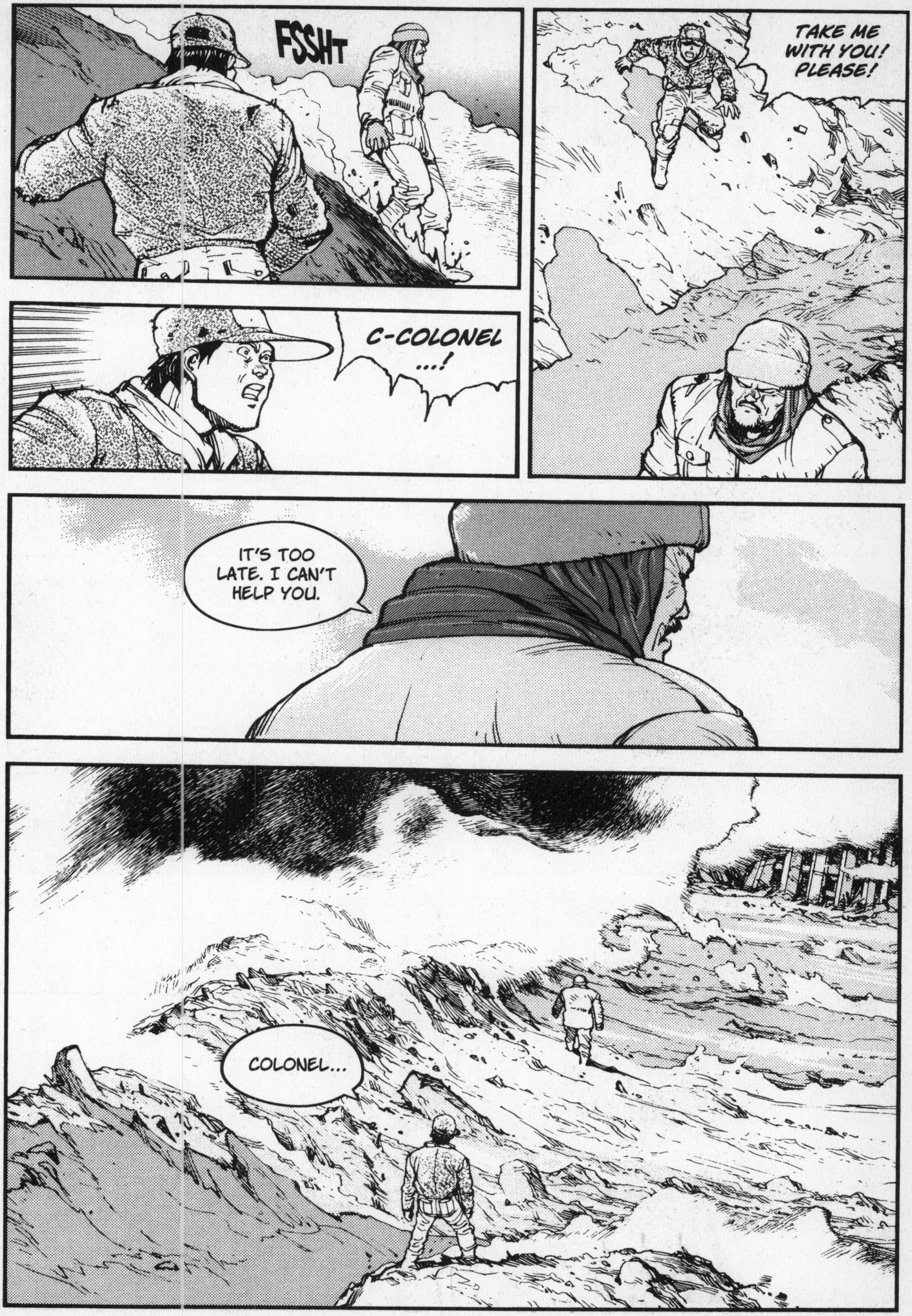
FSSHT
C-COLONEL ...!
TAKE ME WITH YOU! PLEASE!
IT'S TOO LATE. I CAN'T HELP YOU.
COLONEL...

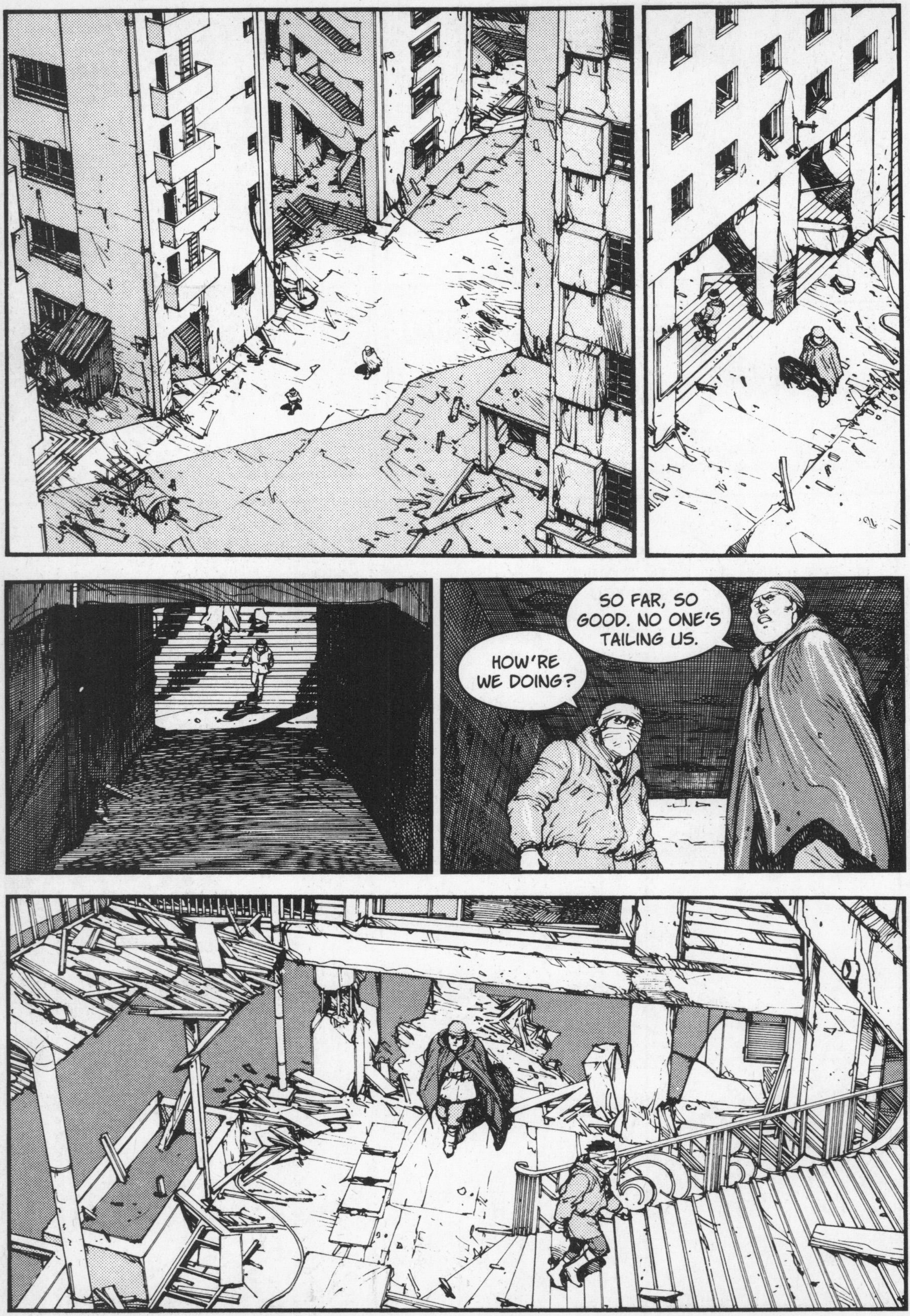
HOW'RE WE DOING?
SO FAR, SO GOOD. NO ONE'S TAILING US.

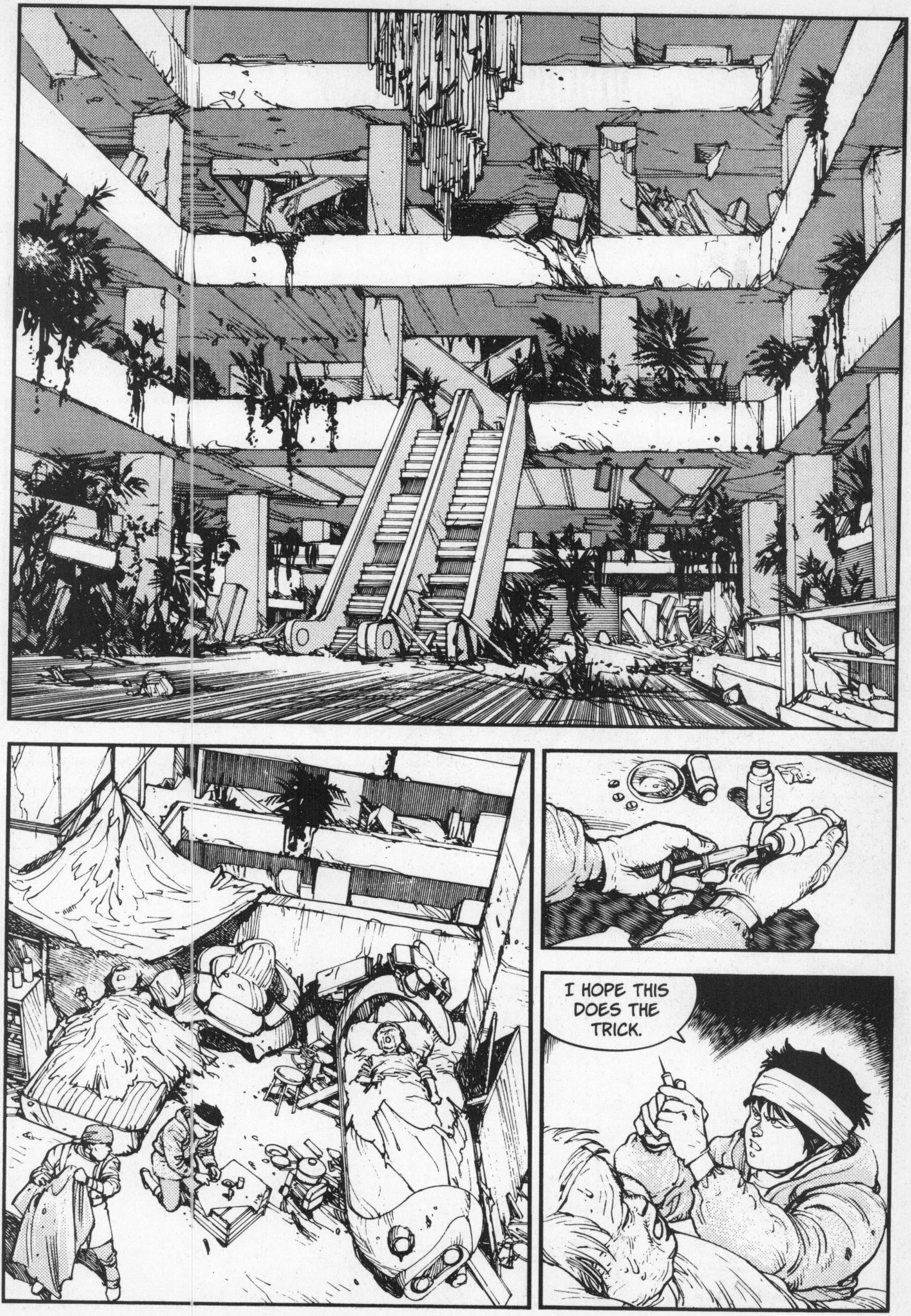
I HOPE THIS DOES THE TRICK.

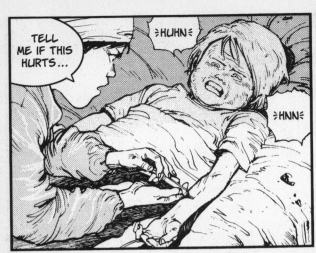

TELL ME IF THIS HURTS...

≶HUHN≶

≶HNN≶

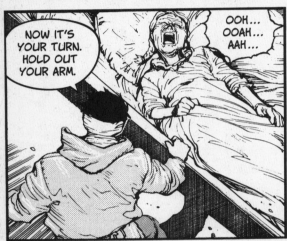

NOW IT'S YOUR TURN. HOLD OUT YOUR ARM.

OOH... OOAH... AAH...

IT'S ALMOST GONE...

THIS IS ALL I HAVE...

WHAT?! WHAT ARE YOU TRYING TO TELL ME?

...N-NU...

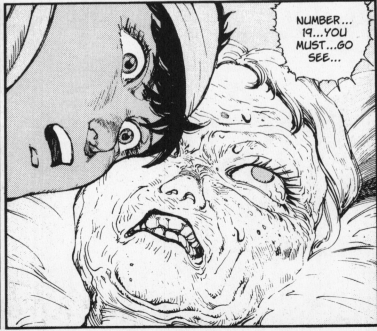

NUMBER... 19...YOU MUST...GO SEE...

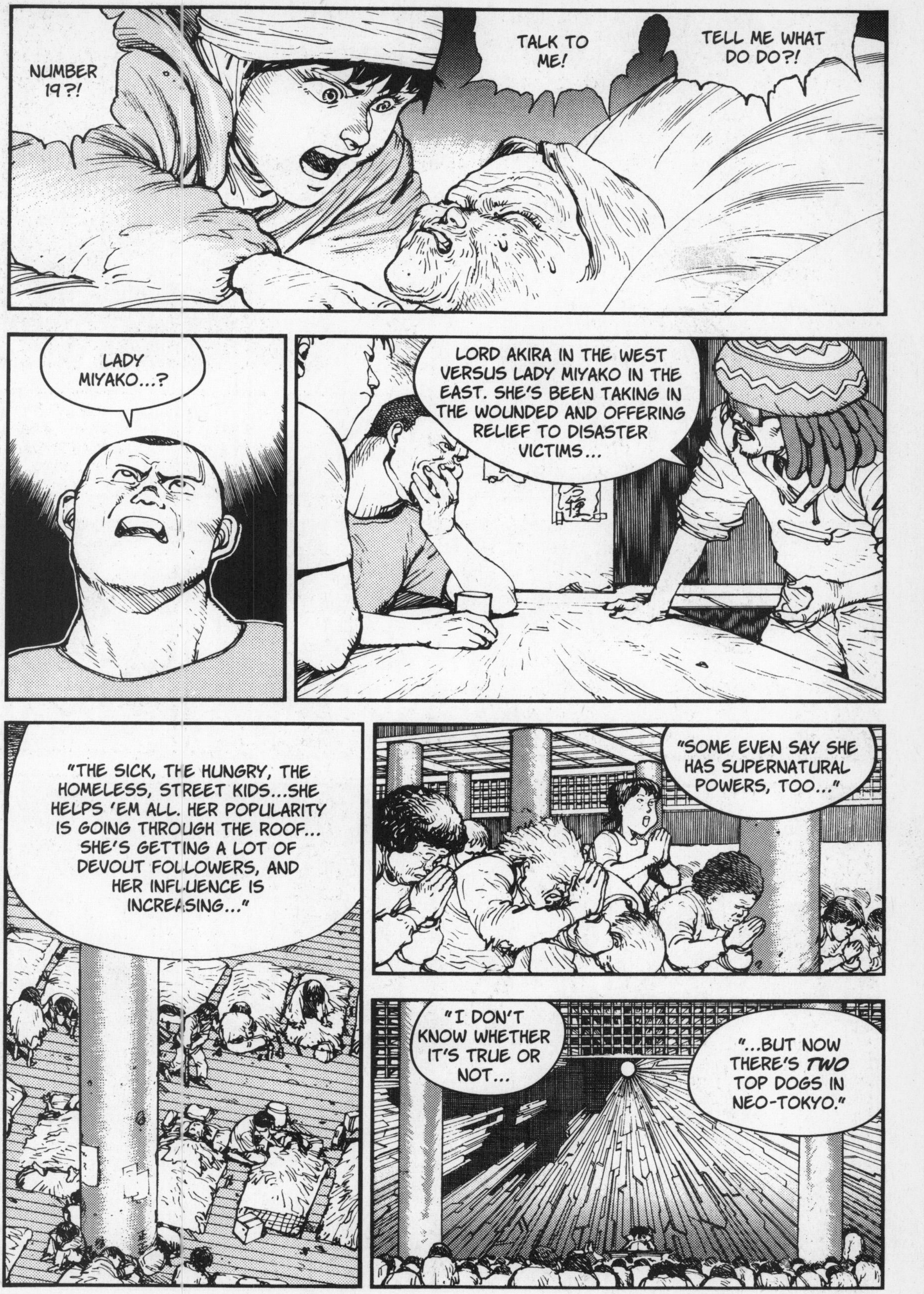
NUMBER 19?!
TALK TO ME!
TELL ME WHAT DO DO?!
LADY MIYAKO...?
LORD AKIRA IN THE WEST VERSUS LADY MIYAKO IN THE EAST. SHE'S BEEN TAKING IN THE WOUNDED AND OFFERING RELIEF TO DISASTER VICTIMS...
"THE SICK, THE HUNGRY, THE HOMELESS, STREET KIDS...SHE HELPS 'EM ALL. HER POPULARITY IS GOING THROUGH THE ROOF... SHE'S GETTING A LOT OF DEVOUT FOLLOWERS, AND HER INFLUENCE IS INCREASING..."
"SOME EVEN SAY SHE HAS SUPERNATURAL POWERS, TOO..."
"I DON'T KNOW WHETHER IT'S TRUE OR NOT...
"...BUT NOW THERE'S *TWO* TOP DOGS IN NEO-TOKYO."

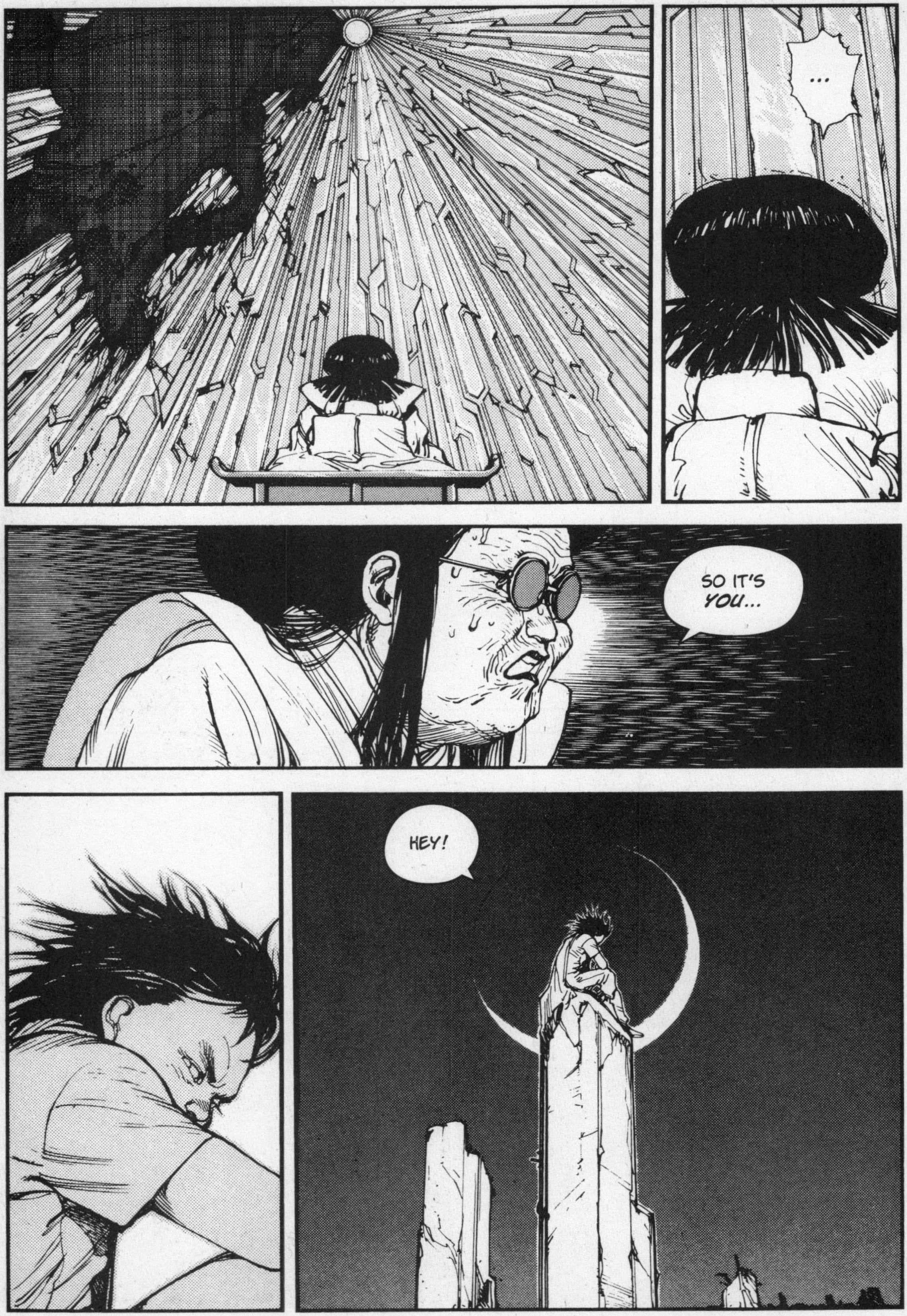
...
SO IT'S YOU...
HEY!

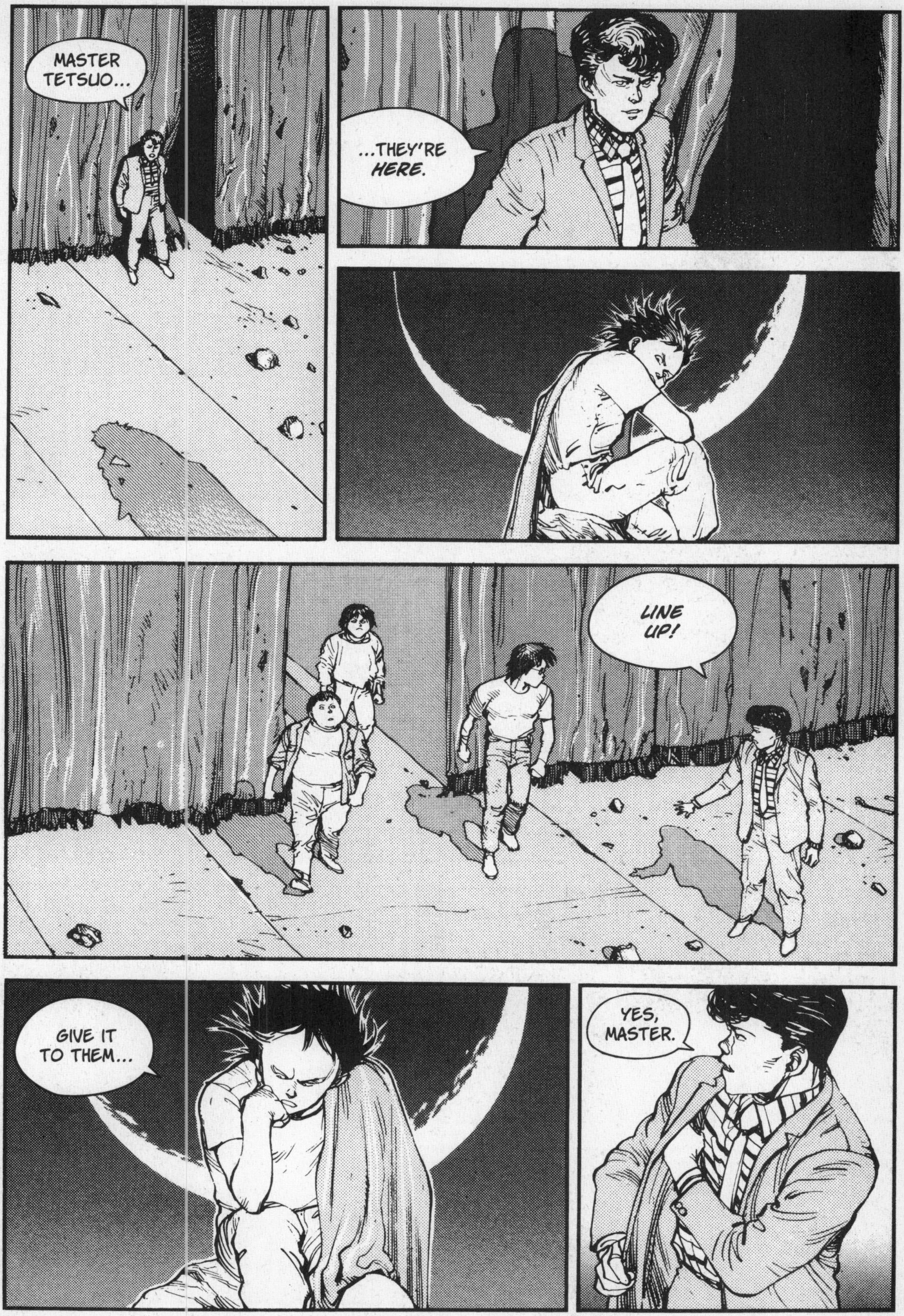
MASTER TETSUO...
...THEY'RE *HERE.*
*LINE UP!*
GIVE IT TO THEM...
YES, MASTER.

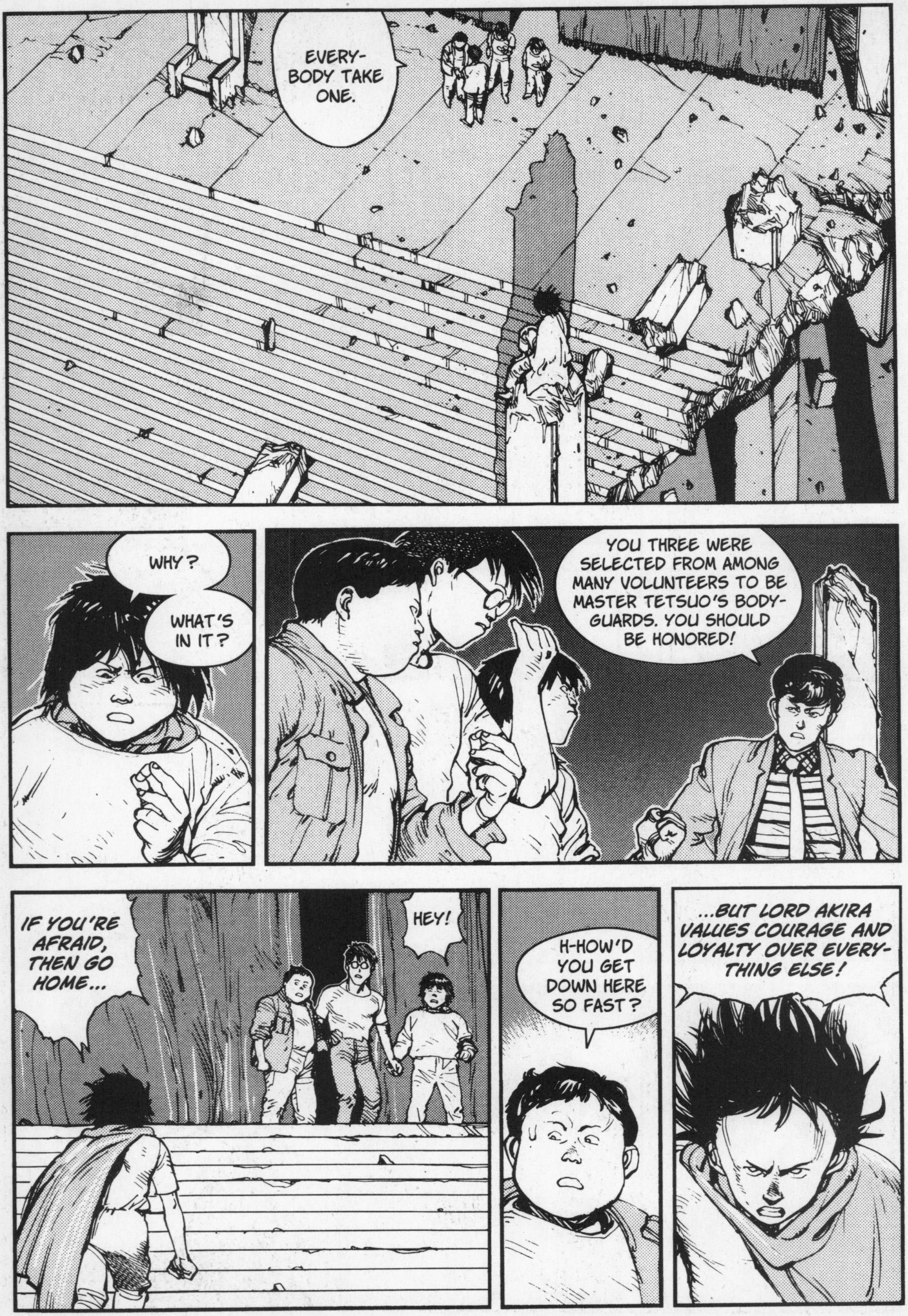
EVERY-BODY TAKE ONE.
WHY?
WHAT'S IN IT?
YOU THREE WERE SELECTED FROM AMONG MANY VOLUNTEERS TO BE MASTER TETSUO'S BODY-GUARDS. YOU SHOULD BE HONORED!
IF YOU'RE AFRAID, THEN GO HOME...
HEY!
H-HOW'D YOU GET DOWN HERE SO FAST?
...BUT LORD AKIRA VALUES COURAGE AND LOYALTY OVER EVERY-THING ELSE!

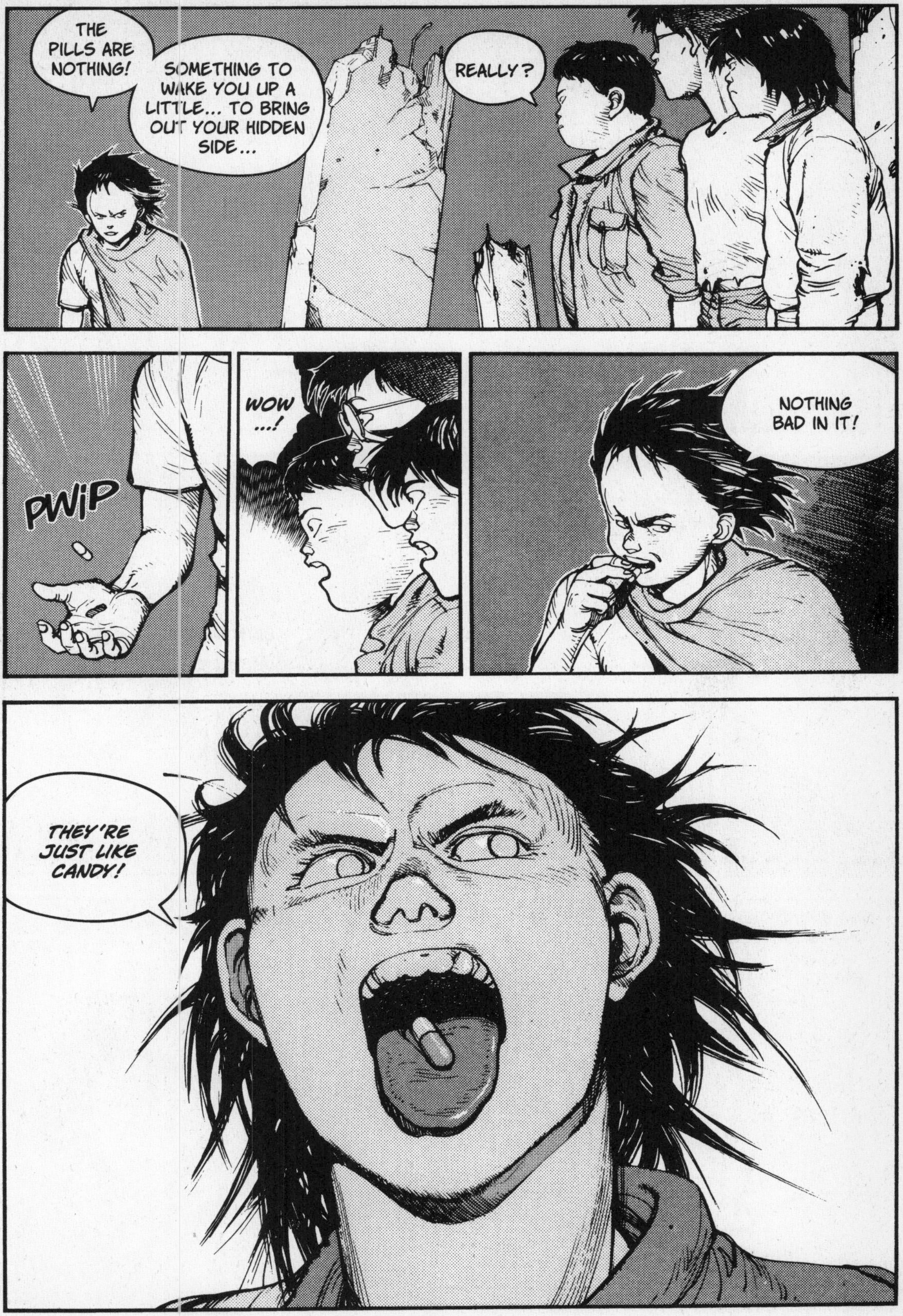
THE PILLS ARE NOTHING!
SOMETHING TO WAKE YOU UP A LITTLE... TO BRING OUT YOUR HIDDEN SIDE...
REALLY?
PWIP
WOW ...!
NOTHING BAD IN IT!
THEY'RE JUST LIKE CANDY!

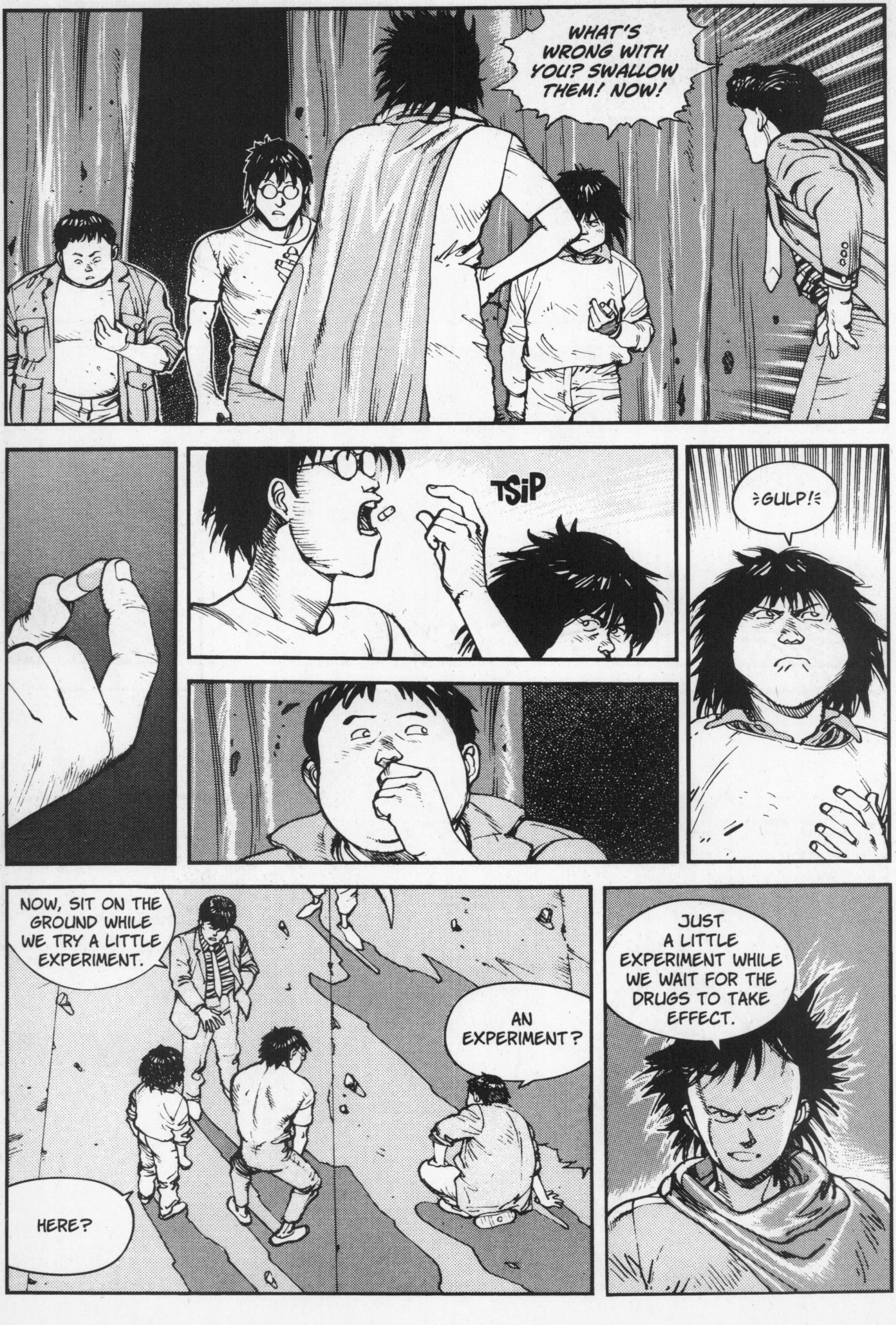
WHAT'S WRONG WITH YOU? SWALLOW THEM! NOW!
TSIP
GULP!
NOW, SIT ON THE GROUND WHILE WE TRY A LITTLE EXPERIMENT.
AN EXPERIMENT?
HERE?
JUST A LITTLE EXPERIMENT WHILE WE WAIT FOR THE DRUGS TO TAKE EFFECT.

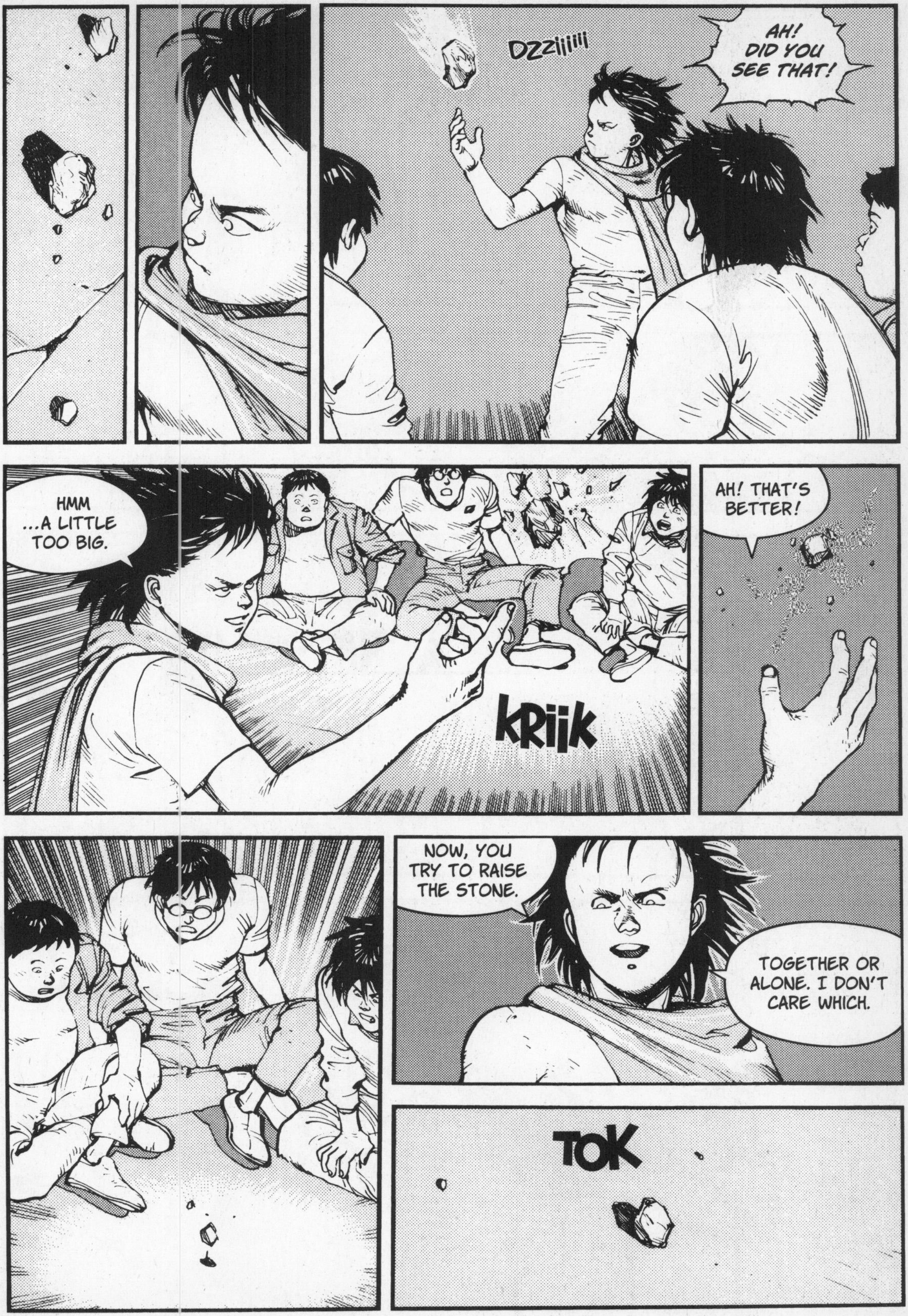
DZZIIIIII
AH! DID YOU SEE THAT!
HMM ...A LITTLE TOO BIG.
KRIIK
AH! THAT'S BETTER!
NOW, YOU TRY TO RAISE THE STONE.
TOGETHER OR ALONE. I DON'T CARE WHICH.
TOK

EMPTY YOUR MIND. TRY TO FOCUS THE POWER OF YOUR SPIRIT.

MMMMM... HMM...

THERE'S NO WAY TO DO THAT WITHOUT TOUCHING IT, GUYS.

HMMM...

I MEAN, SURE, I'VE BENT A SPOON OR TWO IN MY TIME, BUT A STONE--

≥UHN≥

DOOM

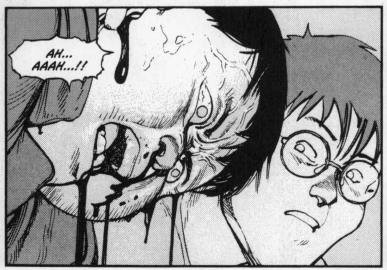

AH... AAAH...!!

DODOM

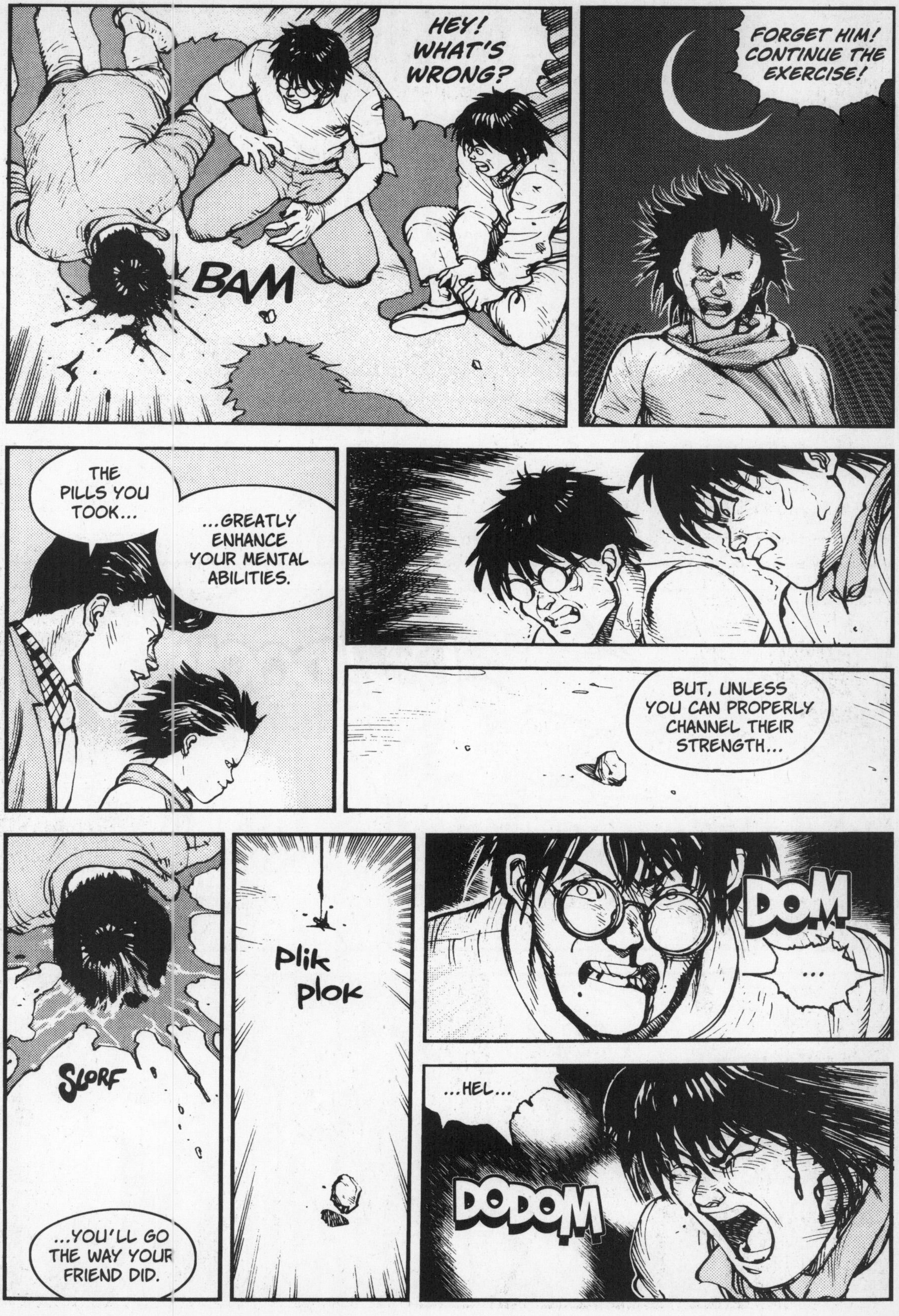
HEY! WHAT'S WRONG?
BAM
FORGET HIM! CONTINUE THE EXERCISE!
THE PILLS YOU TOOK...
...GREATLY ENHANCE YOUR MENTAL ABILITIES.
BUT, UNLESS YOU CAN PROPERLY CHANNEL THEIR STRENGTH...
SLORF
...YOU'LL GO THE WAY YOUR FRIEND DID.
plik plok
DOM
...
...HEL...
DODOM

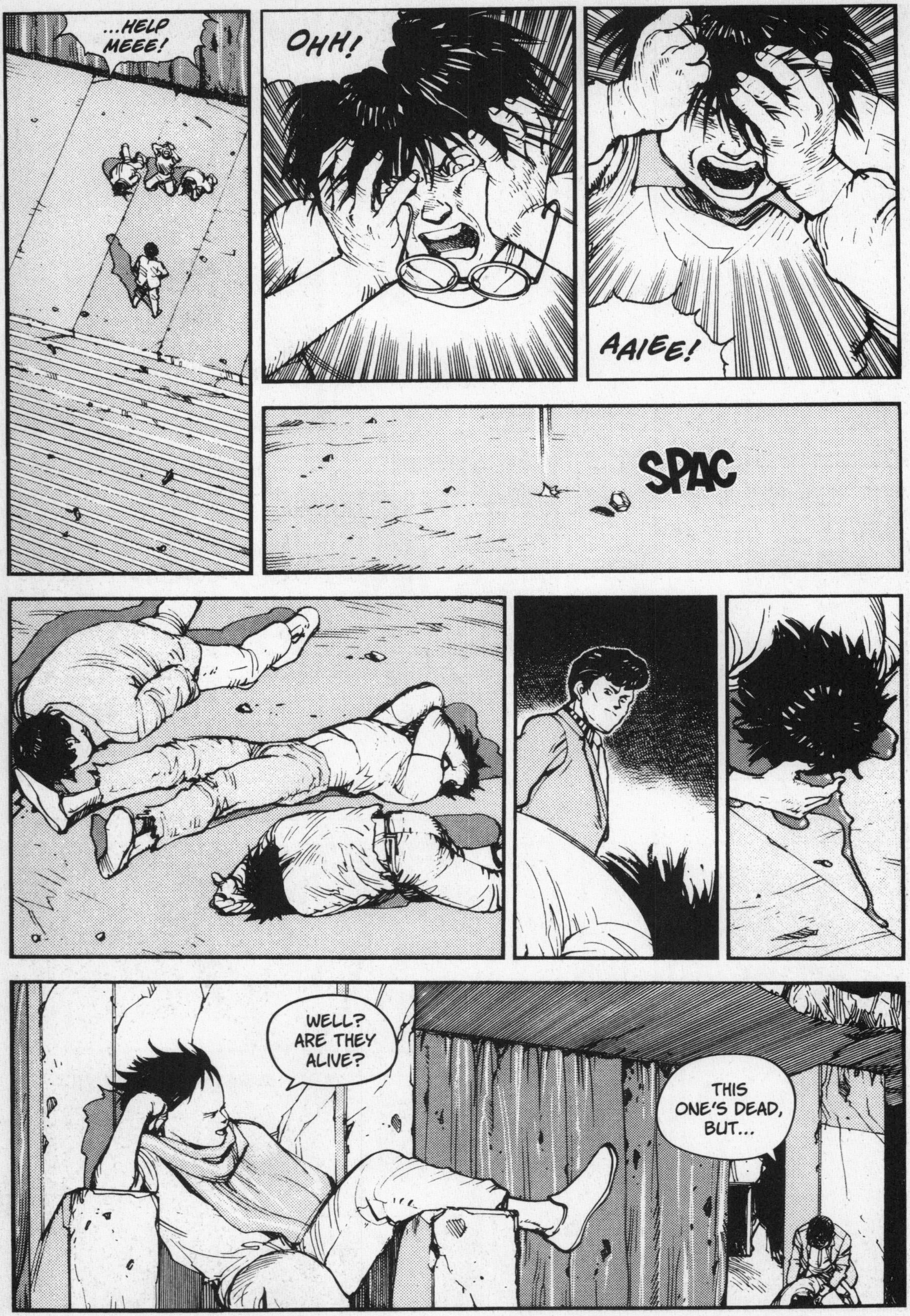
...HELP MEEE!
OHH!
AAIEE!
SPAC
WELL? ARE THEY ALIVE?
THIS ONE'S DEAD, BUT...

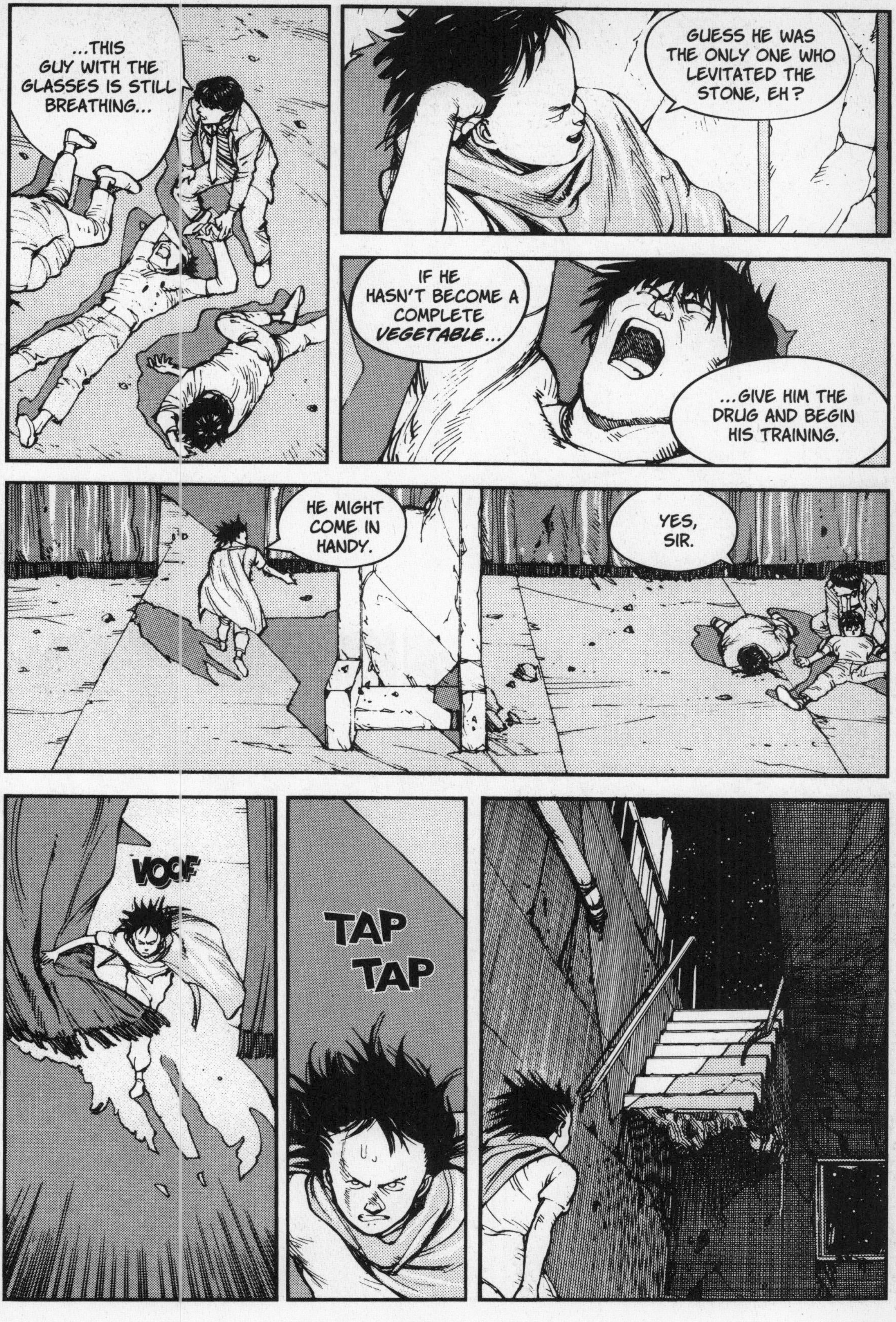
...THIS GUY WITH THE GLASSES IS STILL BREATHING...
GUESS HE WAS THE ONLY ONE WHO LEVITATED THE STONE, EH?
IF HE HASN'T BECOME A COMPLETE *VEGETABLE*...
...GIVE HIM THE DRUG AND BEGIN HIS TRAINING.
HE MIGHT COME IN HANDY.
YES, SIR.
VOOF
TAP
TAP

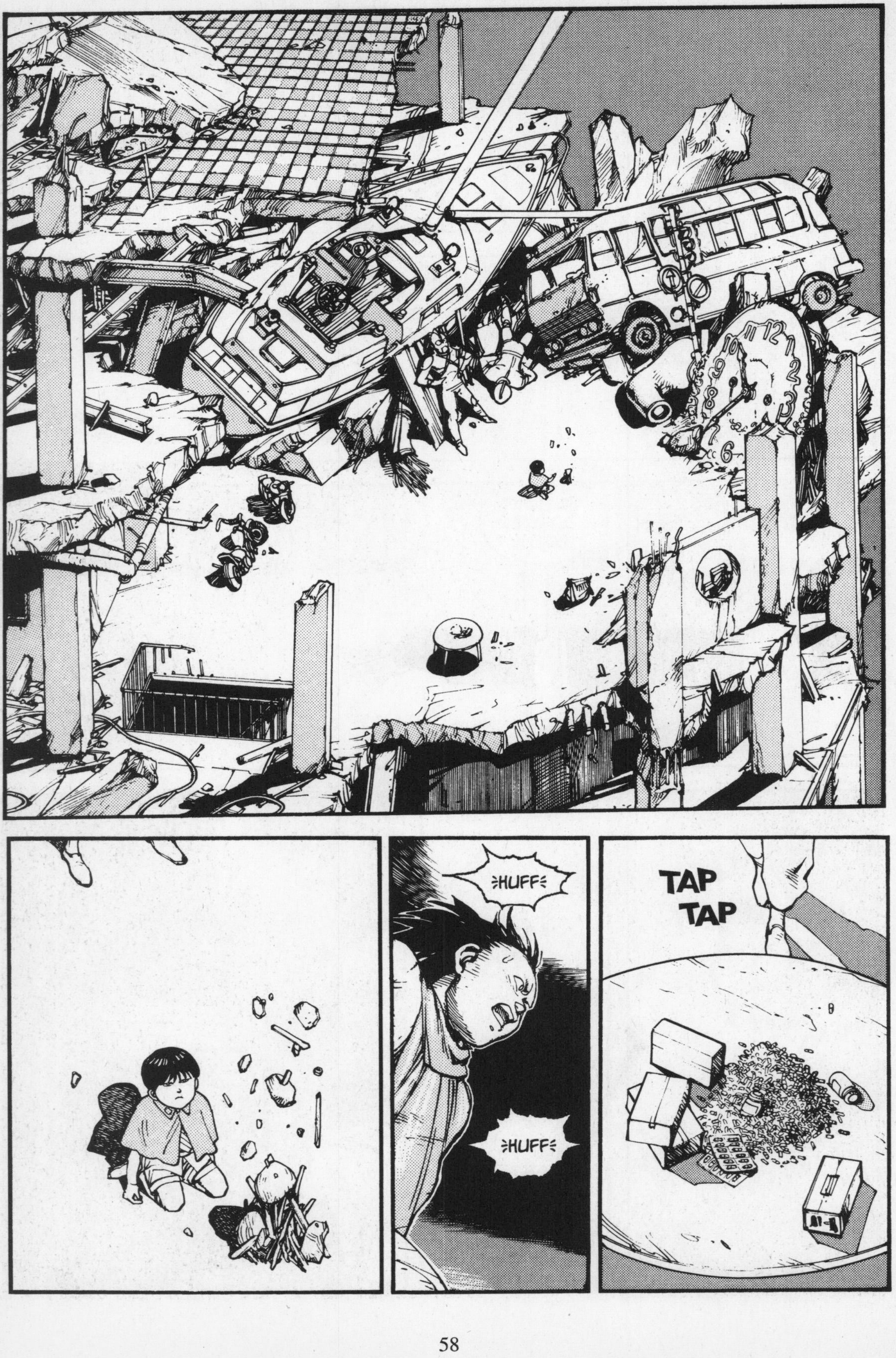
HUFF
HUFF
TAP
TAP

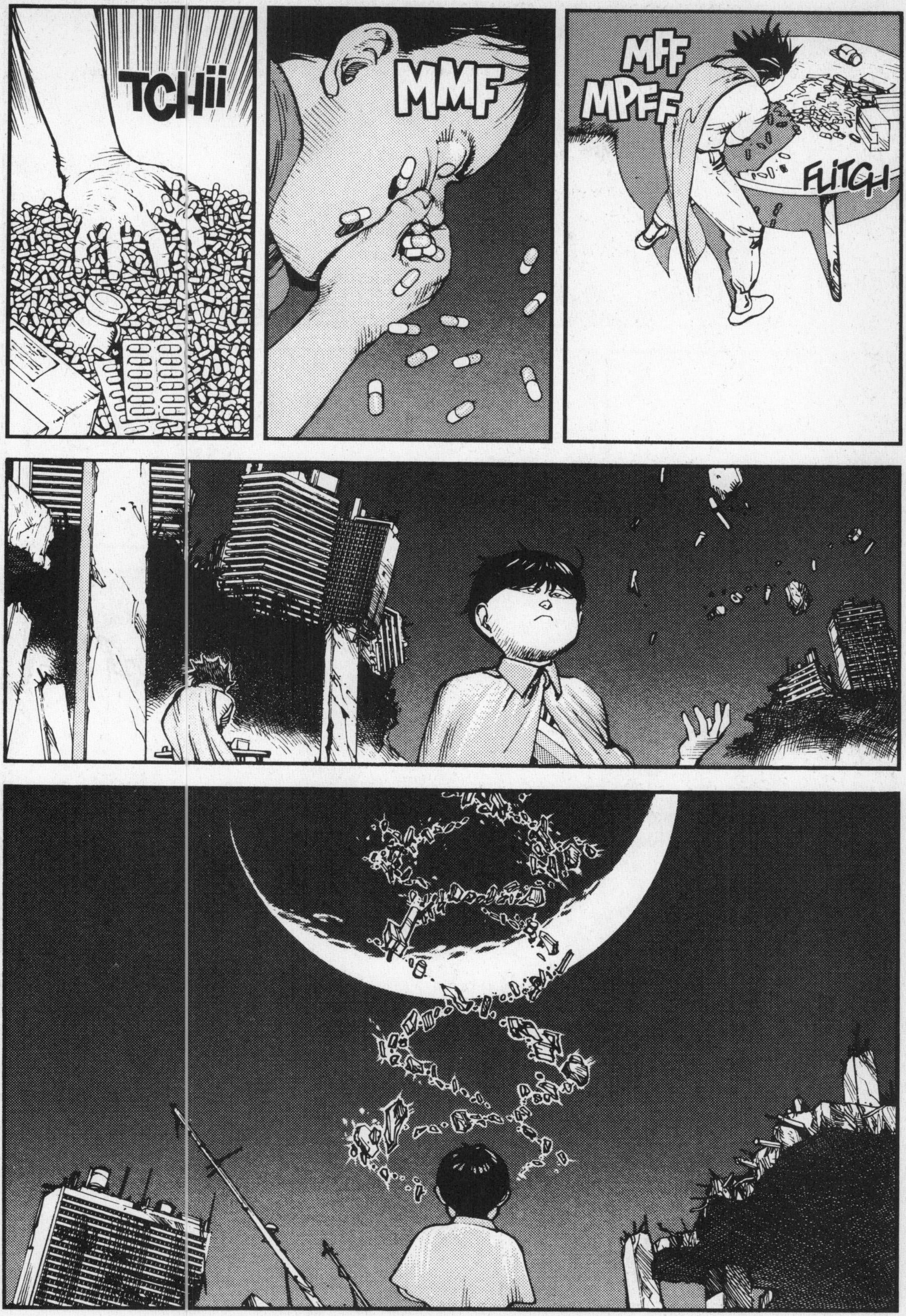
TCHii
MMF
MFF
MPFF
FLITCH

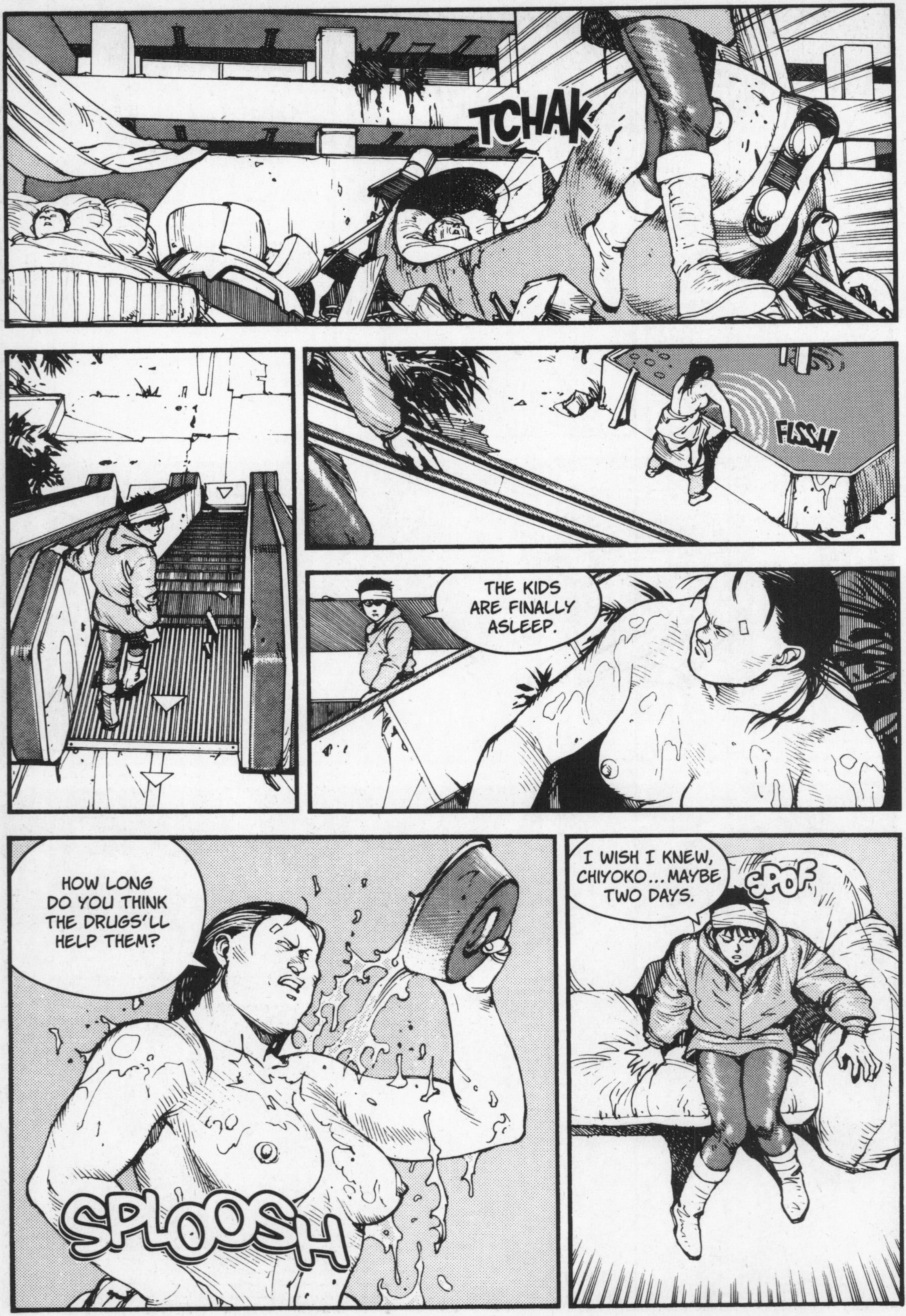
TCHAK
FLSSH
THE KIDS ARE FINALLY ASLEEP.
HOW LONG DO YOU THINK THE DRUGS'LL HELP THEM?
SPLOOSH
I WISH I KNEW, CHIYOKO... MAYBE TWO DAYS.
SPOF

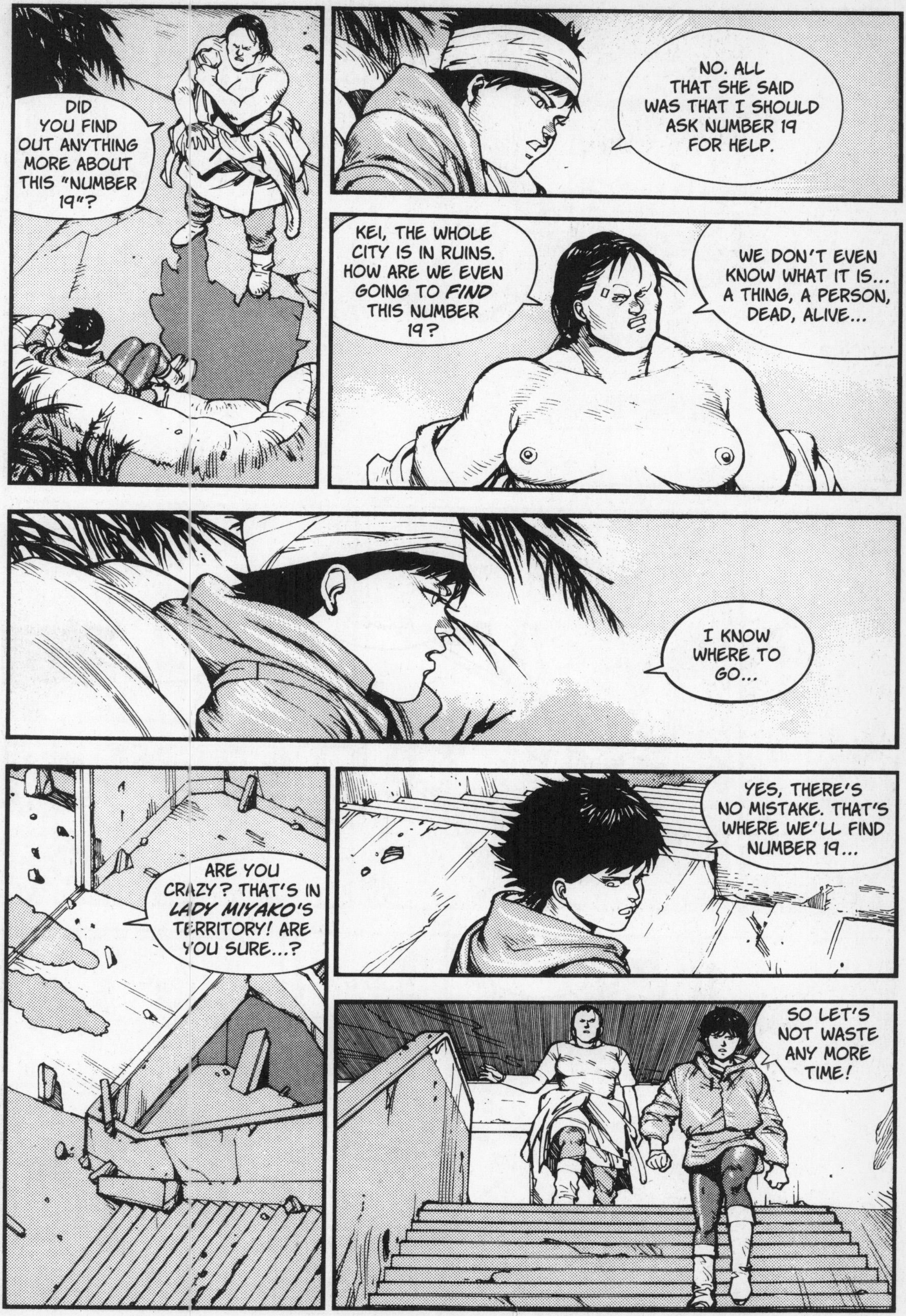
DID YOU FIND OUT ANYTHING MORE ABOUT THIS "NUMBER 19"?
NO. ALL THAT SHE SAID WAS THAT I SHOULD ASK NUMBER 19 FOR HELP.
KEI, THE WHOLE CITY IS IN RUINS. HOW ARE WE EVEN GOING TO FIND THIS NUMBER 19?
WE DON'T EVEN KNOW WHAT IT IS... A THING, A PERSON, DEAD, ALIVE...
I KNOW WHERE TO GO...
ARE YOU CRAZY? THAT'S IN LADY MIYAKO'S TERRITORY! ARE YOU SURE...?
YES, THERE'S NO MISTAKE. THAT'S WHERE WE'LL FIND NUMBER 19...
SO LET'S NOT WASTE ANY MORE TIME!

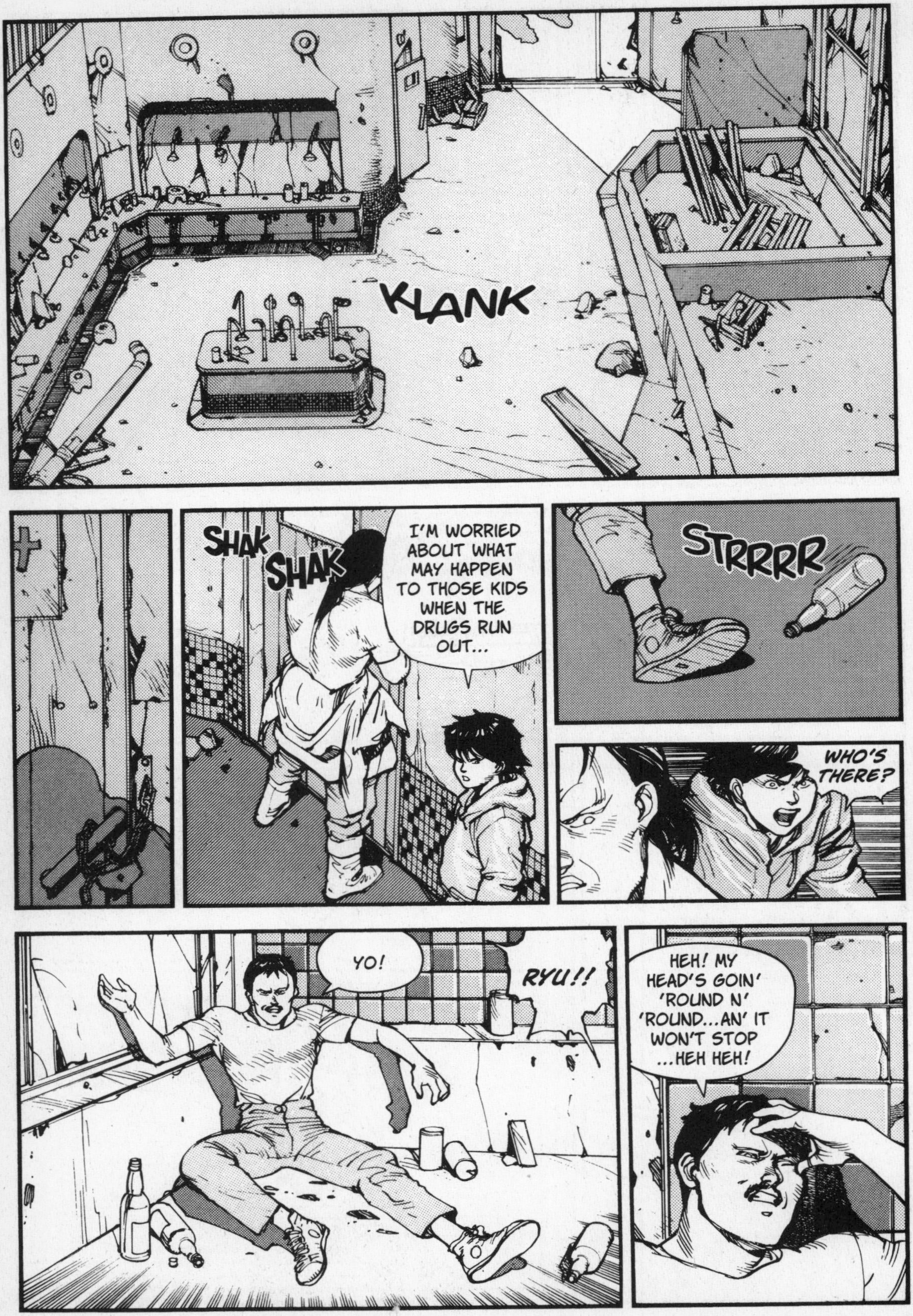
KLANK
SHAK SHAK
I'M WORRIED ABOUT WHAT MAY HAPPEN TO THOSE KIDS WHEN THE DRUGS RUN OUT...
STRRRR
WHO'S THERE?
YO!
RYU!!
HEH! MY HEAD'S GOIN' 'ROUND N' 'ROUND...AN' IT WON'T STOP ...HEH HEH!

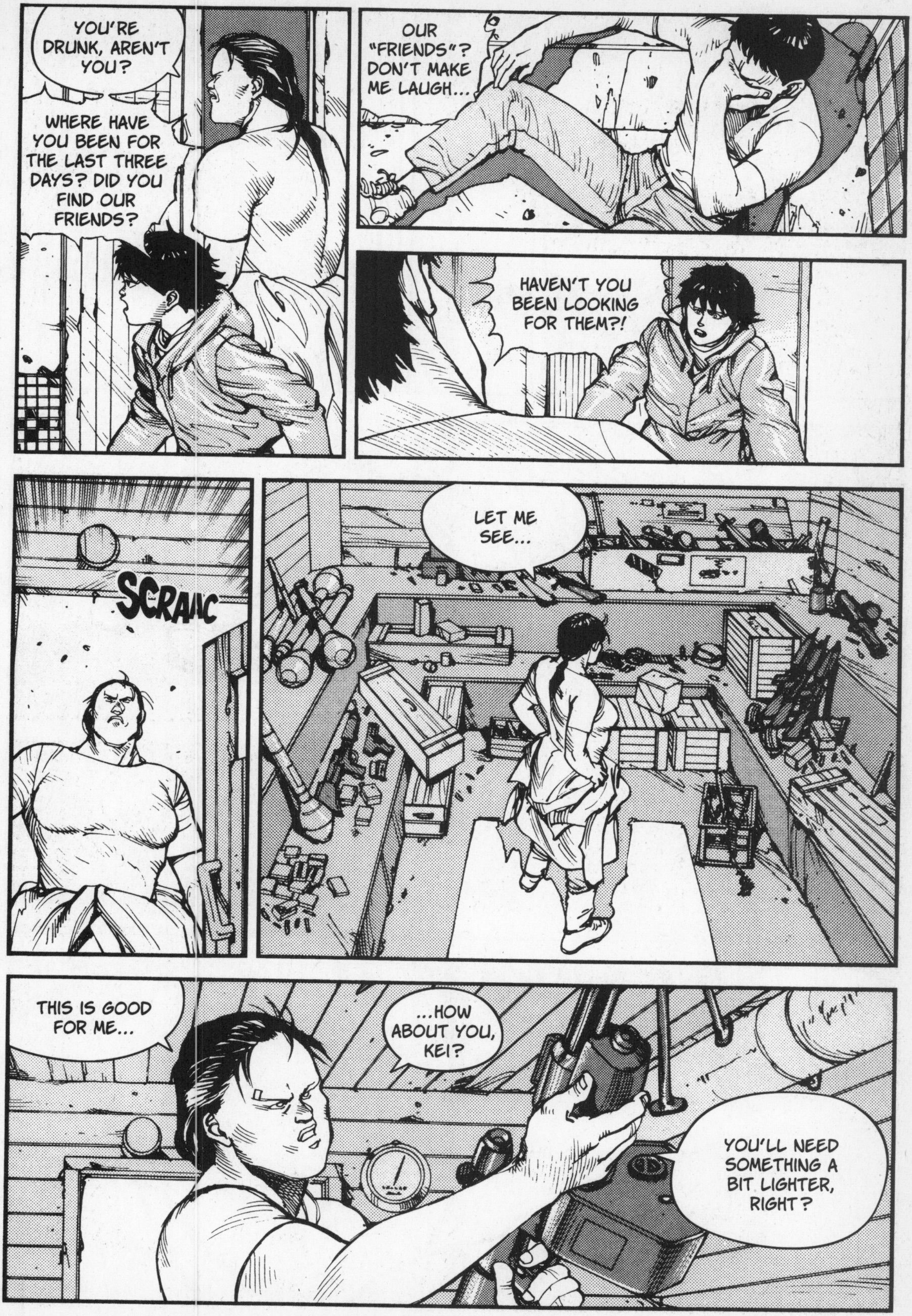
YOU'RE DRUNK, AREN'T YOU?
WHERE HAVE YOU BEEN FOR THE LAST THREE DAYS? DID YOU FIND OUR FRIENDS?
OUR "FRIENDS"? DON'T MAKE ME LAUGH...
HAVEN'T YOU BEEN LOOKING FOR THEM?!
SCRANC
LET ME SEE...
THIS IS GOOD FOR ME...
...HOW ABOUT YOU, KEI?
YOU'LL NEED SOMETHING A BIT LIGHTER, RIGHT?

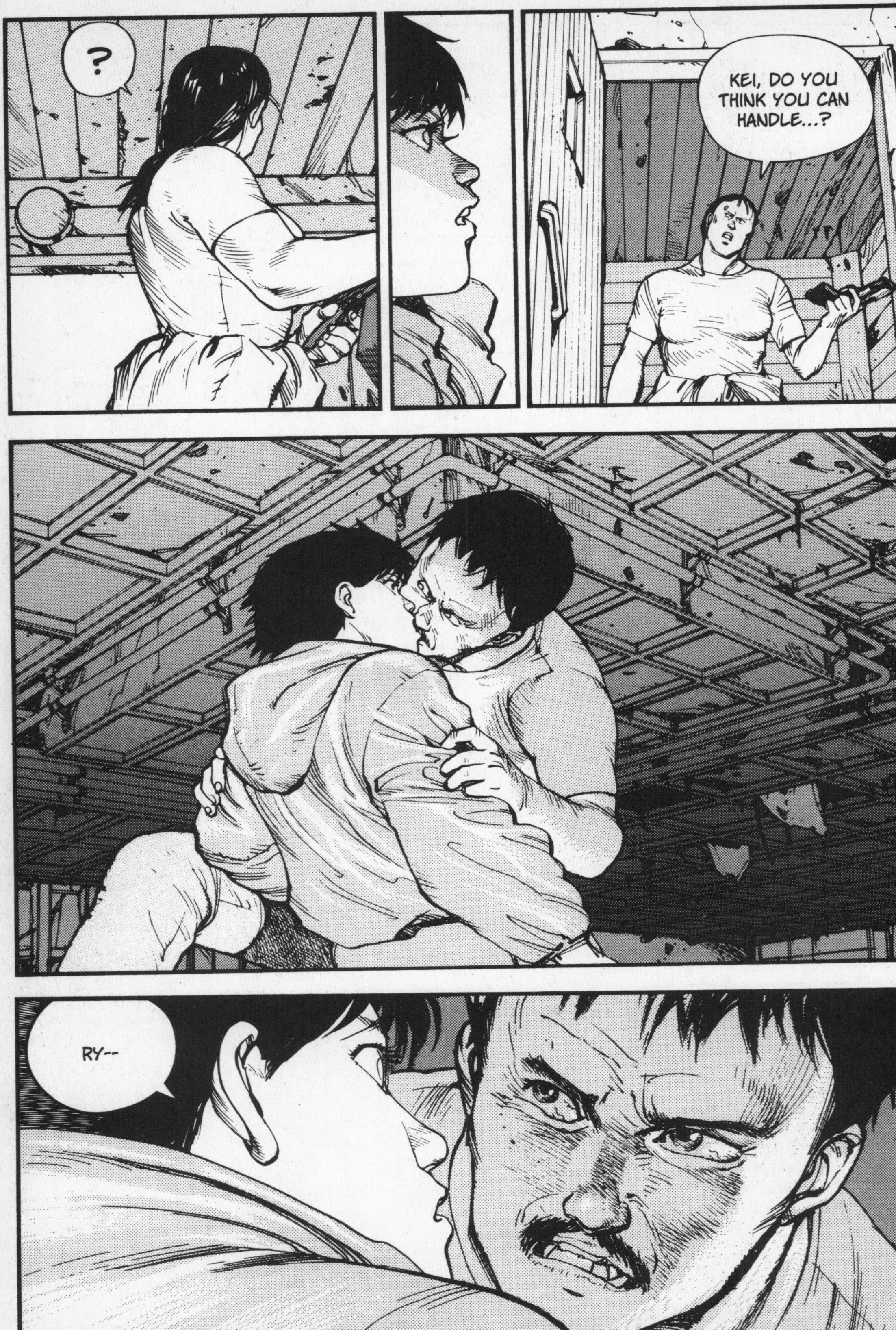
?
KEI, DO YOU THINK YOU CAN HANDLE...?
RY--

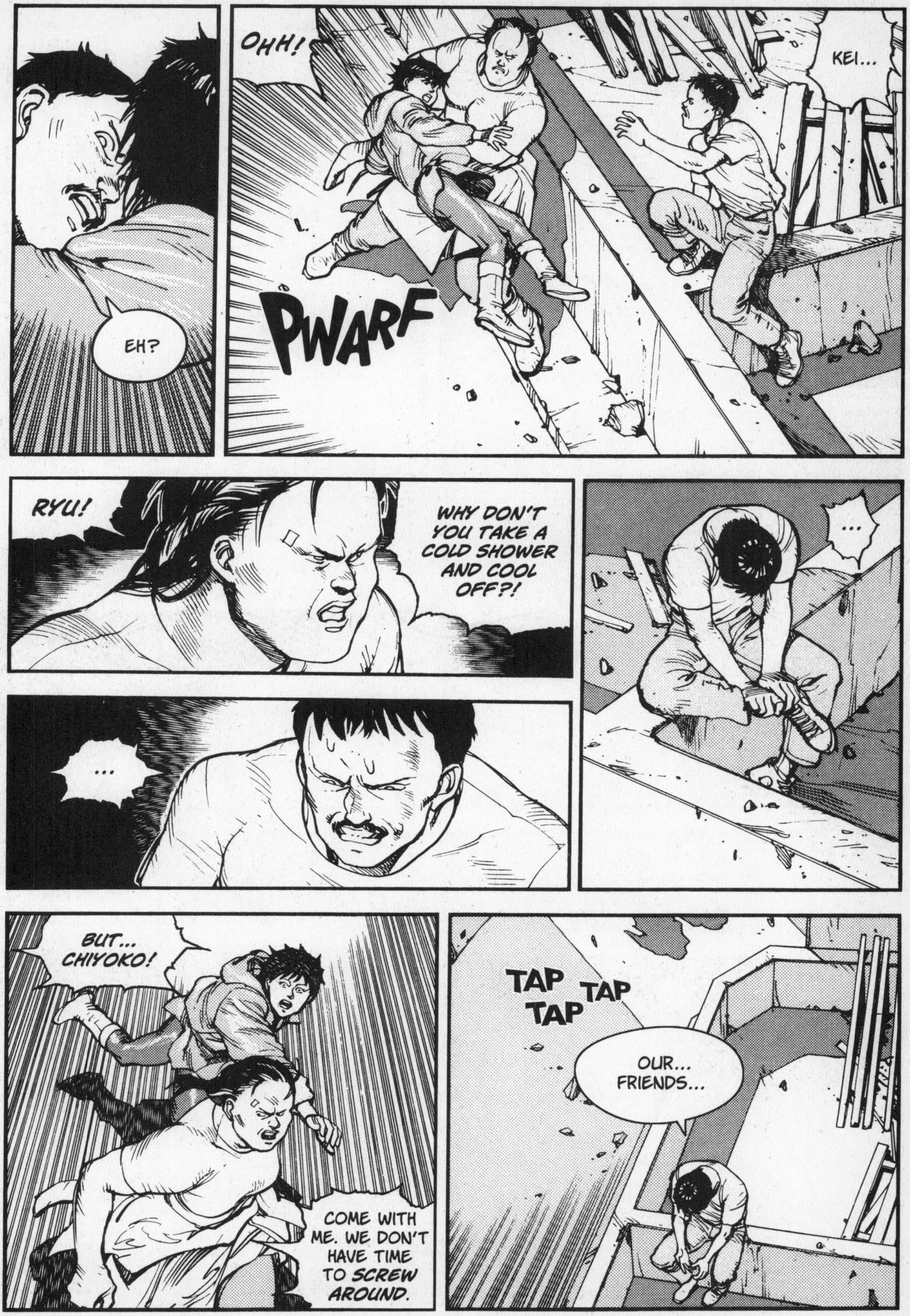
EH?
OHH!
PWARF
KEI...
RYU!
WHY DON'T YOU TAKE A COLD SHOWER AND COOL OFF?!
...
...
BUT... CHIYOKO!
COME WITH ME. WE DON'T HAVE TIME TO SCREW AROUND.
TAP TAP TAP
OUR... FRIENDS...

BUT ...I LOVE HIM!

I HAVE FOR A LONG TIME...

IF THERE'S ANYTHING I CAN DO TO HELP HIM...

WHAT?!

SMAK

FOOL! YOU'RE WASTING YOUR TIME ON HIM!

OUR FRIENDS...ALL OF THEM...

...ALL DEAD!!

HE'S JUST A DRUNKEN BUM!

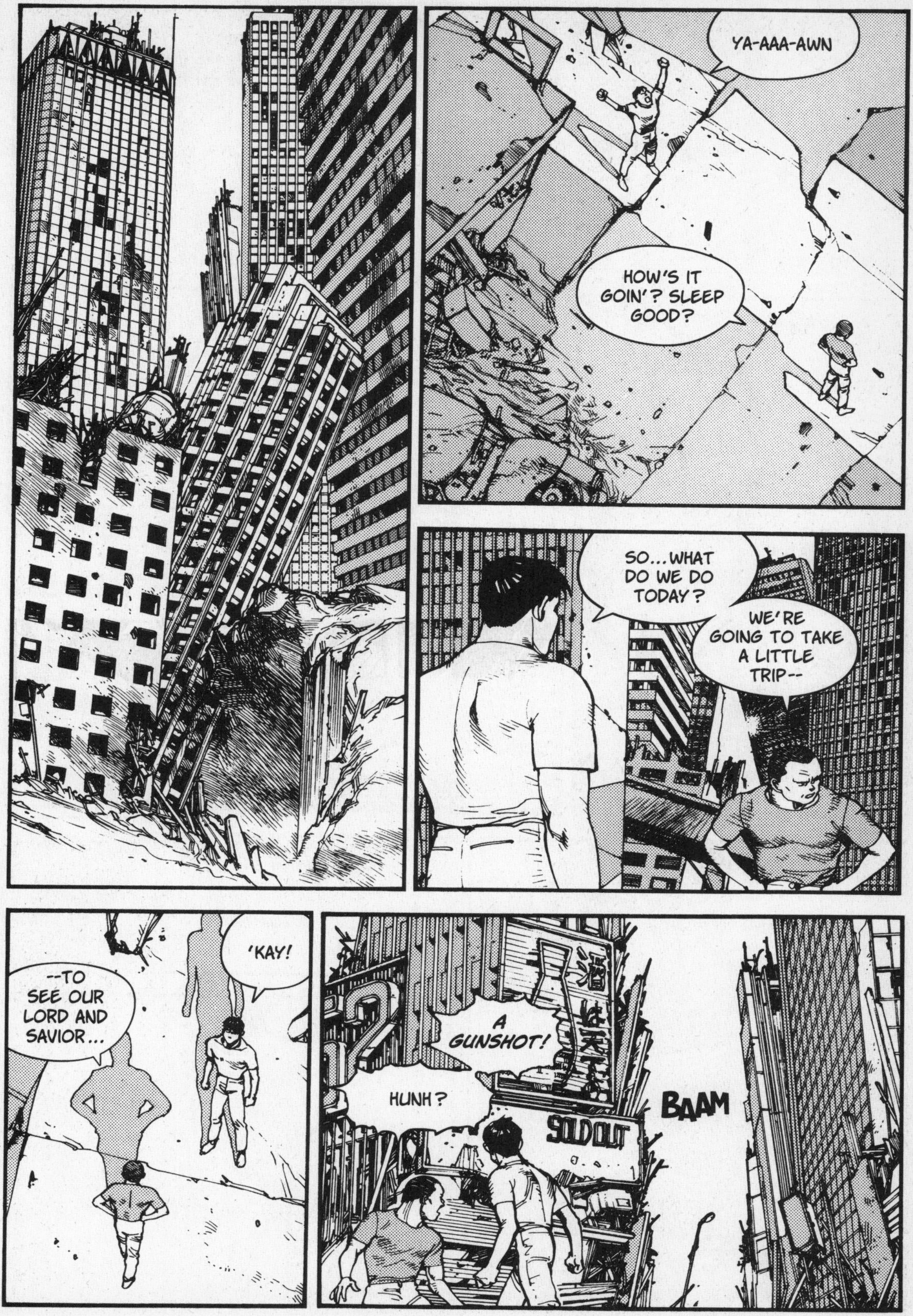
YA-AAA-AWN
HOW'S IT GOIN'? SLEEP GOOD?
SO...WHAT DO WE DO TODAY?
WE'RE GOING TO TAKE A LITTLE TRIP--
--TO SEE OUR LORD AND SAVIOR...
'KAY!
A GUNSHOT!
HUNH?
BAAM
SOLD OUT

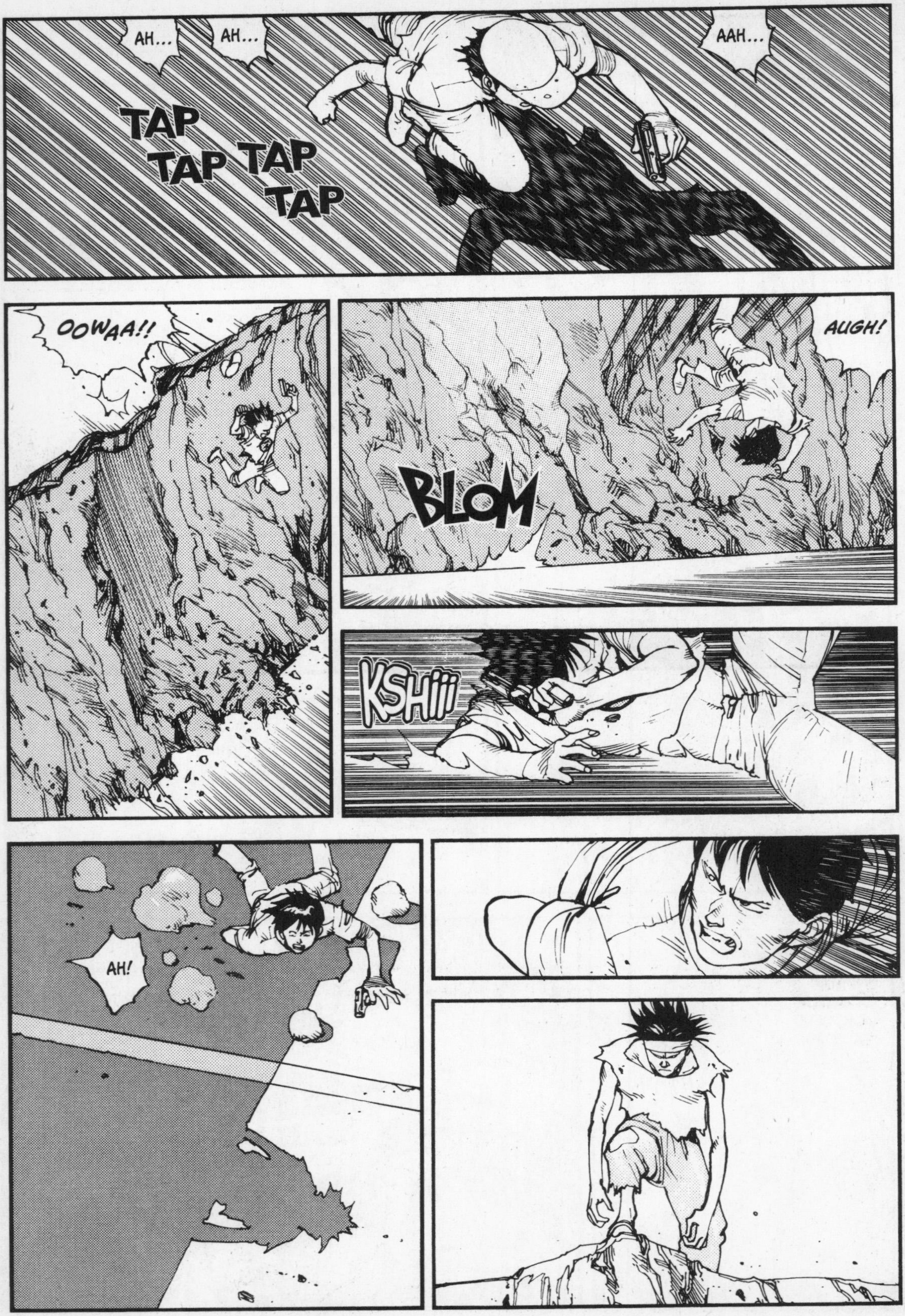
AH...
AH...
AAH...
TAP
TAP
TAP
TAP
OOWAA!!
AUGH!
BLOM
KSHiii
AH!

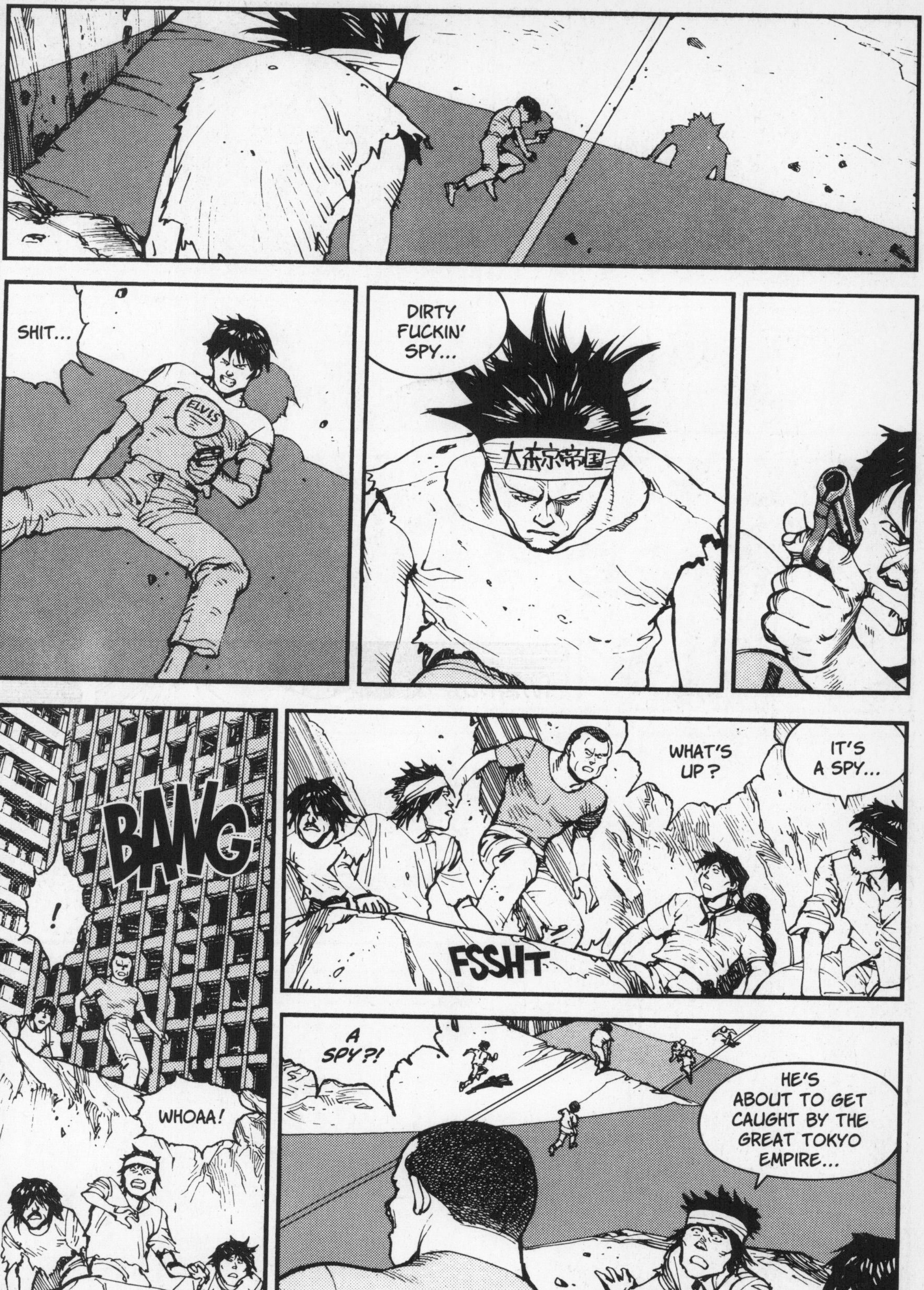
SHIT...
DIRTY FUCKIN' SPY...
BANG
!
WHOAA!
WHAT'S UP?
IT'S A SPY...
FSSHT
A SPY?!
HE'S ABOUT TO GET CAUGHT BY THE GREAT TOKYO EMPIRE...

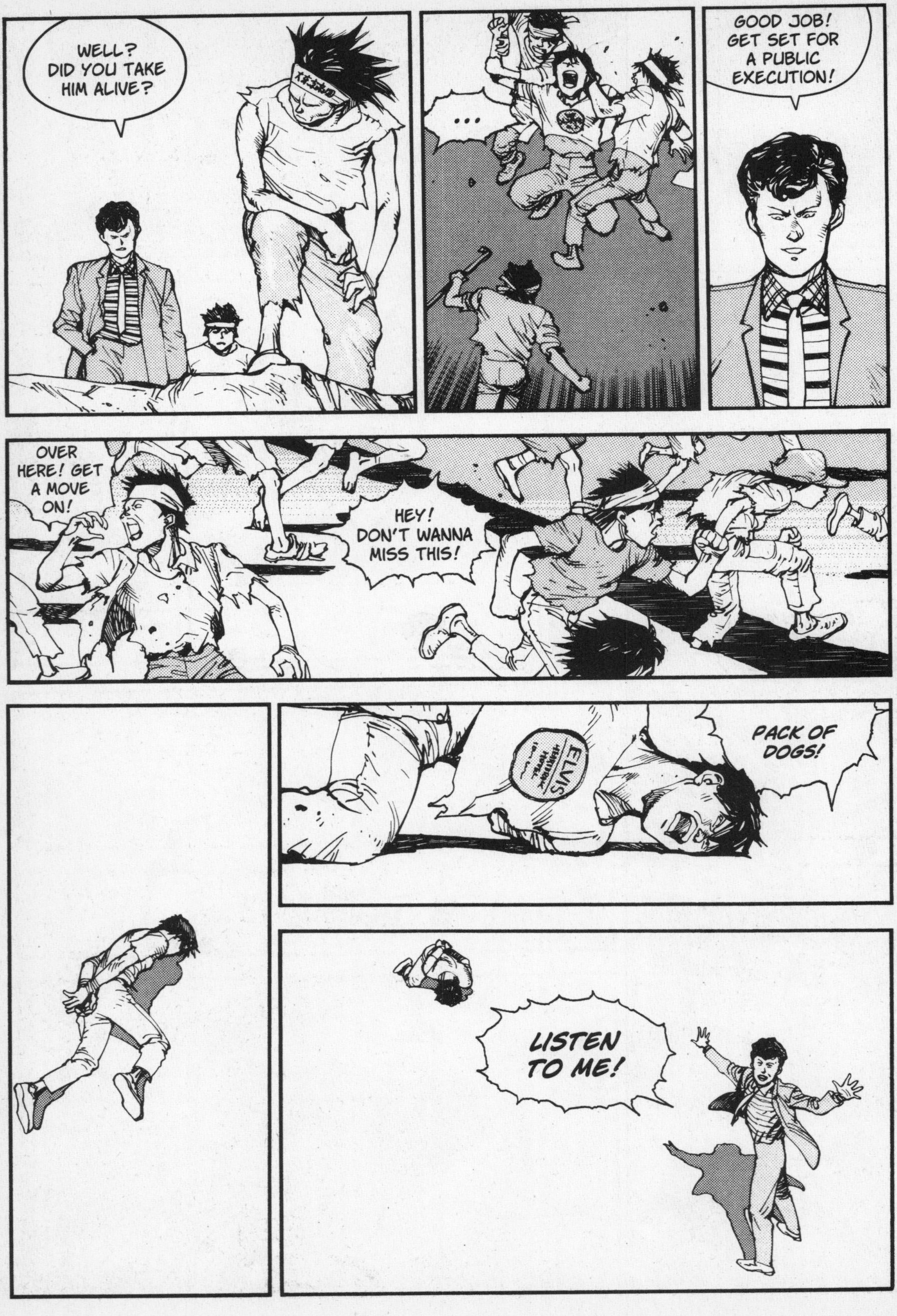
WELL? DID YOU TAKE HIM ALIVE?
...
GOOD JOB! GET SET FOR A PUBLIC EXECUTION!
OVER HERE! GET A MOVE ON!
HEY! DON'T WANNA MISS THIS!
ELVIS
PACK OF DOGS!
LISTEN TO ME!

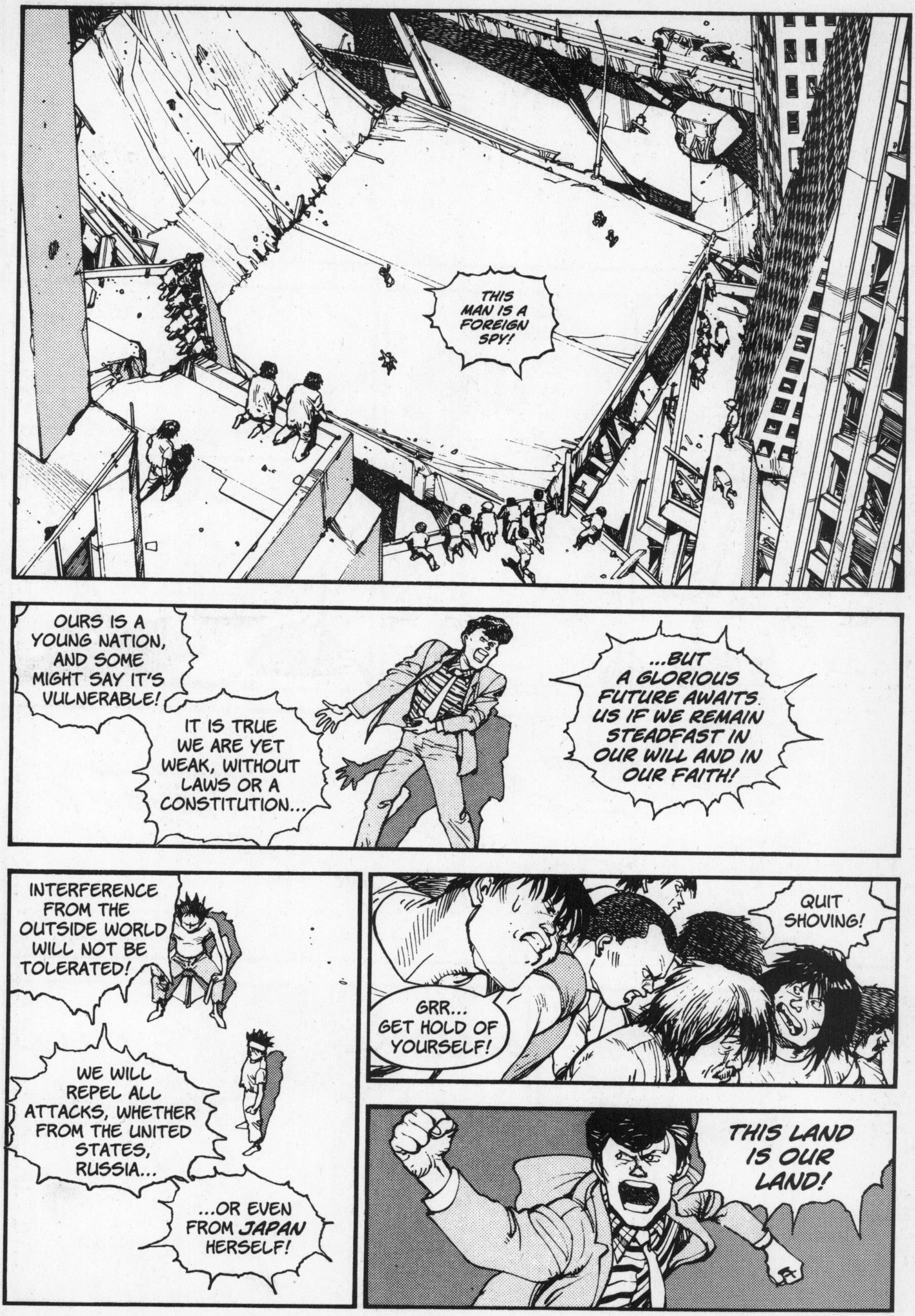
THIS MAN IS A FOREIGN SPY!
OURS IS A YOUNG NATION, AND SOME MIGHT SAY IT'S VULNERABLE!
IT IS TRUE WE ARE YET WEAK, WITHOUT LAWS OR A CONSTITUTION...
...BUT A GLORIOUS FUTURE AWAITS US IF WE REMAIN STEADFAST IN OUR WILL AND IN OUR FAITH!
INTERFERENCE FROM THE OUTSIDE WORLD WILL NOT BE TOLERATED!
WE WILL REPEL ALL ATTACKS, WHETHER FROM THE UNITED STATES, RUSSIA...
...OR EVEN FROM JAPAN HERSELF!
QUIT SHOVING!
GRR... GET HOLD OF YOURSELF!
THIS LAND IS OUR LAND!

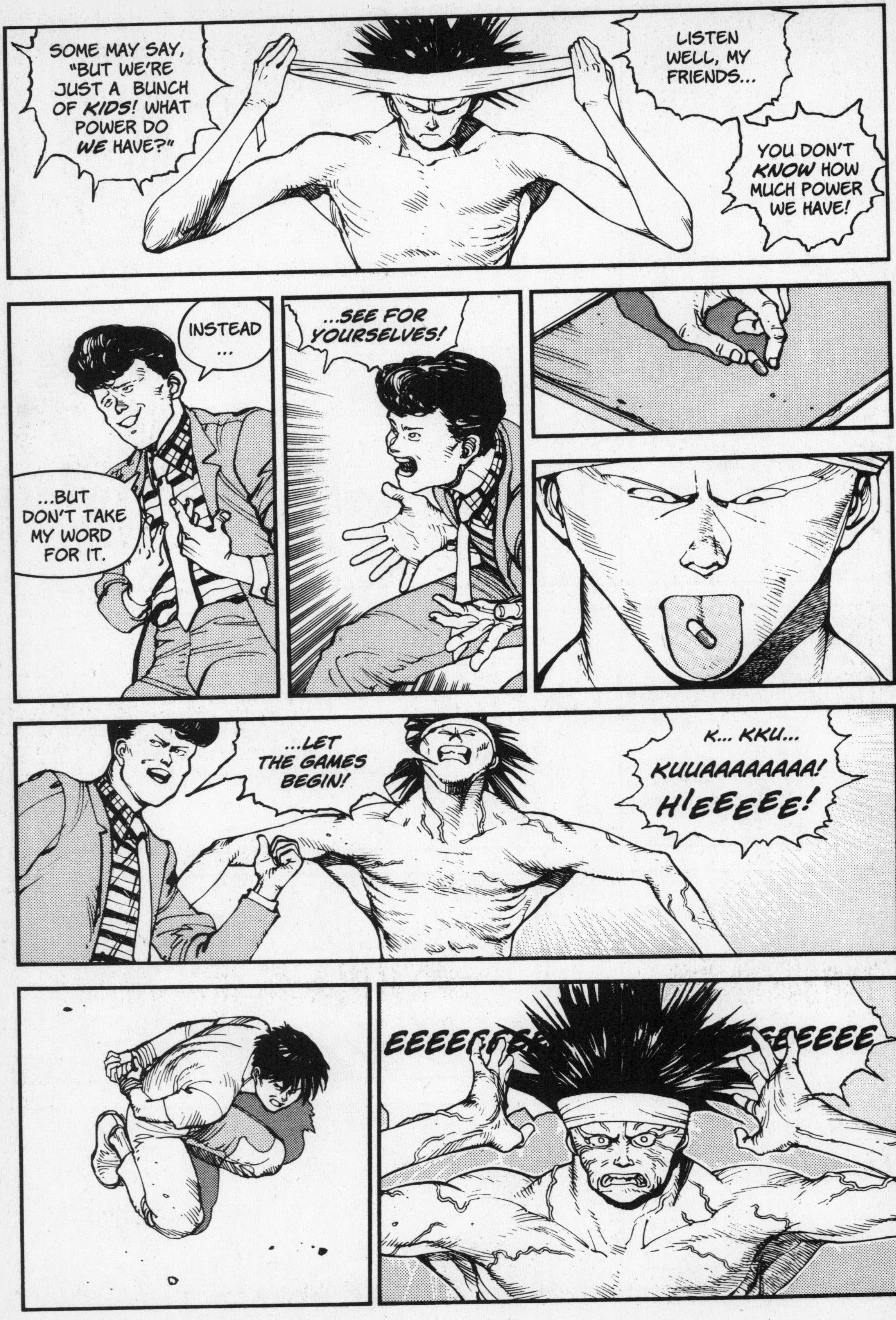
SOME MAY SAY, "BUT WE'RE JUST A BUNCH OF *KIDS*! WHAT POWER DO *WE* HAVE?"
LISTEN WELL, MY FRIENDS...
YOU DON'T *KNOW* HOW MUCH POWER WE HAVE!
INSTEAD ...
...BUT DON'T TAKE MY WORD FOR IT.
...SEE FOR YOURSELVES!
...LET THE GAMES BEGIN!
K... KKU...
KUUAAAAAAAA!
H'EEEEEE!

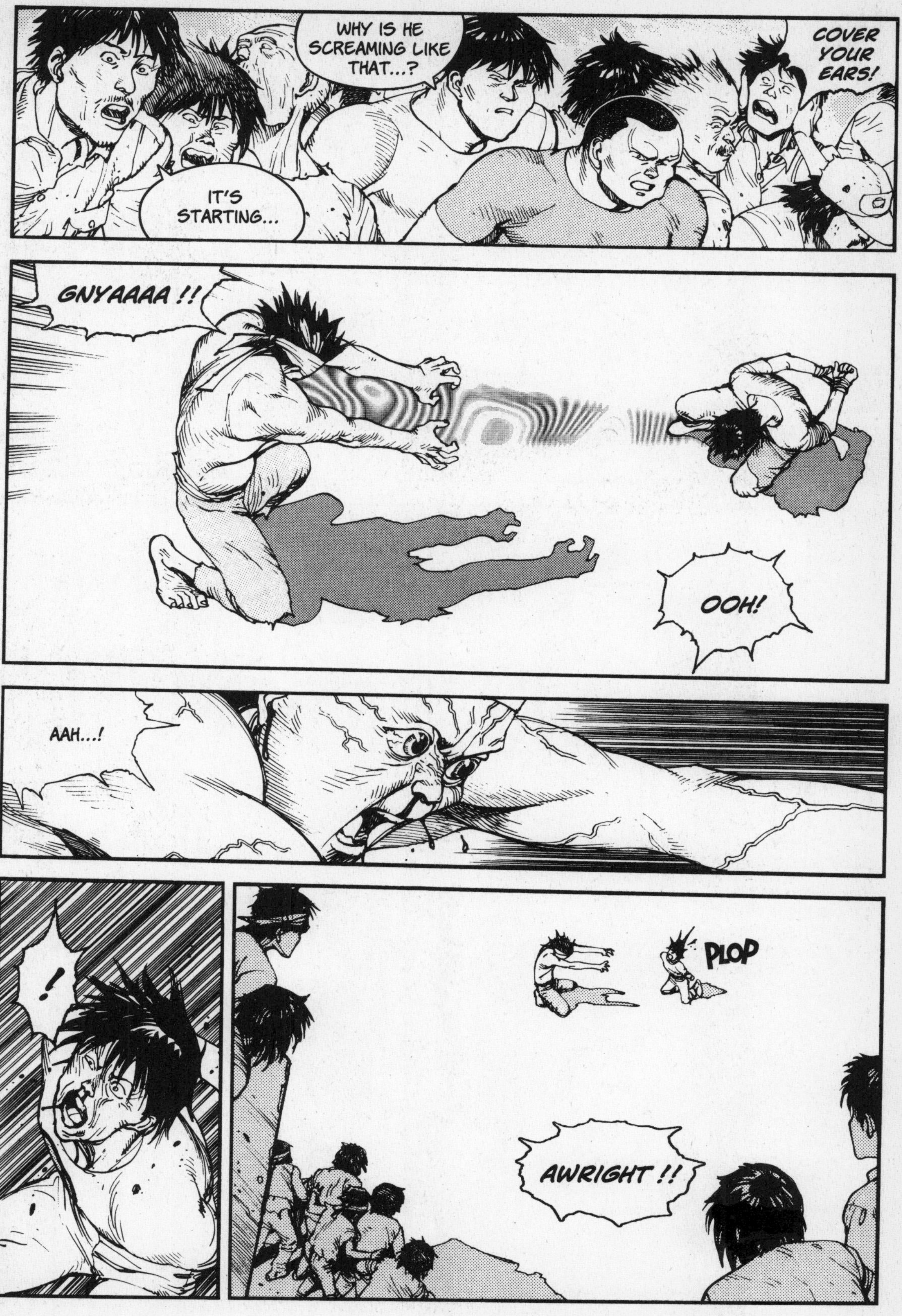
WHY IS HE SCREAMING LIKE THAT...?
IT'S STARTING...
COVER YOUR EARS!
GNYAAAA !!
OOH!
AAH...!
!
PLOP
AWRIGHT !!

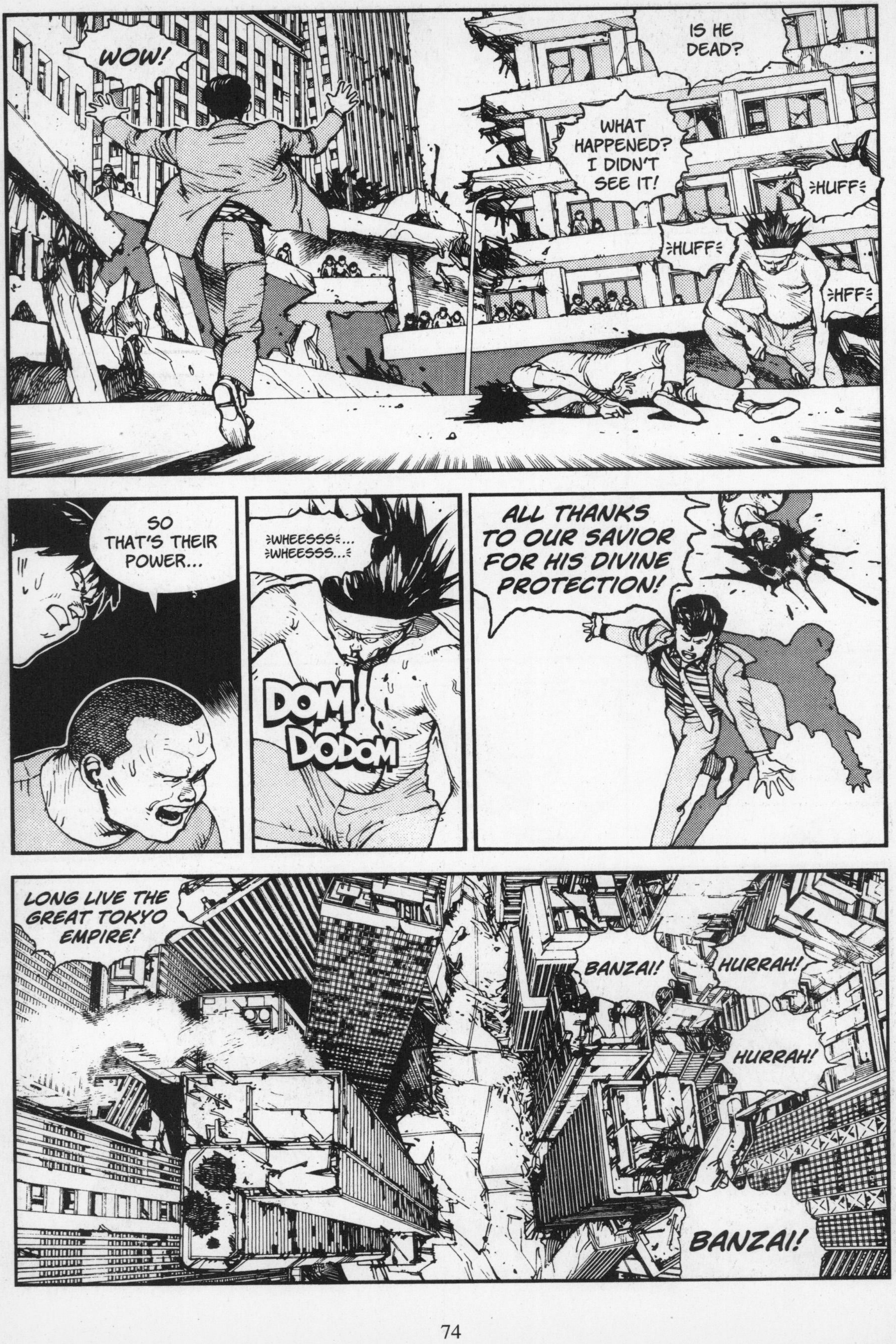
WOW!
IS HE DEAD?
WHAT HAPPENED? I DIDN'T SEE IT!
HUFF
HUFF
HFF
SO THAT'S THEIR POWER...
WHEESSS... WHEESSS...
DOM DODOM
ALL THANKS TO OUR SAVIOR FOR HIS DIVINE PROTECTION!
LONG LIVE THE GREAT TOKYO EMPIRE!
BANZAI!
HURRAH!
HURRAH!
BANZAI!

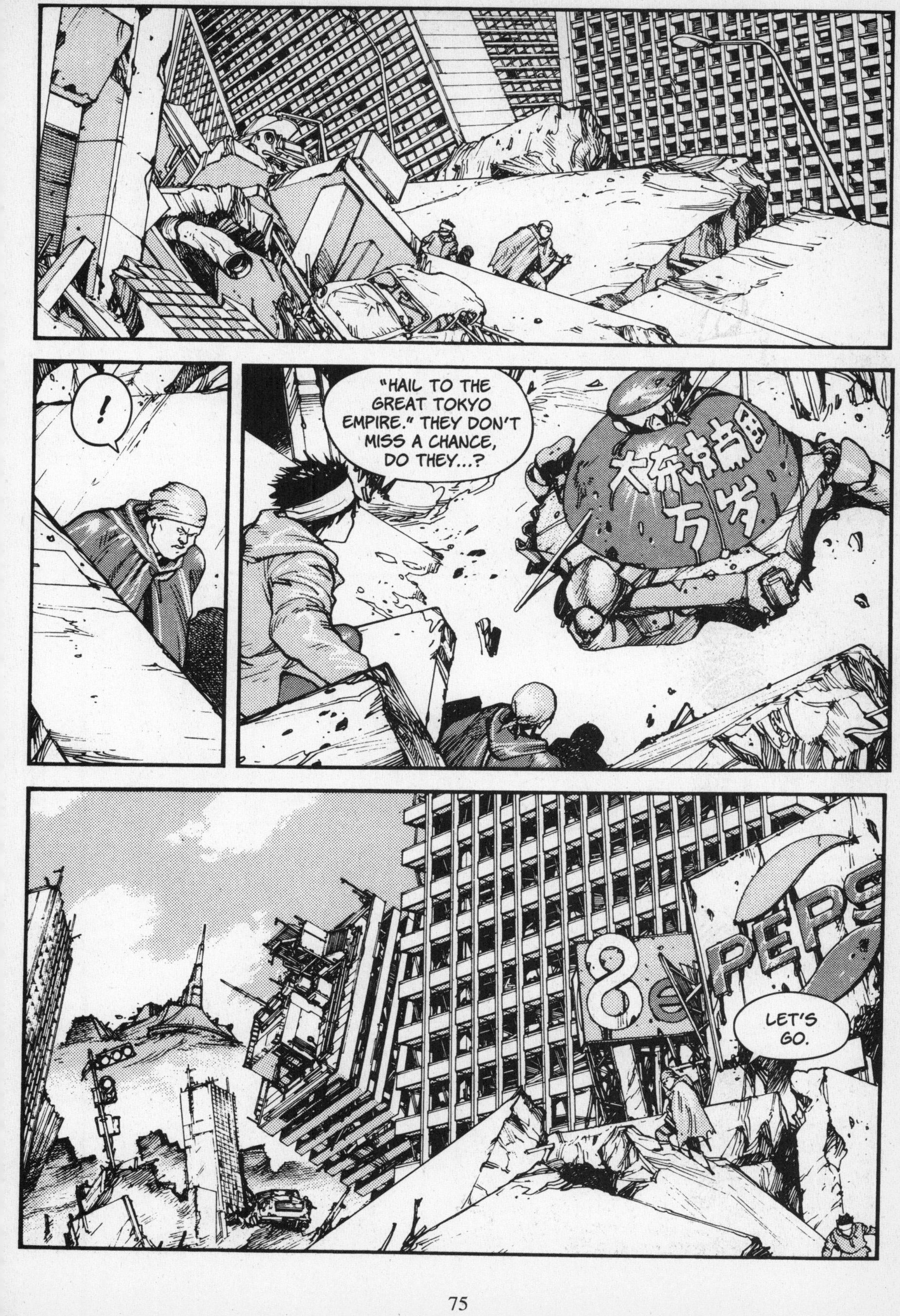
!
"HAIL TO THE GREAT TOKYO EMPIRE." THEY DON'T MISS A CHANCE, DO THEY...?
8e
PEPS
LET'S GO.

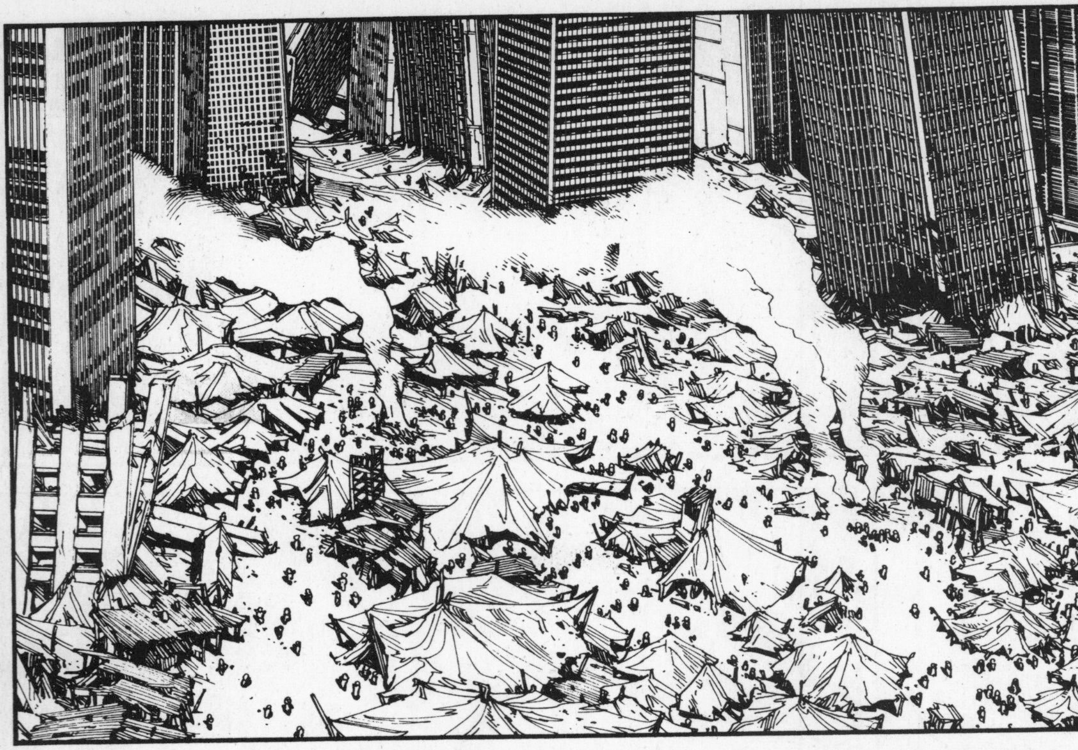

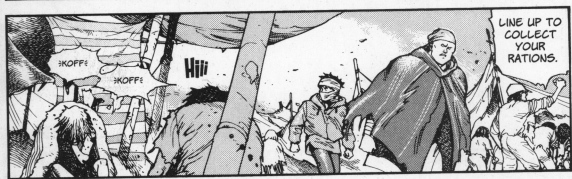

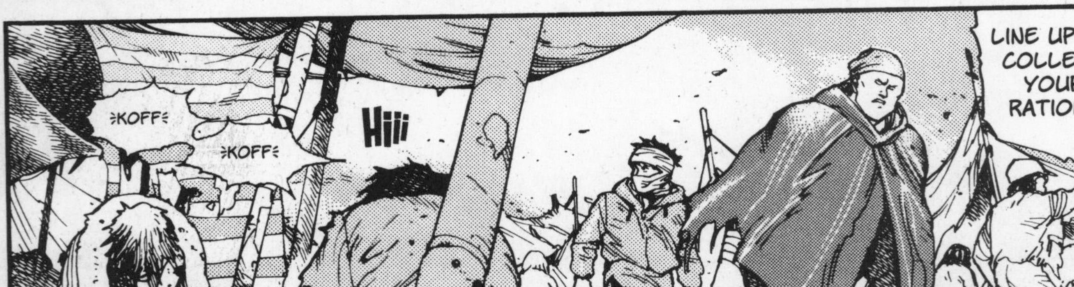
*KOFF*
*KOFF*
HIII
LINE UP TO COLLECT YOUR RATIONS.

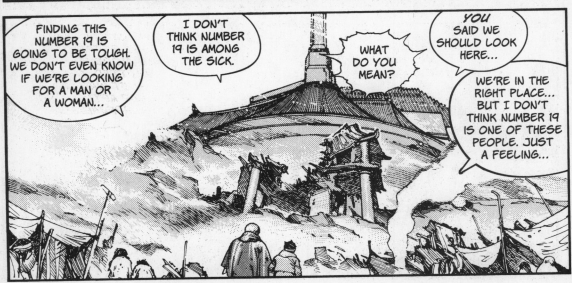

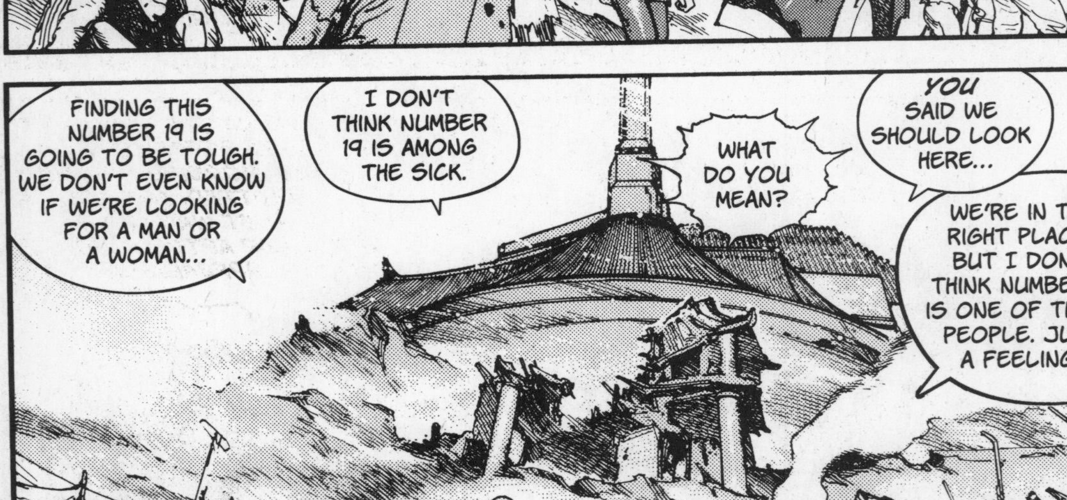
FINDING THIS NUMBER 19 IS GOING TO BE TOUGH. WE DON'T EVEN KNOW IF WE'RE LOOKING FOR A MAN OR A WOMAN...
I DON'T THINK NUMBER 19 IS AMONG THE SICK.
WHAT DO YOU MEAN?
YOU SAID WE SHOULD LOOK HERE...
WE'RE IN THE RIGHT PLACE... BUT I DON'T THINK NUMBER 19 IS ONE OF THESE PEOPLE. JUST A FEELING...

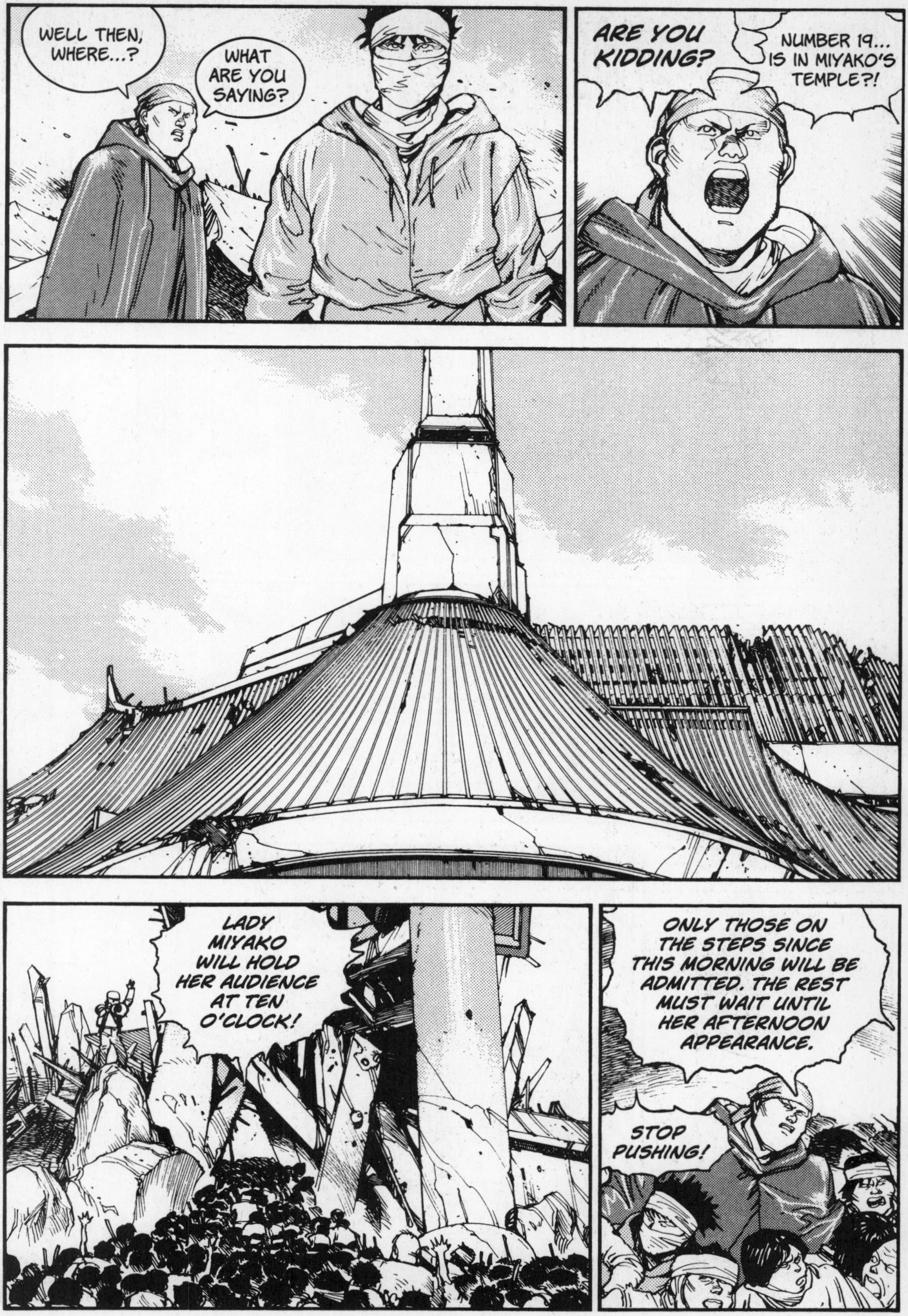
WELL THEN, WHERE...?
WHAT ARE YOU SAYING?
ARE YOU KIDDING?
NUMBER 19... IS IN MIYAKO'S TEMPLE?!
LADY MIYAKO WILL HOLD HER AUDIENCE AT TEN O'CLOCK!
ONLY THOSE ON THE STEPS SINCE THIS MORNING WILL BE ADMITTED. THE REST MUST WAIT UNTIL HER AFTERNOON APPEARANCE.
STOP PUSHING!

PLEASE STOP SHOVING! STAY CALM!

YOU WILL ALL GET YOUR TURN!

ALL OF THE SICK LINE UP HERE!

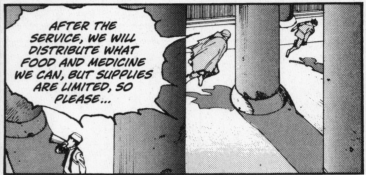

AFTER THE SERVICE, WE WILL DISTRIBUTE WHAT FOOD AND MEDICINE WE CAN, BUT SUPPLIES ARE LIMITED, SO PLEASE...

LOOKS LIKE THE COAST IS CLEAR.

THIS WAY.

KEI! HOW DID YOU ...?

I DON'T KNOW HOW I KNOW...

...BUT I KNOW THIS IS THE WAY!

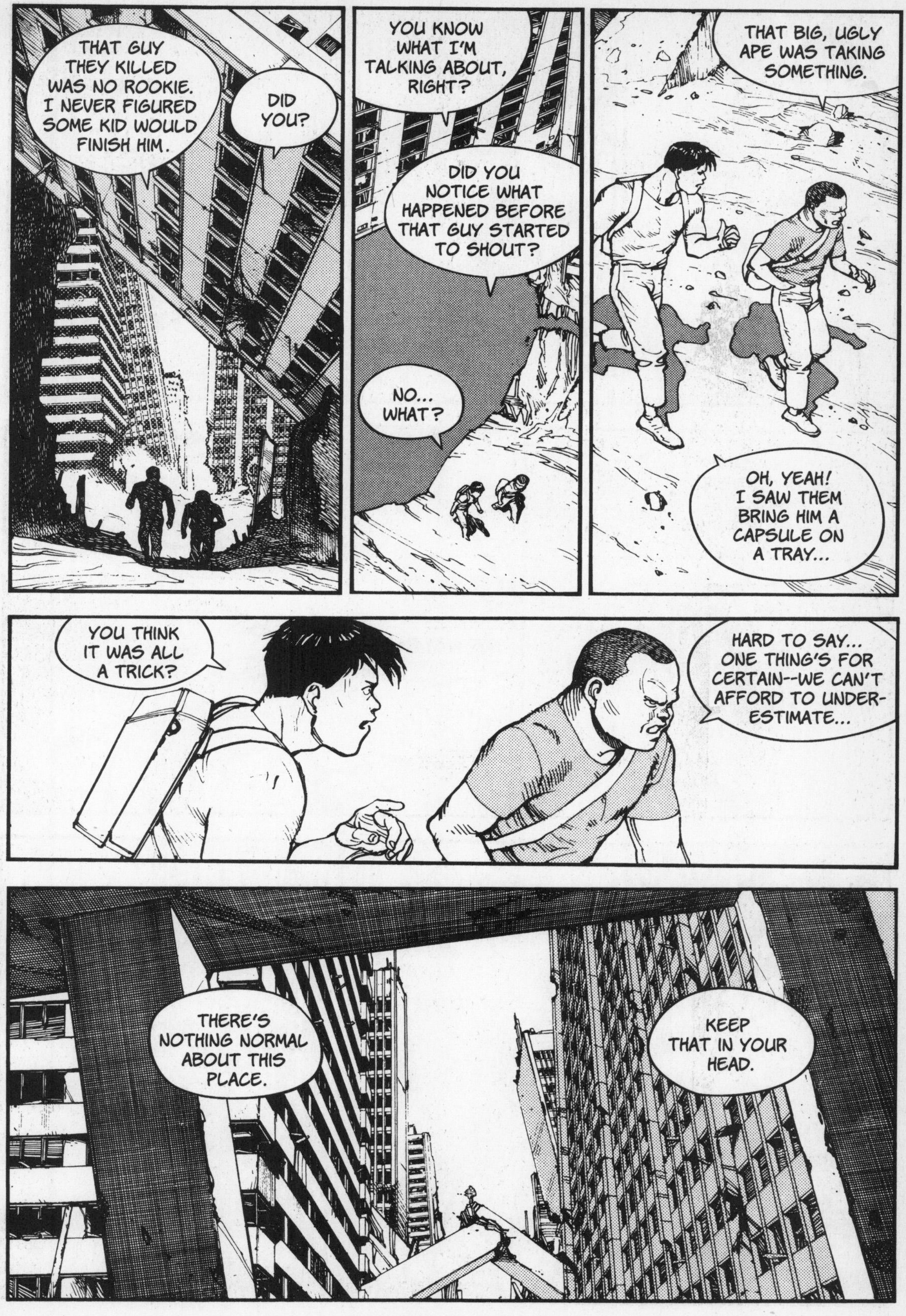
THAT GUY THEY KILLED WAS NO ROOKIE. I NEVER FIGURED SOME KID WOULD FINISH HIM.
DID YOU?
YOU KNOW WHAT I'M TALKING ABOUT, RIGHT?
DID YOU NOTICE WHAT HAPPENED BEFORE THAT GUY STARTED TO SHOUT?
NO... WHAT?
THAT BIG, UGLY APE WAS TAKING SOMETHING.
OH, YEAH! I SAW THEM BRING HIM A CAPSULE ON A TRAY...
YOU THINK IT WAS ALL A TRICK?
HARD TO SAY... ONE THING'S FOR CERTAIN--WE CAN'T AFFORD TO UNDER-ESTIMATE...
THERE'S NOTHING NORMAL ABOUT THIS PLACE.
KEEP THAT IN YOUR HEAD.

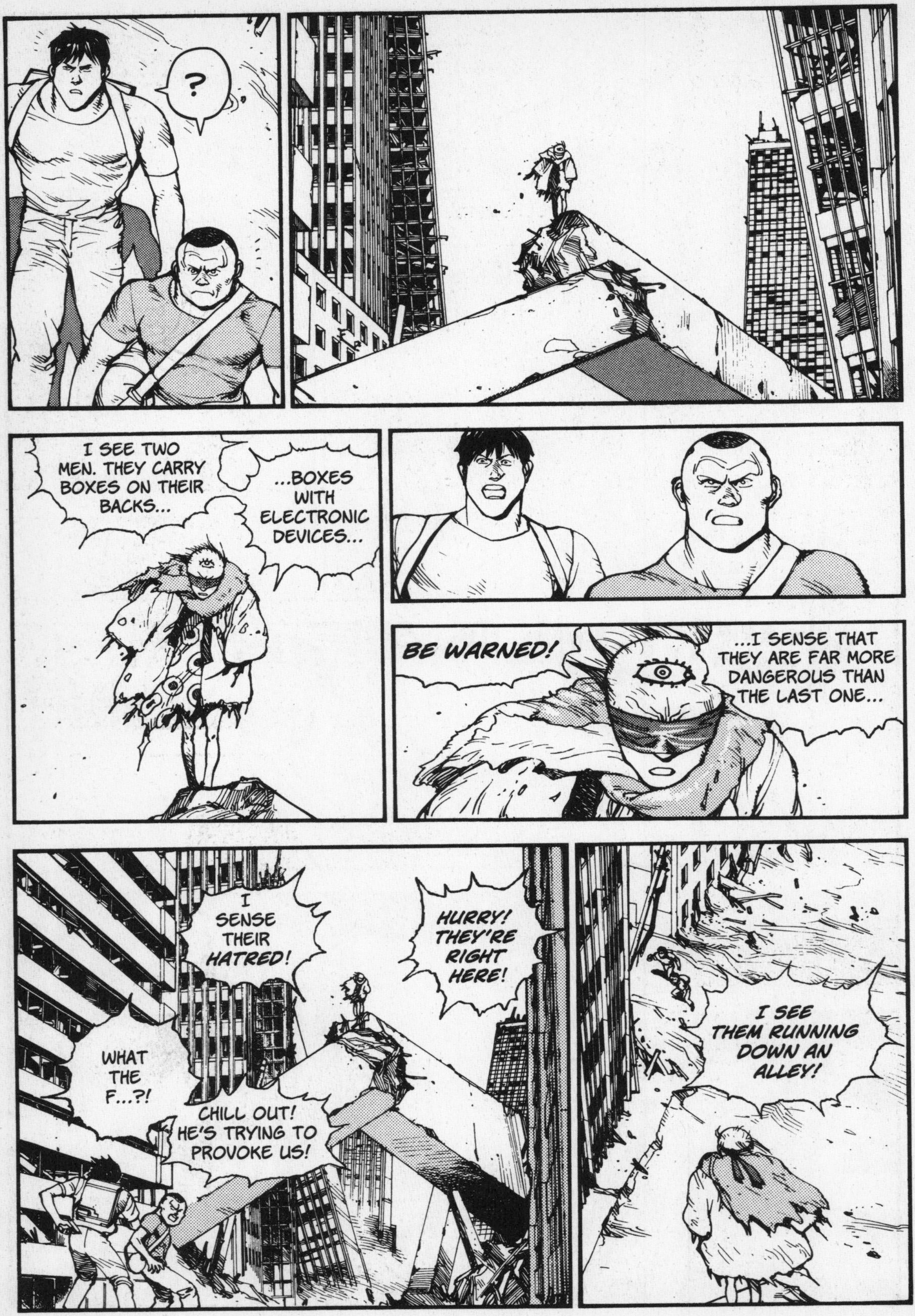
?
I SEE TWO MEN. THEY CARRY BOXES ON THEIR BACKS...
...BOXES WITH ELECTRONIC DEVICES...
BE WARNED!
...I SENSE THAT THEY ARE FAR MORE DANGEROUS THAN THE LAST ONE...
I SENSE THEIR HATRED!
HURRY! THEY'RE RIGHT HERE!
WHAT THE F...?!
CHILL OUT! HE'S TRYING TO PROVOKE US!
I SEE THEM RUNNING DOWN AN ALLEY!

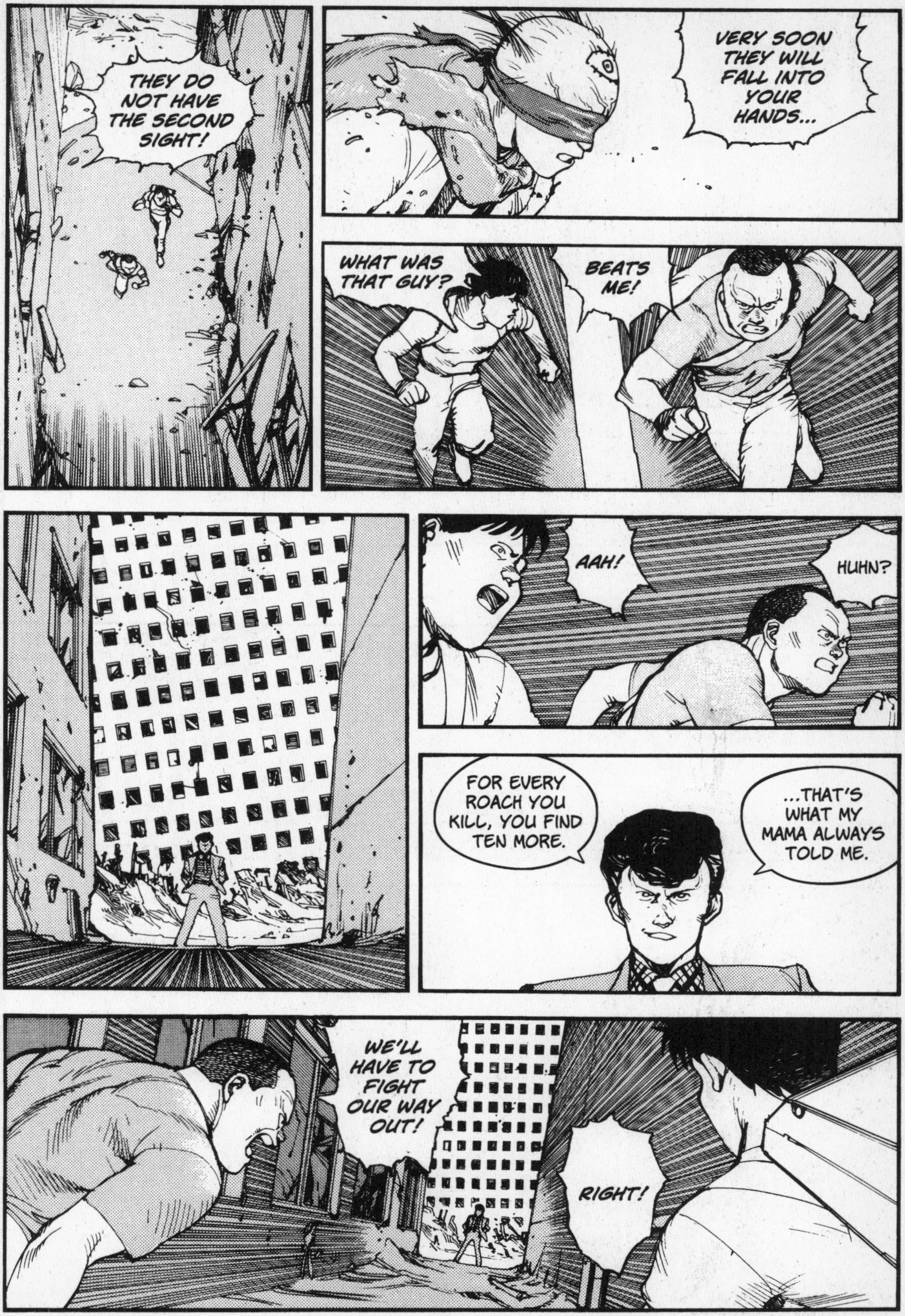
THEY DO NOT HAVE THE SECOND SIGHT!
VERY SOON THEY WILL FALL INTO YOUR HANDS...
WHAT WAS THAT GUY?
BEATS ME!
AAH!
HUHN?
FOR EVERY ROACH YOU KILL, YOU FIND TEN MORE.
...THAT'S WHAT MY MAMA ALWAYS TOLD ME.
WE'LL HAVE TO FIGHT OUR WAY OUT!
RIGHT!

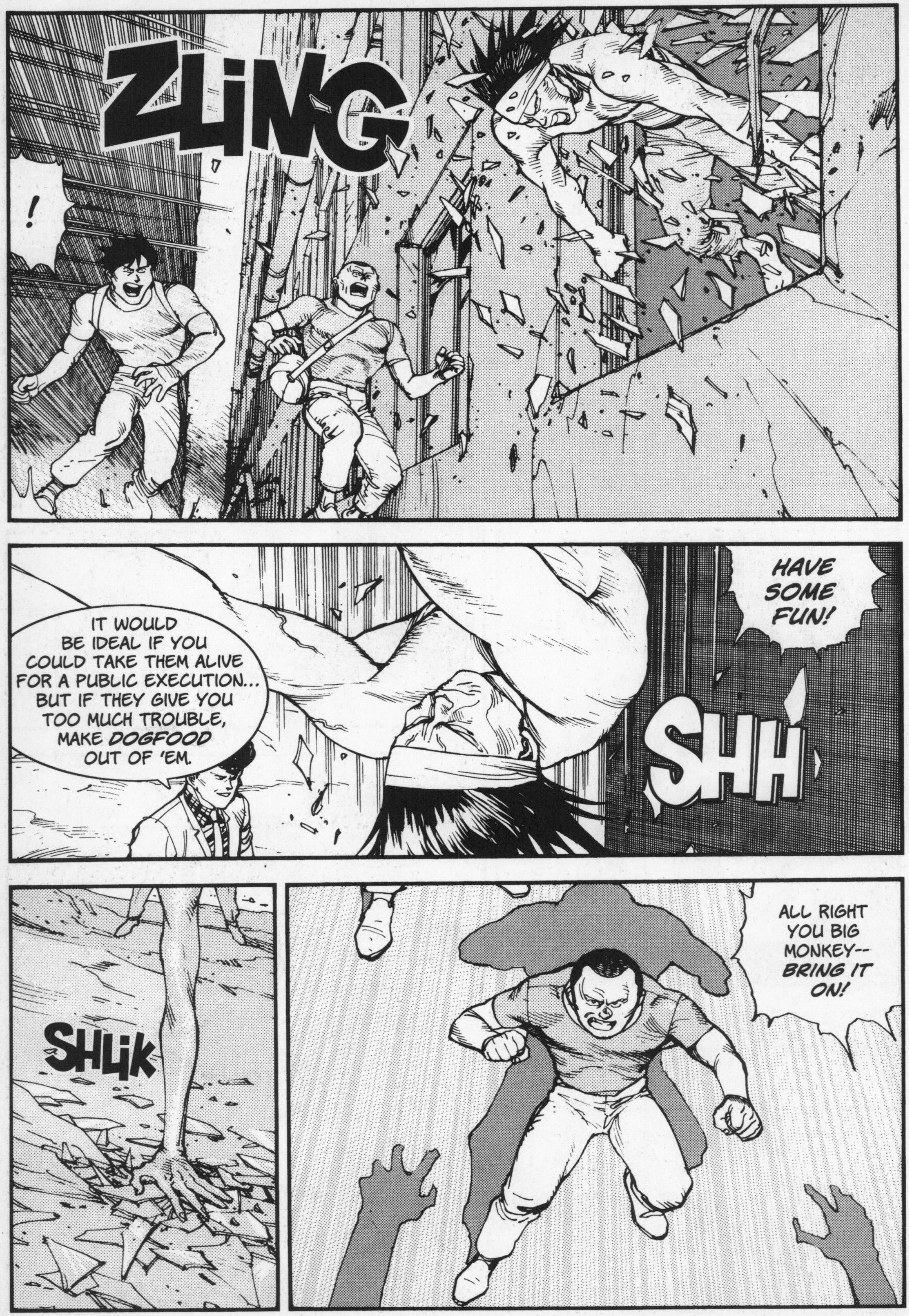
ZLING
!
IT WOULD BE IDEAL IF YOU COULD TAKE THEM ALIVE FOR A PUBLIC EXECUTION... BUT IF THEY GIVE YOU TOO MUCH TROUBLE, MAKE DOGFOOD OUT OF 'EM.
HAVE SOME FUN!
SHH
SHLIK
ALL RIGHT YOU BIG MONKEY-- BRING IT ON!

WOOOOOOOOOOO!!
GZWiiii
AGH!
AAYAAH!
SLAP
BAP
!

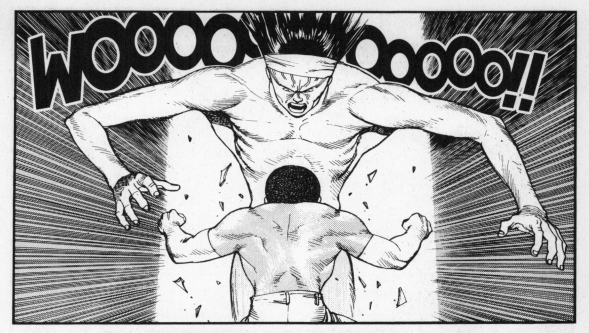

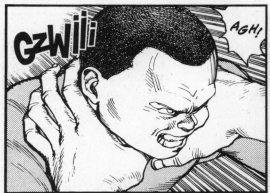

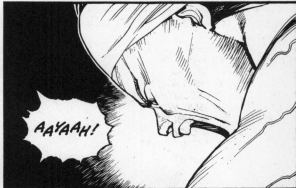

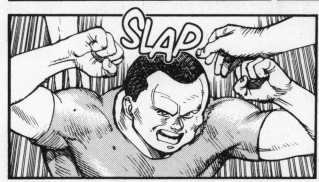

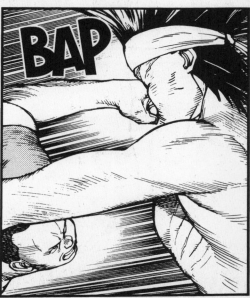

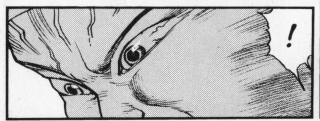

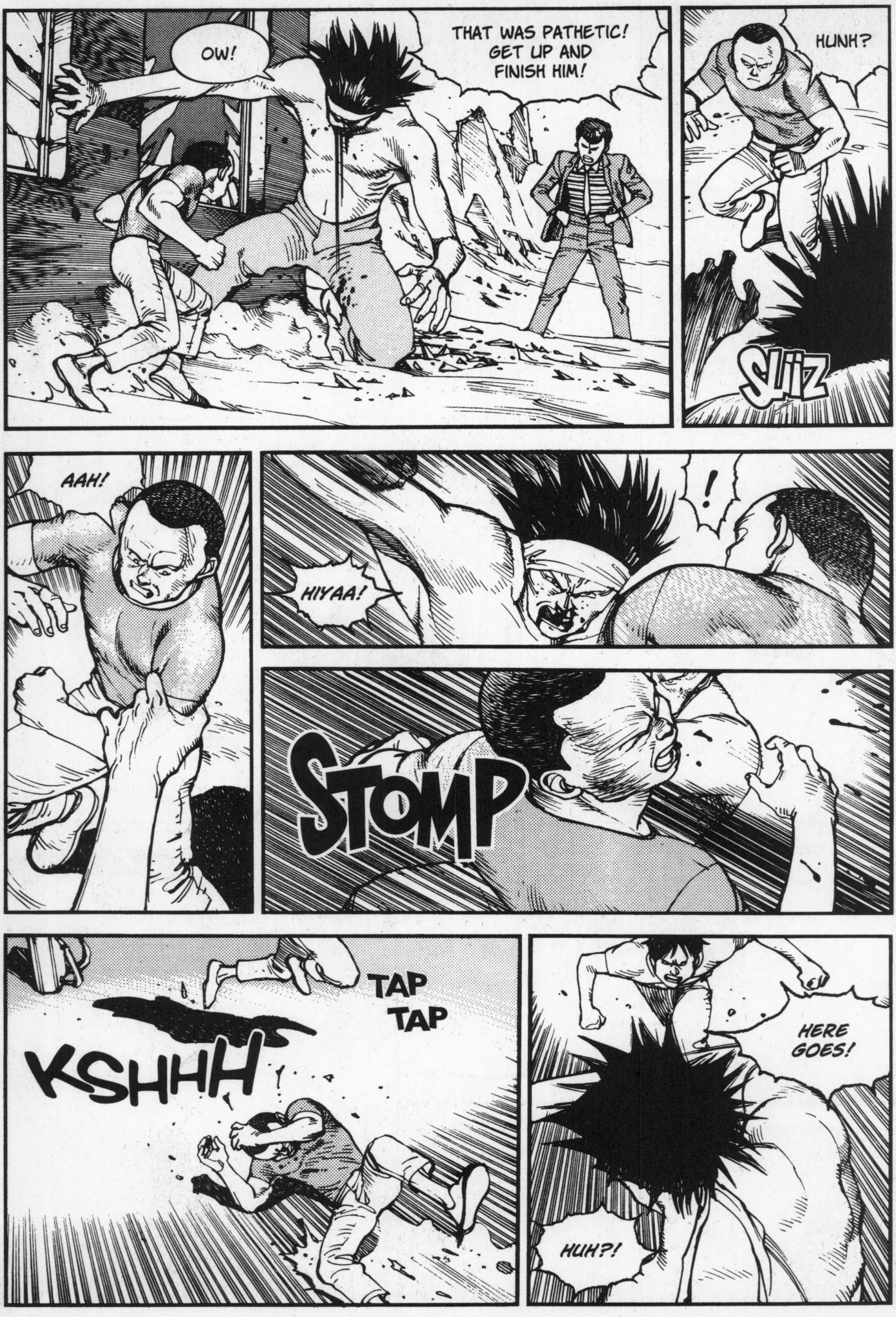
OW!
THAT WAS PATHETIC! GET UP AND FINISH HIM!
HUNH?
SLIIZ
AAH!
HIYAA!
!
STOMP
TAP
TAP
KSHHH
HERE GOES!
HUH?!

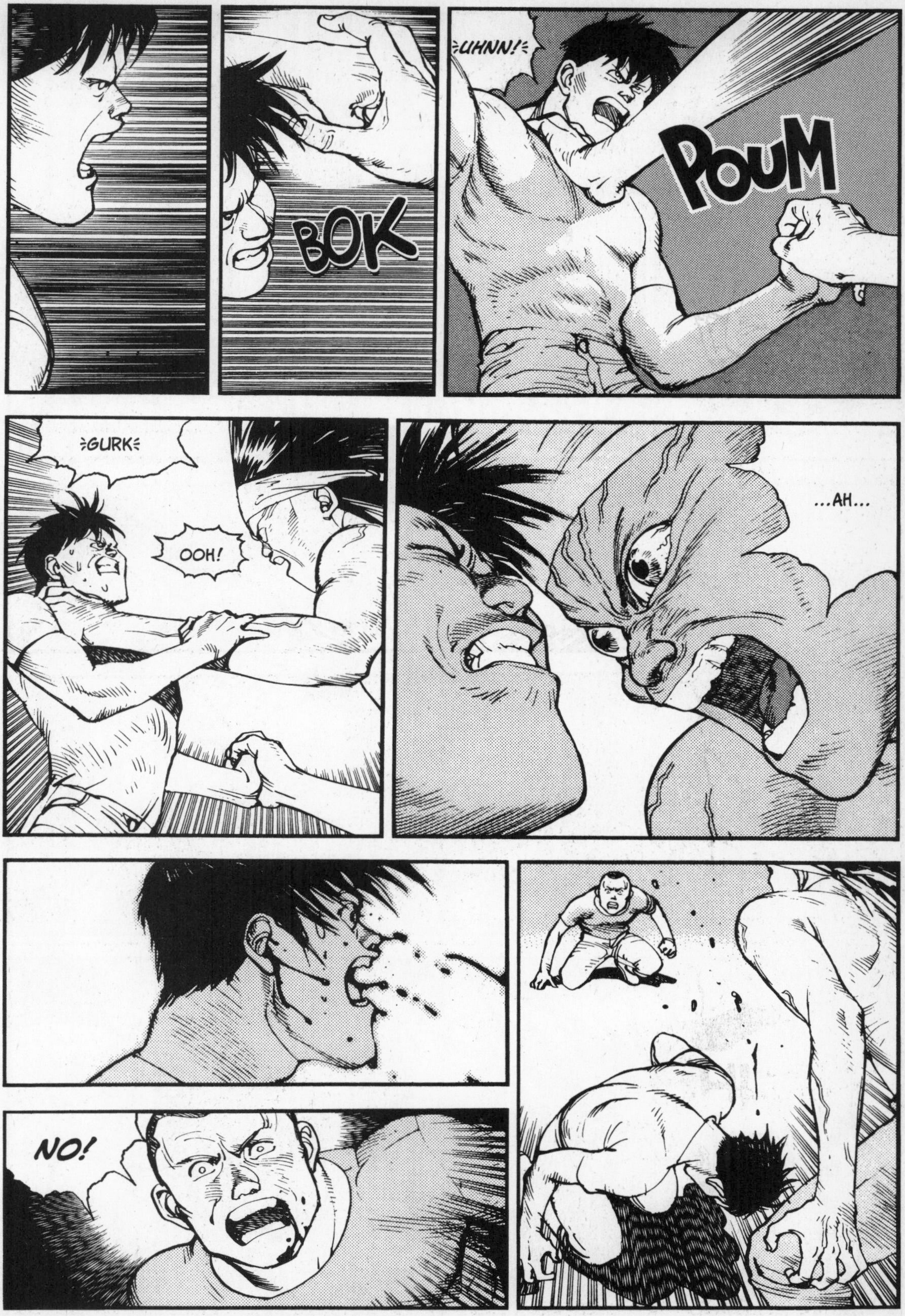
BOK
UHNN!
POUM
GURK
OOH!
...AH...
NO!

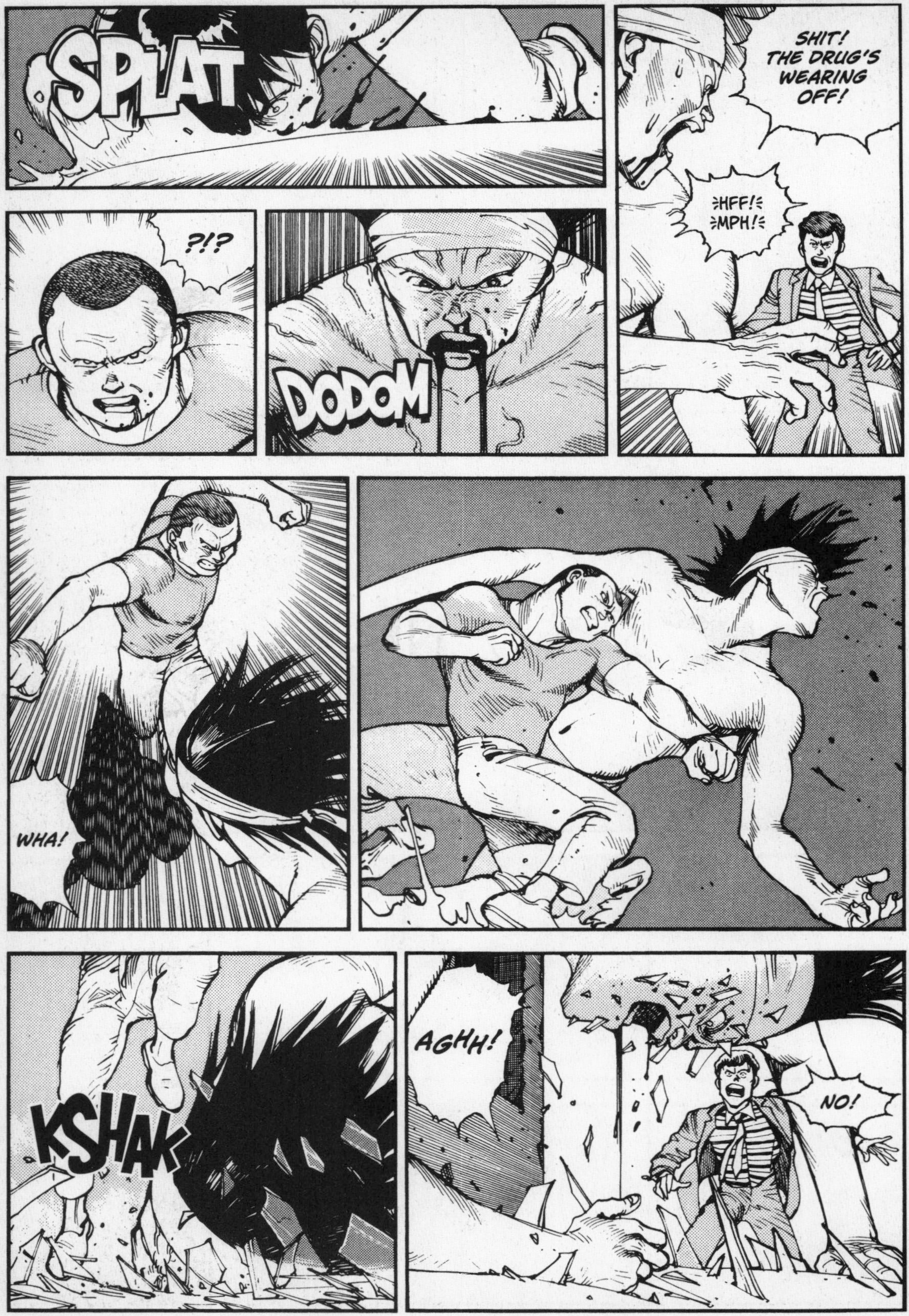
SPLAT
SHIT! THE DRUG'S WEARING OFF!
?!?
DODOM
HFF! MPH!
WHA!
KSHAK
AGHH!
NO!

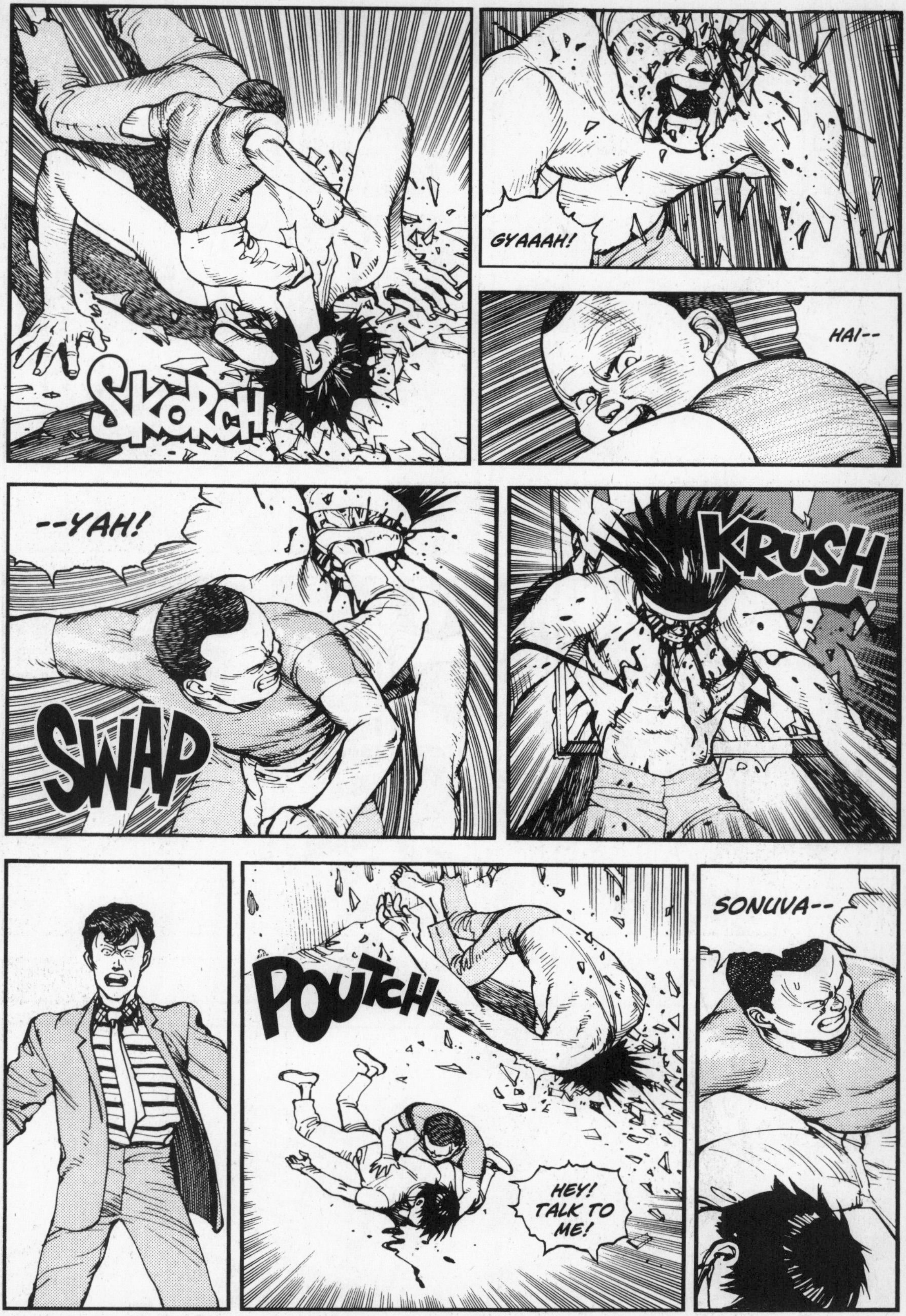
SKORCH
GYAAAH!
HAI--
--YAH!
SWAP
KRUSH
POUTCH
HEY! TALK TO ME!
SONUVA--

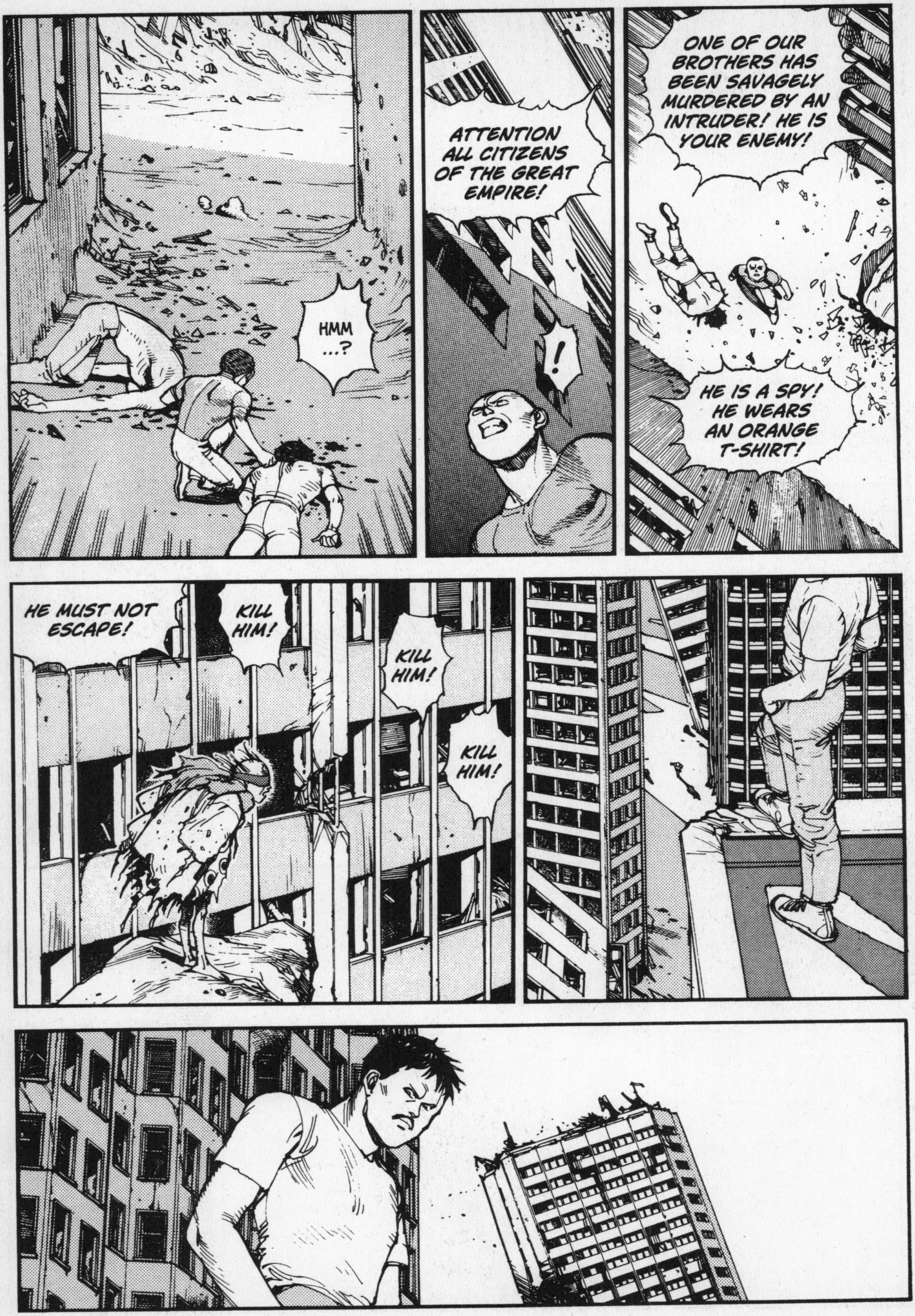
HMM ...?
ATTENTION ALL CITIZENS OF THE GREAT EMPIRE!
!
ONE OF OUR BROTHERS HAS BEEN SAVAGELY MURDERED BY AN INTRUDER! HE IS YOUR ENEMY!
HE IS A SPY! HE WEARS AN ORANGE T-SHIRT!
HE MUST NOT ESCAPE!
KILL HIM!
KILL HIM!
KILL HIM!

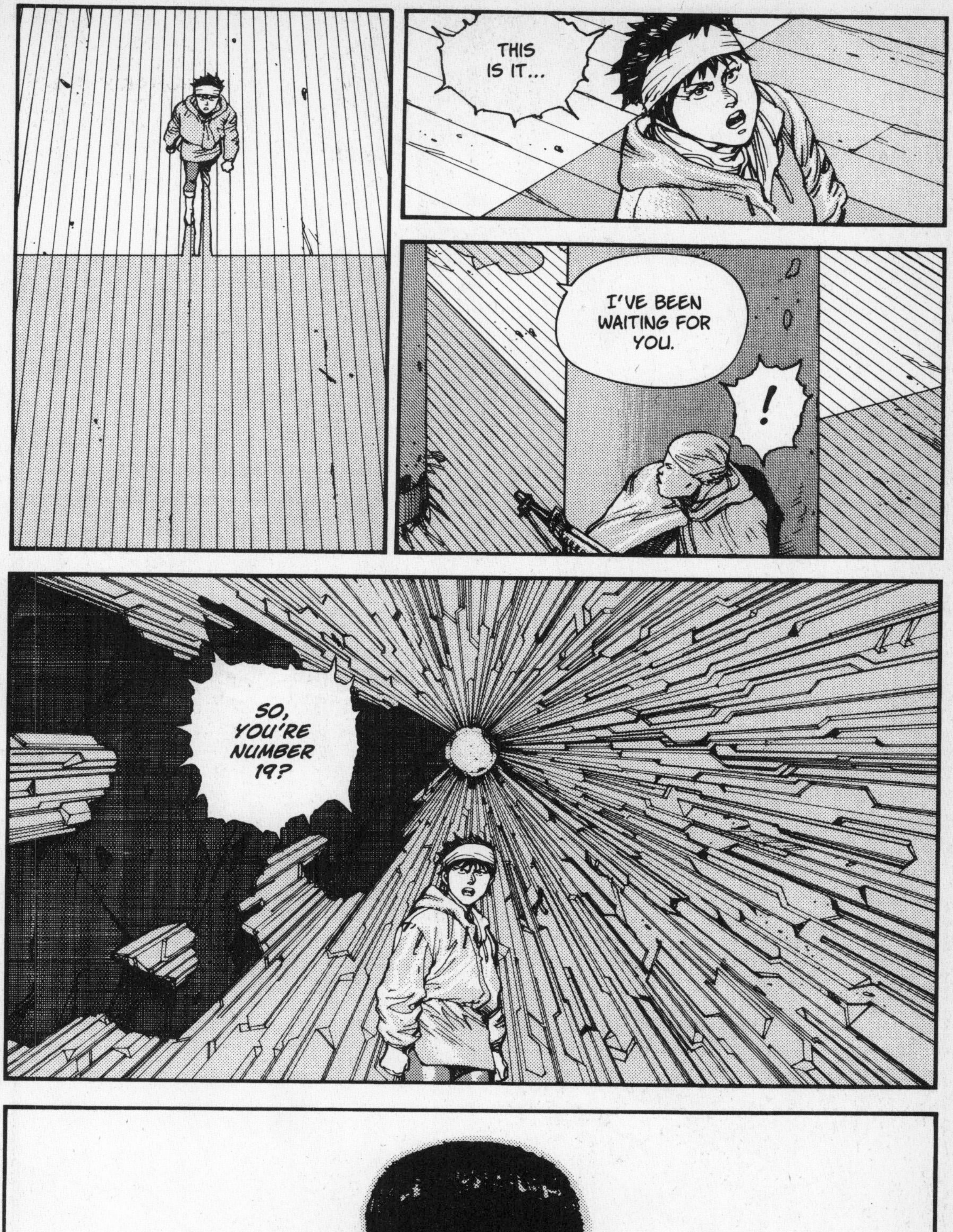
THIS IS IT...
I'VE BEEN WAITING FOR YOU.
!
SO, YOU'RE NUMBER 19?

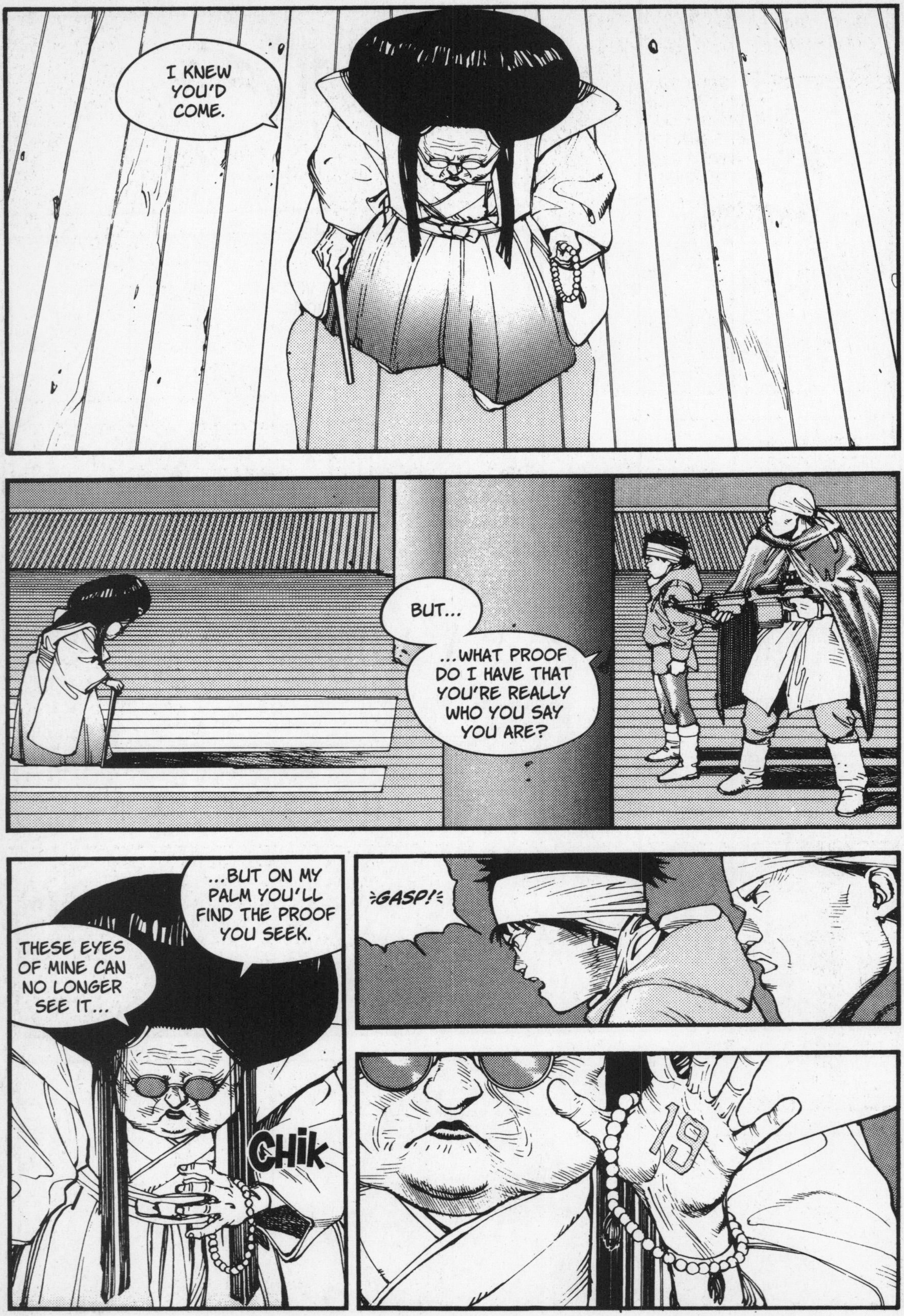

I KNEW YOU'D COME.
BUT...
...WHAT PROOF DO I HAVE THAT YOU'RE REALLY WHO YOU SAY YOU ARE?
THESE EYES OF MINE CAN NO LONGER SEE IT...
...BUT ON MY PALM YOU'LL FIND THE PROOF YOU SEEK.
CHIK
GASP!
19

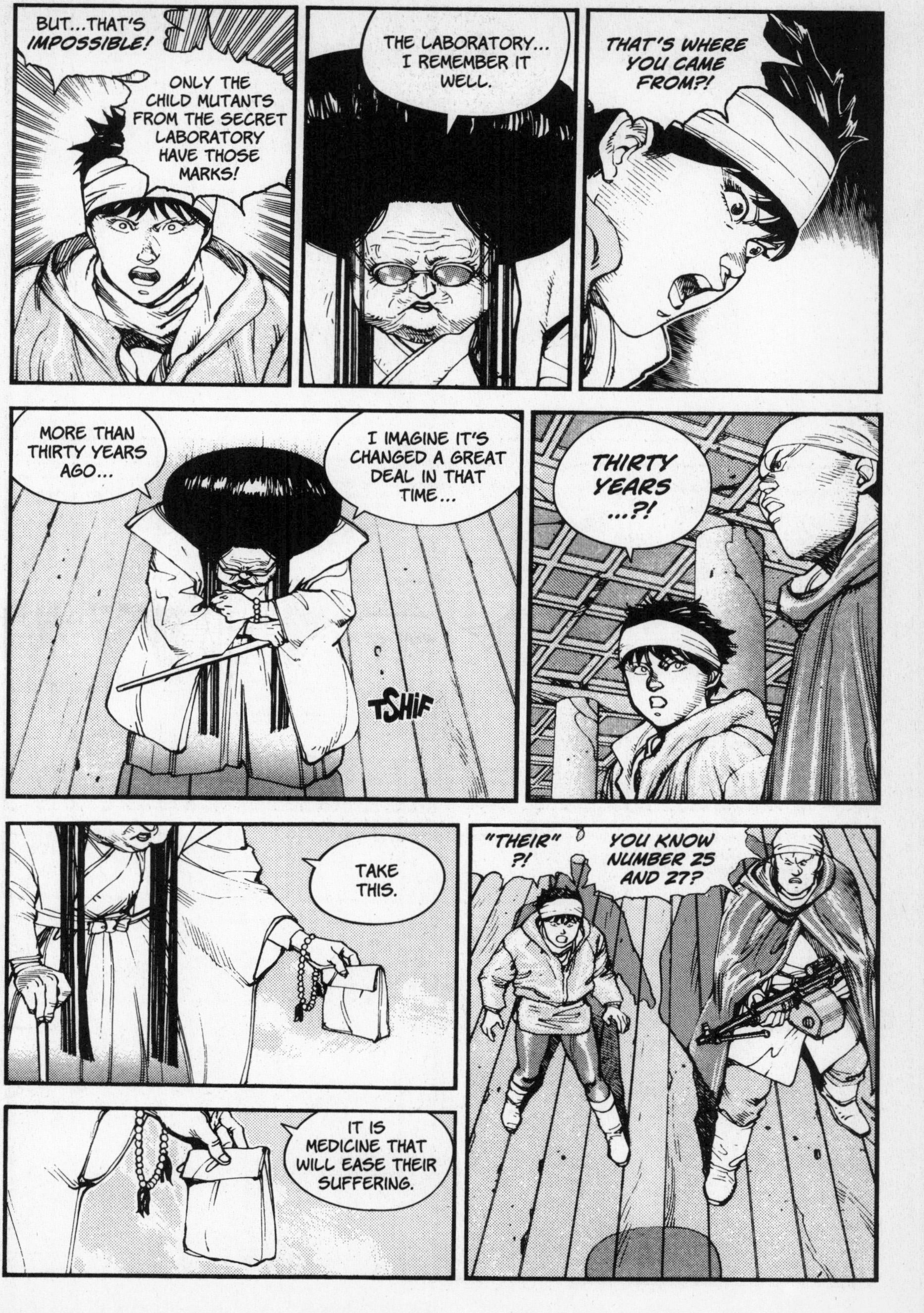
BUT...THAT'S IMPOSSIBLE!
ONLY THE CHILD MUTANTS FROM THE SECRET LABORATORY HAVE THOSE MARKS!
THE LABORATORY... I REMEMBER IT WELL.
THAT'S WHERE YOU CAME FROM?!
MORE THAN THIRTY YEARS AGO...
I IMAGINE IT'S CHANGED A GREAT DEAL IN THAT TIME...
TSHIF
THIRTY YEARS ...?!
TAKE THIS.
IT IS MEDICINE THAT WILL EASE THEIR SUFFERING.
"THEIR" ?!
YOU KNOW NUMBER 25 AND 27?

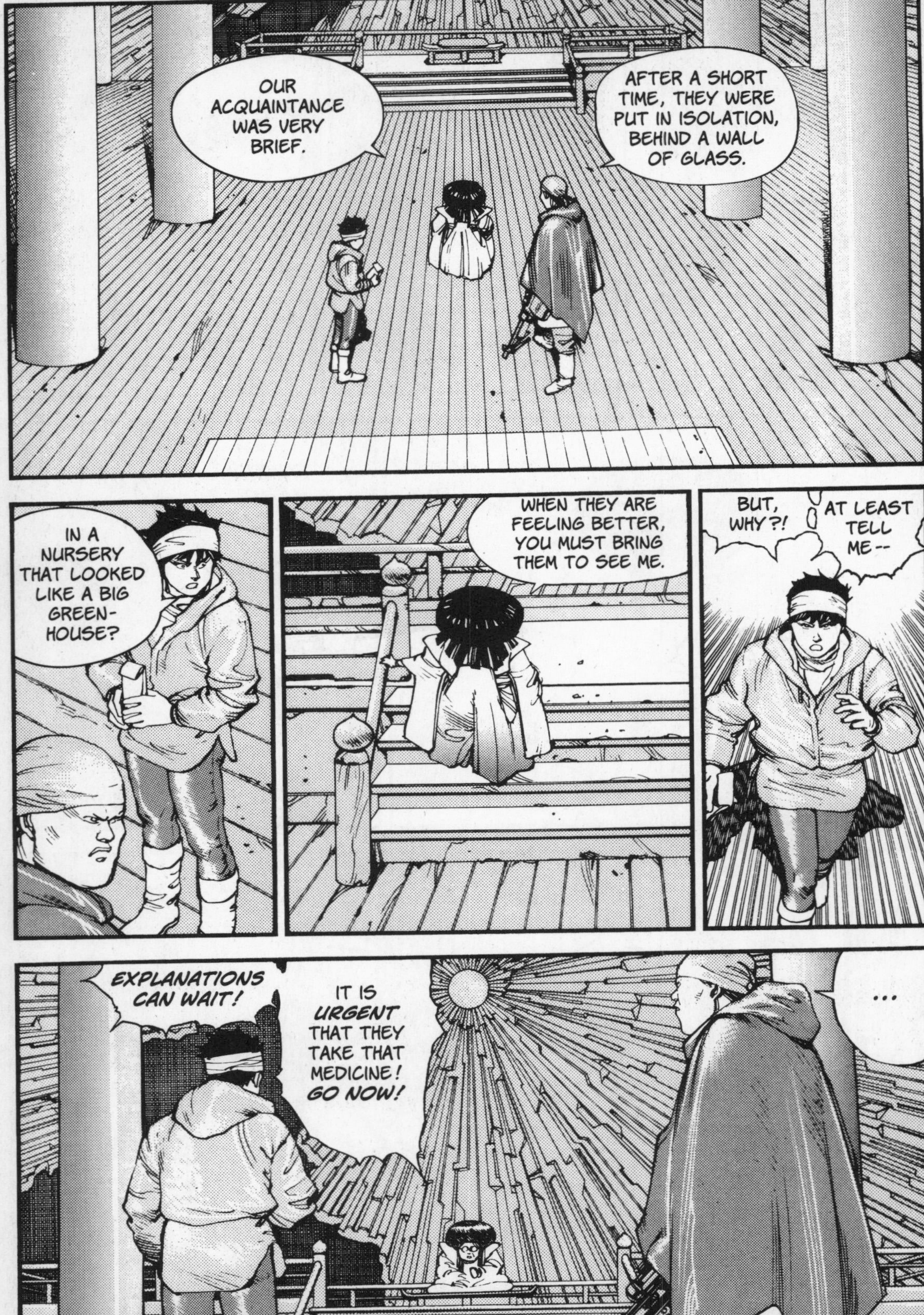
OUR ACQUAINTANCE WAS VERY BRIEF.
AFTER A SHORT TIME, THEY WERE PUT IN ISOLATION, BEHIND A WALL OF GLASS.
IN A NURSERY THAT LOOKED LIKE A BIG GREEN-HOUSE?
WHEN THEY ARE FEELING BETTER, YOU MUST BRING THEM TO SEE ME.
BUT, WHY?!
AT LEAST TELL ME--
EXPLANATIONS CAN WAIT!
IT IS URGENT THAT THEY TAKE THAT MEDICINE! GO NOW!
...

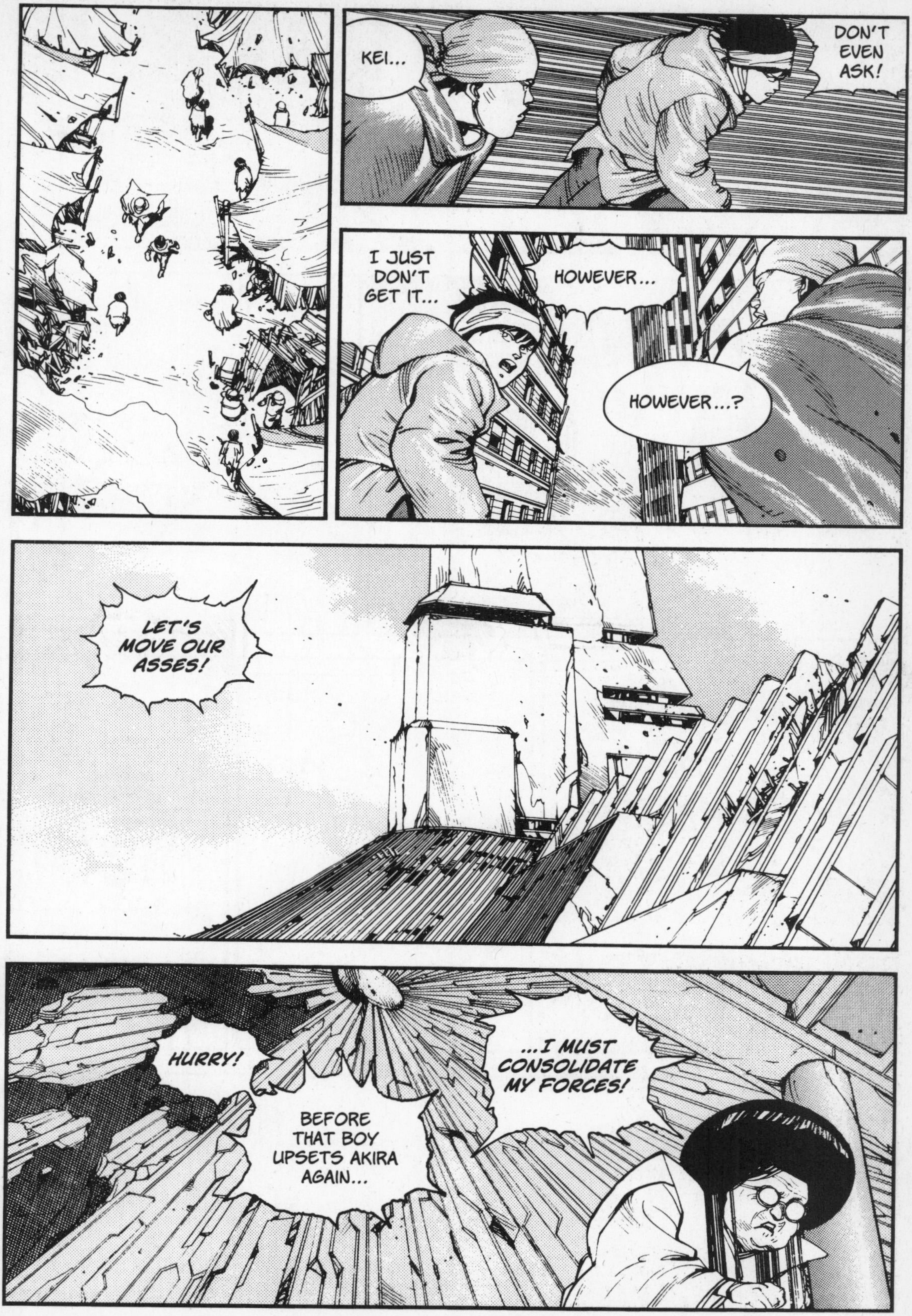
KEI...
DON'T EVEN ASK!
I JUST DON'T GET IT...
HOWEVER...
HOWEVER...?
LET'S MOVE OUR ASSES!
HURRY!
...I MUST CONSOLIDATE MY FORCES!
BEFORE THAT BOY UPSETS AKIRA AGAIN...

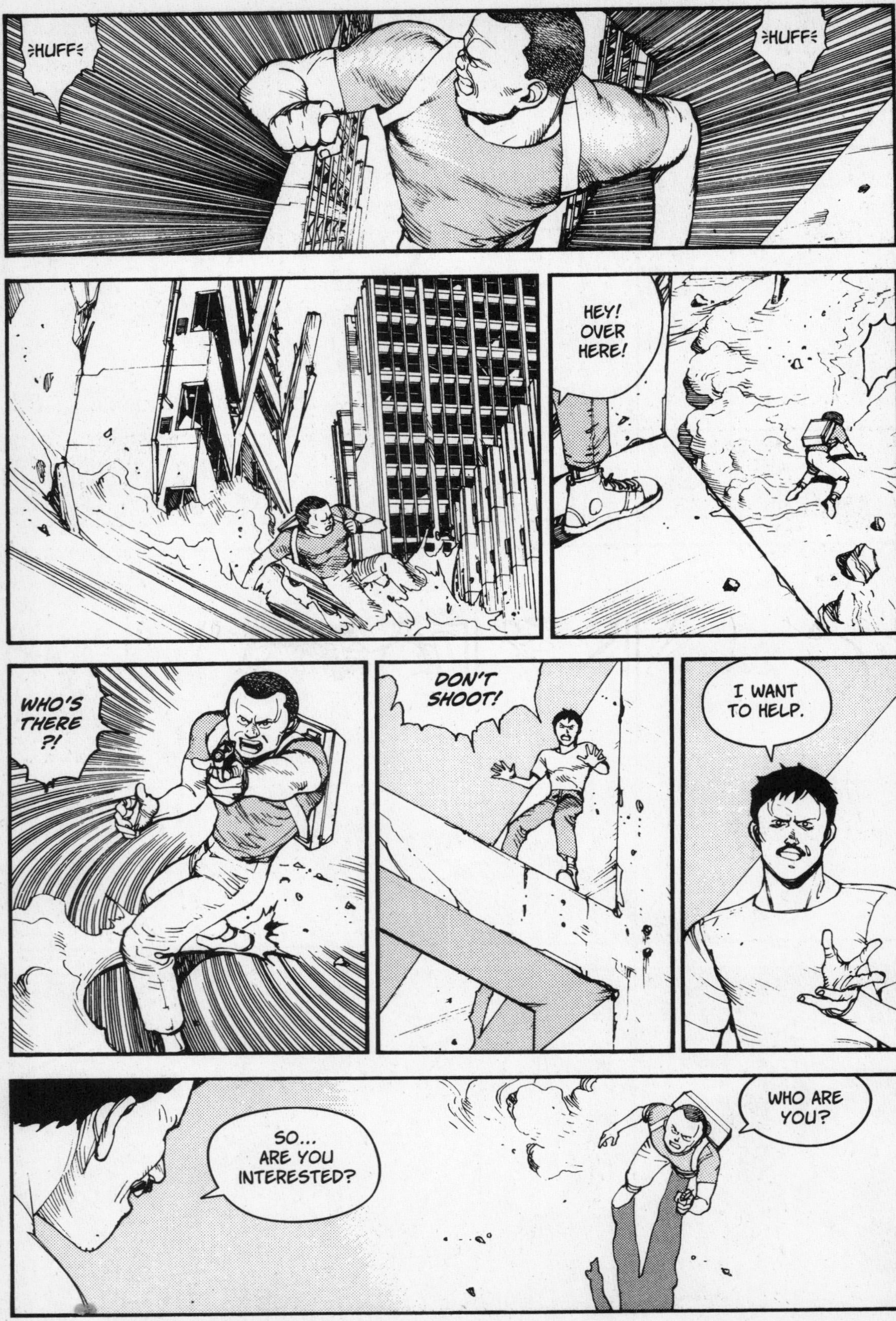
HUFF
HUFF
HEY! OVER HERE!
WHO'S THERE ?!
DON'T SHOOT!
I WANT TO HELP.
SO... ARE YOU INTERESTED?
WHO ARE YOU?

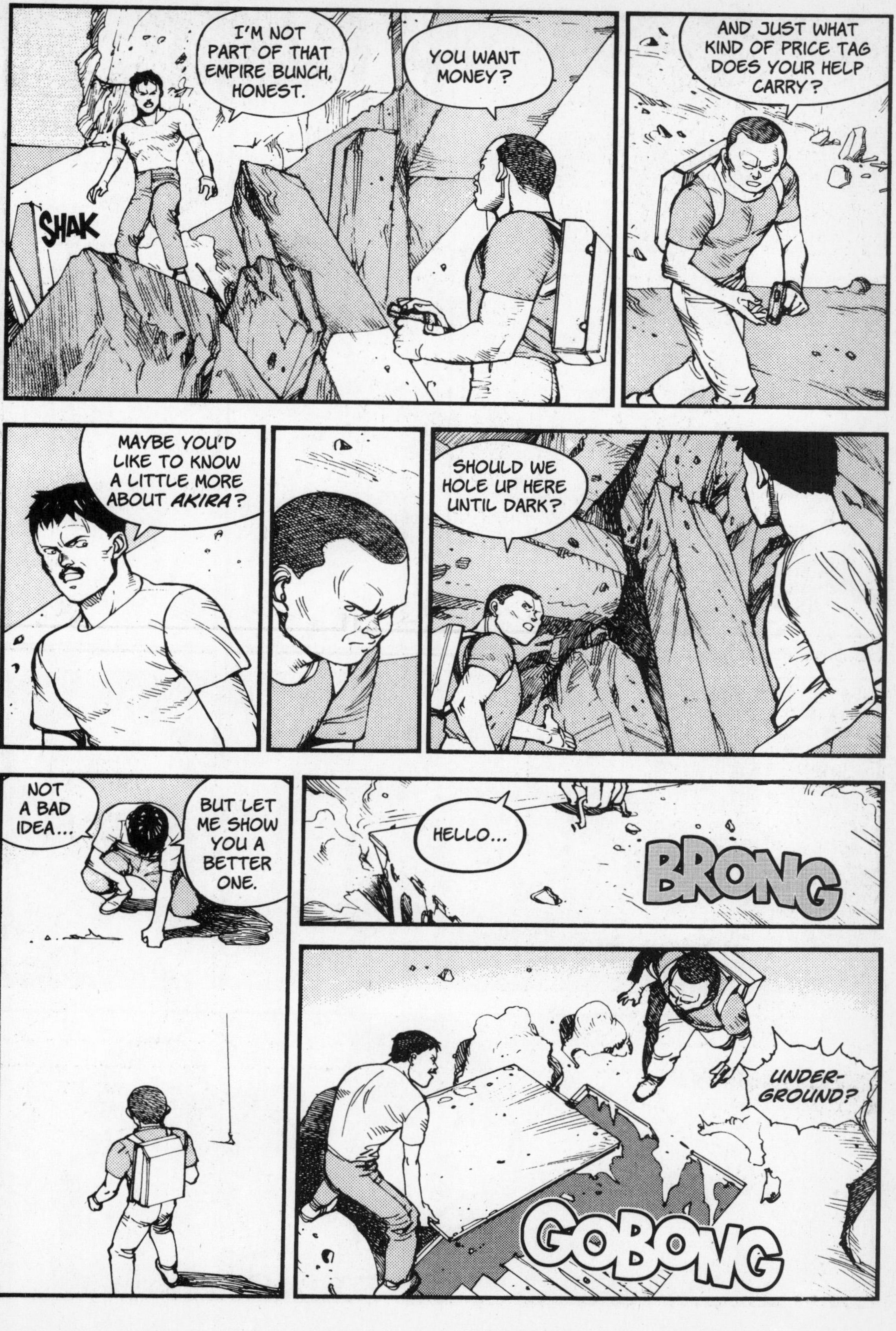
I'M NOT PART OF THAT EMPIRE BUNCH, HONEST.
SHAK
YOU WANT MONEY?
AND JUST WHAT KIND OF PRICE TAG DOES YOUR HELP CARRY?
MAYBE YOU'D LIKE TO KNOW A LITTLE MORE ABOUT *AKIRA*?
SHOULD WE HOLE UP HERE UNTIL DARK?
NOT A BAD IDEA...
BUT LET ME SHOW YOU A BETTER ONE.
HELLO...
BRONG
UNDER-GROUND?
GOBONG

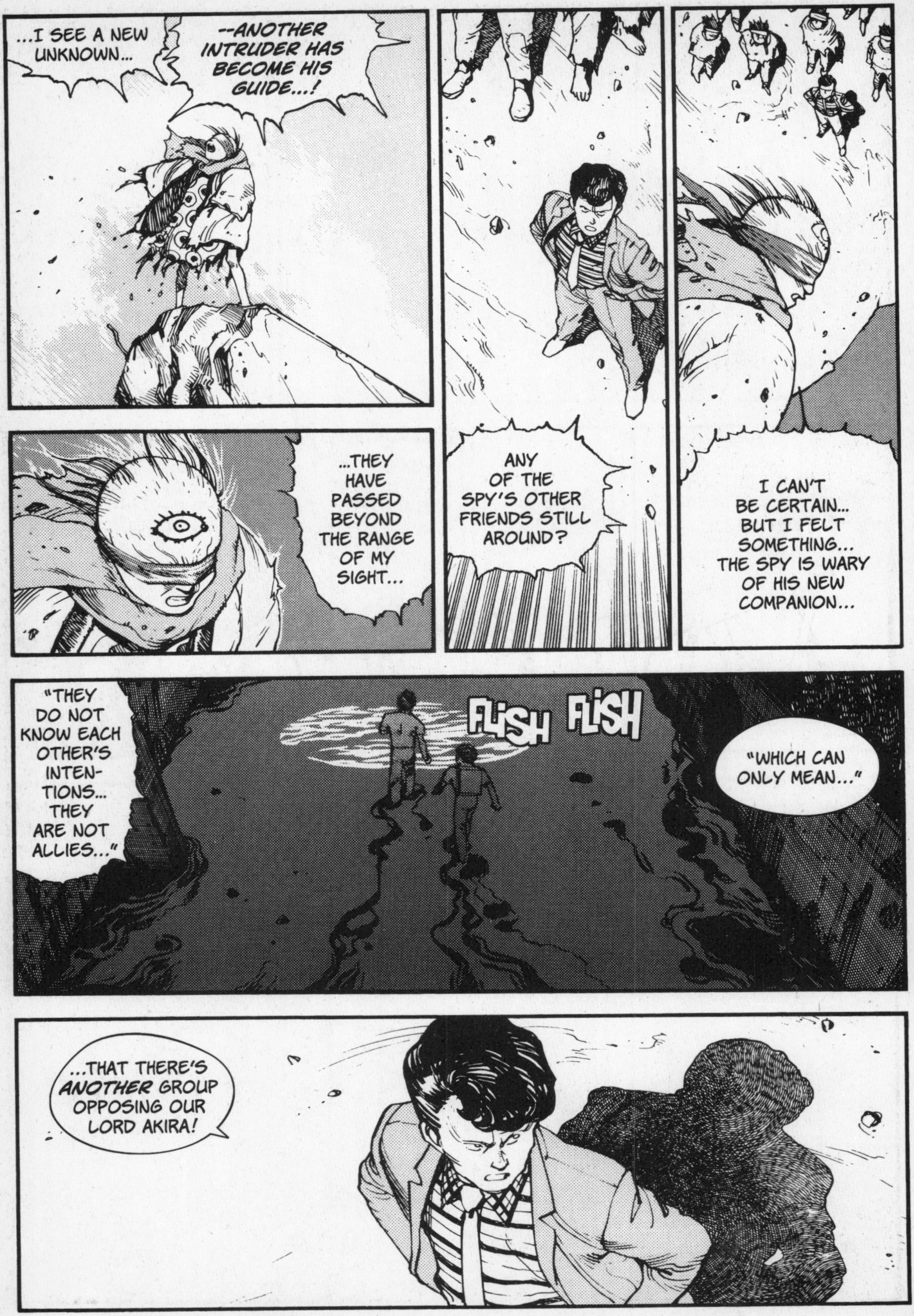
...I SEE A NEW UNKNOWN...
--ANOTHER INTRUDER HAS BECOME HIS GUIDE...!
...THEY HAVE PASSED BEYOND THE RANGE OF MY SIGHT...
ANY OF THE SPY'S OTHER FRIENDS STILL AROUND?
I CAN'T BE CERTAIN... BUT I FELT SOMETHING... THE SPY IS WARY OF HIS NEW COMPANION...
"THEY DO NOT KNOW EACH OTHER'S INTENTIONS... THEY ARE NOT ALLIES..."
FLISH FLISH
"WHICH CAN ONLY MEAN..."
...THAT THERE'S ANOTHER GROUP OPPOSING OUR LORD AKIRA!

HAIL OUR SAVIOR! LORD AKIRA!
LONG LIFE TO YOU, NOBLE AKIRA!
HAIL!
BANZAI!
BANZAI!
AKIRA
30
大覚
AKIRA
LONG LIVE OUR SAVIOR!

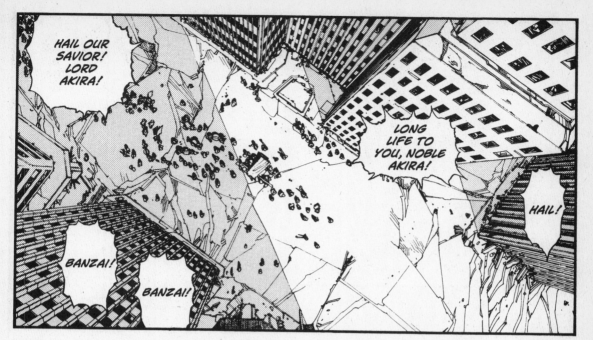

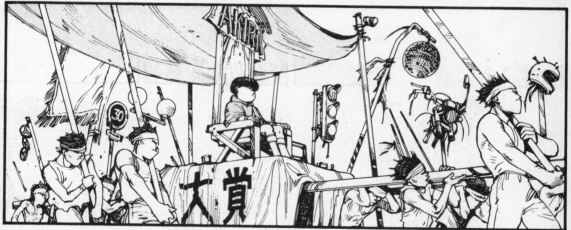

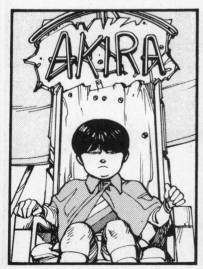

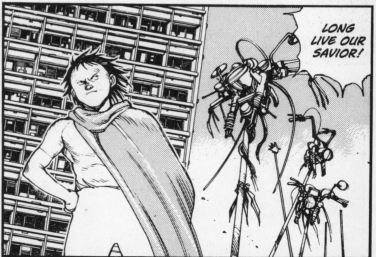

LORD AKIRA, IN HIS INFINITE MERCY, HAS DECREED THAT WE DISTRIBUTE FOOD TO YOU!

THANK YOU, LORD!

HURRAY FOR THE NOBLE AKIRA!

HURRAY!

FILTHY PIGS.

FROSH

HA HA! IN THE NAME OF OUR GREAT LORD AKIRA...

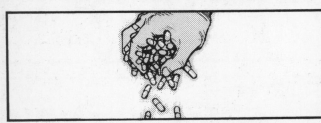

IT'S HERE! PLEASE!

LINE UP!

AIEE!

98

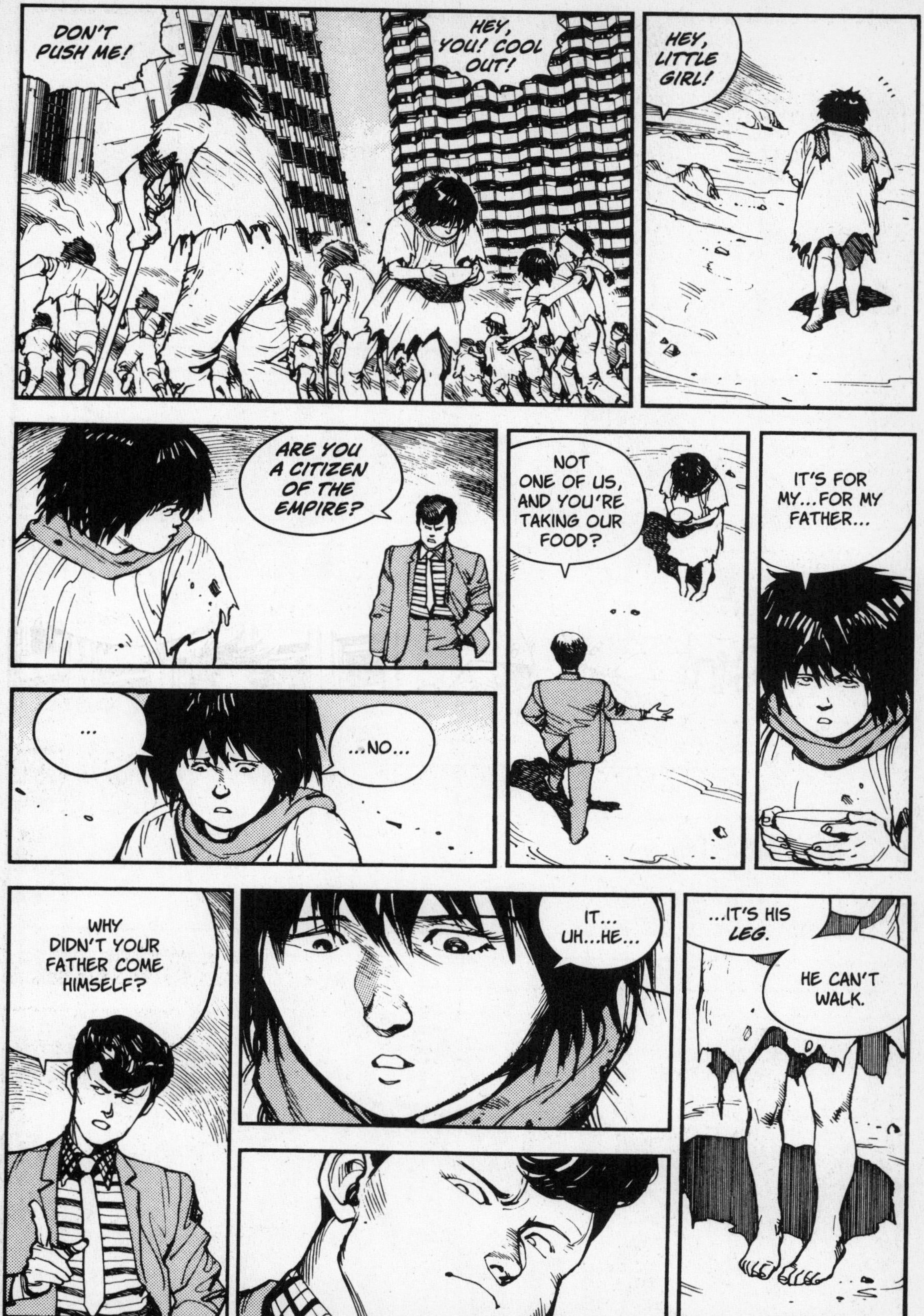
DON'T PUSH ME!
HEY, YOU! COOL OUT!
HEY, LITTLE GIRL!
ARE YOU A CITIZEN OF THE EMPIRE?
...
...NO...
NOT ONE OF US, AND YOU'RE TAKING OUR FOOD?
IT'S FOR MY...FOR MY FATHER...
WHY DIDN'T YOUR FATHER COME HIMSELF?
IT... UH...HE...
...IT'S HIS LEG.
HE CAN'T WALK.

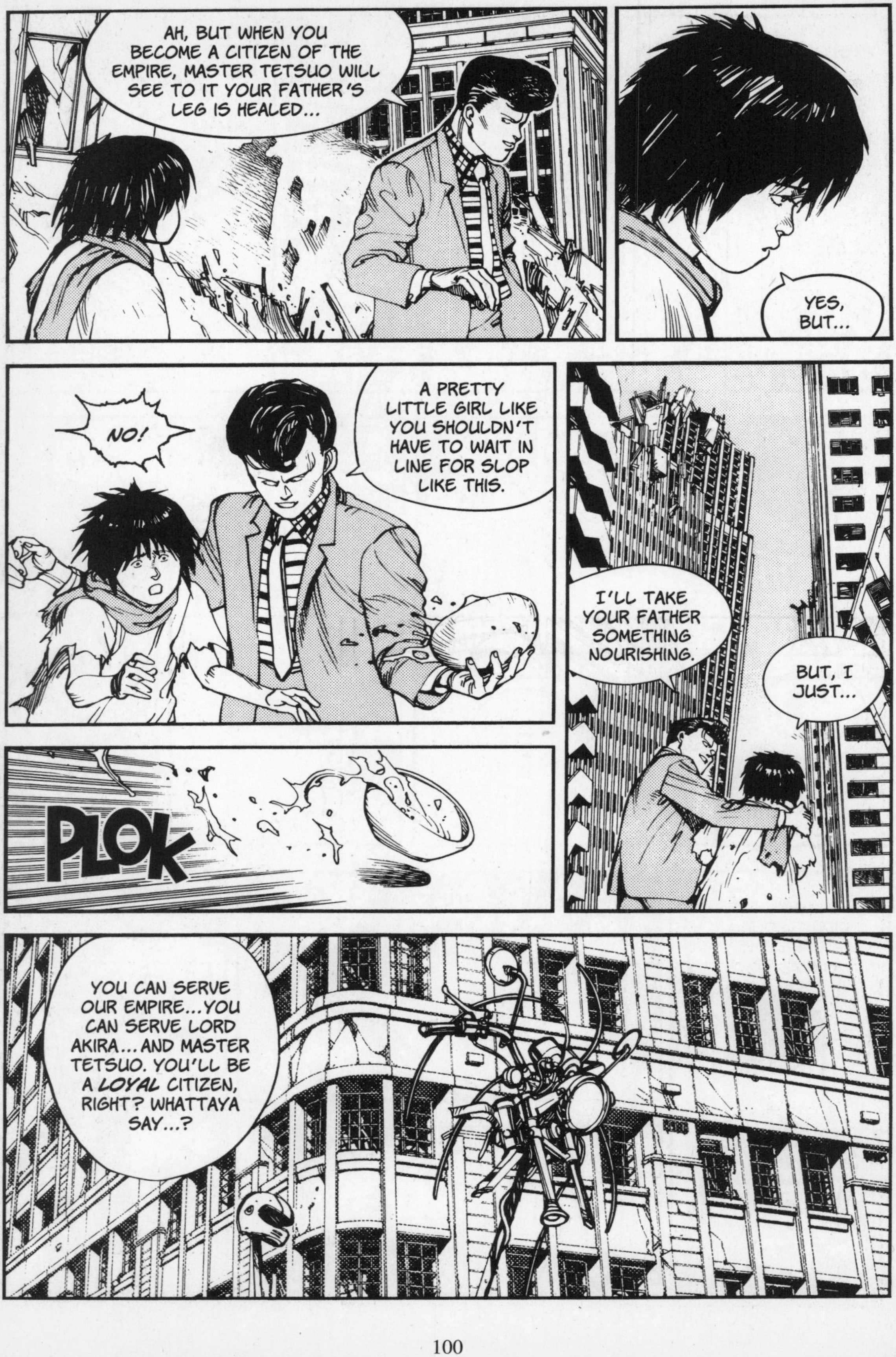
AH, BUT WHEN YOU BECOME A CITIZEN OF THE EMPIRE, MASTER TETSUO WILL SEE TO IT YOUR FATHER'S LEG IS HEALED...
YES, BUT...
NO!
A PRETTY LITTLE GIRL LIKE YOU SHOULDN'T HAVE TO WAIT IN LINE FOR SLOP LIKE THIS.
PLOK
I'LL TAKE YOUR FATHER SOMETHING NOURISHING.
BUT, I JUST...
YOU CAN SERVE OUR EMPIRE...YOU CAN SERVE LORD AKIRA...AND MASTER TETSUO. YOU'LL BE A *LOYAL* CITIZEN, RIGHT? WHATTAYA SAY...?

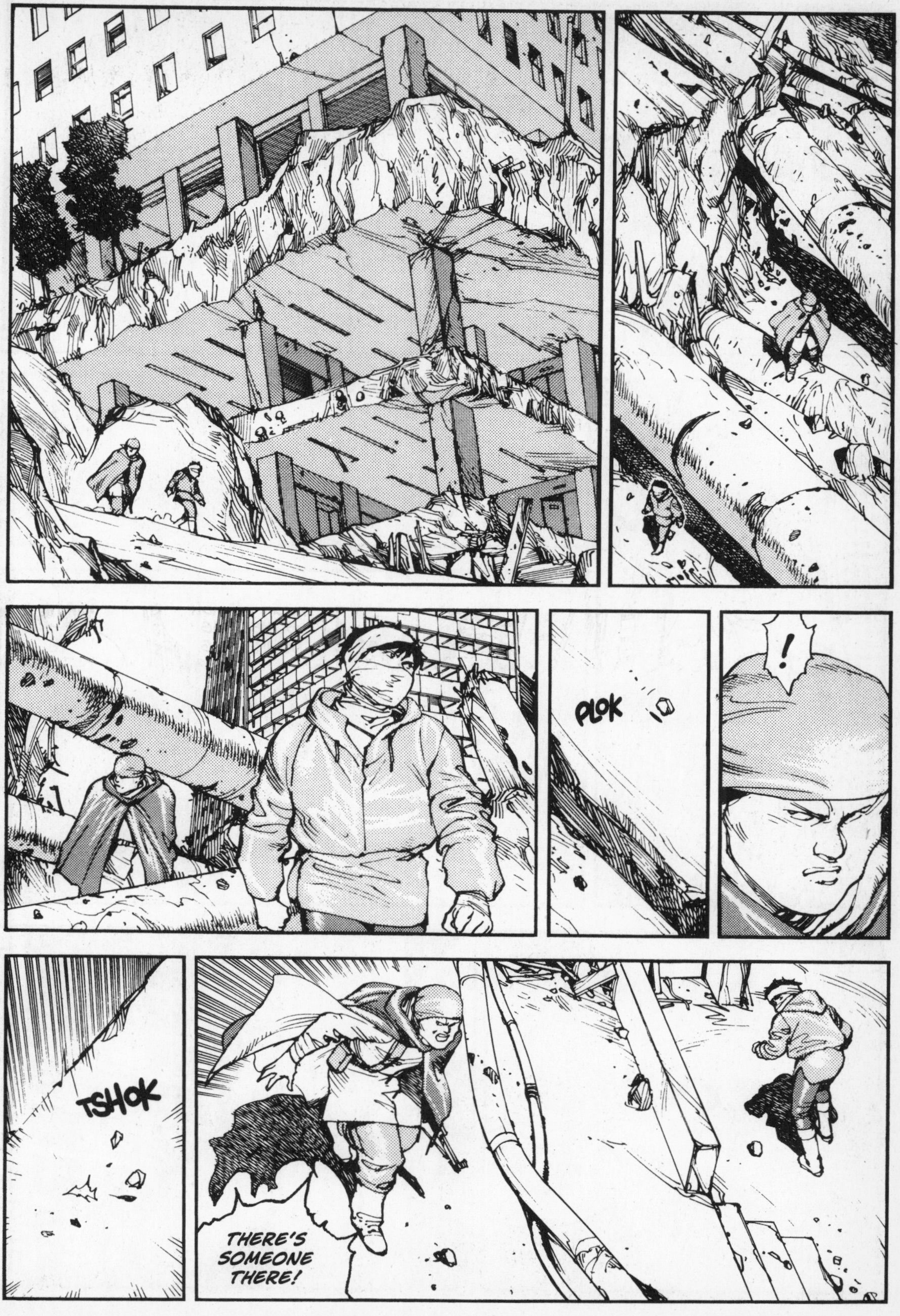
PLOK
!
TSHOK
THERE'S SOMEONE THERE!

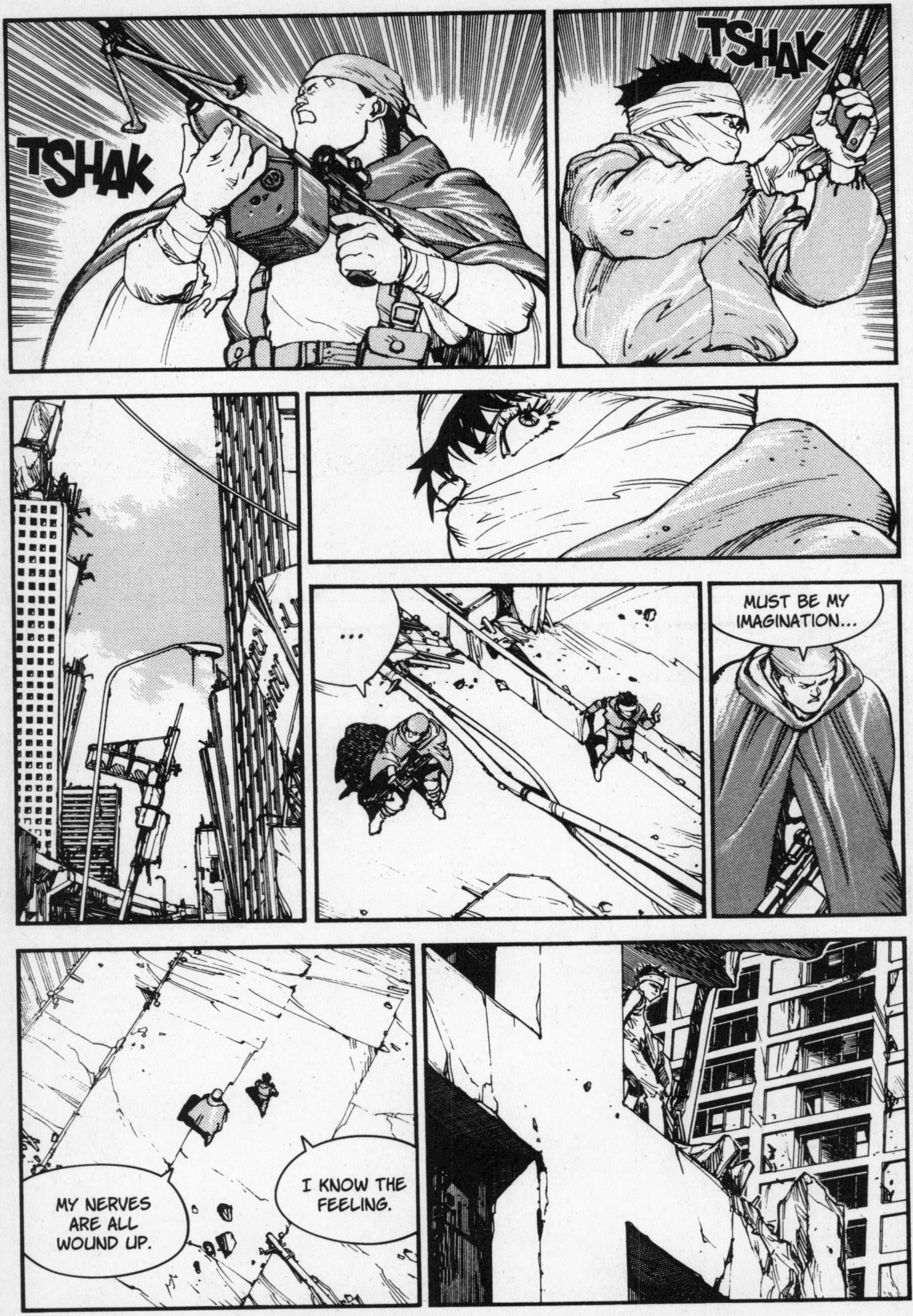
TSHAK
TSHAK
...
MUST BE MY IMAGINATION...
MY NERVES ARE ALL WOUND UP.
I KNOW THE FEELING.

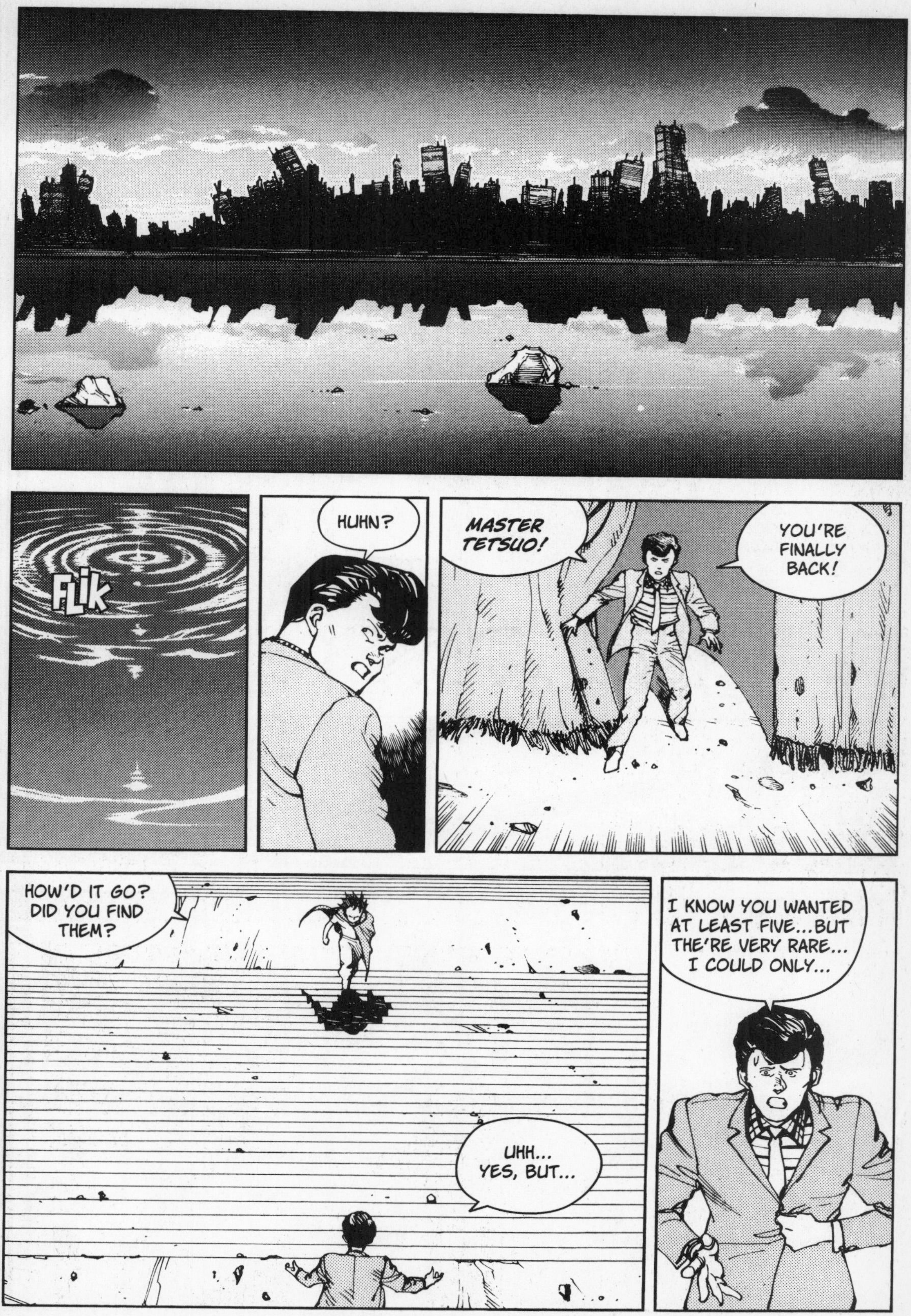
FLIK
HUHN?
MASTER TETSUO!
YOU'RE FINALLY BACK!
HOW'D IT GO? DID YOU FIND THEM?
UHH... YES, BUT...
I KNOW YOU WANTED AT LEAST FIVE...BUT THE'RE VERY RARE... I COULD ONLY...

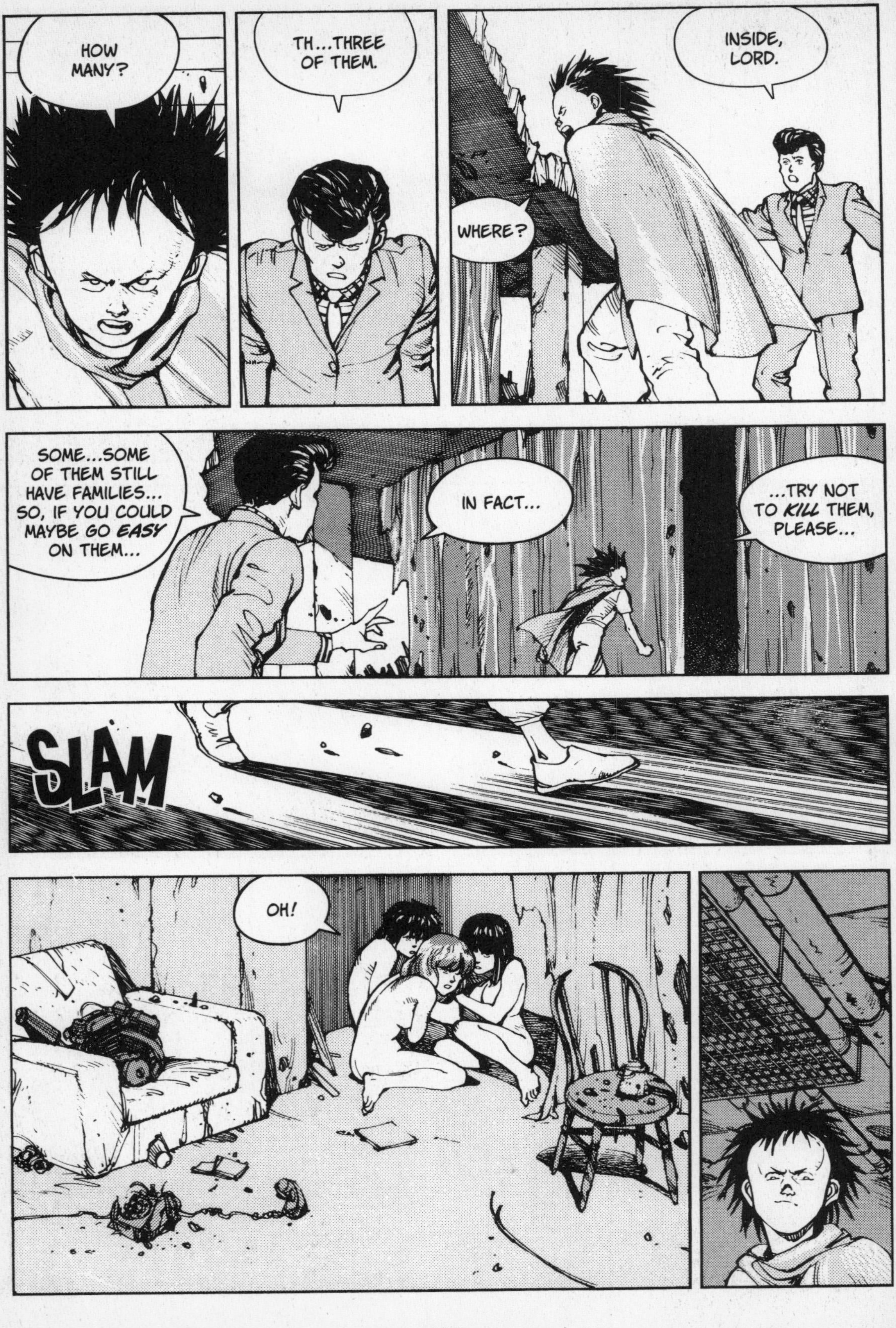
HOW MANY?
TH...THREE OF THEM.
INSIDE, LORD.
WHERE?
SOME...SOME OF THEM STILL HAVE FAMILIES... SO, IF YOU COULD MAYBE GO EASY ON THEM...
IN FACT...
...TRY NOT TO KILL THEM, PLEASE...
SLAM
OH!

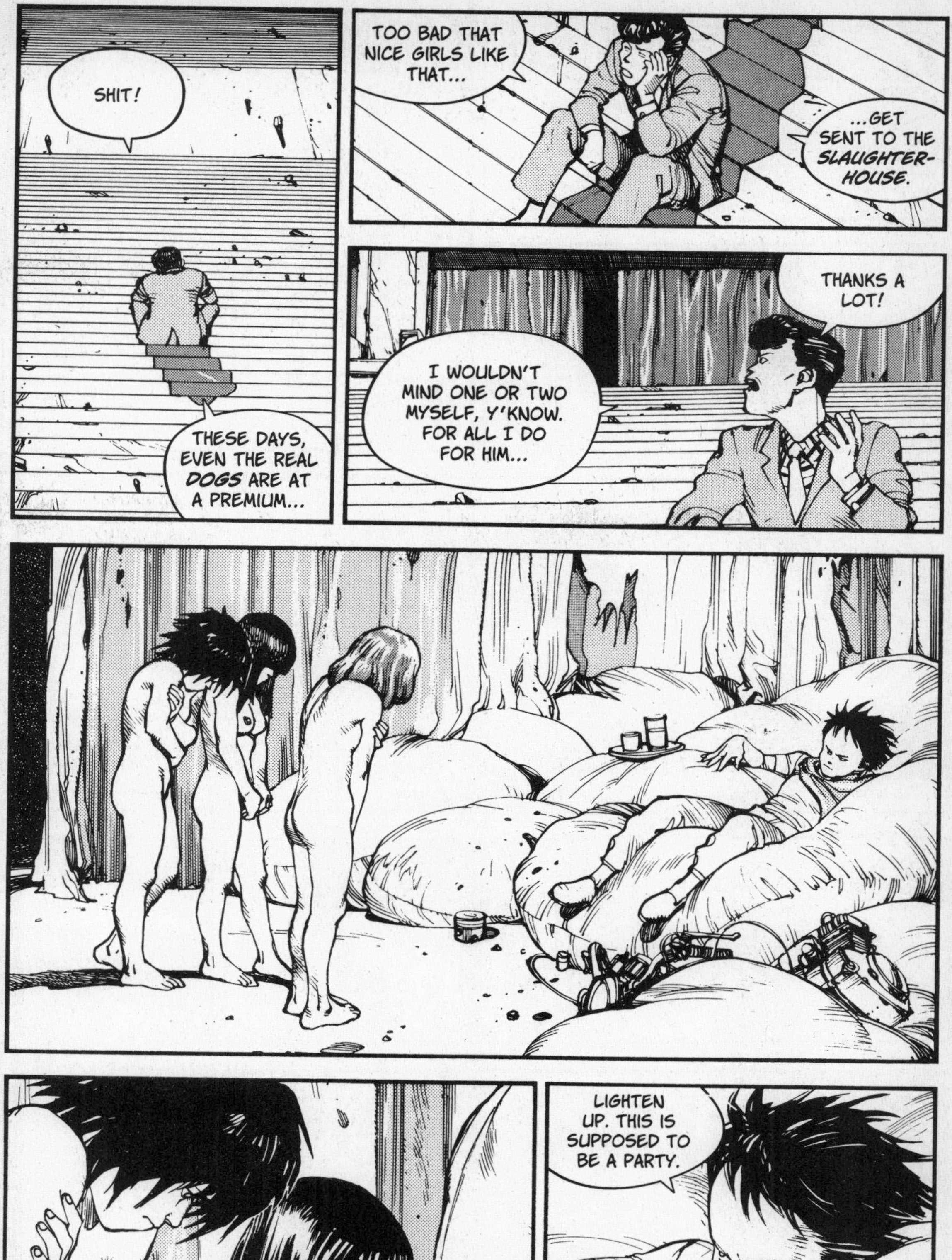
SHIT!
THESE DAYS, EVEN THE REAL *DOGS* ARE AT A PREMIUM...
TOO BAD THAT NICE GIRLS LIKE THAT...
...GET SENT TO THE *SLAUGHTER-HOUSE.*
THANKS A LOT!
I WOULDN'T MIND ONE OR TWO MYSELF, Y'KNOW. FOR ALL I DO FOR HIM...
LIGHTEN UP. THIS IS SUPPOSED TO BE A PARTY.

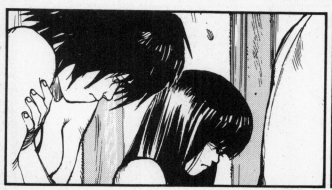

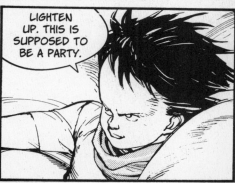

...AND I BROUGHT THE FAVORS!

DON'T WORRY... THEY AREN'T FULL STRENGTH. JUST ENOUGH TO MAKE YOU RELAX.

SLIF

OH!

...

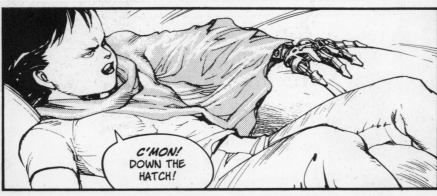

C'MON! DOWN THE HATCH!

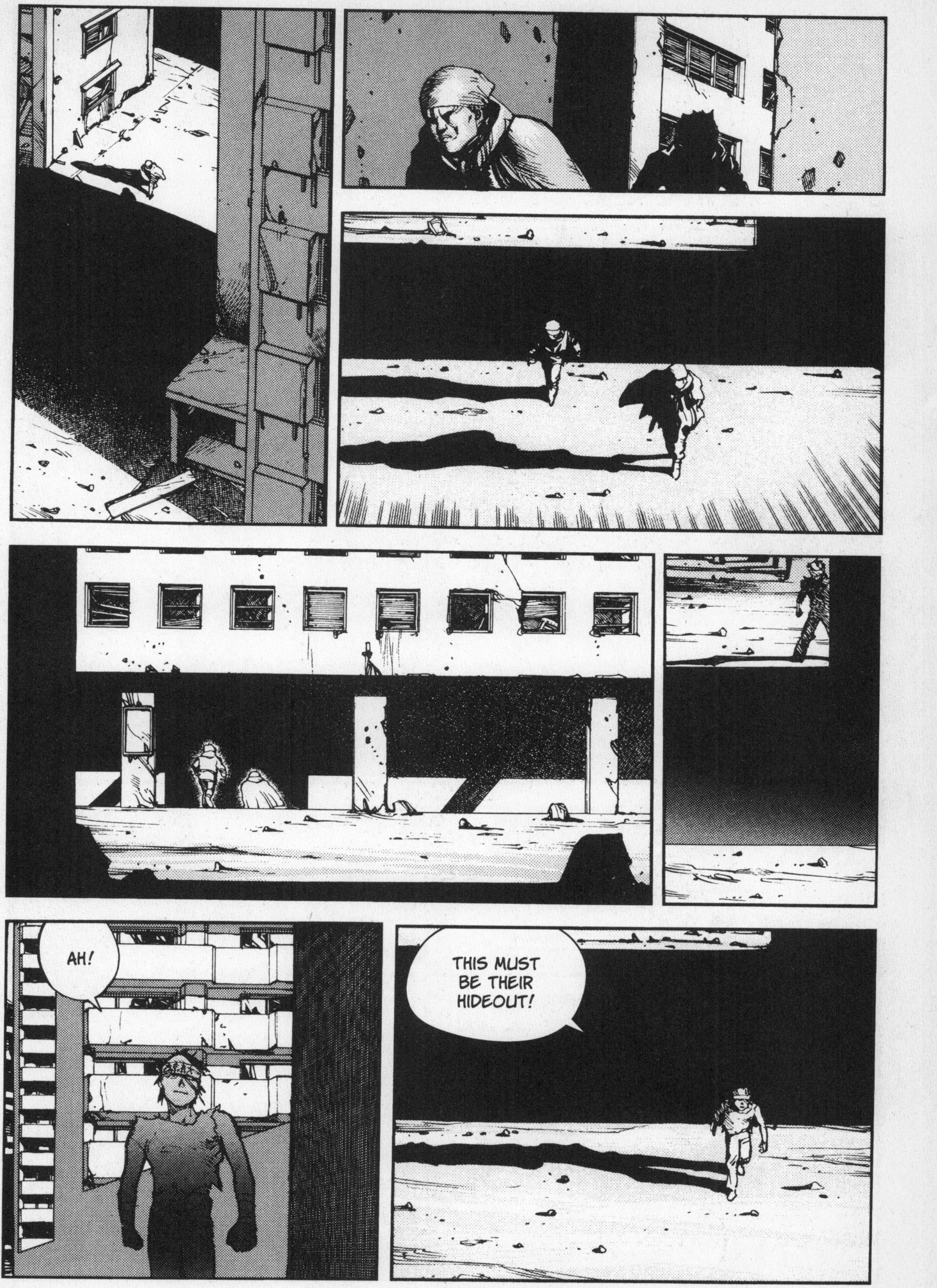
AH!
THIS MUST BE THEIR HIDEOUT!

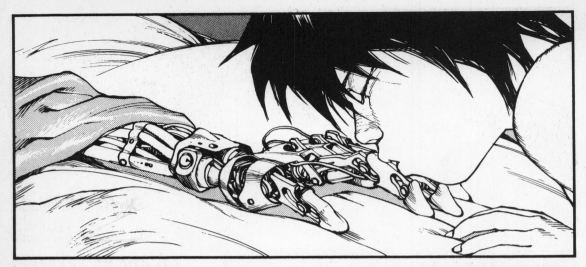

KLic

OH!

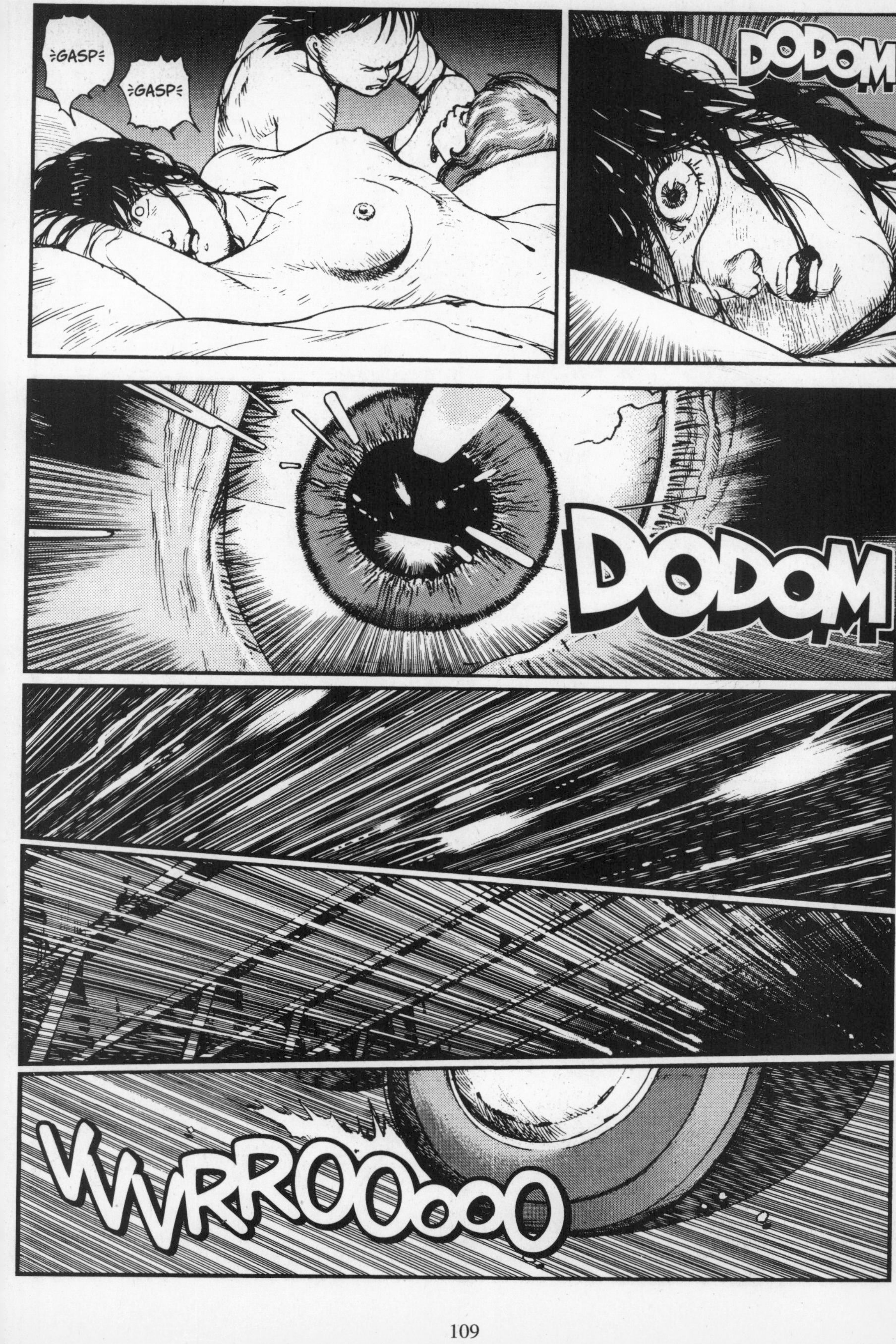
GASP
GASP
DODOM
DODOM
VVVRROOooo

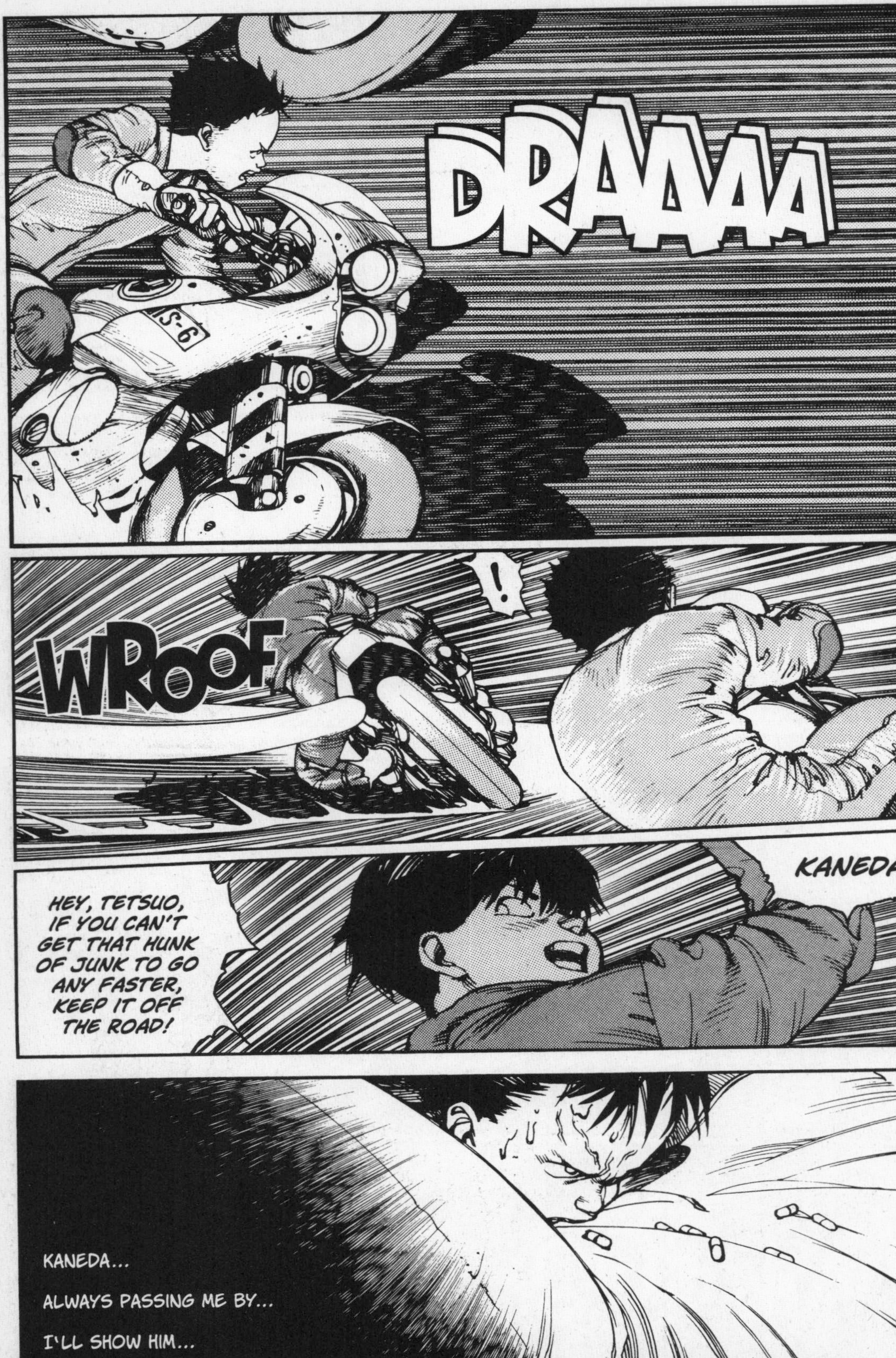
DRAAAAA
WROOF
!
HEY, TETSUO, IF YOU CAN'T GET THAT HUNK OF JUNK TO GO ANY FASTER, KEEP IT OFF THE ROAD!
KANEDA!
KANEDA...
ALWAYS PASSING ME BY...
I'LL SHOW HIM...

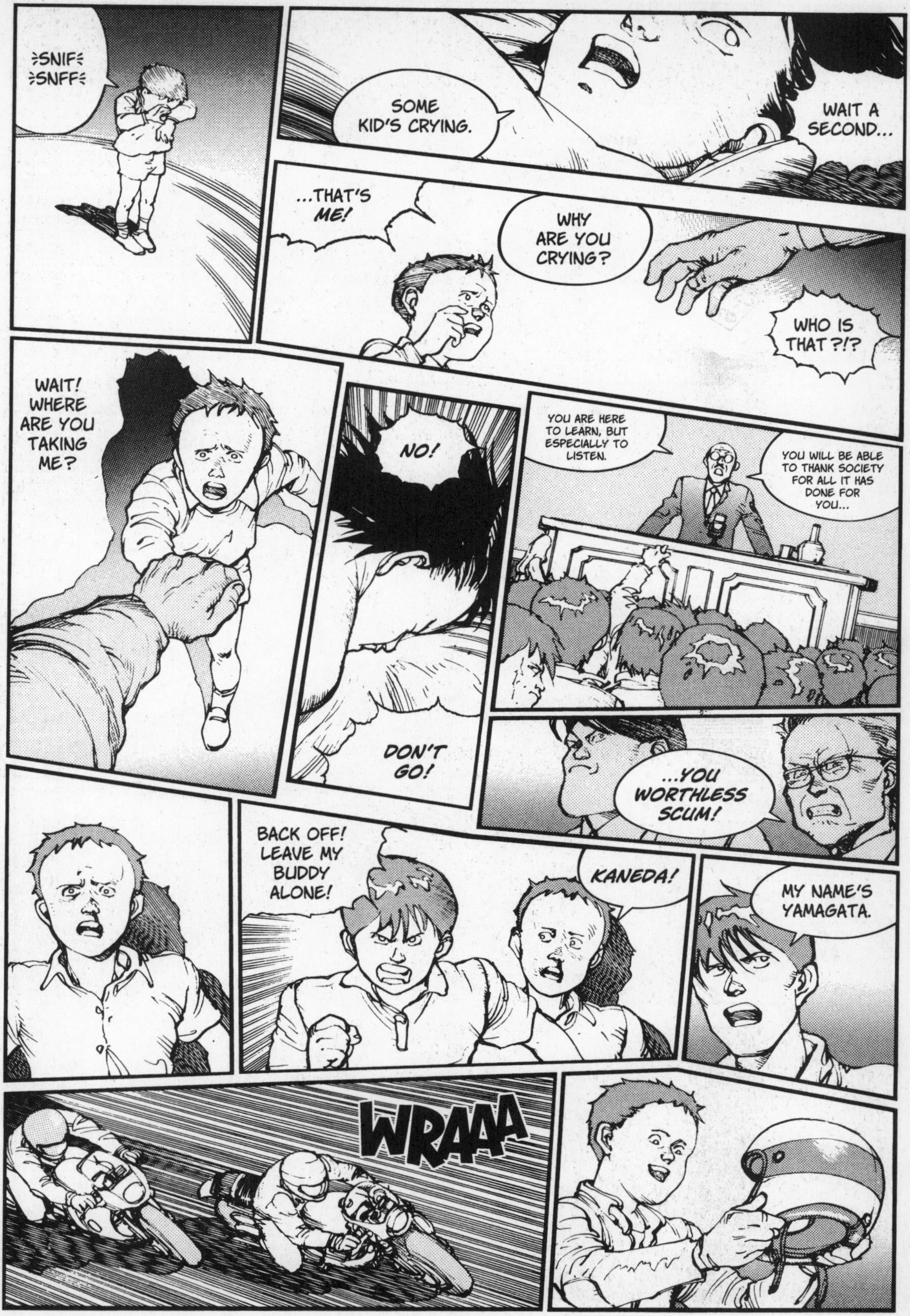

⫶SNIF⫶
⫶SNFF⫶
SOME KID'S CRYING.
WAIT A SECOND...
...THAT'S *ME!*
WHY ARE YOU CRYING?
WHO IS THAT?!?
WAIT! WHERE ARE YOU TAKING ME?
*NO!*
*DON'T GO!*
YOU ARE HERE TO LEARN, BUT ESPECIALLY TO LISTEN.
YOU WILL BE ABLE TO THANK SOCIETY FOR ALL IT HAS DONE FOR YOU...
*...YOU WORTHLESS SCUM!*
BACK OFF! LEAVE MY BUDDY ALONE!
*KANEDA!*
MY NAME'S YAMAGATA.
WRAAA

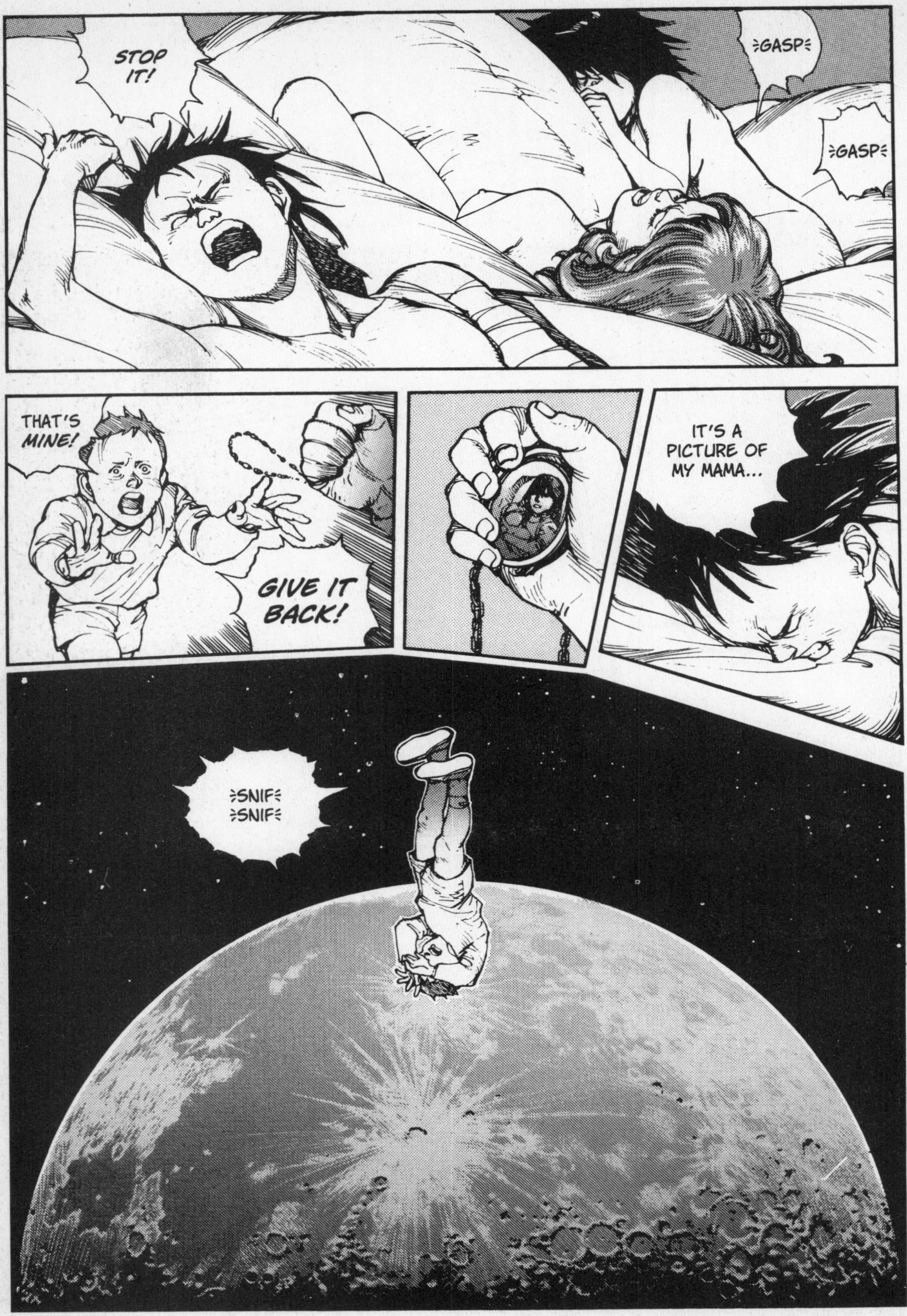
STOP IT!
≑GASP≑
≑GASP≑
THAT'S MINE!
GIVE IT BACK!
IT'S A PICTURE OF MY MAMA...
≑SNIF≑
≑SNIF≑

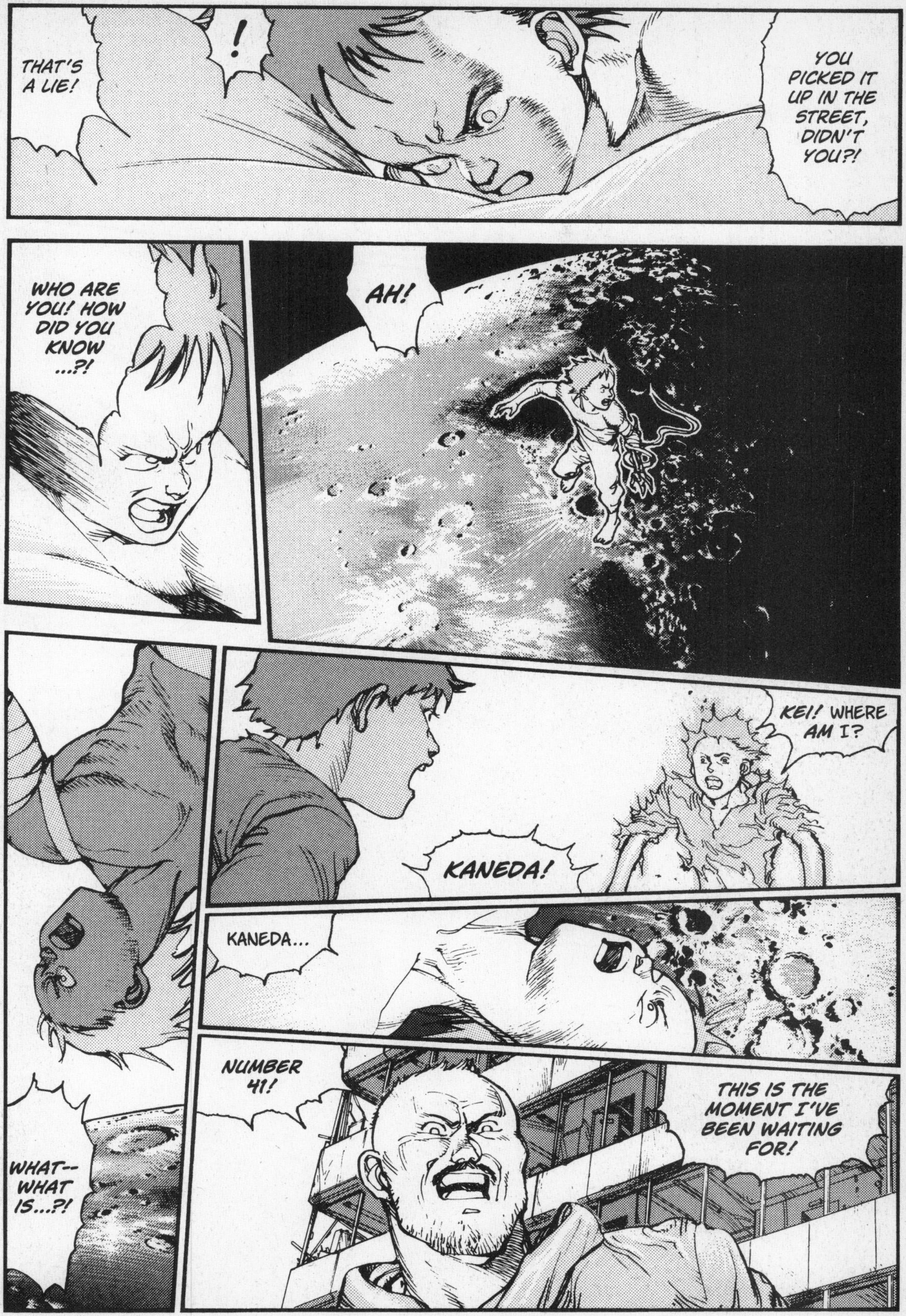
THAT'S A LIE!
!
YOU PICKED IT UP IN THE STREET, DIDN'T YOU?!
WHO ARE YOU! HOW DID YOU KNOW ...?!
AH!
WHAT-- WHAT IS...?!
KEI! WHERE AM I?
KANEDA!
KANEDA...
NUMBER 41!
THIS IS THE MOMENT I'VE BEEN WAITING FOR!

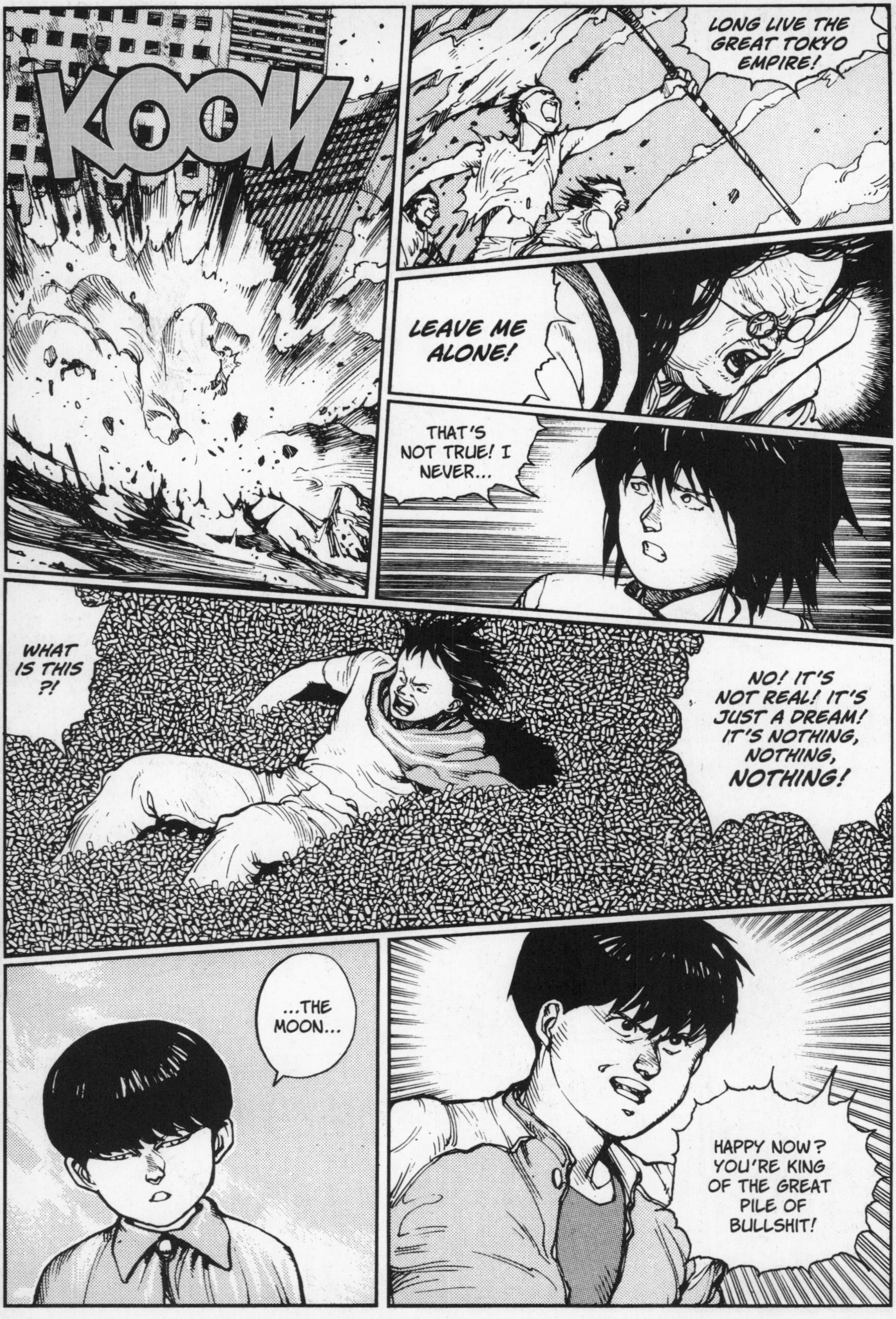
KOOM
LONG LIVE THE GREAT TOKYO EMPIRE!
LEAVE ME ALONE!
THAT'S NOT TRUE! I NEVER...
WHAT IS THIS ?!
NO! IT'S NOT REAL! IT'S JUST A DREAM! IT'S NOTHING, NOTHING, NOTHING!
...THE MOON...
HAPPY NOW? YOU'RE KING OF THE GREAT PILE OF BULLSHIT!

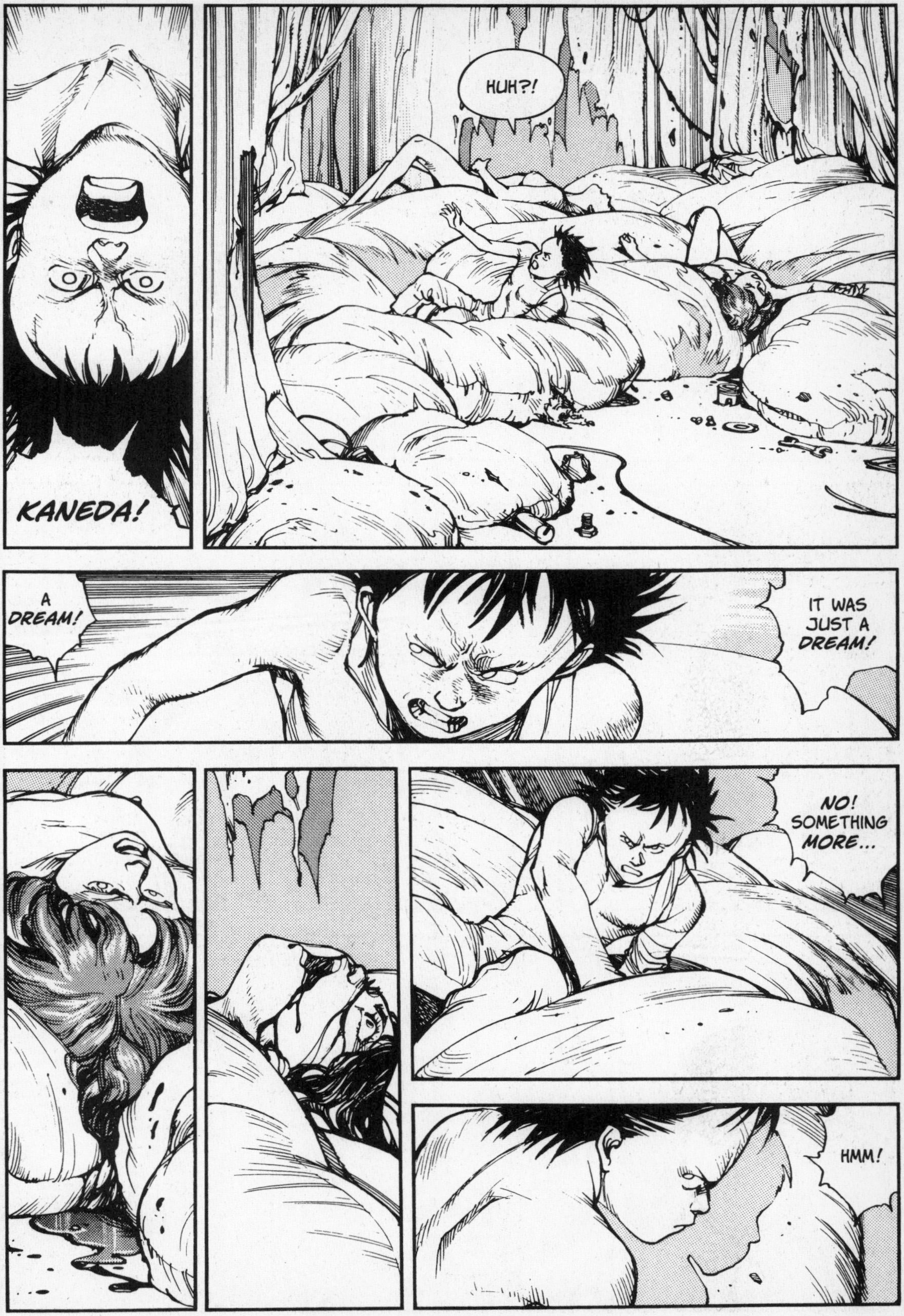
KANEDA!
HUH?!
A DREAM!
IT WAS JUST A DREAM!
NO! SOMETHING MORE...
HMM!

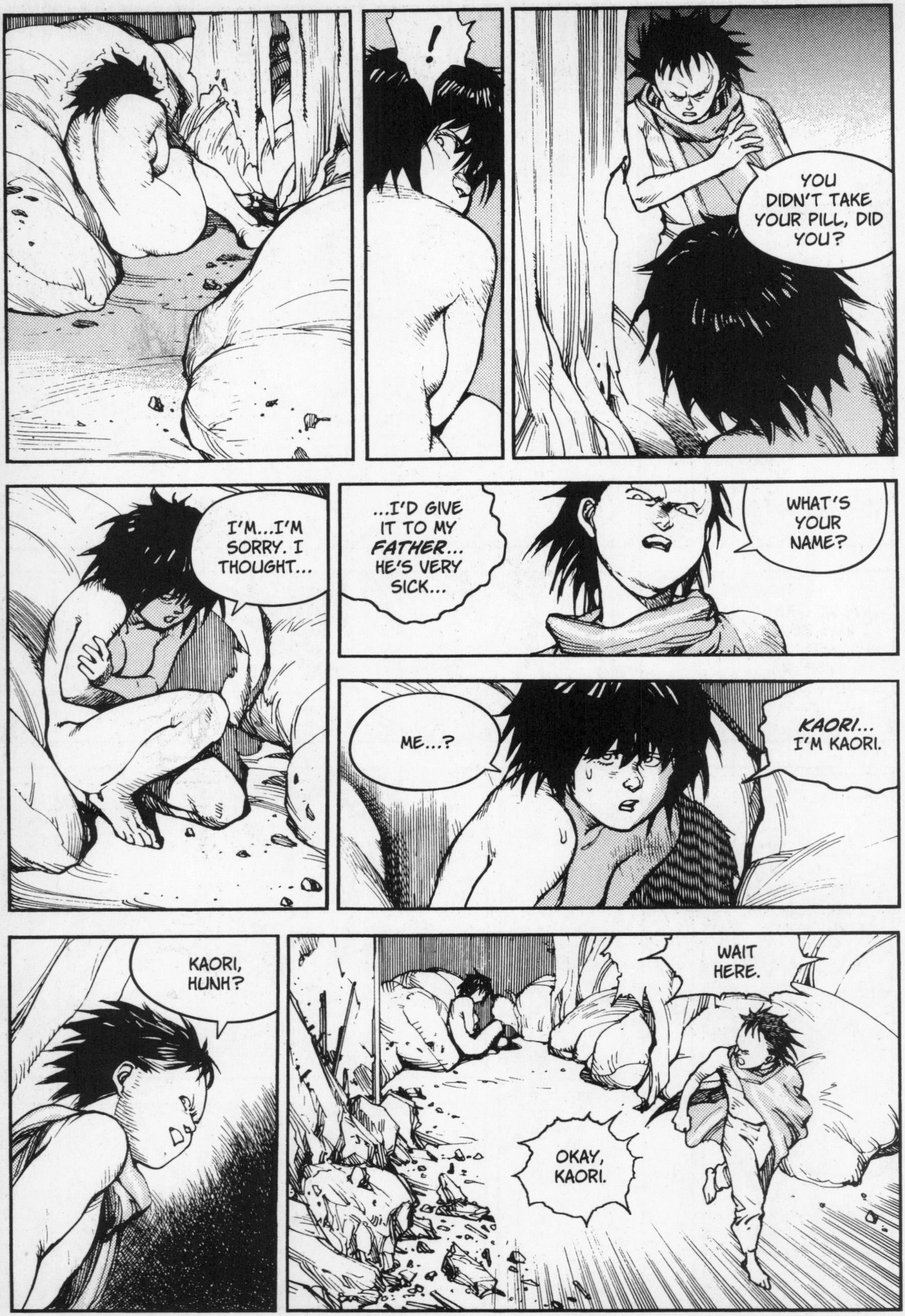
!
YOU DIDN'T TAKE YOUR PILL, DID YOU?
I'M...I'M SORRY. I THOUGHT...
...I'D GIVE IT TO MY *FATHER*... HE'S VERY SICK...
WHAT'S YOUR NAME?
ME...?
*KAORI*... I'M KAORI.
KAORI, HUNH?
WAIT HERE.
OKAY, KAORI.

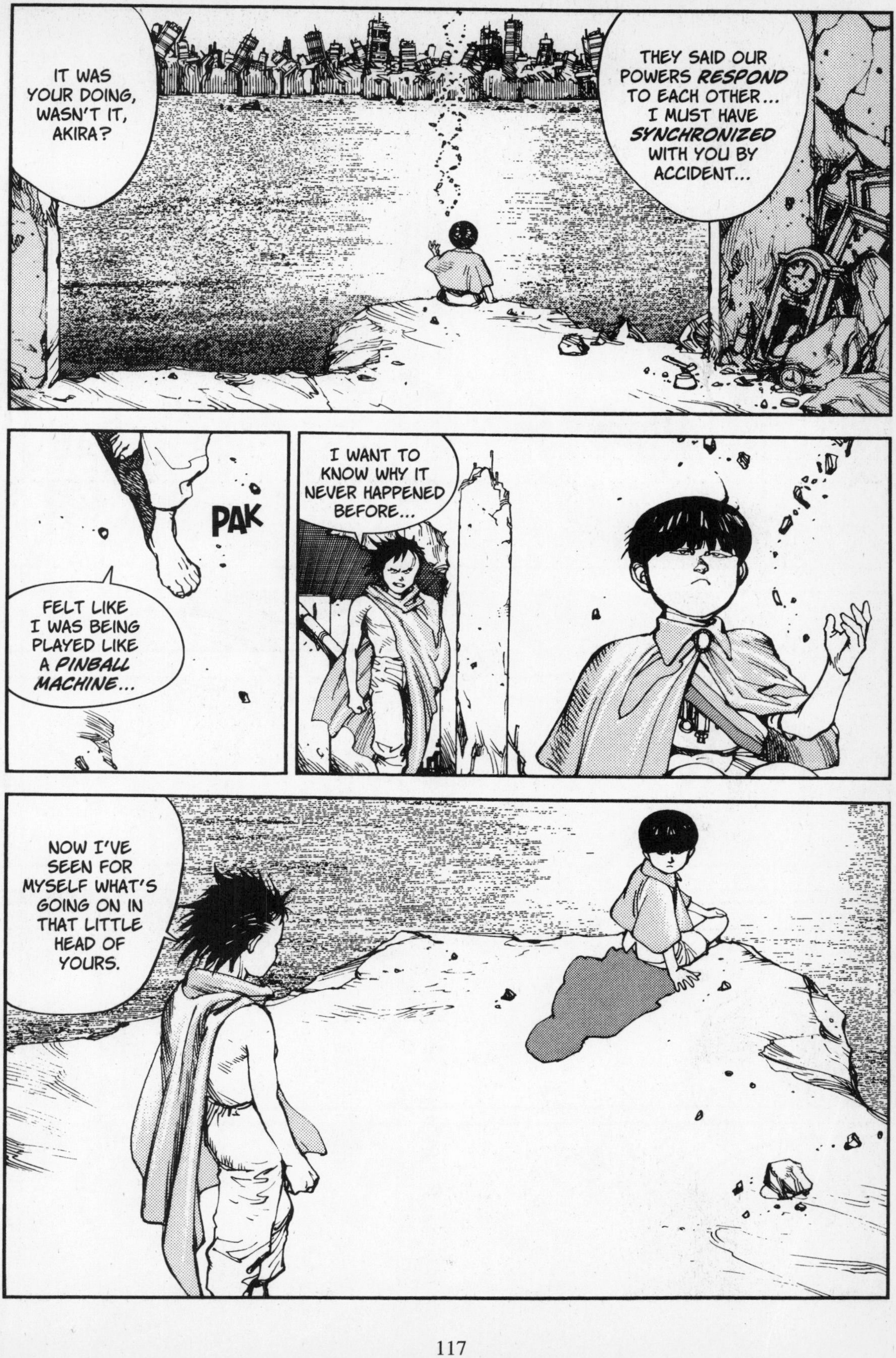
IT WAS YOUR DOING, WASN'T IT, AKIRA?
THEY SAID OUR POWERS *RESPOND* TO EACH OTHER... I MUST HAVE *SYNCHRONIZED* WITH YOU BY ACCIDENT...
PAK
FELT LIKE I WAS BEING PLAYED LIKE A *PINBALL MACHINE*...
I WANT TO KNOW WHY IT NEVER HAPPENED BEFORE...
NOW I'VE SEEN FOR MYSELF WHAT'S GOING ON IN THAT LITTLE HEAD OF YOURS.

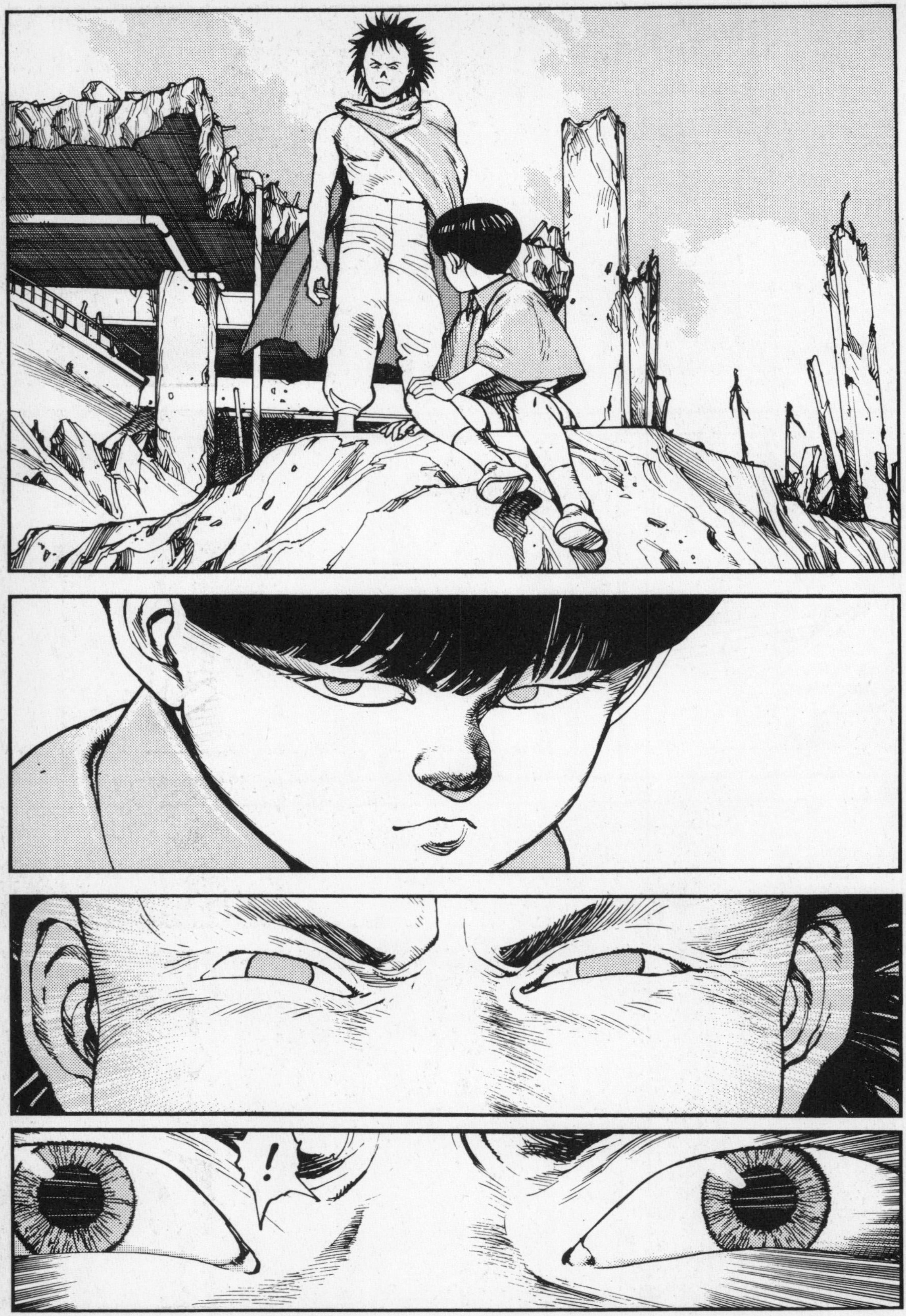
!

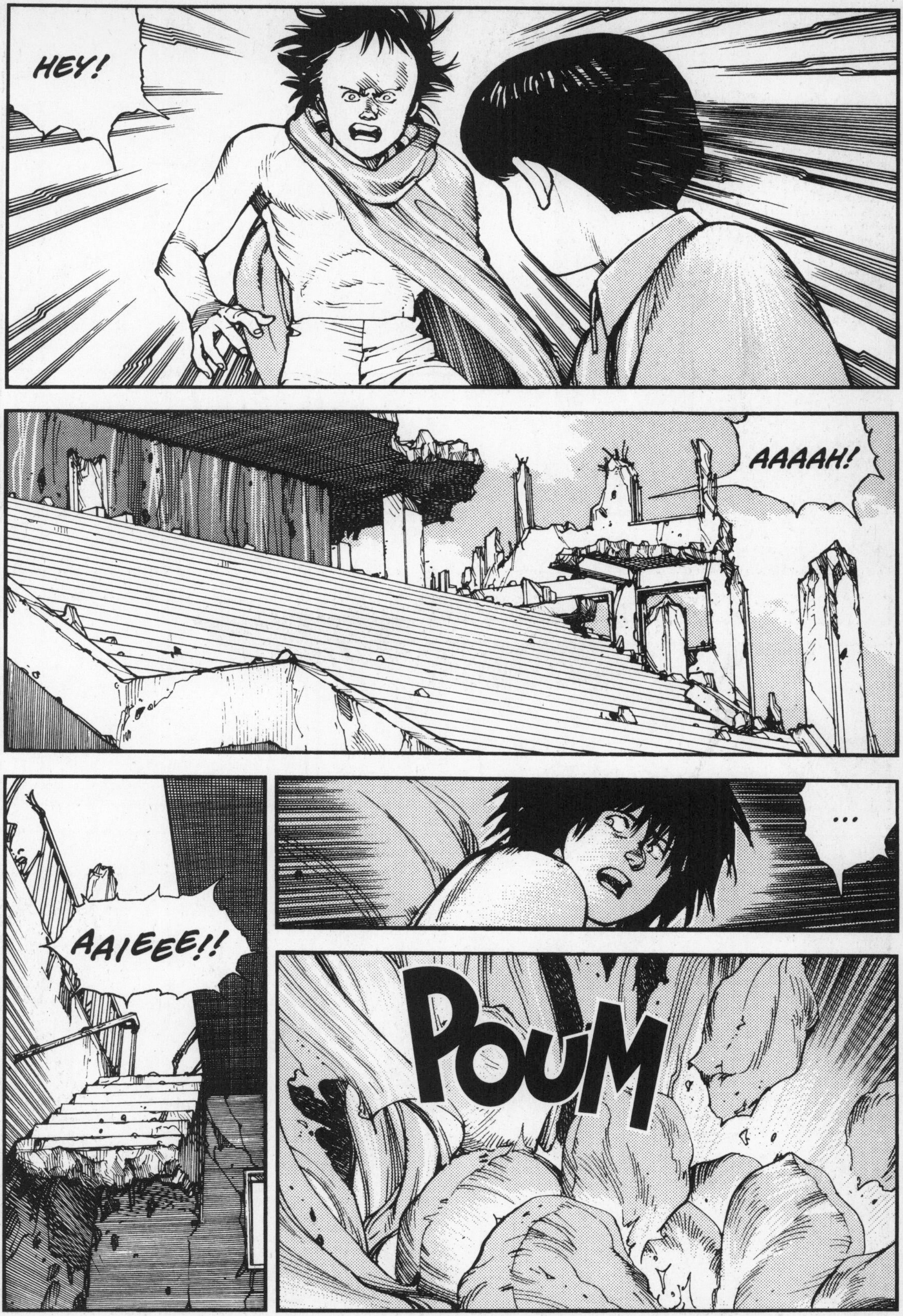
HEY!
AAAAH!
AAIEEE!!
...
POUM

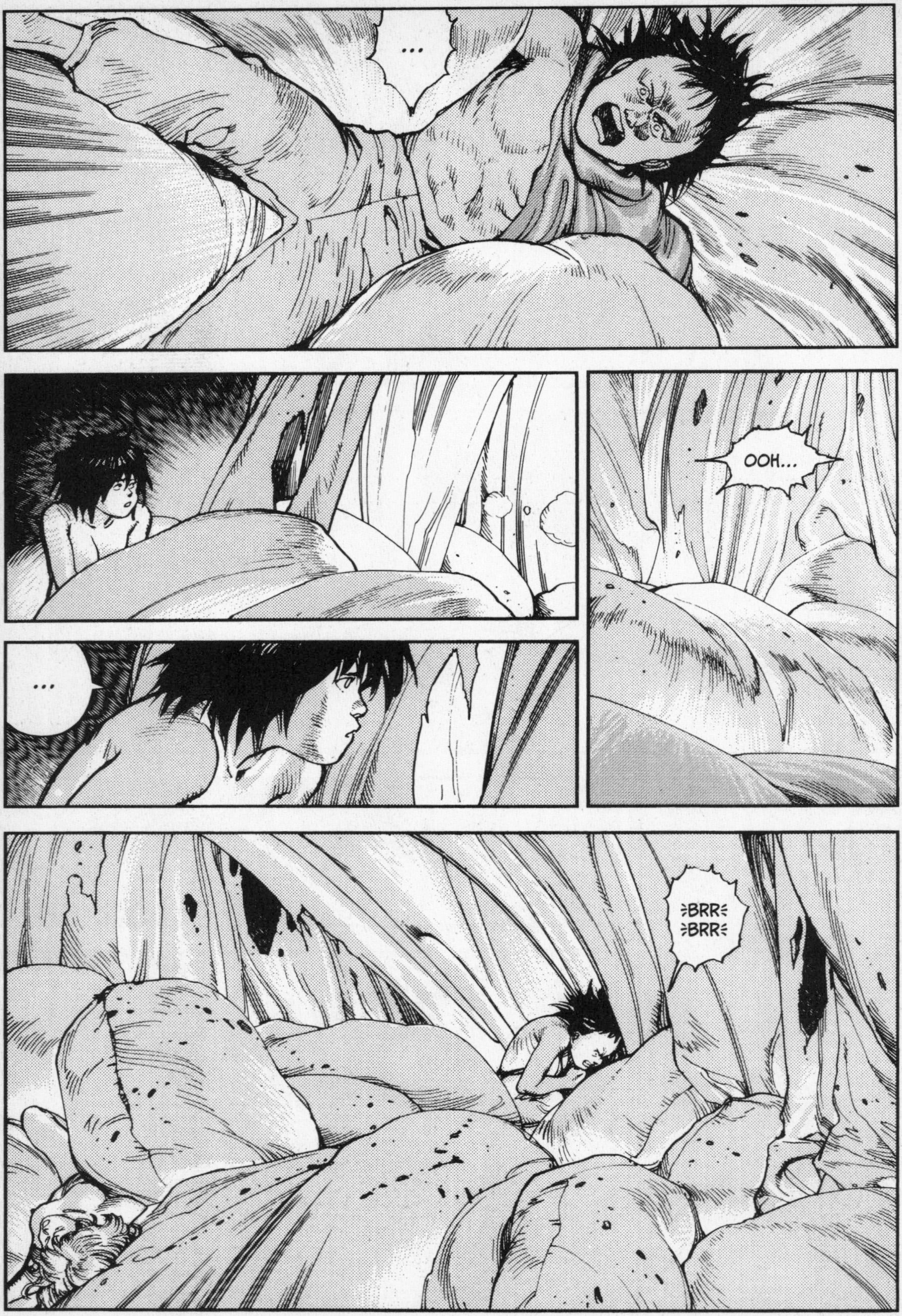
...
OOH...
...
BRR BRR

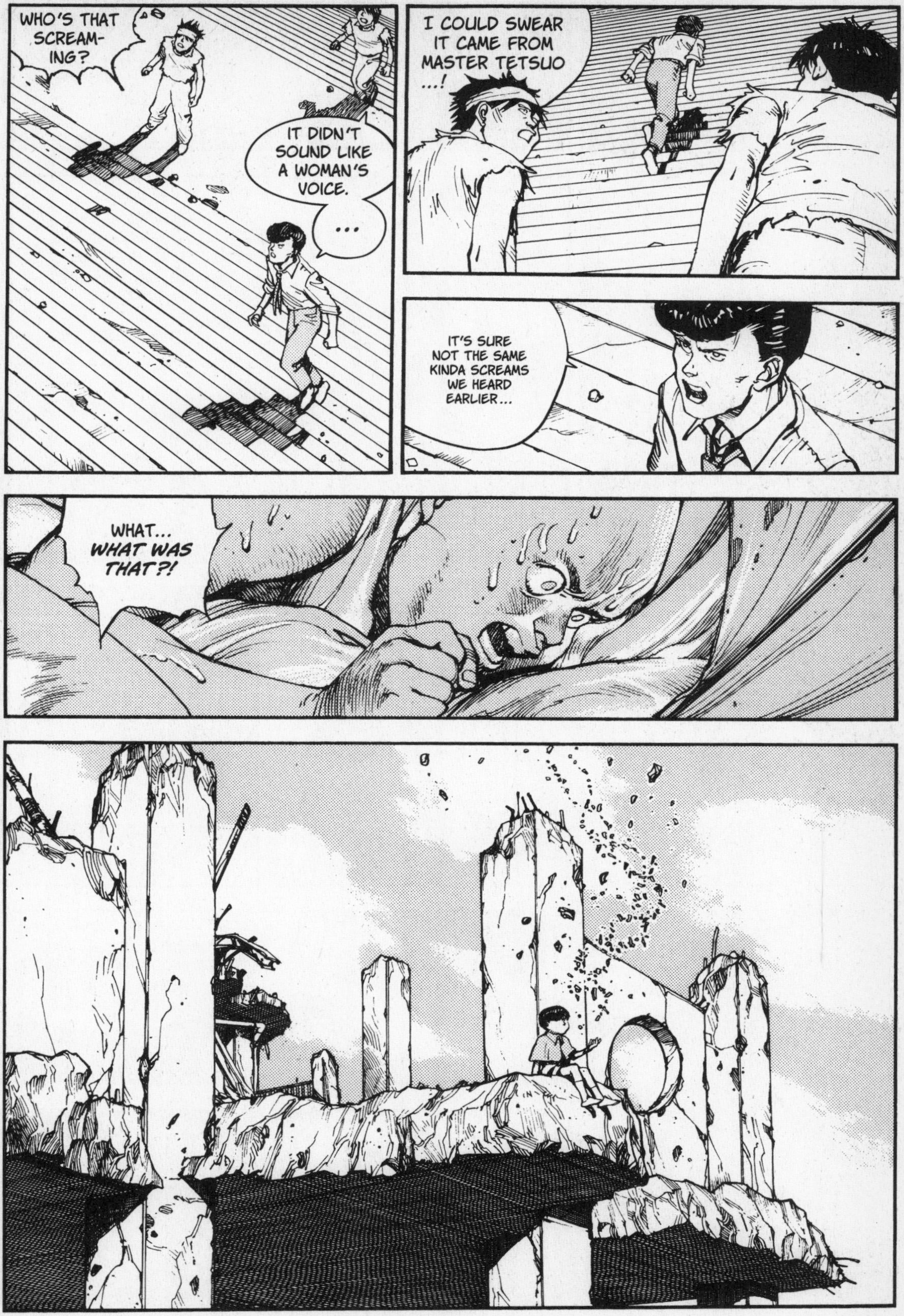
WHO'S THAT SCREAM-ING?
IT DIDN'T SOUND LIKE A WOMAN'S VOICE.
...
I COULD SWEAR IT CAME FROM MASTER TETSUO ...!
IT'S SURE NOT THE SAME KINDA SCREAMS WE HEARD EARLIER...
WHAT... *WHAT WAS THAT?!*

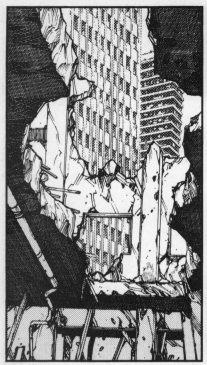

THIS FOOD STASH IS AN OLD BAG LADY'S LEGACY.

I THINK SHE WAS AFRAID TO BORROW A CAN OPENER IN CASE ANYONE GUESSED SHE WAS HOARDING.

HER DENTURES WERE IN HER HAND WHEN I FOUND HER.

...SHE STARVED WITHOUT OPENING A SINGLE CAN.

THERE A MORAL TO THAT STORY?

NAH. NOT UNLESS THERE'S SOMETHING YOU CAN LEARN FROM IT.

I GET IT. YOU WANT MY THANKS FOR SAVING ME.

SWAP

KEEP YOUR GRATITUDE. I WANT TO KNOW WHAT'S BEEN GOING ON IN THE OUTSIDE WORLD.

BLINK

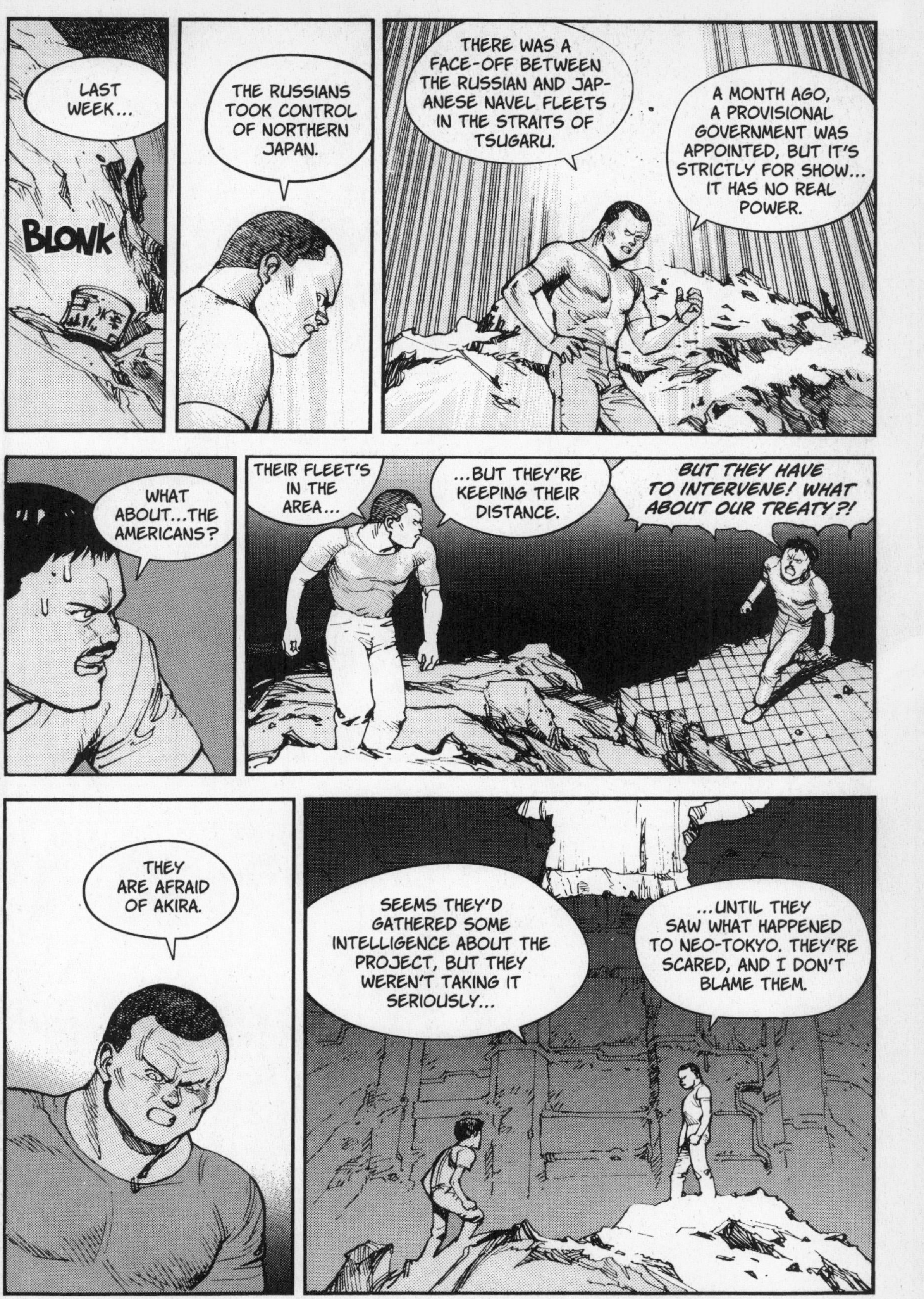
LAST WEEK...
BLONK
THE RUSSIANS TOOK CONTROL OF NORTHERN JAPAN.
THERE WAS A FACE-OFF BETWEEN THE RUSSIAN AND JAPANESE NAVEL FLEETS IN THE STRAITS OF TSUGARU.
A MONTH AGO, A PROVISIONAL GOVERNMENT WAS APPOINTED, BUT IT'S STRICTLY FOR SHOW... IT HAS NO REAL POWER.
WHAT ABOUT...THE AMERICANS?
THEIR FLEET'S IN THE AREA...
...BUT THEY'RE KEEPING THEIR DISTANCE.
BUT THEY HAVE TO INTERVENE! WHAT ABOUT OUR TREATY?!
THEY ARE AFRAID OF AKIRA.
SEEMS THEY'D GATHERED SOME INTELLIGENCE ABOUT THE PROJECT, BUT THEY WEREN'T TAKING IT SERIOUSLY...
...UNTIL THEY SAW WHAT HAPPENED TO NEO-TOKYO. THEY'RE SCARED, AND I DON'T BLAME THEM.

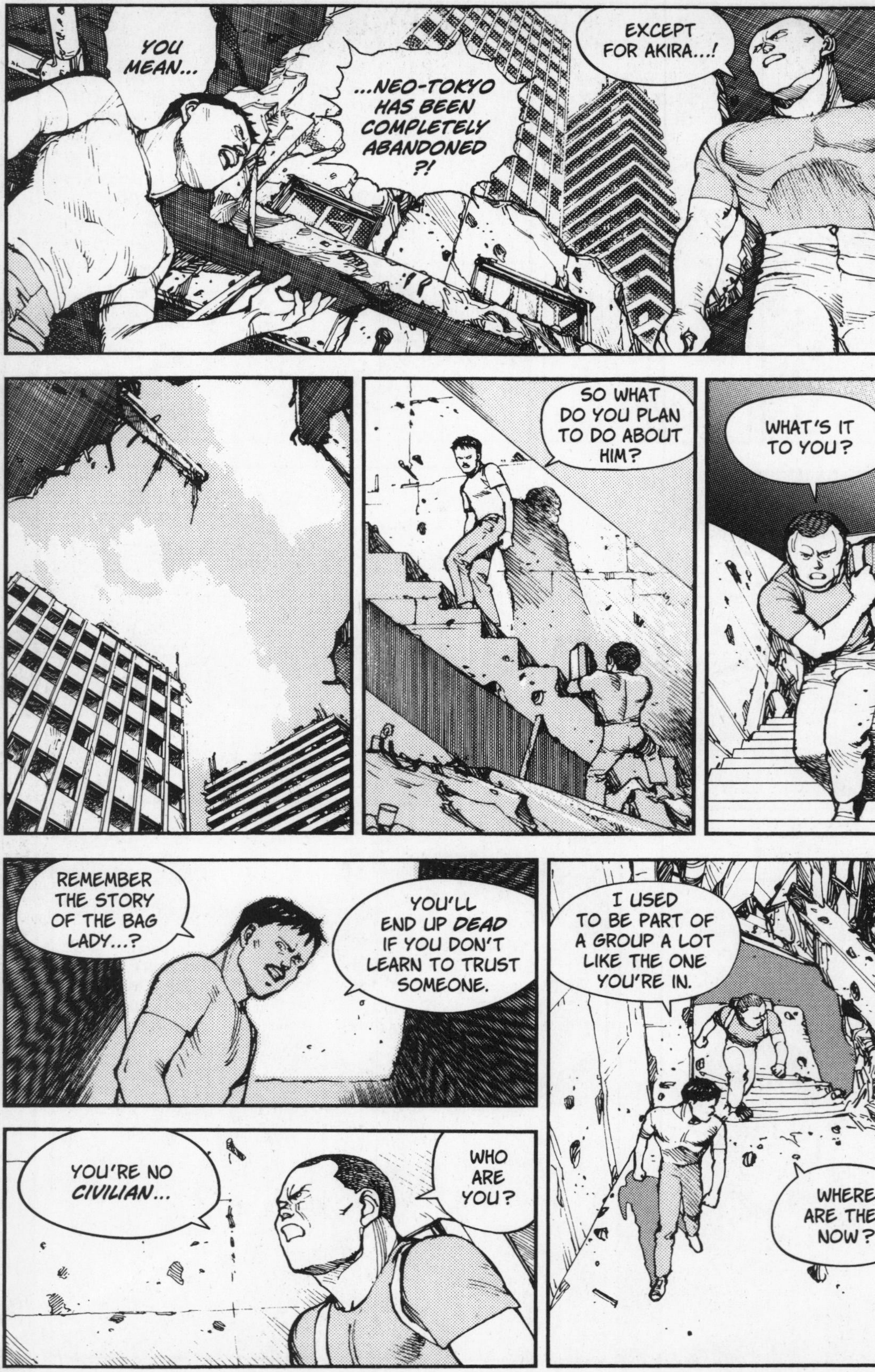
YOU MEAN...
...NEO-TOKYO HAS BEEN COMPLETELY ABANDONED ?!
EXCEPT FOR AKIRA...!
SO WHAT DO YOU PLAN TO DO ABOUT HIM?
WHAT'S IT TO YOU?
REMEMBER THE STORY OF THE BAG LADY...?
YOU'LL END UP DEAD IF YOU DON'T LEARN TO TRUST SOMEONE.
YOU'RE NO CIVILIAN...
WHO ARE YOU?
I USED TO BE PART OF A GROUP A LOT LIKE THE ONE YOU'RE IN.
WHERE ARE THEY NOW?

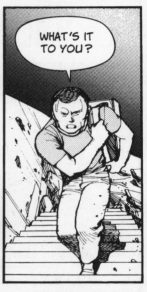

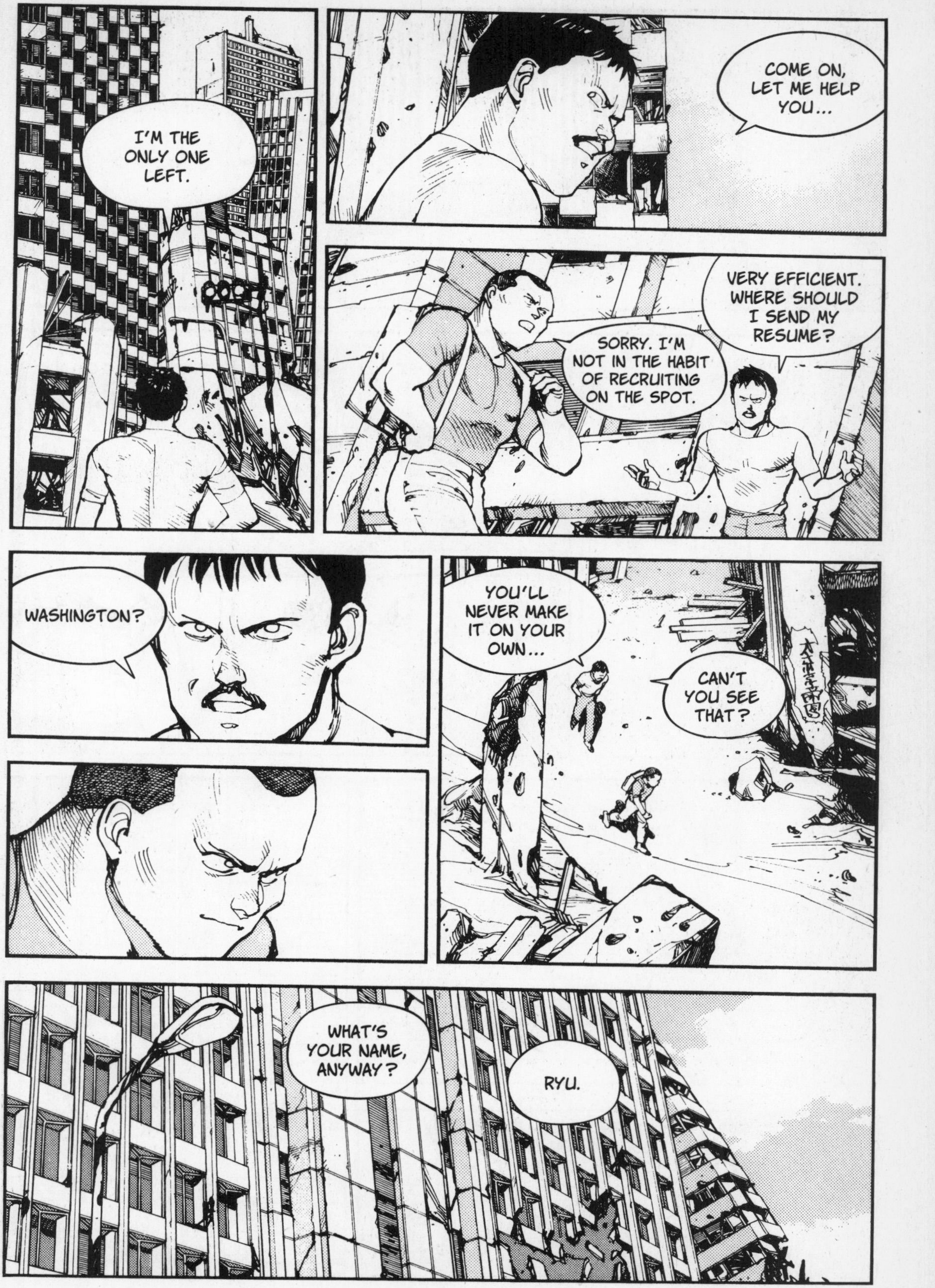
I'M THE ONLY ONE LEFT.
COME ON, LET ME HELP YOU...
SORRY. I'M NOT IN THE HABIT OF RECRUITING ON THE SPOT.
VERY EFFICIENT. WHERE SHOULD I SEND MY RESUME?
WASHINGTON?
YOU'LL NEVER MAKE IT ON YOUR OWN...
CAN'T YOU SEE THAT?
WHAT'S YOUR NAME, ANYWAY?
RYU.

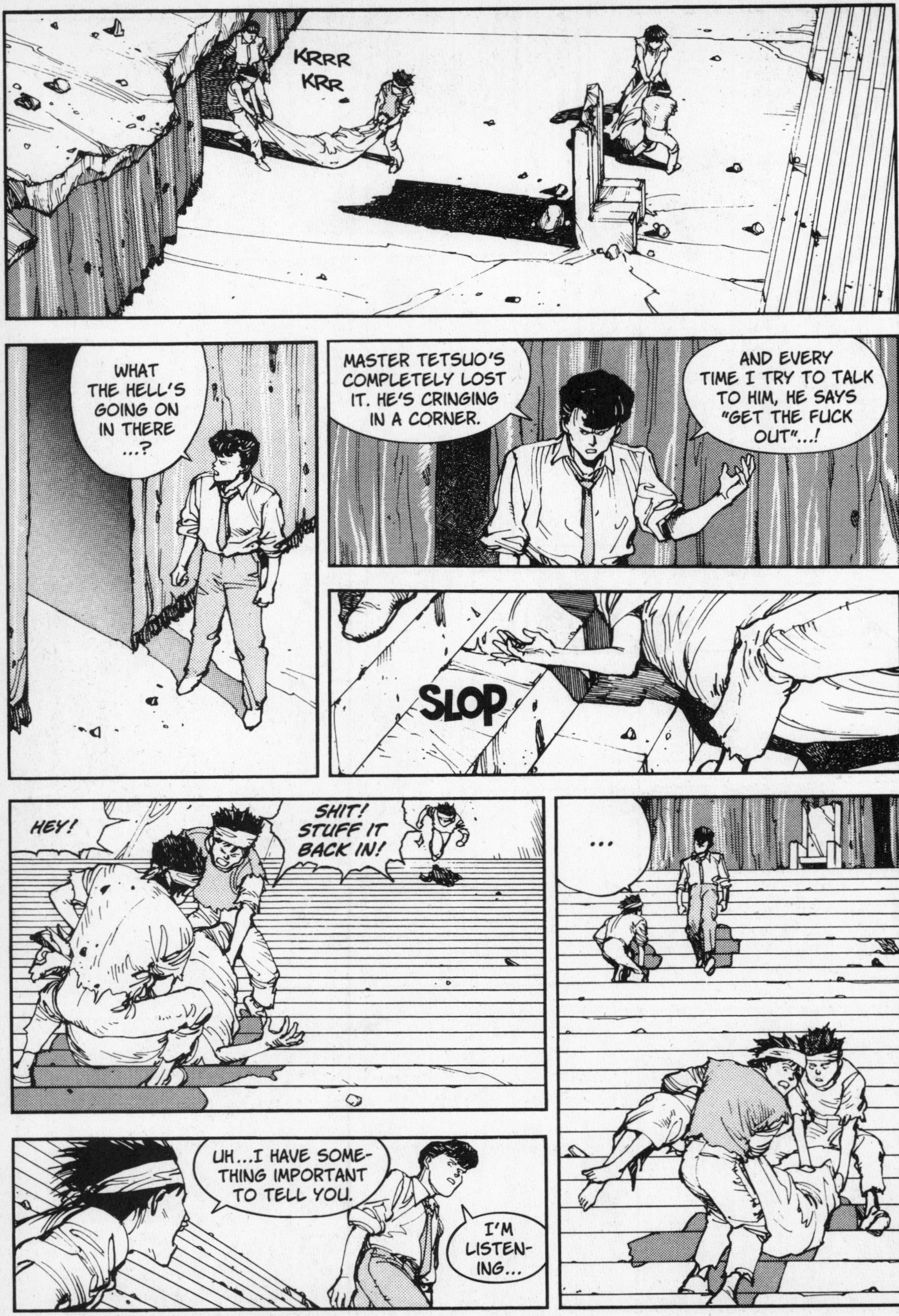
KRRR
KRR
WHAT THE HELL'S GOING ON IN THERE ...?
MASTER TETSUO'S COMPLETELY LOST IT. HE'S CRINGING IN A CORNER.
AND EVERY TIME I TRY TO TALK TO HIM, HE SAYS "GET THE FUCK OUT"...!
SLOP
HEY!
SHIT! STUFF IT BACK IN!
UH...I HAVE SOME-THING IMPORTANT TO TELL YOU.
I'M LISTEN-ING...
...

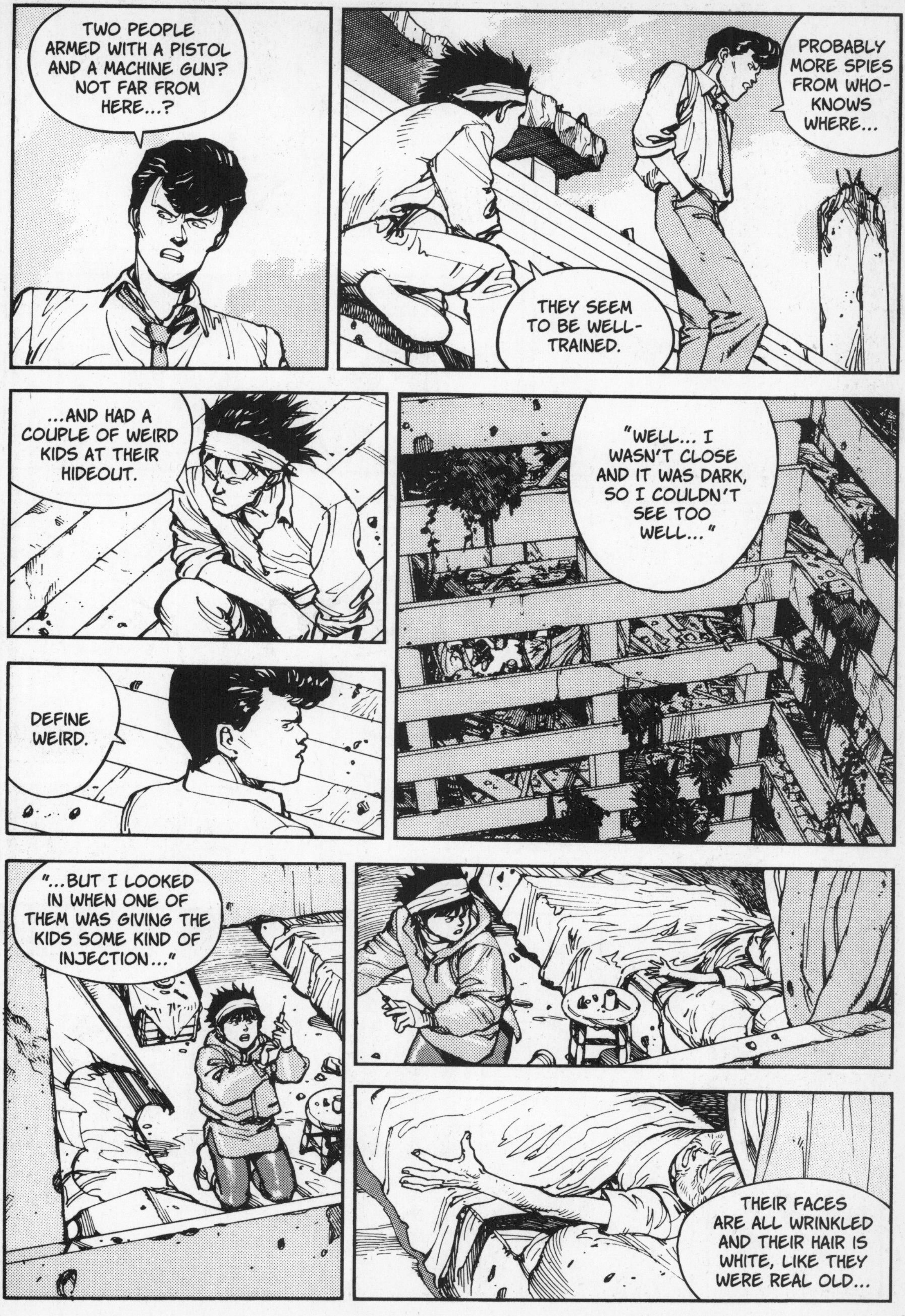
TWO PEOPLE ARMED WITH A PISTOL AND A MACHINE GUN? NOT FAR FROM HERE...?
PROBABLY MORE SPIES FROM WHO-KNOWS WHERE...
THEY SEEM TO BE WELL-TRAINED.
...AND HAD A COUPLE OF WEIRD KIDS AT THEIR HIDEOUT.
DEFINE WEIRD.
"WELL... I WASN'T CLOSE AND IT WAS DARK, SO I COULDN'T SEE TOO WELL..."
"...BUT I LOOKED IN WHEN ONE OF THEM WAS GIVING THE KIDS SOME KIND OF INJECTION..."
THEIR FACES ARE ALL WRINKLED AND THEIR HAIR IS WHITE, LIKE THEY WERE REAL OLD...

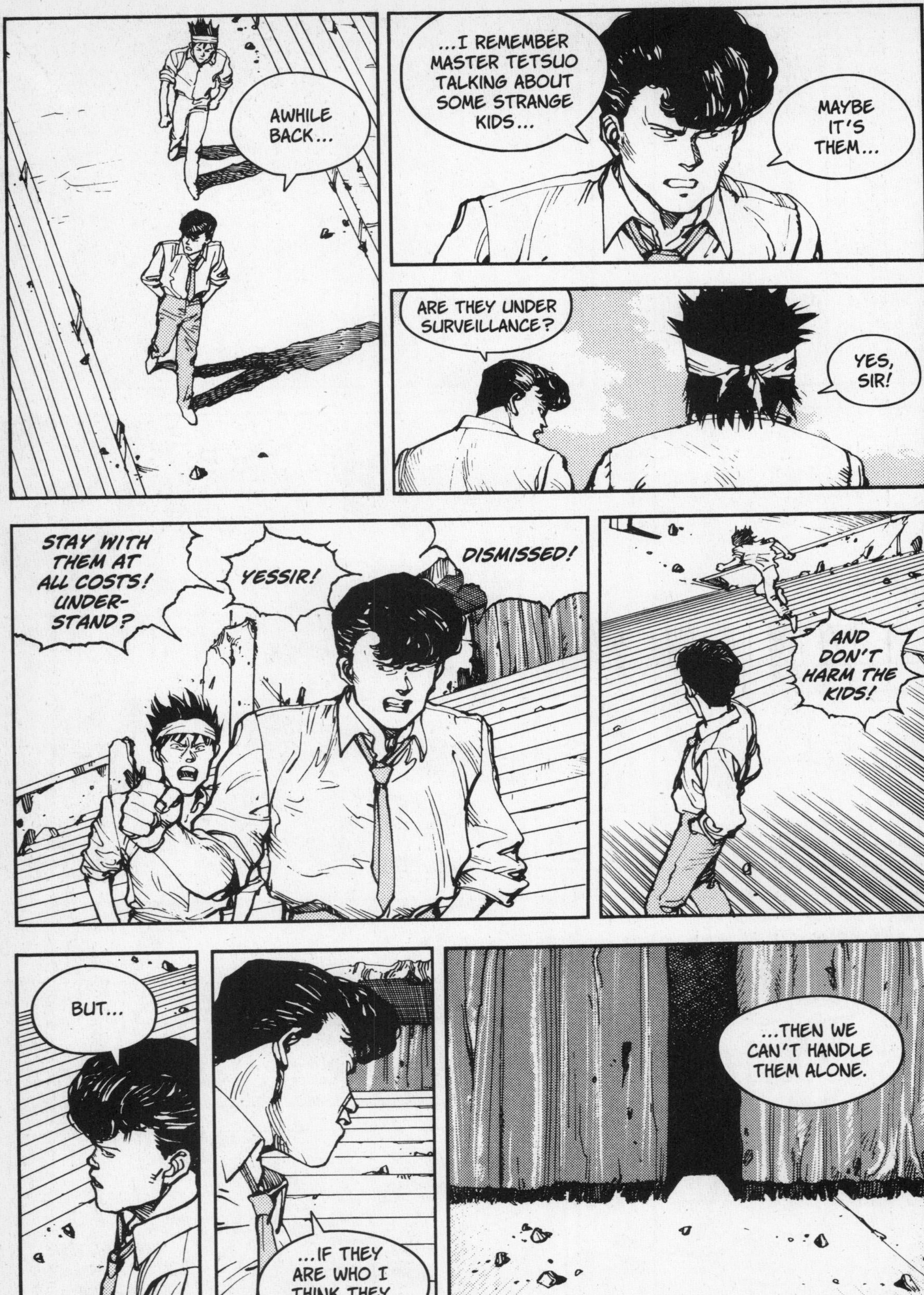
AWHILE BACK...
...I REMEMBER MASTER TETSUO TALKING ABOUT SOME STRANGE KIDS...
MAYBE IT'S THEM...
ARE THEY UNDER SURVEILLANCE?
YES, SIR!
STAY WITH THEM AT ALL COSTS! UNDER-STAND?
YESSIR!
DISMISSED!
AND DON'T HARM THE KIDS!
BUT...
...IF THEY ARE WHO I THINK THEY ARE...
...THEN WE CAN'T HANDLE THEM ALONE.

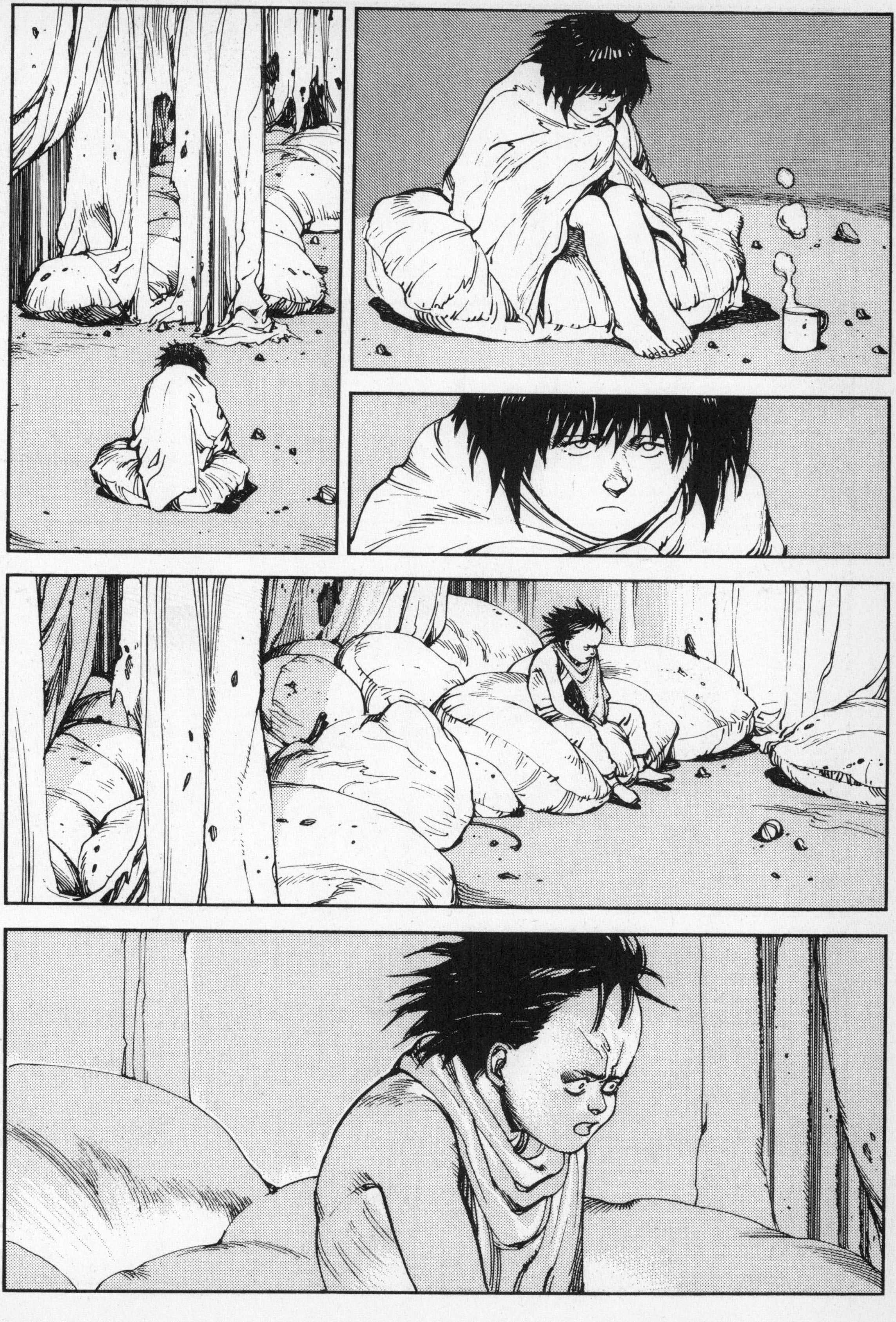

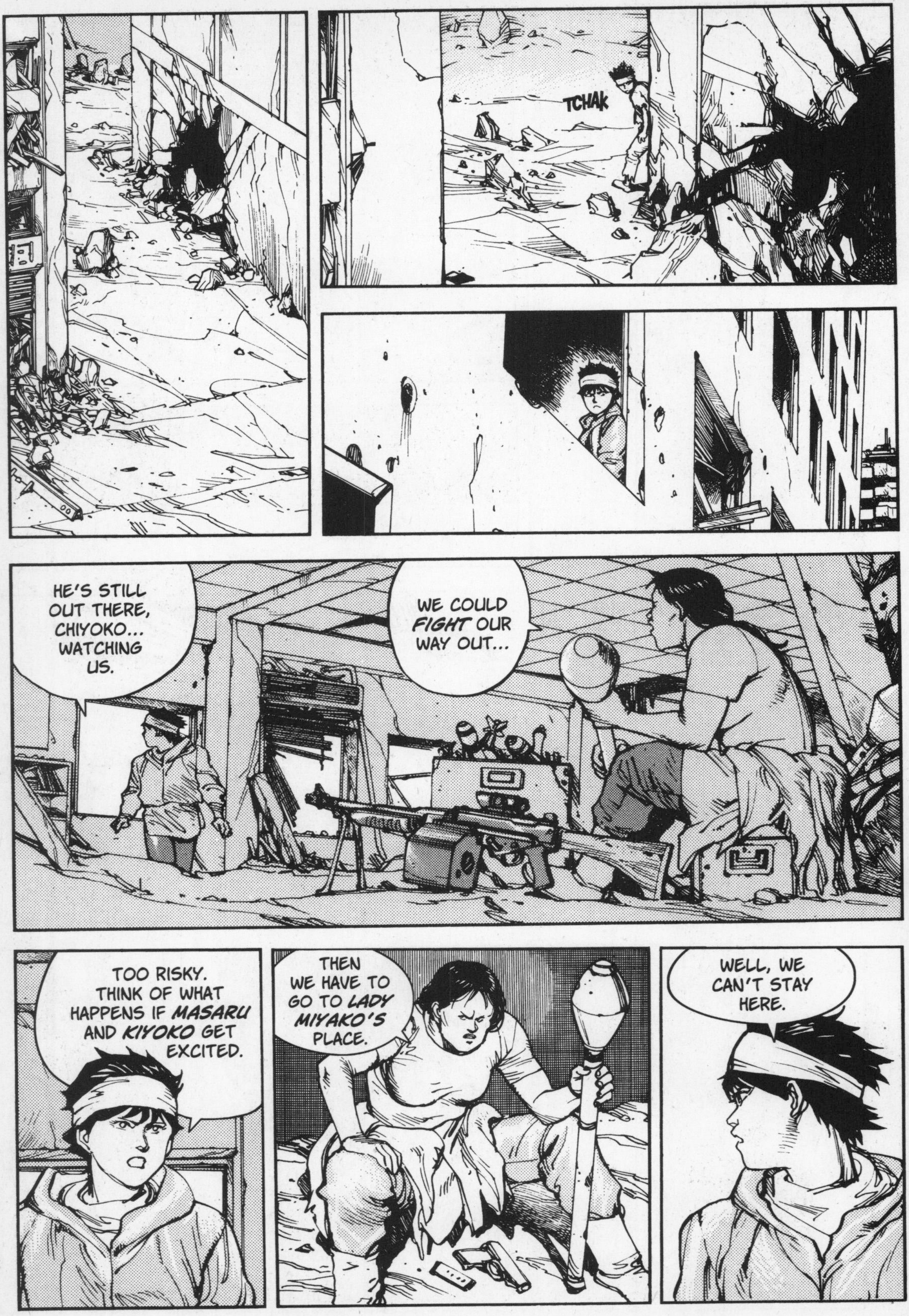
TCHAK
HE'S STILL OUT THERE, CHIYOKO... WATCHING US.
WE COULD FIGHT OUR WAY OUT...
TOO RISKY. THINK OF WHAT HAPPENS IF MASARU AND KIYOKO GET EXCITED.
THEN WE HAVE TO GO TO LADY MIYAKO'S PLACE.
WELL, WE CAN'T STAY HERE.

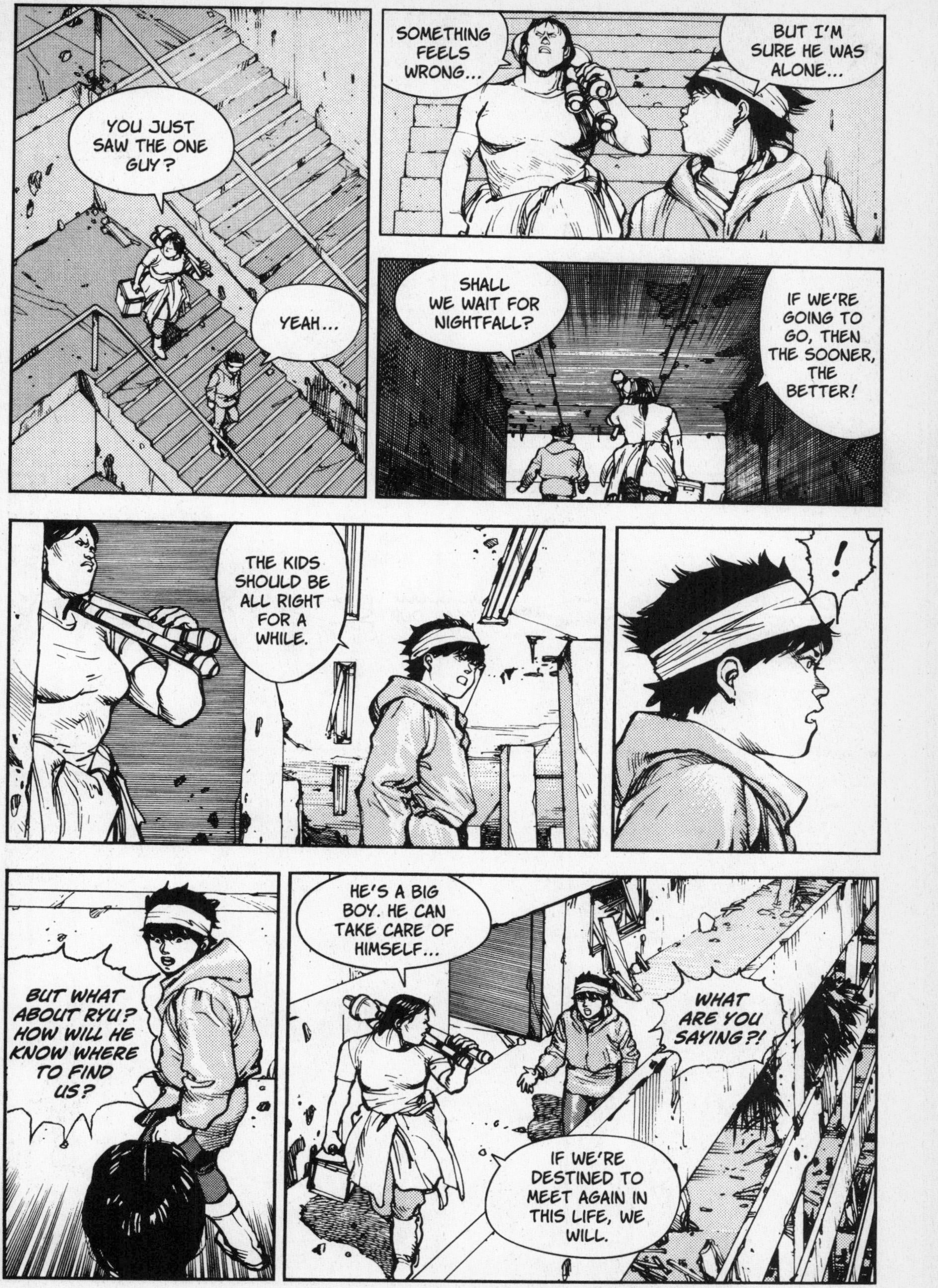
YOU JUST SAW THE ONE GUY?
YEAH...
SOMETHING FEELS WRONG...
BUT I'M SURE HE WAS ALONE...
SHALL WE WAIT FOR NIGHTFALL?
IF WE'RE GOING TO GO, THEN THE SOONER, THE BETTER!
THE KIDS SHOULD BE ALL RIGHT FOR A WHILE.
!
BUT WHAT ABOUT RYU? HOW WILL HE KNOW WHERE TO FIND US?
HE'S A BIG BOY. HE CAN TAKE CARE OF HIMSELF...
WHAT ARE YOU SAYING?!
IF WE'RE DESTINED TO MEET AGAIN IN THIS LIFE, WE WILL.

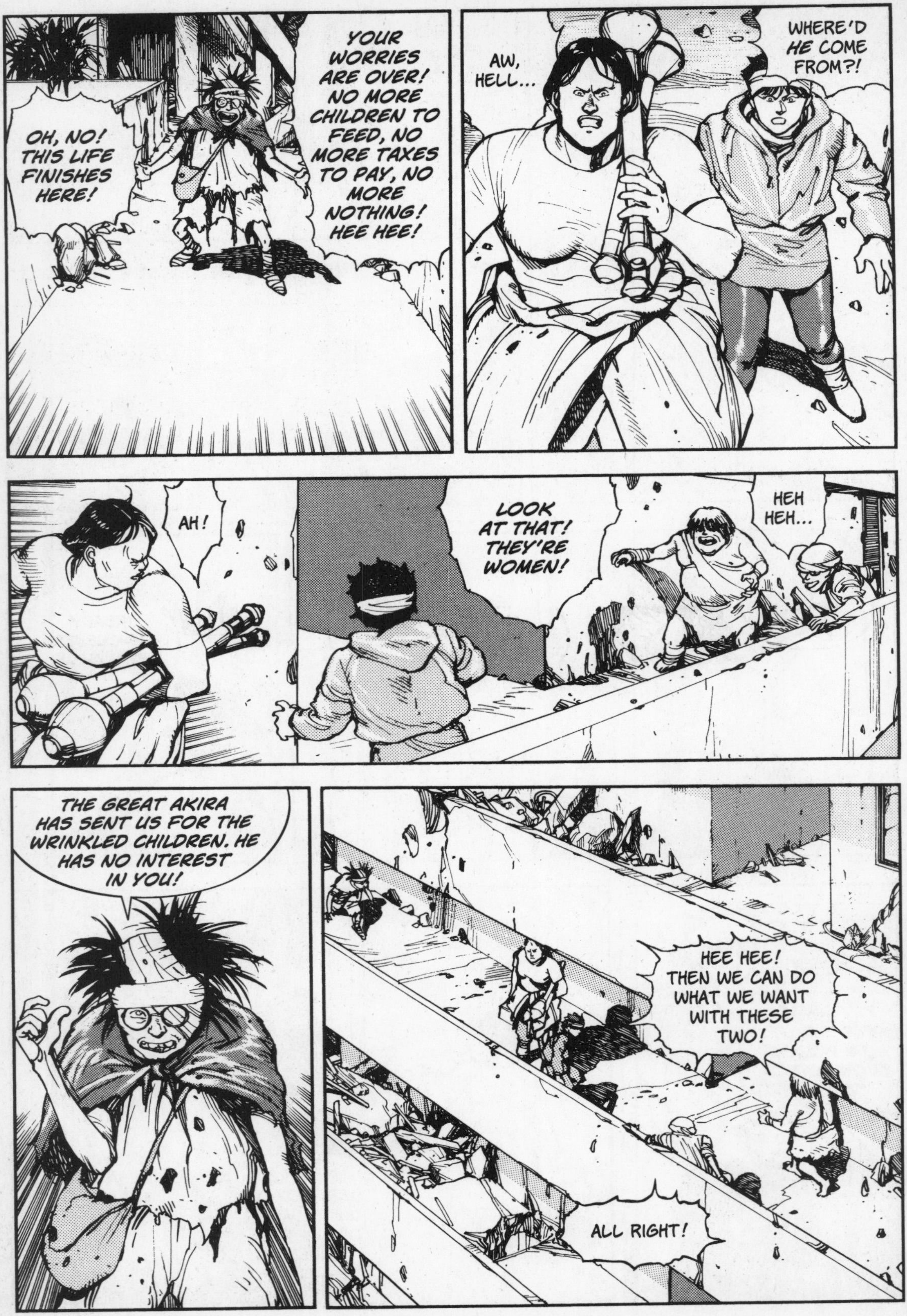

OH, NO! THIS LIFE FINISHES HERE!
YOUR WORRIES ARE OVER! NO MORE CHILDREN TO FEED, NO MORE TAXES TO PAY, NO MORE NOTHING! HEE HEE!
AW, HELL...
WHERE'D HE COME FROM?!
AH!
LOOK AT THAT! THEY'RE WOMEN!
HEH HEH...
THE GREAT AKIRA HAS SENT US FOR THE WRINKLED CHILDREN. HE HAS NO INTEREST IN YOU!
HEE HEE! THEN WE CAN DO WHAT WE WANT WITH THESE TWO!
ALL RIGHT!

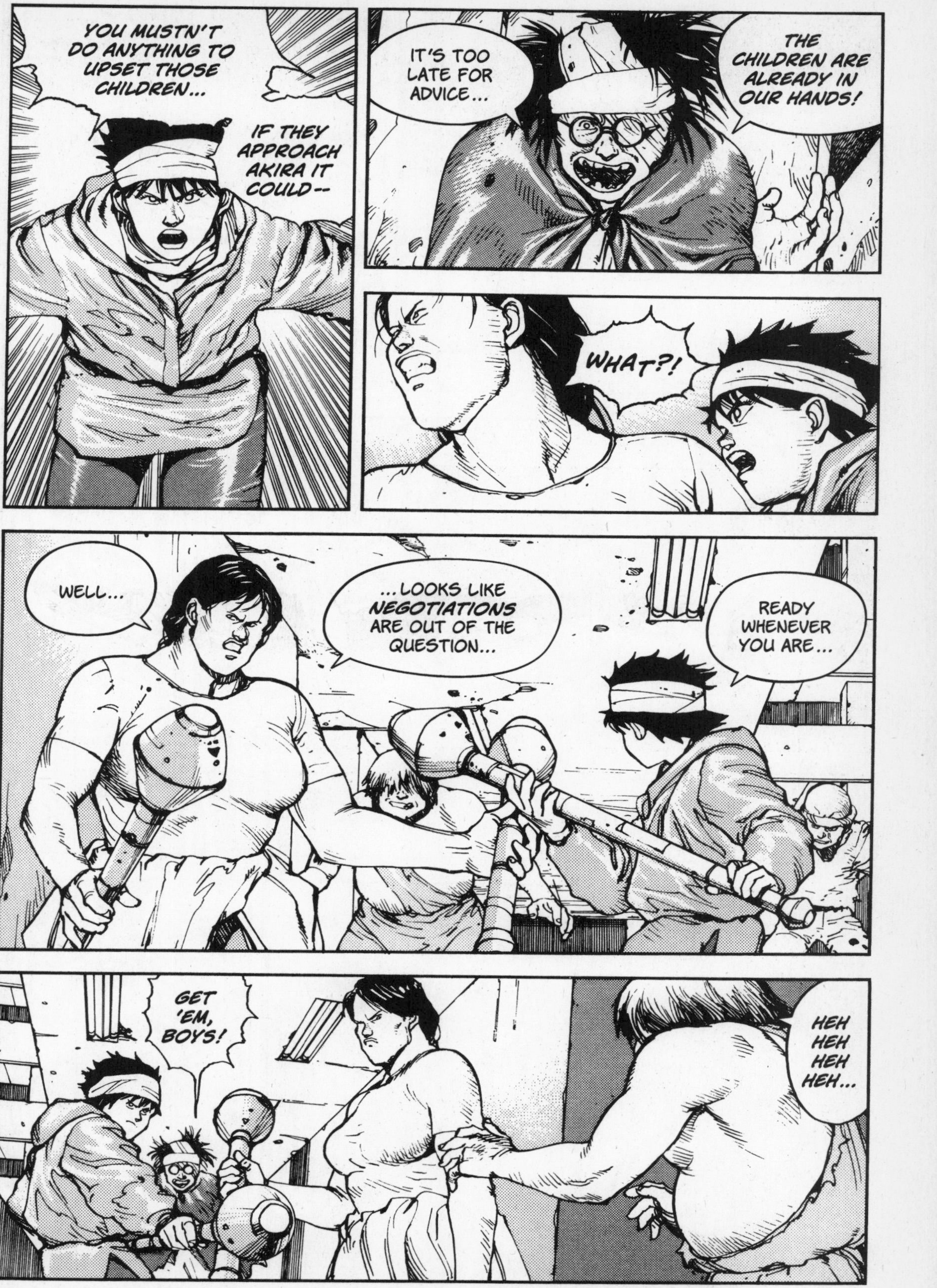
YOU MUSTN'T DO ANYTHING TO UPSET THOSE CHILDREN...
IF THEY APPROACH AKIRA IT COULD--
IT'S TOO LATE FOR ADVICE...
THE CHILDREN ARE ALREADY IN OUR HANDS!
WHAT?!
WELL...
...LOOKS LIKE NEGOTIATIONS ARE OUT OF THE QUESTION...
READY WHENEVER YOU ARE...
GET 'EM, BOYS!
HEH HEH HEH HEH...

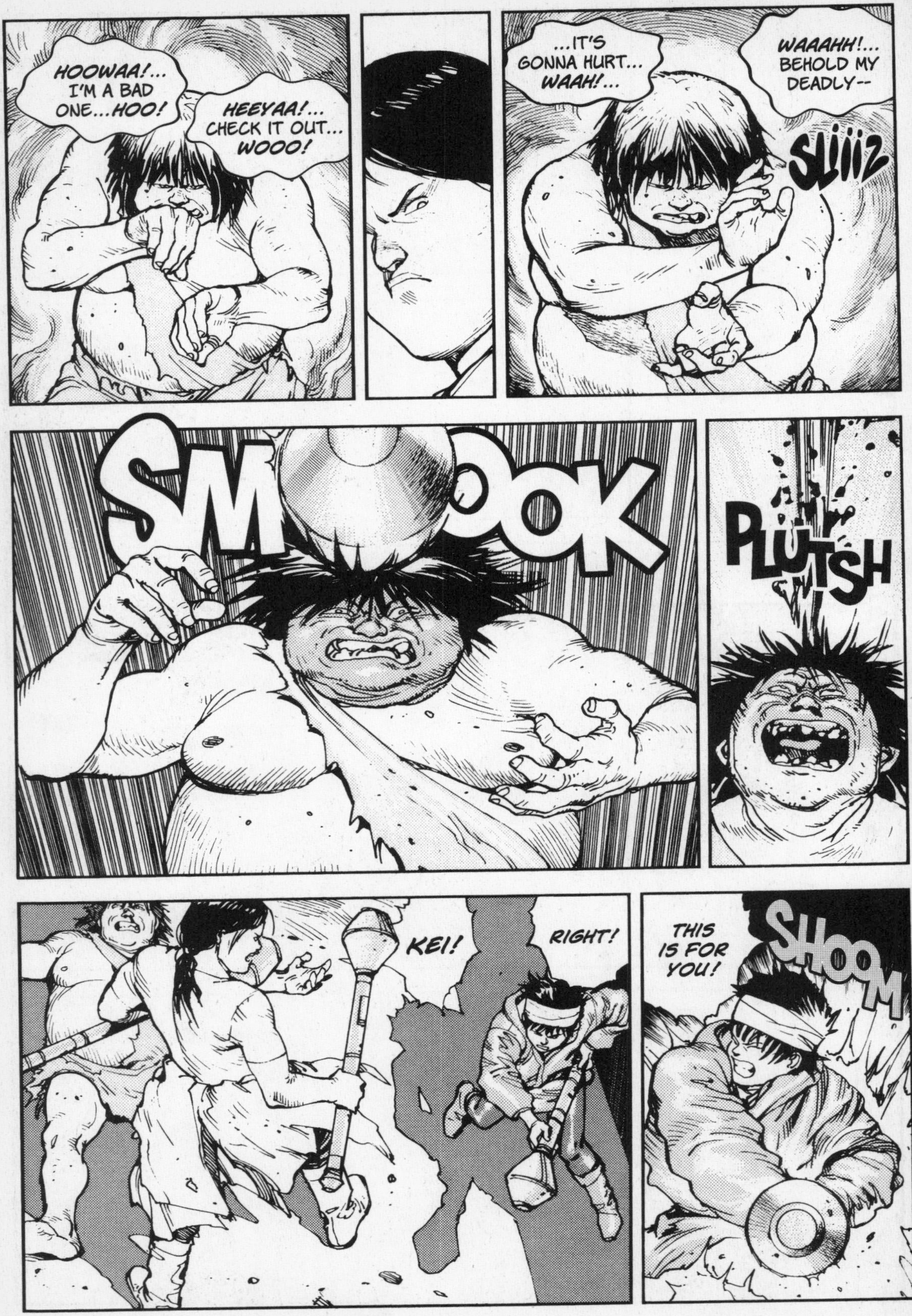
HOOWAA!... I'M A BAD ONE...HOO!
HEEYAA!... CHECK IT OUT... WOOO!
...IT'S GONNA HURT... WAAH!...
WAAAHH!... BEHOLD MY DEADLY--
SLIIIZ
SMOOOK
PLUTSH
KEI!
RIGHT!
THIS IS FOR YOU!
SHOOM

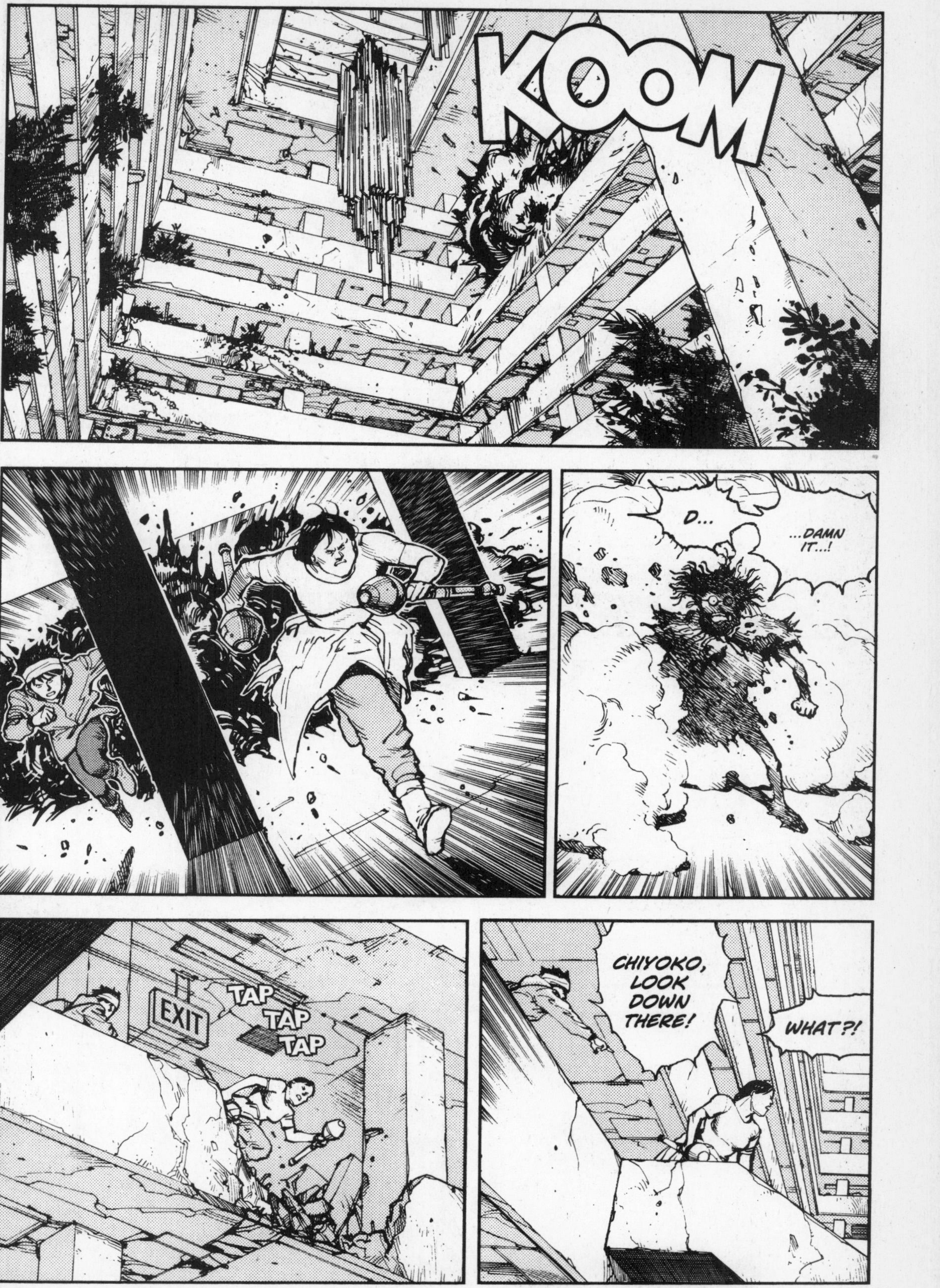
KOOM
D...
...DAMN IT...!
EXIT
TAP
TAP
TAP
CHIYOKO, LOOK DOWN THERE!
WHAT?!

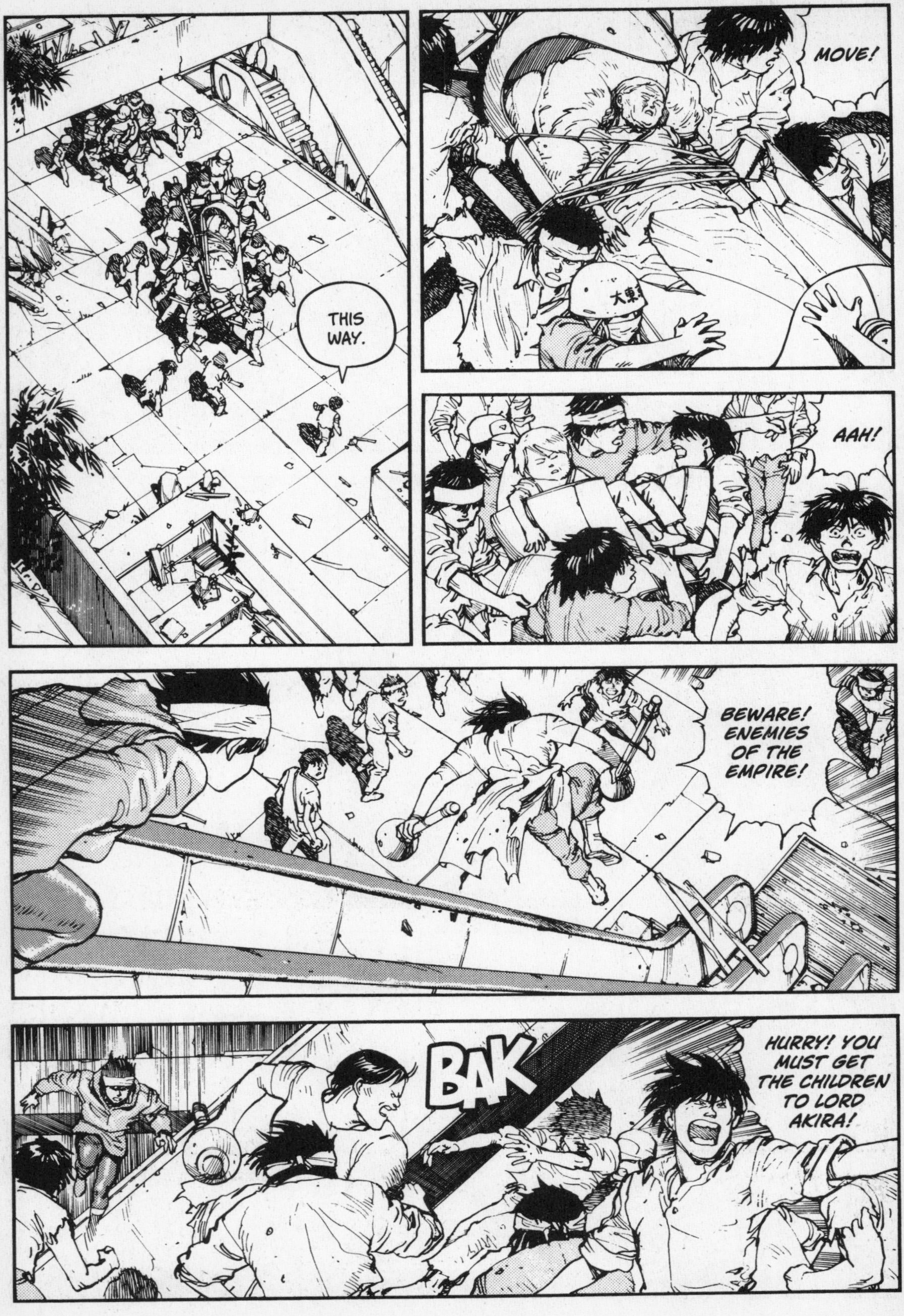
THIS WAY.
MOVE!
AAH!
BEWARE! ENEMIES OF THE EMPIRE!
BAK
HURRY! YOU MUST GET THE CHILDREN TO LORD AKIRA!

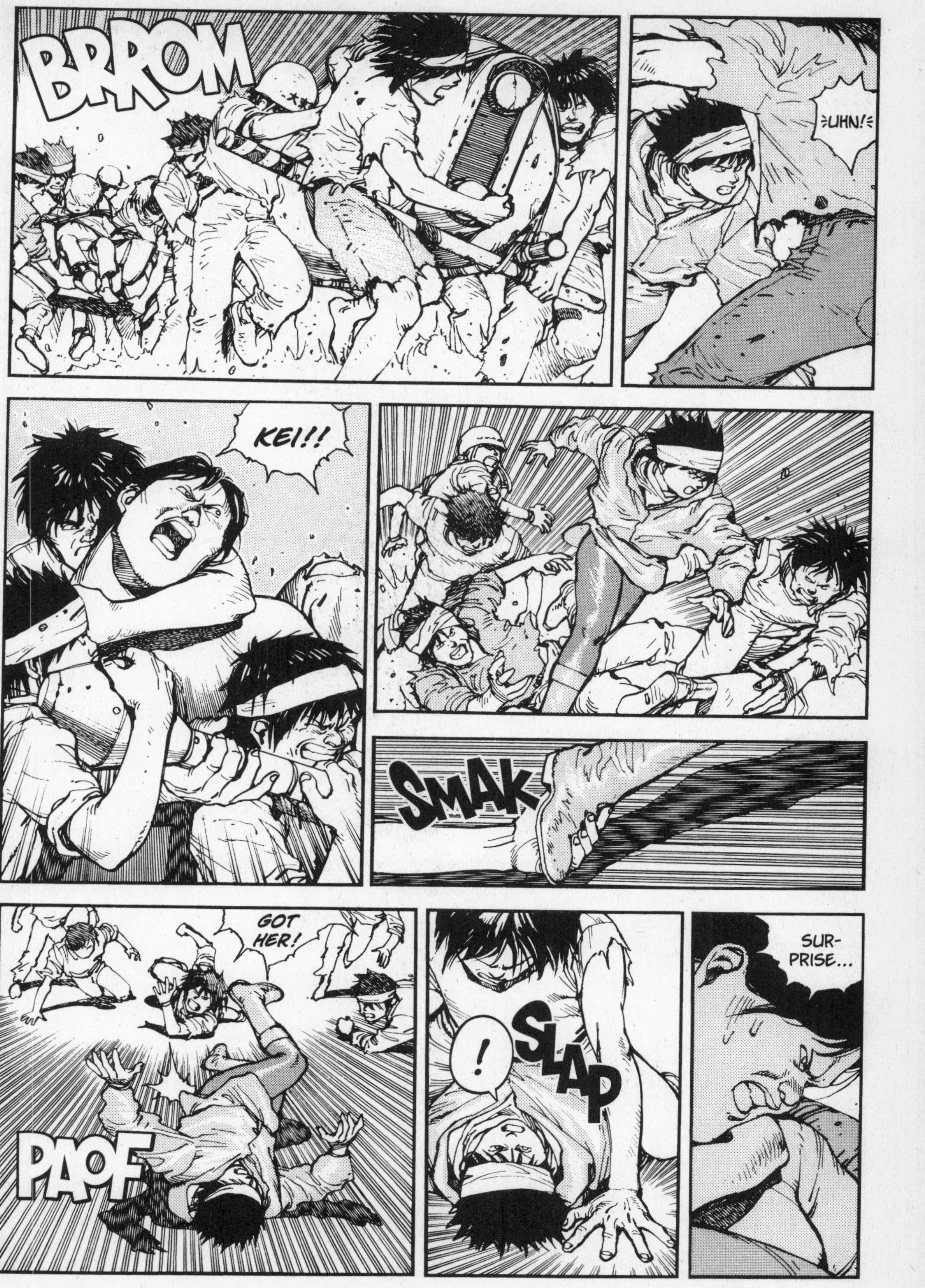
BRROM
UHN!
KEI!!
SMAK
GOT HER!
PAOF
!
SLAP
SUR-PRISE...

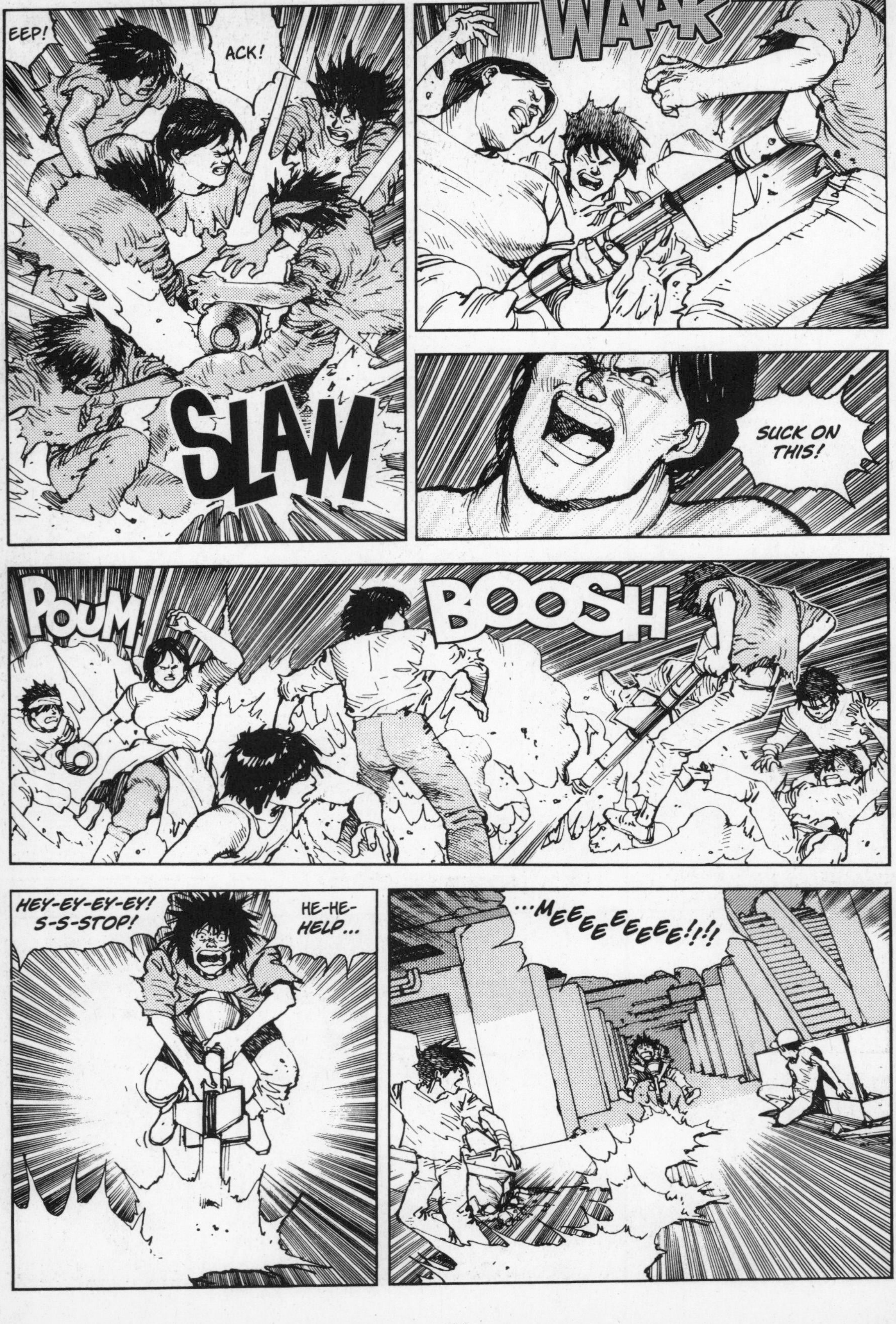
EEP!
ACK!
SLAM
WAAK
SUCK ON THIS!
POUM
BOOSH
HEY-EY-EY-EY! S-S-STOP!
HE-HE-HELP...
...MEEEEEEEEE!!!!

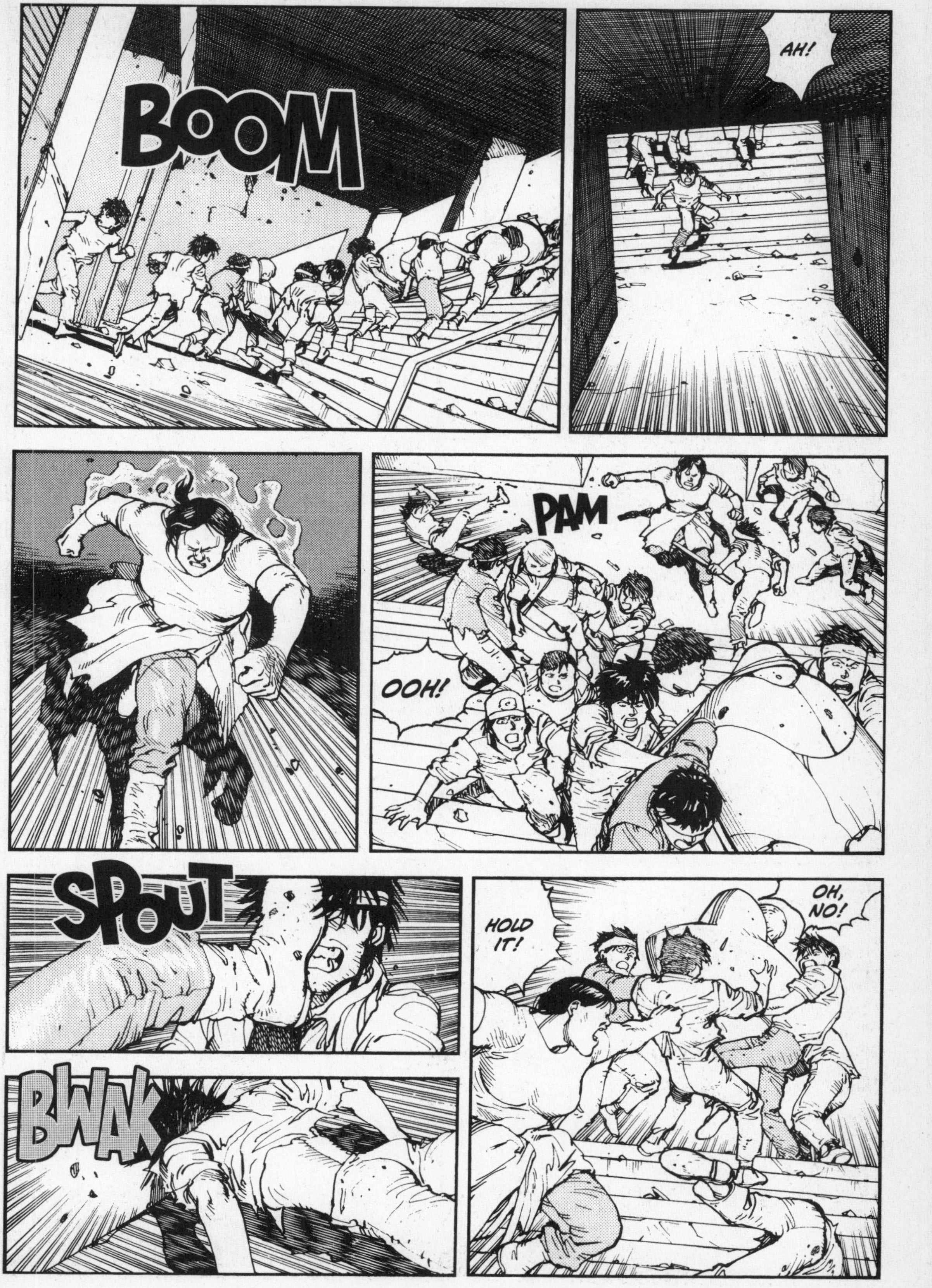
BOOM
AH!
PAM
OOH!
SPOUT
HOLD IT!
OH, NO!
BWAK

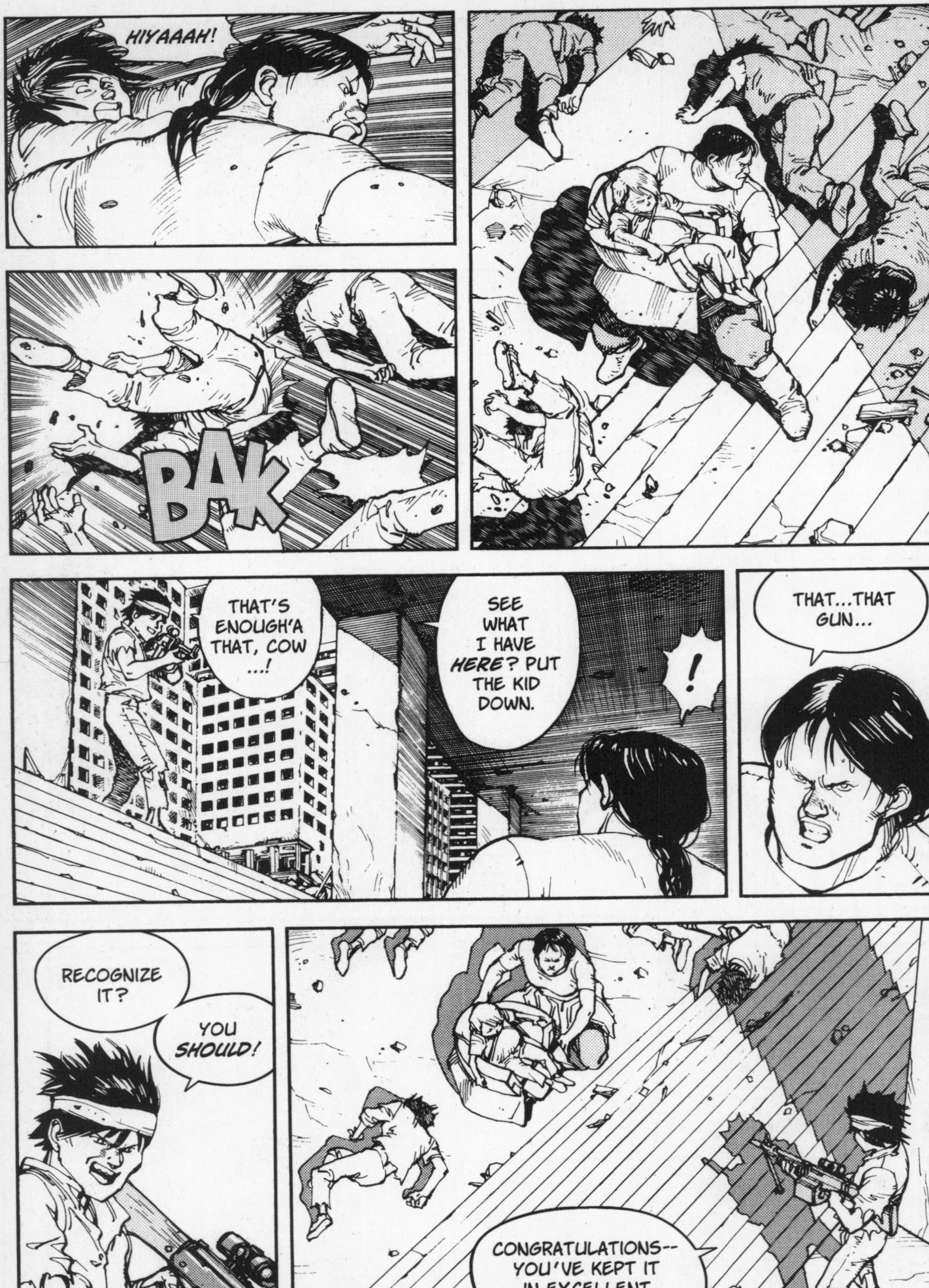
HIYAAAH!
BAK
THAT'S ENOUGH'A THAT, COW ...!
SEE WHAT I HAVE *HERE*? PUT THE KID DOWN.
!
THAT...THAT GUN...
RECOGNIZE IT?
YOU *SHOULD!*
CONGRATULATIONS-- YOU'VE KEPT IT IN EXCELLENT CONDITION!

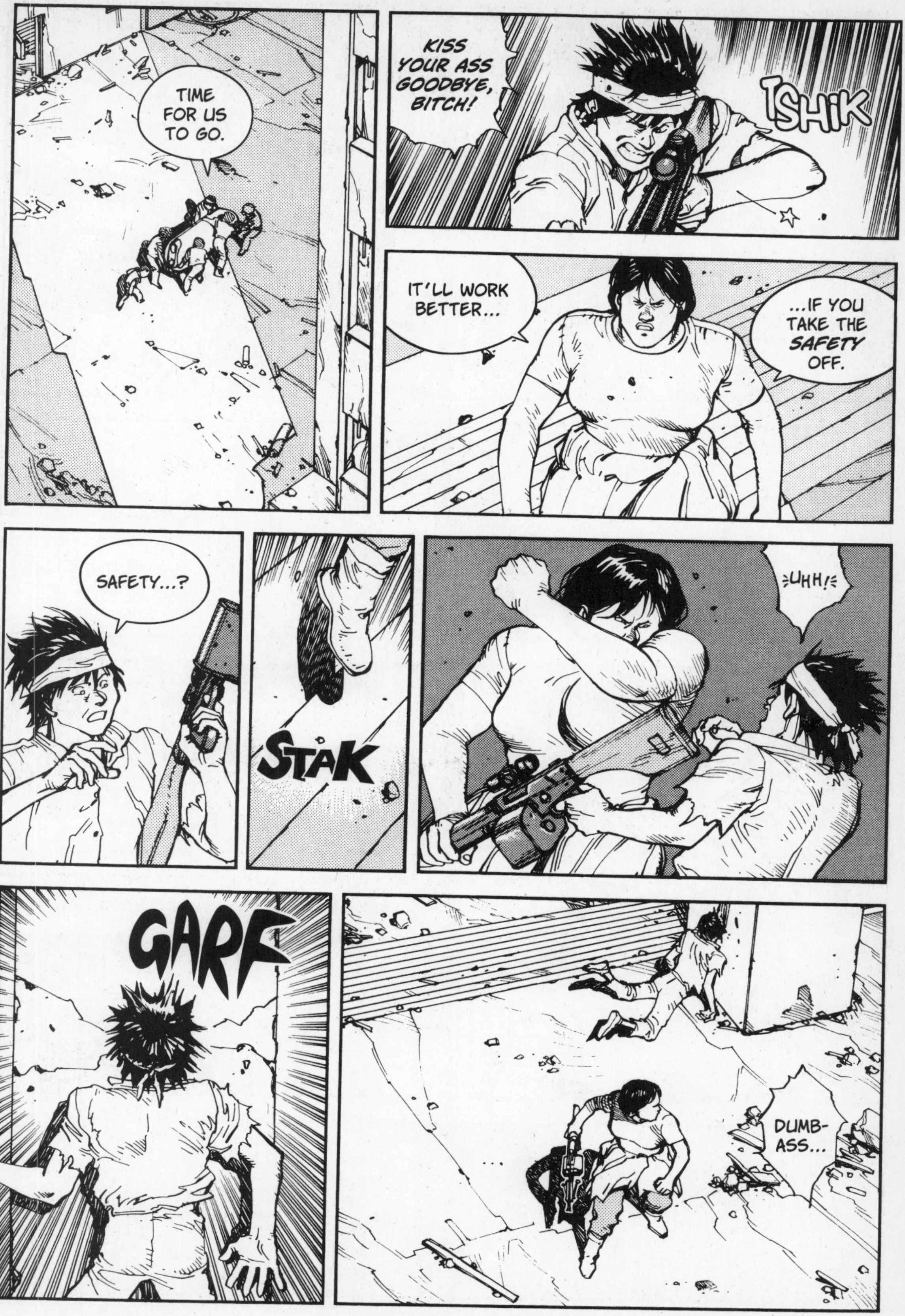
TIME FOR US TO GO.
KISS YOUR ASS GOODBYE, BITCH!
TSHIK
IT'LL WORK BETTER...
...IF YOU TAKE THE SAFETY OFF.
SAFETY...?
STAK
UHH!
GARF
...
DUMB-ASS...

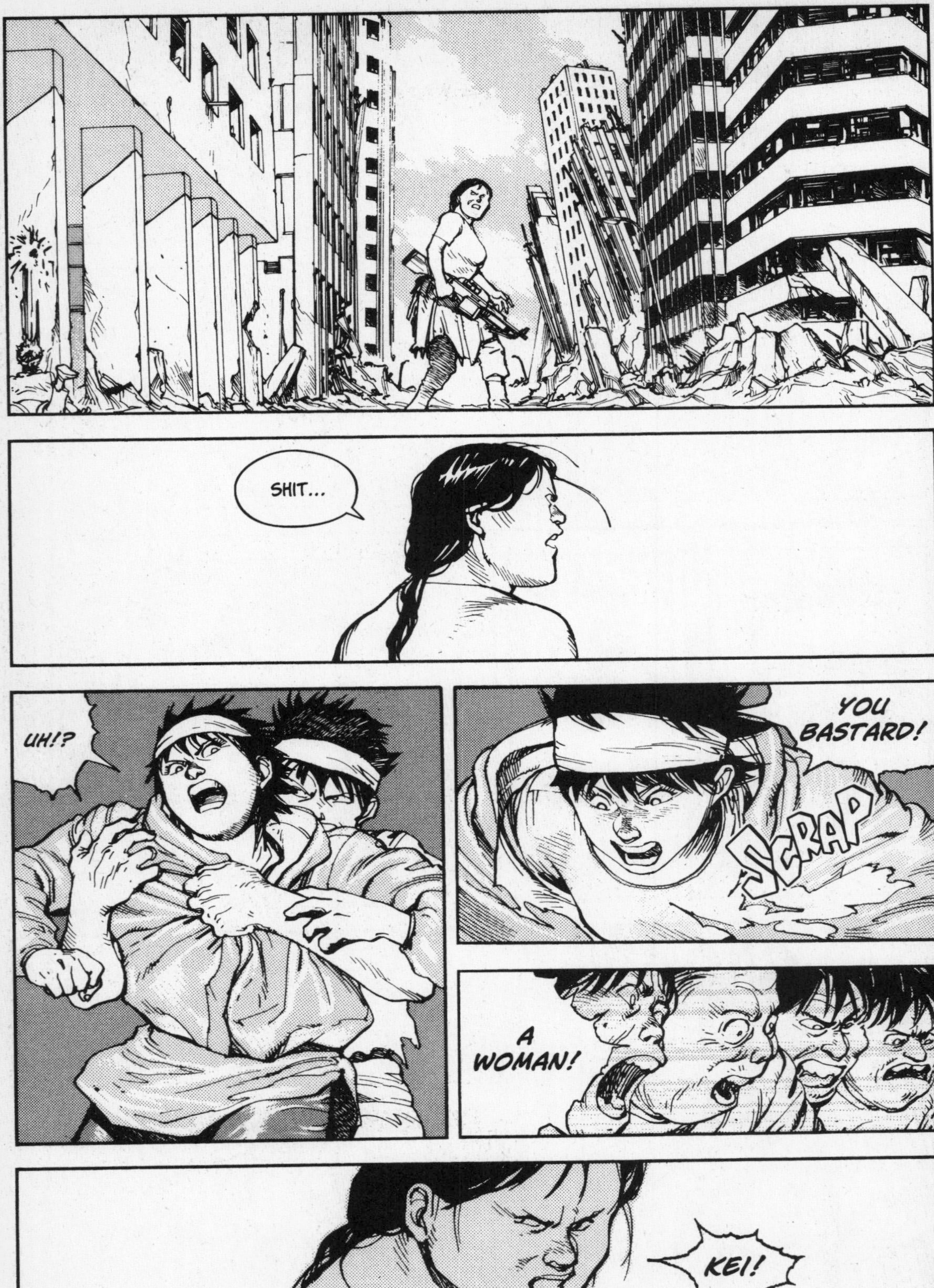
SHIT...
UH!?
YOU BASTARD!
SCRAP
A WOMAN!
KEI!

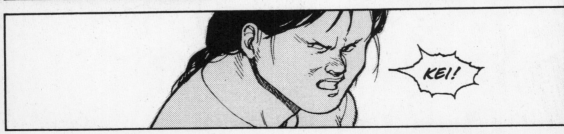

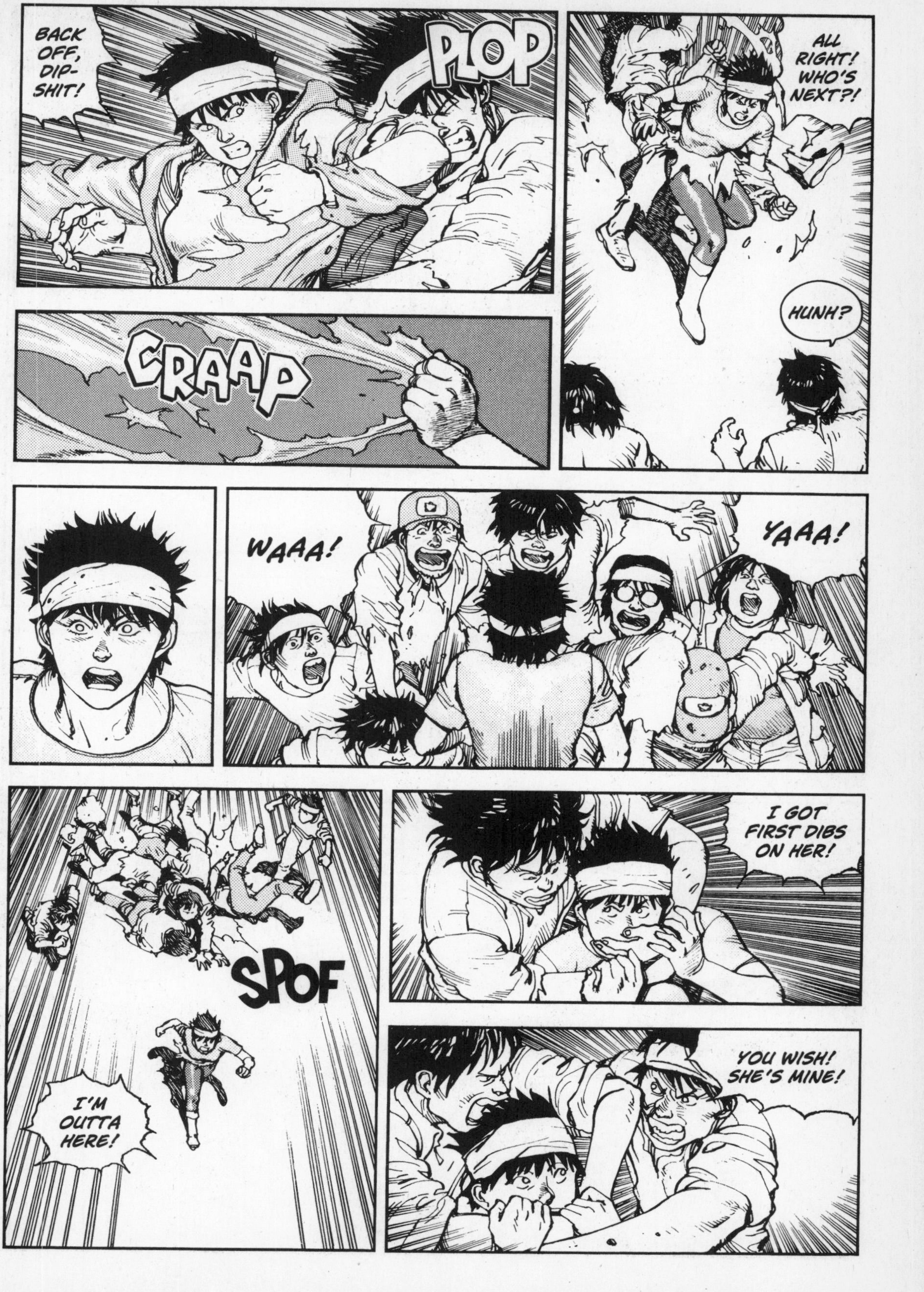
BACK OFF, DIP-SHIT!
PLOP
ALL RIGHT! WHO'S NEXT?!
CRAAP
HUNH?
WAAA!
YAAA!
SPOF
I'M OUTTA HERE!
I GOT FIRST DIBS ON HER!
YOU WISH! SHE'S MINE!

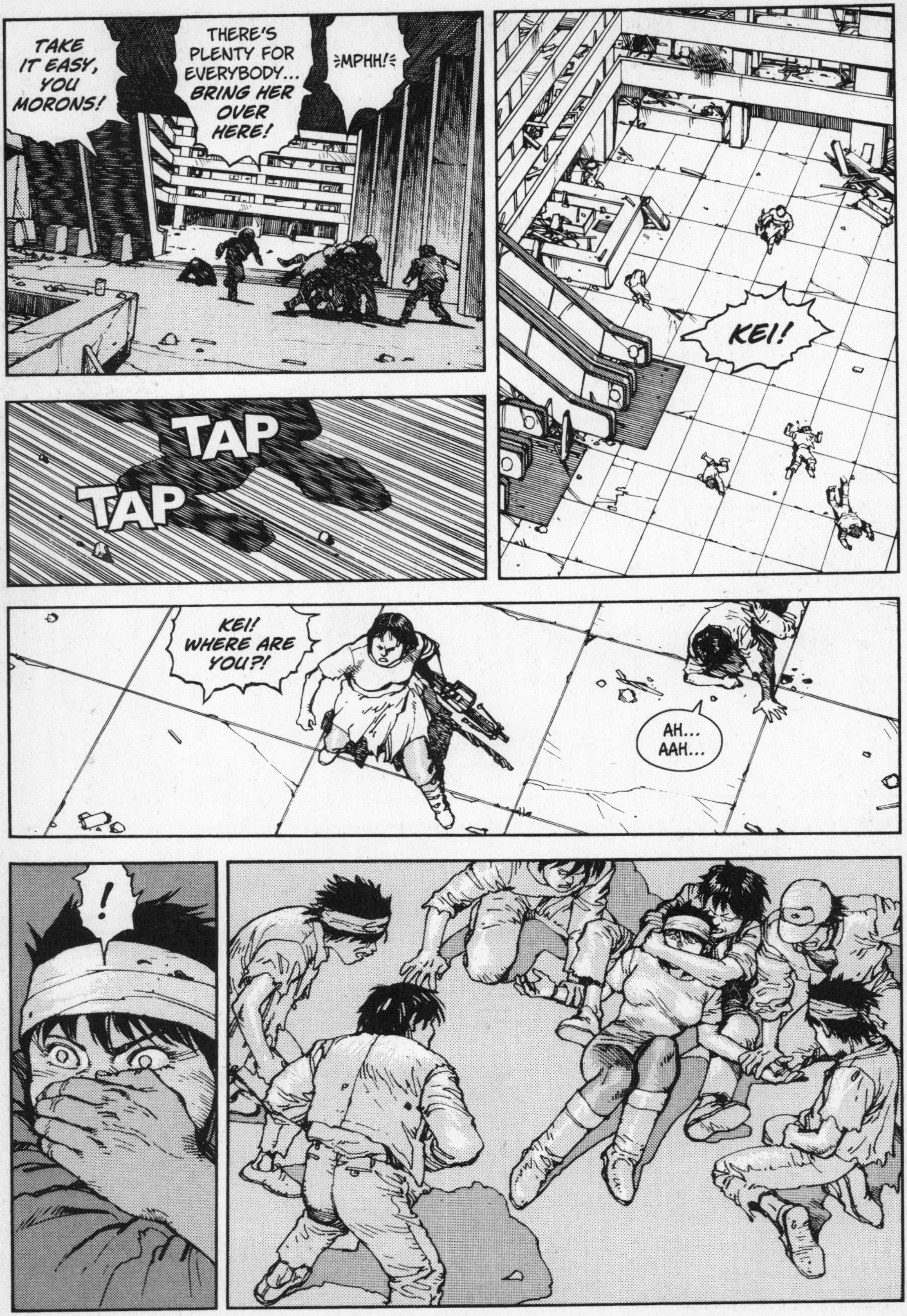
TAKE IT EASY, YOU MORONS!
THERE'S PLENTY FOR EVERYBODY... BRING HER OVER HERE!
MPHH!
KEI!
TAP
TAP
KEI! WHERE ARE YOU?!
AH... AAH...
!

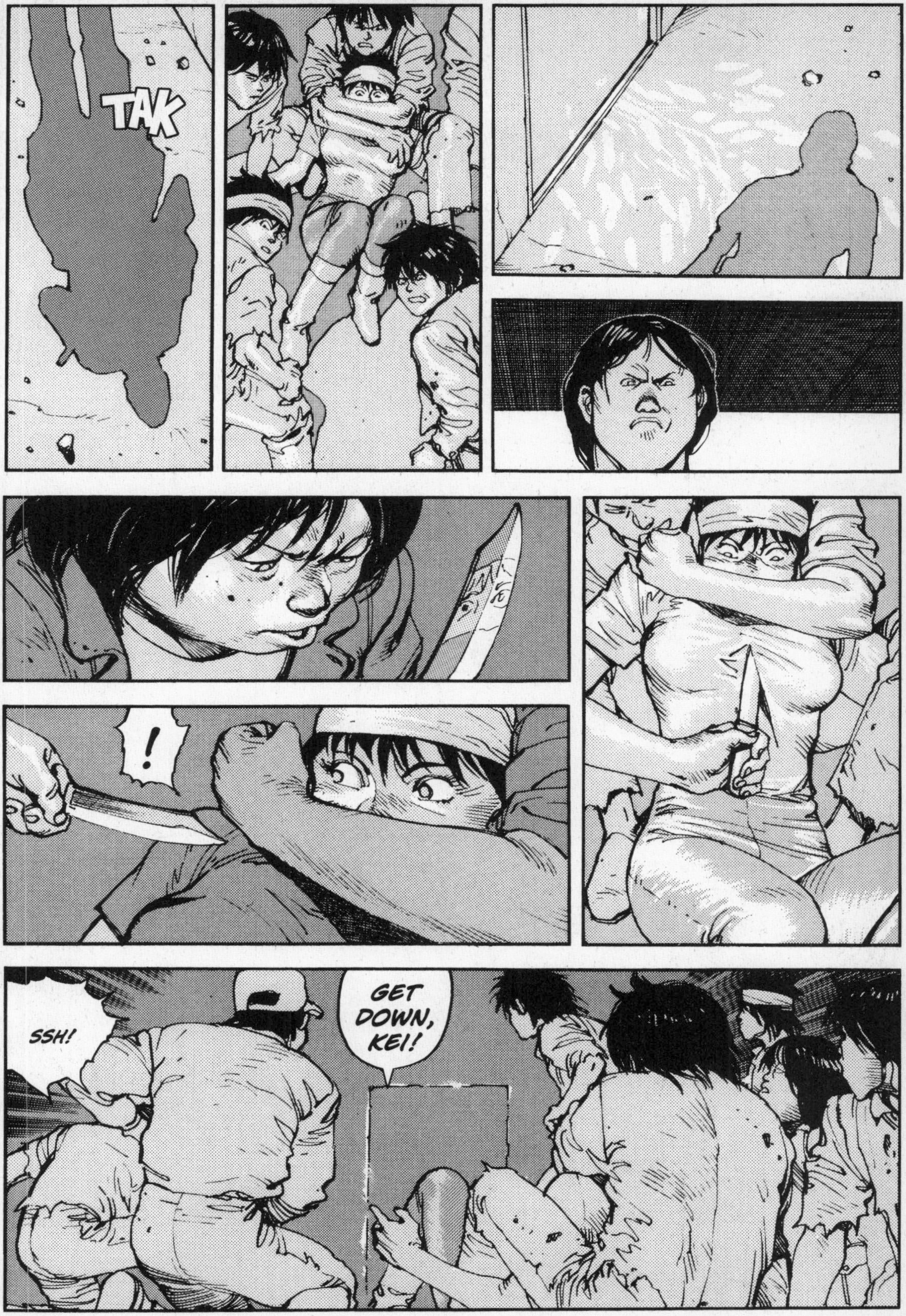
TAK
!
SSH!
GET DOWN, KEI!

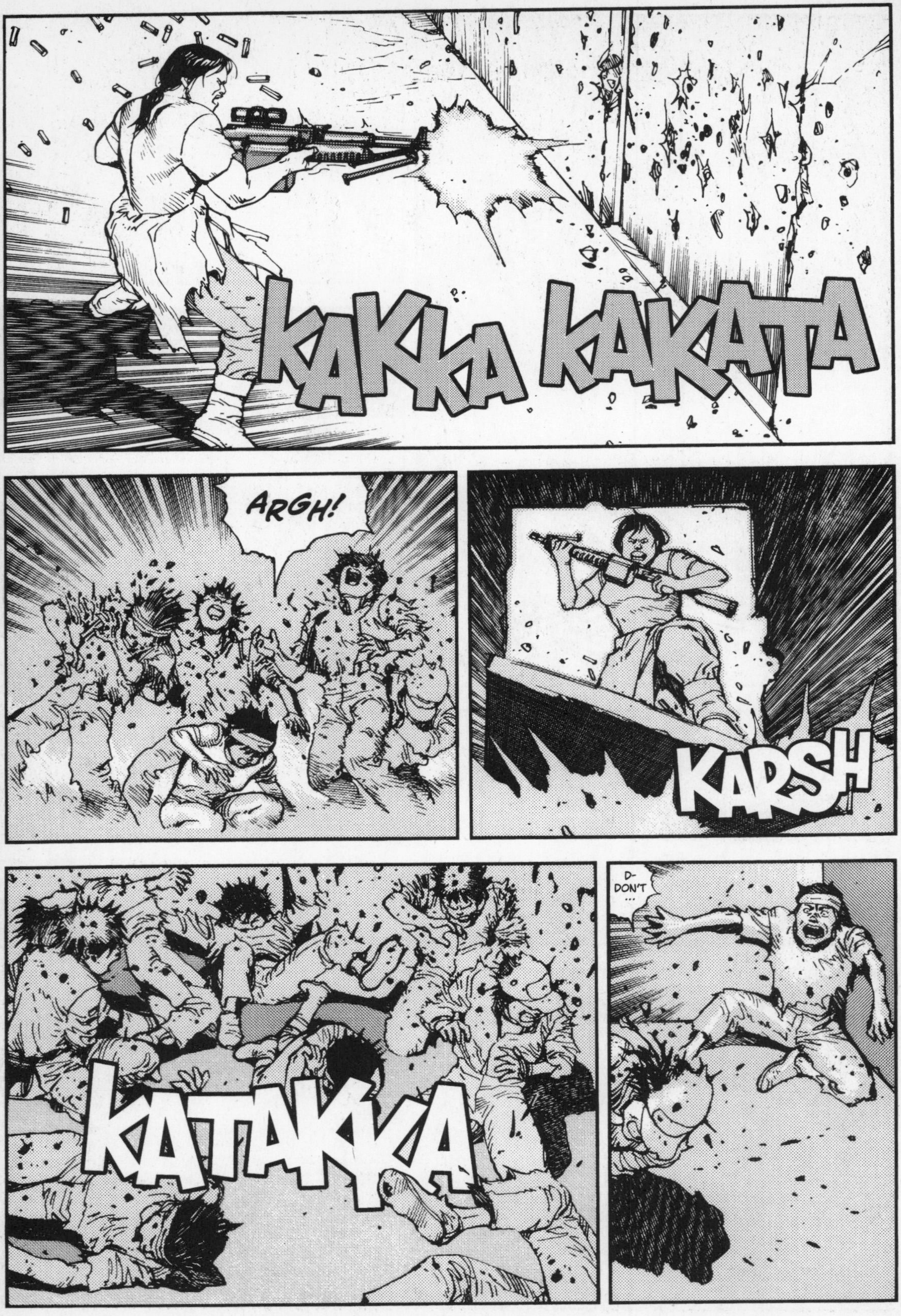
KAKKA KAKATA
ARGH!
KARSH
KATAKKA
D-DON'T...

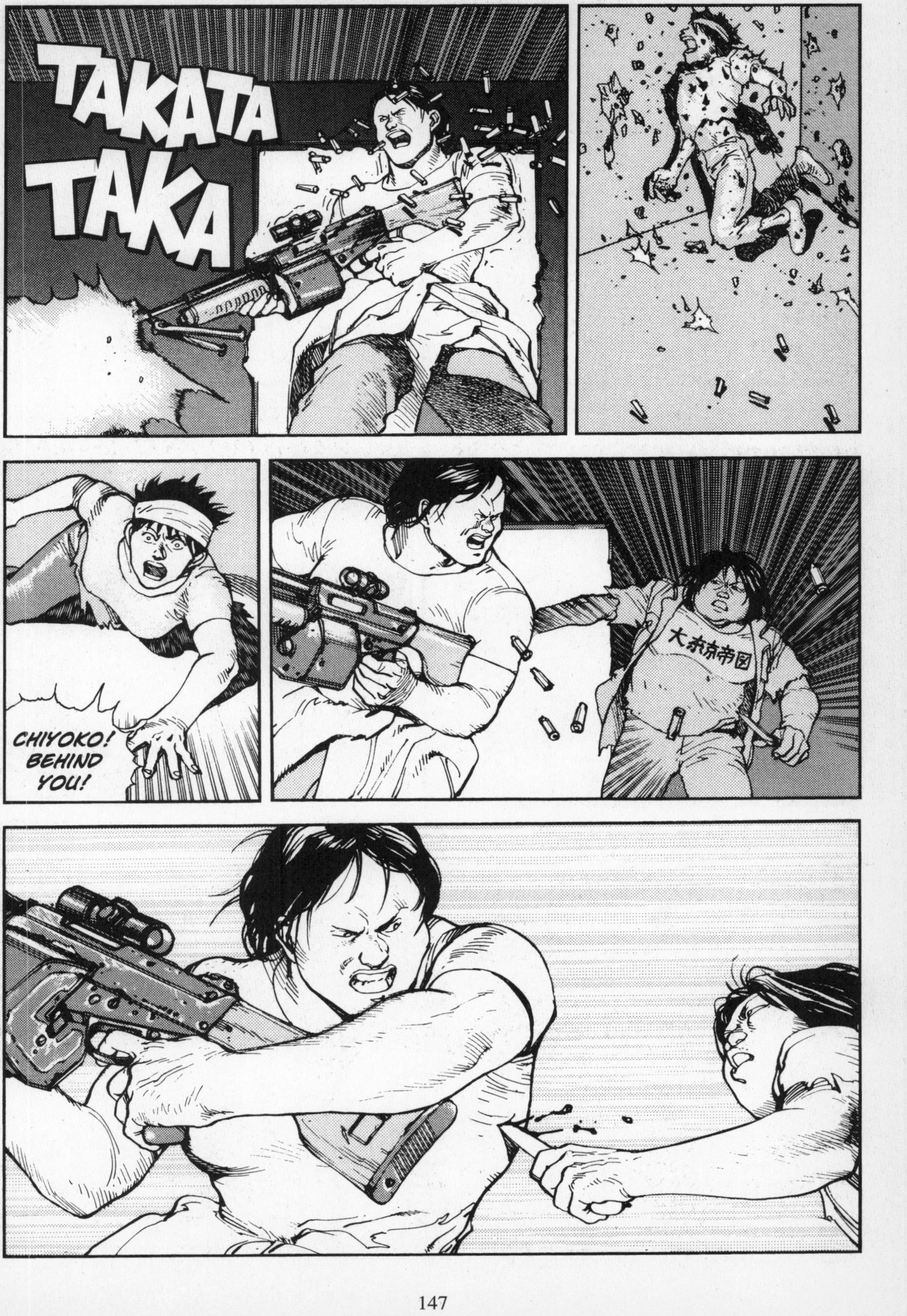
TAKATA
TAKA
CHIYOKO! BEHIND YOU!

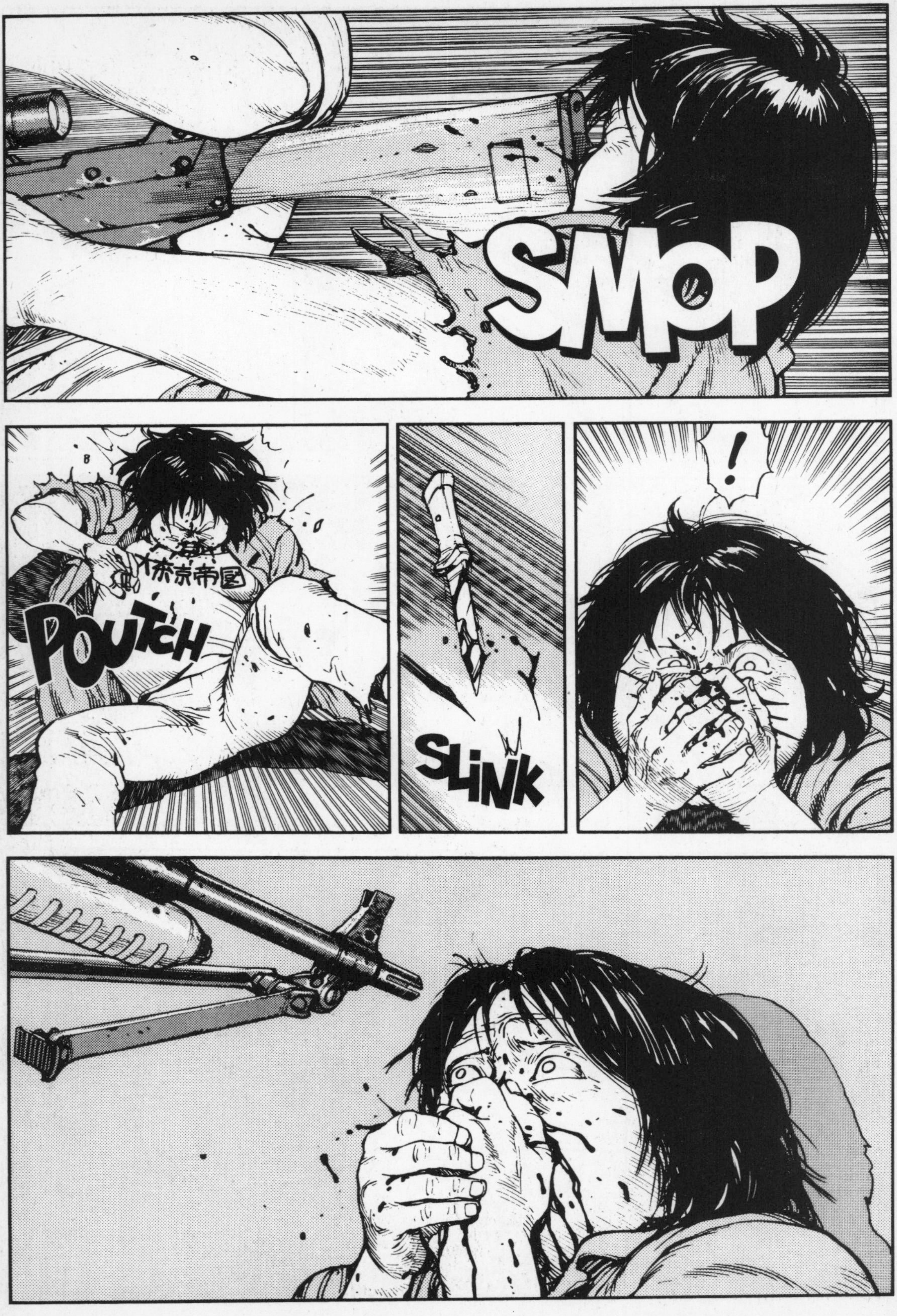
SMOP
POUTCH
SLINK
!

KSHAKAKA KAKAKA

SHUIIN

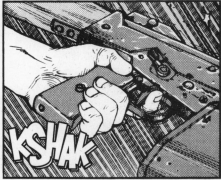

KSHAK

DID THEY... DO ANYTHING TO YOU?

CHIYOKO! YOU'RE WOUNDED!

IT'S JUST A SCRATCH. *FORGET* ABOUT IT...

WE GOT *URGENT* BUSINESS.

KLIC

TCHOK

KLANG

TAP TAP

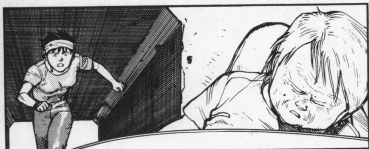

HE'S OKAY. THE MEDICATION HASN'T WORN OFF...

...

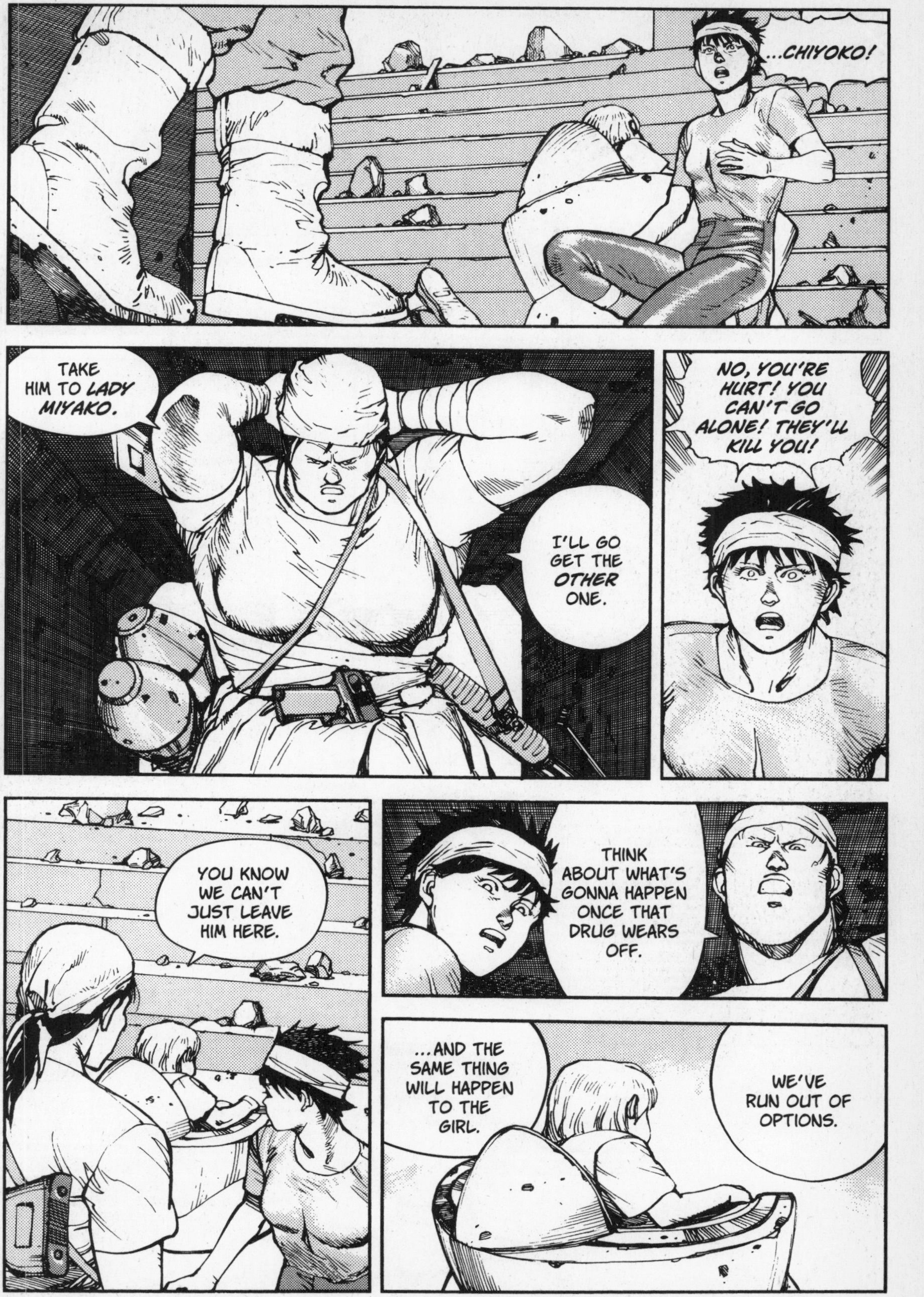
...CHIYOKO!
TAKE HIM TO LADY MIYAKO.
I'LL GO GET THE OTHER ONE.
NO, YOU'RE HURT! YOU CAN'T GO ALONE! THEY'LL KILL YOU!
YOU KNOW WE CAN'T JUST LEAVE HIM HERE.
THINK ABOUT WHAT'S GONNA HAPPEN ONCE THAT DRUG WEARS OFF.
...AND THE SAME THING WILL HAPPEN TO THE GIRL.
WE'VE RUN OUT OF OPTIONS.

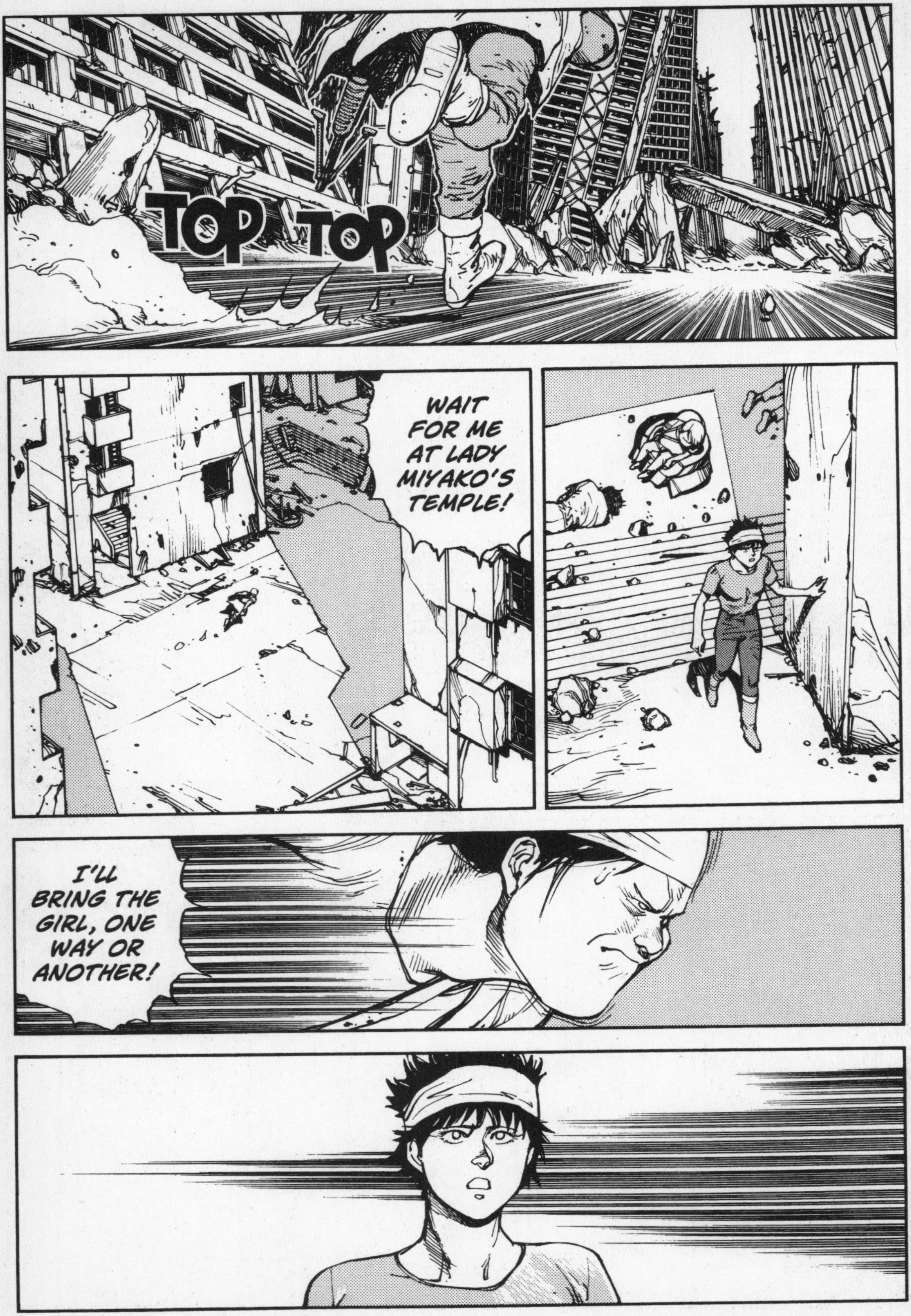
TOP TOP
WAIT FOR ME AT LADY MIYAKO'S TEMPLE!
I'LL BRING THE GIRL, ONE WAY OR ANOTHER!

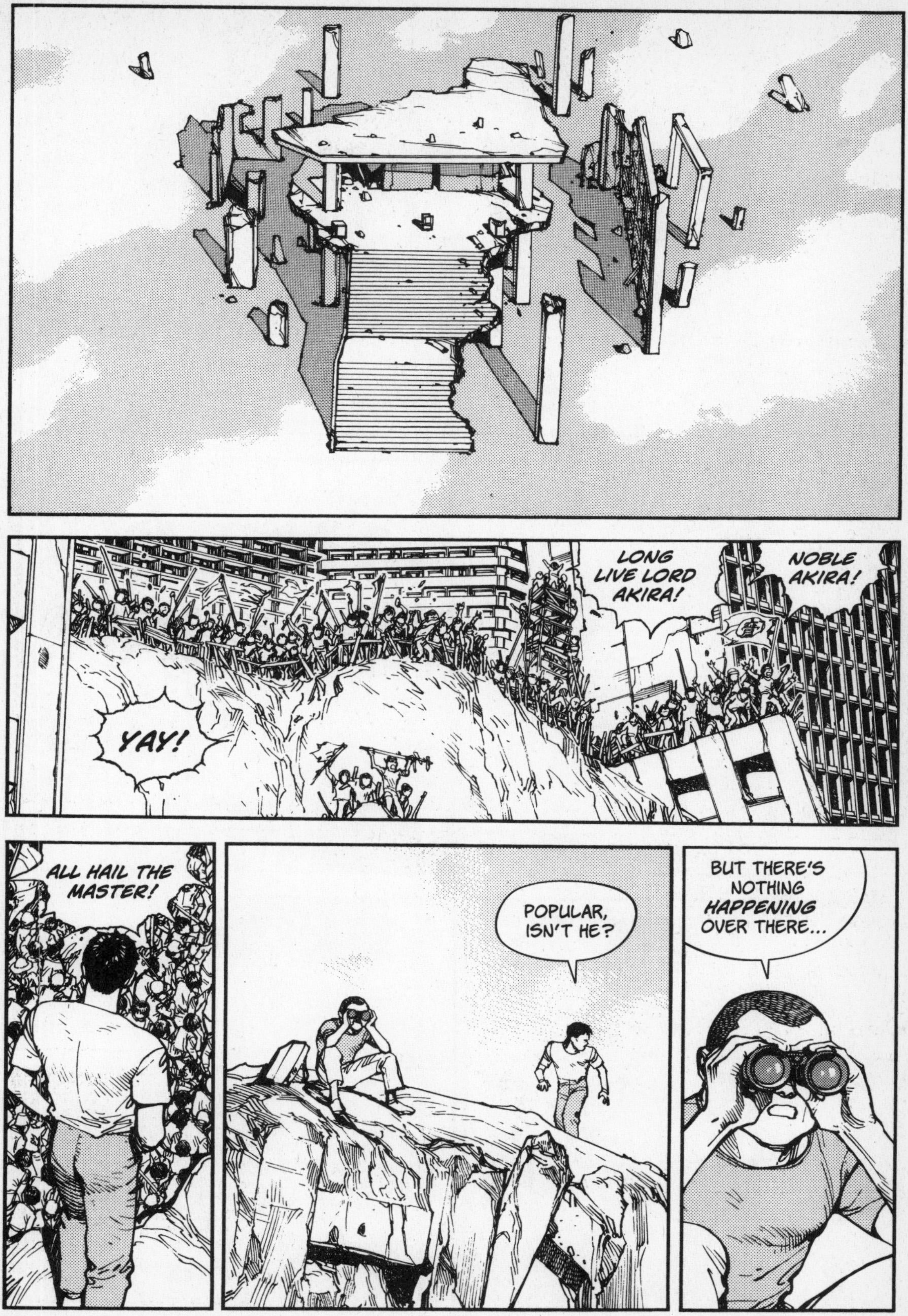
LONG LIVE LORD AKIRA!
NOBLE AKIRA!
YAY!
ALL HAIL THE MASTER!
POPULAR, ISN'T HE?
BUT THERE'S NOTHING HAPPENING OVER THERE...

RUMOR HAS IT HE APPEARS BEFORE THE FAITHFUL TWICE A DAY.

THEN I INTEND TO STICK AROUND AND GET A GOOD LOOK AT HIS EXHALTED PRESENCE...

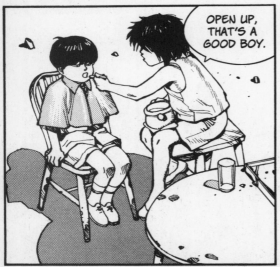

OPEN UP, THAT'S A GOOD BOY.

COME ON... IT'S NOT SO BAD. COULDN'T YOU SMILE JUST A LITTLE?

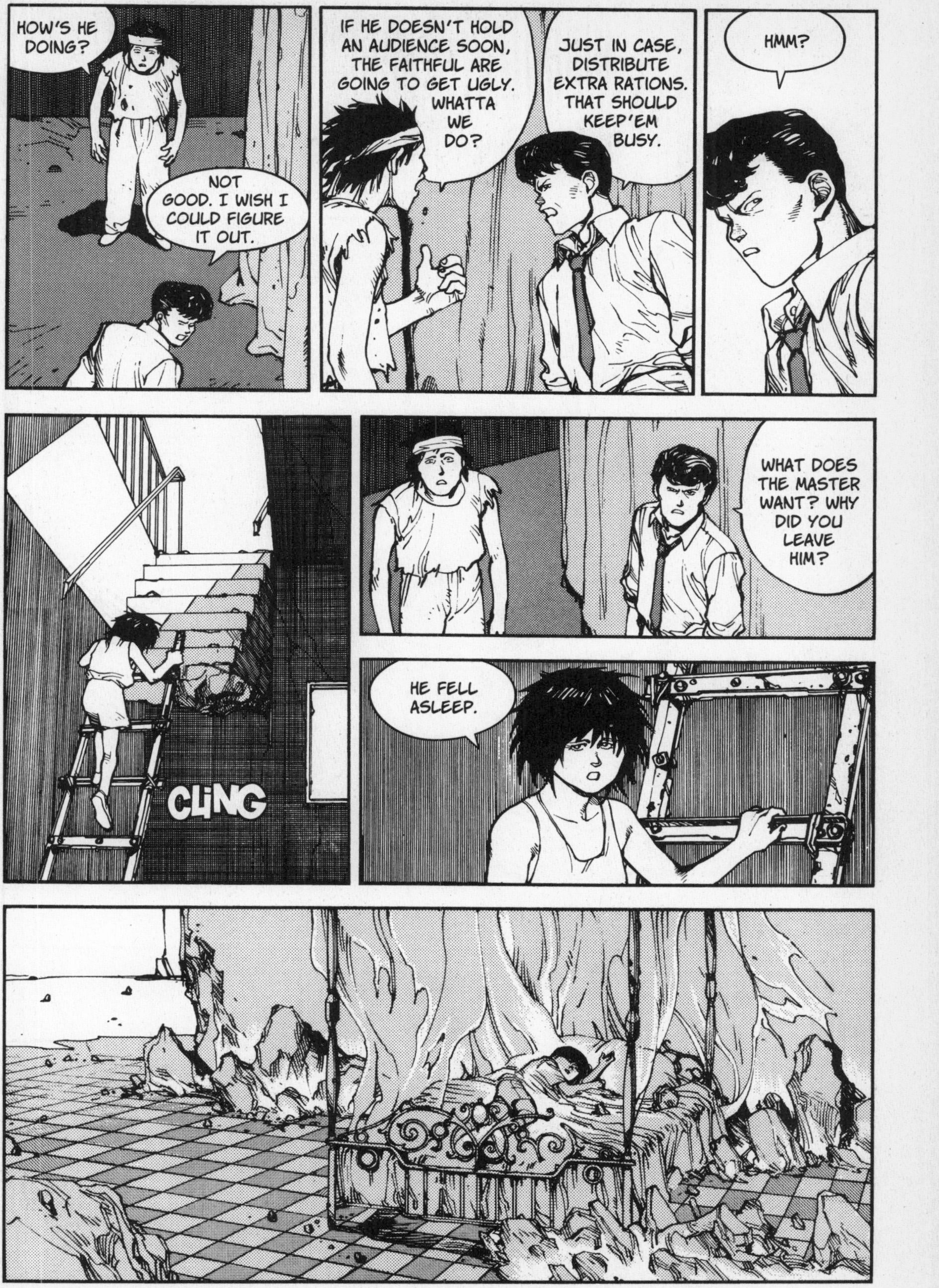
HOW'S HE DOING?
NOT GOOD. I WISH I COULD FIGURE IT OUT.
IF HE DOESN'T HOLD AN AUDIENCE SOON, THE FAITHFUL ARE GOING TO GET UGLY. WHATTA WE DO?
JUST IN CASE, DISTRIBUTE EXTRA RATIONS. THAT SHOULD KEEP'EM BUSY.
HMM?
CLiNG
WHAT DOES THE MASTER WANT? WHY DID YOU LEAVE HIM?
HE FELL ASLEEP.

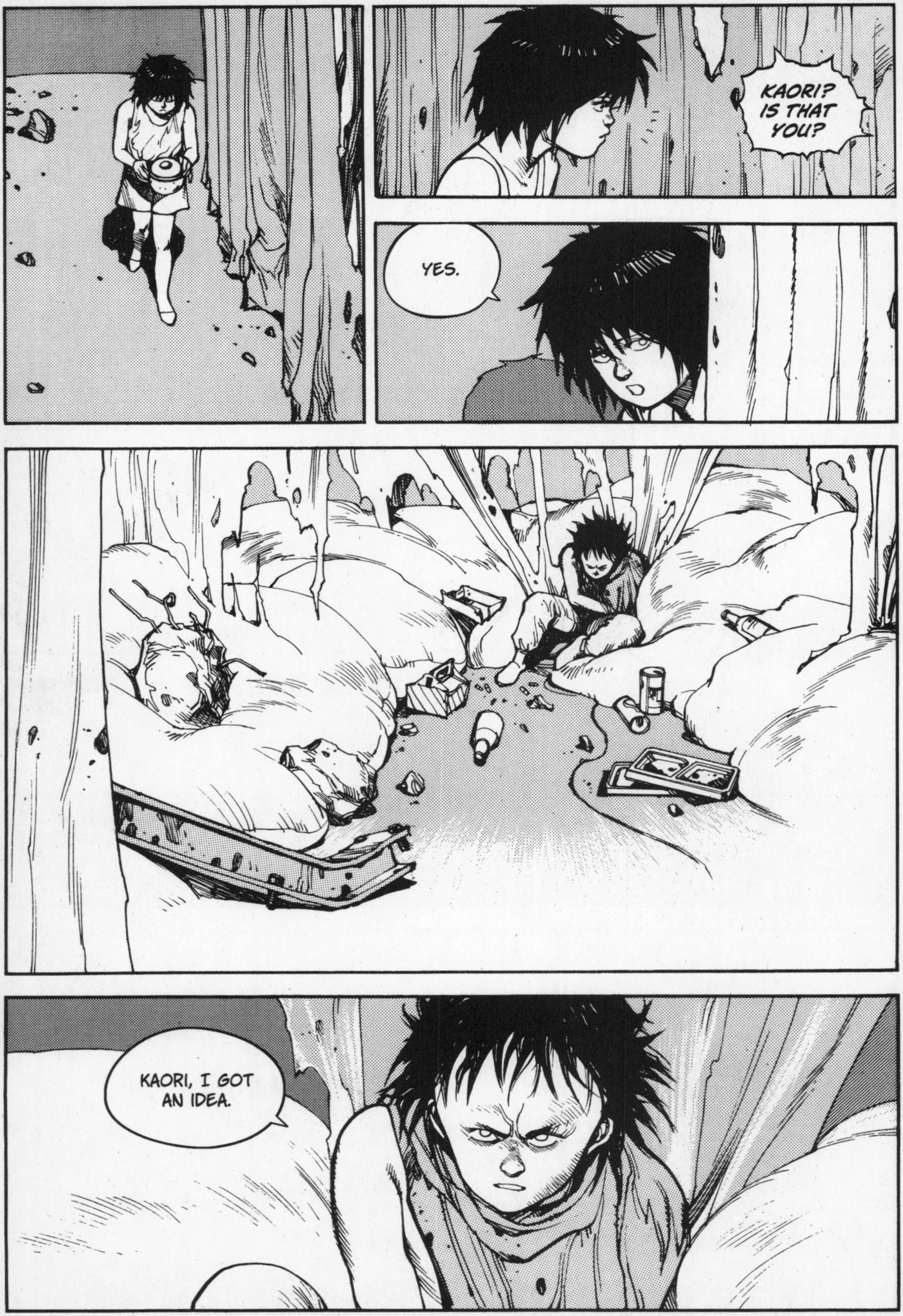
KAORI? IS THAT YOU?
YES.
KAORI, I GOT AN IDEA.

THEN... YOU DON'T REMEMBER?

... I BROUGHT YOU SOME FOOD...

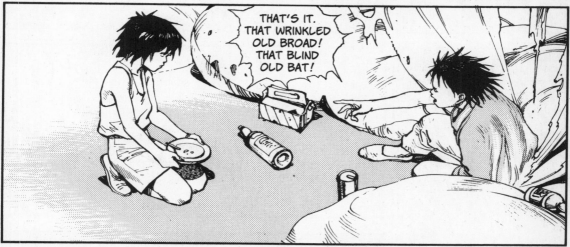

THAT'S IT. THAT WRINKLED OLD BROAD! THAT BLIND OLD BAT!

FOR SOMEONE WHO CAN'T SEE...SHE KNOWS A HELL OF A LOT...

I'M SURE...YEAH, SHE CAN EXPLAIN IT TO ME!

HELP ME UP!

I HAVE TO GO SEE HER.

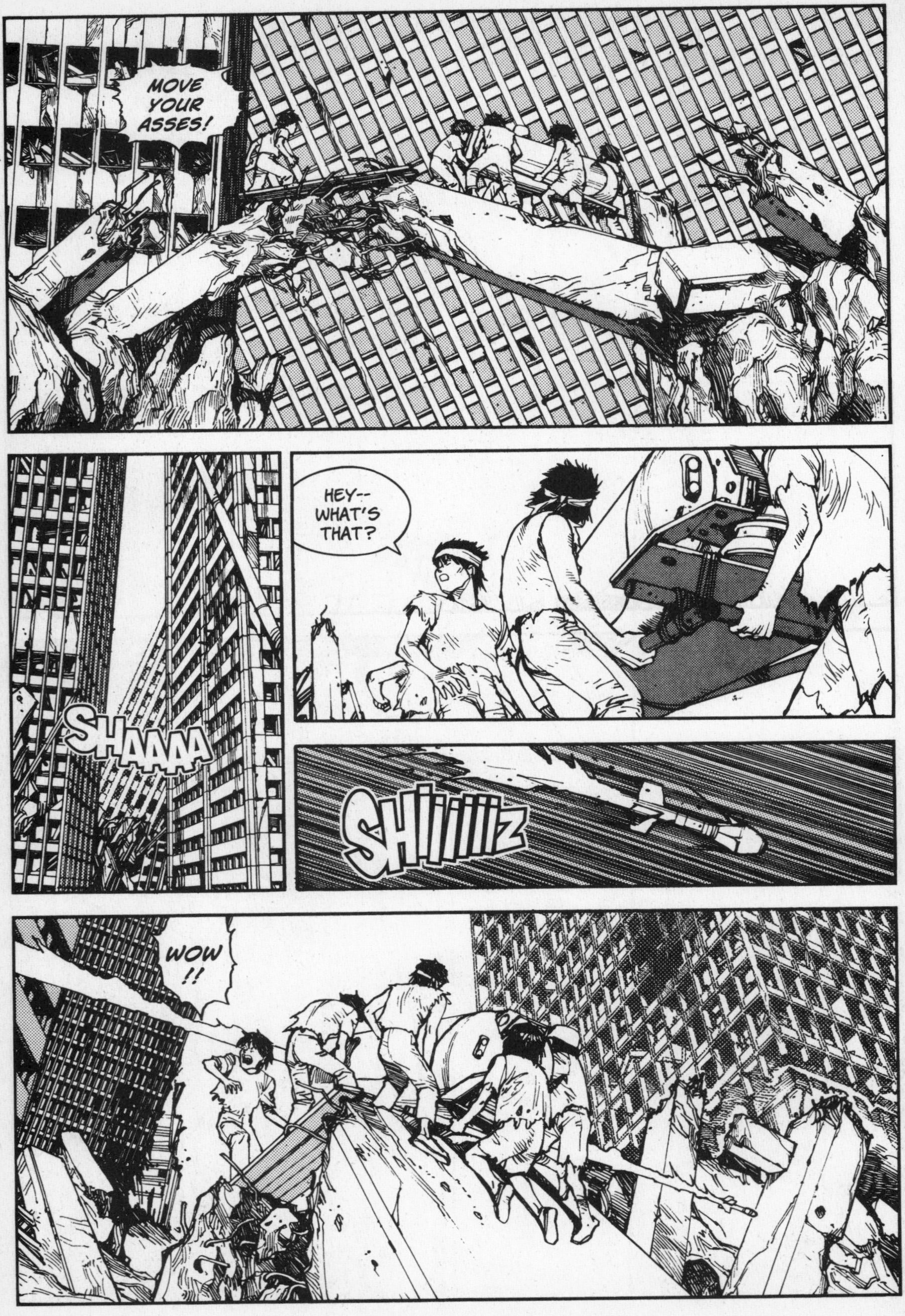
MOVE YOUR ASSES!
SHAAAA
HEY-- WHAT'S THAT?
SHIIIIIIZ
WOW !!

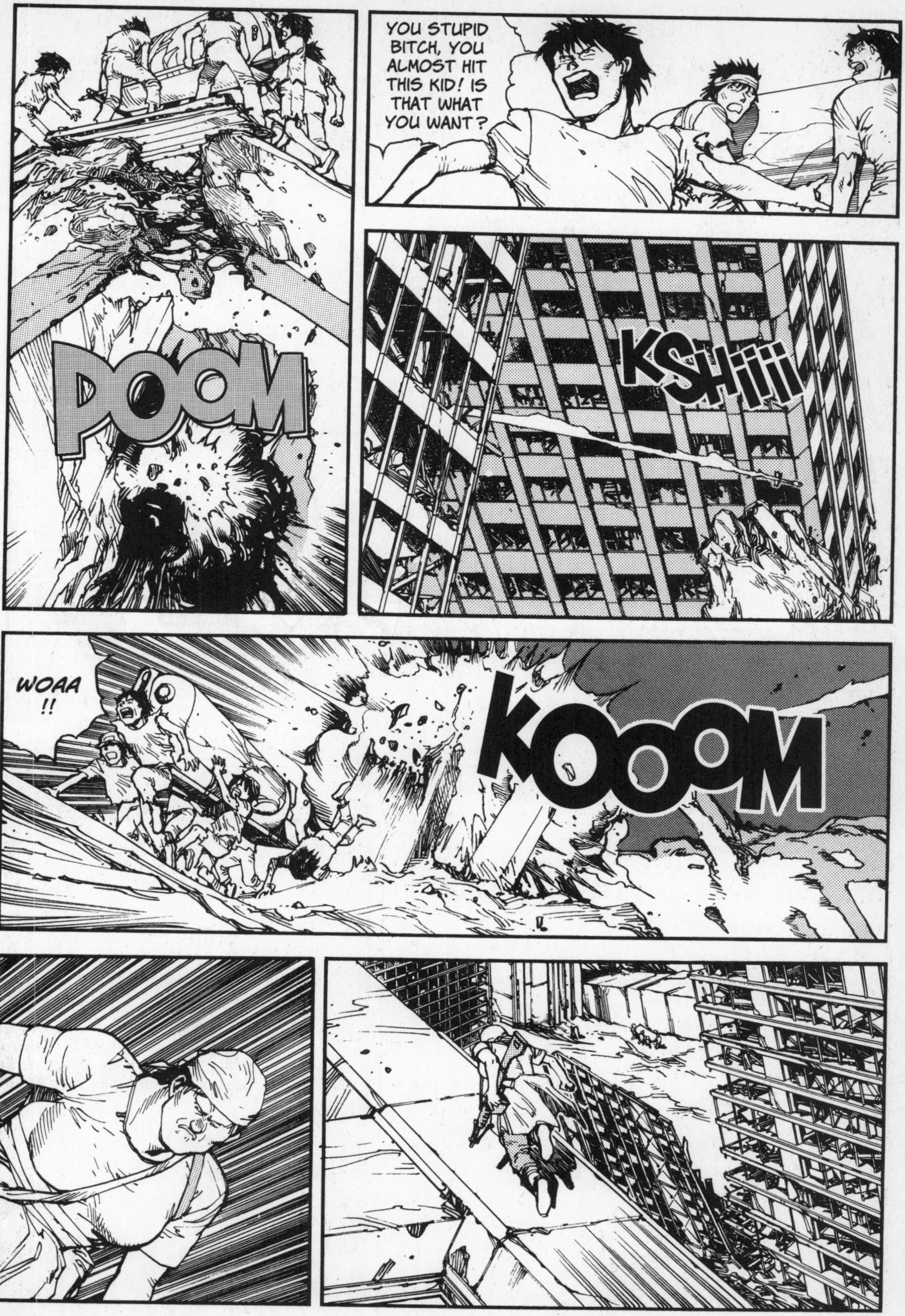
POOM
YOU STUPID BITCH, YOU ALMOST HIT THIS KID! IS THAT WHAT YOU WANT?
KSHIiii
WOAA !!
KOOOM

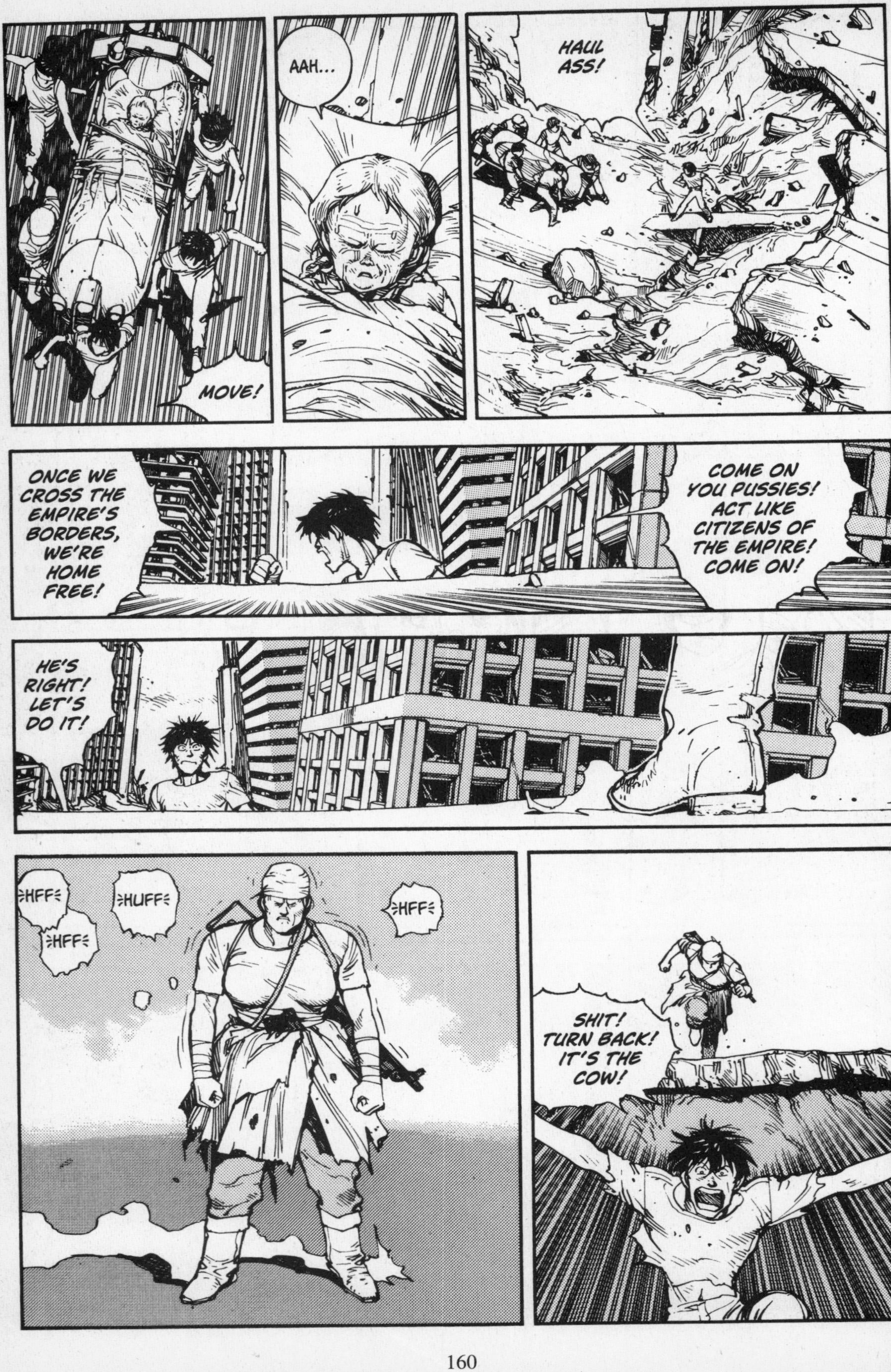
MOVE!
AAH...
HAUL ASS!
ONCE WE CROSS THE EMPIRE'S BORDERS, WE'RE HOME FREE!
COME ON YOU PUSSIES! ACT LIKE CITIZENS OF THE EMPIRE! COME ON!
HE'S RIGHT! LET'S DO IT!
HFF
HFF
HUFF
HFF
SHIT! TURN BACK! IT'S THE COW!

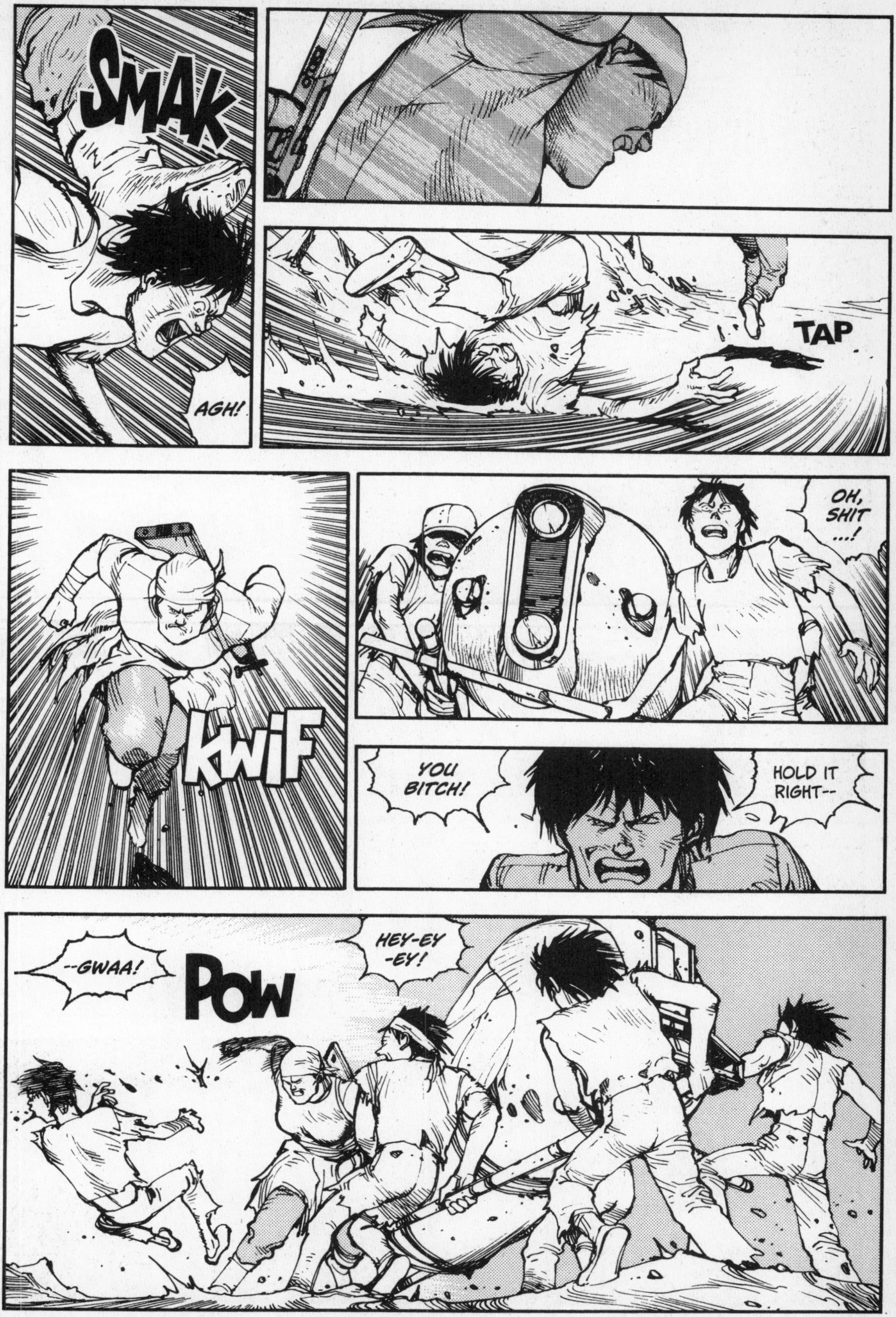
SMAK
AGH!
TAP
KWIF
OH, SHIT ...!
YOU BITCH!
HOLD IT RIGHT--
--GWAA!
POW
HEY-EY -EY!

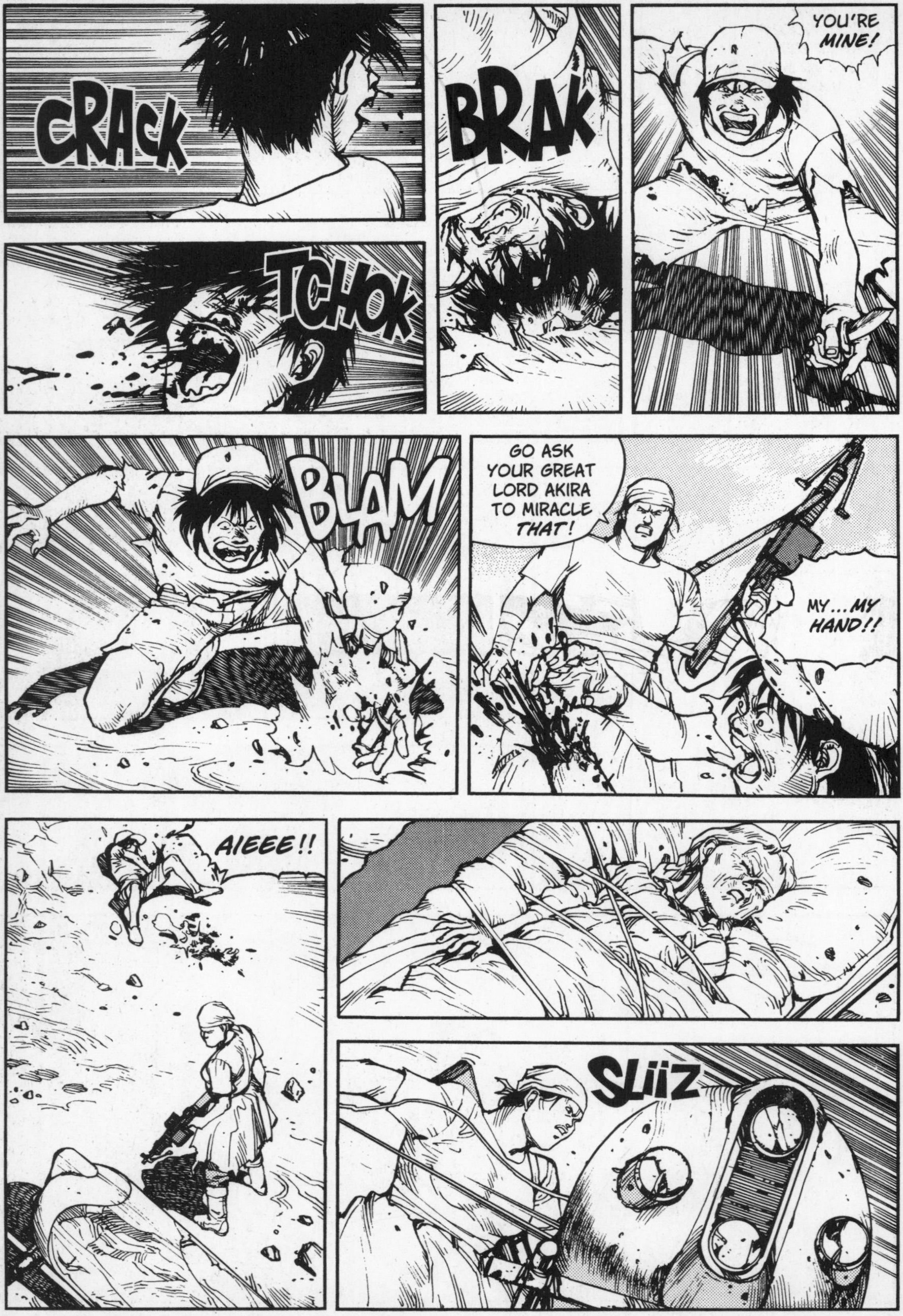
CRACK
BRAK
YOU'RE MINE!
TCHOK
BLAM
GO ASK YOUR GREAT LORD AKIRA TO MIRACLE THAT!
MY... MY HAND!!
AIEEE!!
SLIIZ

OUR BROTHERS HAVE BEEN FELLED BY A WOMAN OF THE ENEMY!

SHE HAS TAKEN THE CHILD!

SHE IS JUST BEYOND OUR EASTERN BORDER.

ALL MEN MUST GO FORTH TO RECOVER THE CHILD!

BUT BEWARE! SHE IS HEAVILY ARMED! SHE IS QUICK AND CLEVER!

DON'T UNDER-ESTIMATE HER!

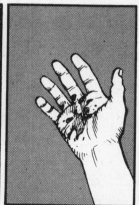

LET'S GO...

WE'RE RUNNING OUT OF TIME...

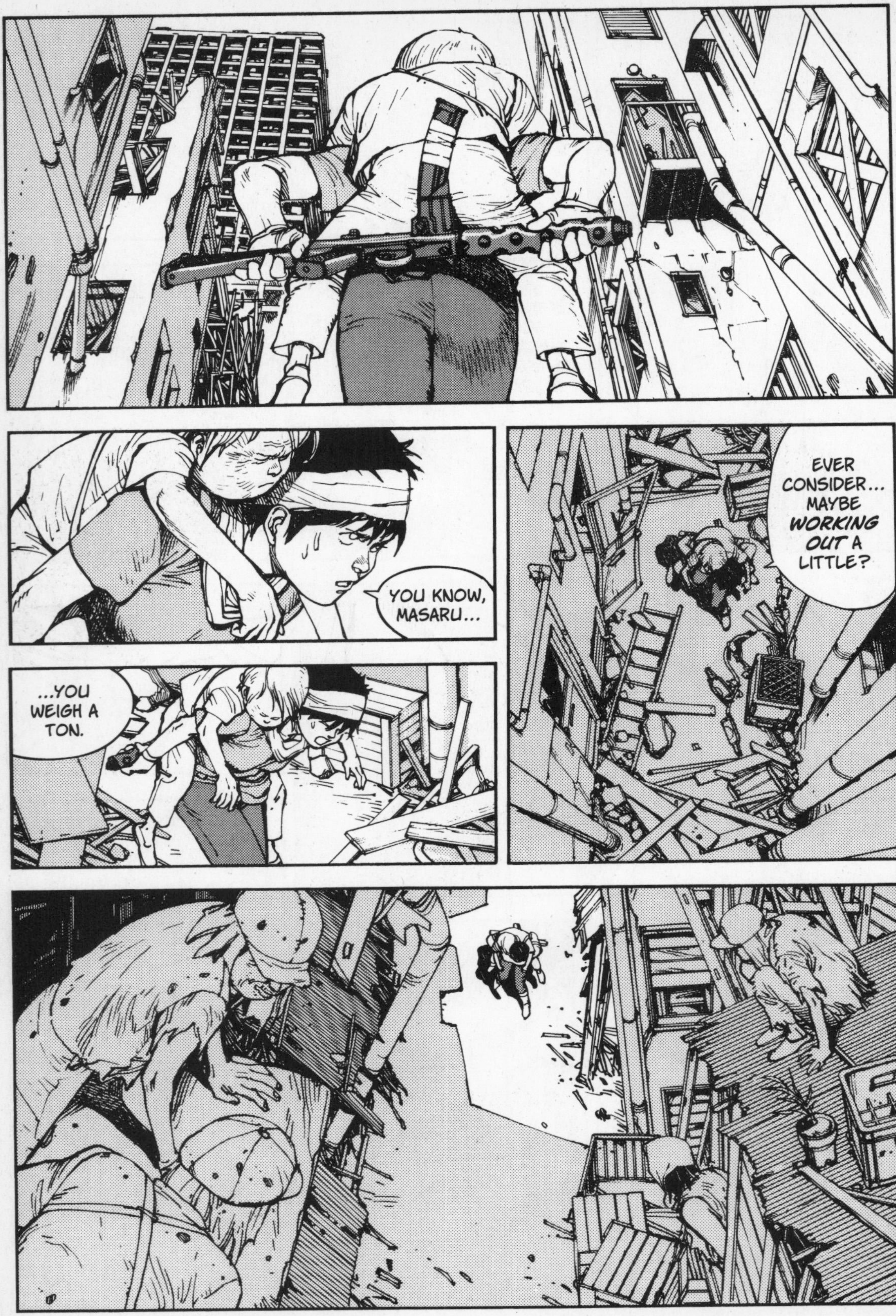
YOU KNOW, MASARU...
...YOU WEIGH A TON.
EVER CONSIDER... MAYBE WORKING OUT A LITTLE?

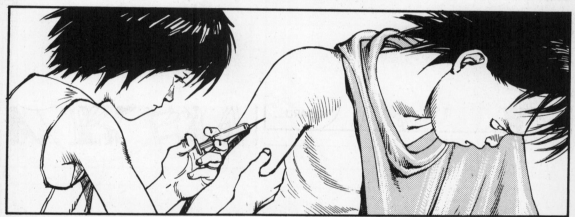

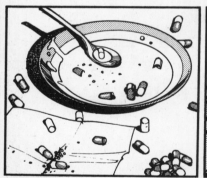

ARE YOU
FEELING
BETTER?

HUHN
HUHN
KLING
KAORI...
YES?
I'M GOING.
!

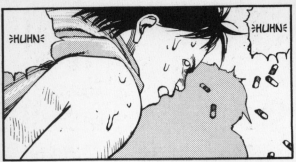

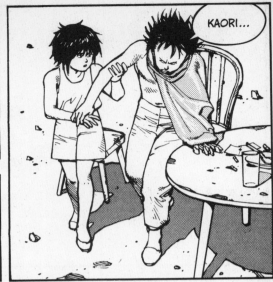

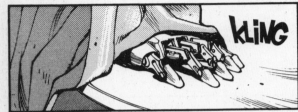

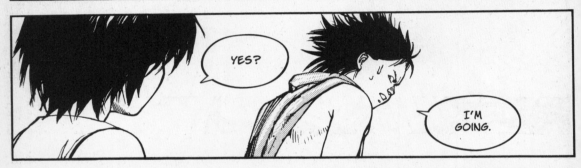

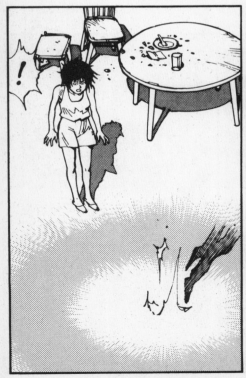

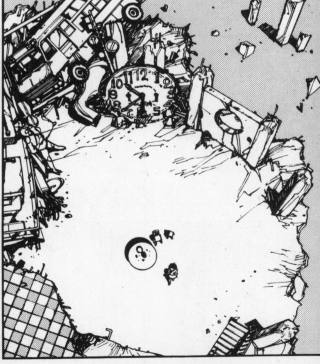

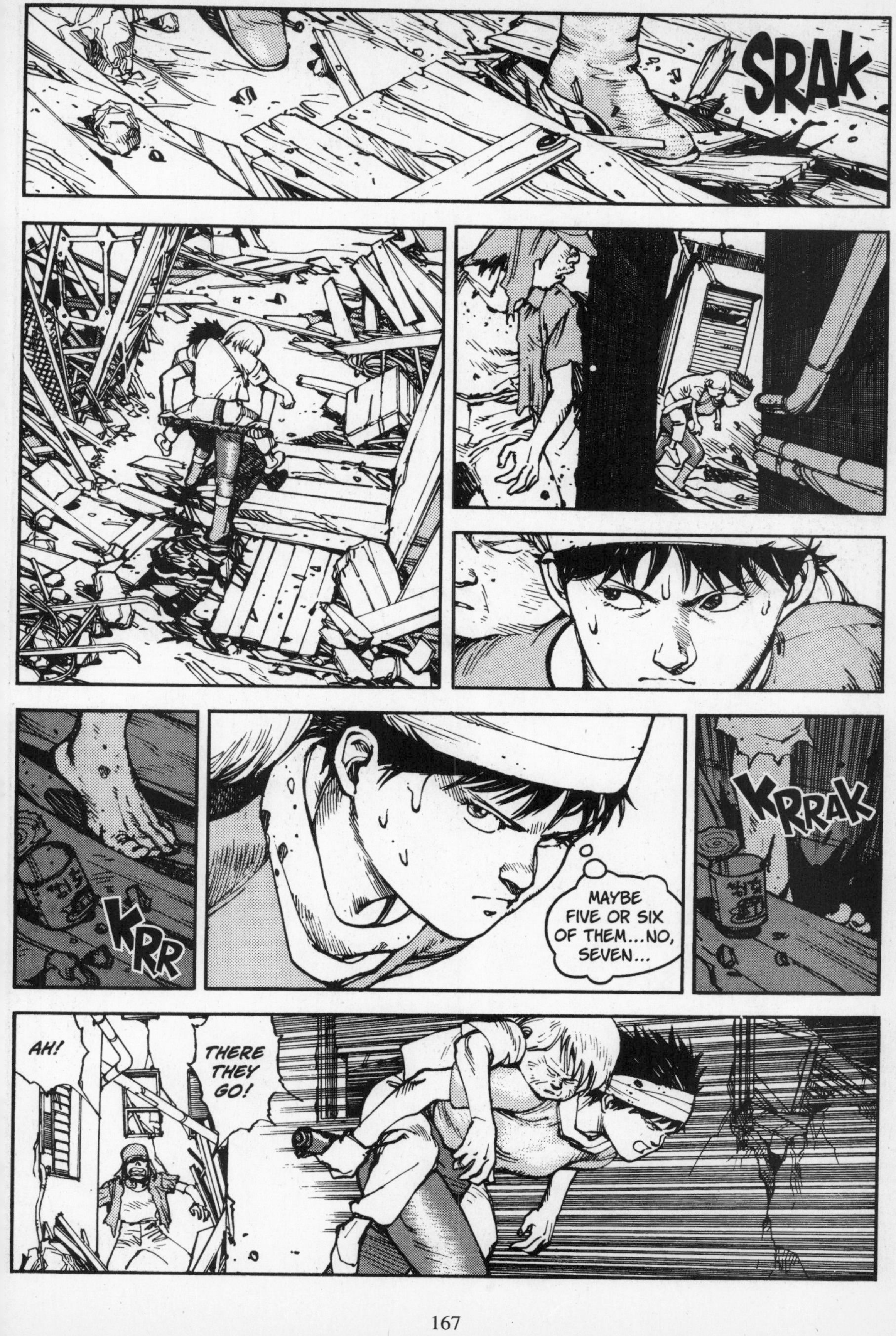
SRAK
KRR
MAYBE FIVE OR SIX OF THEM...NO, SEVEN...
KRRAK
AH!
THERE THEY GO!

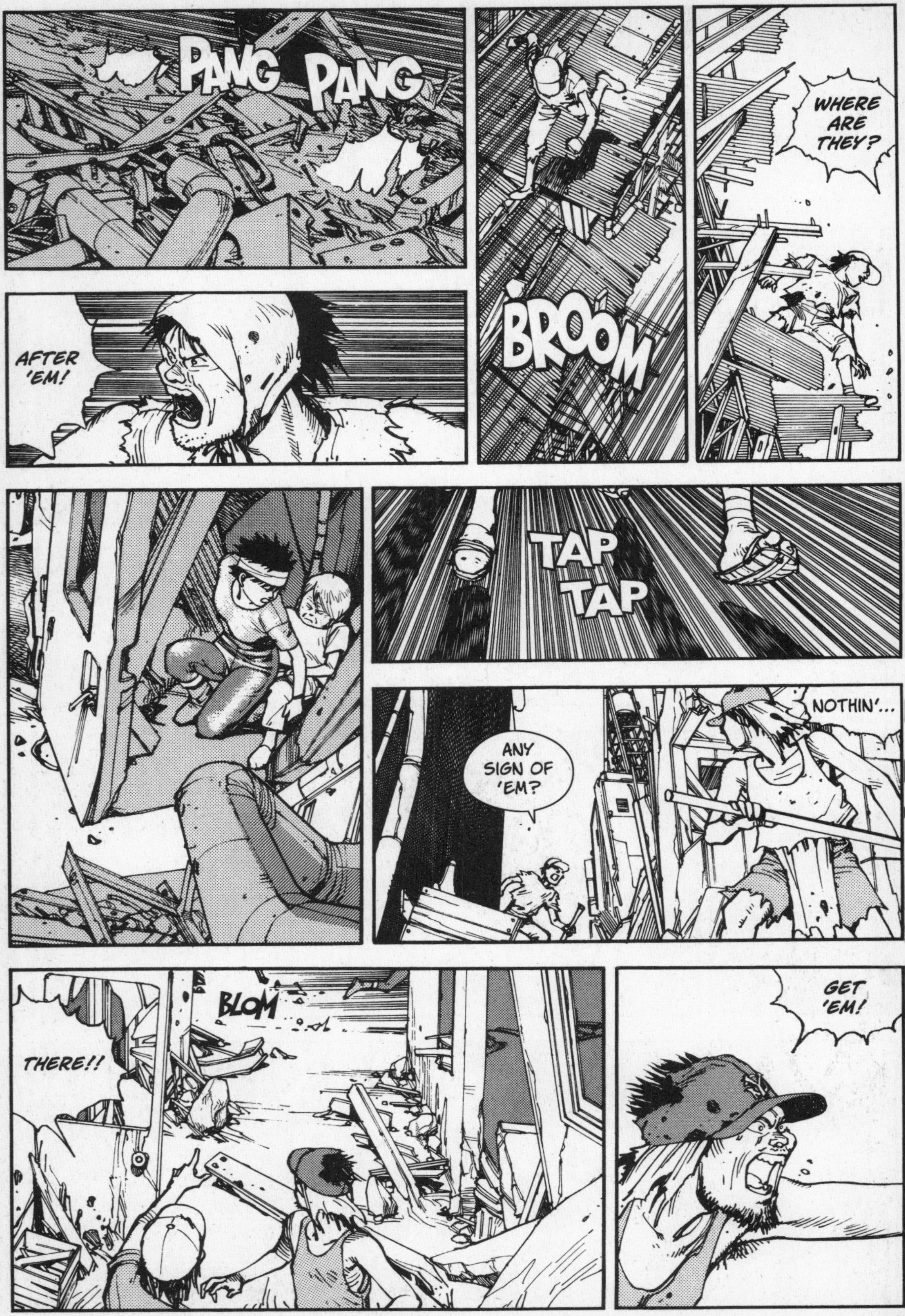
PANG PANG
AFTER 'EM!
BROOM
WHERE ARE THEY?
TAP TAP
ANY SIGN OF 'EM?
NOTHIN'...
BLOM
THERE!!
GET 'EM!

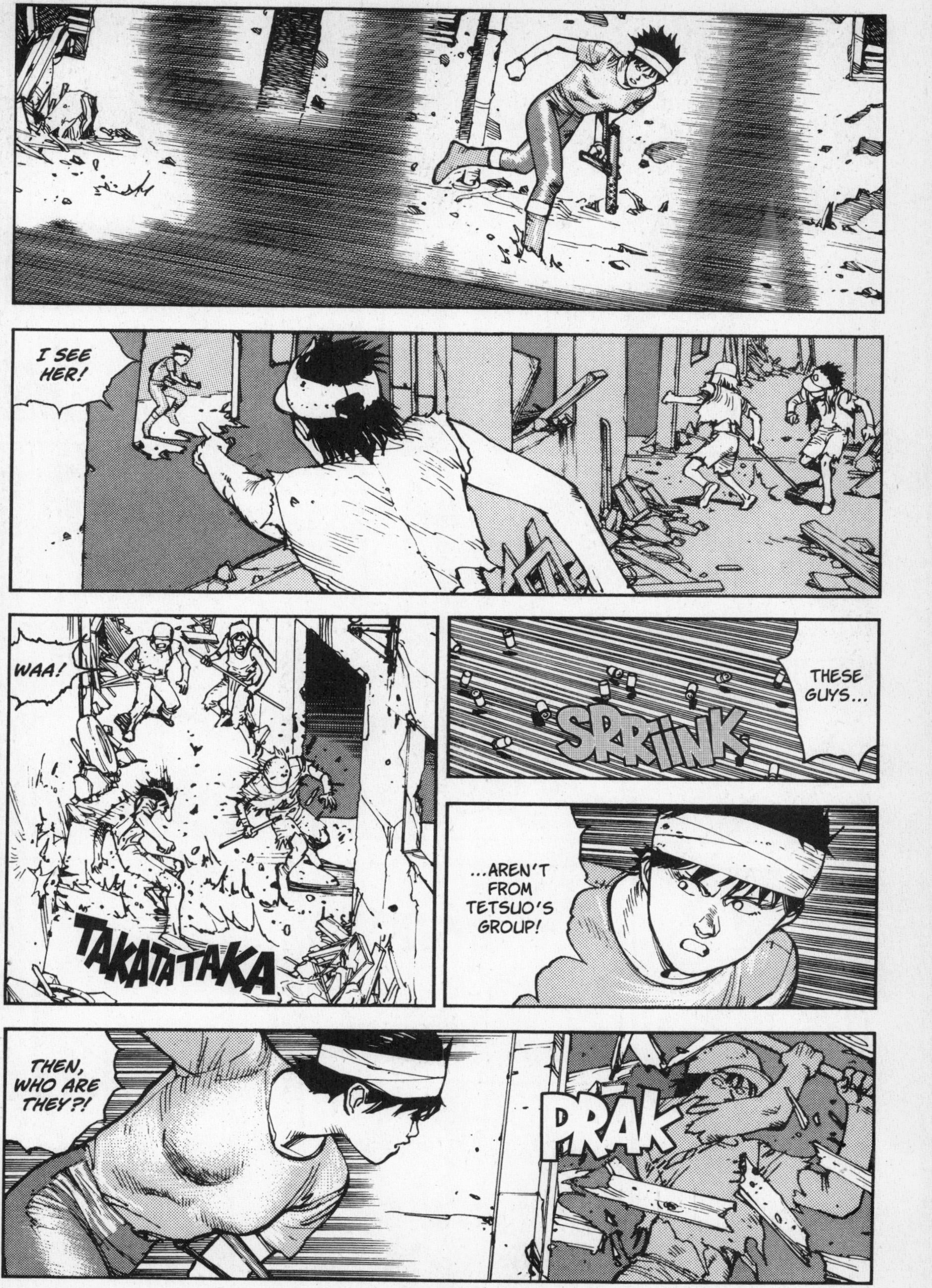
I SEE HER!
WAA!
TAKATATAKA
SRRIINK
THESE GUYS...
...AREN'T FROM TETSUO'S GROUP!
THEN, WHO ARE THEY?!
PRAK

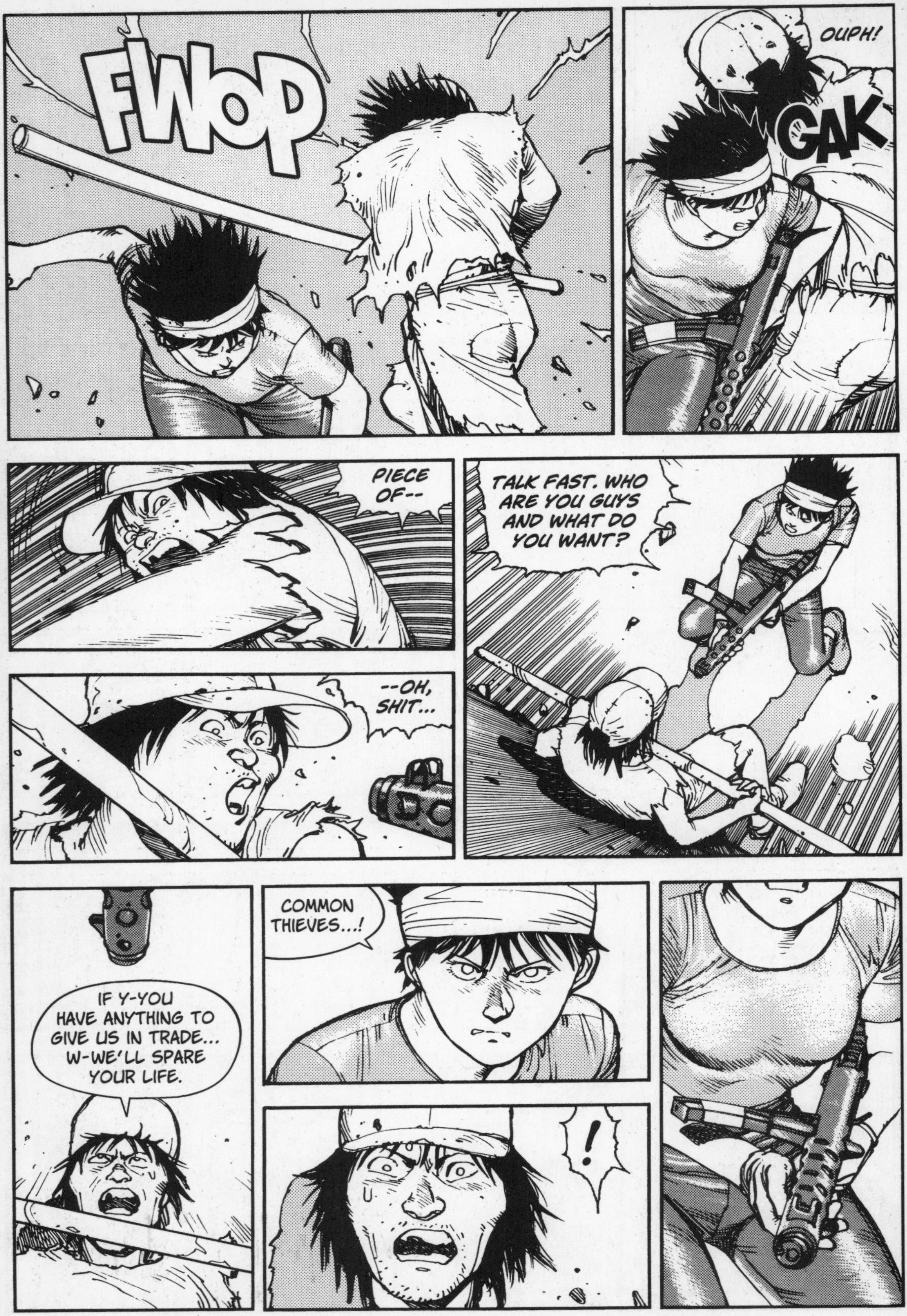
FWOP
OUPH!
GAK
PIECE OF--
TALK FAST. WHO ARE YOU GUYS AND WHAT DO YOU WANT?
--OH, SHIT...
IF Y-YOU HAVE ANYTHING TO GIVE US IN TRADE... W-WE'LL SPARE YOUR LIFE.
COMMON THIEVES...!
!

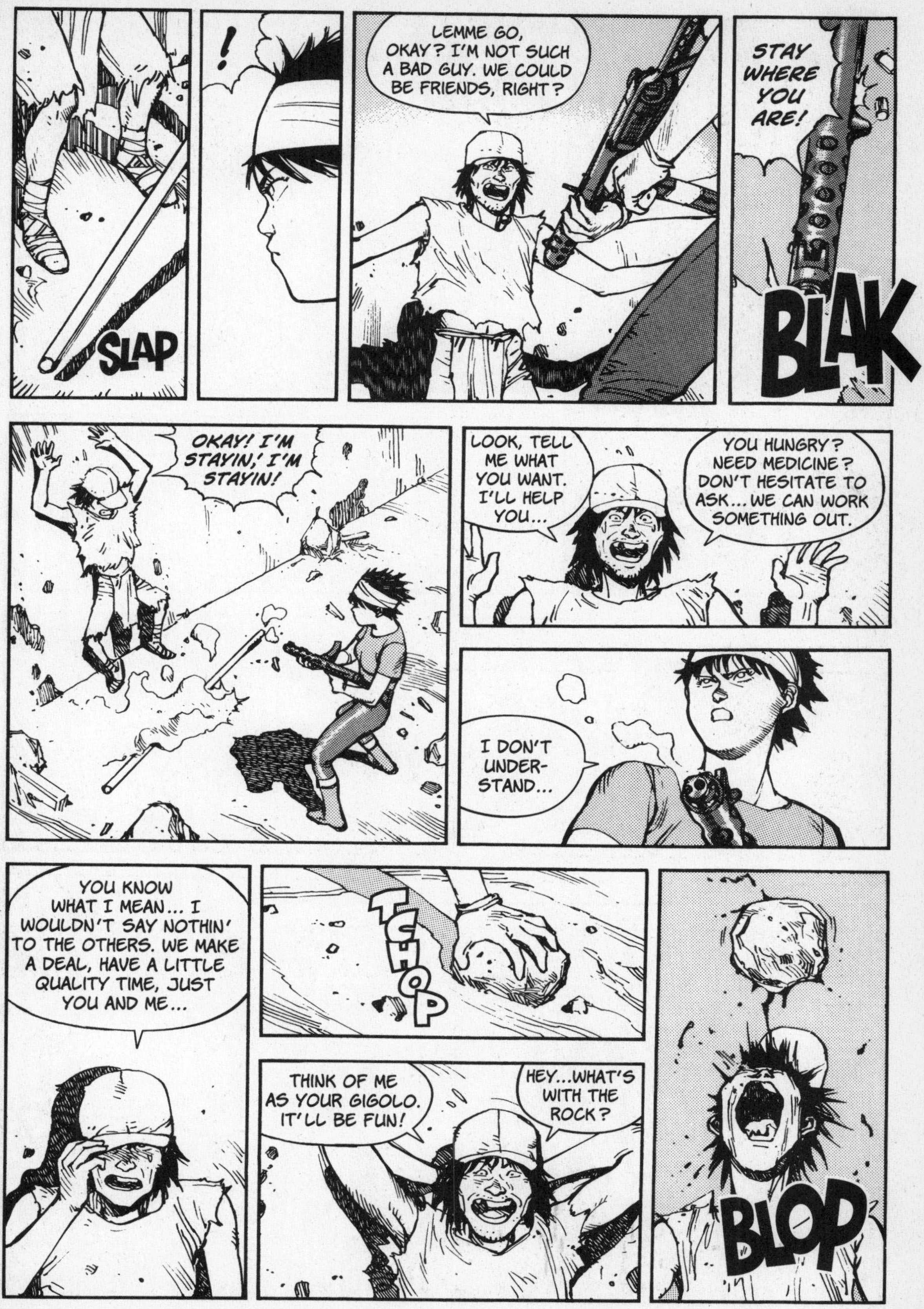
SLAP
!
LEMME GO, OKAY? I'M NOT SUCH A BAD GUY. WE COULD BE FRIENDS, RIGHT?
STAY WHERE YOU ARE!
BLAK
OKAY! I'M STAYIN,' I'M STAYIN!
LOOK, TELL ME WHAT YOU WANT. I'LL HELP YOU...
YOU HUNGRY? NEED MEDICINE? DON'T HESITATE TO ASK... WE CAN WORK SOMETHING OUT.
I DON'T UNDER-STAND...
YOU KNOW WHAT I MEAN... I WOULDN'T SAY NOTHIN' TO THE OTHERS. WE MAKE A DEAL, HAVE A LITTLE QUALITY TIME, JUST YOU AND ME...
TCHOP
THINK OF ME AS YOUR GIGOLO. IT'LL BE FUN!
HEY...WHAT'S WITH THE ROCK?
BLOP

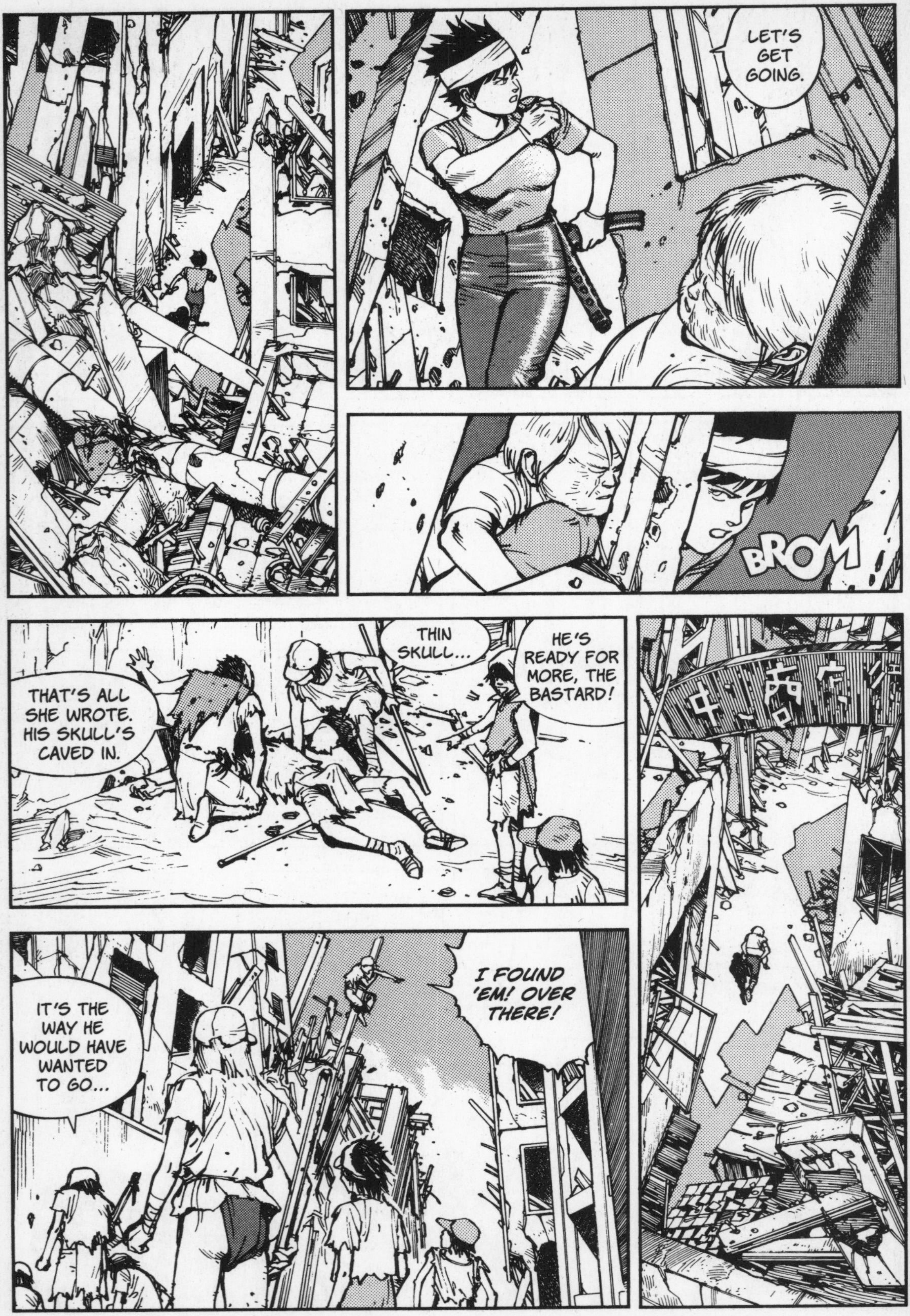
LET'S GET GOING.
BROM
THAT'S ALL SHE WROTE. HIS SKULL'S CAVED IN.
THIN SKULL...
HE'S READY FOR MORE, THE BASTARD!
IT'S THE WAY HE WOULD HAVE WANTED TO GO...
I FOUND 'EM! OVER THERE!

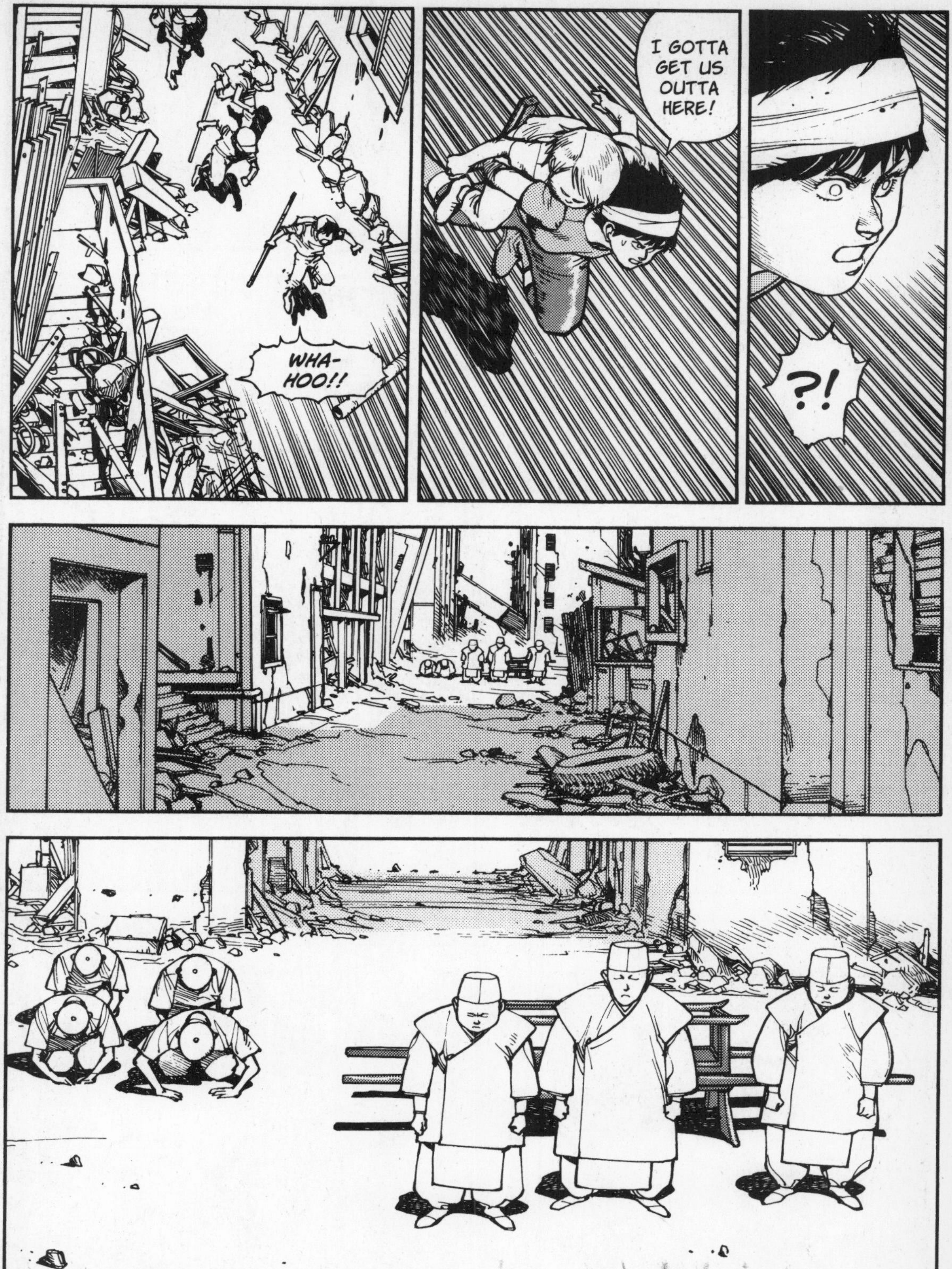
WHA-HOO!!
I GOTTA GET US OUTTA HERE!
?!

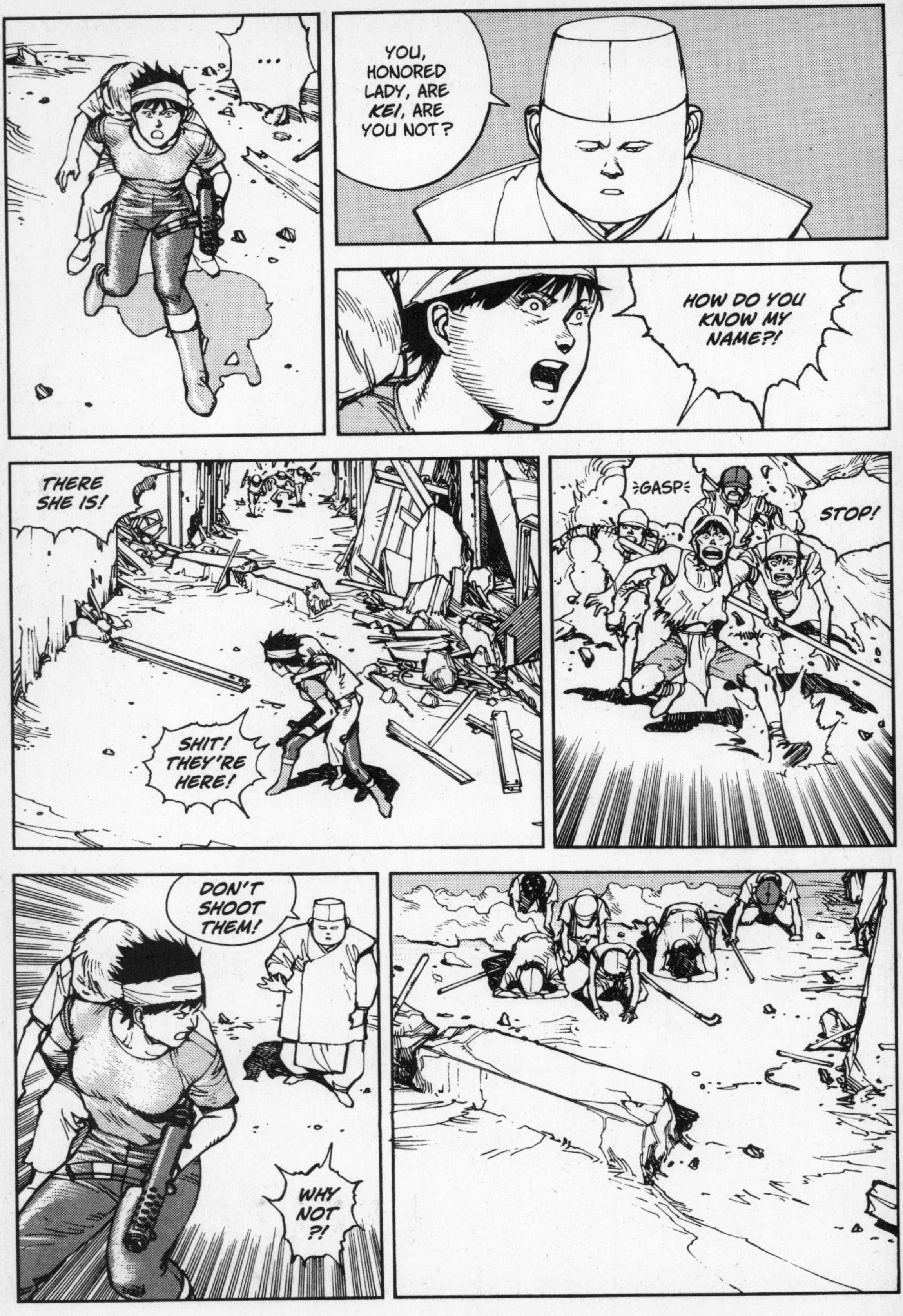
...
YOU, HONORED LADY, ARE KEI, ARE YOU NOT?
HOW DO YOU KNOW MY NAME?!
THERE SHE IS!
SHIT! THEY'RE HERE!
GASP
STOP!
DON'T SHOOT THEM!
WHY NOT ?!

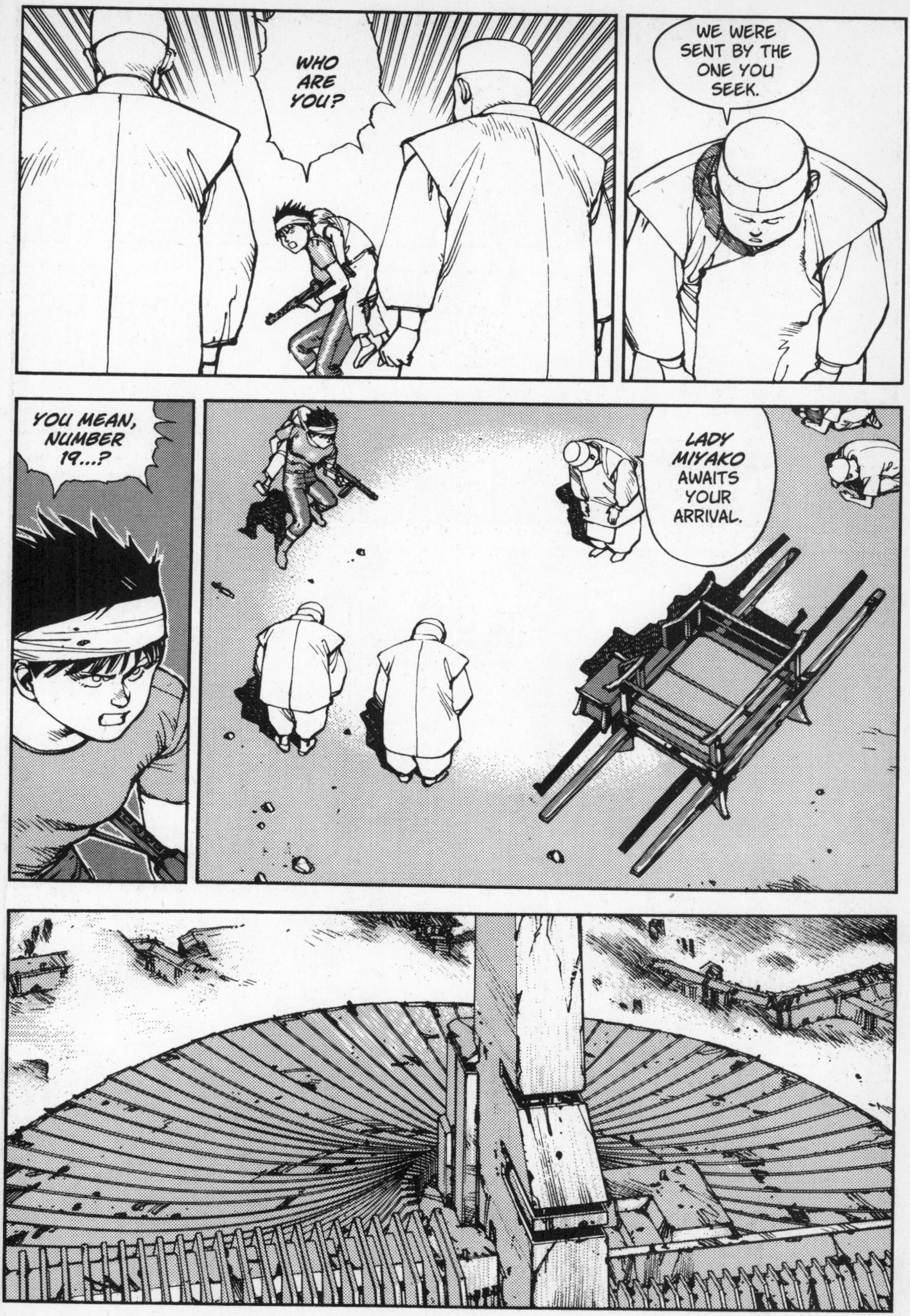
WHO ARE YOU?
WE WERE SENT BY THE ONE YOU SEEK.
YOU MEAN, NUMBER 19...?
LADY MIYAKO AWAITS YOUR ARRIVAL.

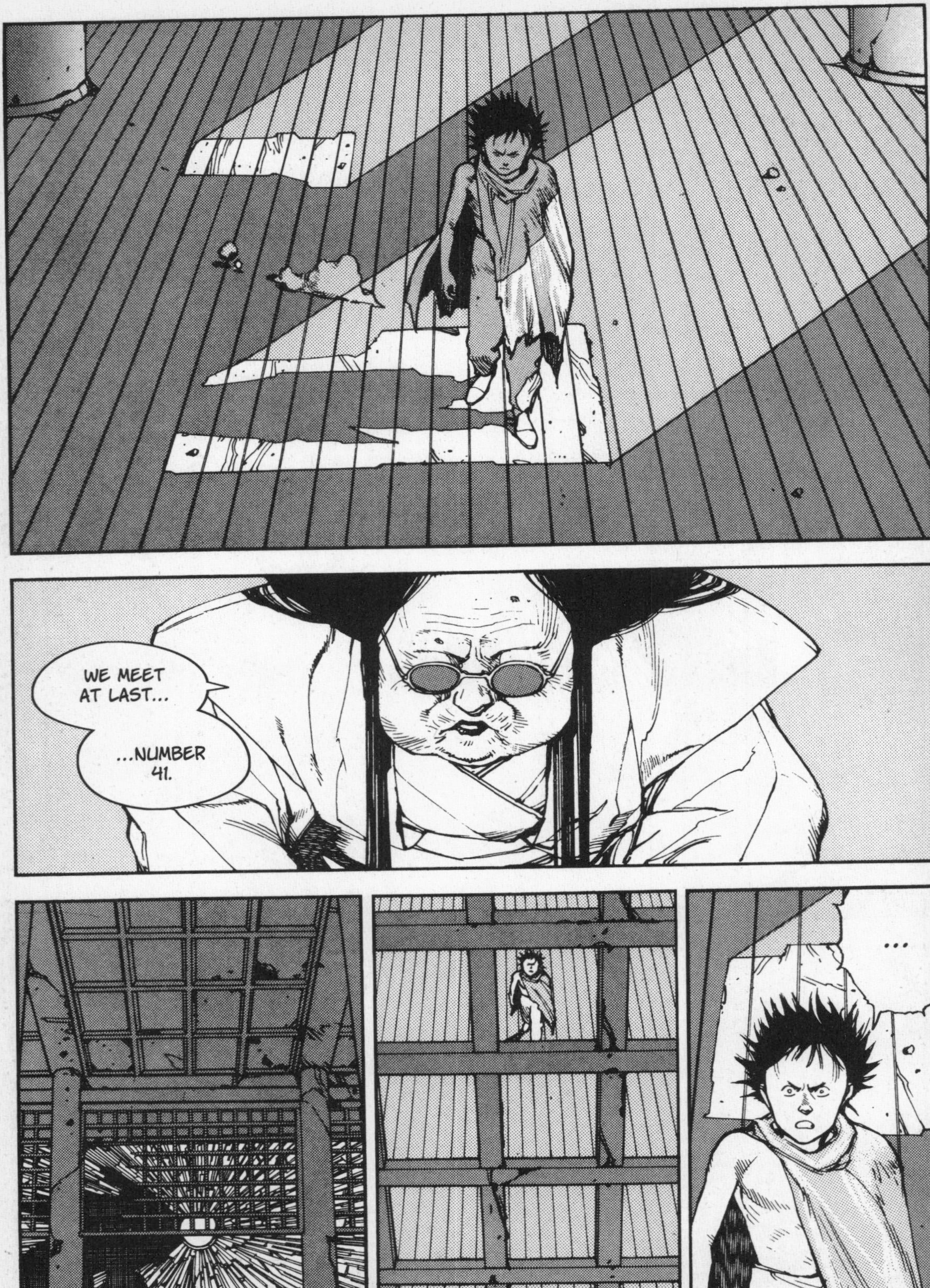
WE MEET AT LAST...
...NUMBER 41.
...

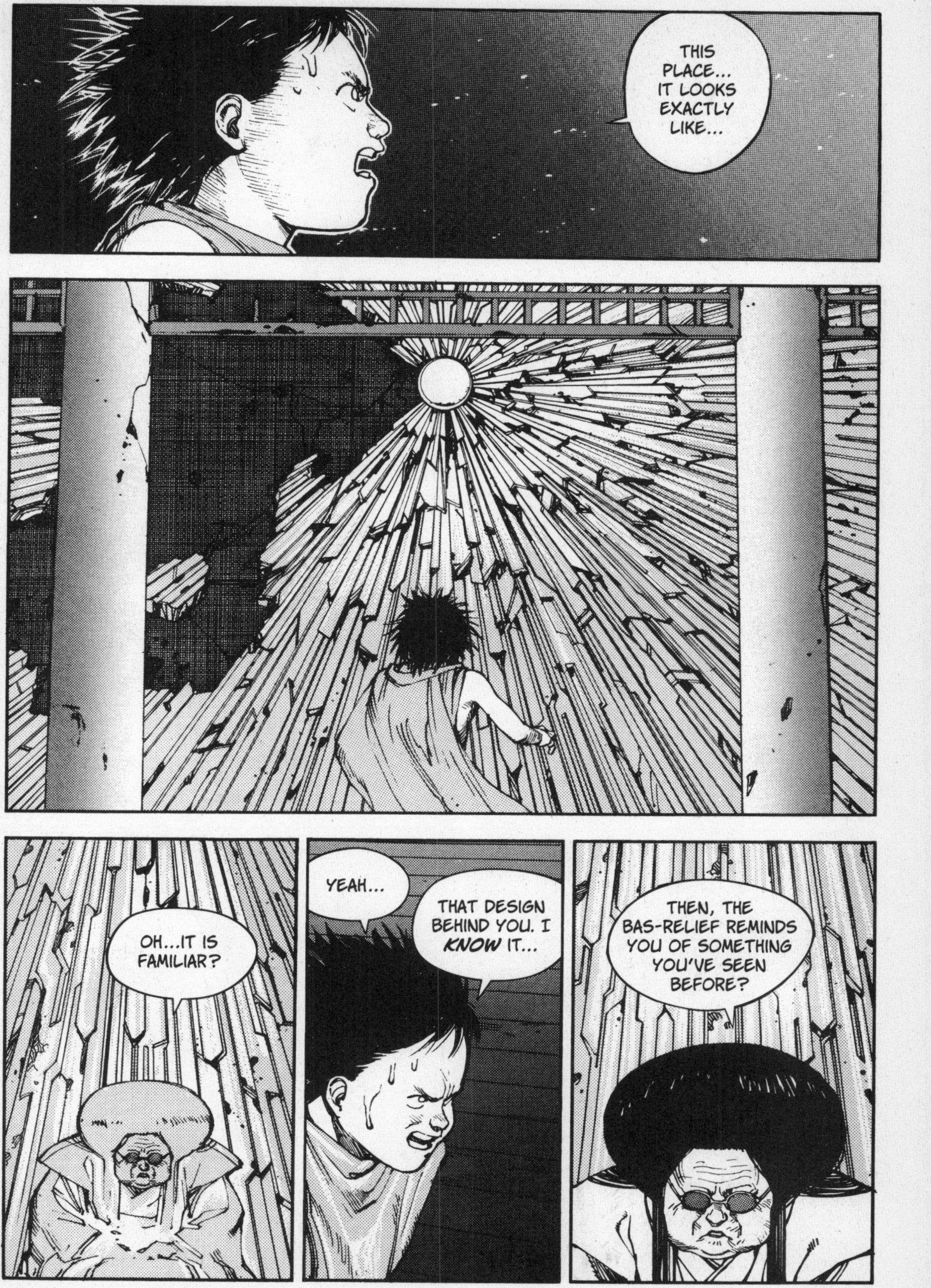
THIS PLACE... IT LOOKS EXACTLY LIKE...
OH...IT IS FAMILIAR?
YEAH...
THAT DESIGN BEHIND YOU. I *KNOW* IT...
THEN, THE BAS-RELIEF REMINDS YOU OF SOMETHING YOU'VE SEEN BEFORE?

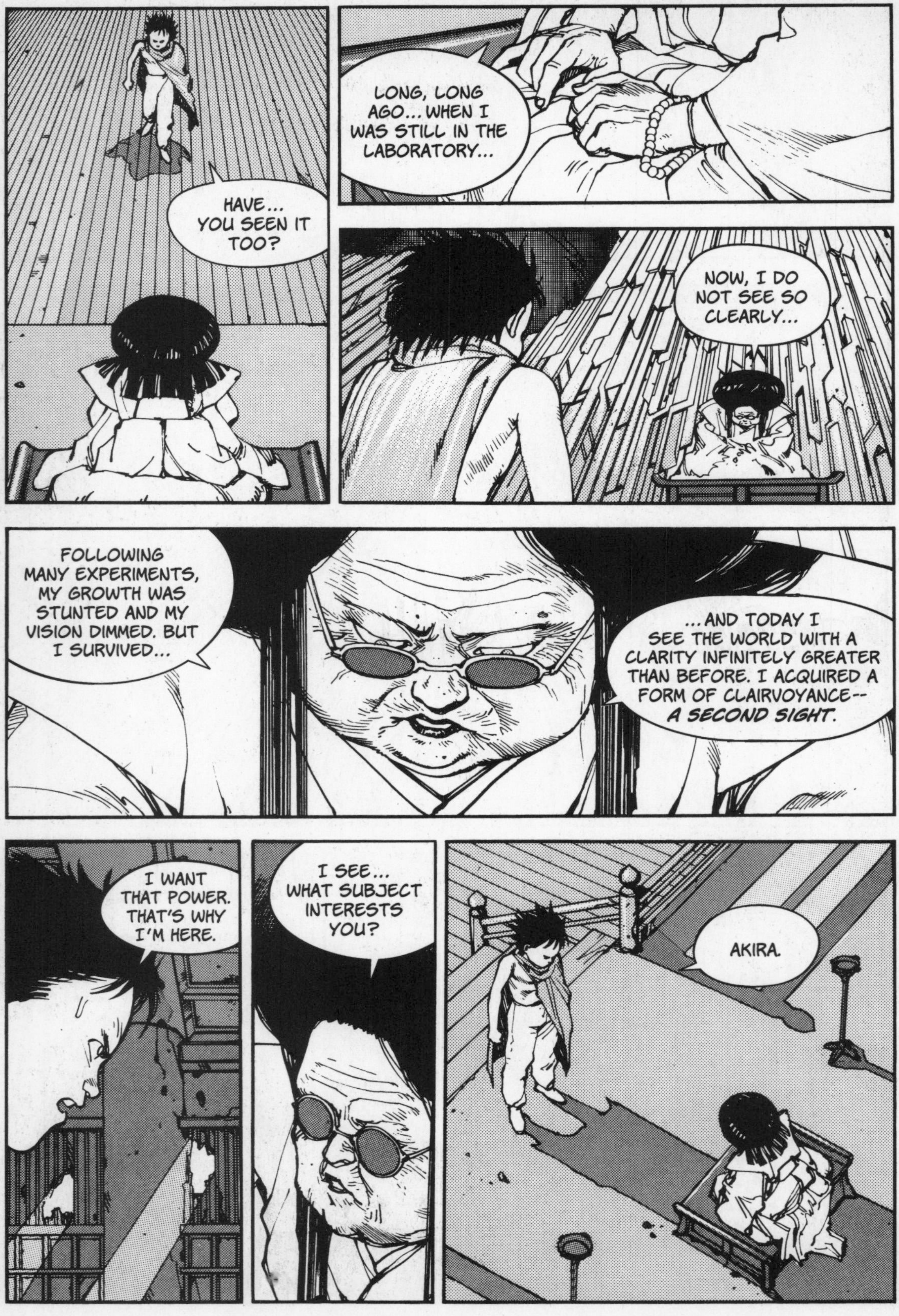
HAVE... YOU SEEN IT TOO?
LONG, LONG AGO... WHEN I WAS STILL IN THE LABORATORY...
NOW, I DO NOT SEE SO CLEARLY...
FOLLOWING MANY EXPERIMENTS, MY GROWTH WAS STUNTED AND MY VISION DIMMED. BUT I SURVIVED...
...AND TODAY I SEE THE WORLD WITH A CLARITY INFINITELY GREATER THAN BEFORE. I ACQUIRED A FORM OF CLAIRVOYANCE-- *A SECOND SIGHT*.
I WANT THAT POWER. THAT'S WHY I'M HERE.
I SEE... WHAT SUBJECT INTERESTS YOU?
AKIRA.

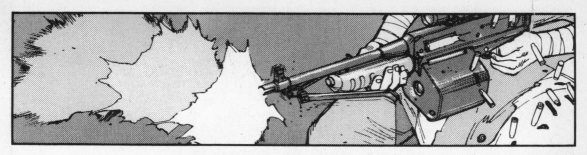

VRAKAKA TAKA

HEAVE!

KRRR KRR

!

DIIIEE!

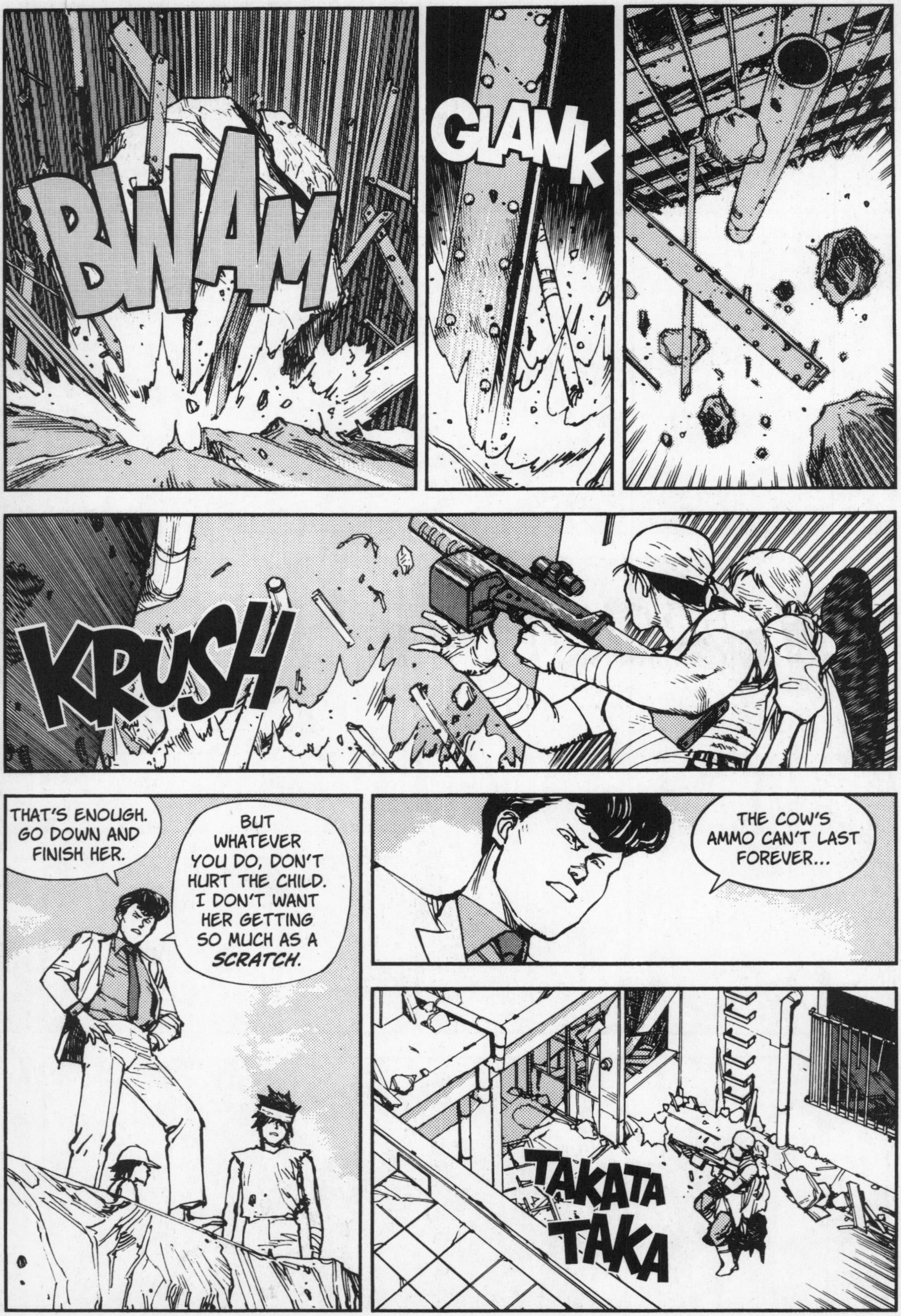
BWAM
GLANK
KRUSH
THAT'S ENOUGH. GO DOWN AND FINISH HER.
BUT WHATEVER YOU DO, DON'T HURT THE CHILD. I DON'T WANT HER GETTING SO MUCH AS A *SCRATCH*.
THE COW'S AMMO CAN'T LAST FOREVER...
TAKATA TAKA

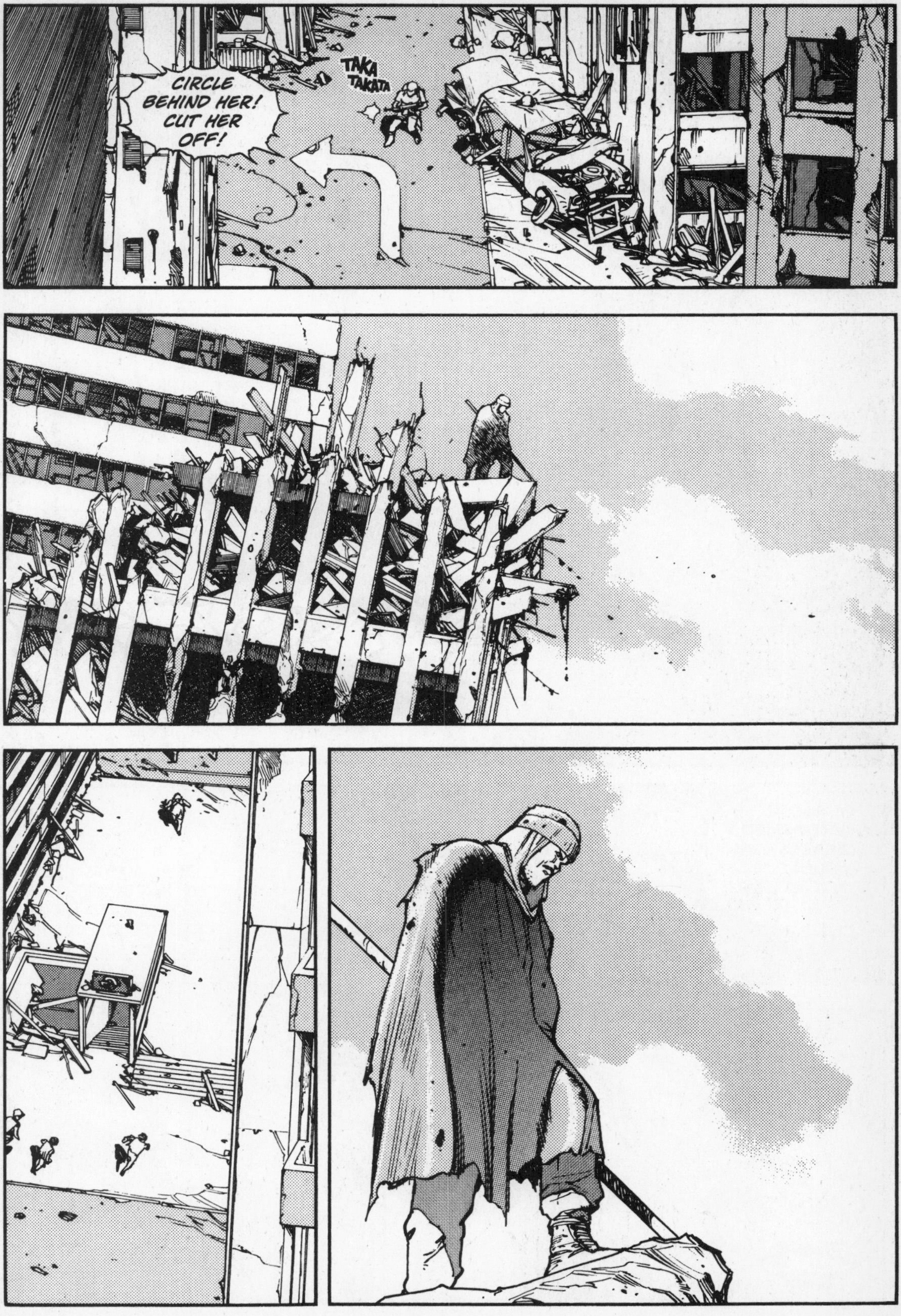
CIRCLE BEHIND HER! CUT HER OFF!
TAKA TAKATA

IT BEGAN IN THE 1960'S...A SMALL PROJECT WITHOUT EVEN A CODE NAME...JUST "THE PROJECT."

AT FIRST, JUST A HANDFUL OF PEOPLE IN THE MINISTRY OF DEFENSE, COLLATING DATA AND ANALYZING IT...

BY THE 1970'S, BASED ON THEIR FINDINGS, A GROUP OF PEOPLE THOUGHT TO HAVE PARTICULAR TRAITS WERE BROUGHT TOGETHER.

THE SCIENTISTS PERFORMED ALL MANNER OF EXPERIMENTS ON THEIR SUBJECTS AND DEVELOPED NEW TRAINING TECHNIQUES...

A CERTAIN HIGHLY CONTROVERSIAL SCHOLAR JOINED THE PROJECT.

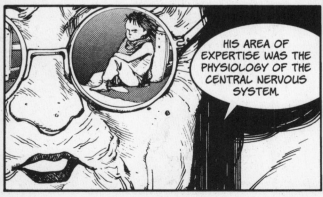

HIS AREA OF EXPERTISE WAS THE PHYSIOLOGY OF THE CENTRAL NERVOUS SYSTEM.

SPECIALISTS FROM OTHER DISCIPLINES CONSIDERED HIM AN ECCENTRIC... AND HIS COLLEAGUES TOOK A DIM VIEW OF HIS FINDINGS...

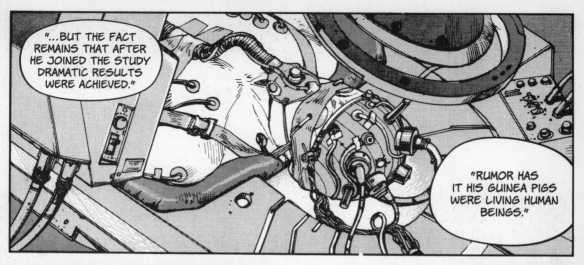

"...BUT THE FACT REMAINS THAT AFTER HE JOINED THE STUDY DRAMATIC RESULTS WERE ACHIEVED."

"RUMOR HAS IT HIS GUINEA PIGS WERE LIVING HUMAN BEINGS."

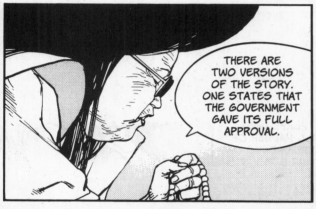

THERE ARE TWO VERSIONS OF THE STORY. ONE STATES THAT THE GOVERNMENT GAVE ITS FULL APPROVAL.

THE OTHER IS THAT THE SCHOLAR WAS SOLELY RESPONSIBLE. AS NO ONE KNOWS THE TRUTH, YOU MAY BELIEVE WHICHEVER SATISFIES YOU.

THESE EXPERIMENTS... WHAT DID THEY USE? SURGERY? NEW DRUGS?

HMM... HOW BEST TO EXPLAIN...?

USING A GLASS-LIKE MATERIAL, THEY MANUFACTUR-ED TUBES, FINER THAN THE DIAMETER OF THE SMALLEST BLOOD VESSEL...

...AND FILLED THESE TUBES WITH A SALT WATER SOLUTION.

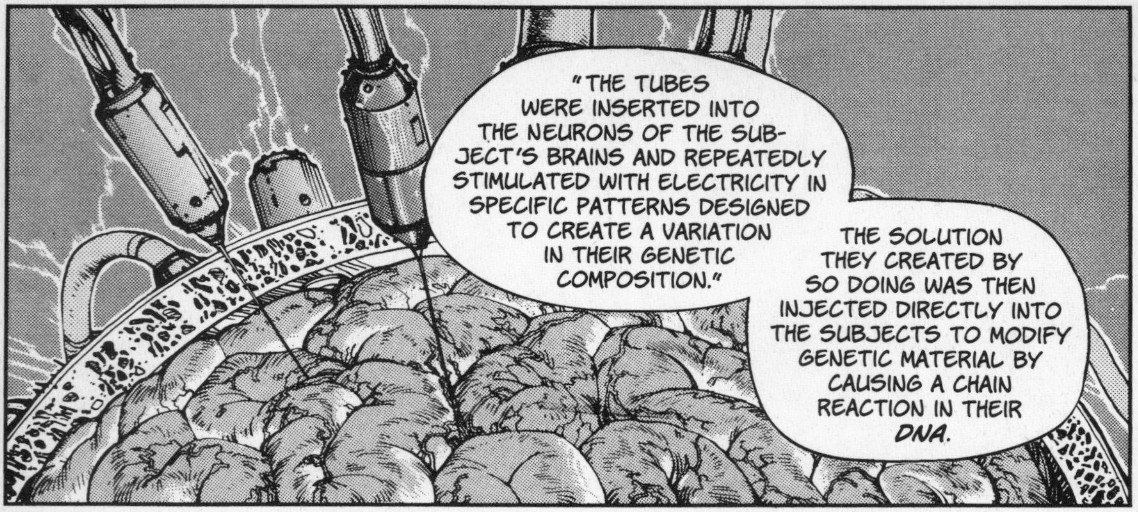
"THE TUBES WERE INSERTED INTO THE NEURONS OF THE SUB-JECT'S BRAINS AND REPEATEDLY STIMULATED WITH ELECTRICITY IN SPECIFIC PATTERNS DESIGNED TO CREATE A VARIATION IN THEIR GENETIC COMPOSITION."
THE SOLUTION THEY CREATED BY SO DOING WAS THEN INJECTED DIRECTLY INTO THE SUBJECTS TO MODIFY GENETIC MATERIAL BY CAUSING A CHAIN REACTION IN THEIR *DNA*.
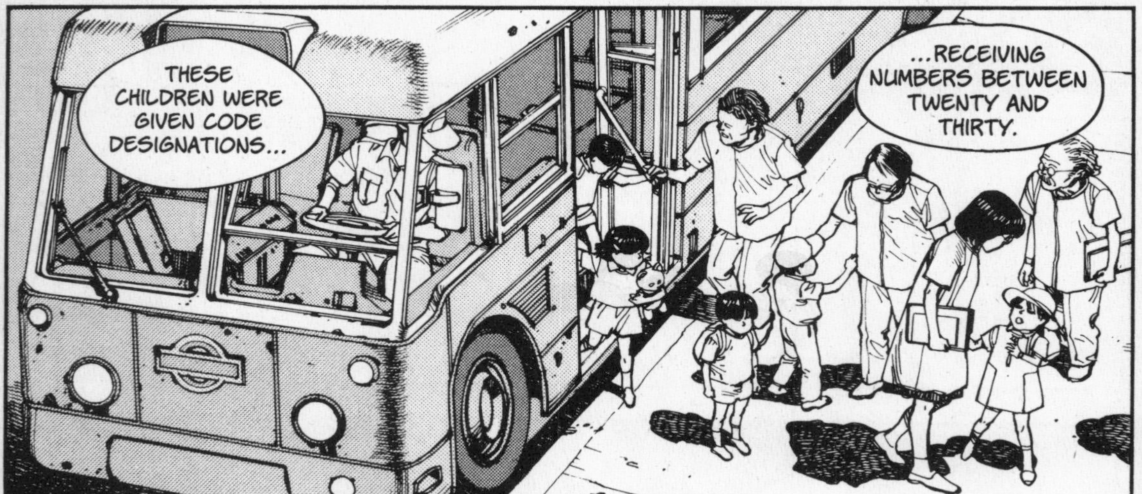
THESE CHILDREN WERE GIVEN CODE DESIGNATIONS...
...RECEIVING NUMBERS BETWEEN TWENTY AND THIRTY.
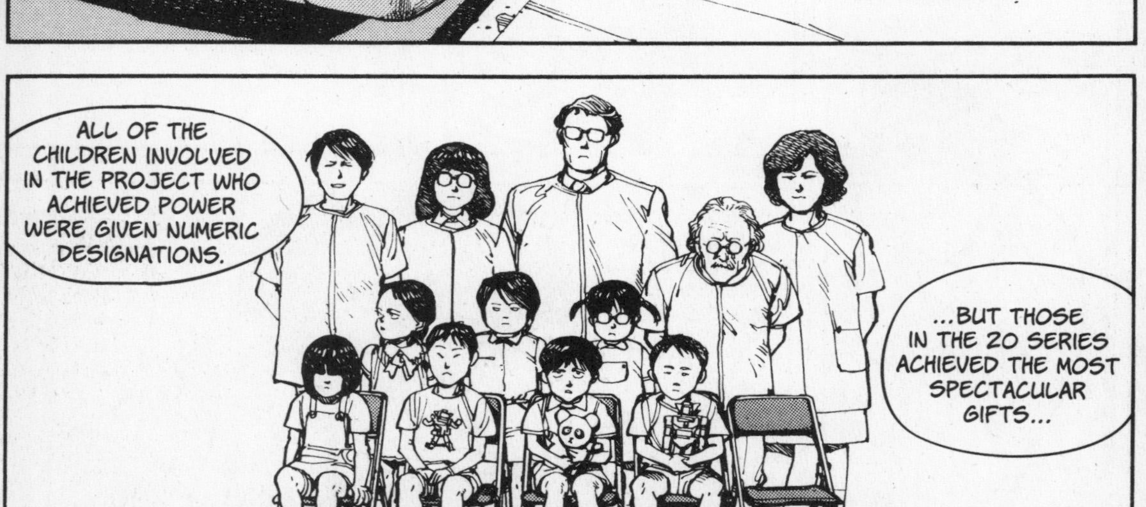
ALL OF THE CHILDREN INVOLVED IN THE PROJECT WHO ACHIEVED POWER WERE GIVEN NUMERIC DESIGNATIONS.
...BUT THOSE IN THE 20 SERIES ACHIEVED THE MOST SPECTACULAR GIFTS...

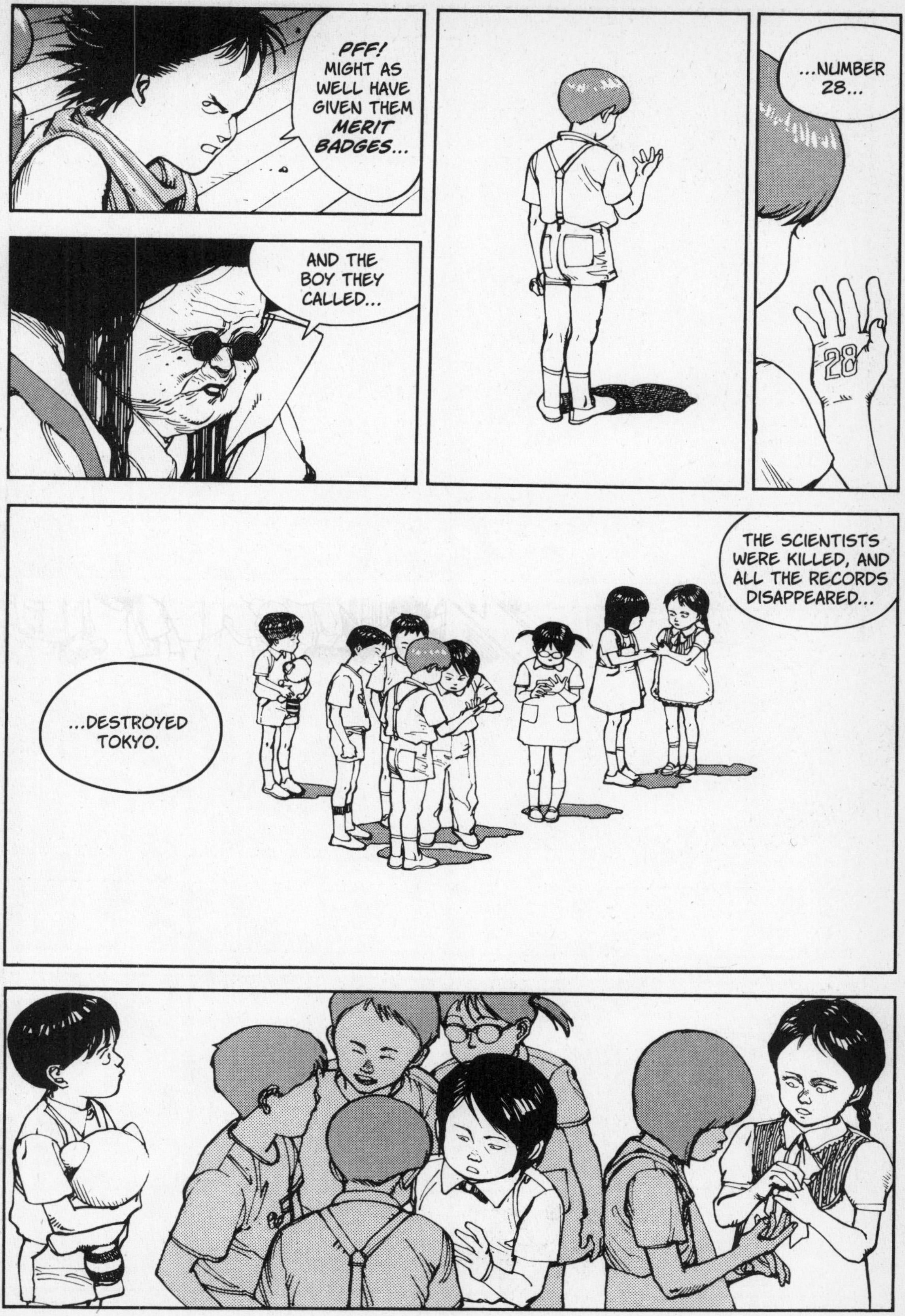
PFF! MIGHT AS WELL HAVE GIVEN THEM MERIT BADGES...
AND THE BOY THEY CALLED...
...NUMBER 28...
28
...DESTROYED TOKYO.
THE SCIENTISTS WERE KILLED, AND ALL THE RECORDS DISAPPEARED...

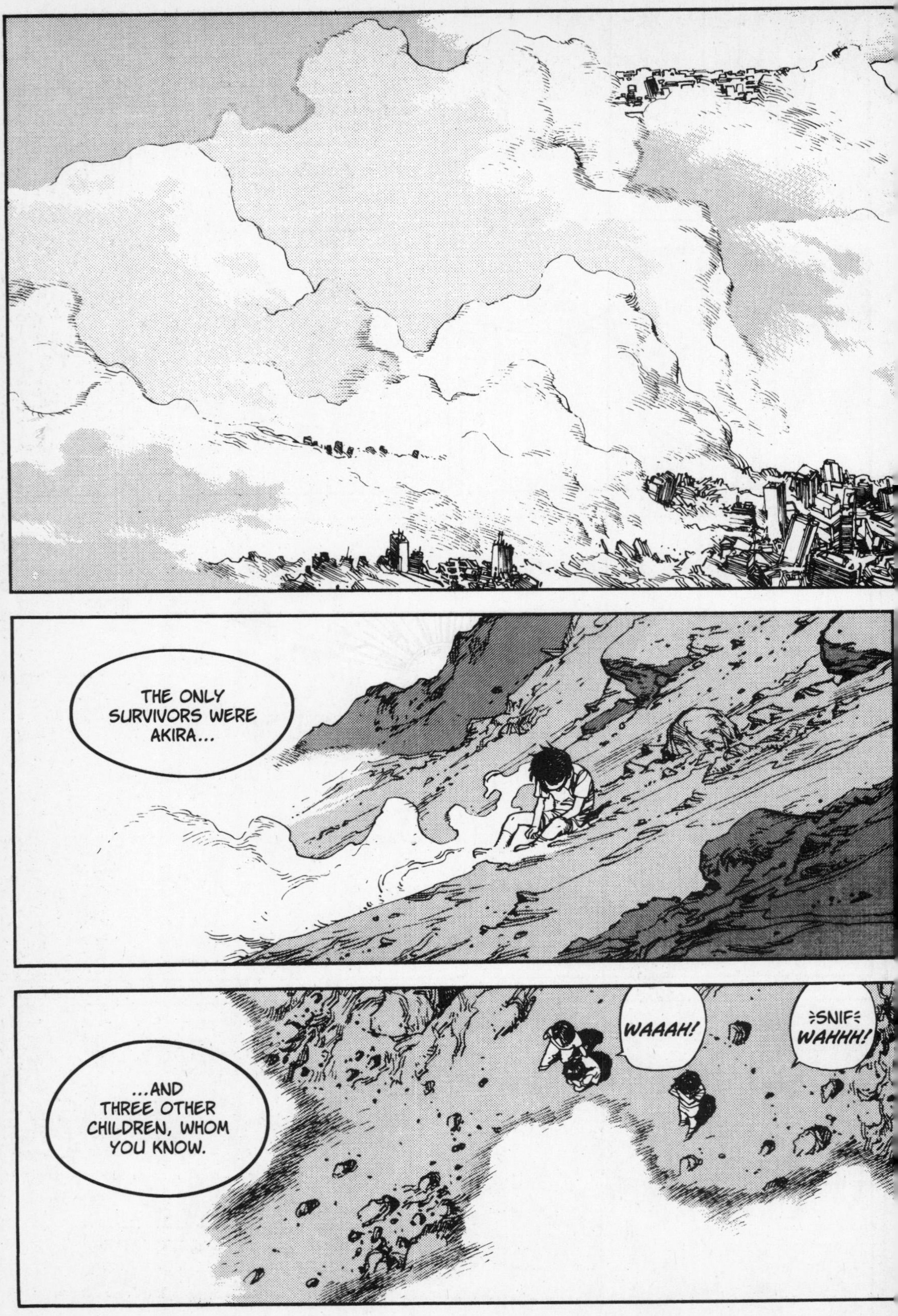
THE ONLY SURVIVORS WERE AKIRA...
...AND THREE OTHER CHILDREN, WHOM YOU KNOW.
WAAAH!
SNIF WAHHH!

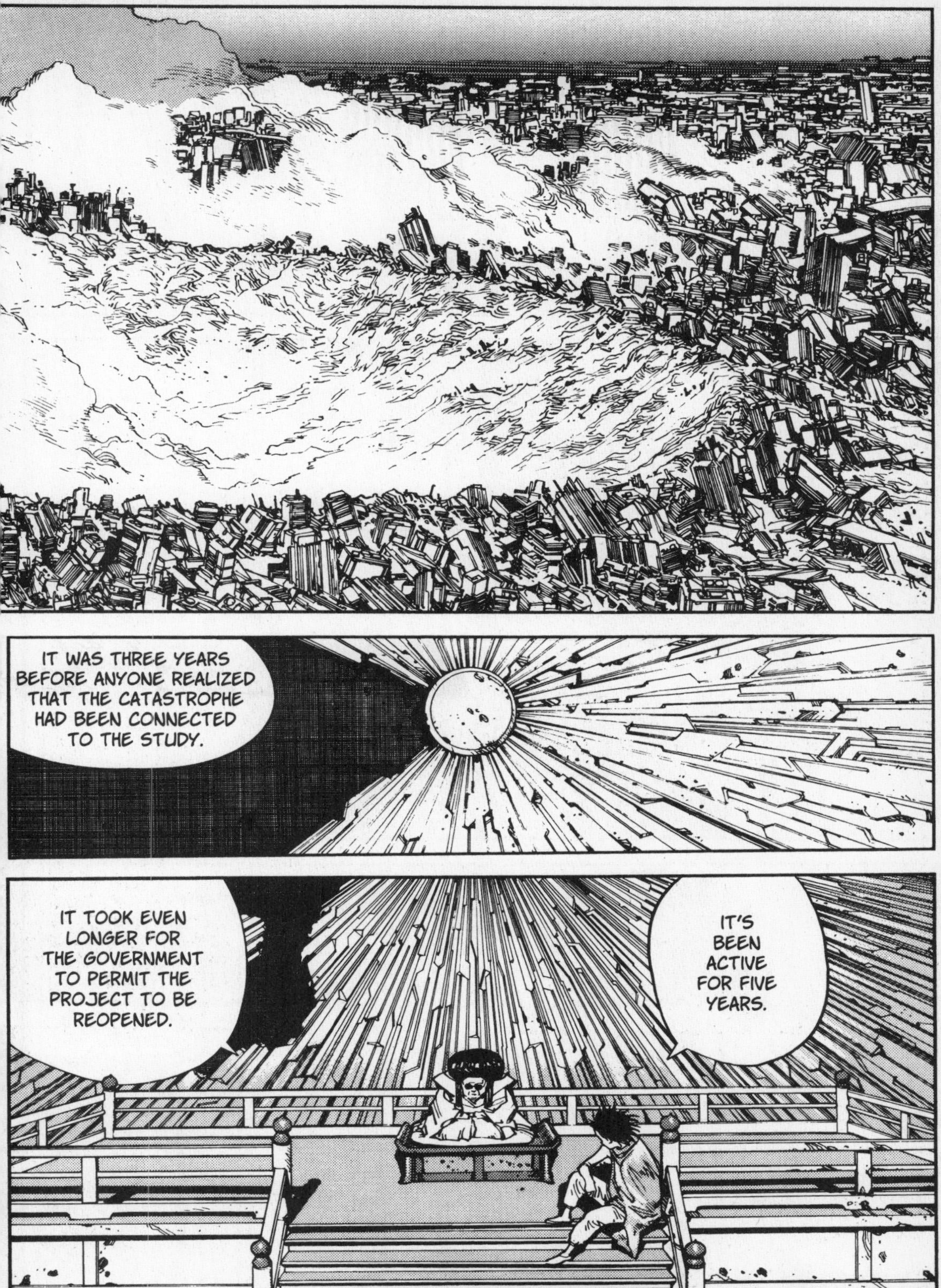
IT WAS THREE YEARS BEFORE ANYONE REALIZED THAT THE CATASTROPHE HAD BEEN CONNECTED TO THE STUDY.
IT TOOK EVEN LONGER FOR THE GOVERNMENT TO PERMIT THE PROJECT TO BE REOPENED.
IT'S BEEN ACTIVE FOR FIVE YEARS.

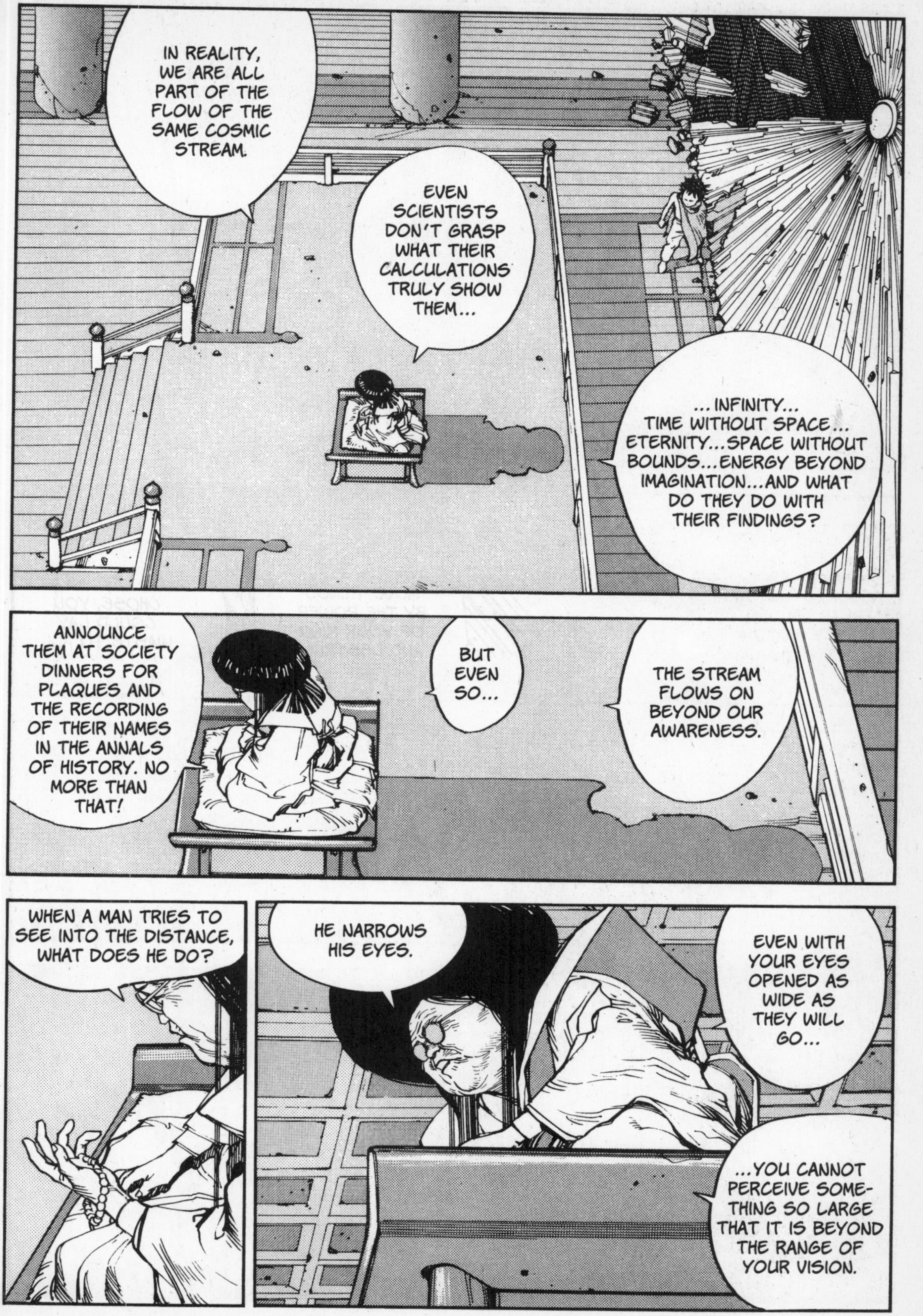
IN REALITY, WE ARE ALL PART OF THE FLOW OF THE SAME COSMIC STREAM.
EVEN SCIENTISTS DON'T GRASP WHAT THEIR CALCULATIONS TRULY SHOW THEM...
...INFINITY... TIME WITHOUT SPACE... ETERNITY...SPACE WITHOUT BOUNDS...ENERGY BEYOND IMAGINATION...AND WHAT DO THEY DO WITH THEIR FINDINGS?
ANNOUNCE THEM AT SOCIETY DINNERS FOR PLAQUES AND THE RECORDING OF THEIR NAMES IN THE ANNALS OF HISTORY. NO MORE THAN THAT!
BUT EVEN SO...
THE STREAM FLOWS ON BEYOND OUR AWARENESS.
WHEN A MAN TRIES TO SEE INTO THE DISTANCE, WHAT DOES HE DO?
HE NARROWS HIS EYES.
EVEN WITH YOUR EYES OPENED AS WIDE AS THEY WILL GO...
...YOU CANNOT PERCEIVE SOMETHING SO LARGE THAT IT IS BEYOND THE RANGE OF YOUR VISION.

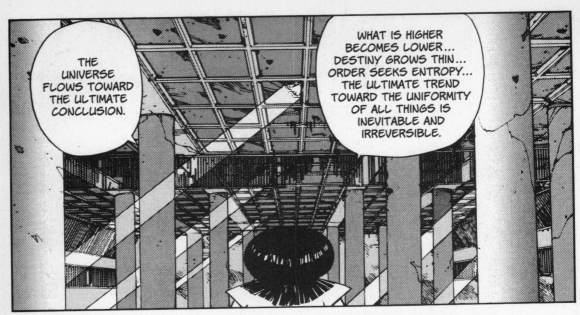

THE UNIVERSE FLOWS TOWARD THE ULTIMATE CONCLUSION.

WHAT IS HIGHER BECOMES LOWER... DESTINY GROWS THIN... ORDER SEEKS ENTROPY... THE ULTIMATE TREND TOWARD THE UNIFORMITY OF ALL THINGS IS INEVITABLE AND IRREVERSIBLE.

MEN GATHER TOGETHER AS THOUGH THEY WOULD REVERSE THE COSMIC STREAM, BUT IN TRUTH THEY ARE ONLY DRIFTWOOD.

YET, EVEN AS THE STREAM SWEEPS THEM ALONG...

...THEY POSSESS ONE POWER CAPABLE OF STOPPING THE STREAM.

WHEN THIS POWER IS USED, THE STREAM WILL STOP FOR AN INSTANT... AND THEN RESUME ITS COURSE WITH REDOUBLED INTENSITY.

WHEN IT IS BEFORE THEM, PEOPLE RECOGNIZE THE STREAM FOR WHAT IT IS AND FEAR ITS POWER...

...AS YOU'VE ALREADY SEEN.

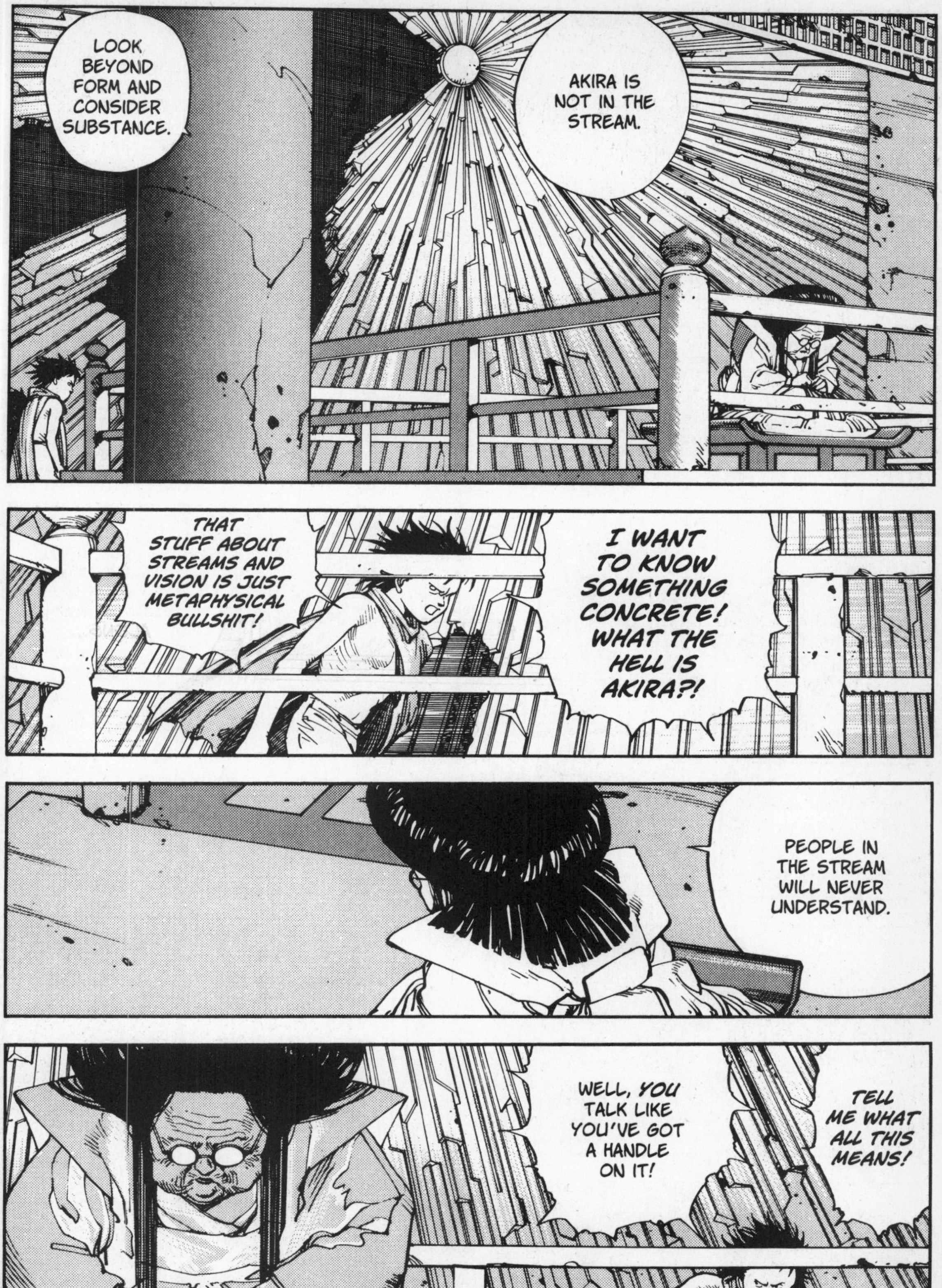
LOOK BEYOND FORM AND CONSIDER SUBSTANCE.
AKIRA IS NOT IN THE STREAM.
THAT STUFF ABOUT STREAMS AND VISION IS JUST METAPHYSICAL BULLSHIT!
I WANT TO KNOW SOMETHING CONCRETE! WHAT THE HELL IS AKIRA?!
PEOPLE IN THE STREAM WILL NEVER UNDERSTAND.
WELL, YOU TALK LIKE YOU'VE GOT A HANDLE ON IT!
TELL ME WHAT ALL THIS MEANS!

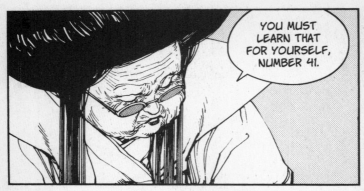

YOU MUST LEARN THAT FOR YOURSELF, NUMBER 41.

YOU HEARD ME. ONLY YOU CAN FIND THE ANSWERS. TO DO SO IS YOUR DESTINY.

WHAT?!

BUT...

...WHY ME?

I DON'T WANT THE JOB! I CAN'T DO IT!

ONE LOOK INSIDE HIS MIND WAS PLENTY! I ALMOST GOT BLOWN AWAY!

HO HO HO... WHY, NUMBER 41, THIS DOESN'T SOUND LIKE YOU AT ALL.

ARE YOU AFRAID?

CALL IT WHATEVER YOU LIKE, BUT THAT WAS THE LAST LOOK I'LL EVER TAKE INSIDE HIS HEAD! I'LL NEVER DO IT AGAIN!

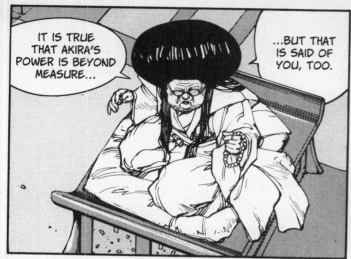

IT IS TRUE THAT AKIRA'S POWER IS BEYOND MEASURE...

...BUT THAT IS SAID OF YOU, TOO.

ALTHOUGH, I DO SEE YOUR POINT. AT YOUR *INHIBITED* LEVEL OF POWER, IT WOULD BE BEYOND YOU. AS A PSYCHIC, YOU GROVEL AT AKIRA'S FEET.

INHIBITED ...?

SURELY YOU MUST REALIZE THAT THE DRUGS YOU TAKE SLOW THE DEVELOPMENT OF YOUR POWER.

MIND YOUR OWN BUSINESS!

IT'S TRUE, THEY EXPEDITE RELEASE OF SOME OF YOUR MENTAL ENERGIES, BUT THEY CREATE A SORT OF SHORT-CIRCUIT...

...THAT PREVENTS YOU FROM BECOMING ALL YOU COULD BE.

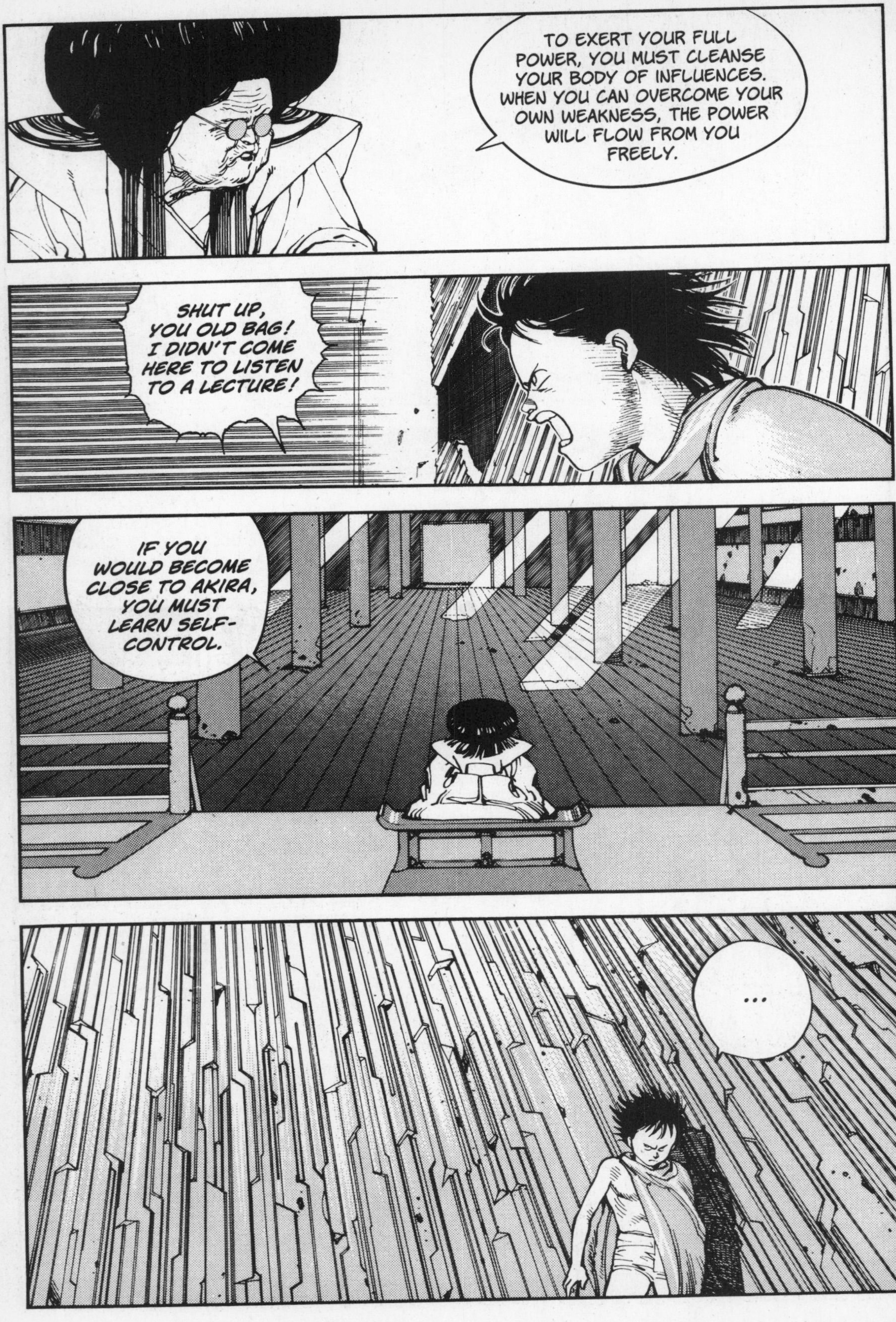
TO EXERT YOUR FULL POWER, YOU MUST CLEANSE YOUR BODY OF INFLUENCES. WHEN YOU CAN OVERCOME YOUR OWN WEAKNESS, THE POWER WILL FLOW FROM YOU FREELY.
SHUT UP, YOU OLD BAG! I DIDN'T COME HERE TO LISTEN TO A LECTURE!
IF YOU WOULD BECOME CLOSE TO AKIRA, YOU MUST LEARN SELF-CONTROL.
...

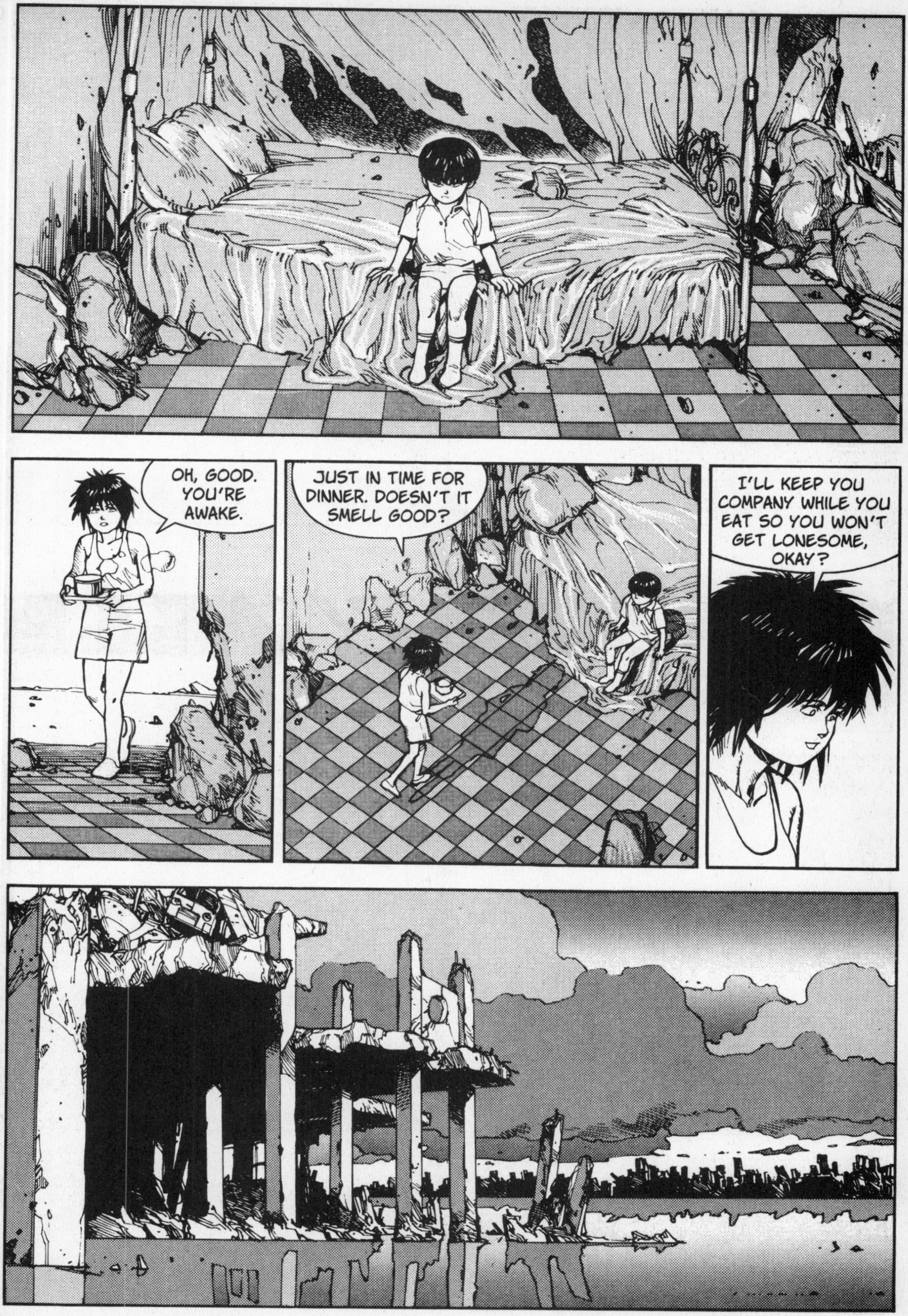
OH, GOOD. YOU'RE AWAKE.
JUST IN TIME FOR DINNER. DOESN'T IT SMELL GOOD?
I'LL KEEP YOU COMPANY WHILE YOU EAT SO YOU WON'T GET LONESOME, OKAY?

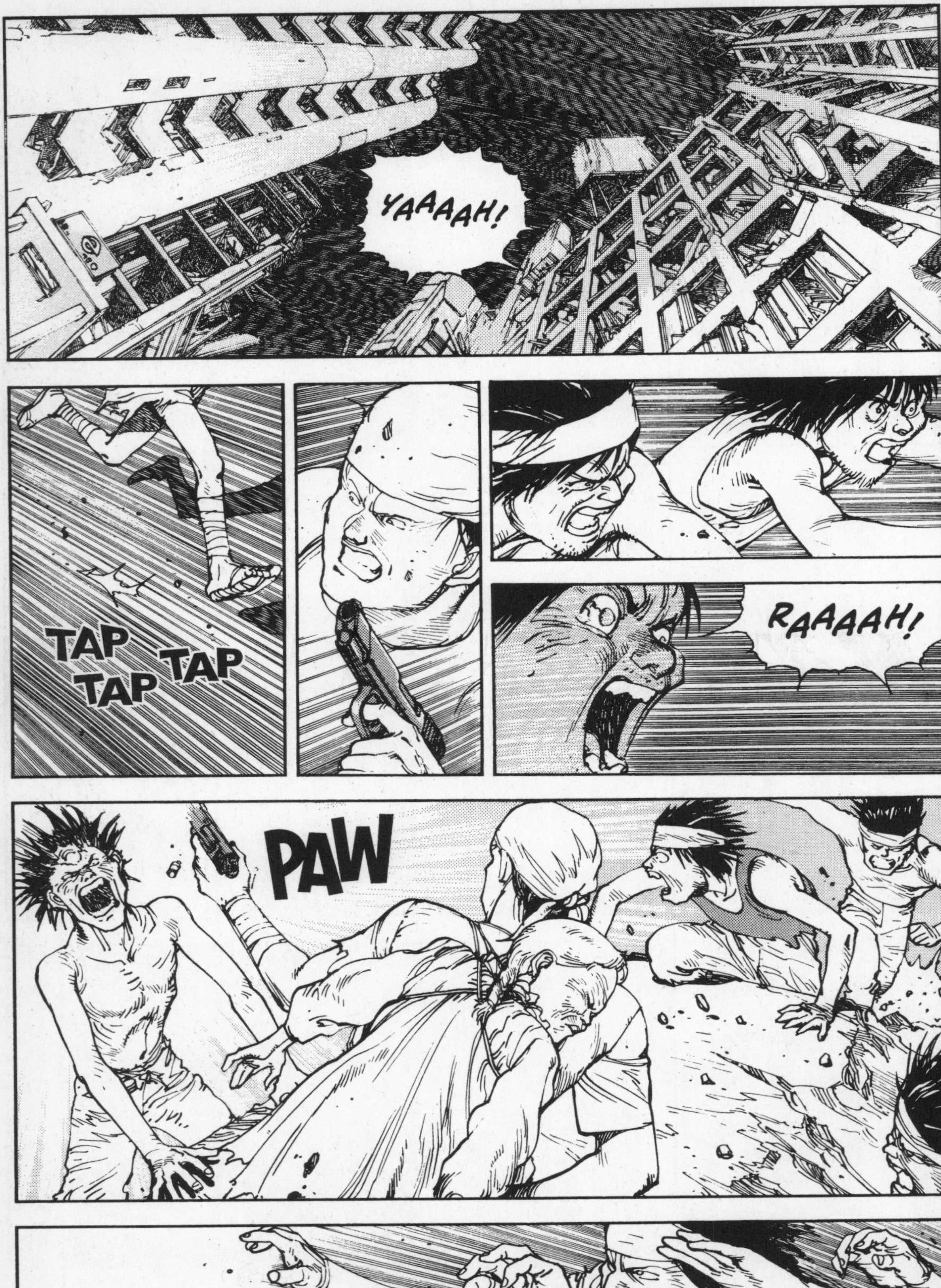
YAAAAH!
TAP TAP TAP
RAAAAH!
PAW

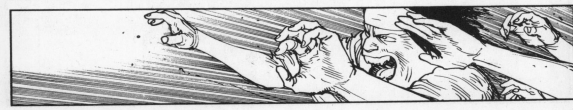

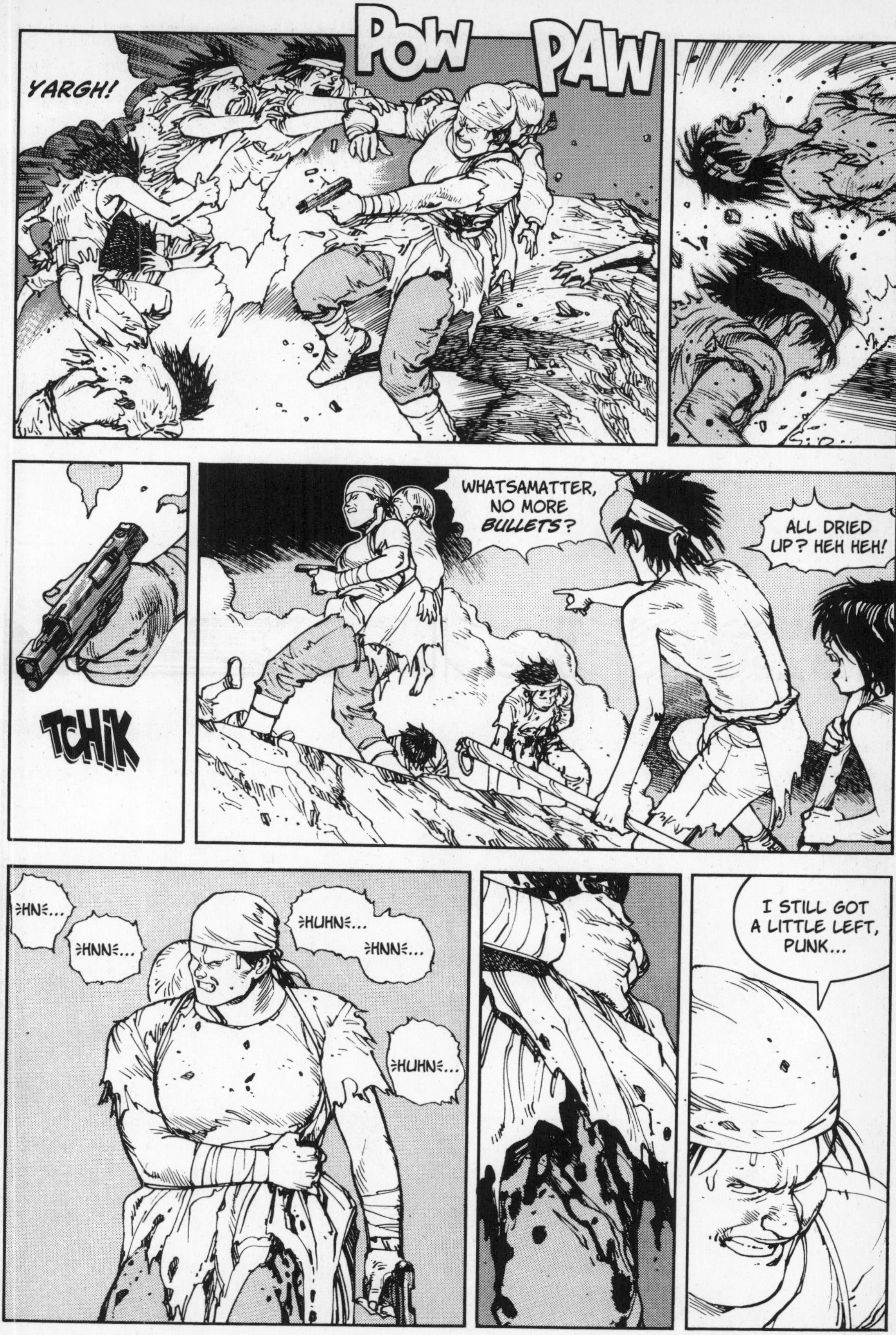
POW
PAW
YARGH!
TCHIK
WHATSAMATTER, NO MORE BULLETS?
ALL DRIED UP? HEH HEH!
≶HN≷...
≶HNN≷...
≶HUHN≷...
≶HNN≷...
≶HUHN≷...
I STILL GOT A LITTLE LEFT, PUNK...

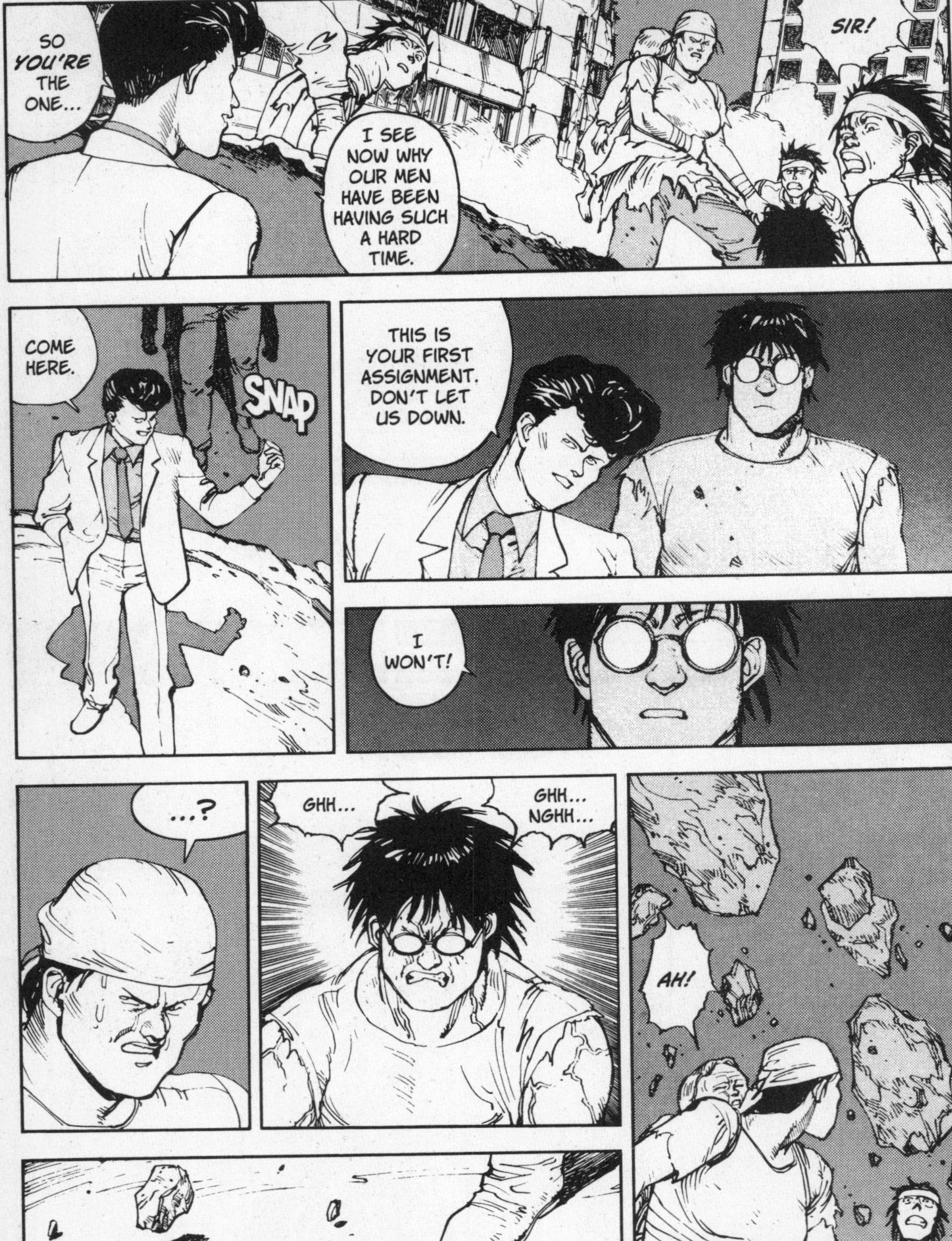

SO *YOU'RE* THE ONE...
I SEE NOW WHY OUR MEN HAVE BEEN HAVING SUCH A HARD TIME.
SIR!
COME HERE.
SNAP
THIS IS YOUR FIRST ASSIGNMENT. DON'T LET US DOWN.
I WON'T!
...?
GHH...
GHH... NGHH...
AH!

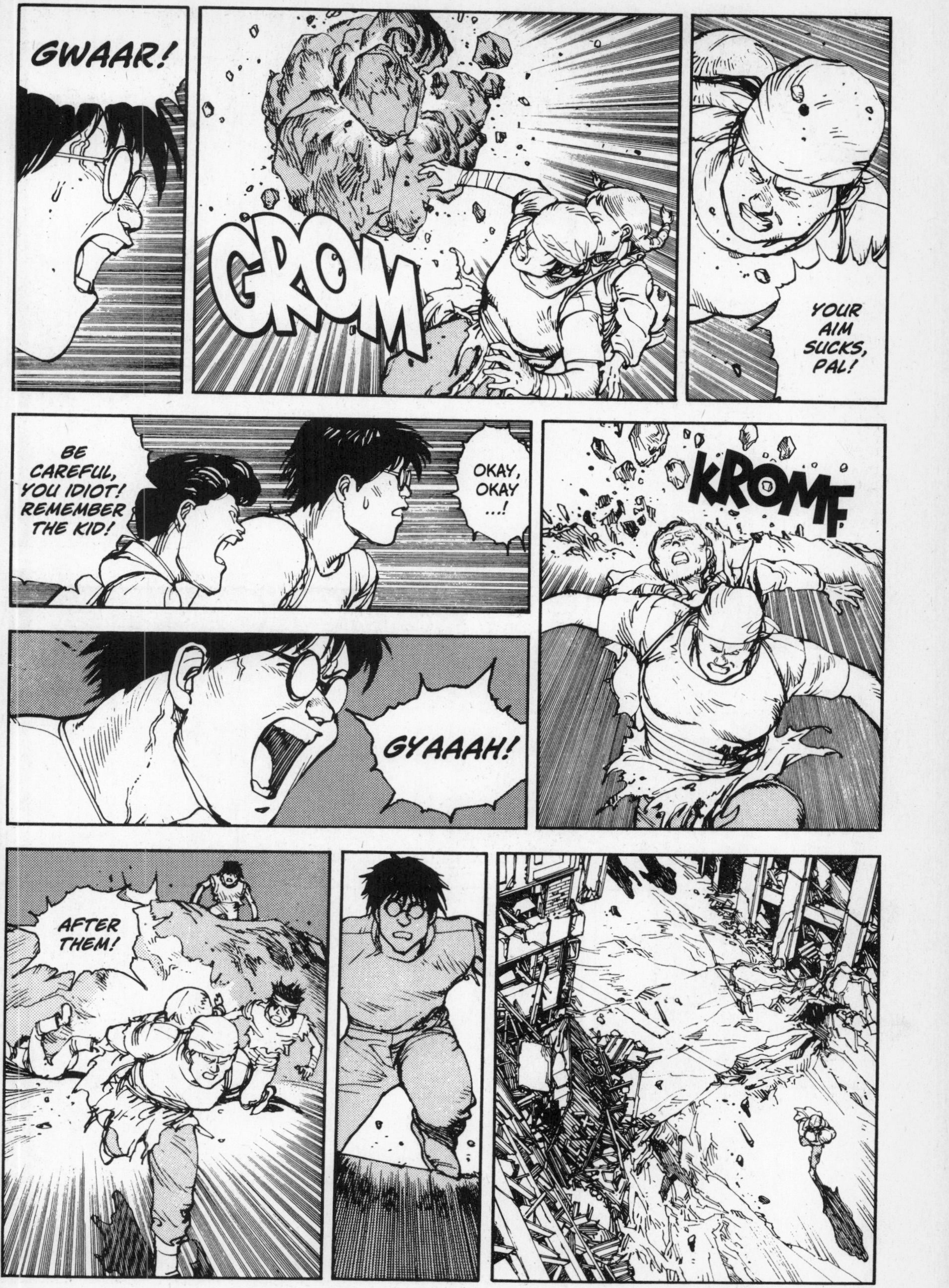
GWAAR!
GROM
YOUR AIM SUCKS, PAL!
BE CAREFUL, YOU IDIOT! REMEMBER THE KID!
OKAY, OKAY ...!
KROMF
GYAAAH!
AFTER THEM!

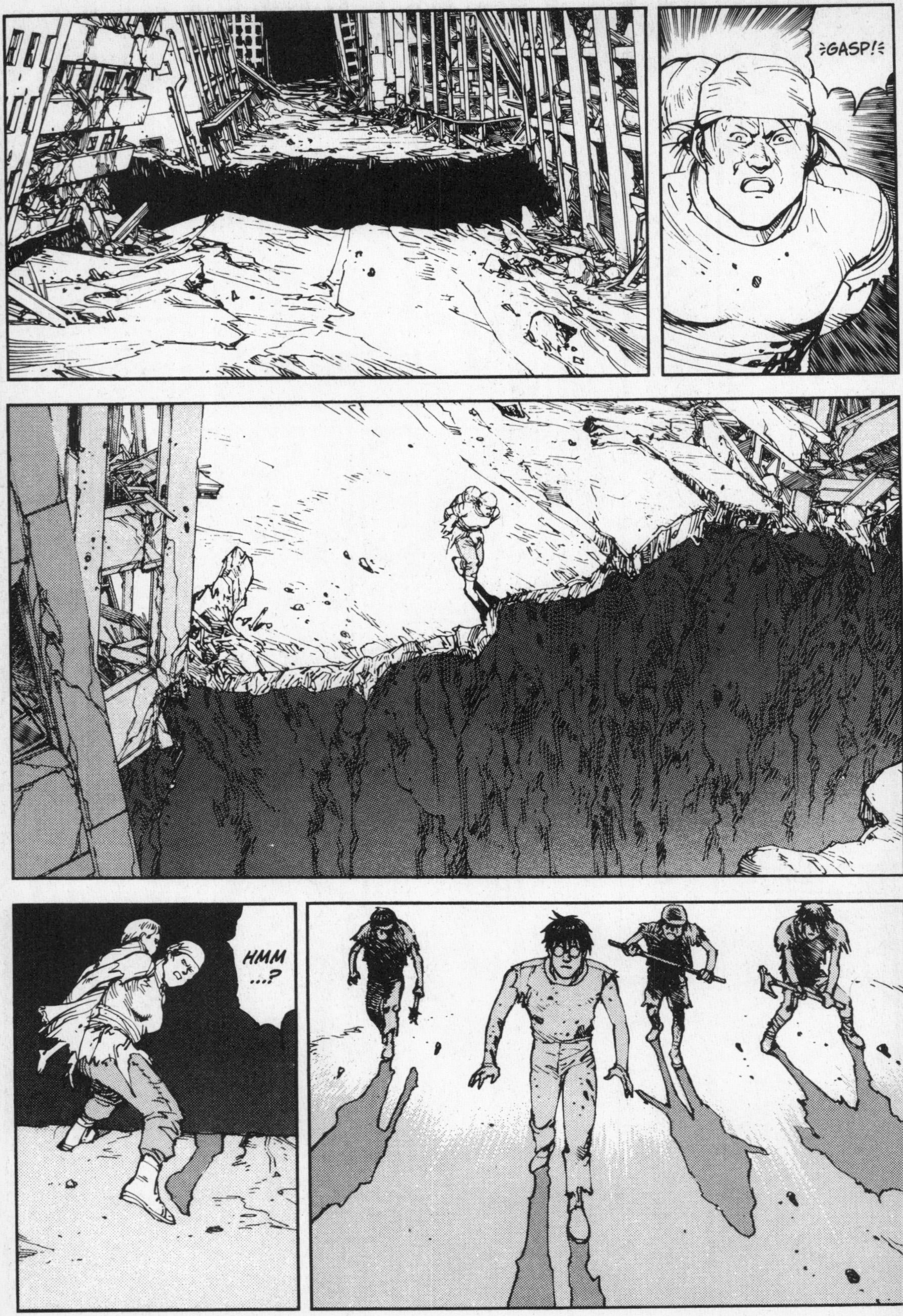
GASP!
HMM ...?

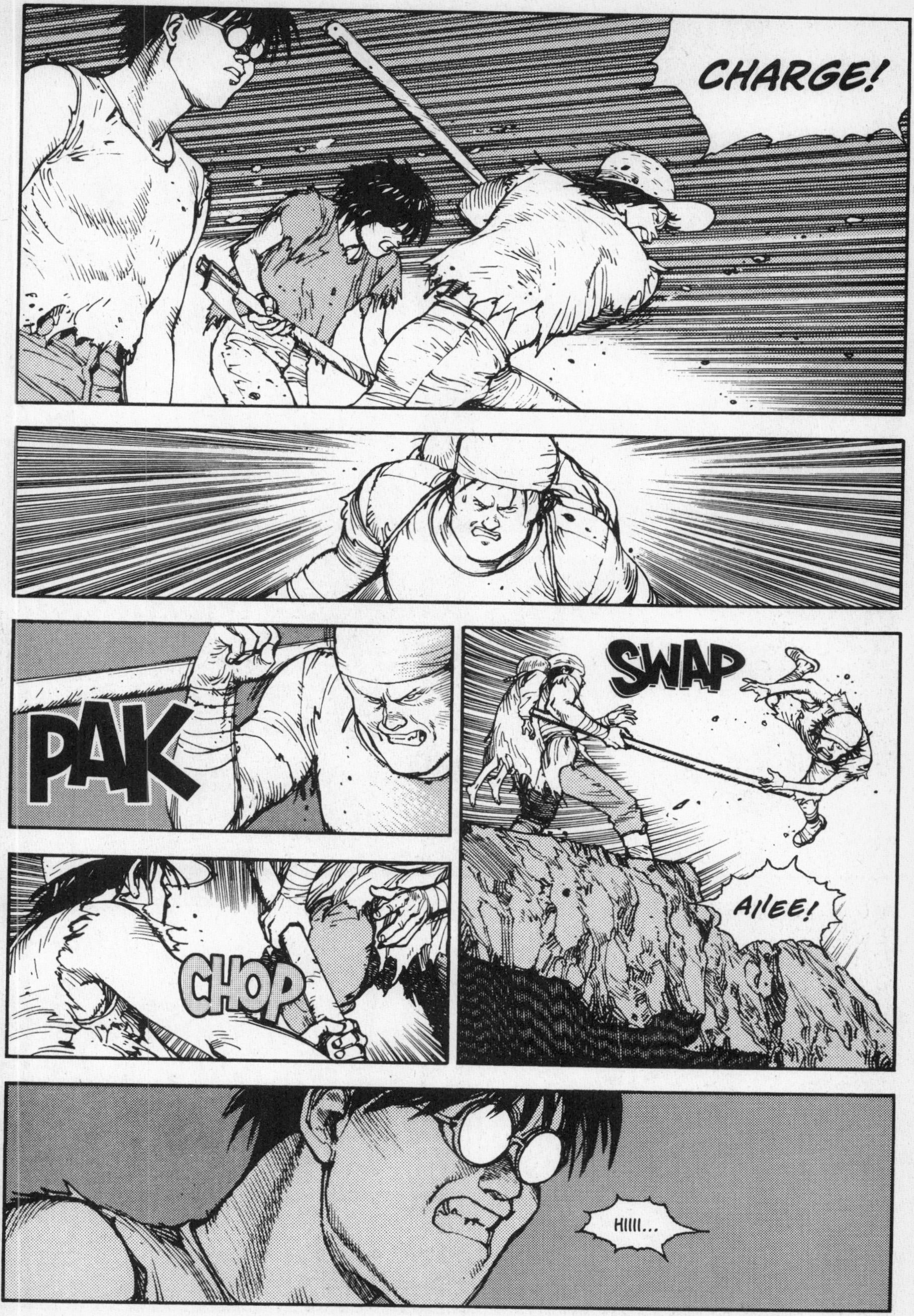
CHARGE!
PAK
SWAP
AIIEE!
CHOP
HIIII...

TSHAF
EAT THIS!
KLAW
GWAARR!
!
AGH!
OH--!
SHRAK

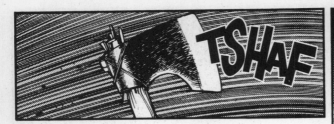

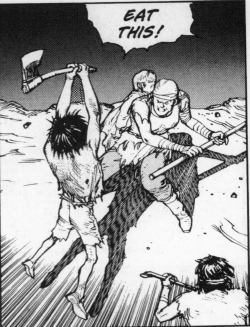

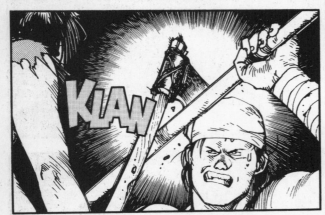

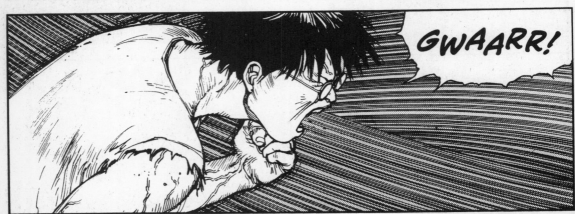

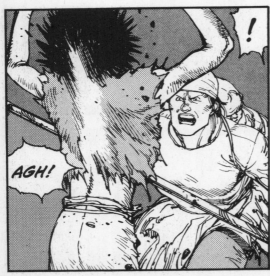

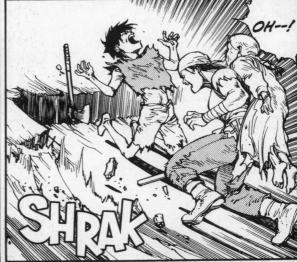

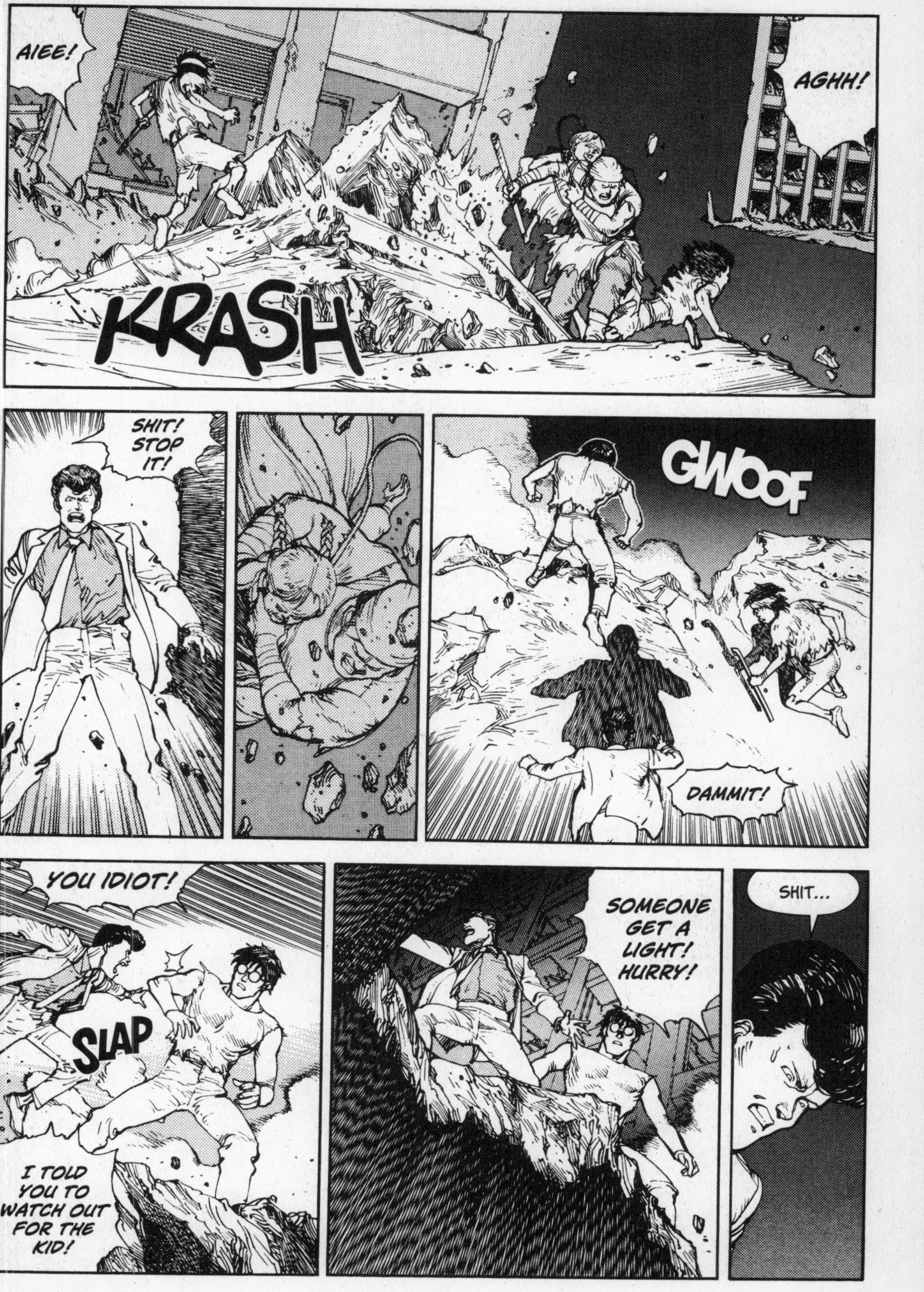
AIEE!
AGHH!
KRASH
SHIT! STOP IT!
GWOOF
DAMMIT!
YOU IDIOT!
SLAP
I TOLD YOU TO WATCH OUT FOR THE KID!
SOMEONE GET A LIGHT! HURRY!
SHIT...

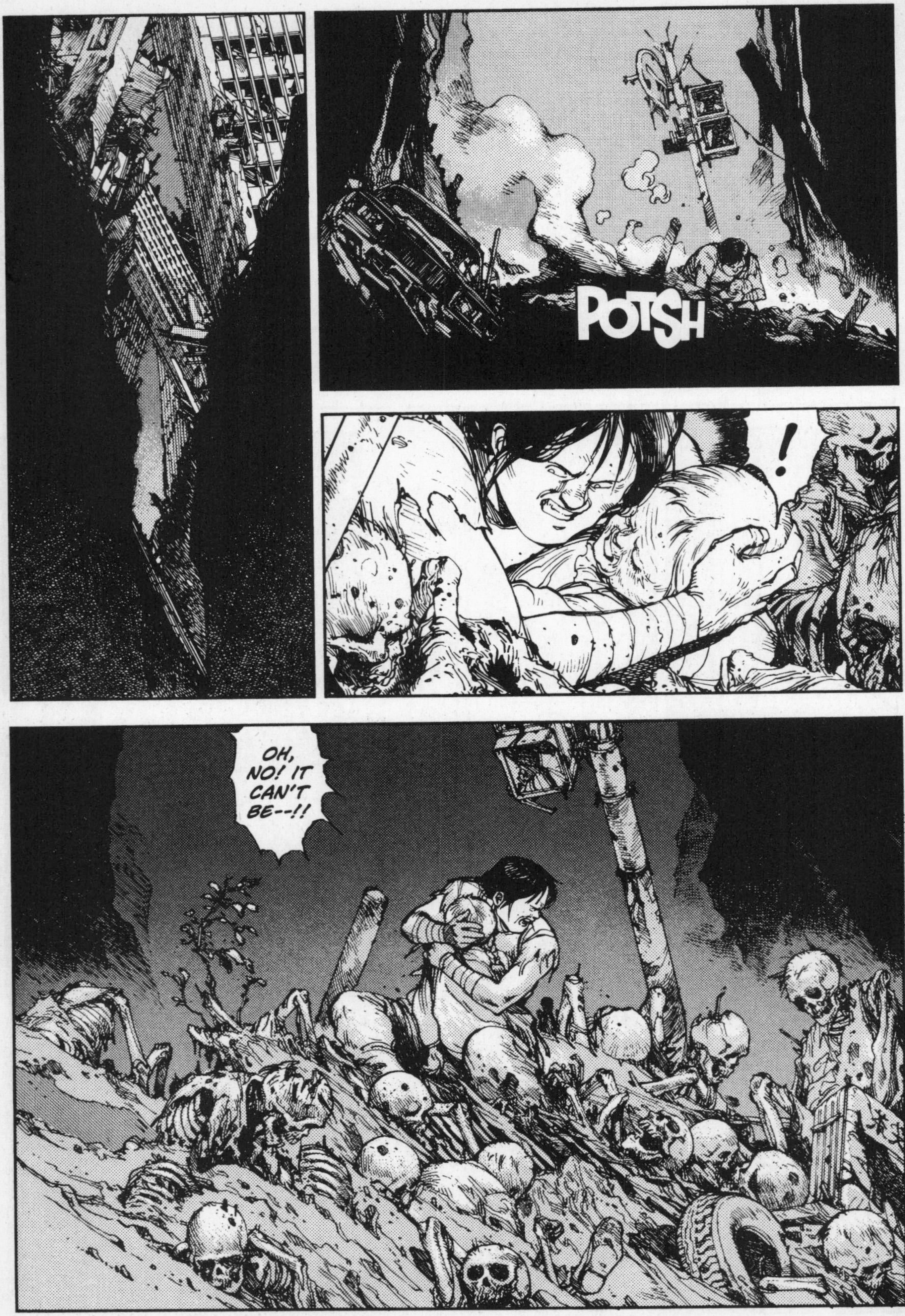
POTSH
!
OH, NO! IT CAN'T BE--!!

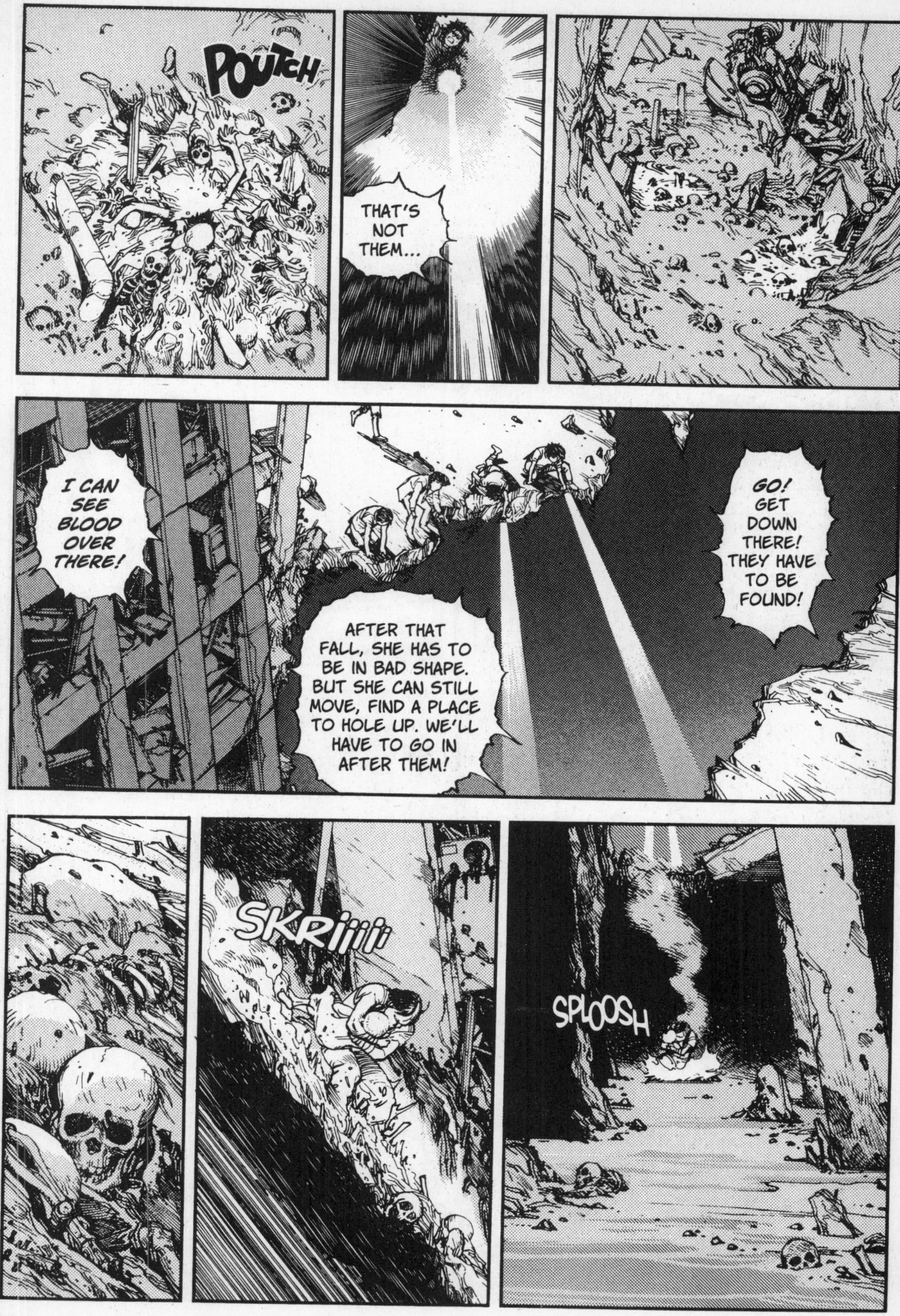
POUTCH
THAT'S NOT THEM...
I CAN SEE BLOOD OVER THERE!
AFTER THAT FALL, SHE HAS TO BE IN BAD SHAPE. BUT SHE CAN STILL MOVE, FIND A PLACE TO HOLE UP. WE'LL HAVE TO GO IN AFTER THEM!
GO! GET DOWN THERE! THEY HAVE TO BE FOUND!
SKRIiiii
SPLOOSH

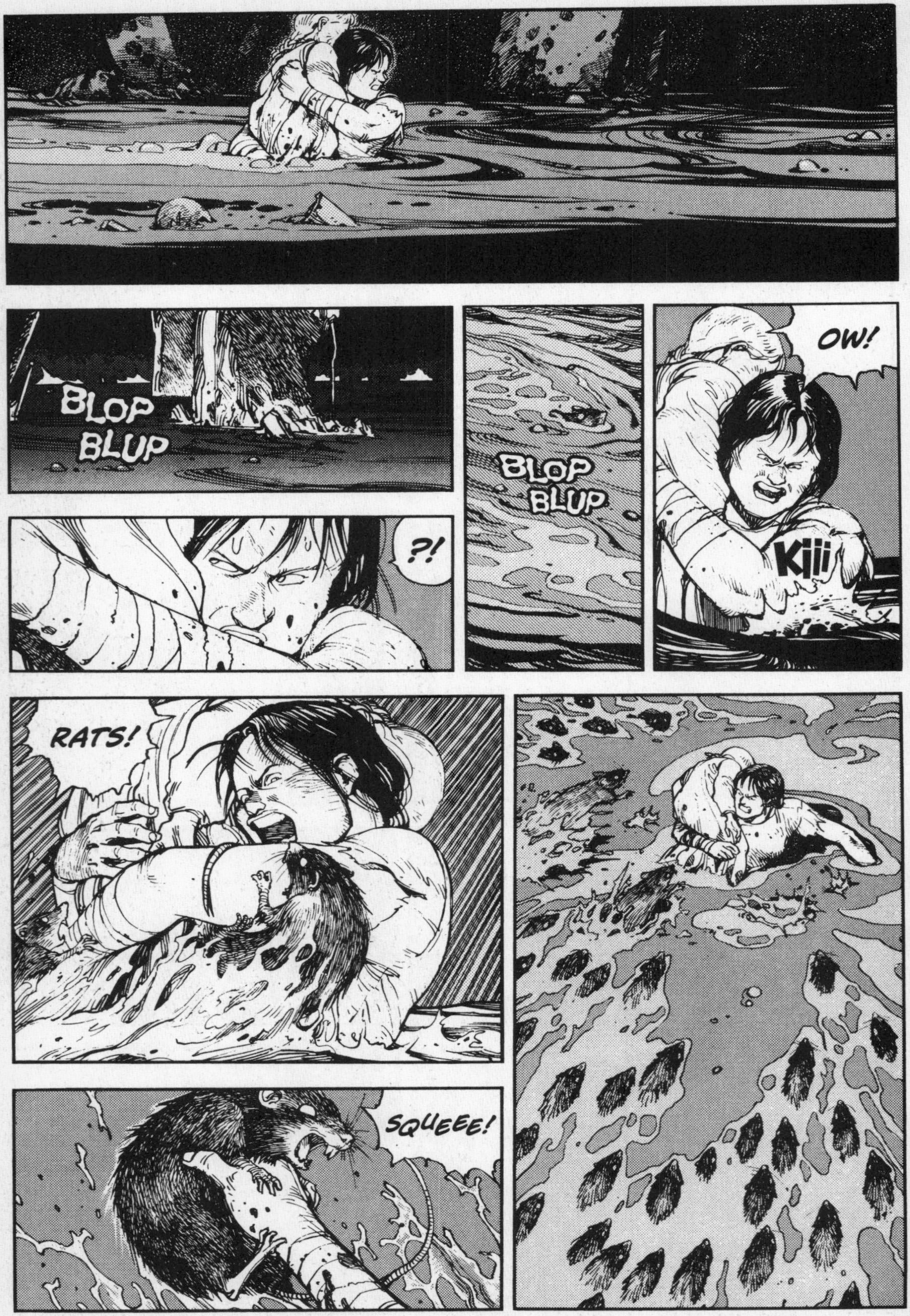
BLOP
BLUP
BLOP
BLUP
OW!
KJII
?!
RATS!
SQUEEE!

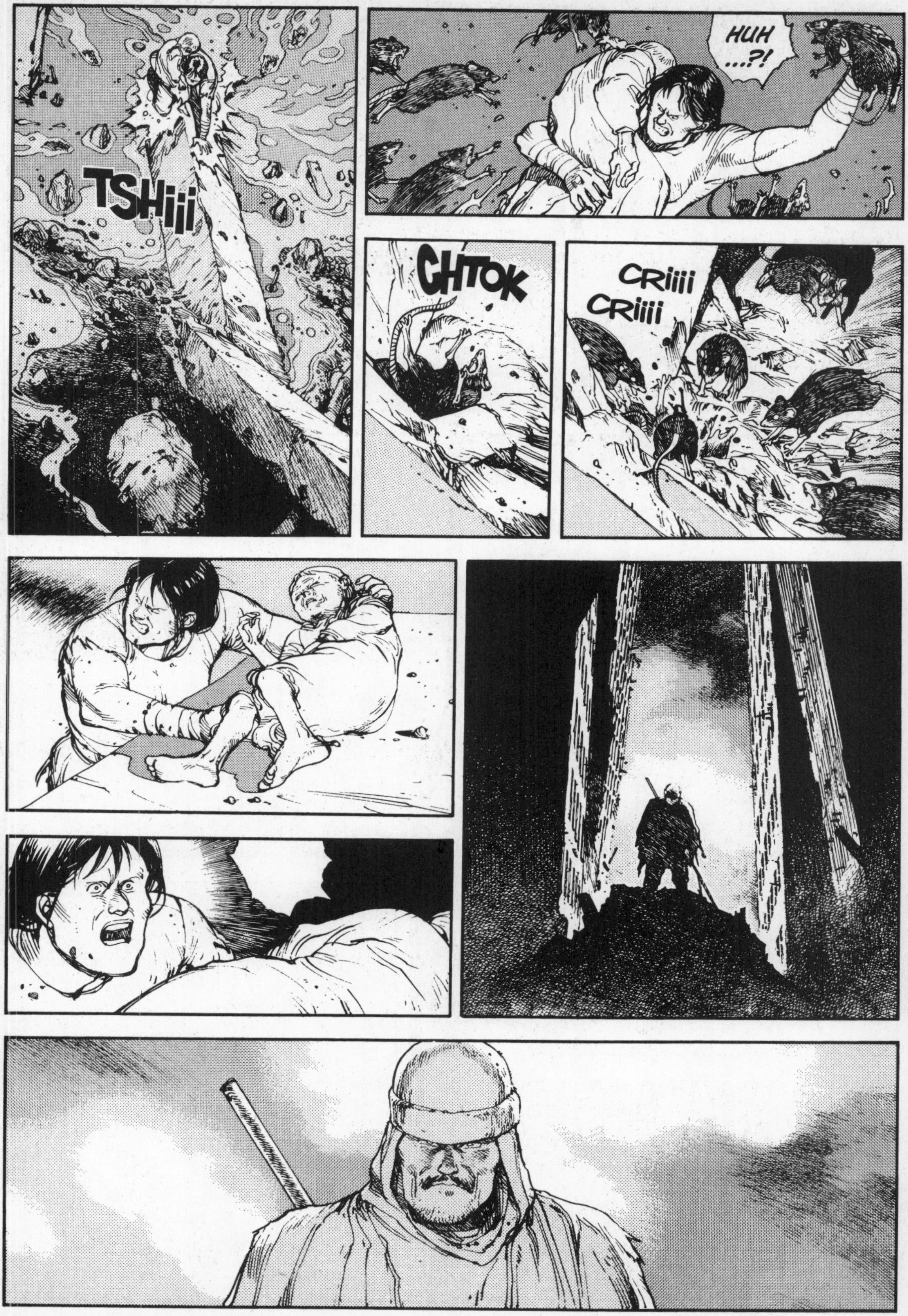
TSHiiii
HUH ...?!
CHTOK
CRiiii
CRiiii

COME ON, IF YOU GOT THE GUTS!

?!

WE MEET AGAIN.

I'M DREAM- ING...! YOU'RE...

...THE COLONEL!

HUHN?

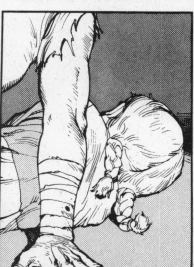

KIYOKO ?!

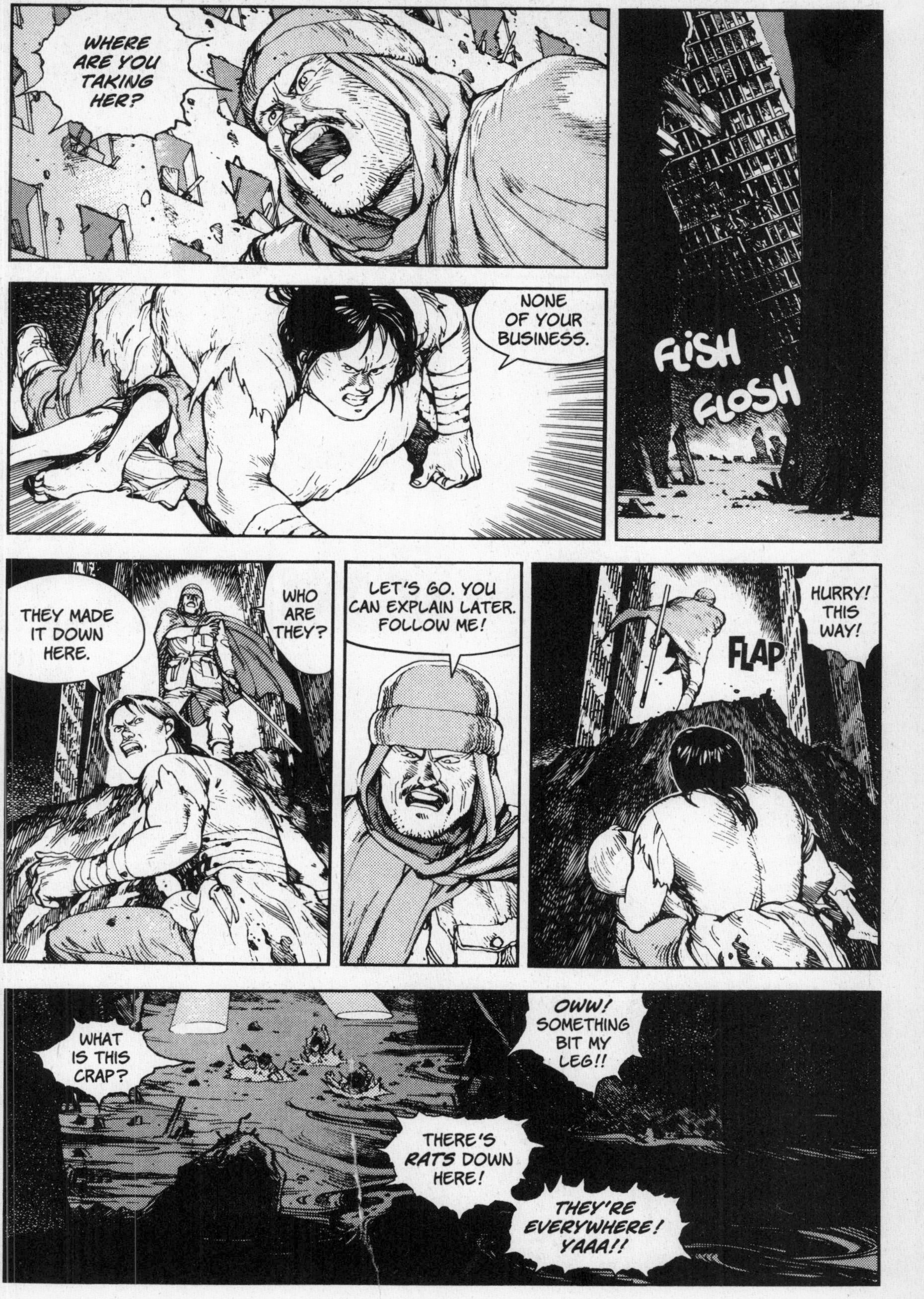
WHERE ARE YOU TAKING HER?
NONE OF YOUR BUSINESS.
FLISH
FLOSH
THEY MADE IT DOWN HERE.
WHO ARE THEY?
LET'S GO. YOU CAN EXPLAIN LATER. FOLLOW ME!
HURRY! THIS WAY!
FLAP
WHAT IS THIS CRAP?
OWW! SOMETHING BIT MY LEG!!
THERE'S RATS DOWN HERE!
THEY'RE EVERYWHERE! YAAA!!

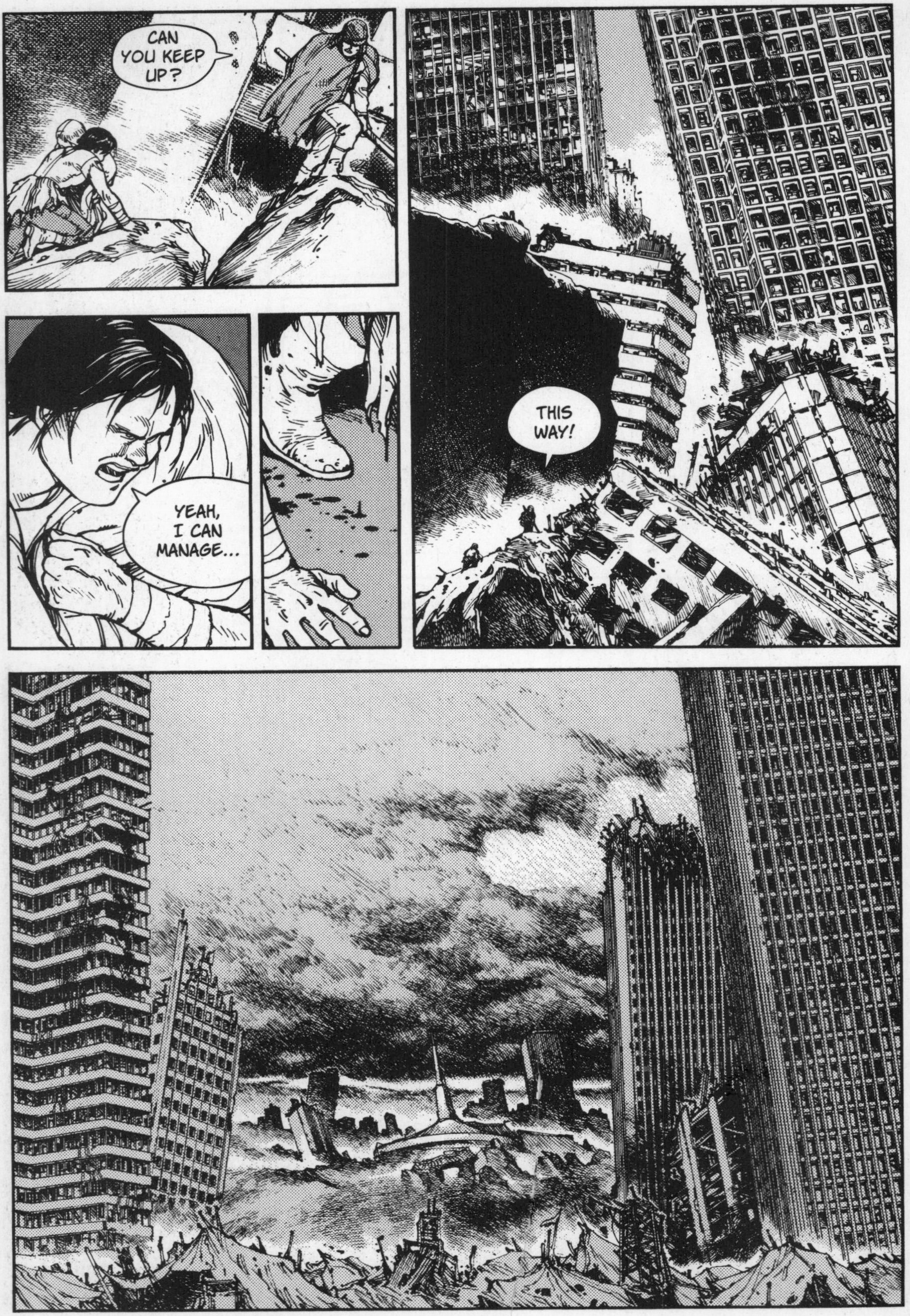
CAN YOU KEEP UP?
YEAH, I CAN MANAGE...
THIS WAY!

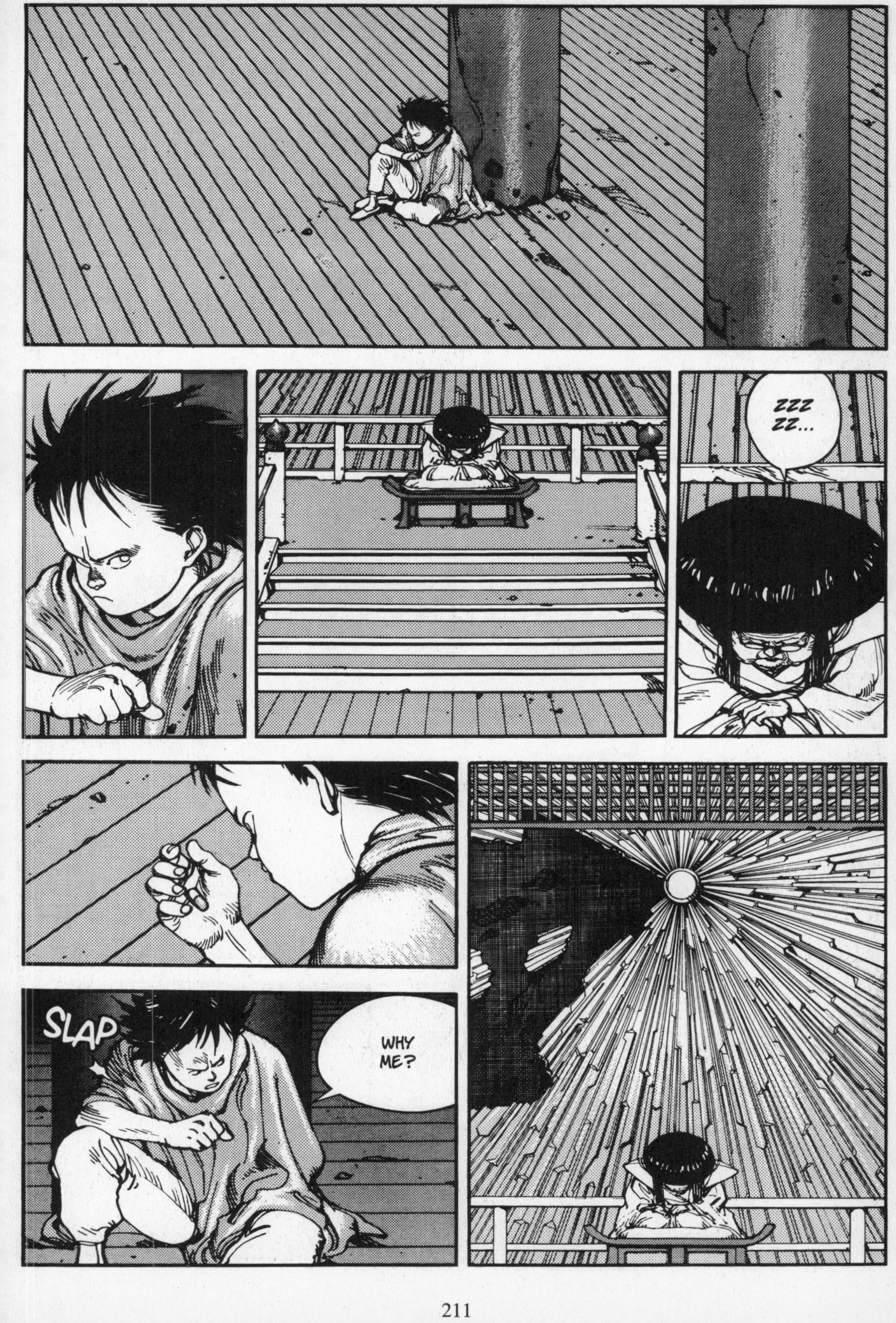
ZZZ
ZZ...
SLAP
WHY ME?

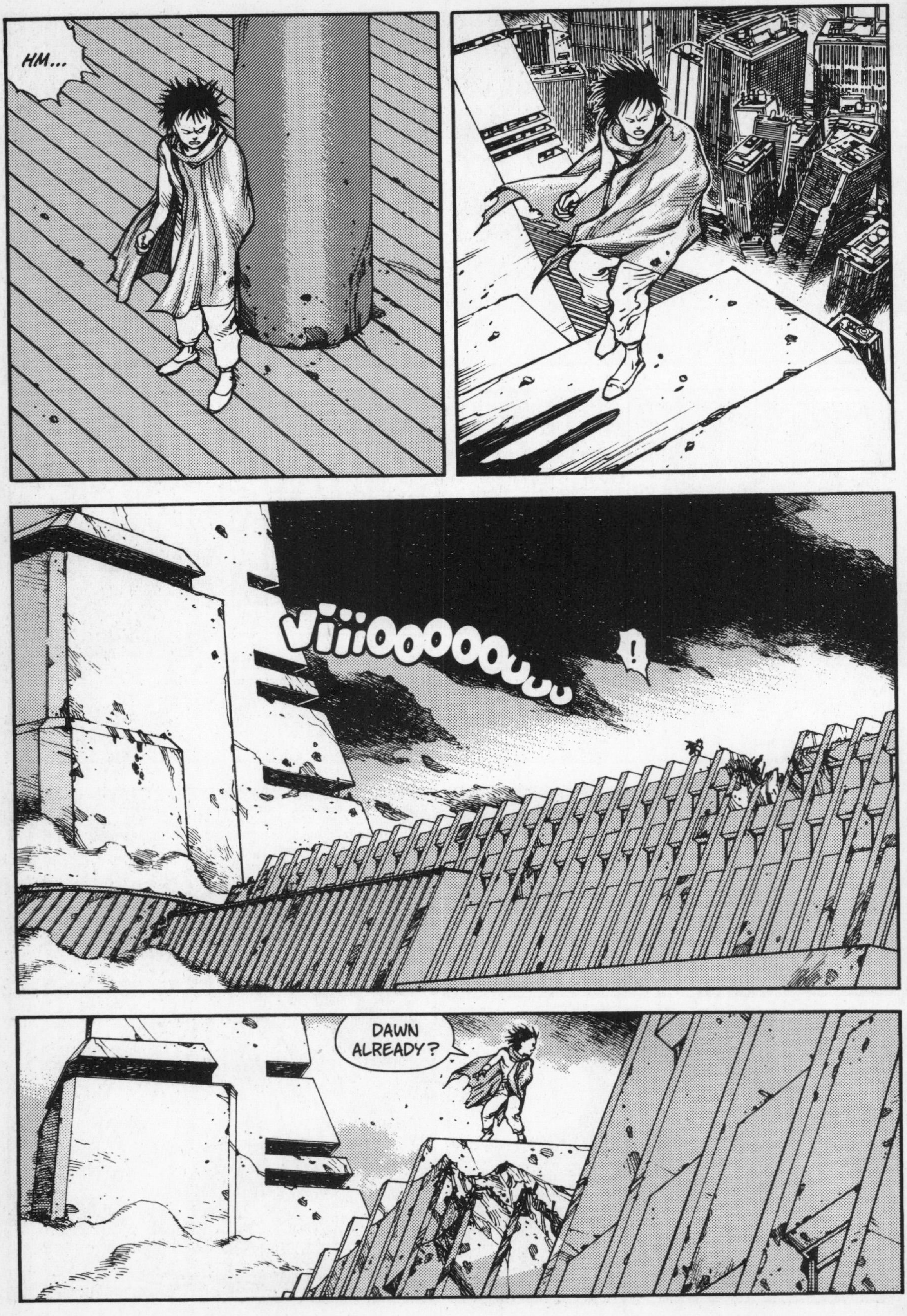
HM...
Viiiooooouuu
!
DAWN ALREADY?

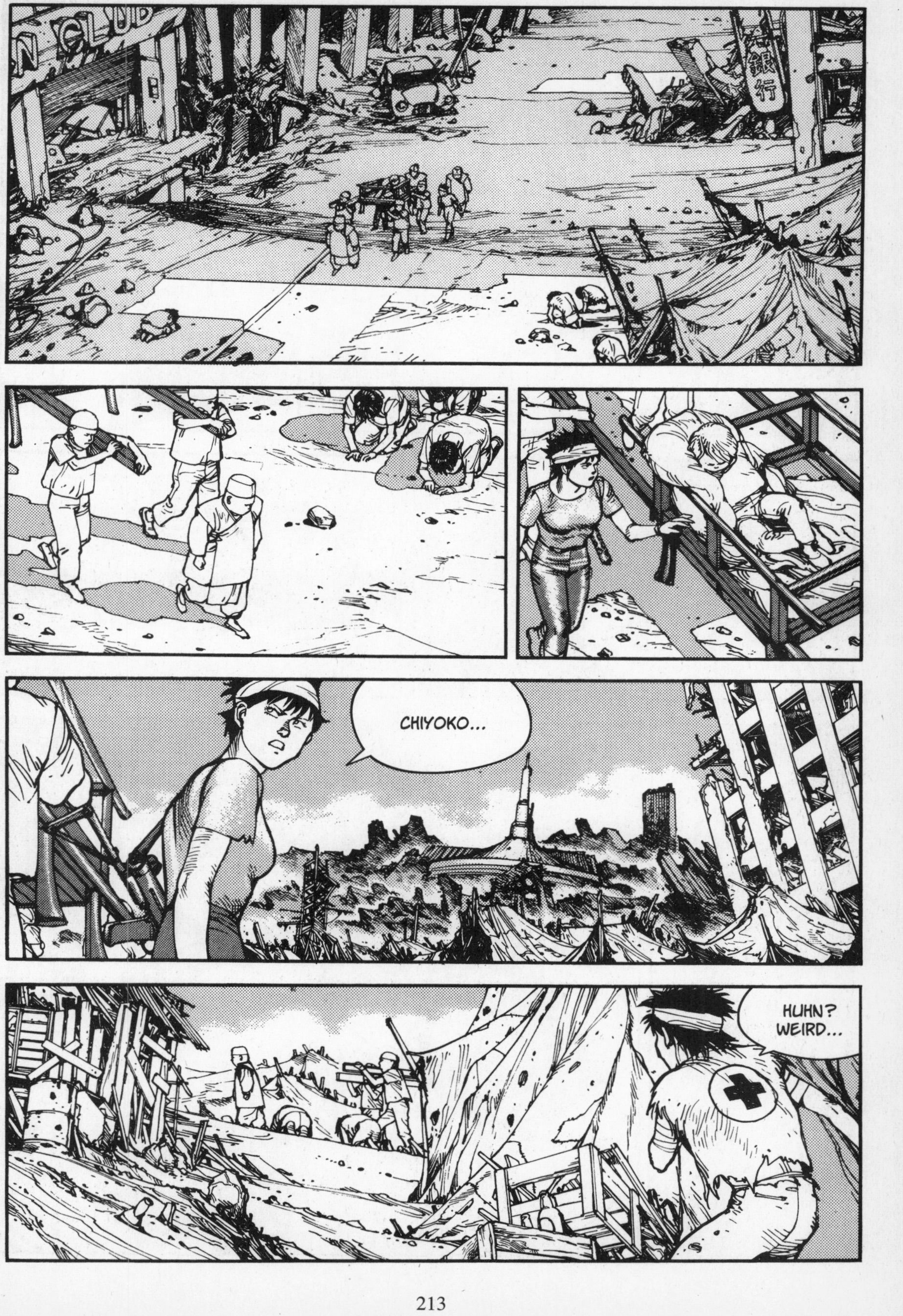
CHIYOKO...
HUHN? WEIRD...

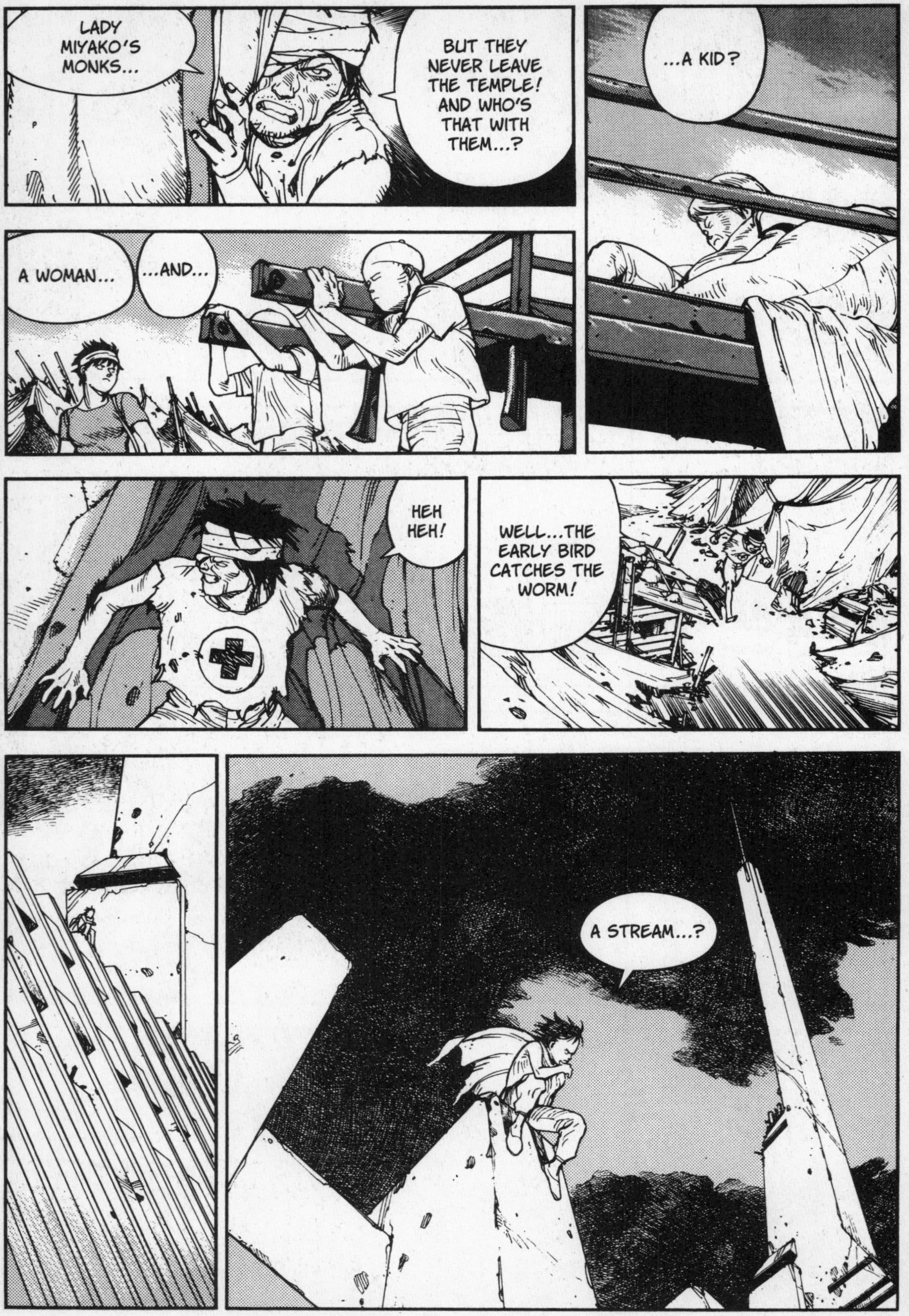
LADY MIYAKO'S MONKS...
BUT THEY NEVER LEAVE THE TEMPLE! AND WHO'S THAT WITH THEM...?
...A KID?
A WOMAN...
...AND...
HEH HEH!
WELL...THE EARLY BIRD CATCHES THE WORM!
A STREAM...?

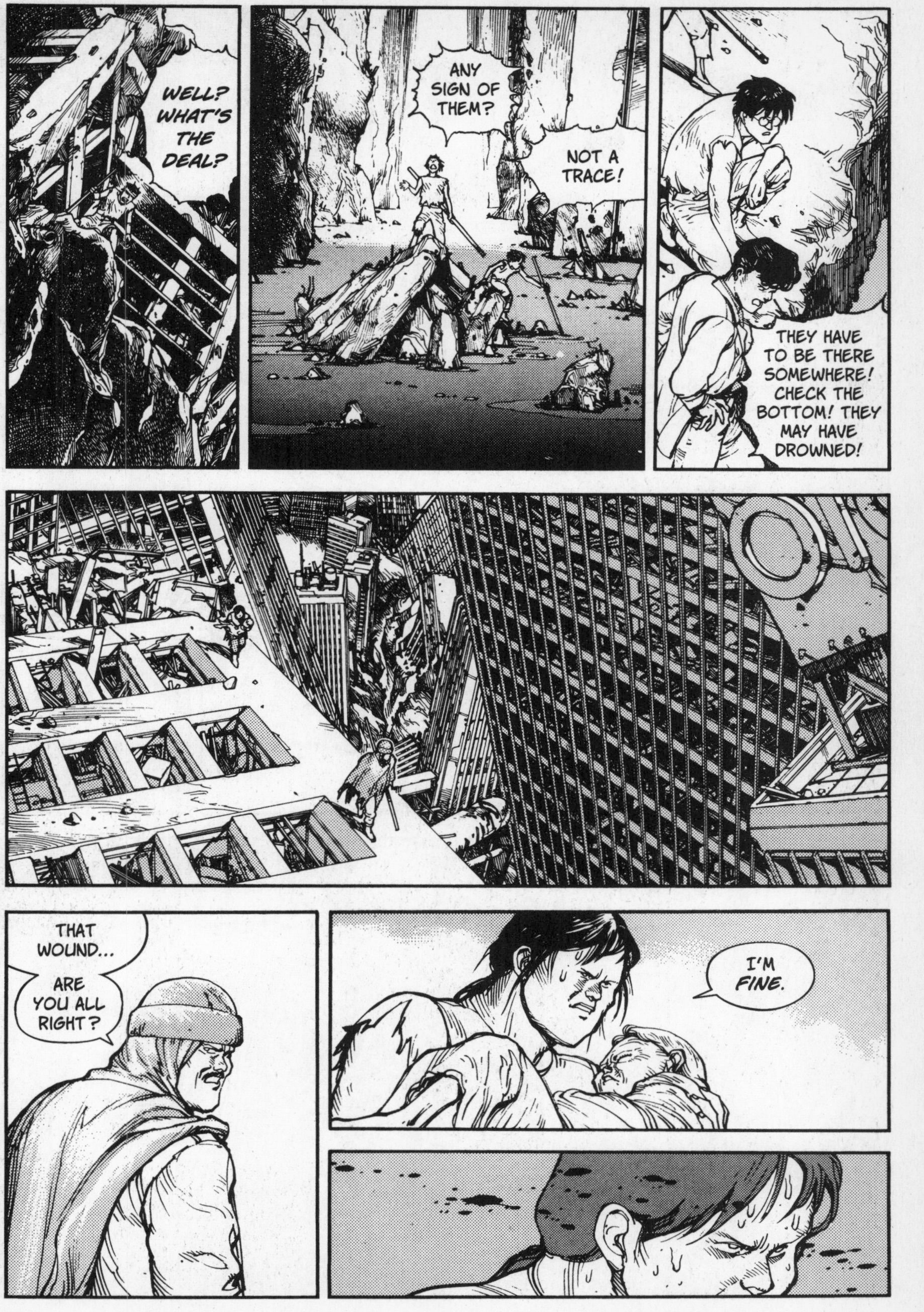
WELL? WHAT'S THE DEAL?
ANY SIGN OF THEM?
NOT A TRACE!
THEY HAVE TO BE THERE SOMEWHERE! CHECK THE BOTTOM! THEY MAY HAVE DROWNED!
THAT WOUND...
ARE YOU ALL RIGHT?
I'M FINE.

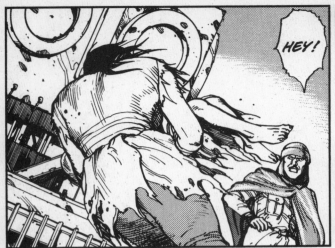

HEY!

THIS ISN'T THE TIME TO QUIT! GET UP!

STAC

NOW!!

216

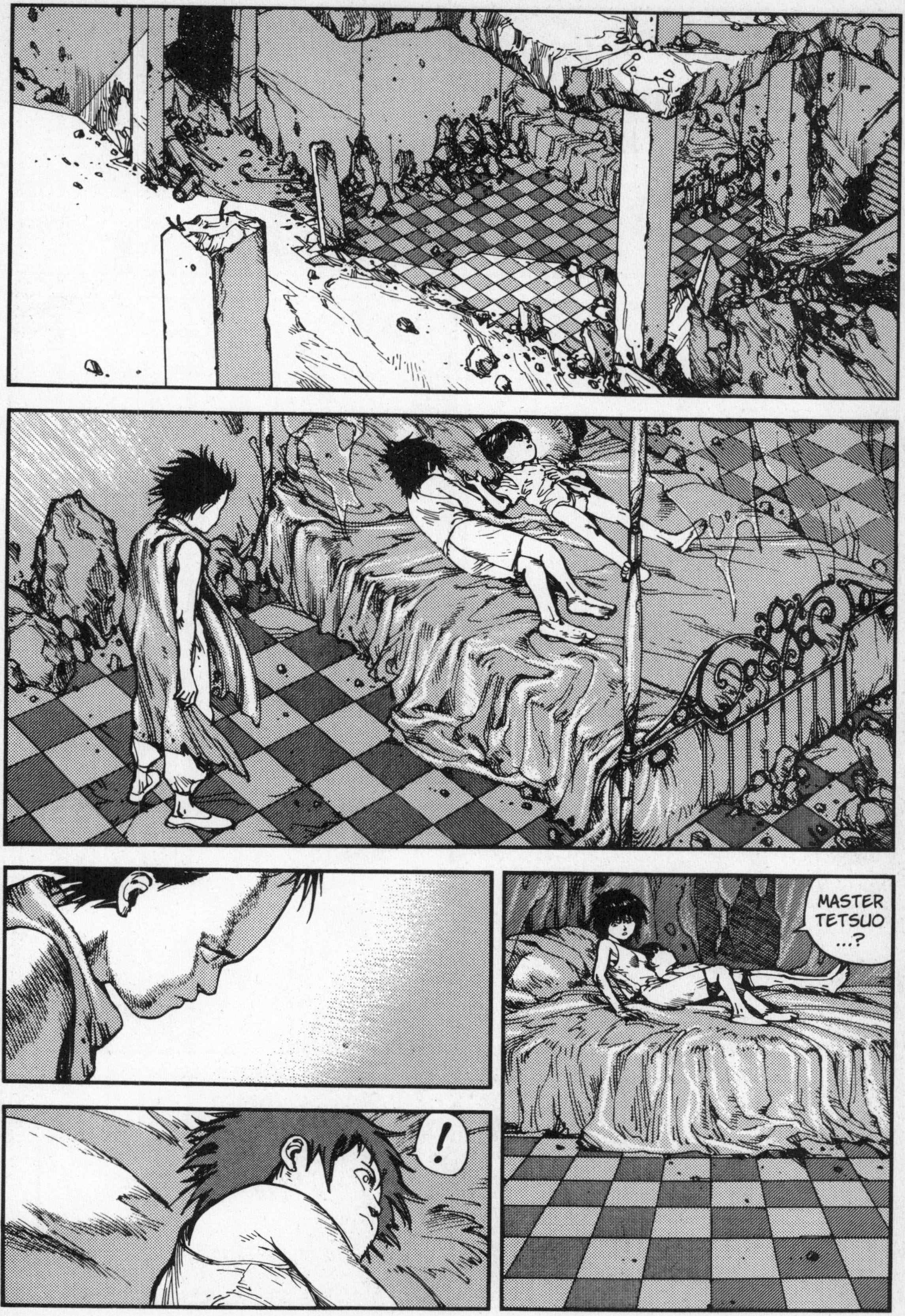
!
MASTER TETSUO ...?

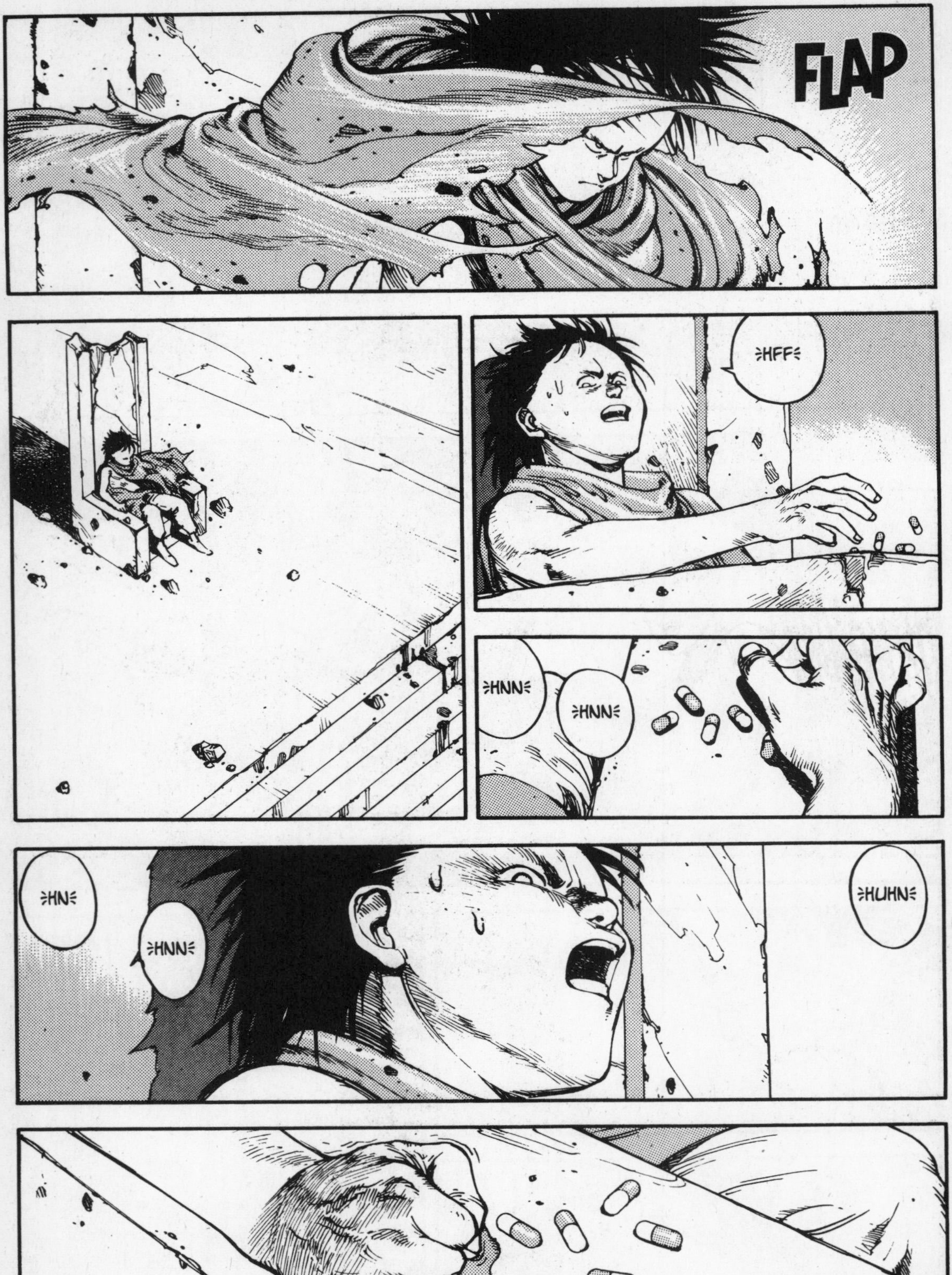
FLAP
HFF
HNN
HNN
HN
HNN
HUHN

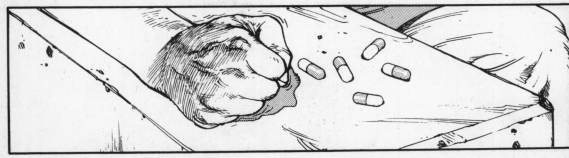

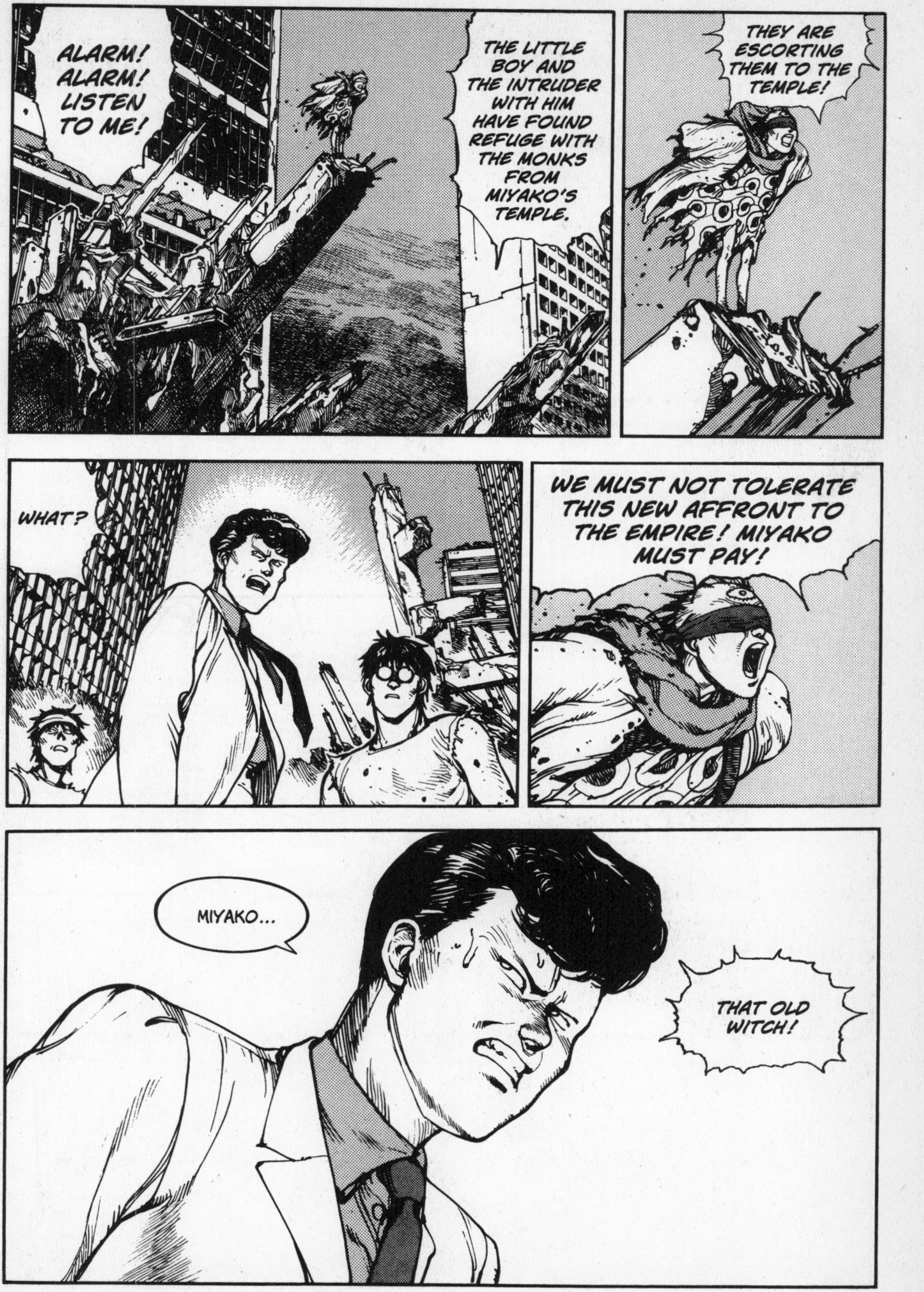
ALARM! ALARM! LISTEN TO ME!
THE LITTLE BOY AND THE INTRUDER WITH HIM HAVE FOUND REFUGE WITH THE MONKS FROM MIYAKO'S TEMPLE.
THEY ARE ESCORTING THEM TO THE TEMPLE!
WHAT?
WE MUST NOT TOLERATE THIS NEW AFFRONT TO THE EMPIRE! MIYAKO MUST PAY!
MIYAKO...
THAT OLD WITCH!

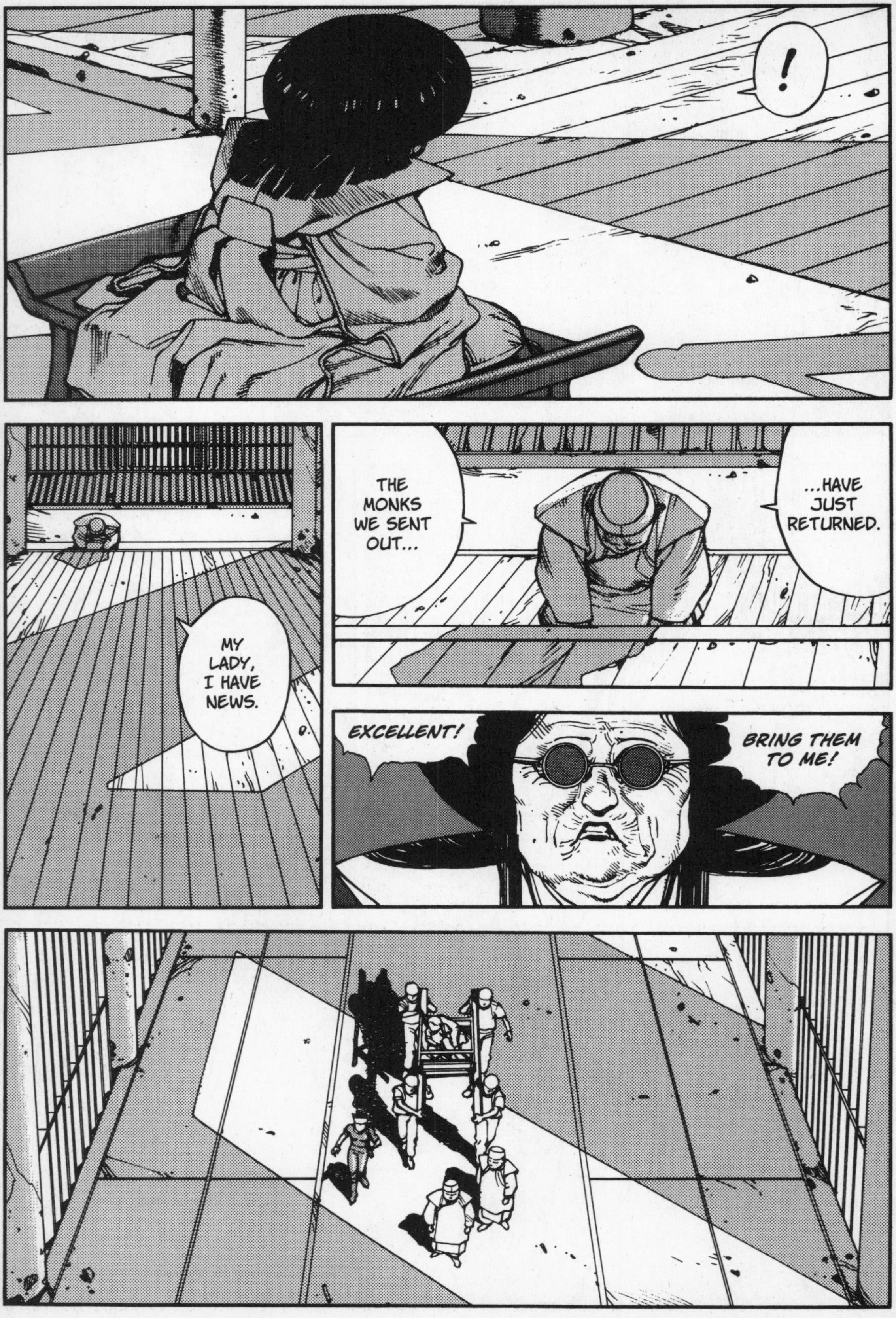
!
MY LADY, I HAVE NEWS.
THE MONKS WE SENT OUT...
...HAVE JUST RETURNED.
EXCELLENT!
BRING THEM TO ME!

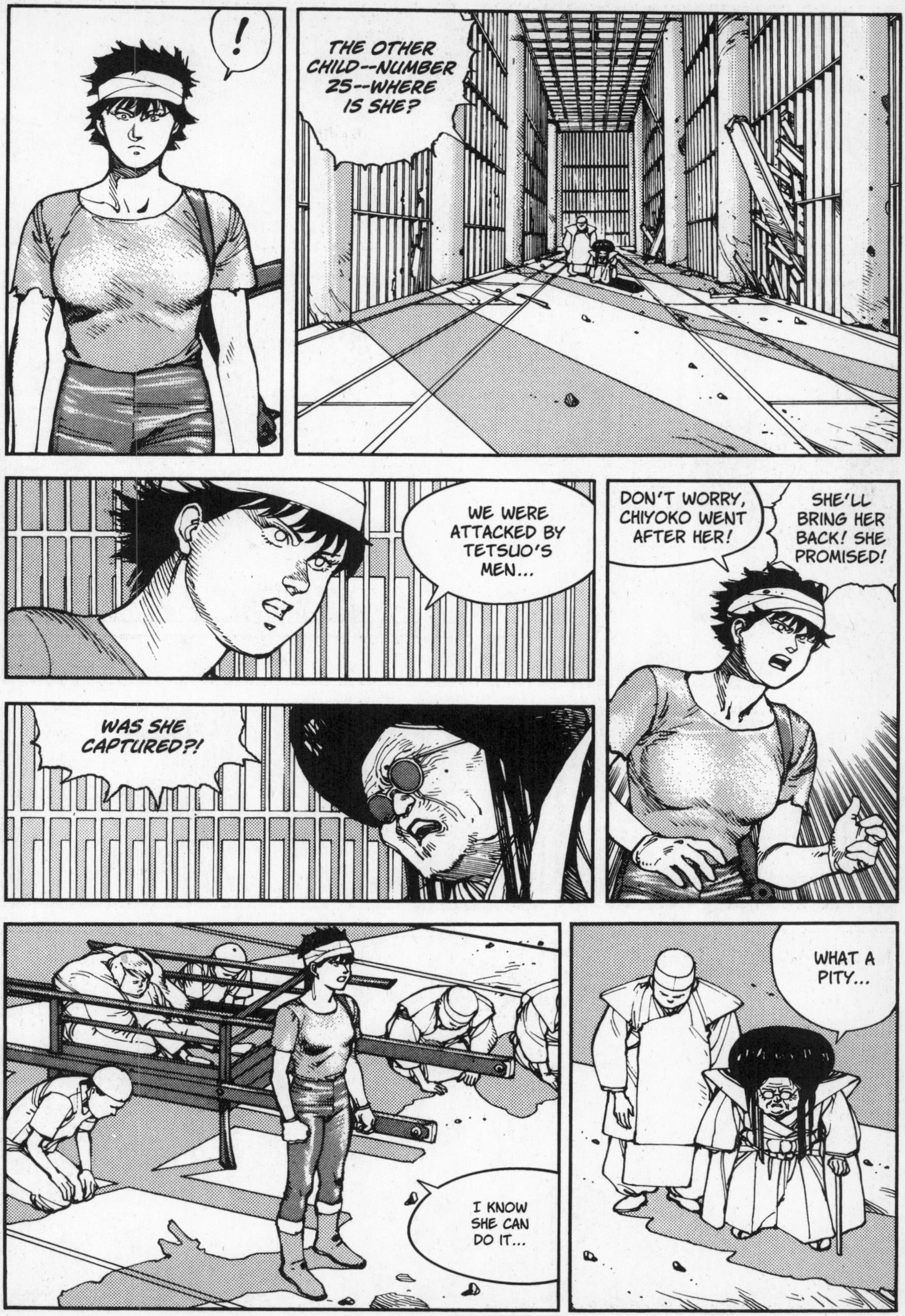
!
THE OTHER CHILD--NUMBER 25--WHERE IS SHE?
WE WERE ATTACKED BY TETSUO'S MEN...
DON'T WORRY, CHIYOKO WENT AFTER HER!
SHE'LL BRING HER BACK! SHE PROMISED!
WAS SHE CAPTURED?!
I KNOW SHE CAN DO IT...
WHAT A PITY...

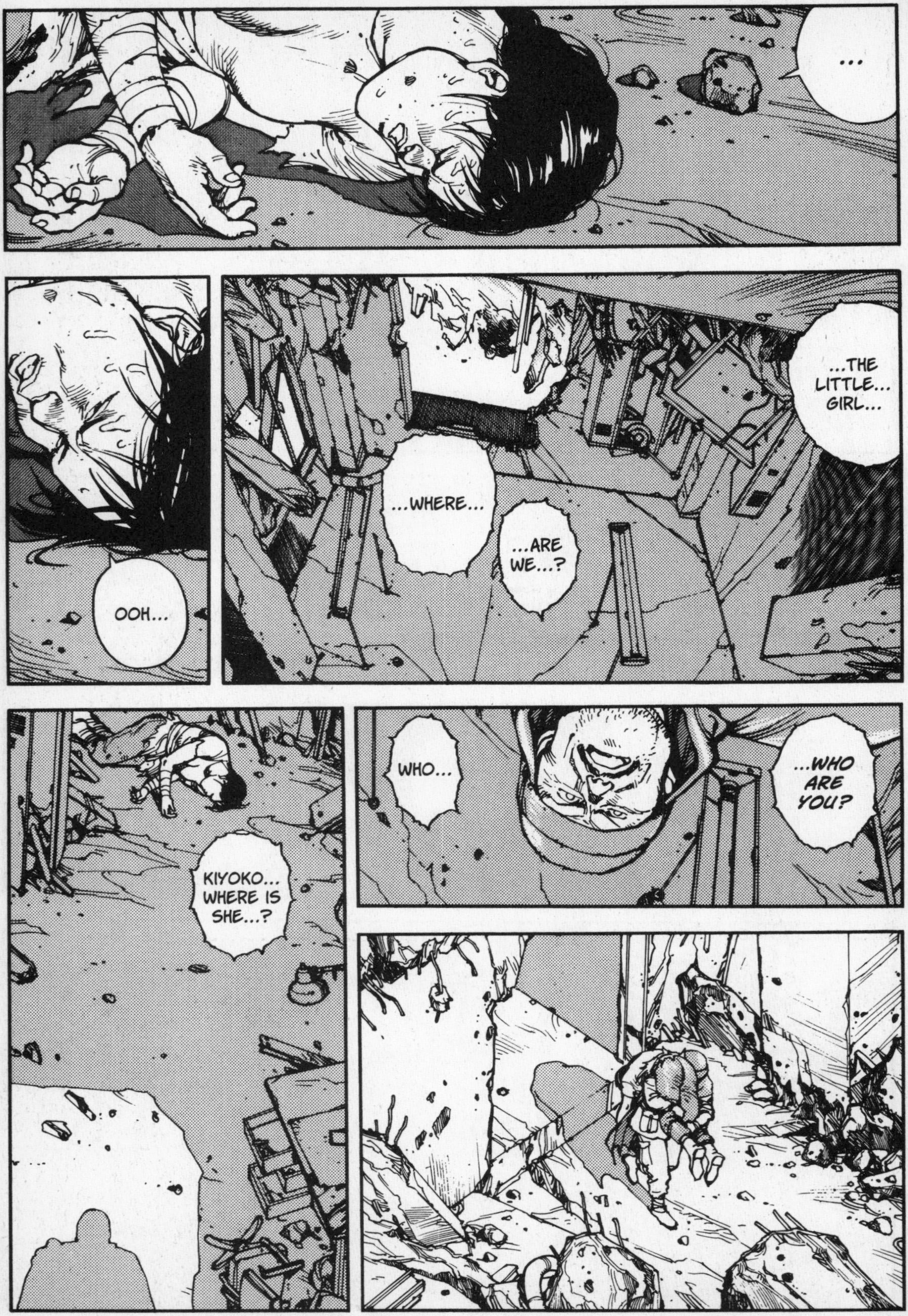
...
OOH...
...WHERE...
...ARE WE...?
...THE LITTLE... GIRL...
KIYOKO... WHERE IS SHE...?
WHO...
...WHO ARE YOU?

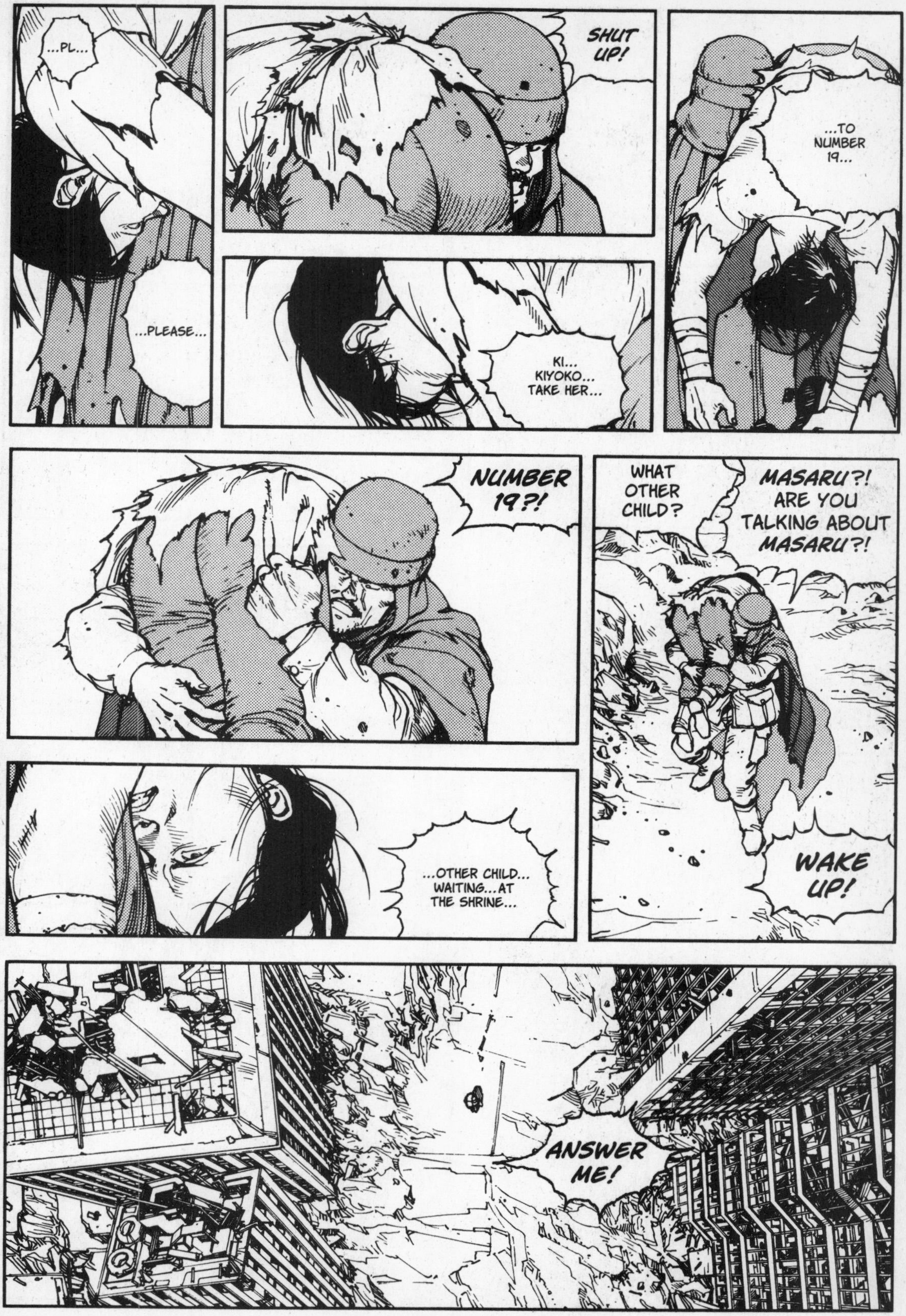
...PL...
...PLEASE...
SHUT UP!
KI... KIYOKO... TAKE HER...
...TO NUMBER 19...
NUMBER 19?!
...OTHER CHILD... WAITING...AT THE SHRINE...
WHAT OTHER CHILD?
MASARU?! ARE YOU TALKING ABOUT MASARU?!
WAKE UP!
ANSWER ME!

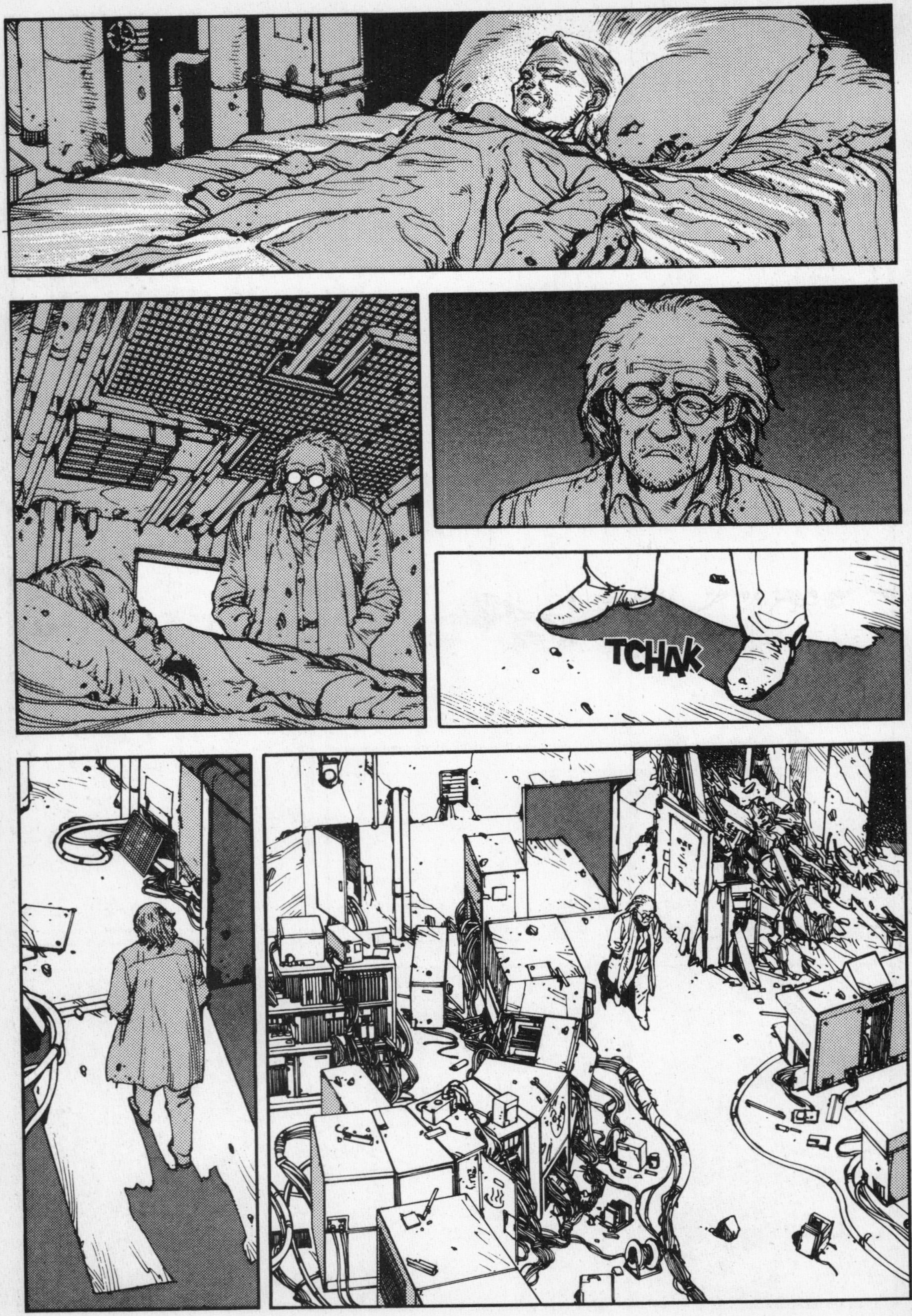
TCHAK

SOL
PFFF
SOL
MATCHES...
WHERE'D I PUT THOSE GODDAMN *MATCHES*?

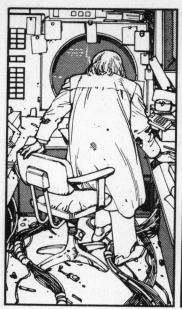

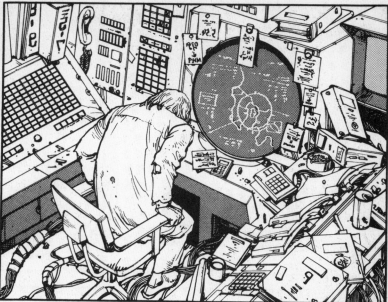

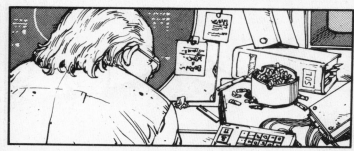

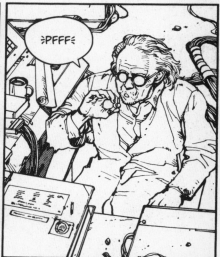

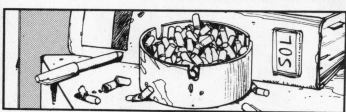

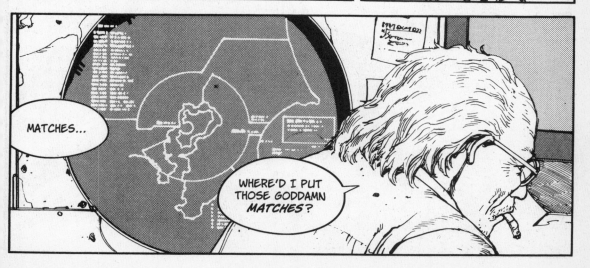

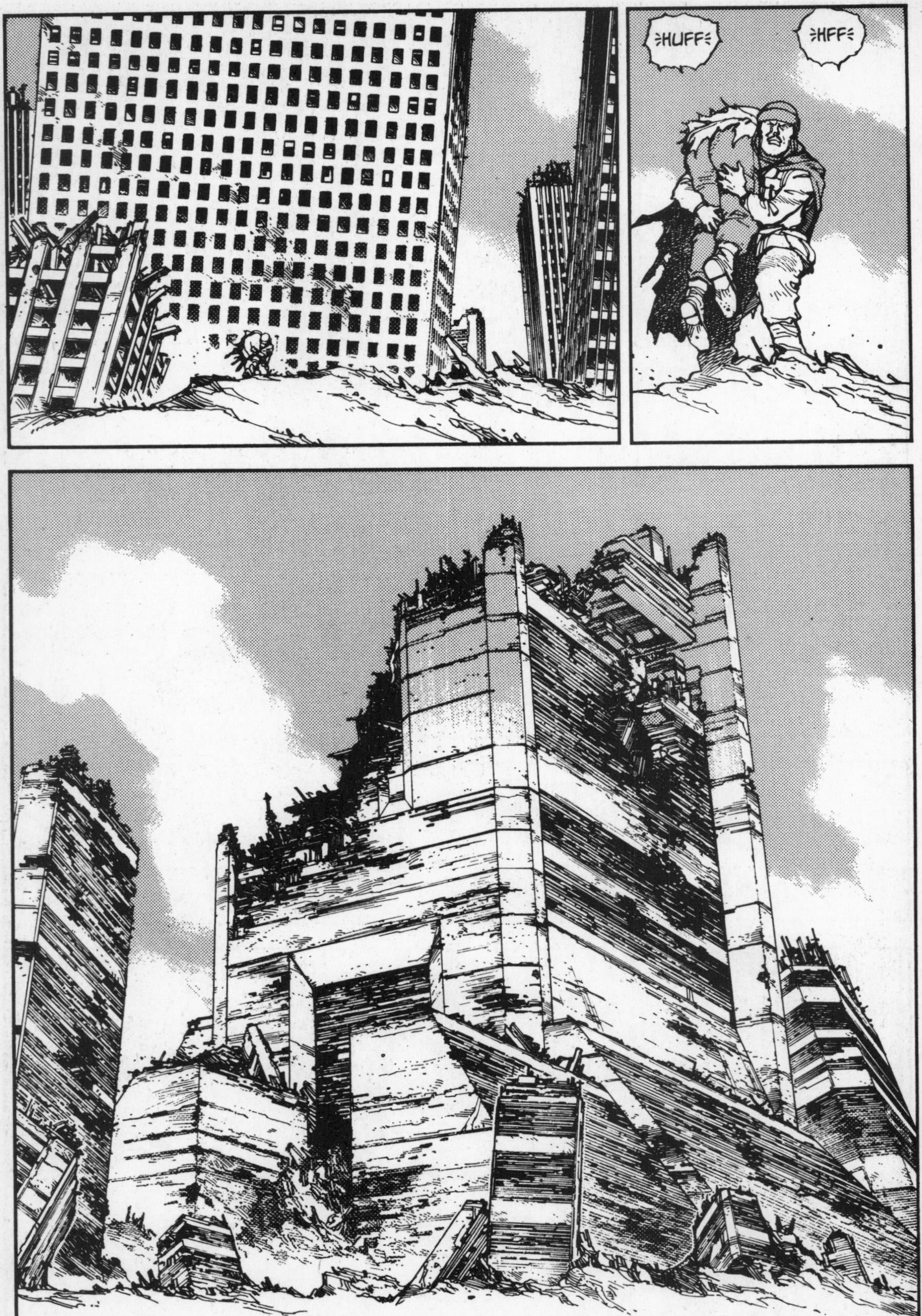
HUFF
HFF

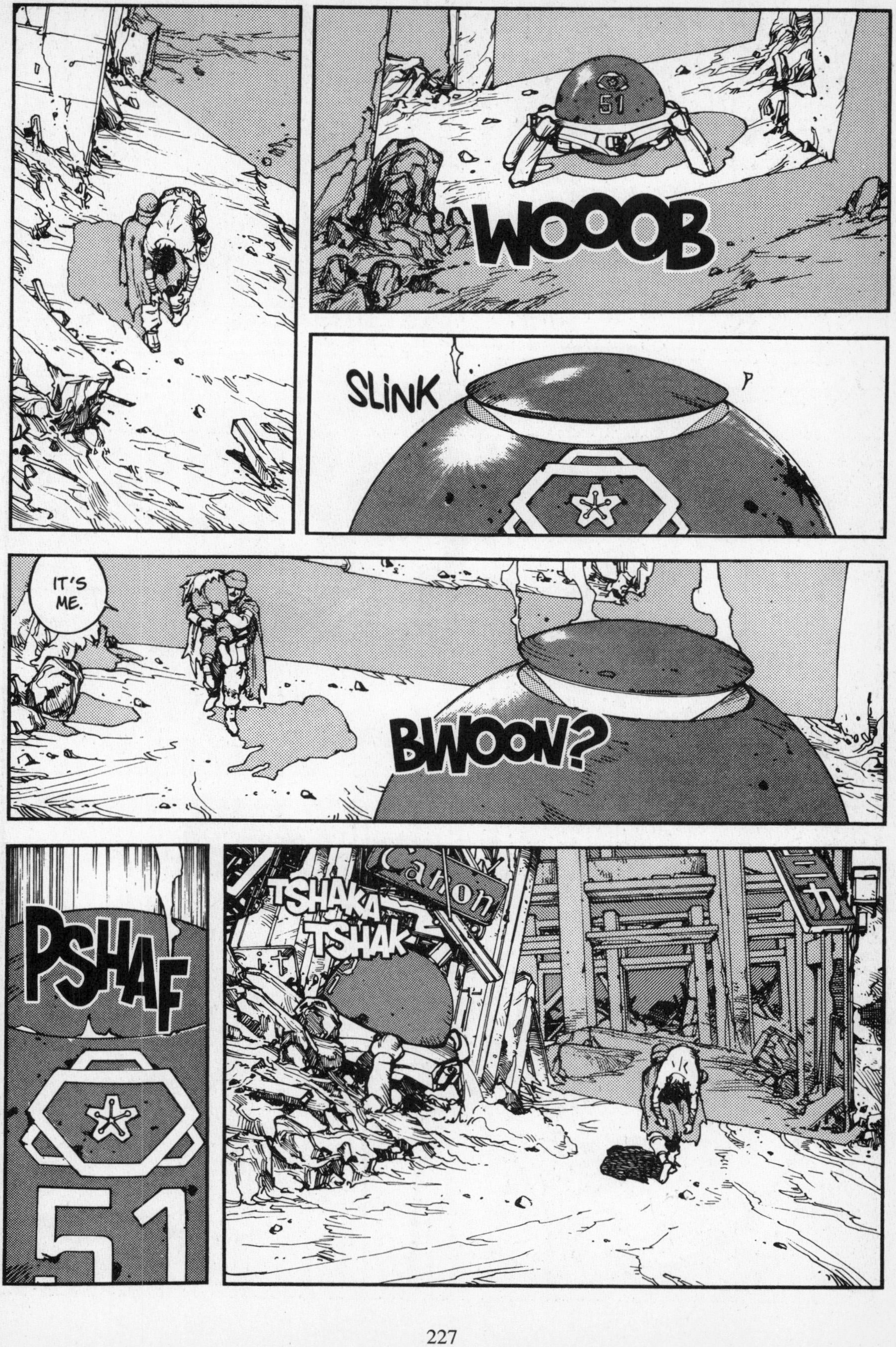
WOOOB
SLINK
IT'S ME.
BIWOON?
PSHAF
Canon
TSHAKA TSHAK

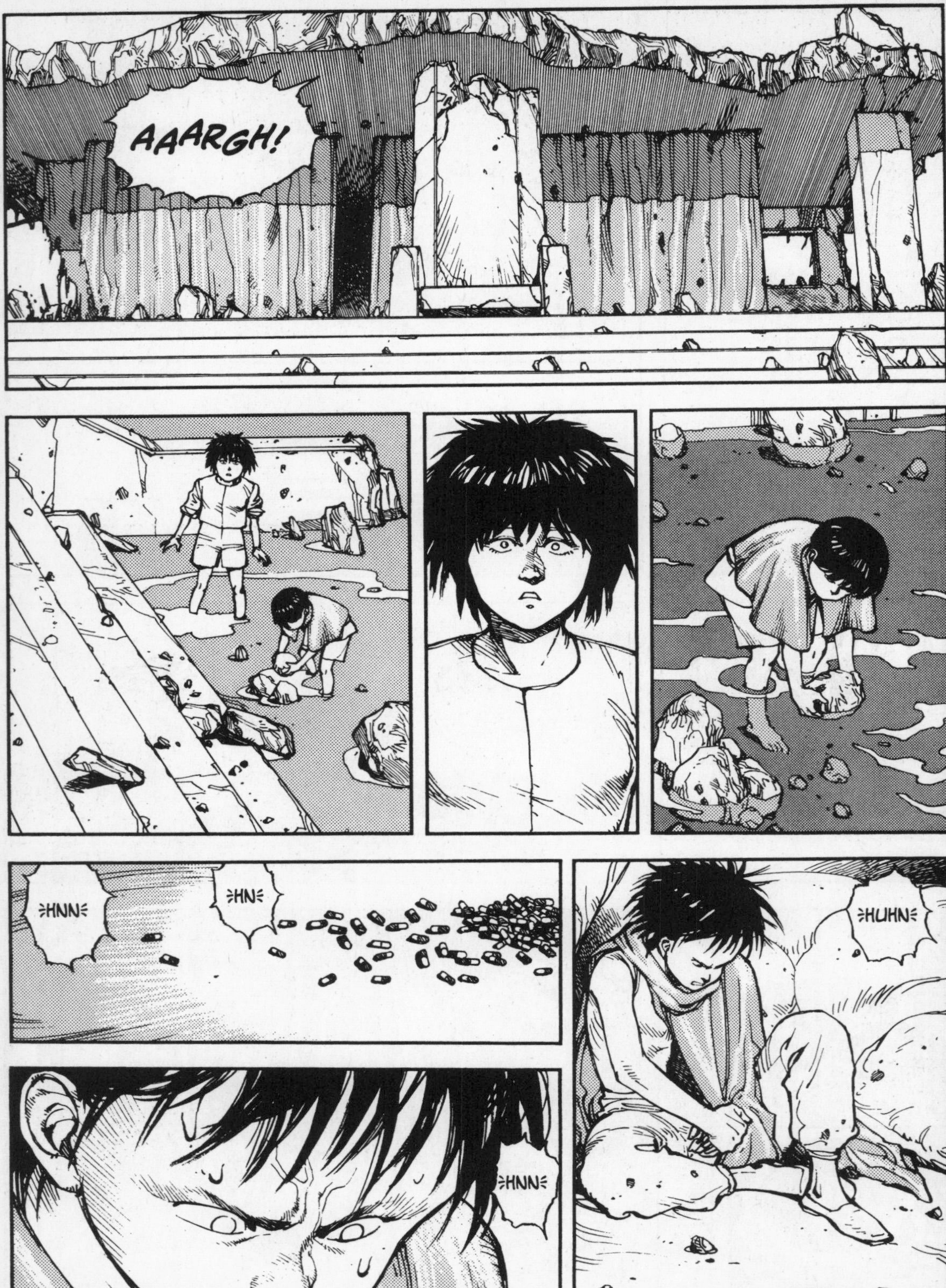
AAARGH!
HNN
HN
HUHN
HNN

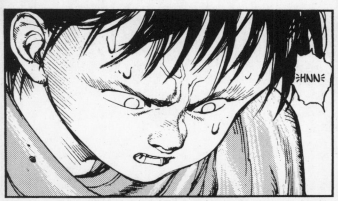

≈HNN≈ ≈HN≈

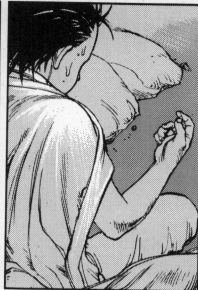

PLOP

SO, FRIEND, YOU FIGURE OUT WHAT THAT SCREAM WAS?

NOPE.

LOOKS PRETTY PEACEFUL, DOESN'T IT? LITTLE AKIRA, PLAYING IN THE WATER, LIKE ANY NORMAL KID...

YOU WON'T, SITTING ALL THE WAY OVER HERE, LOOKING THROUGH BINOCULARS. WHY DON'T YOU GO AND SEE?

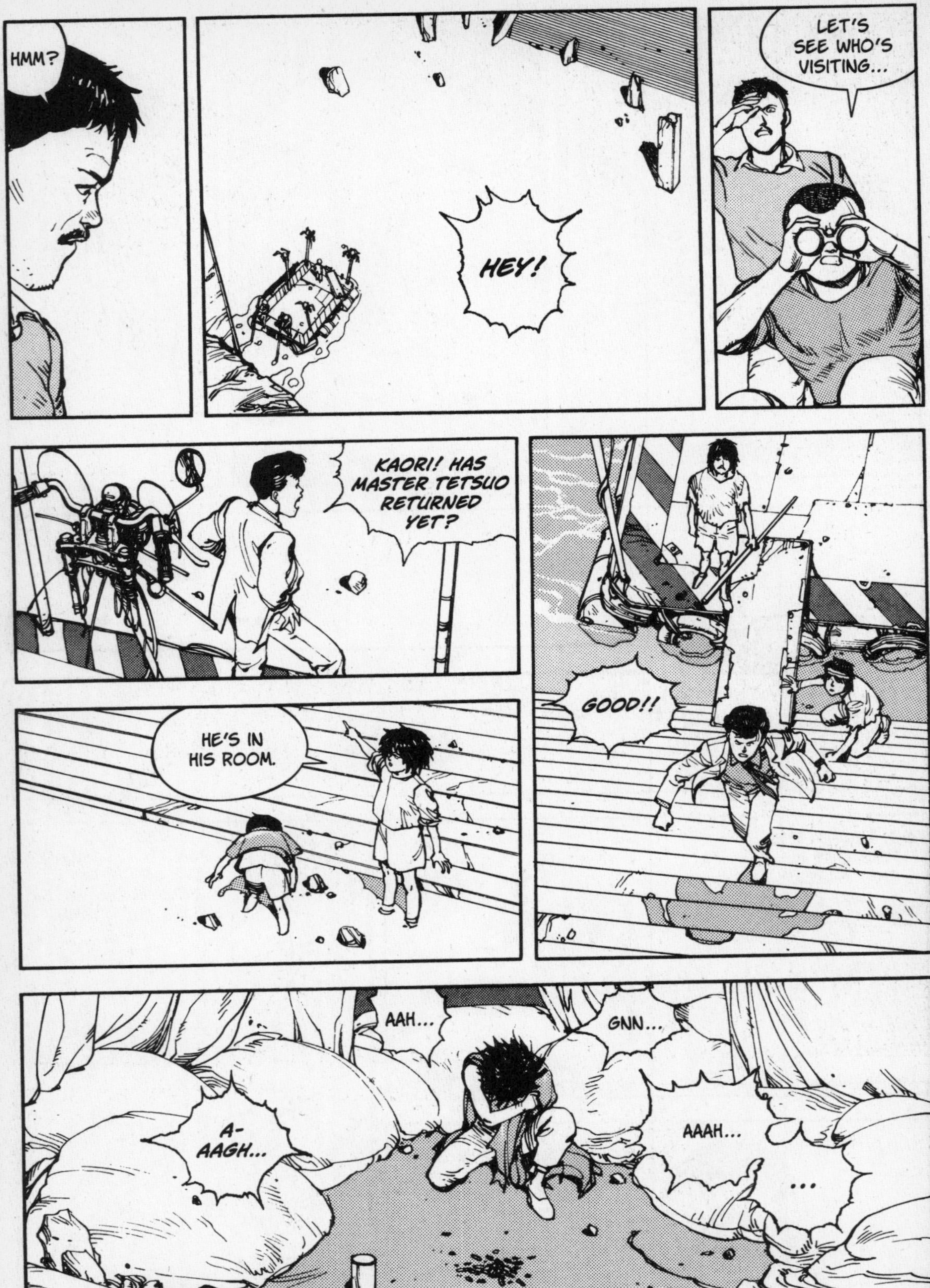
HMM?
HEY!
LET'S SEE WHO'S VISITING...
KAORI! HAS MASTER TETSUO RETURNED YET?
HE'S IN HIS ROOM.
GOOD!!
AAH...
GNN...
A- AAGH...
AAAH...
...

DODOM

GNN...
GNNNN...

AAUGH!

TCHOOF

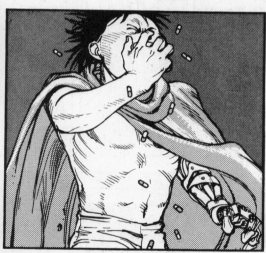

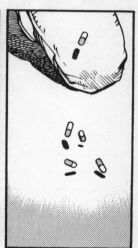

231

WHAT DO YOU WANT?!

IT...IT'S ABOUT THOSE KIDS WE WERE AFTER...

GET LOST.

BUT, MASTER TETSUO, ONE OF THEM... ...IS IN THE HANDS OF MIYAKO'S MONKS.

GET YOUR ASS OUT OF HERE!

Y-YESSIR!

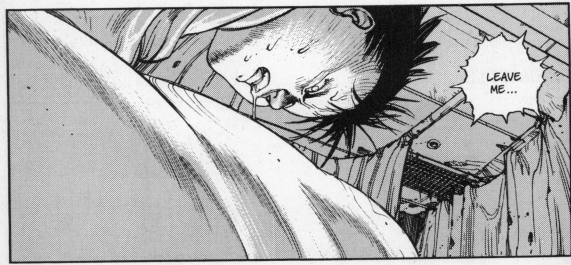
LEAVE ME...

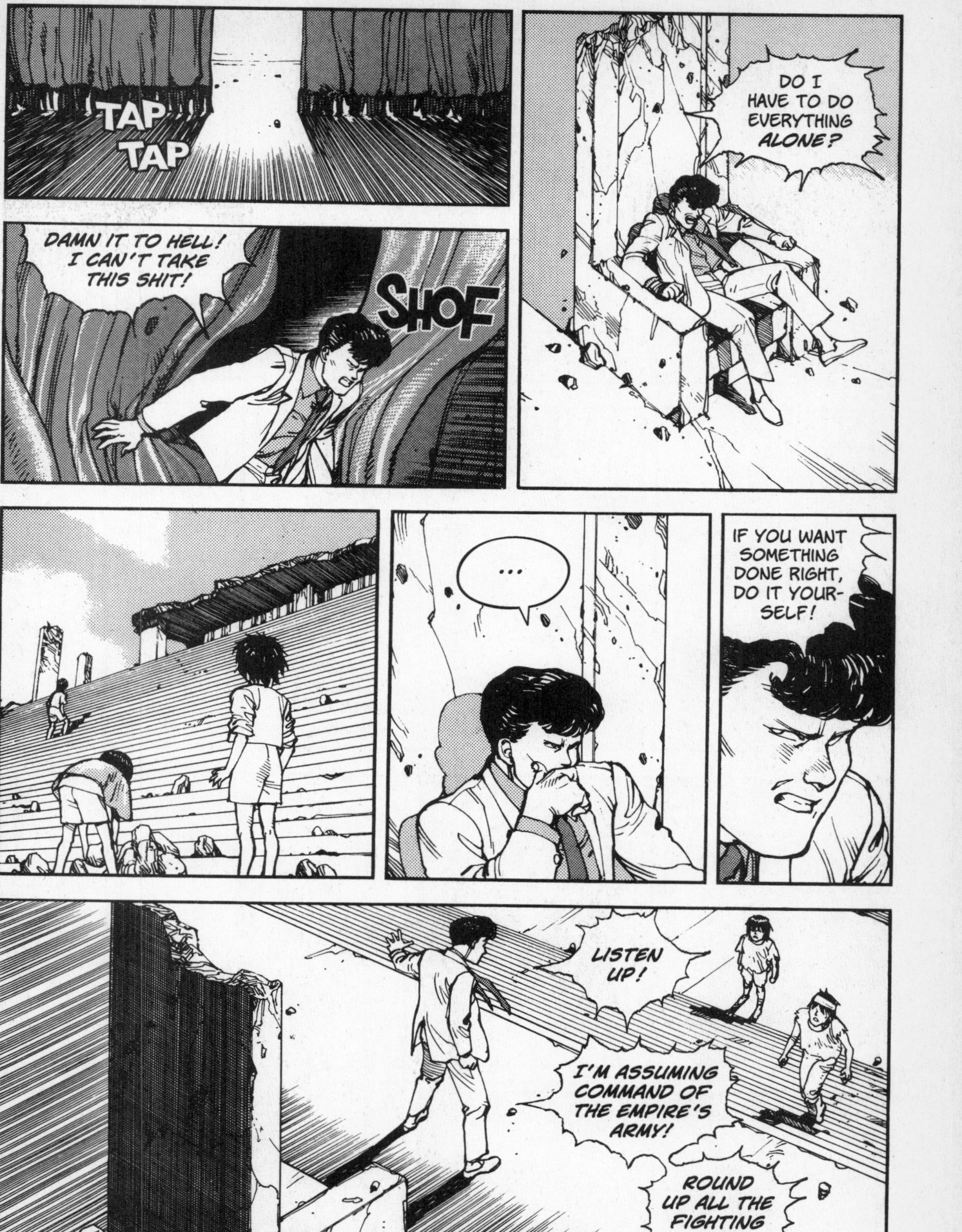
TAP
TAP
DO I HAVE TO DO EVERYTHING ALONE?
DAMN IT TO HELL! I CAN'T TAKE THIS SHIT!
SHOF
...
IF YOU WANT SOMETHING DONE RIGHT, DO IT YOUR-SELF!
LISTEN UP!
I'M ASSUMING COMMAND OF THE EMPIRE'S ARMY!
ROUND UP ALL THE FIGHTING MEN!

DID YOU REMEMBER MY CIGARETTES?

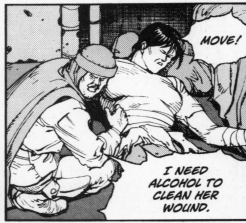
MOVE!

I NEED ALCOHOL TO CLEAN HER WOUND.

A FEW CIGARETTES ISN'T SO MUCH TO ASK FOR...

SRiiiC

...YOU ALWAYS FORGET MY CIGA-RETTES...AND YOU PROMISED!

AH ....!

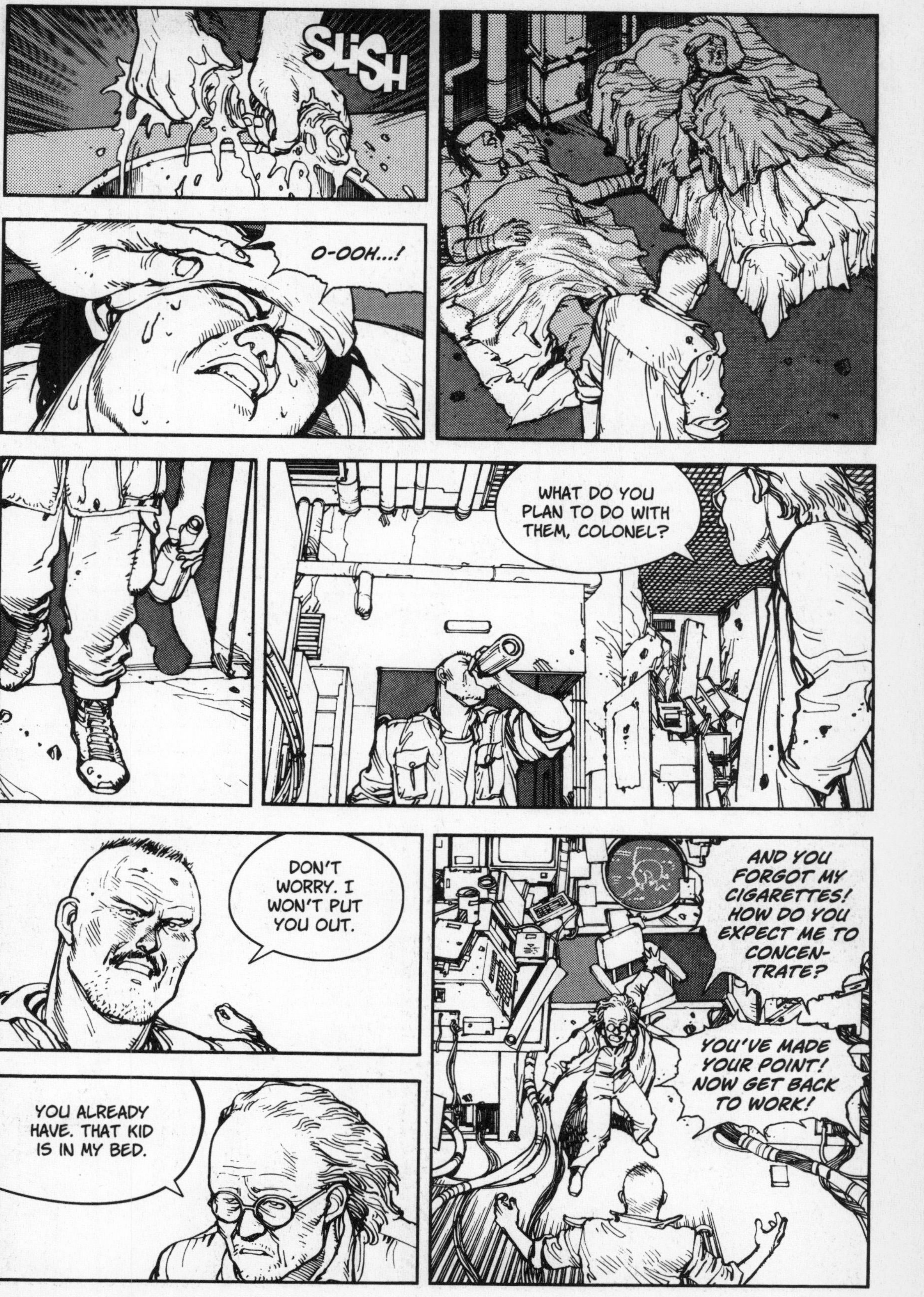
SLISH
O-OOH...!
WHAT DO YOU PLAN TO DO WITH THEM, COLONEL?
DON'T WORRY. I WON'T PUT YOU OUT.
AND YOU FORGOT MY CIGARETTES! HOW DO YOU EXPECT ME TO CONCEN-TRATE?
YOU'VE MADE YOUR POINT! NOW GET BACK TO WORK!
YOU ALREADY HAVE. THAT KID IS IN MY BED.

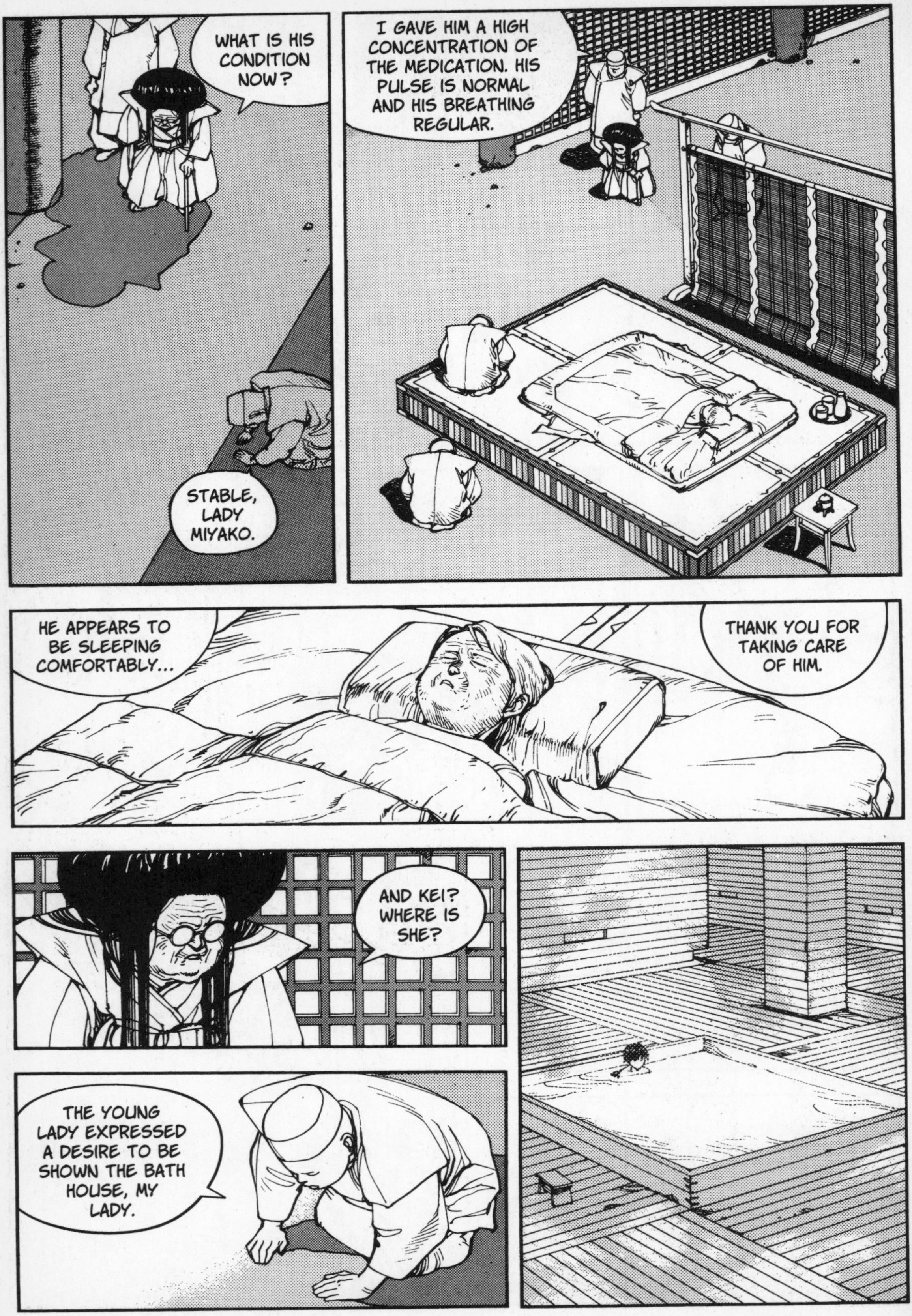
WHAT IS HIS CONDITION NOW?
STABLE, LADY MIYAKO.
I GAVE HIM A HIGH CONCENTRATION OF THE MEDICATION. HIS PULSE IS NORMAL AND HIS BREATHING REGULAR.
HE APPEARS TO BE SLEEPING COMFORTABLY...
THANK YOU FOR TAKING CARE OF HIM.
AND KEI? WHERE IS SHE?
THE YOUNG LADY EXPRESSED A DESIRE TO BE SHOWN THE BATH HOUSE, MY LADY.

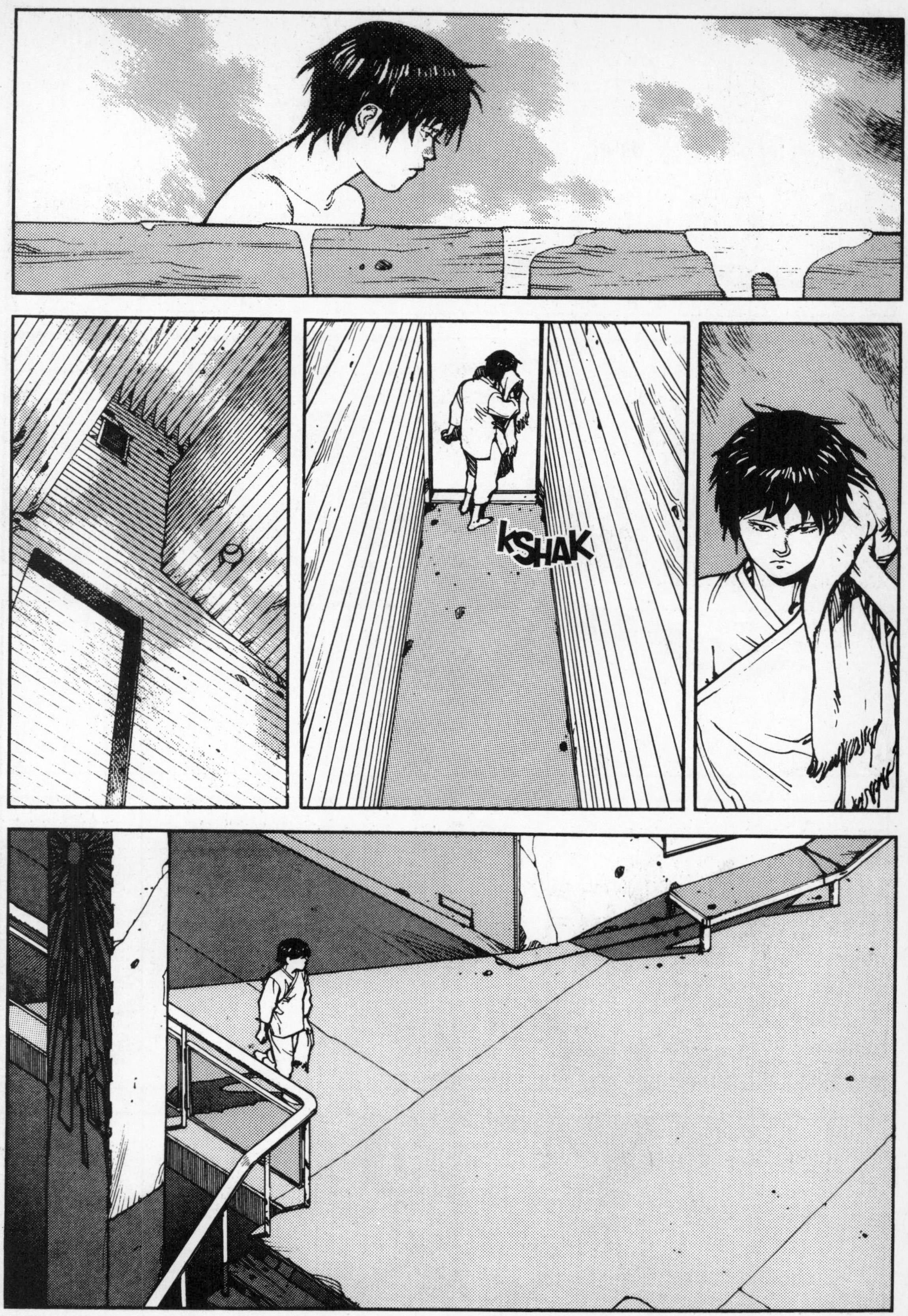
KSHAK

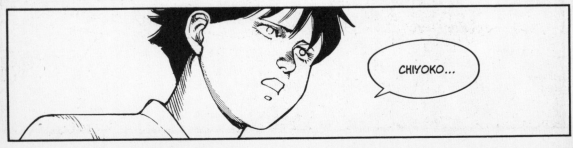

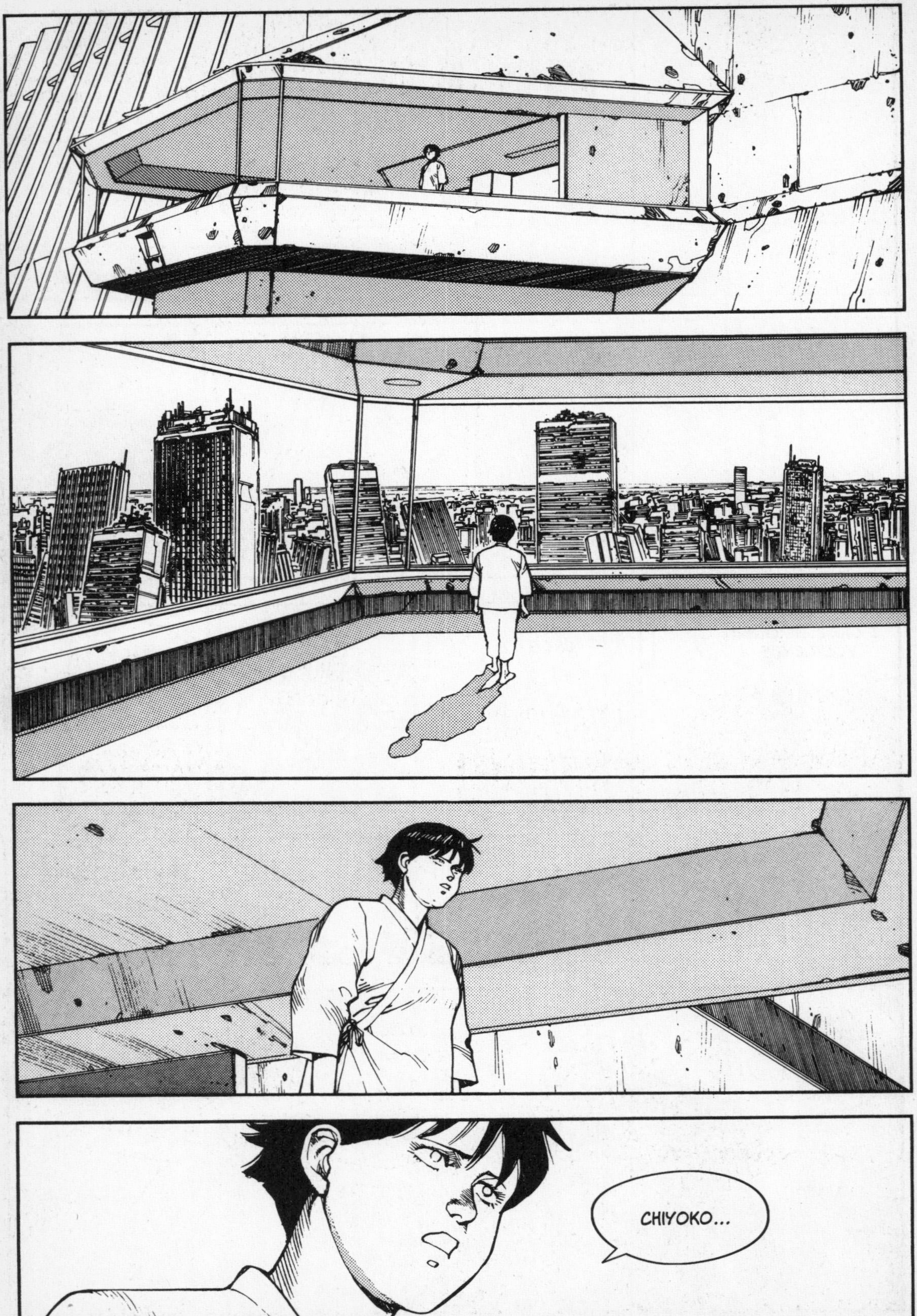
CHIYOKO...

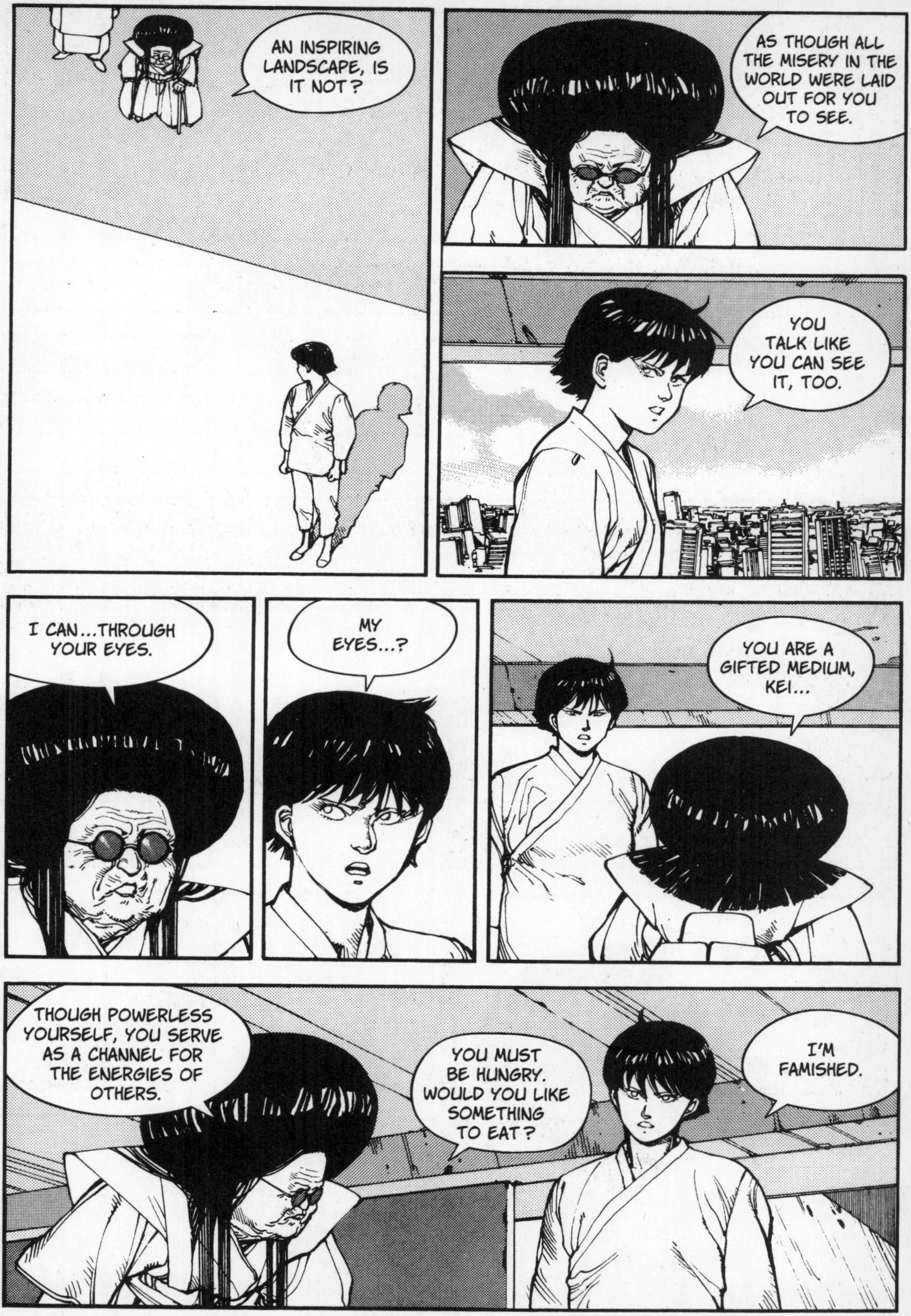
AN INSPIRING LANDSCAPE, IS IT NOT?
AS THOUGH ALL THE MISERY IN THE WORLD WERE LAID OUT FOR YOU TO SEE.
YOU TALK LIKE YOU CAN SEE IT, TOO.
I CAN...THROUGH YOUR EYES.
MY EYES...?
YOU ARE A GIFTED MEDIUM, KEI...
THOUGH POWERLESS YOURSELF, YOU SERVE AS A CHANNEL FOR THE ENERGIES OF OTHERS.
YOU MUST BE HUNGRY. WOULD YOU LIKE SOMETHING TO EAT?
I'M FAMISHED.

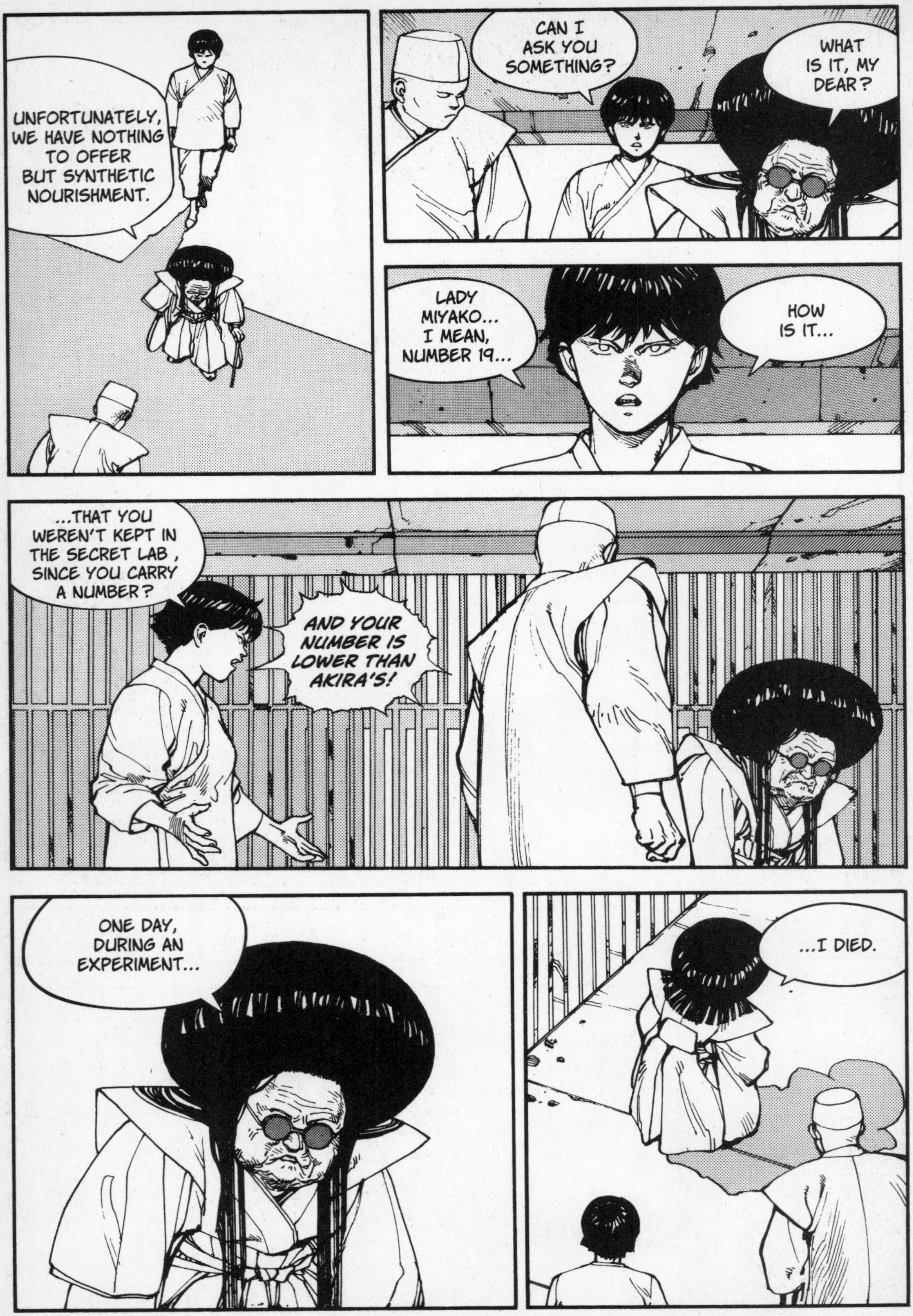
UNFORTUNATELY, WE HAVE NOTHING TO OFFER BUT SYNTHETIC NOURISHMENT.
CAN I ASK YOU SOMETHING?
WHAT IS IT, MY DEAR?
LADY MIYAKO... I MEAN, NUMBER 19...
HOW IS IT...
...THAT YOU WEREN'T KEPT IN THE SECRET LAB , SINCE YOU CARRY A NUMBER?
AND YOUR NUMBER IS LOWER THAN AKIRA'S!
ONE DAY, DURING AN EXPERIMENT...
...I DIED.

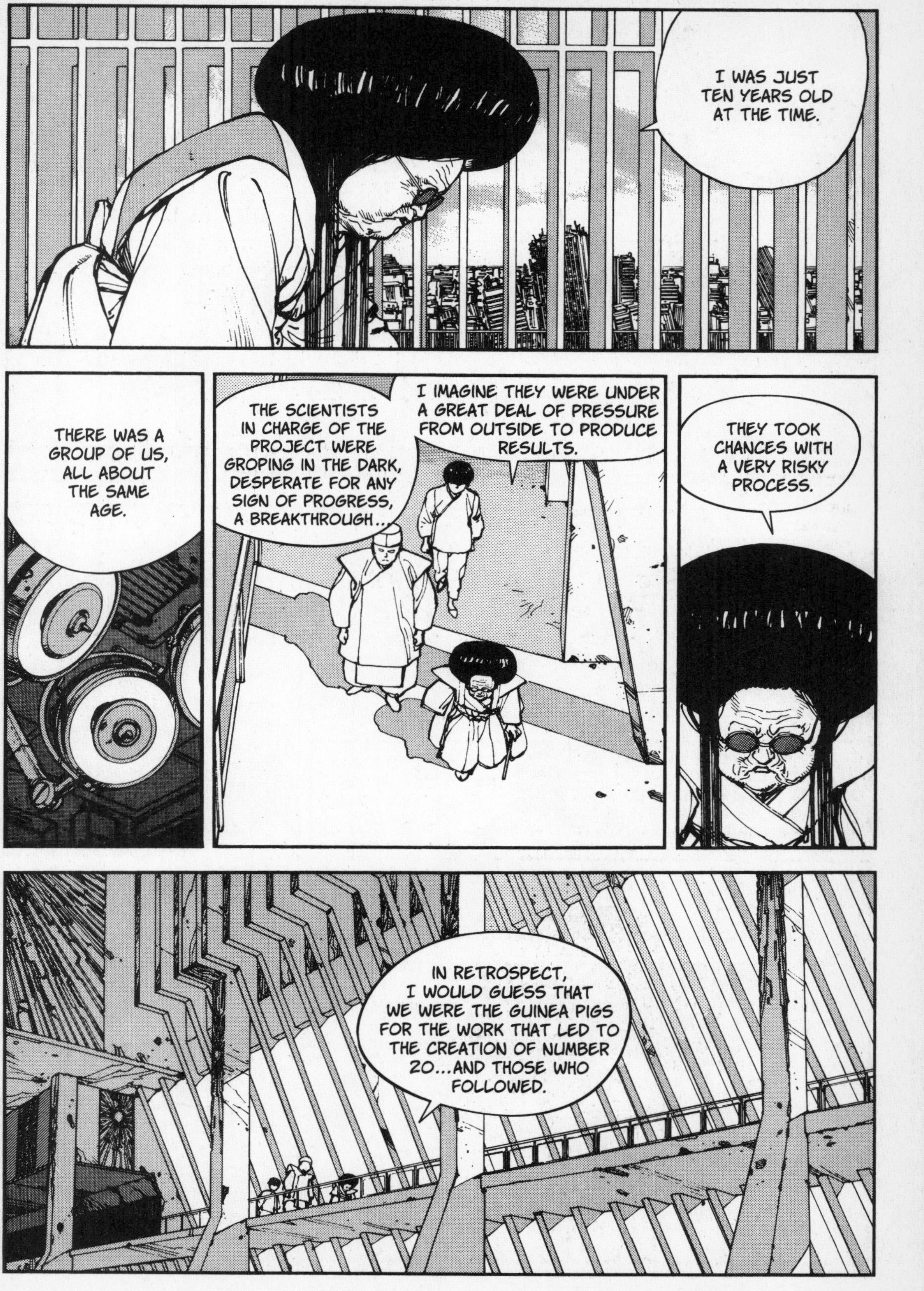
I WAS JUST TEN YEARS OLD AT THE TIME.
THERE WAS A GROUP OF US, ALL ABOUT THE SAME AGE.
THE SCIENTISTS IN CHARGE OF THE PROJECT WERE GROPING IN THE DARK, DESPERATE FOR ANY SIGN OF PROGRESS, A BREAKTHROUGH...
I IMAGINE THEY WERE UNDER A GREAT DEAL OF PRESSURE FROM OUTSIDE TO PRODUCE RESULTS.
THEY TOOK CHANCES WITH A VERY RISKY PROCESS.
IN RETROSPECT, I WOULD GUESS THAT WE WERE THE GUINEA PIGS FOR THE WORK THAT LED TO THE CREATION OF NUMBER 20...AND THOSE WHO FOLLOWED.

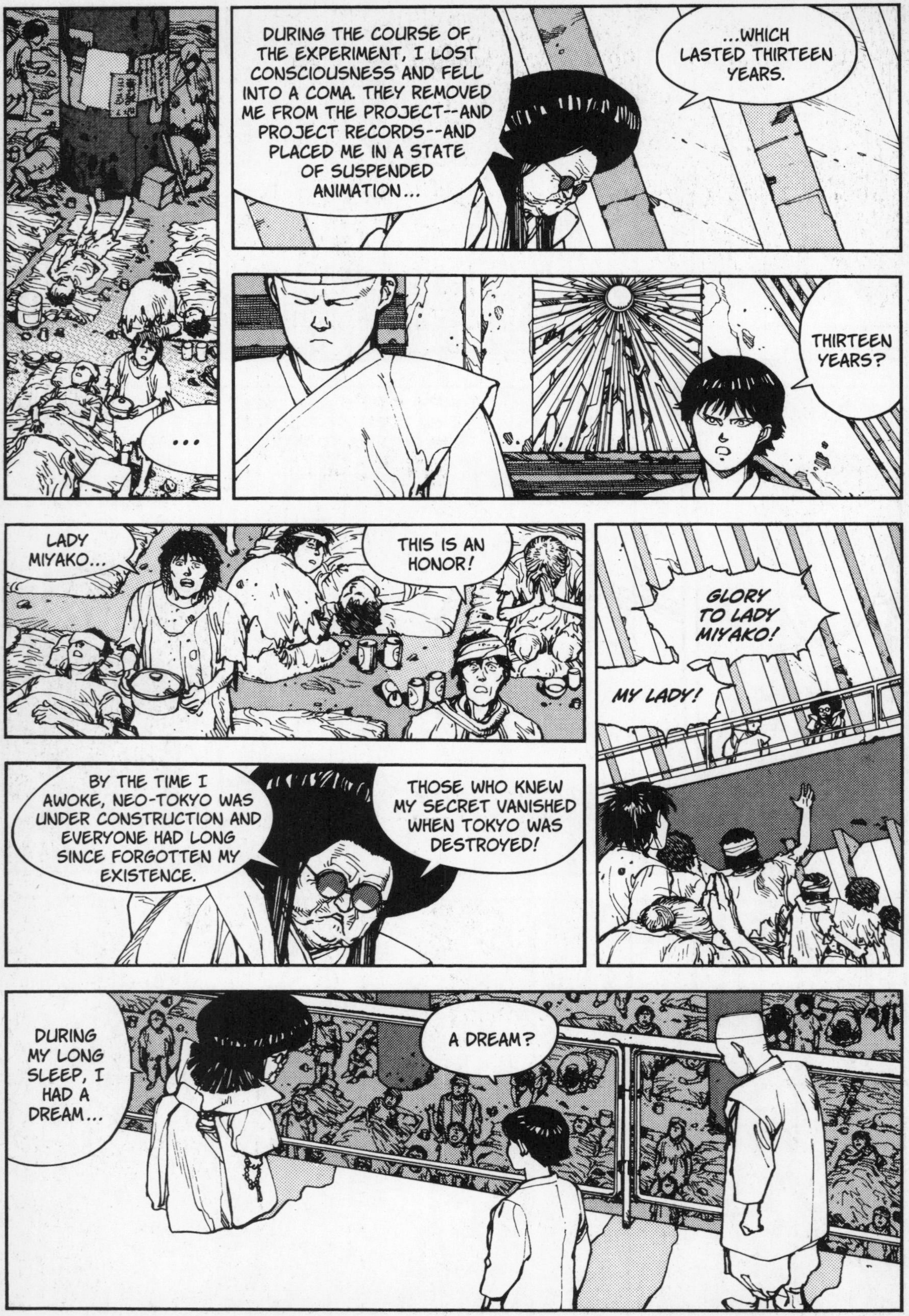
...
DURING THE COURSE OF THE EXPERIMENT, I LOST CONSCIOUSNESS AND FELL INTO A COMA. THEY REMOVED ME FROM THE PROJECT--AND PROJECT RECORDS--AND PLACED ME IN A STATE OF SUSPENDED ANIMATION...
...WHICH LASTED THIRTEEN YEARS.
THIRTEEN YEARS?
LADY MIYAKO...
THIS IS AN HONOR!
BY THE TIME I AWOKE, NEO-TOKYO WAS UNDER CONSTRUCTION AND EVERYONE HAD LONG SINCE FORGOTTEN MY EXISTENCE.
THOSE WHO KNEW MY SECRET VANISHED WHEN TOKYO WAS DESTROYED!
GLORY TO LADY MIYAKO!
MY LADY!
DURING MY LONG SLEEP, I HAD A DREAM...
A DREAM?

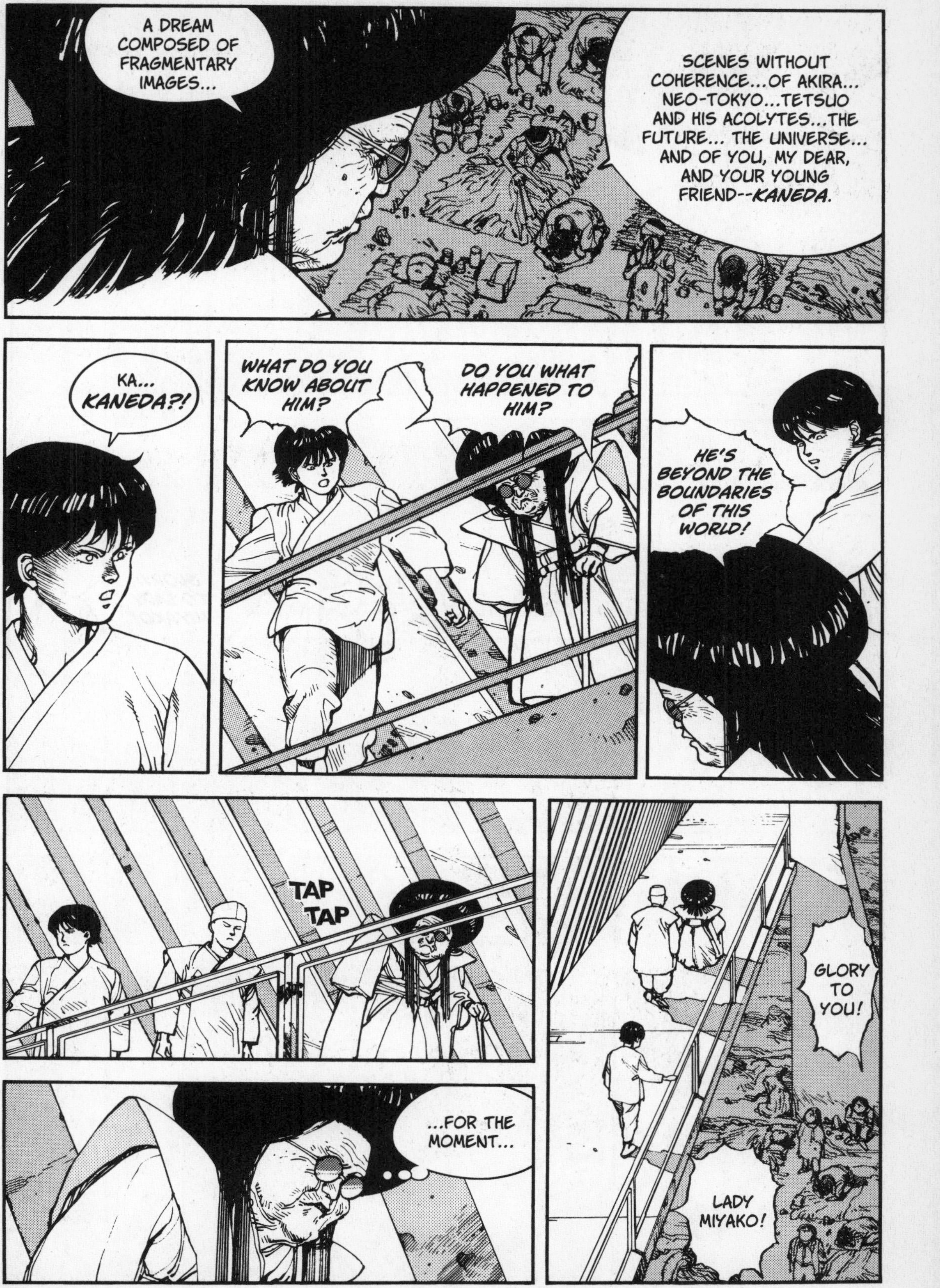
A DREAM COMPOSED OF FRAGMENTARY IMAGES...
SCENES WITHOUT COHERENCE...OF AKIRA... NEO-TOKYO...TETSUO AND HIS ACOLYTES...THE FUTURE... THE UNIVERSE... AND OF YOU, MY DEAR, AND YOUR YOUNG FRIEND--KANEDA.
KA... KANEDA?!
WHAT DO YOU KNOW ABOUT HIM?
DO YOU WHAT HAPPENED TO HIM?
HE'S BEYOND THE BOUNDARIES OF THIS WORLD!
TAP TAP
...FOR THE MOMENT...
GLORY TO YOU!
LADY MIYAKO!

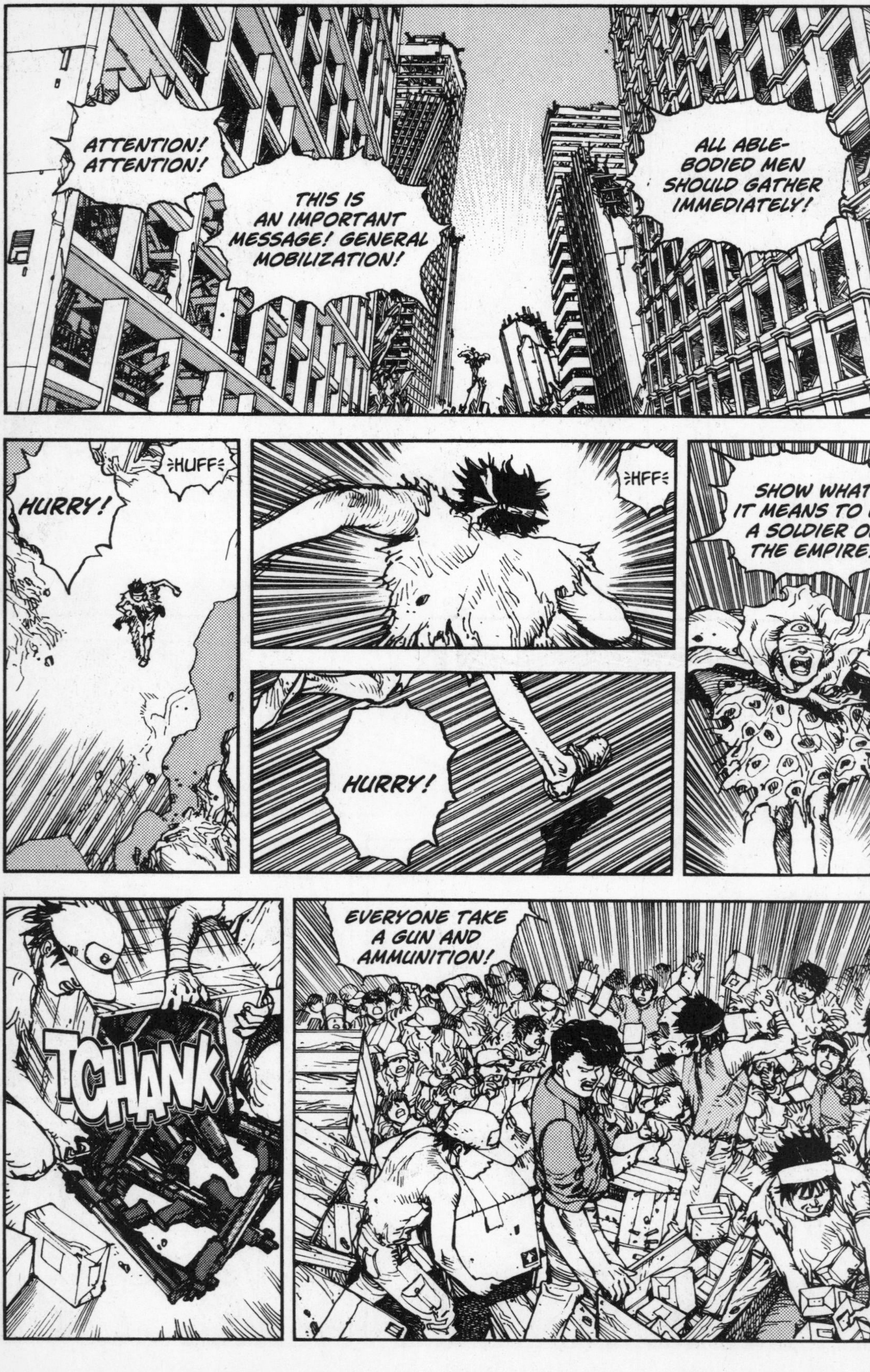
ATTENTION! ATTENTION!
THIS IS AN IMPORTANT MESSAGE! GENERAL MOBILIZATION!
ALL ABLE-BODIED MEN SHOULD GATHER IMMEDIATELY!
HUFF
HURRY!
HFF
SHOW WHAT IT MEANS TO BE A SOLDIER OF THE EMPIRE!
HURRY!
TCHANK
EVERYONE TAKE A GUN AND AMMUNITION!

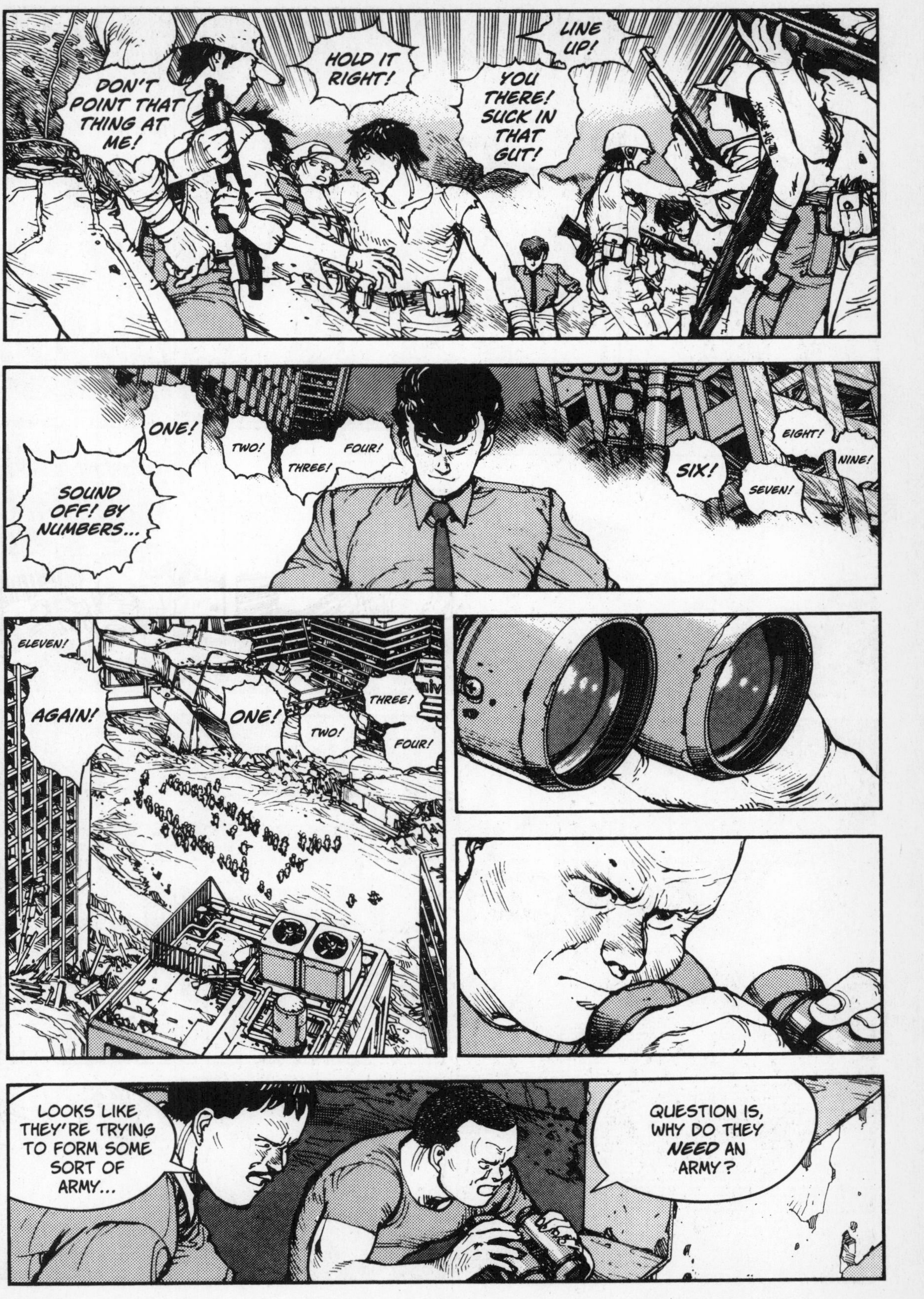
DON'T POINT THAT THING AT ME!
HOLD IT RIGHT!
LINE UP!
YOU THERE! SUCK IN THAT GUT!
SOUND OFF! BY NUMBERS...
ONE!
TWO!
THREE!
FOUR!
SIX!
EIGHT!
SEVEN!
NINE!
ELEVEN!
AGAIN!
ONE!
TWO!
THREE!
FOUR!
LOOKS LIKE THEY'RE TRYING TO FORM SOME SORT OF ARMY...
QUESTION IS, WHY DO THEY *NEED* AN ARMY?

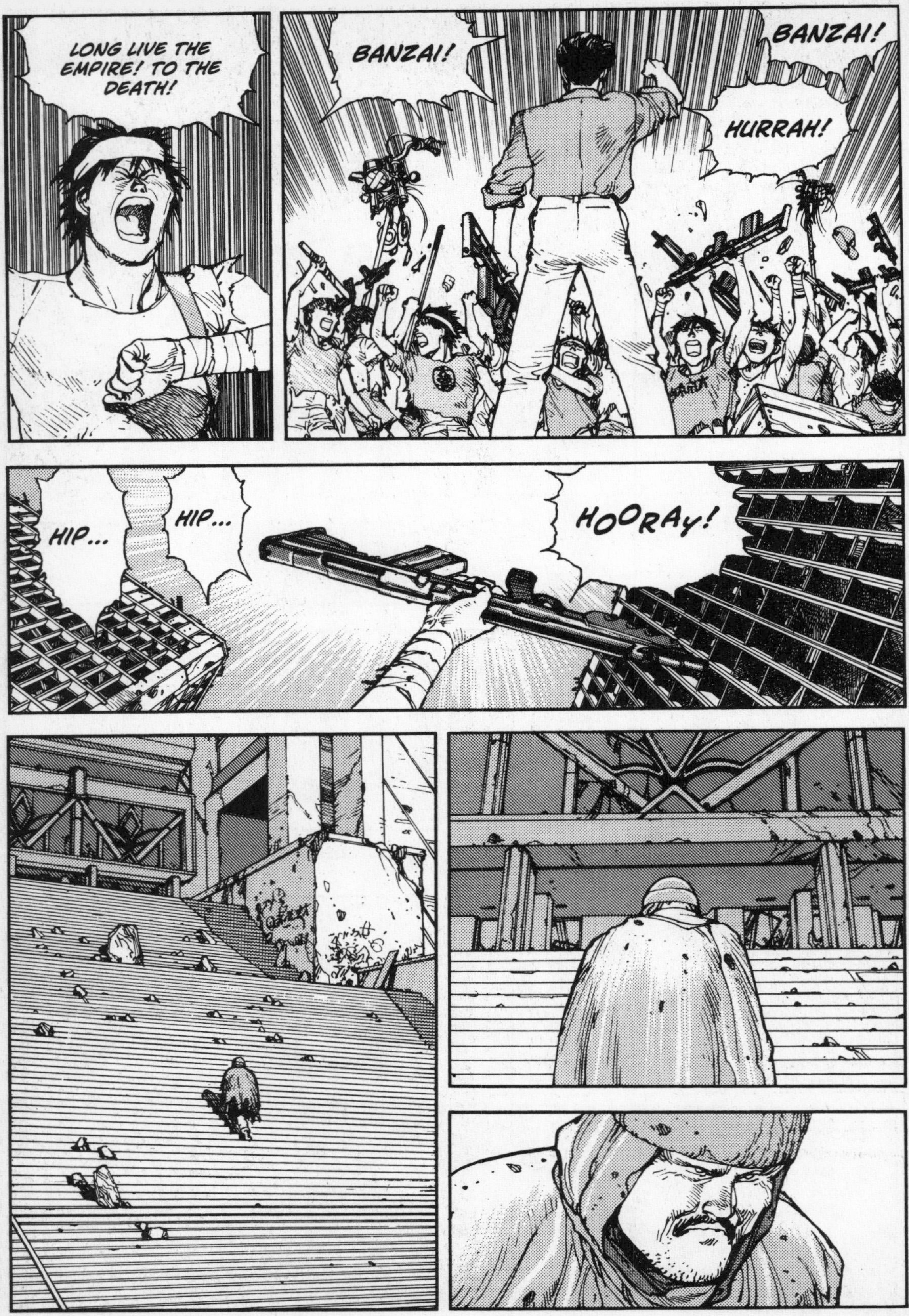
LONG LIVE THE EMPIRE! TO THE DEATH!
BANZAI!
BANZAI!
HURRAH!
HIP...
HIP...
HOORAY!

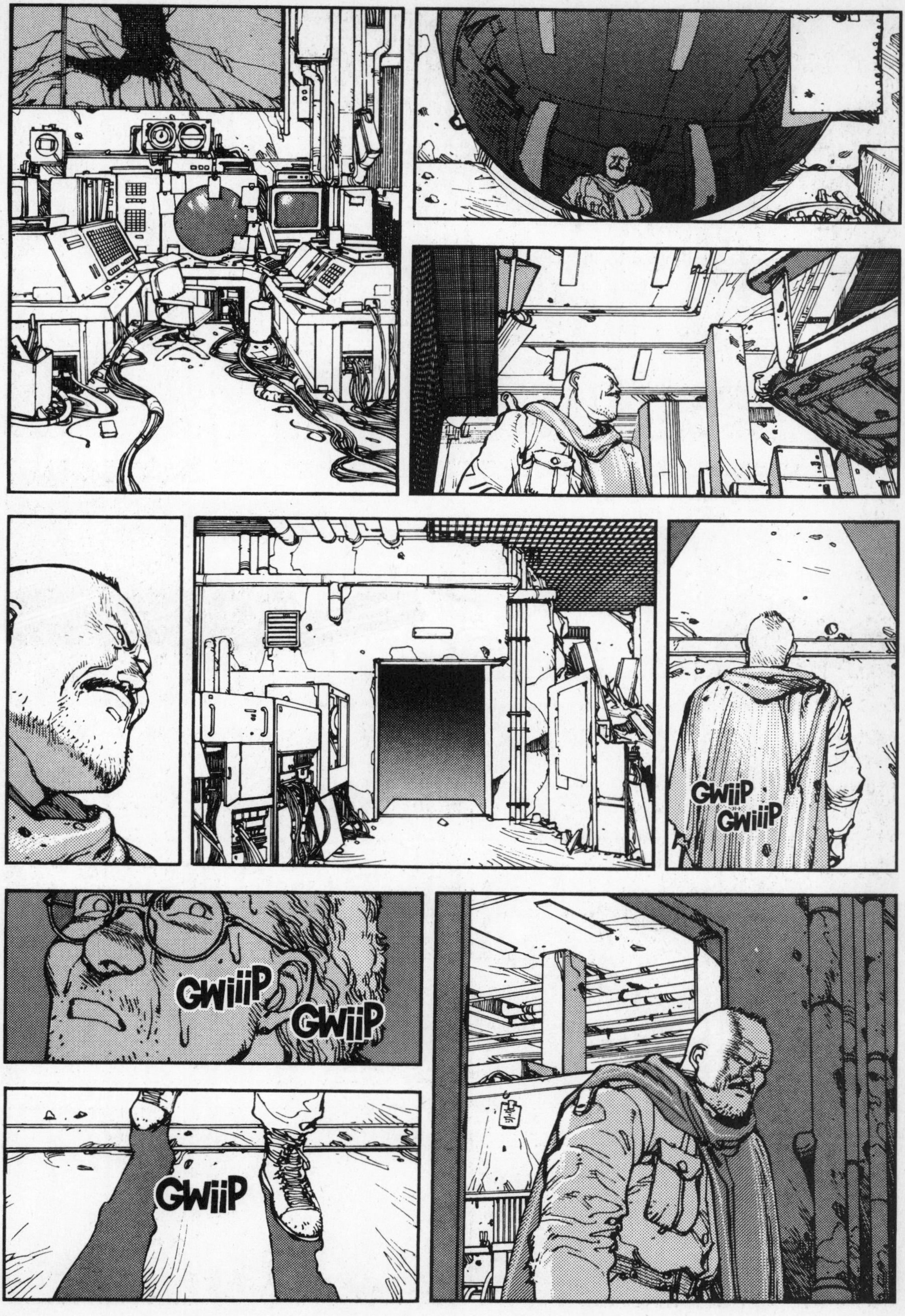
GWiiP
GWiiiP
GWiiiP
GWiiP
GWiiP

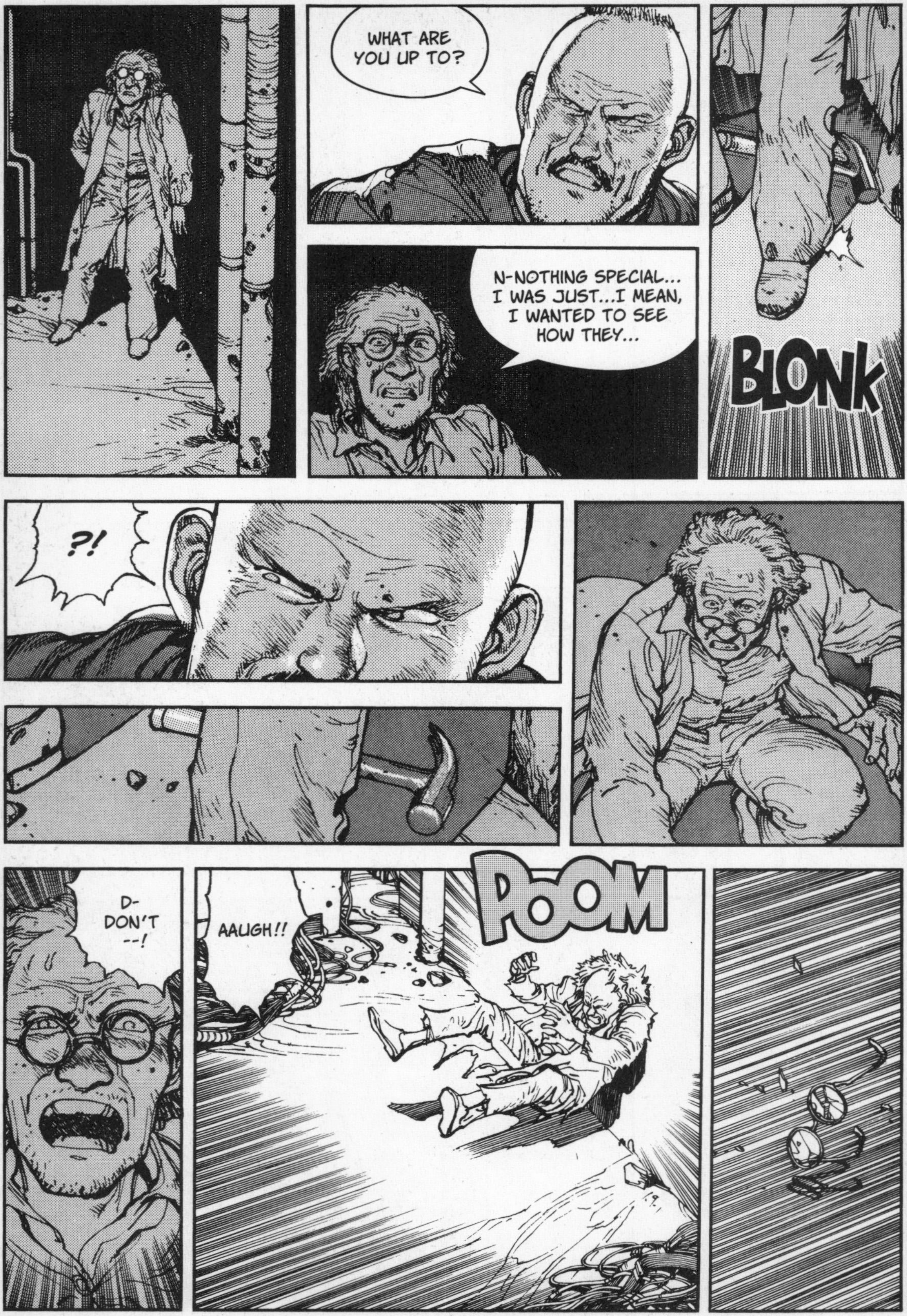
WHAT ARE YOU UP TO?
N-NOTHING SPECIAL... I WAS JUST...I MEAN, I WANTED TO SEE HOW THEY...
BLONK
?!
D-DON'T --!
AAUGH!!
POOM

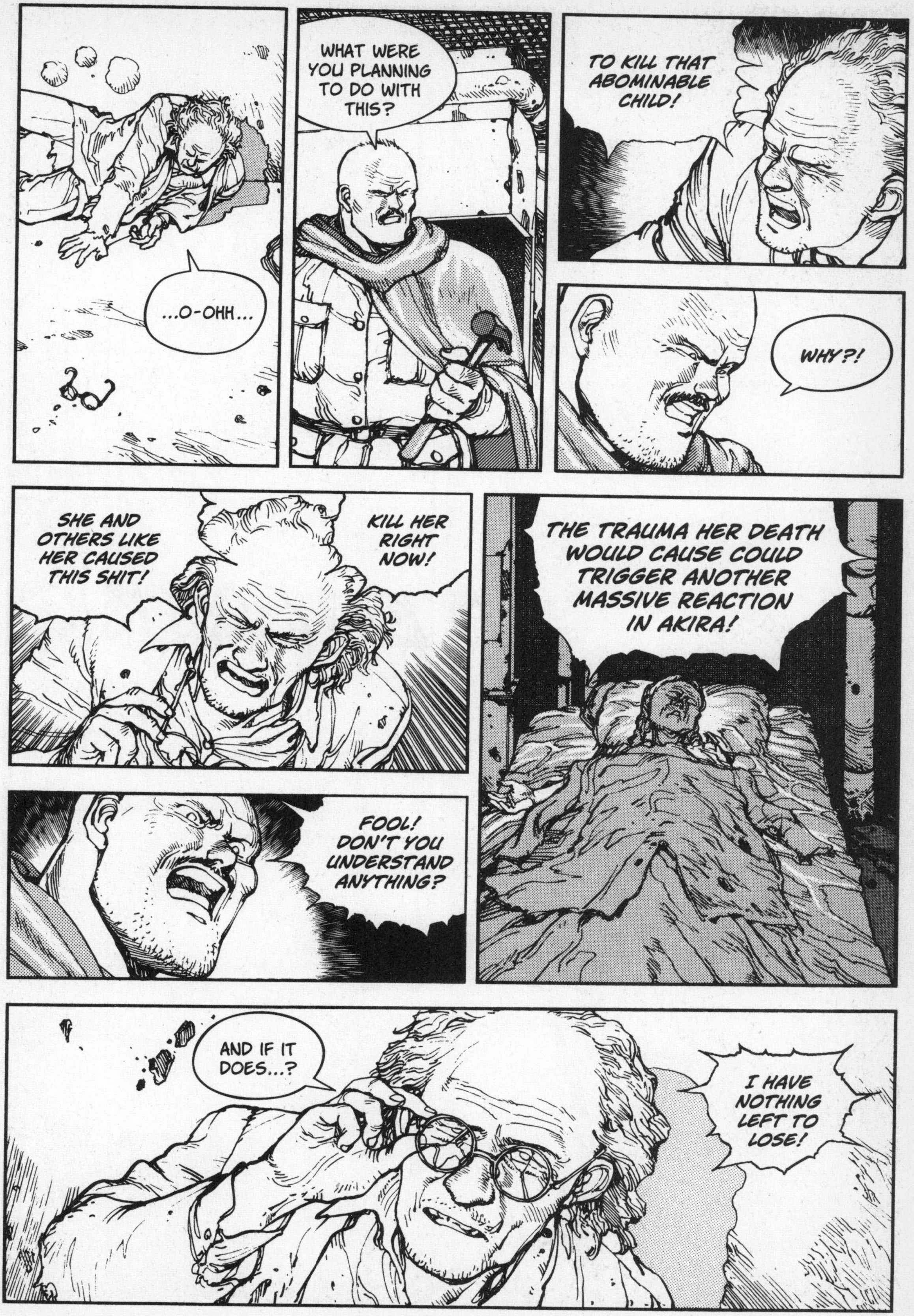
...O-OHH...
WHAT WERE YOU PLANNING TO DO WITH THIS?
TO KILL THAT ABOMINABLE CHILD!
WHY?!
SHE AND OTHERS LIKE HER CAUSED THIS SHIT!
KILL HER RIGHT NOW!
FOOL! DON'T YOU UNDERSTAND ANYTHING?
THE TRAUMA HER DEATH WOULD CAUSE COULD TRIGGER ANOTHER MASSIVE REACTION IN AKIRA!
AND IF IT DOES...?
I HAVE NOTHING LEFT TO LOSE!

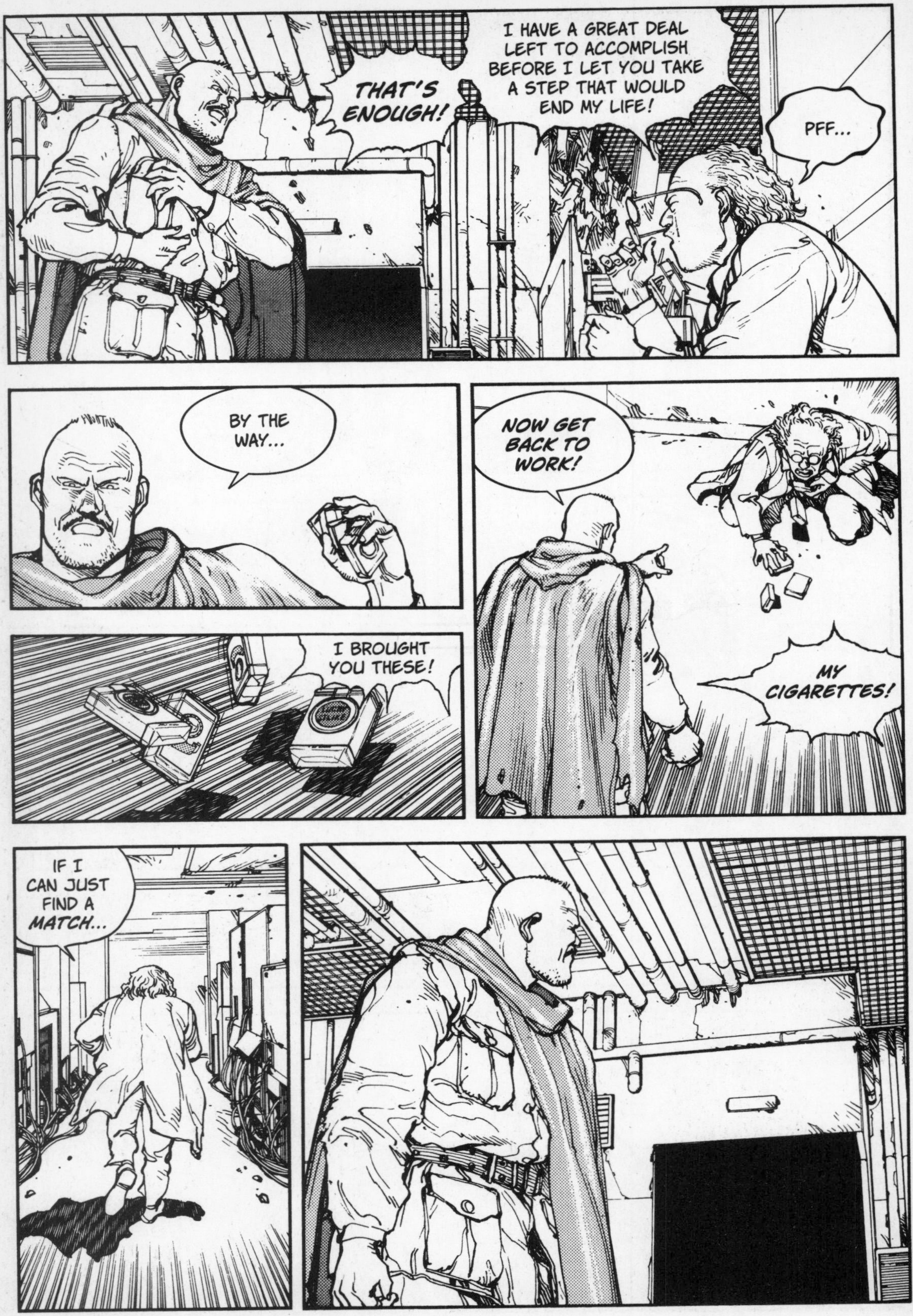
THAT'S ENOUGH!
I HAVE A GREAT DEAL LEFT TO ACCOMPLISH BEFORE I LET YOU TAKE A STEP THAT WOULD END MY LIFE!
PFF...
BY THE WAY...
I BROUGHT YOU THESE!
NOW GET BACK TO WORK!
MY CIGARETTES!
IF I CAN JUST FIND A MATCH...

BOK

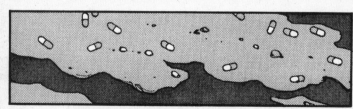

WHAT'S THAT FLOATING IN THE WATER?

251

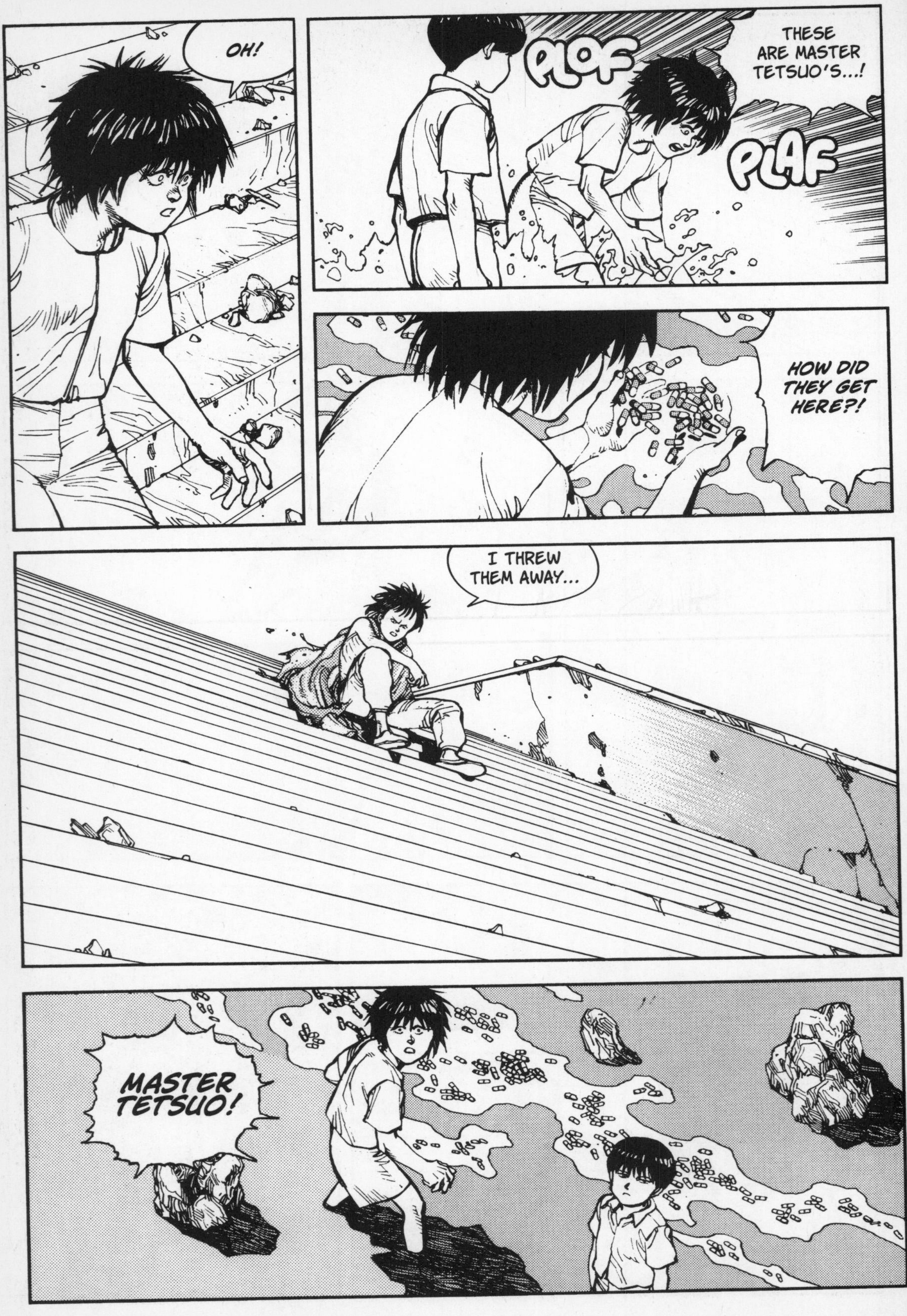
OH!
PLOF
THESE ARE MASTER TETSUO'S...!
PLAF
HOW DID THEY GET HERE?!
I THREW THEM AWAY...
MASTER TETSUO!

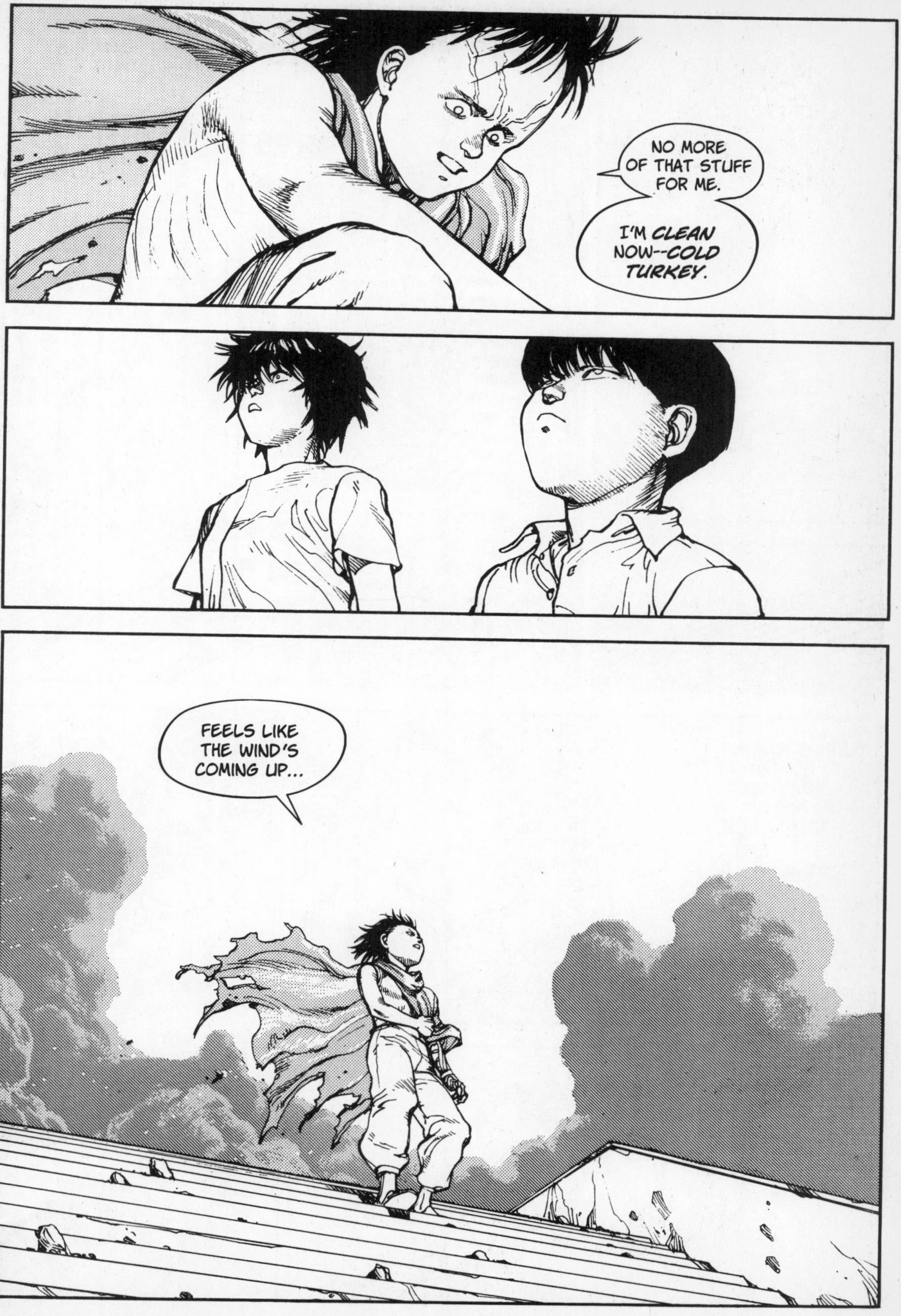
NO MORE OF THAT STUFF FOR ME.
I'M *CLEAN* NOW--*COLD TURKEY*.
FEELS LIKE THE WIND'S COMING UP...

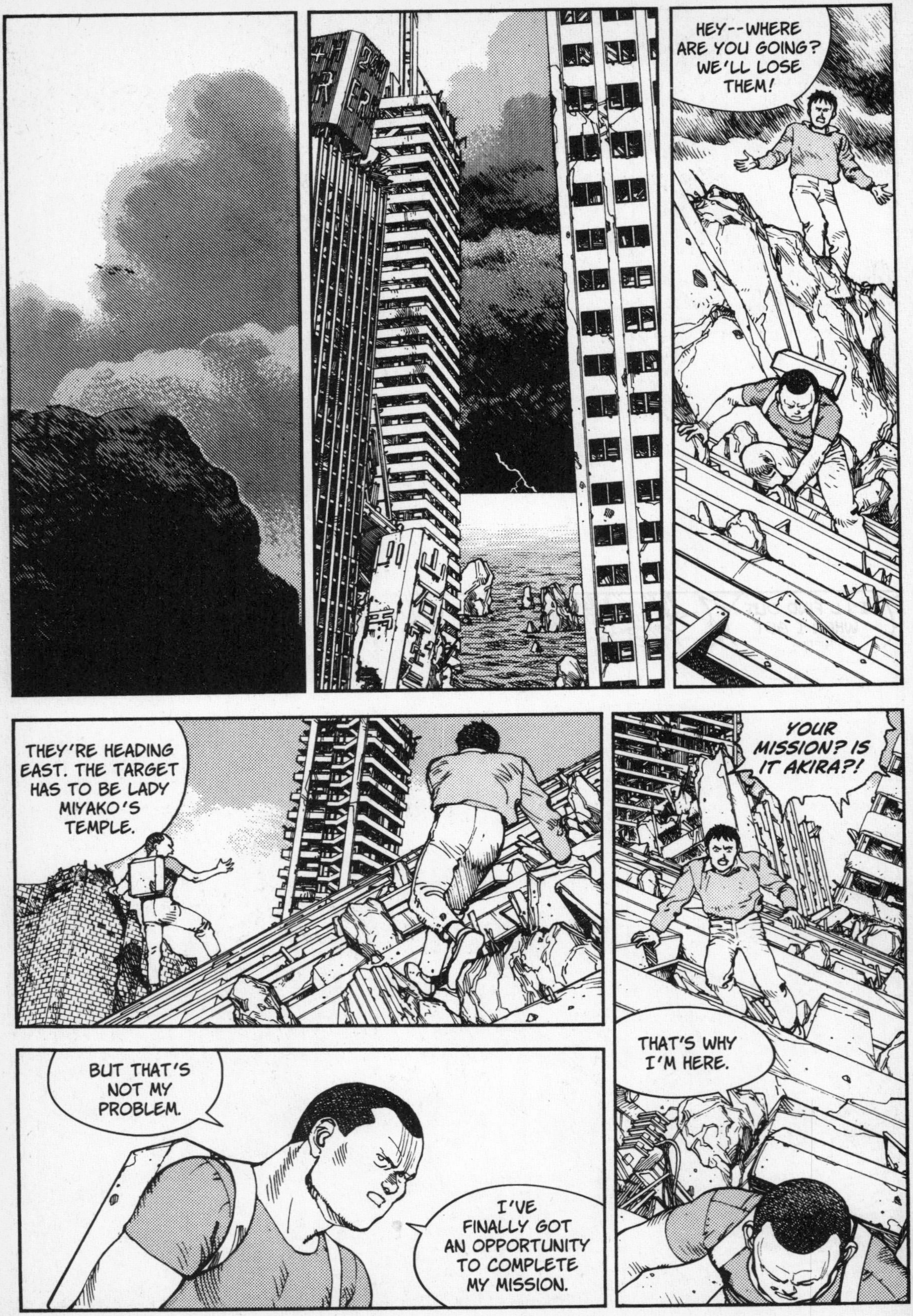
HEY--WHERE ARE YOU GOING? WE'LL LOSE THEM!
THEY'RE HEADING EAST. THE TARGET HAS TO BE LADY MIYAKO'S TEMPLE.
YOUR MISSION? IS IT AKIRA?!
BUT THAT'S NOT MY PROBLEM.
I'VE FINALLY GOT AN OPPORTUNITY TO COMPLETE MY MISSION.
THAT'S WHY I'M HERE.

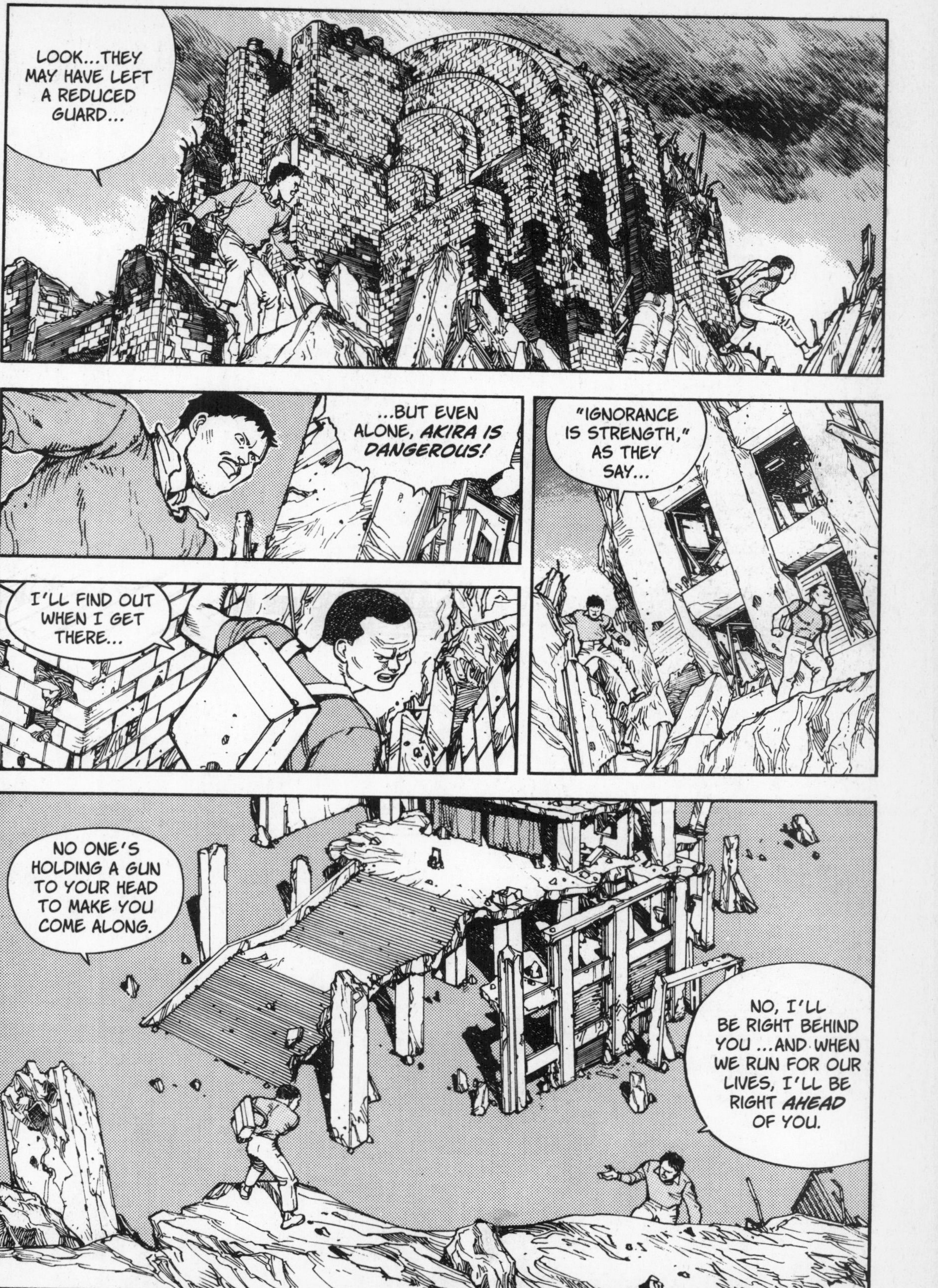
LOOK...THEY MAY HAVE LEFT A REDUCED GUARD...
...BUT EVEN ALONE, AKIRA IS DANGEROUS!
"IGNORANCE IS STRENGTH," AS THEY SAY...
I'LL FIND OUT WHEN I GET THERE...
NO ONE'S HOLDING A GUN TO YOUR HEAD TO MAKE YOU COME ALONG.
NO, I'LL BE RIGHT BEHIND YOU ...AND WHEN WE RUN FOR OUR LIVES, I'LL BE RIGHT AHEAD OF YOU.

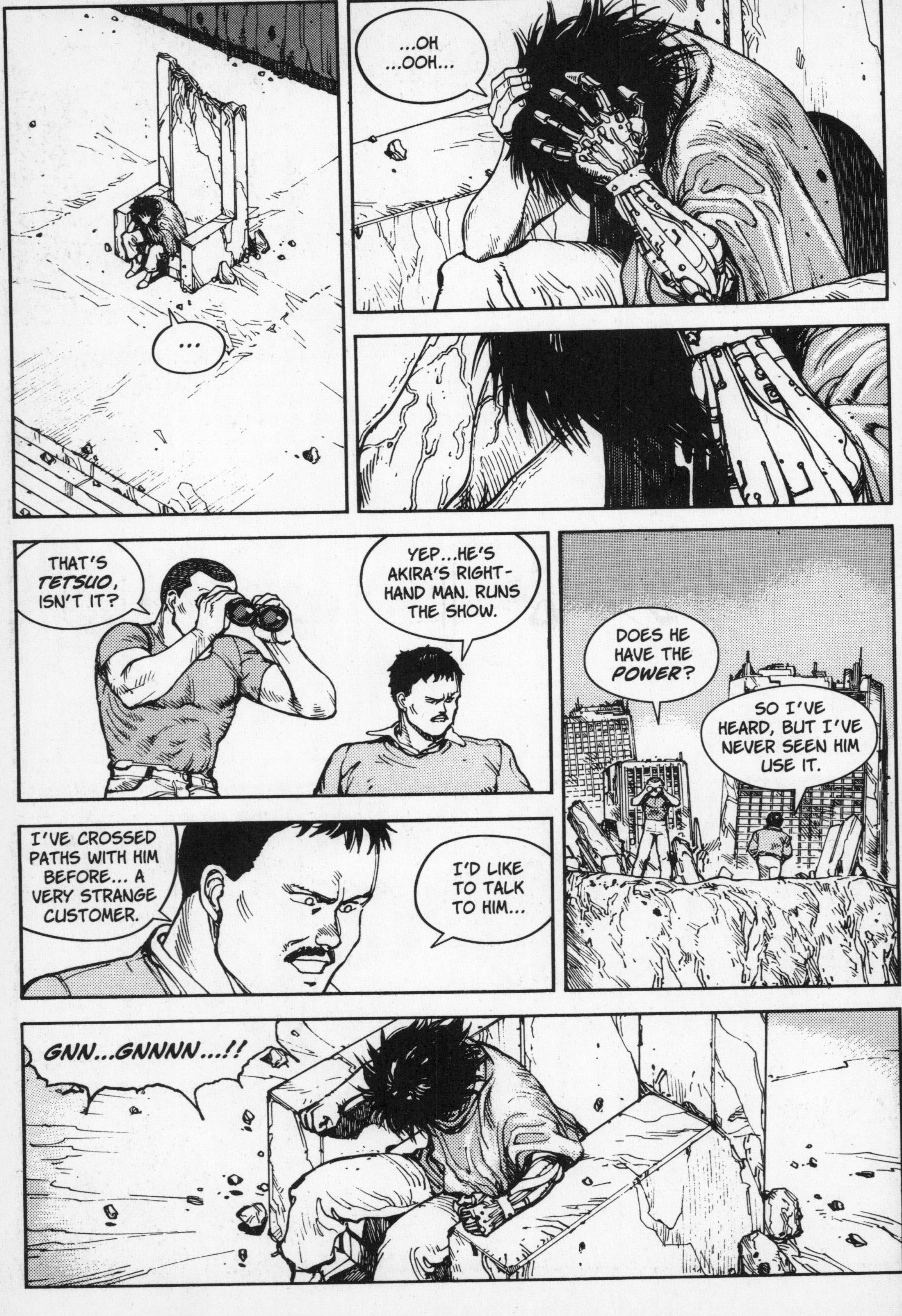
...
...OH
...OOH...
THAT'S *TETSUO*, ISN'T IT?
YEP...HE'S AKIRA'S RIGHT-HAND MAN. RUNS THE SHOW.
I'VE CROSSED PATHS WITH HIM BEFORE... A VERY STRANGE CUSTOMER.
I'D LIKE TO TALK TO HIM...
DOES HE HAVE THE *POWER*?
SO I'VE HEARD, BUT I'VE NEVER SEEN HIM USE IT.
*GNN...GNNNN...!!*

GWAAAH!

BOW

...AAH...

AAAAH!

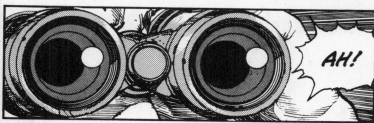

AH!

WHAT'S UP?
YOU SEE A
GHOST?

...

HE...

HE
VANISHED!

257

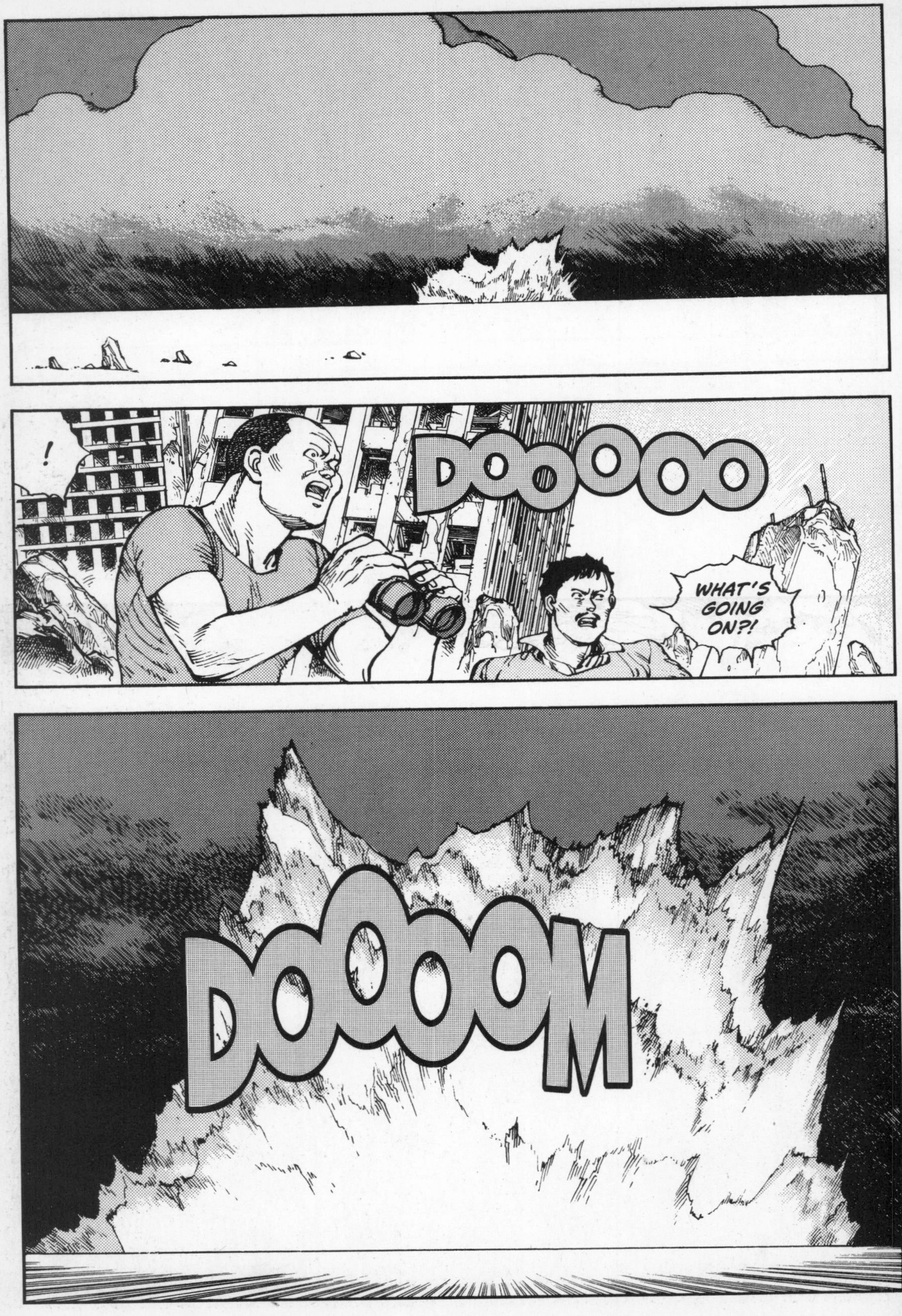
!
DOOOOO
WHAT'S GOING ON?!
DOOOOM

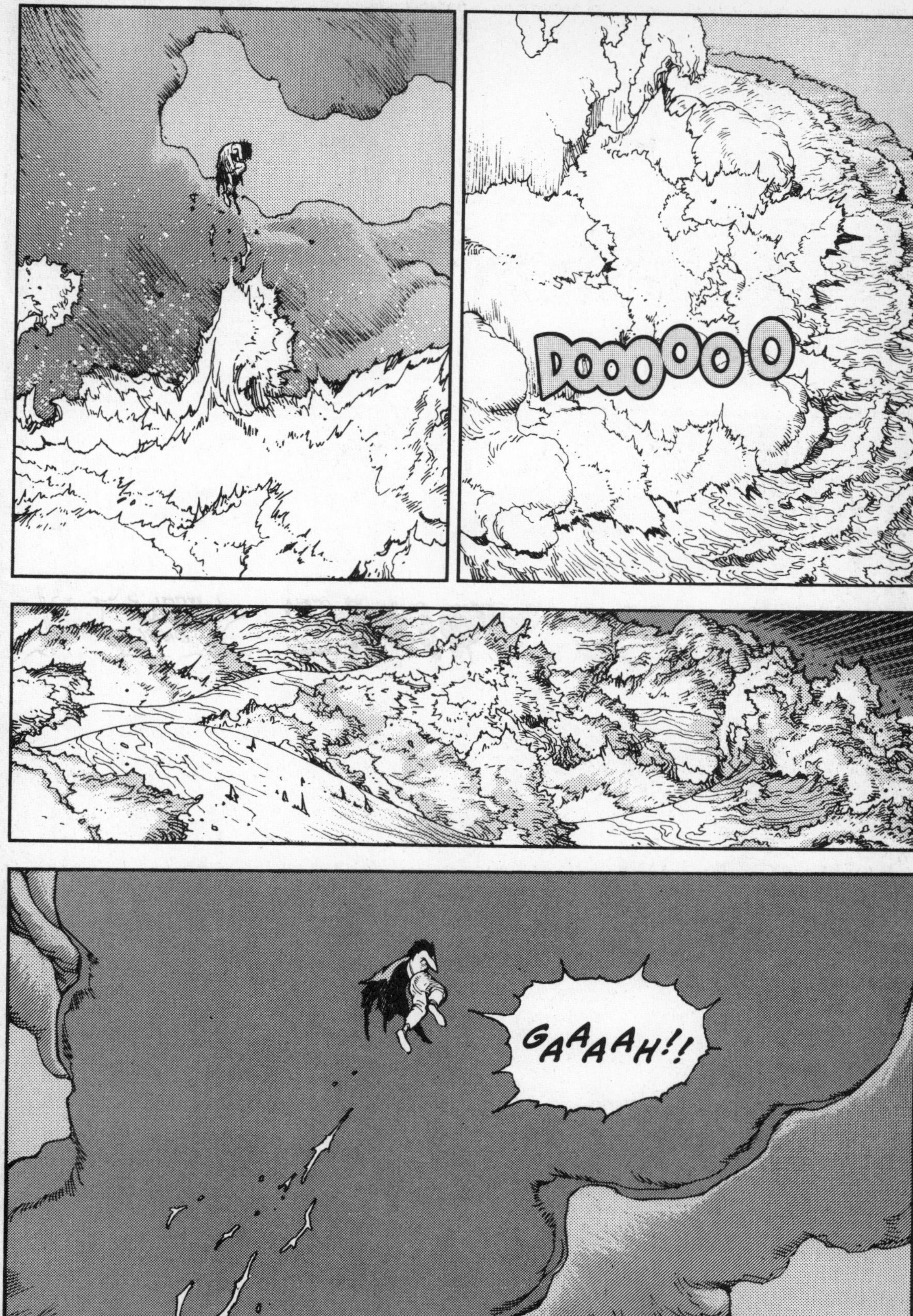
DOOOOOO-O
GAAAAH!!

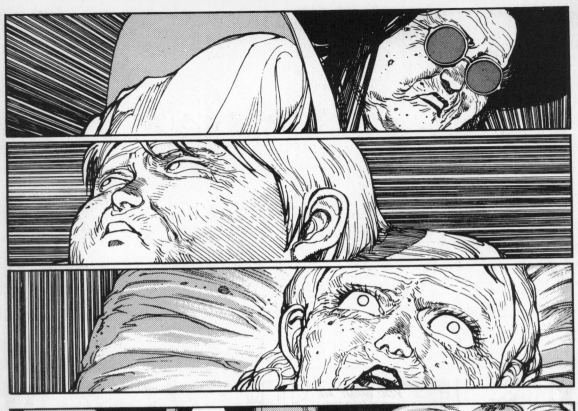

KIYOKO... ARE
YOU AWAKE?

OOOH...
OH...

...

KIYOKO, IT'S ME!
DON'T YOU
RECOGNIZE
ME?!

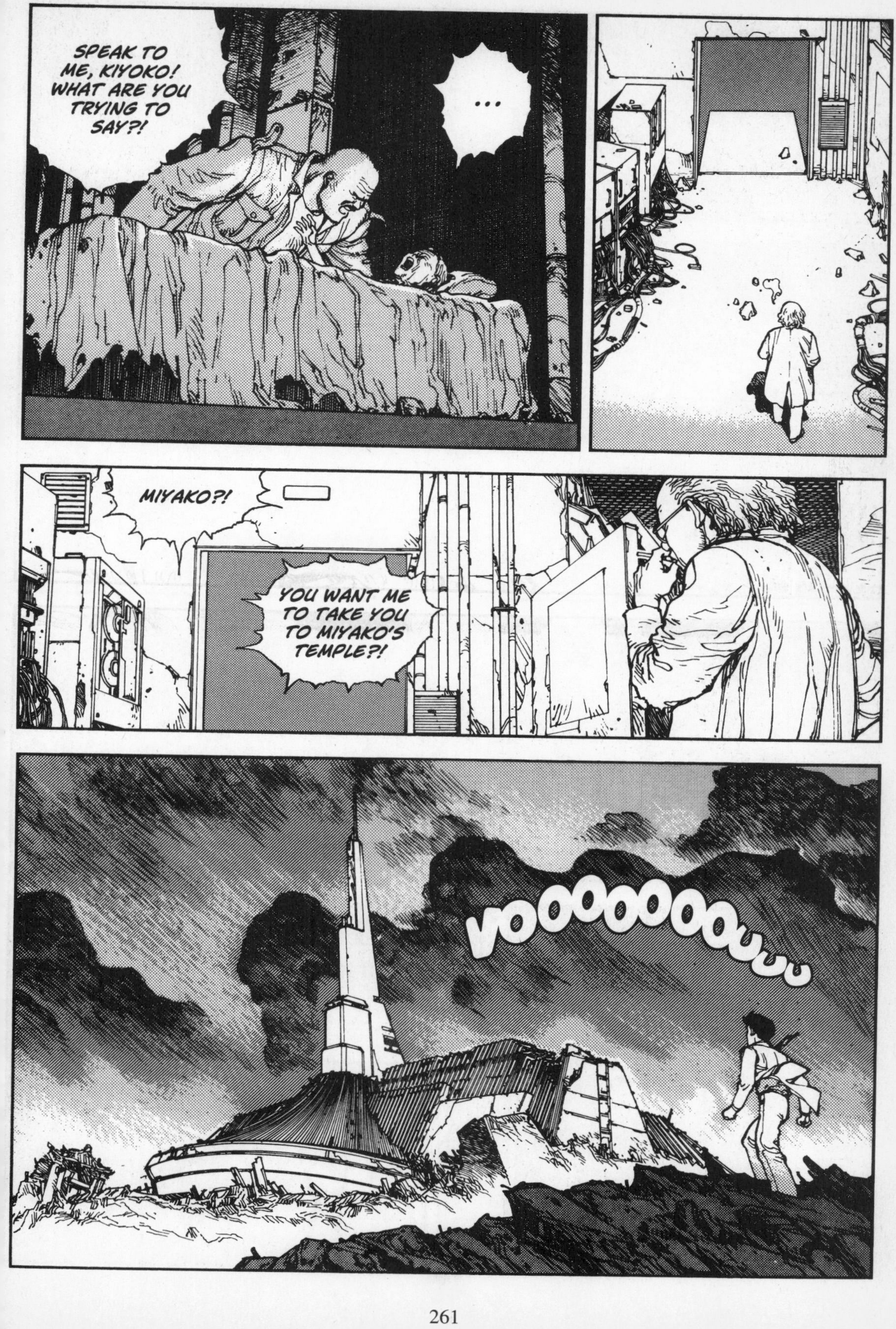
SPEAK TO ME, KIYOKO! WHAT ARE YOU TRYING TO SAY?!
...
MIYAKO?!
YOU WANT ME TO TAKE YOU TO MIYAKO'S TEMPLE?!
VOOOOOOOUUU

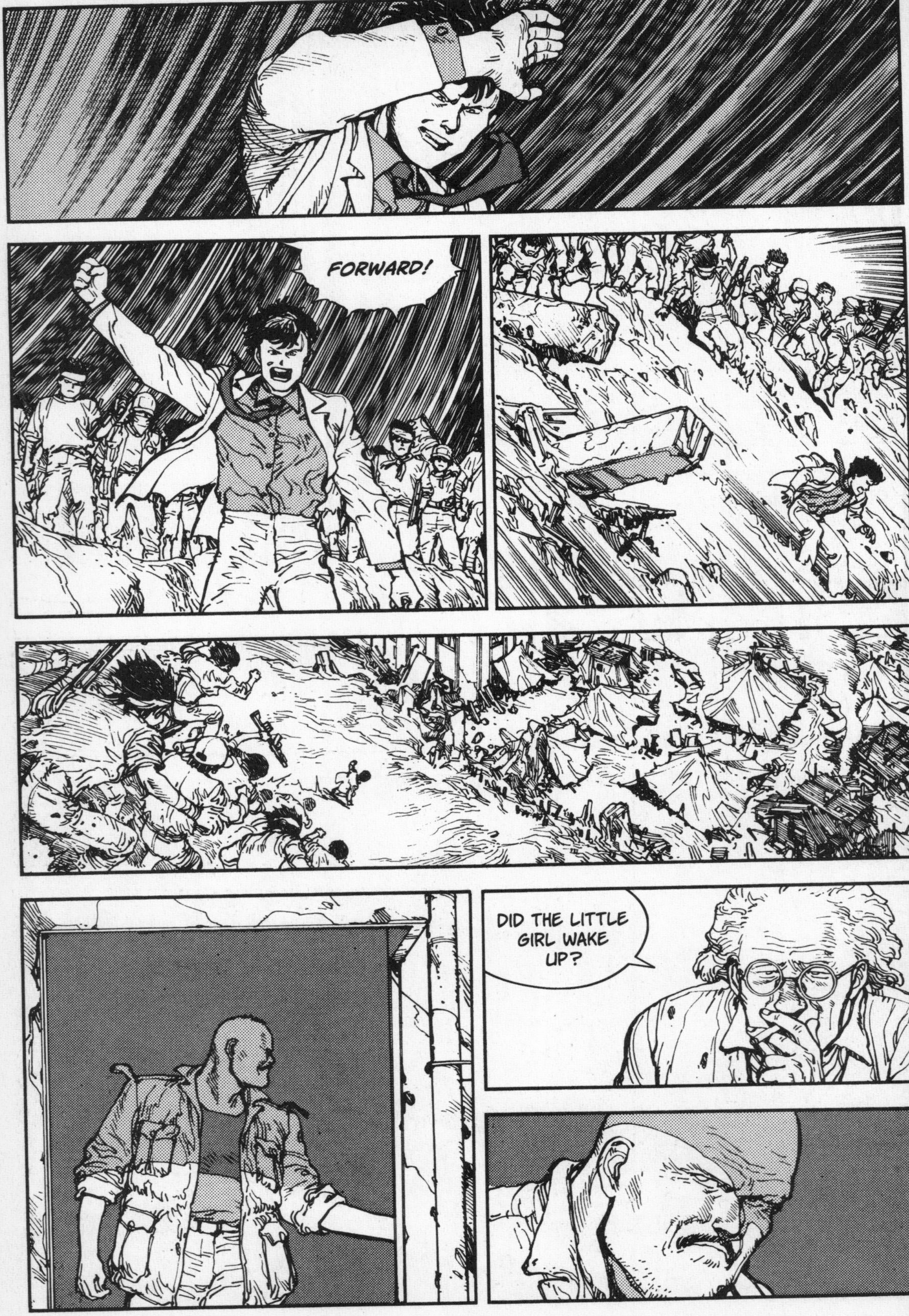
FORWARD!
DID THE LITTLE GIRL WAKE UP?

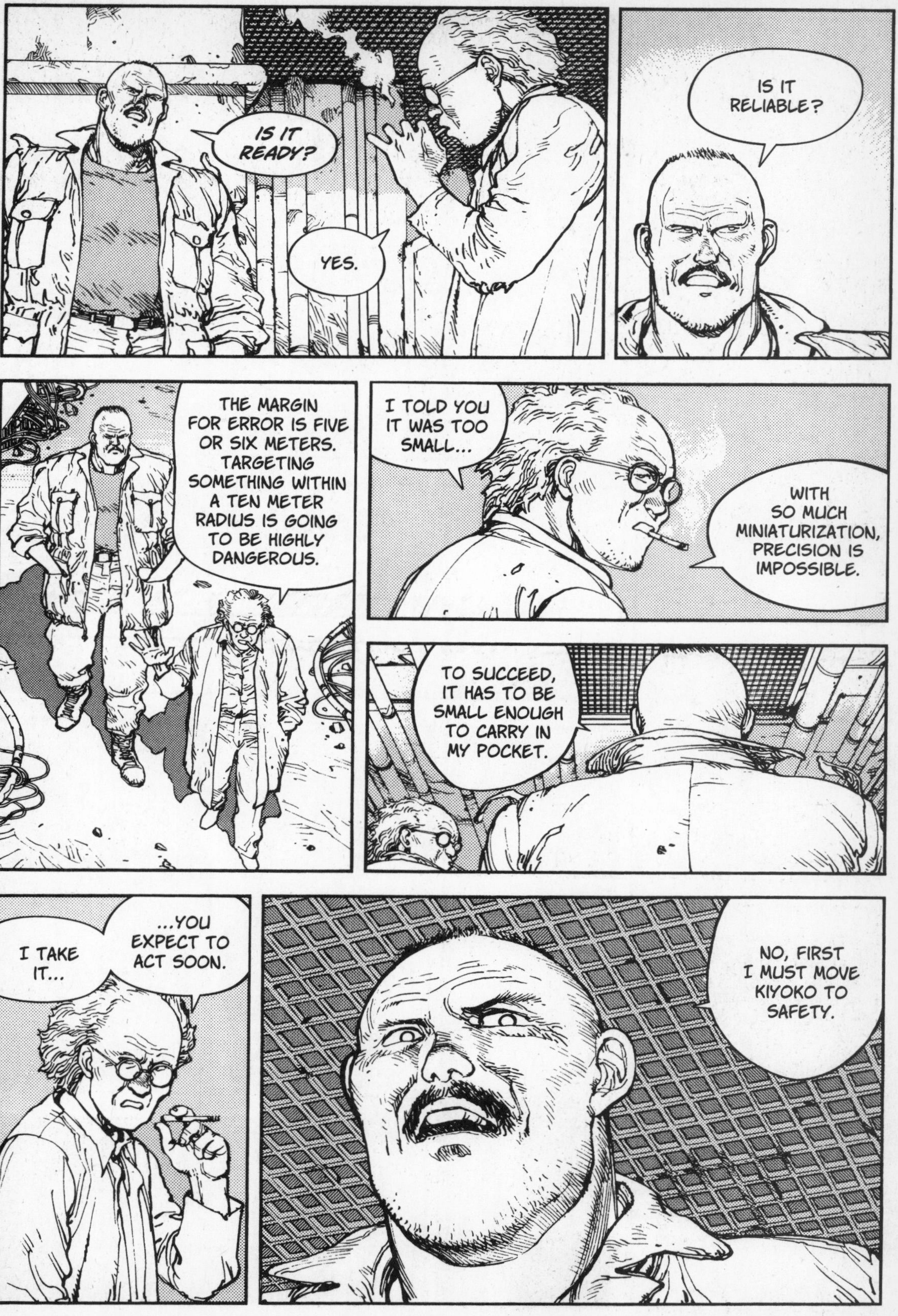
IS IT READY?
YES.
IS IT RELIABLE?
THE MARGIN FOR ERROR IS FIVE OR SIX METERS. TARGETING SOMETHING WITHIN A TEN METER RADIUS IS GOING TO BE HIGHLY DANGEROUS.
I TOLD YOU IT WAS TOO SMALL...
WITH SO MUCH MINIATURIZATION, PRECISION IS IMPOSSIBLE.
TO SUCCEED, IT HAS TO BE SMALL ENOUGH TO CARRY IN MY POCKET.
I TAKE IT...
...YOU EXPECT TO ACT SOON.
NO, FIRST I MUST MOVE KIYOKO TO SAFETY.

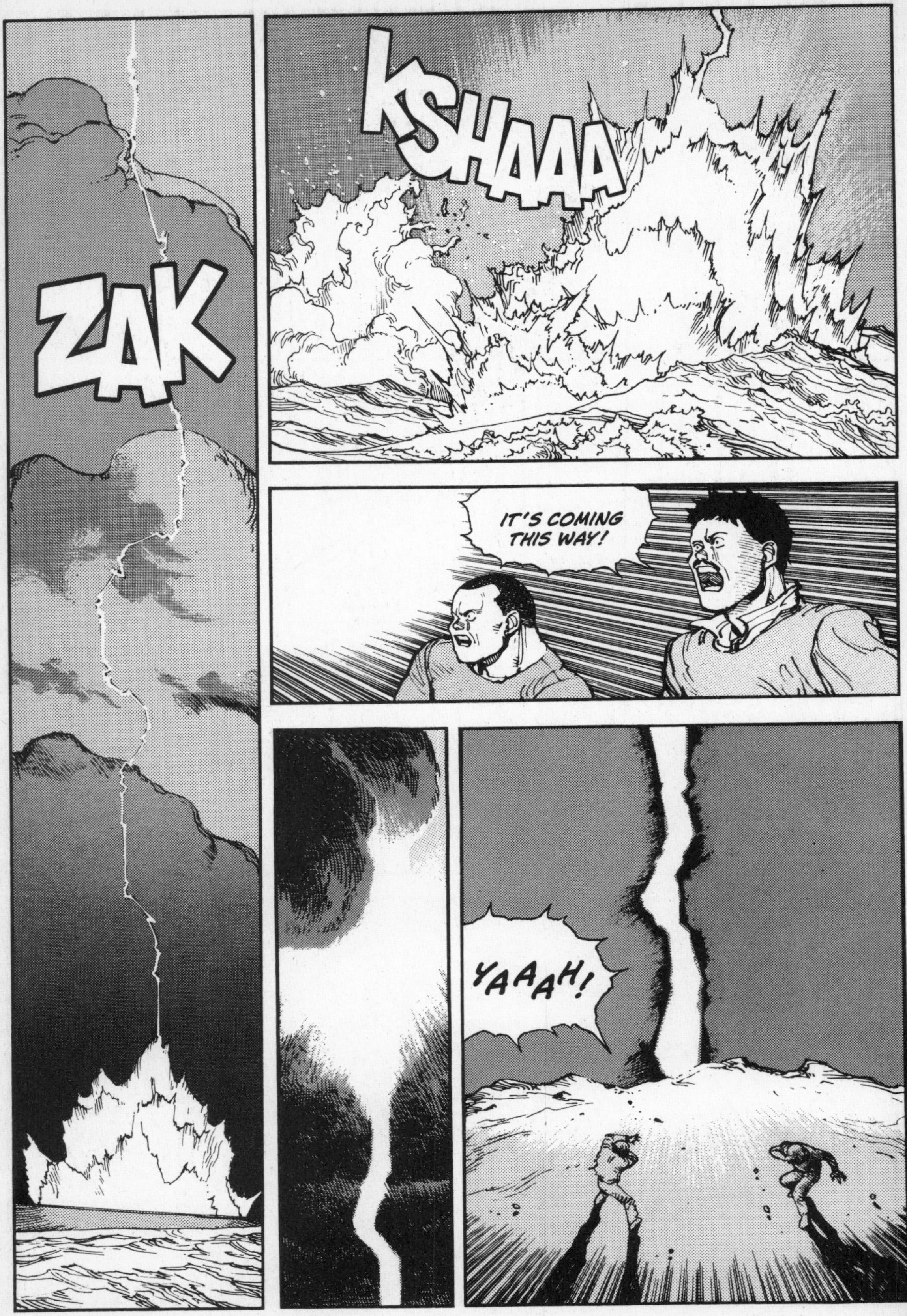
ZAK
KSHAAA
IT'S COMING THIS WAY!
YAAAH!

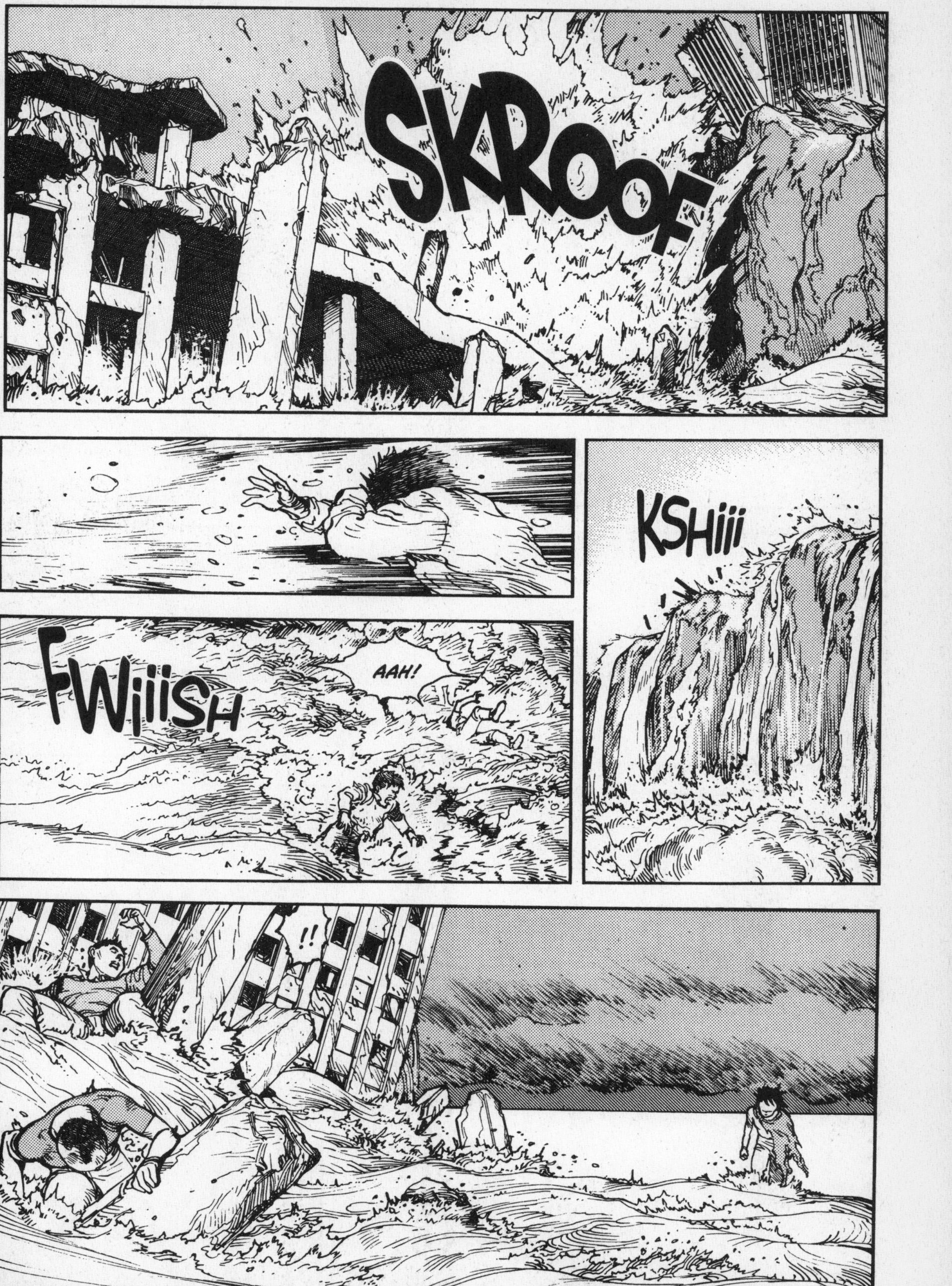
SKROOF
FWiiiSH
AAH!
KSHiiii
!!

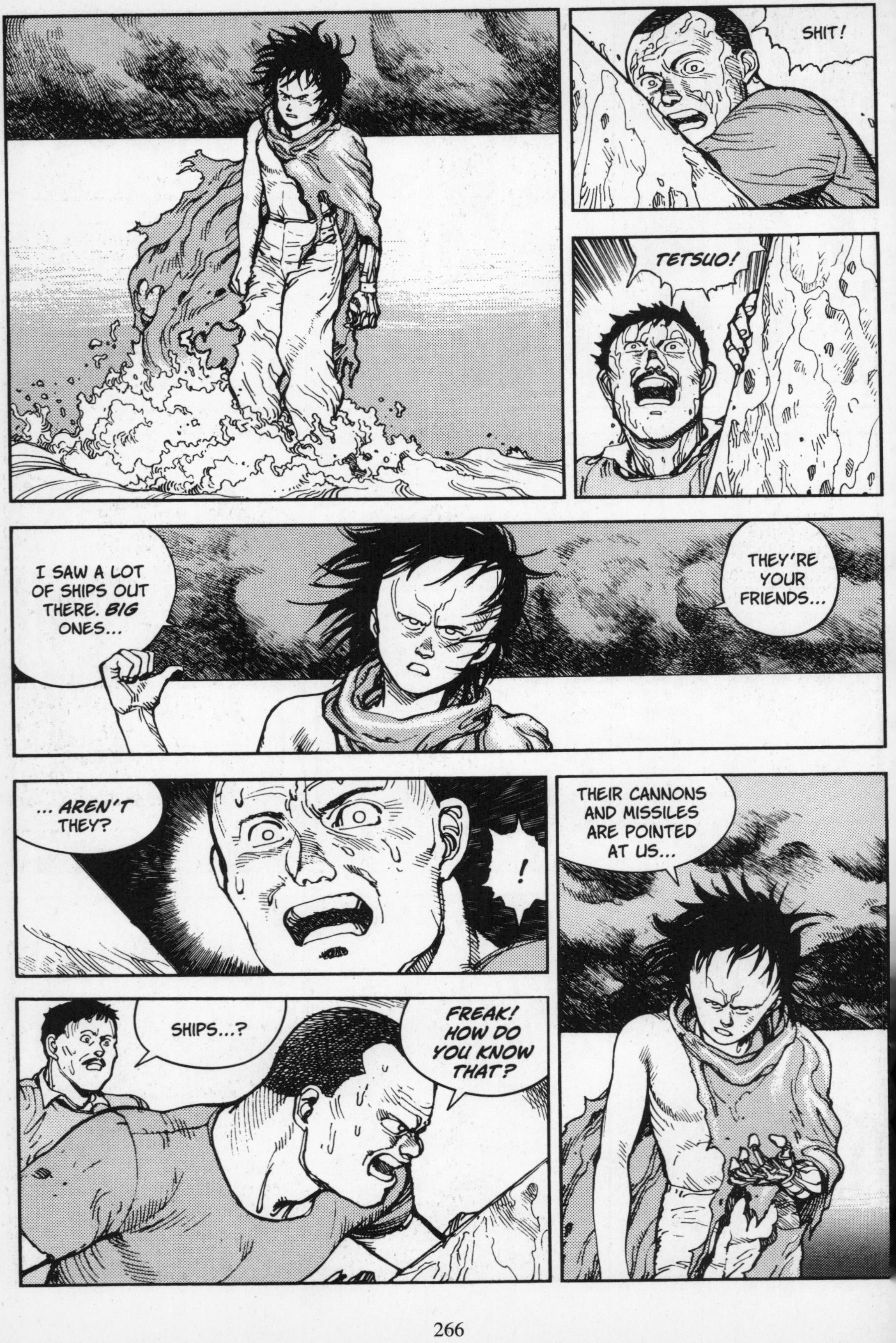
SHIT!
TETSUO!
I SAW A LOT OF SHIPS OUT THERE. BIG ONES...
THEY'RE YOUR FRIENDS...
... AREN'T THEY?
!
SHIPS...?
FREAK! HOW DO YOU KNOW THAT?
THEIR CANNONS AND MISSILES ARE POINTED AT US...

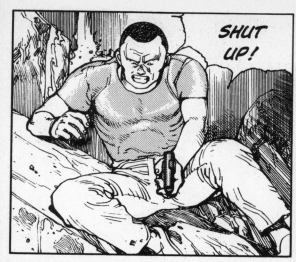 SHUT UP!

 ...

 WHAT THE HELL ARE YOU?

 YOU CAME ALL THIS WAY TO KILL AKIRA, RIGHT?

 ! WHAT?!

 HA HA HA HA!

 ZWAK YAAGH!

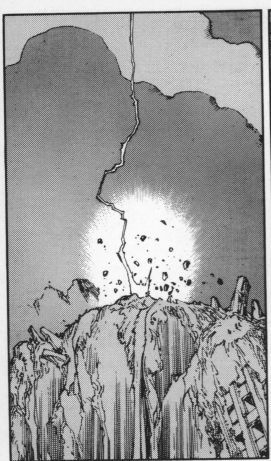
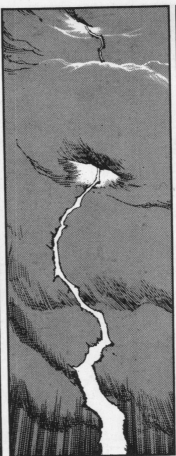

WAK

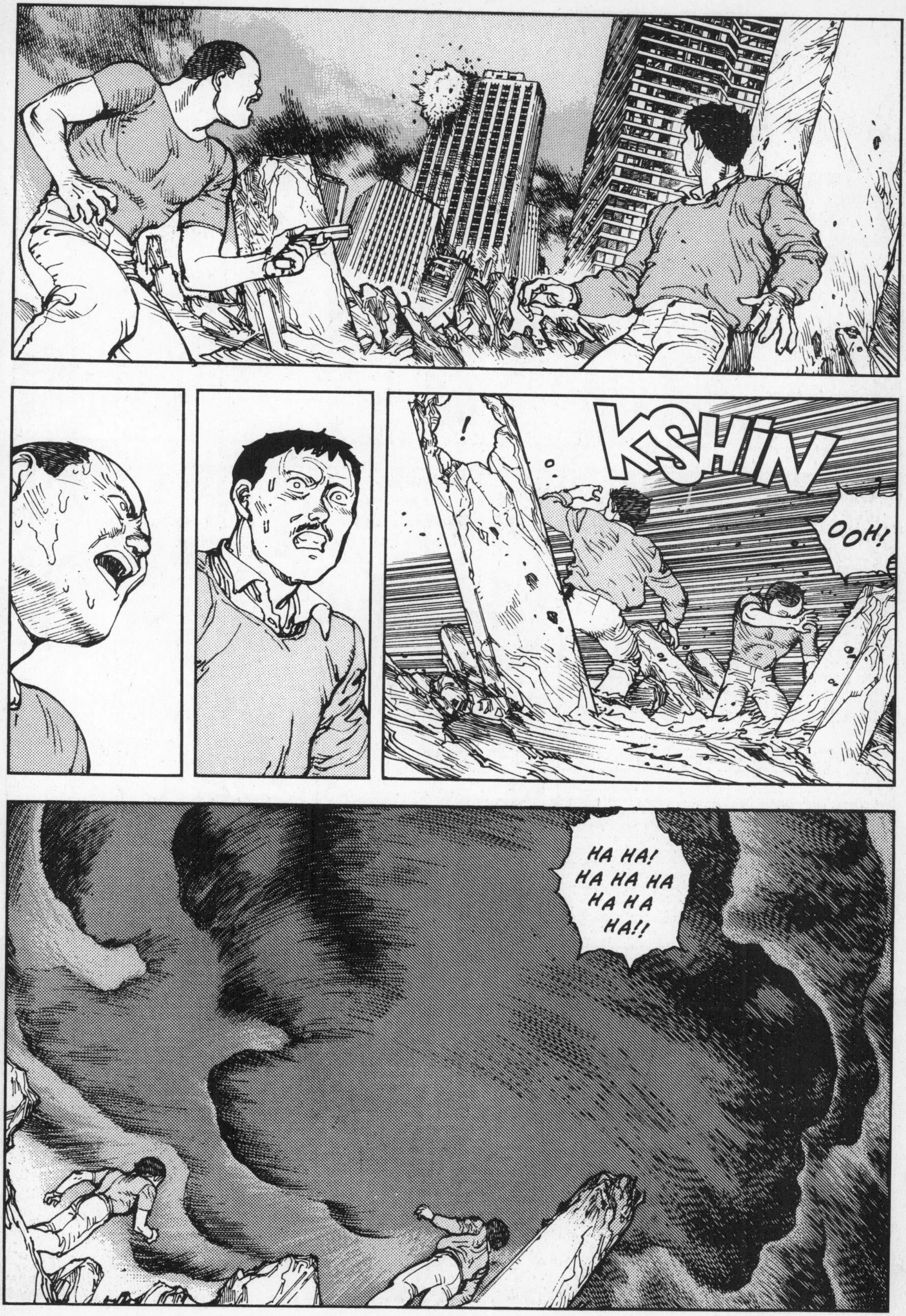
!
KSHIN
OOH!
HA HA! HA HA HA HA HA HA!!

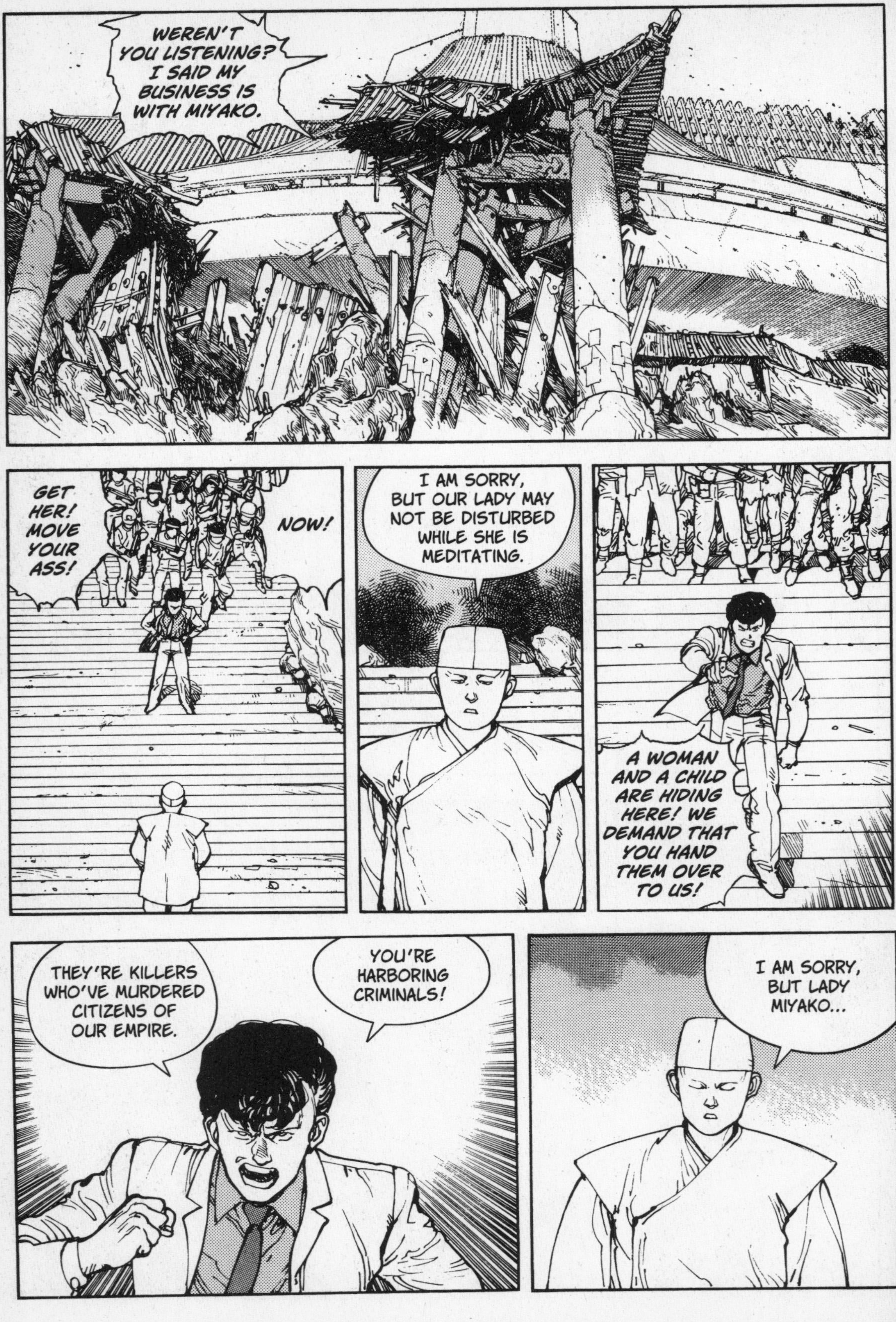
WEREN'T YOU LISTENING? I SAID MY BUSINESS IS WITH MIYAKO.
GET HER! MOVE YOUR ASS!
NOW!
I AM SORRY, BUT OUR LADY MAY NOT BE DISTURBED WHILE SHE IS MEDITATING.
A WOMAN AND A CHILD ARE HIDING HERE! WE DEMAND THAT YOU HAND THEM OVER TO US!
THEY'RE KILLERS WHO'VE MURDERED CITIZENS OF OUR EMPIRE.
YOU'RE HARBORING CRIMINALS!
I AM SORRY, BUT LADY MIYAKO...

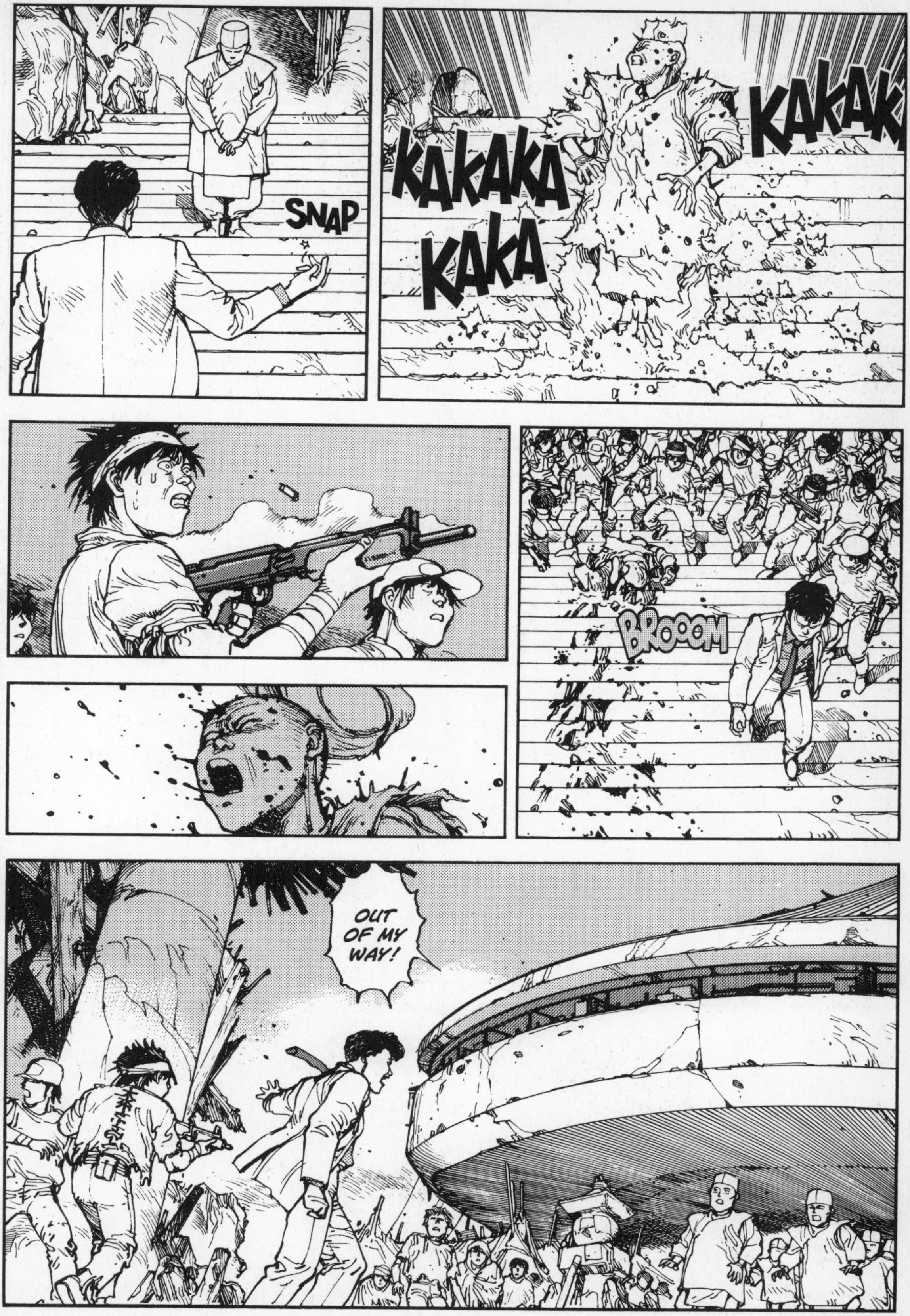
SNAP
KAKAKA
KAKA
KAKAK
BROOOM
OUT OF MY WAY!

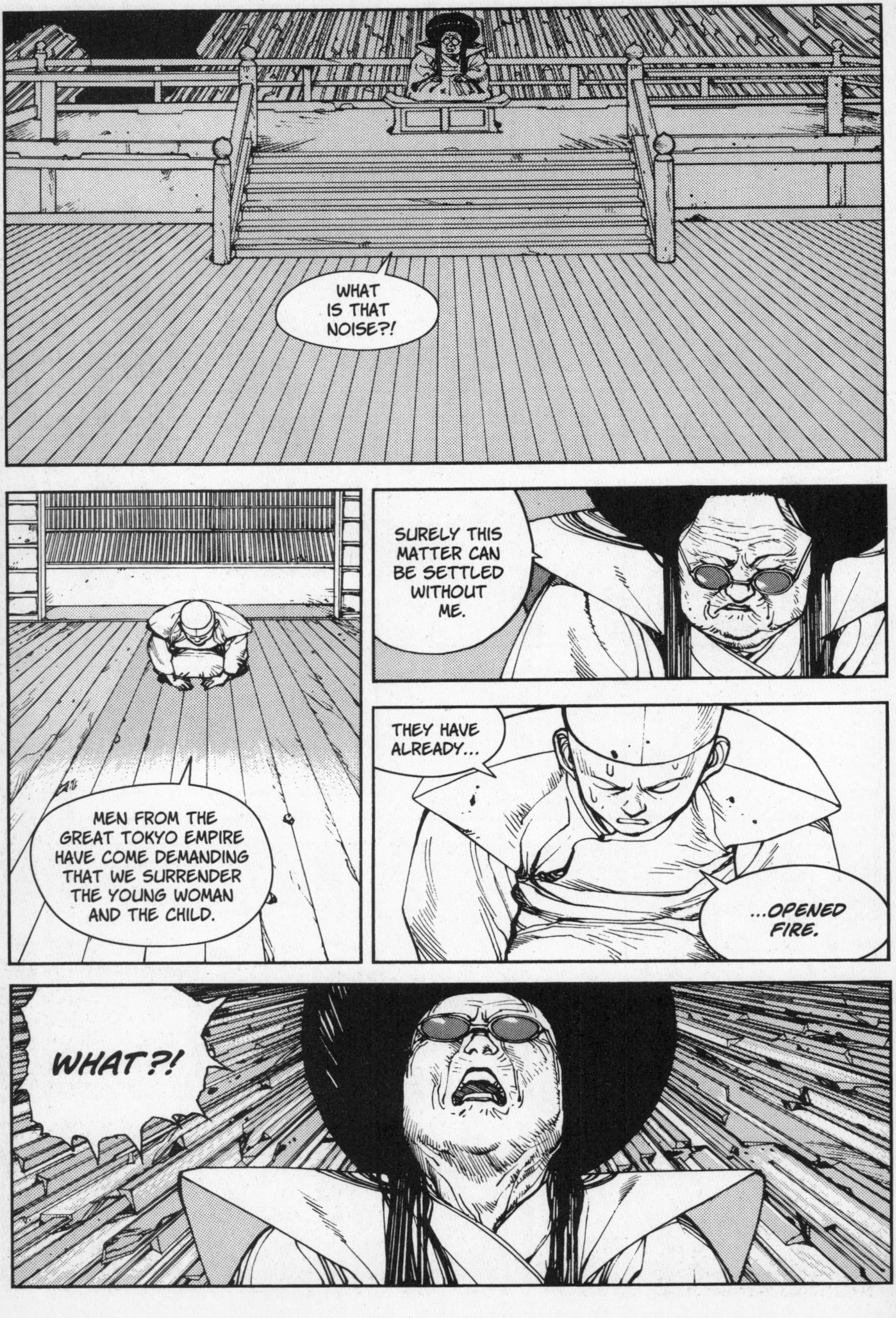
WHAT IS THAT NOISE?!
MEN FROM THE GREAT TOKYO EMPIRE HAVE COME DEMANDING THAT WE SURRENDER THE YOUNG WOMAN AND THE CHILD.
SURELY THIS MATTER CAN BE SETTLED WITHOUT ME.
THEY HAVE ALREADY...
...OPENED FIRE.
WHAT?!

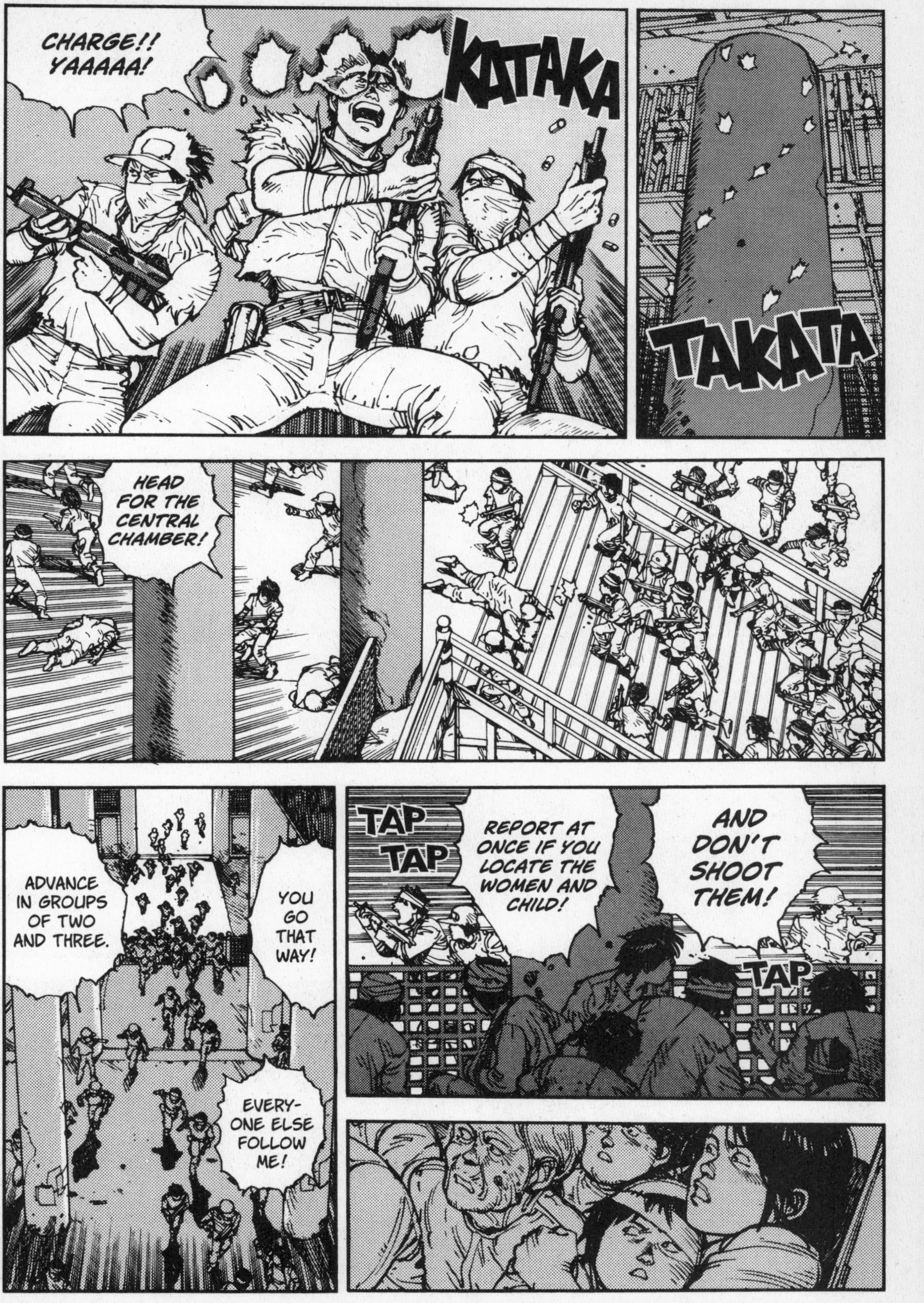
CHARGE!! YAAAAA!
KATAKA
TAKATA
HEAD FOR THE CENTRAL CHAMBER!
ADVANCE IN GROUPS OF TWO AND THREE.
YOU GO THAT WAY!
EVERY-ONE ELSE FOLLOW ME!
TAP TAP
REPORT AT ONCE IF YOU LOCATE THE WOMEN AND CHILD!
AND DON'T SHOOT THEM!
TAP

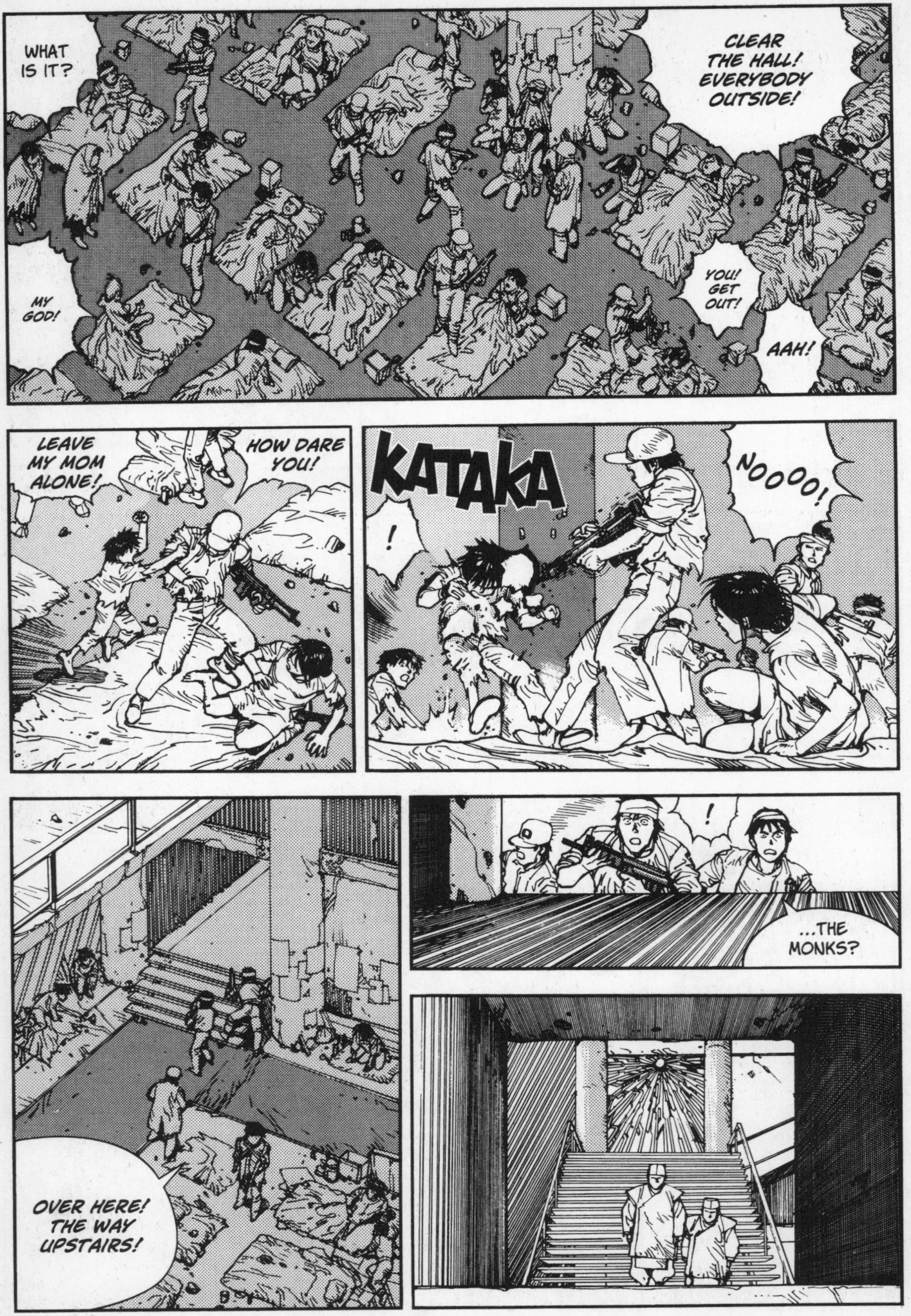
WHAT IS IT?
CLEAR THE HALL! EVERYBODY OUTSIDE!
MY GOD!
YOU! GET OUT!
AAH!
LEAVE MY MOM ALONE!
HOW DARE YOU!
KATAKA
!
NOOOO!
OVER HERE! THE WAY UPSTAIRS!
!
...THE MONKS?

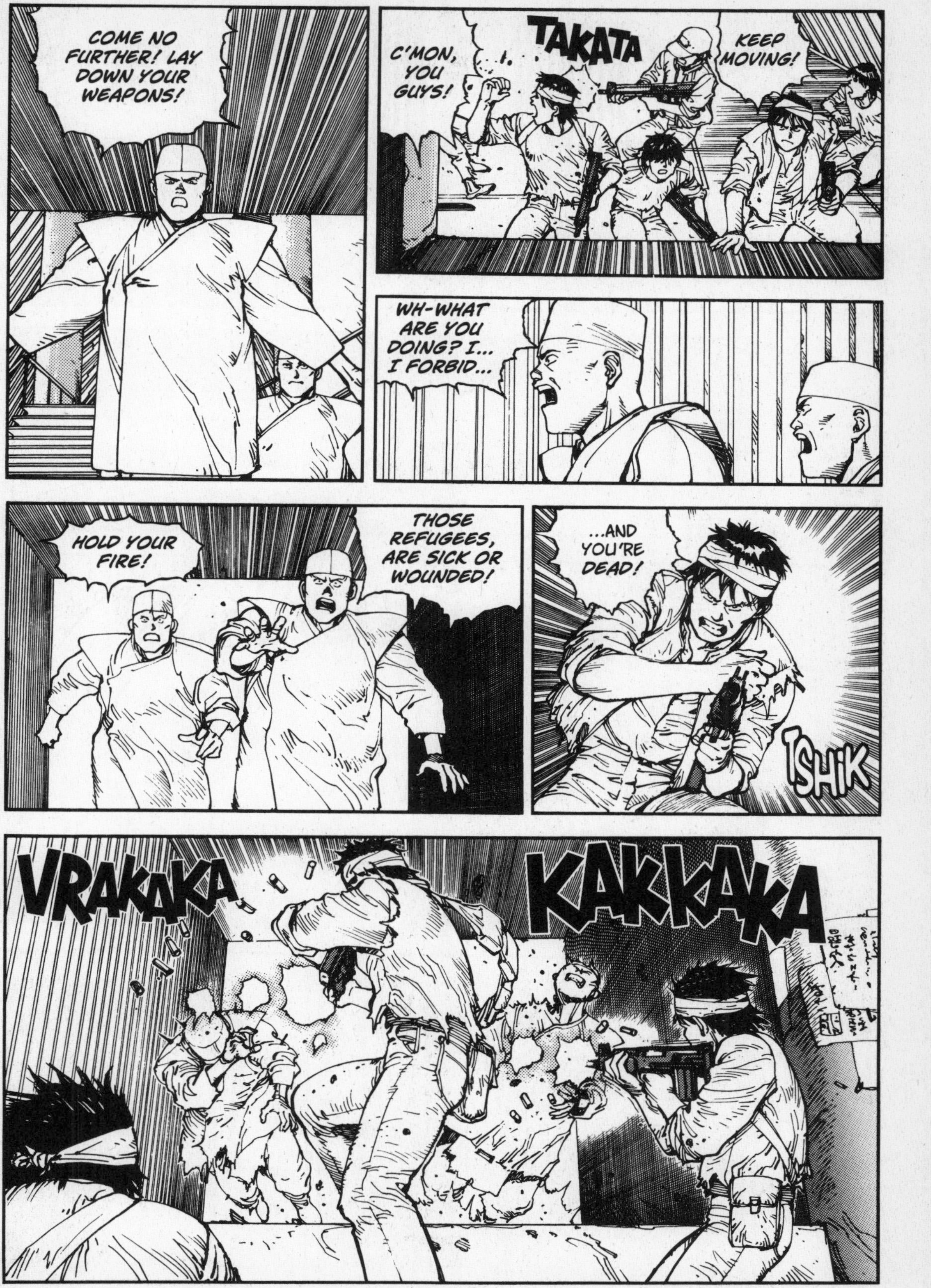
COME NO FURTHER! LAY DOWN YOUR WEAPONS!
C'MON, YOU GUYS!
TAKATA
KEEP MOVING!
WH-WHAT ARE YOU DOING? I... I FORBID...
HOLD YOUR FIRE!
THOSE REFUGEES, ARE SICK OR WOUNDED!
...AND YOU'RE DEAD!
TSHIK
VRAKAKA
KAKKAKA

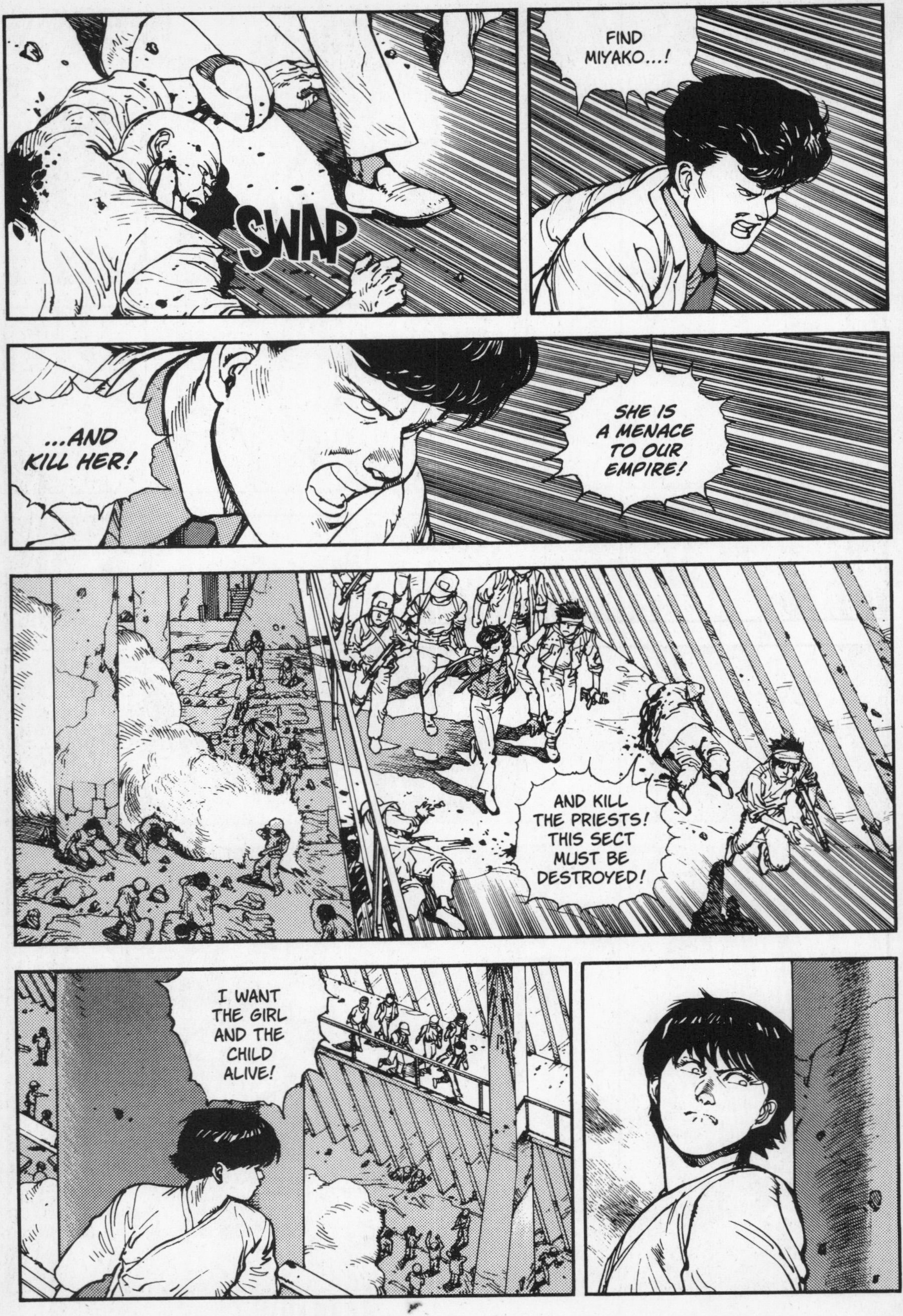
SWAP
FIND MIYAKO...!
...AND KILL HER!
SHE IS A MENACE TO OUR EMPIRE!
AND KILL THE PRIESTS! THIS SECT MUST BE DESTROYED!
I WANT THE GIRL AND THE CHILD ALIVE!

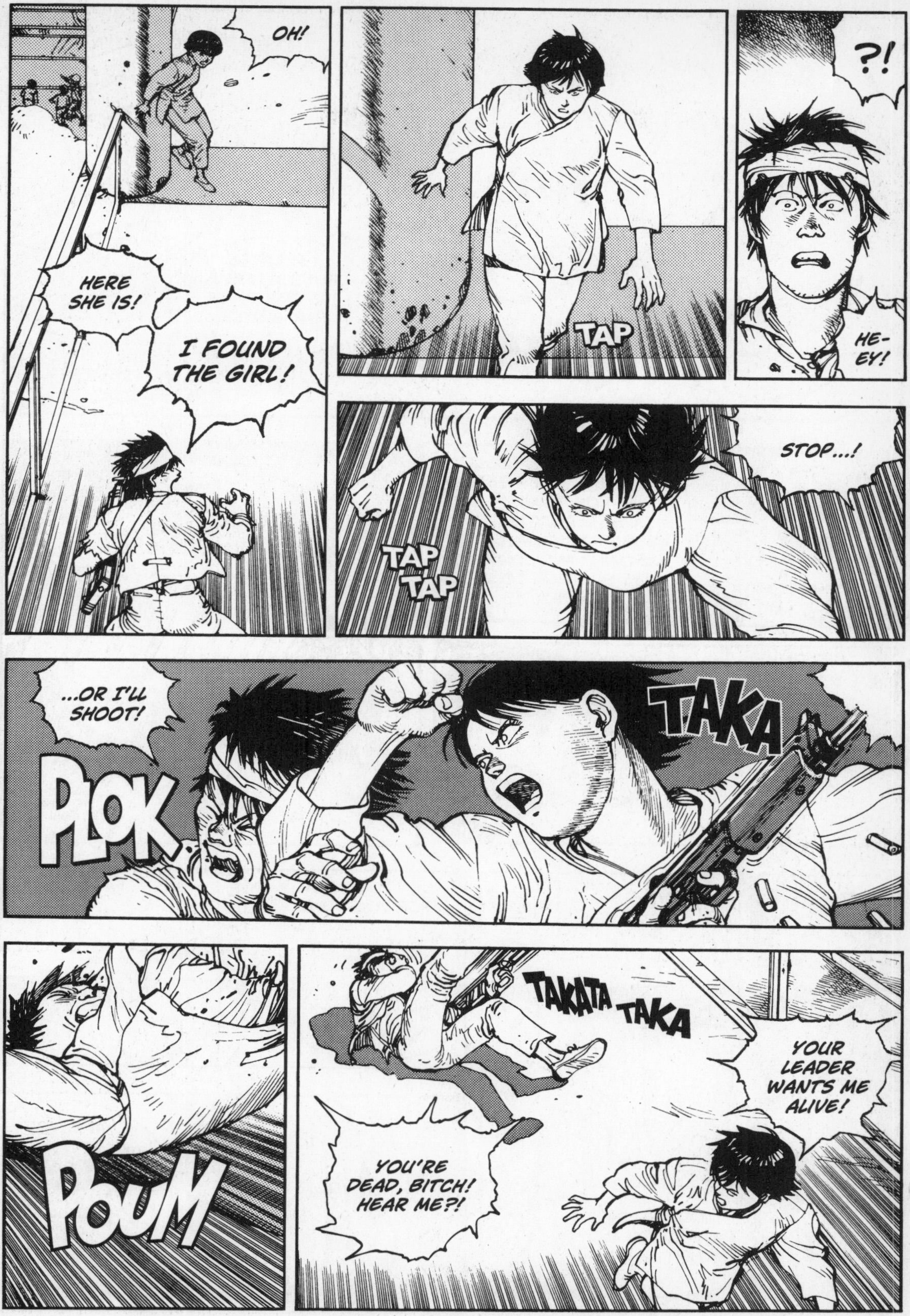
OH!
HERE SHE IS!
I FOUND THE GIRL!
TAP
?!
HE-EY!
STOP...!
TAP TAP
...OR I'LL SHOOT!
PLOK
TAKA
POUM
TAKATA TAKA
YOUR LEADER WANTS ME ALIVE!
YOU'RE DEAD, BITCH! HEAR ME?!

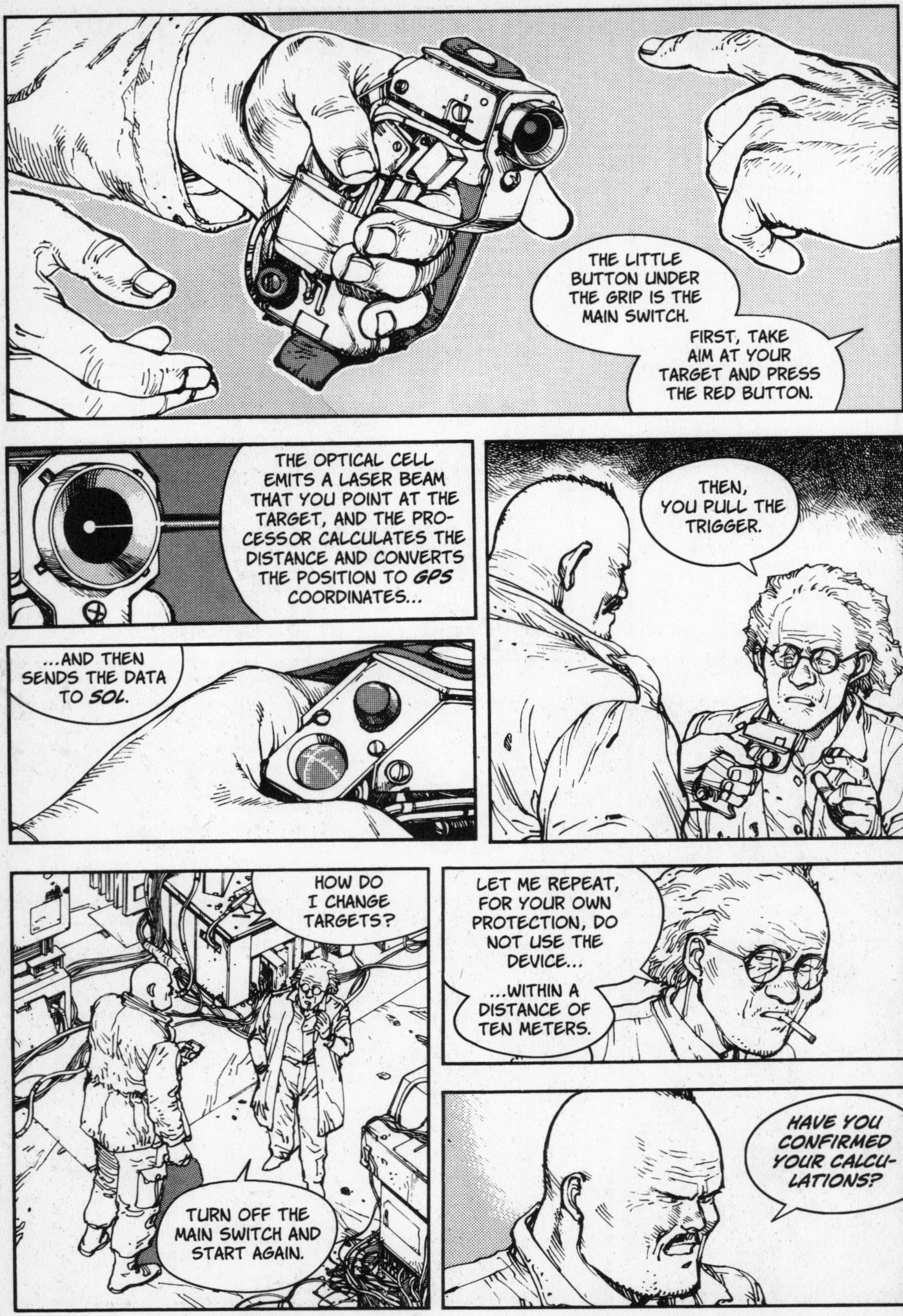
THE LITTLE BUTTON UNDER THE GRIP IS THE MAIN SWITCH.
FIRST, TAKE AIM AT YOUR TARGET AND PRESS THE RED BUTTON.
THE OPTICAL CELL EMITS A LASER BEAM THAT YOU POINT AT THE TARGET, AND THE PROCESSOR CALCULATES THE DISTANCE AND CONVERTS THE POSITION TO GPS COORDINATES...
...AND THEN SENDS THE DATA TO SOL.
THEN, YOU PULL THE TRIGGER.
HOW DO I CHANGE TARGETS?
TURN OFF THE MAIN SWITCH AND START AGAIN.
LET ME REPEAT, FOR YOUR OWN PROTECTION, DO NOT USE THE DEVICE...
...WITHIN A DISTANCE OF TEN METERS.
HAVE YOU CONFIRMED YOUR CALCULATIONS?

GOOD...I HAVE A FEW THINGS TO DO BEFORE I GO...

...THEN I'LL ASSUME I'M SAFE AFTER FIFTEEN METERS.

PFFF...

TEN, FIFTEEN, TWENTY...WHAT DOES IT MATTER WHEN A MAN IS COMMITTING SUICIDE?

TCHAK

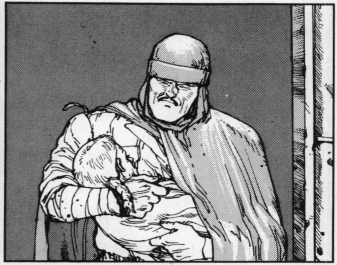

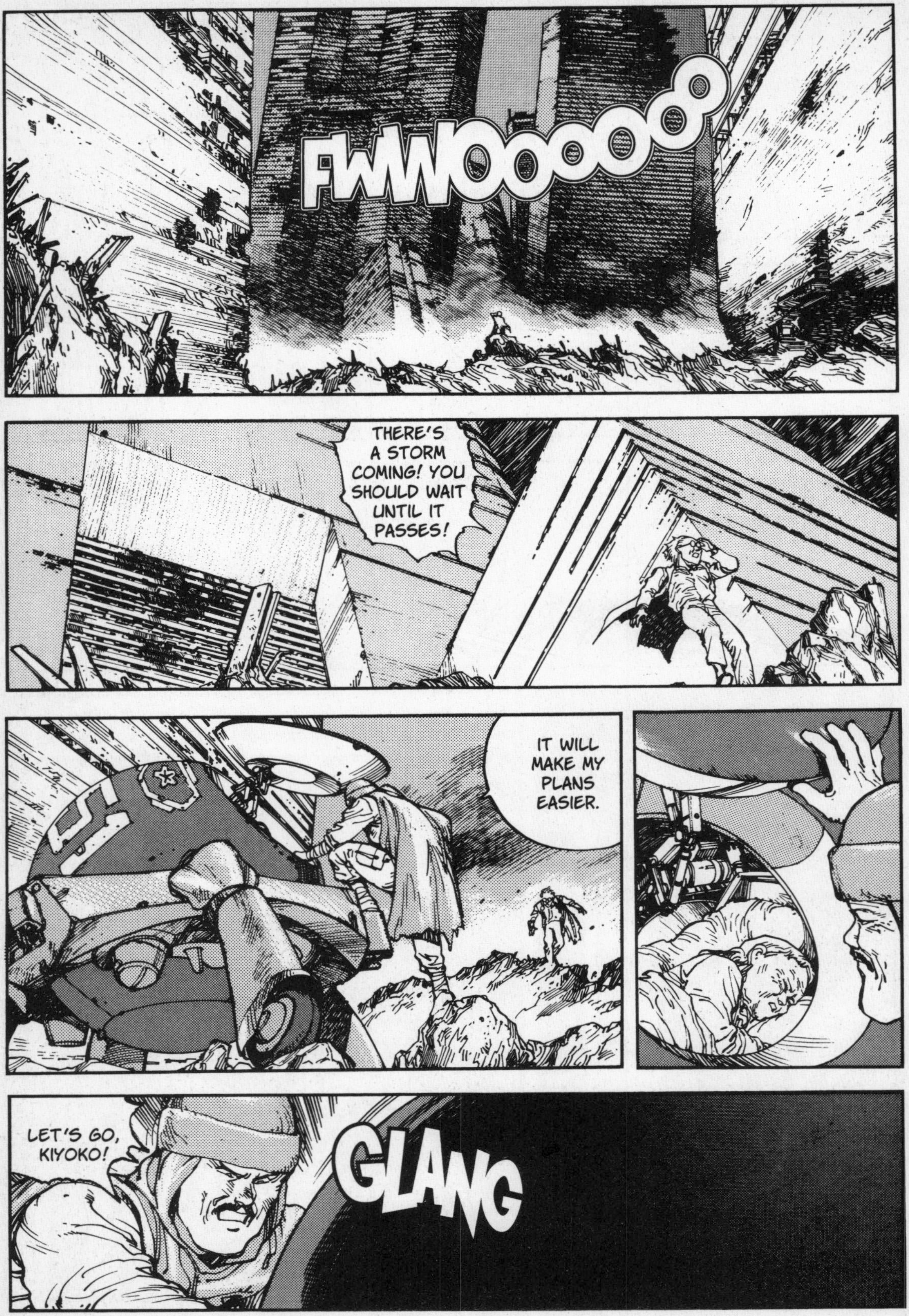
FWWOOOOO
THERE'S A STORM COMING! YOU SHOULD WAIT UNTIL IT PASSES!
IT WILL MAKE MY PLANS EASIER.
LET'S GO, KIYOKO!
GLANG

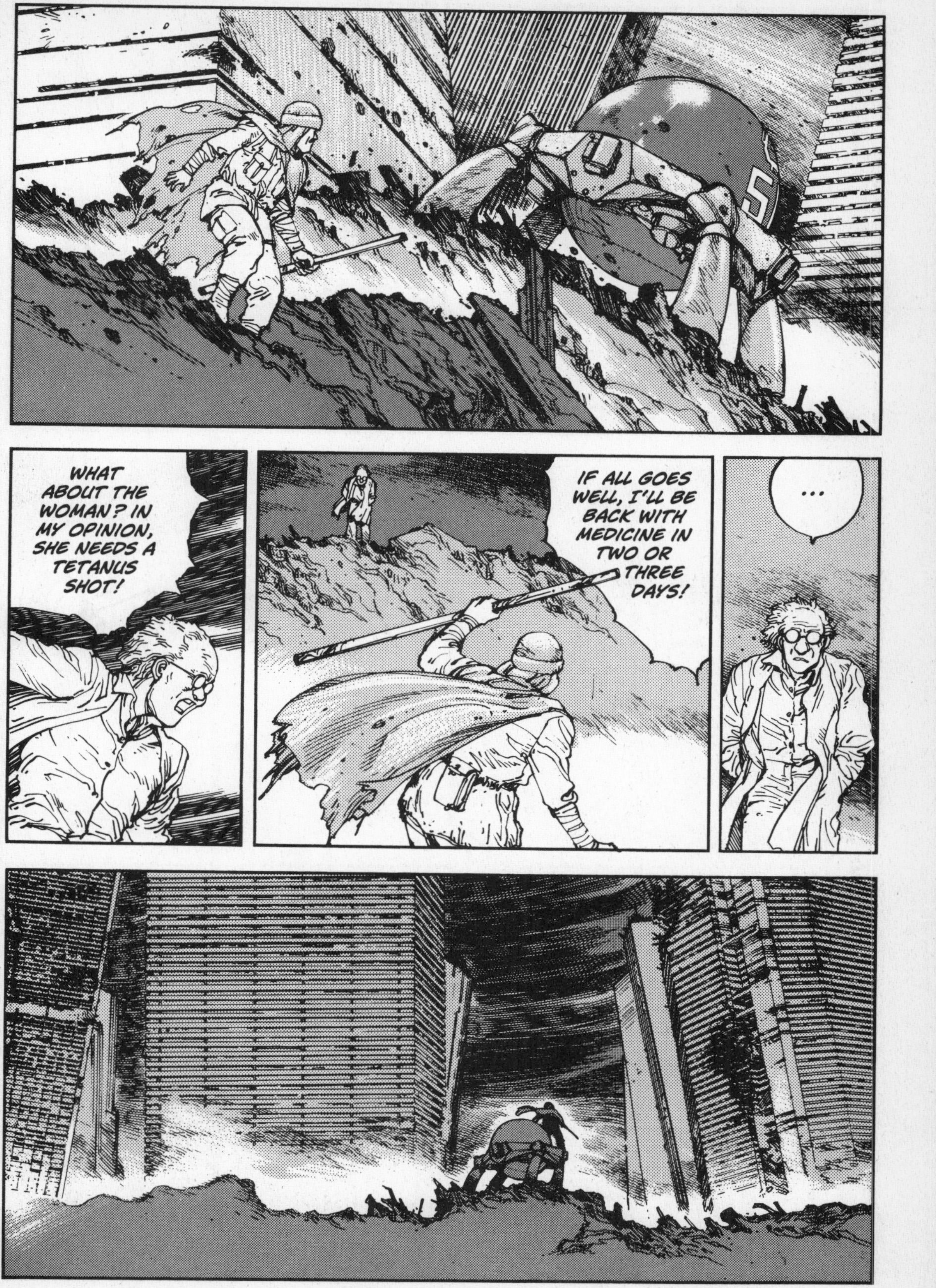
WHAT ABOUT THE WOMAN? IN MY OPINION, SHE NEEDS A TETANUS SHOT!
IF ALL GOES WELL, I'LL BE BACK WITH MEDICINE IN TWO OR THREE DAYS!
...

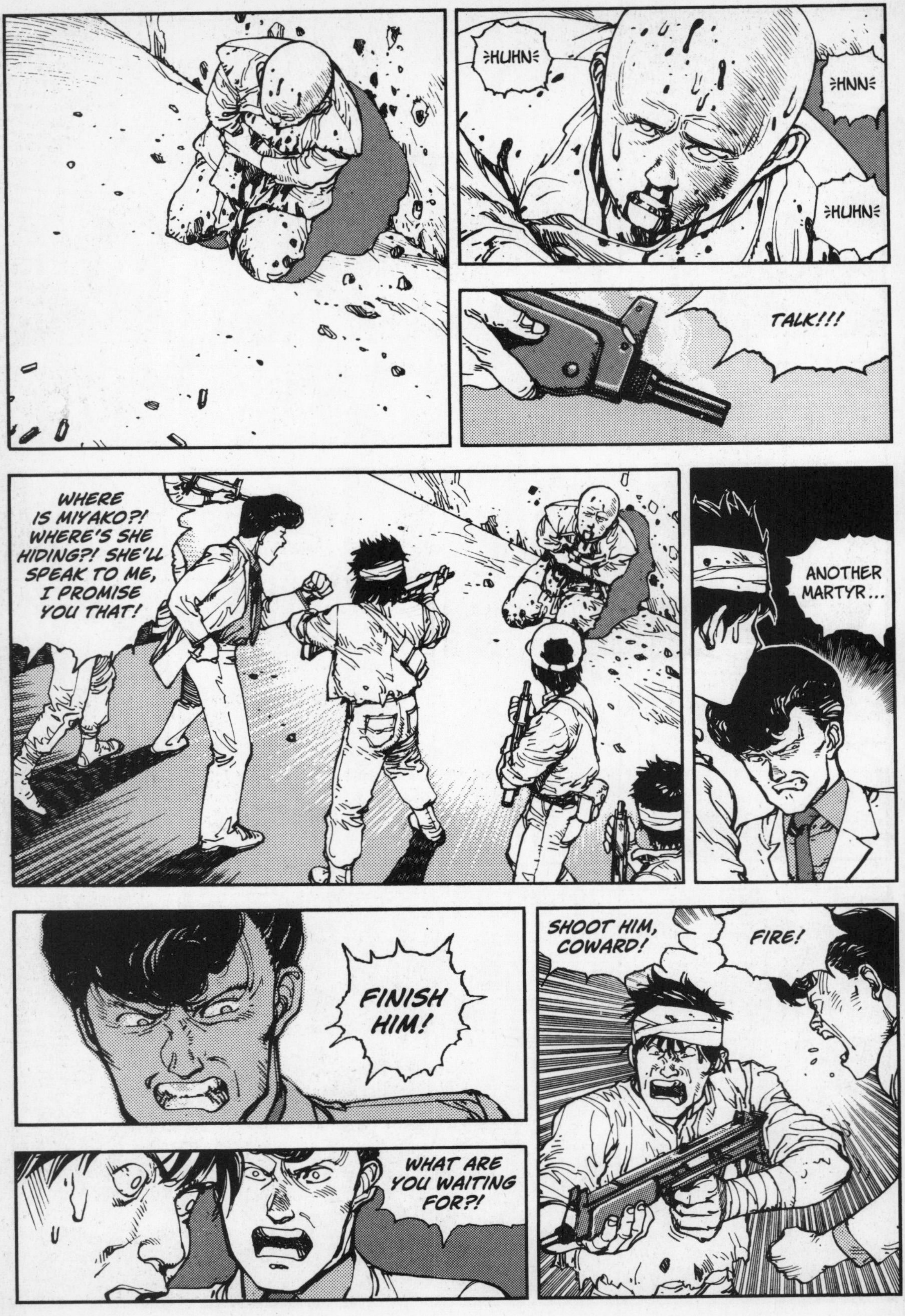

HUHN
HNN
HUHN
TALK!!!
WHERE IS MIYAKO?! WHERE'S SHE HIDING?! SHE'LL SPEAK TO ME, I PROMISE YOU THAT!
ANOTHER MARTYR...
FINISH HIM!
SHOOT HIM, COWARD!
FIRE!
WHAT ARE YOU WAITING FOR?!

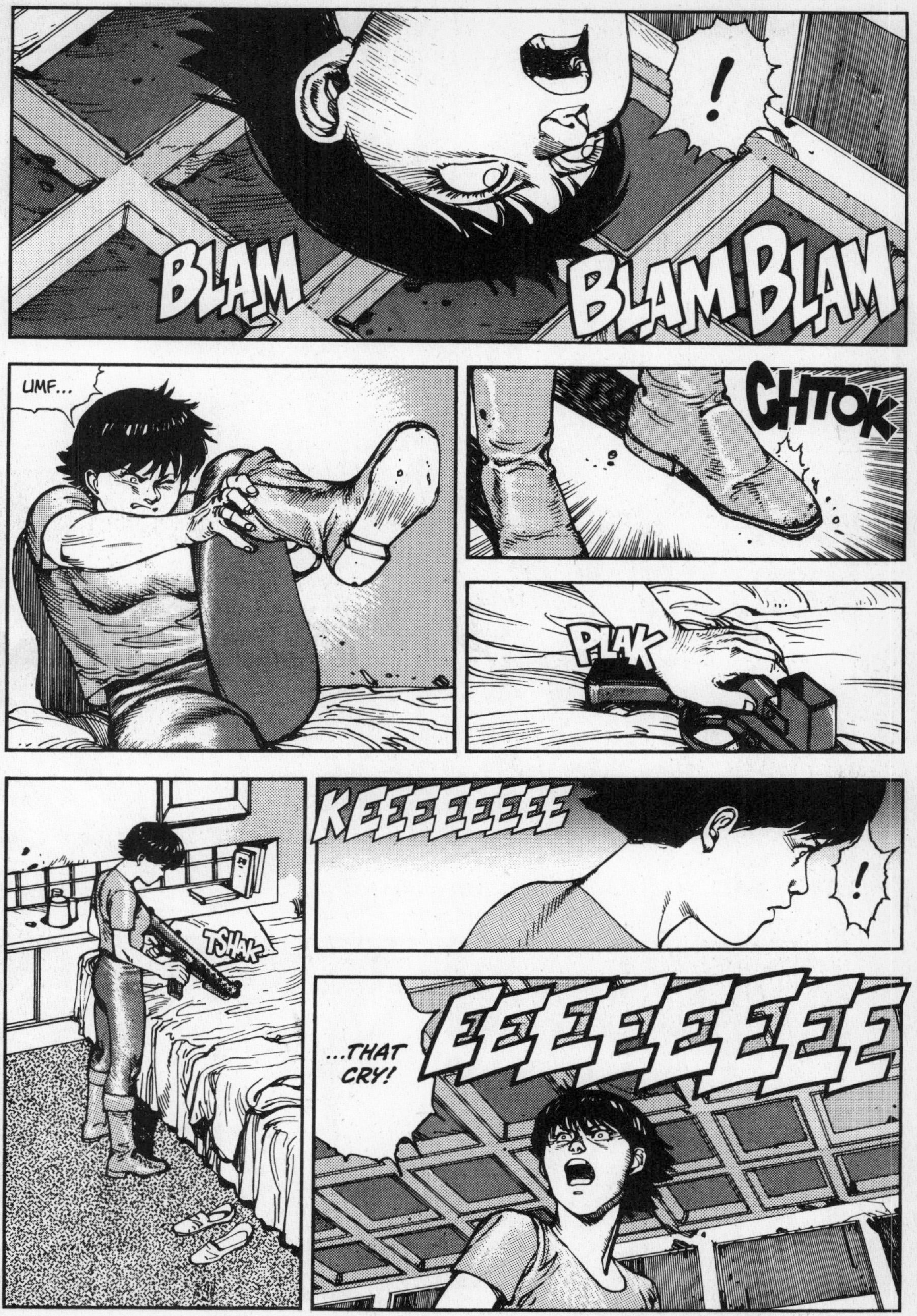
!
BLAM
BLAM BLAM
UMF...
CHTOK
PLAK
TSHAK
KEEEEEEEE
!
...THAT CRY!
EEEEEEEEE

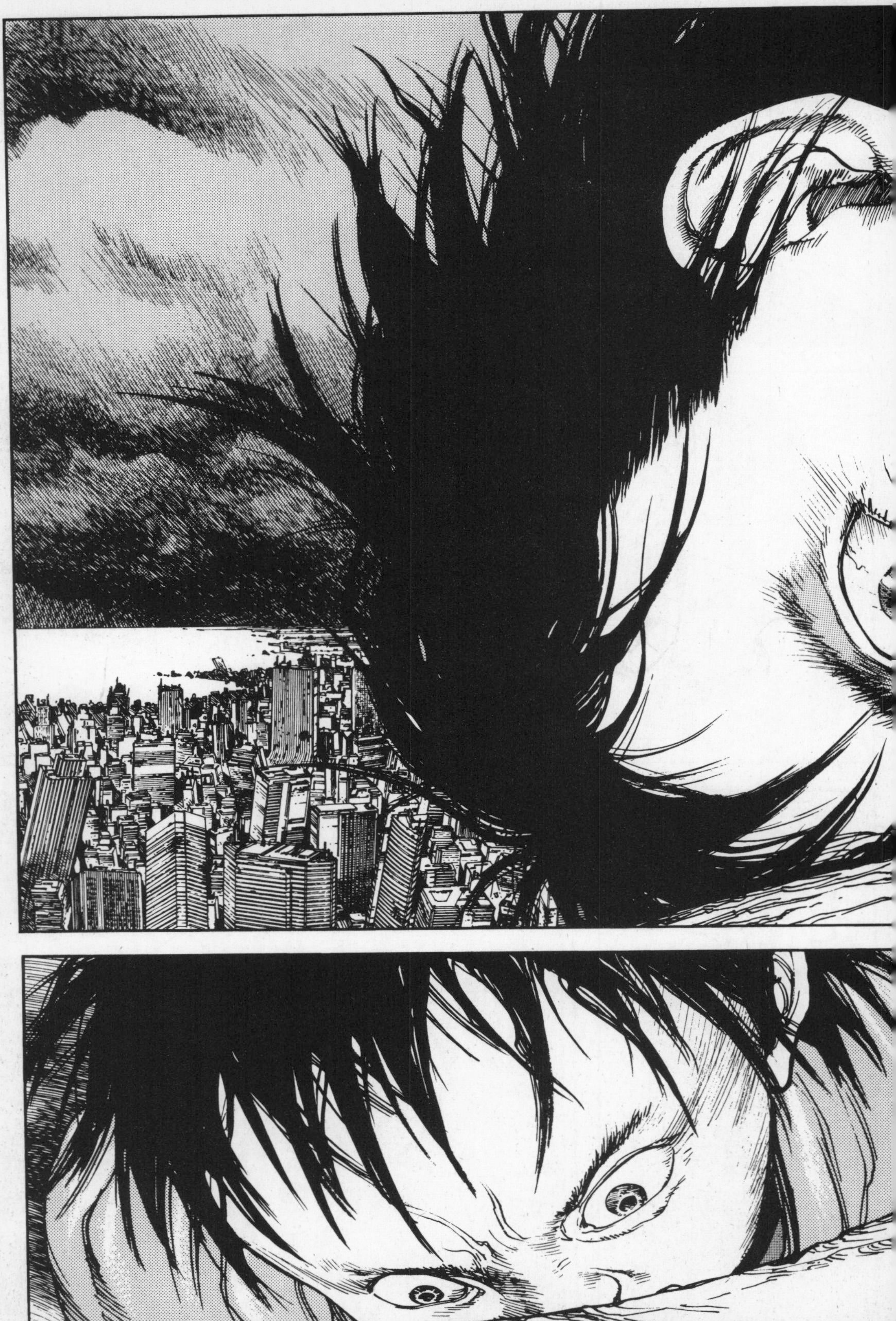

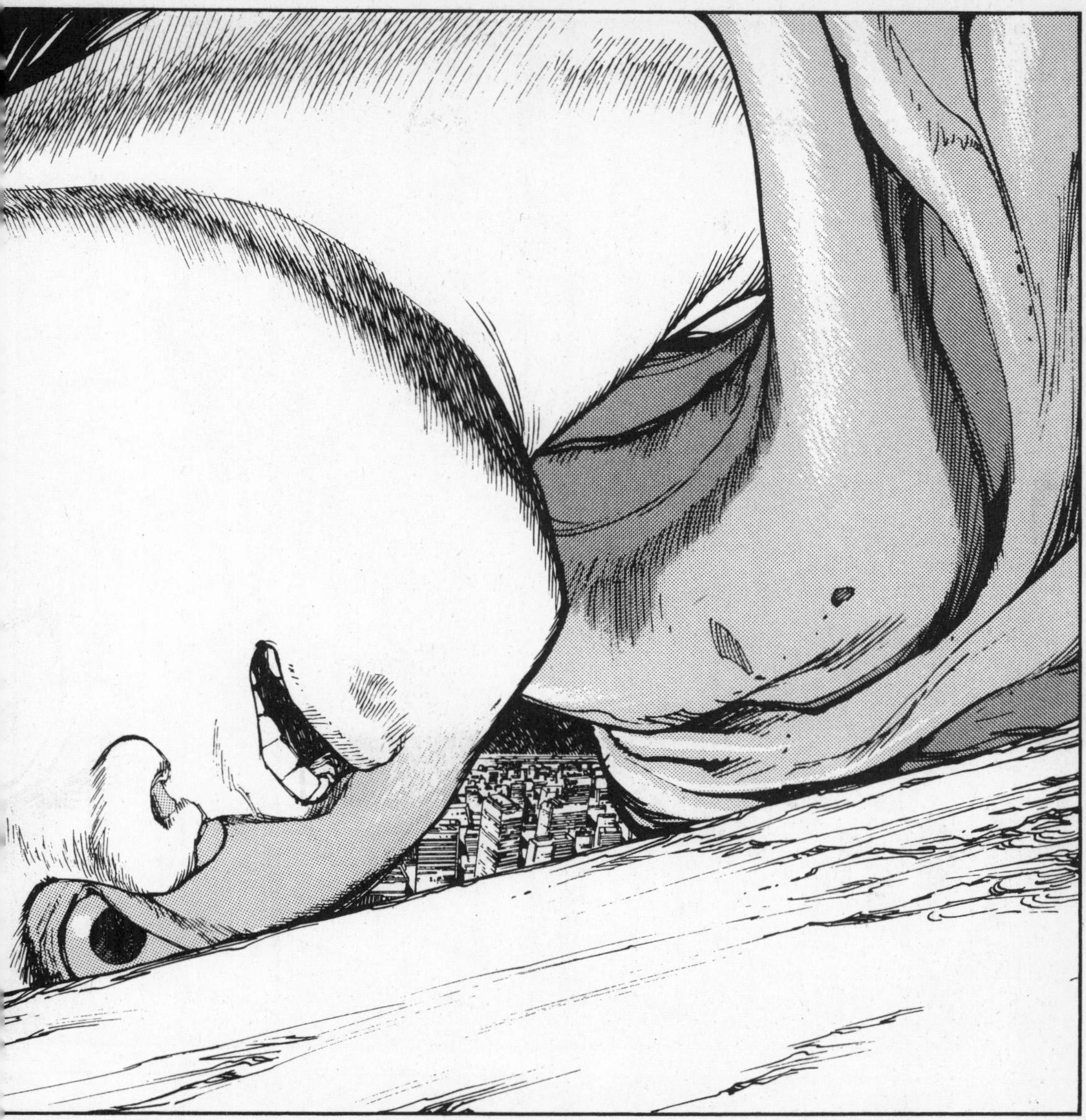

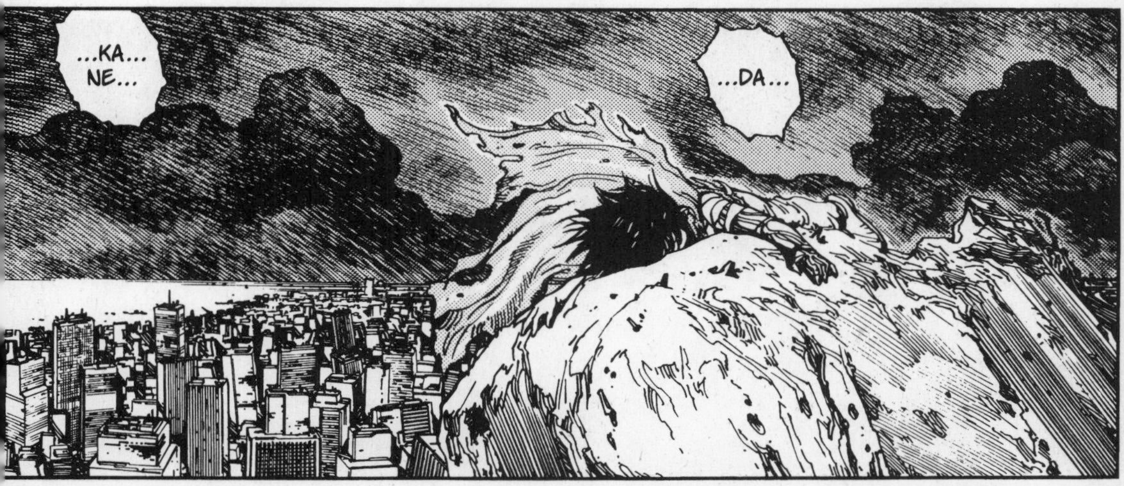

...KA... NE...
...DA...

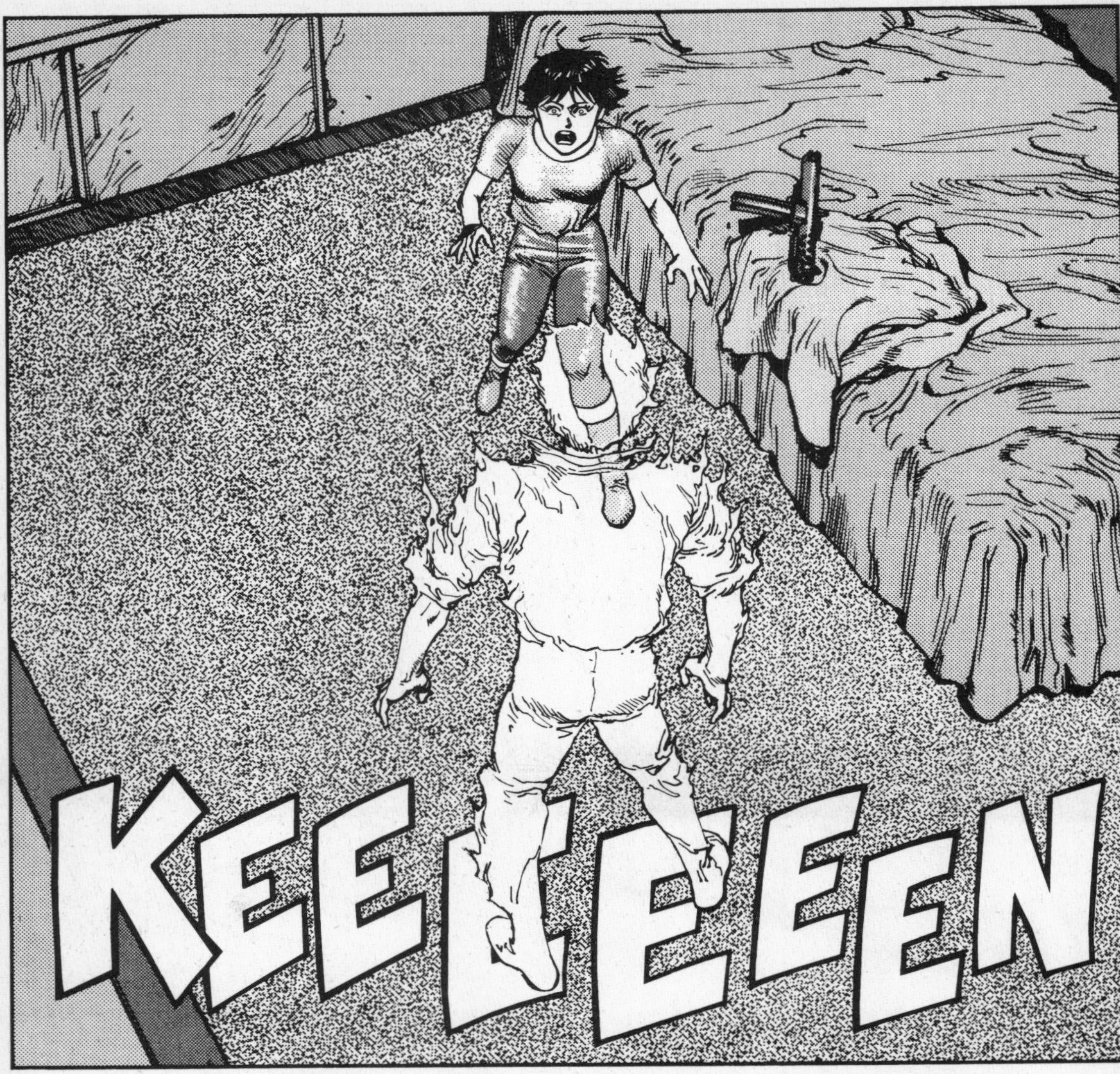
KEEEEEN
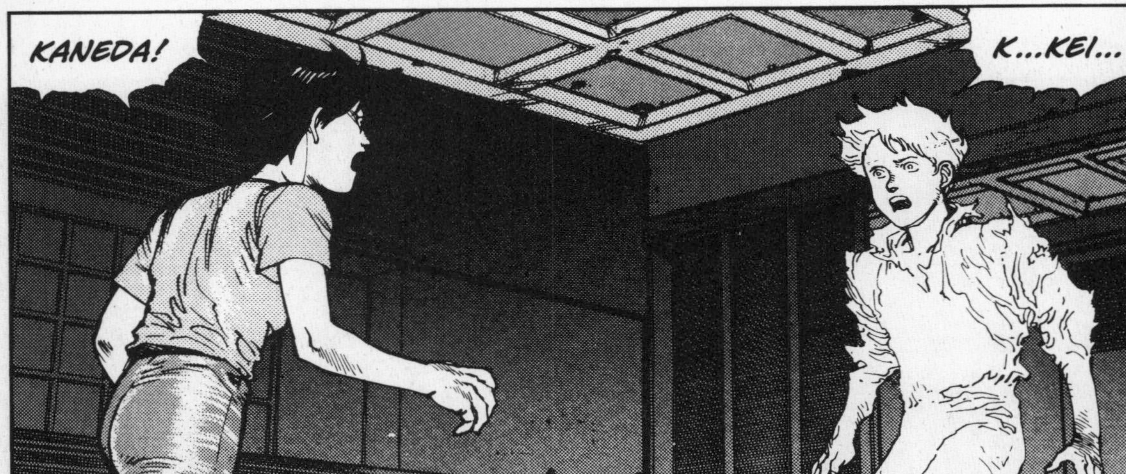
KANEDA!
K...KEI...

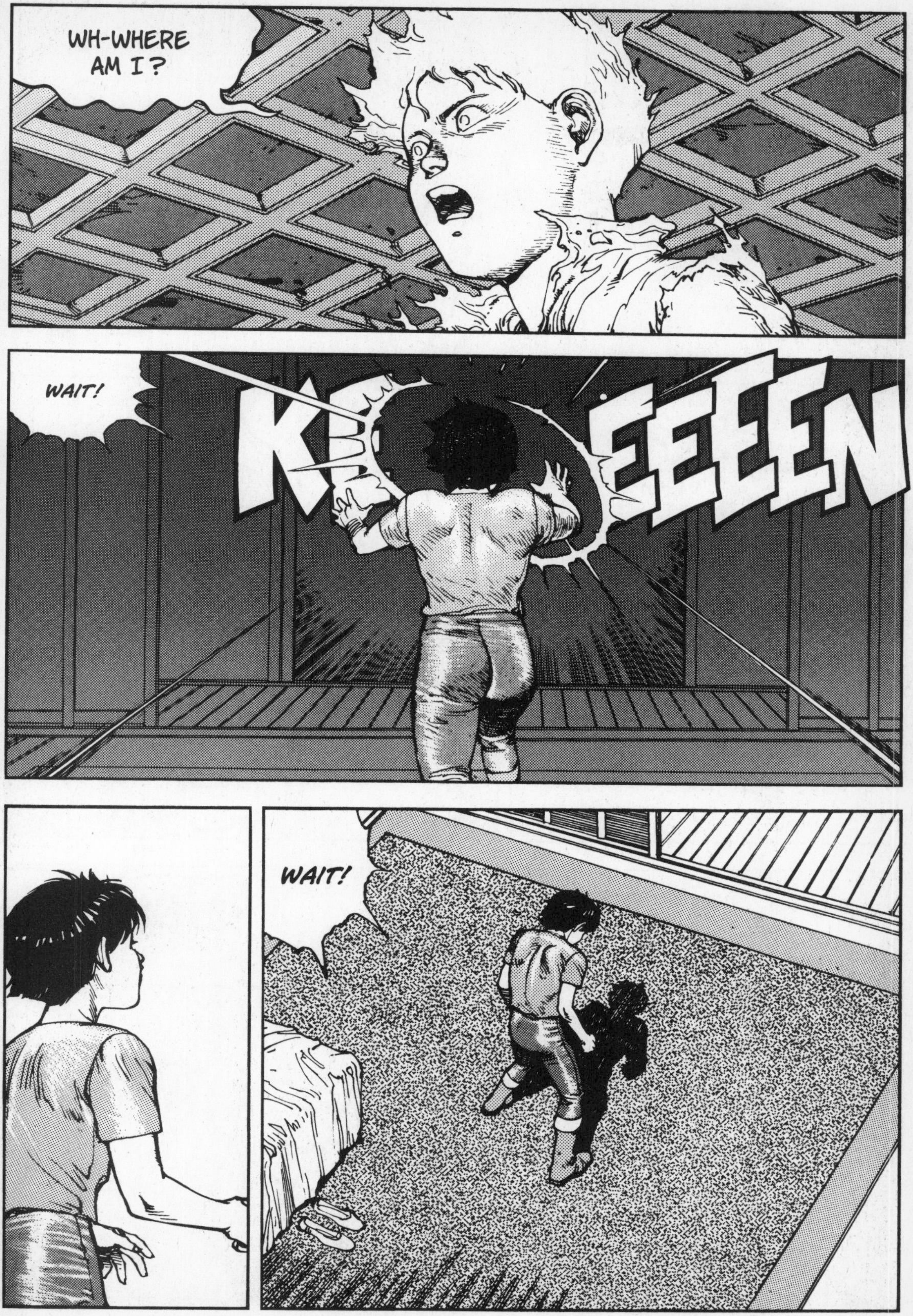
WH-WHERE AM I?
WAIT!
K EEEEN
WAIT!

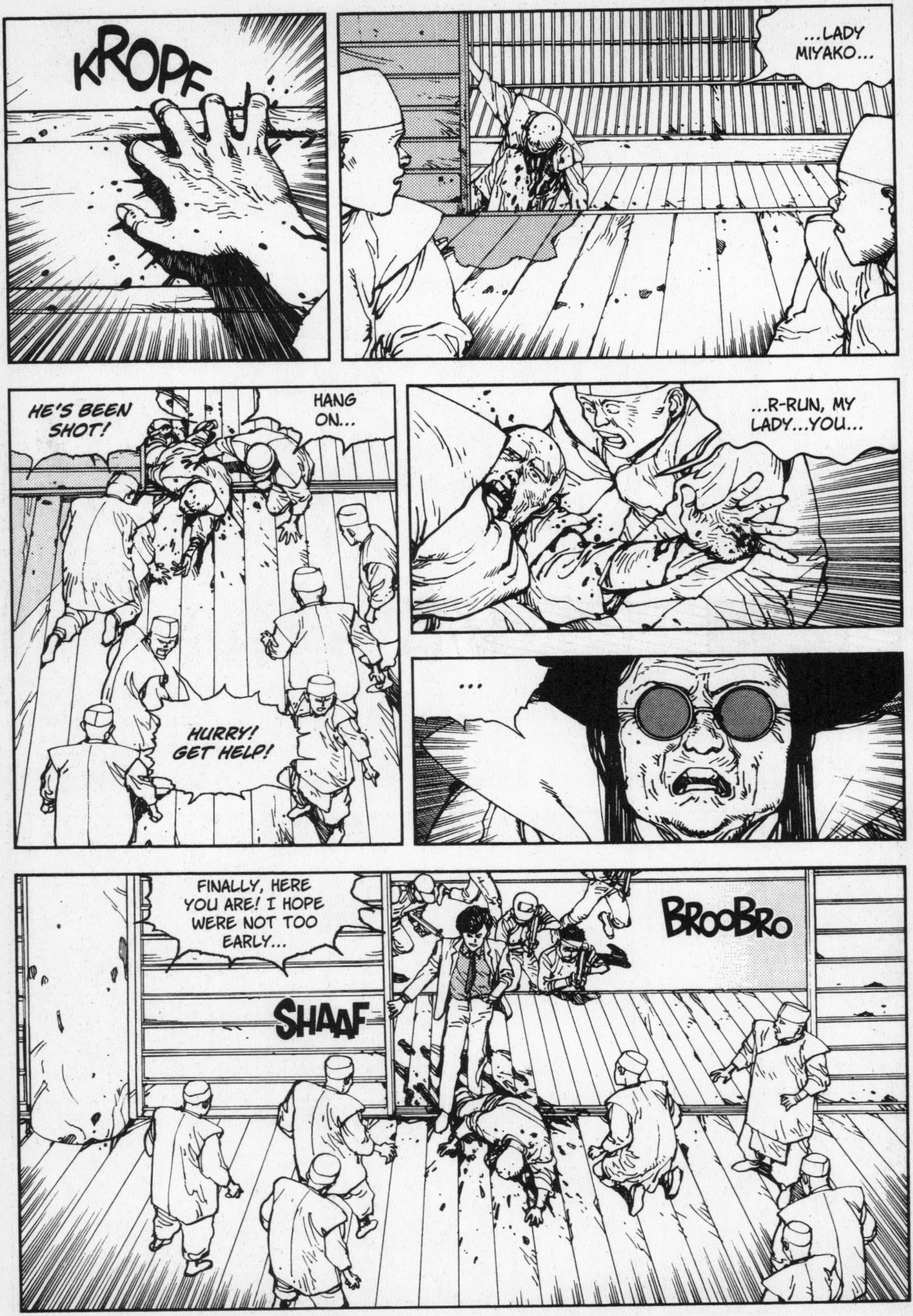
KROPF
...LADY MIYAKO...
HE'S BEEN SHOT!
HANG ON...
HURRY! GET HELP!
...R-RUN, MY LADY...YOU...
...
FINALLY, HERE YOU ARE! I HOPE WERE NOT TOO EARLY...
BROOBRO
SHAAF

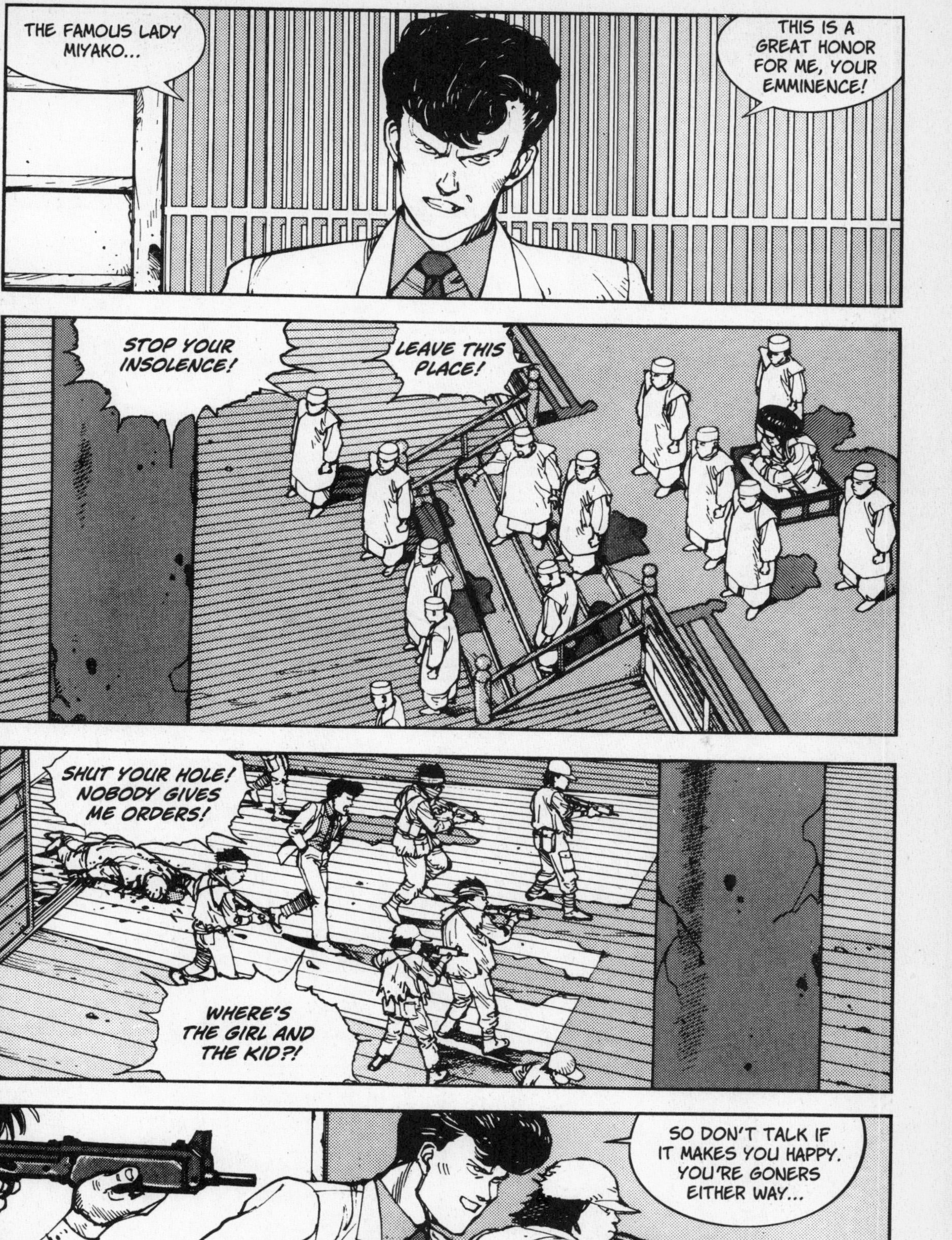
THE FAMOUS LADY MIYAKO...
THIS IS A GREAT HONOR FOR ME, YOUR EMMINENCE!
STOP YOUR INSOLENCE!
LEAVE THIS PLACE!
SHUT YOUR HOLE! NOBODY GIVES ME ORDERS!
WHERE'S THE GIRL AND THE KID?!
SO DON'T TALK IF IT MAKES YOU HAPPY. YOU'RE GONERS EITHER WAY...

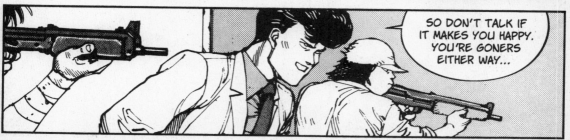

WHAT TO YOU HOPE TO ACHIEVE WITH THIS VIOLENCE?!

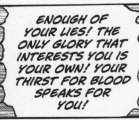

WELL, THE GREATER GLORY OF MY MASTER AKIRA AND OUR LORD TETSUO!

AND YOURS TOO, OF COURSE...

ENOUGH OF YOUR LIES! THE ONLY GLORY THAT INTERESTS YOU IS YOUR OWN! YOUR THIRST FOR BLOOD SPEAKS FOR YOU!

WHAT THE HELL WOULD YOU KNOW ABOUT IT, YOU SENILE FREAK?!

I'VE HAD ENOUGH! WASTE 'EM!

LOVE TO!

SLAK

?

WHAT TH--?!

WHAT'S WRONG WITH THE DAMN' GUNS?

?

SLAK

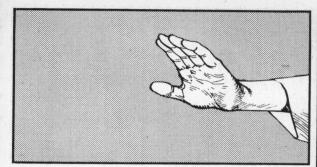

HUHN?!

THEY HAVE THE POWER...

BLAM

AAIEE!

IT BACKFIRED!

TAP

BLAM

STAND YOUR GROUND!

USE YOUR BARE HANDS IF YOU HAVE TO!

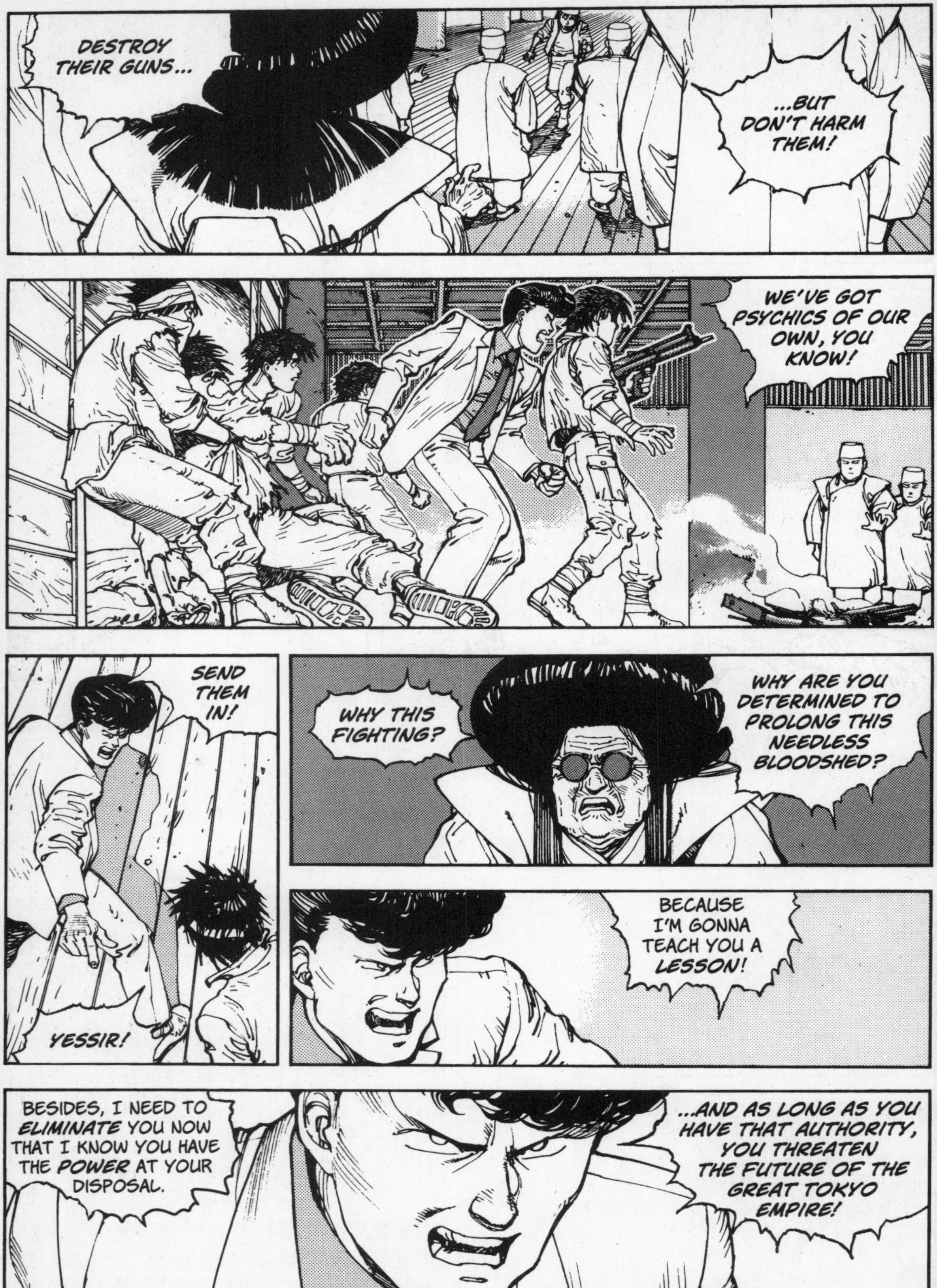

DESTROY THEIR GUNS...
...BUT DON'T HARM THEM!
WE'VE GOT PSYCHICS OF OUR OWN, YOU KNOW!
SEND THEM IN!
YESSIR!
WHY THIS FIGHTING?
WHY ARE YOU DETERMINED TO PROLONG THIS NEEDLESS BLOODSHED?
BECAUSE I'M GONNA TEACH YOU A LESSON!
BESIDES, I NEED TO ELIMINATE YOU NOW THAT I KNOW YOU HAVE THE POWER AT YOUR DISPOSAL.
...AND AS LONG AS YOU HAVE THAT AUTHORITY, YOU THREATEN THE FUTURE OF THE GREAT TOKYO EMPIRE!

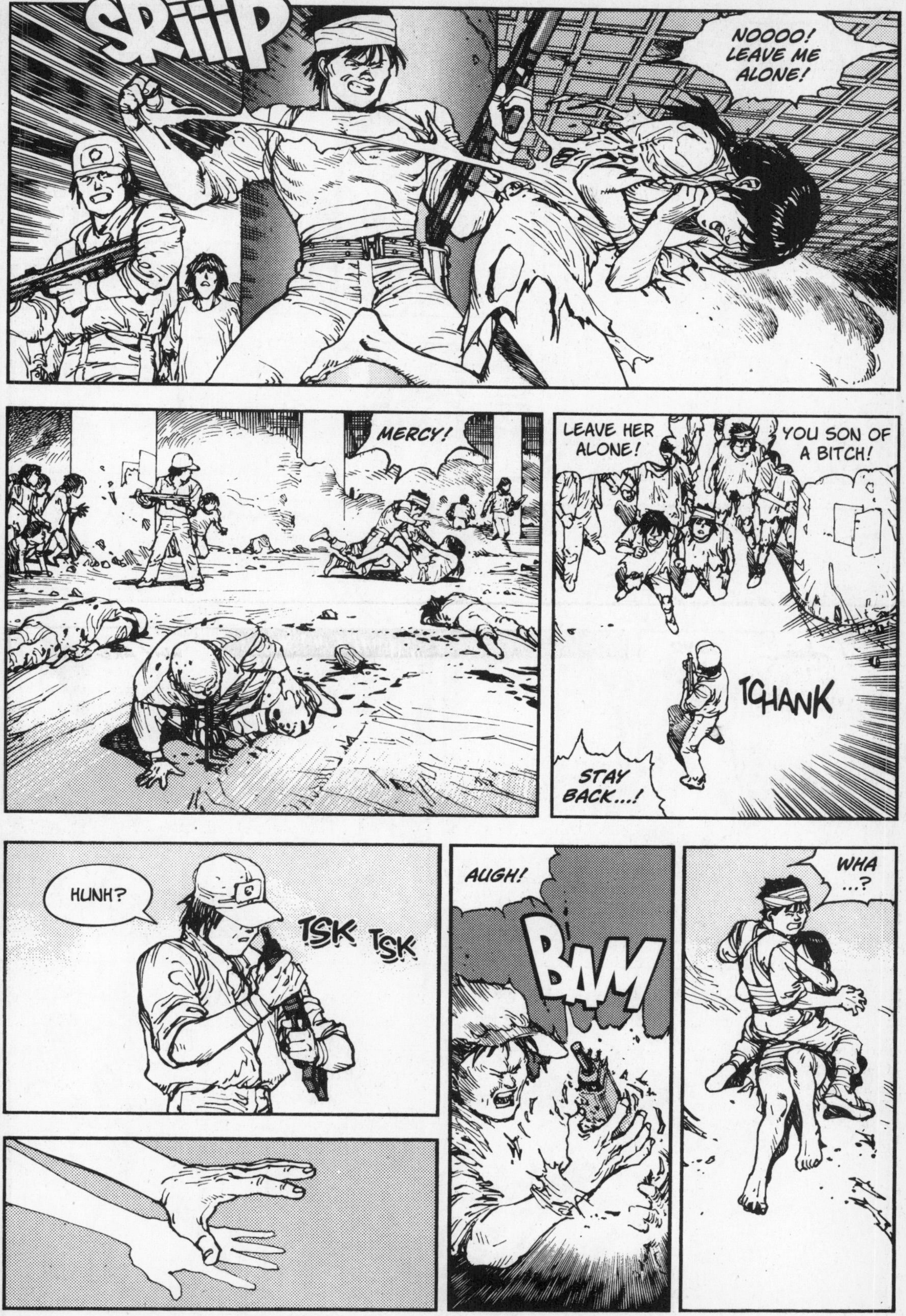
SRiiiP
NOOOO! LEAVE ME ALONE!
MERCY!
LEAVE HER ALONE!
YOU SON OF A BITCH!
TCHANK
STAY BACK...!
HUNH?
TSK TSK
AUGH!
BAM
WHA ...?

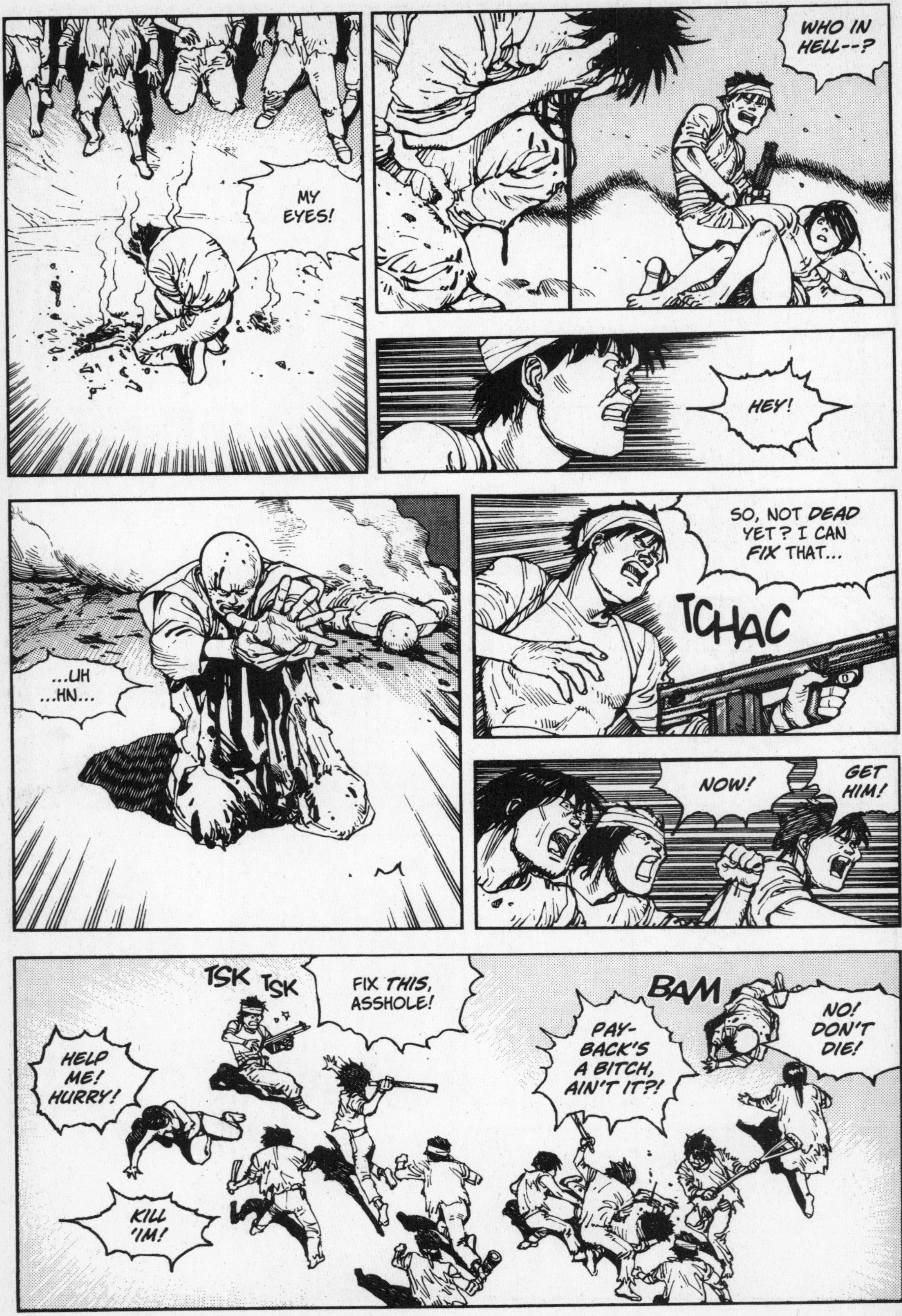
MY EYES!
WHO IN HELL--?
HEY!
...UH ...HN...
SO, NOT DEAD YET? I CAN FIX THAT...
TCHAC
NOW!
GET HIM!
TSK TSK
FIX THIS, ASSHOLE!
HELP ME! HURRY!
KILL 'IM!
BAM
PAY-BACK'S A BITCH, AIN'T IT?!
NO! DON'T DIE!

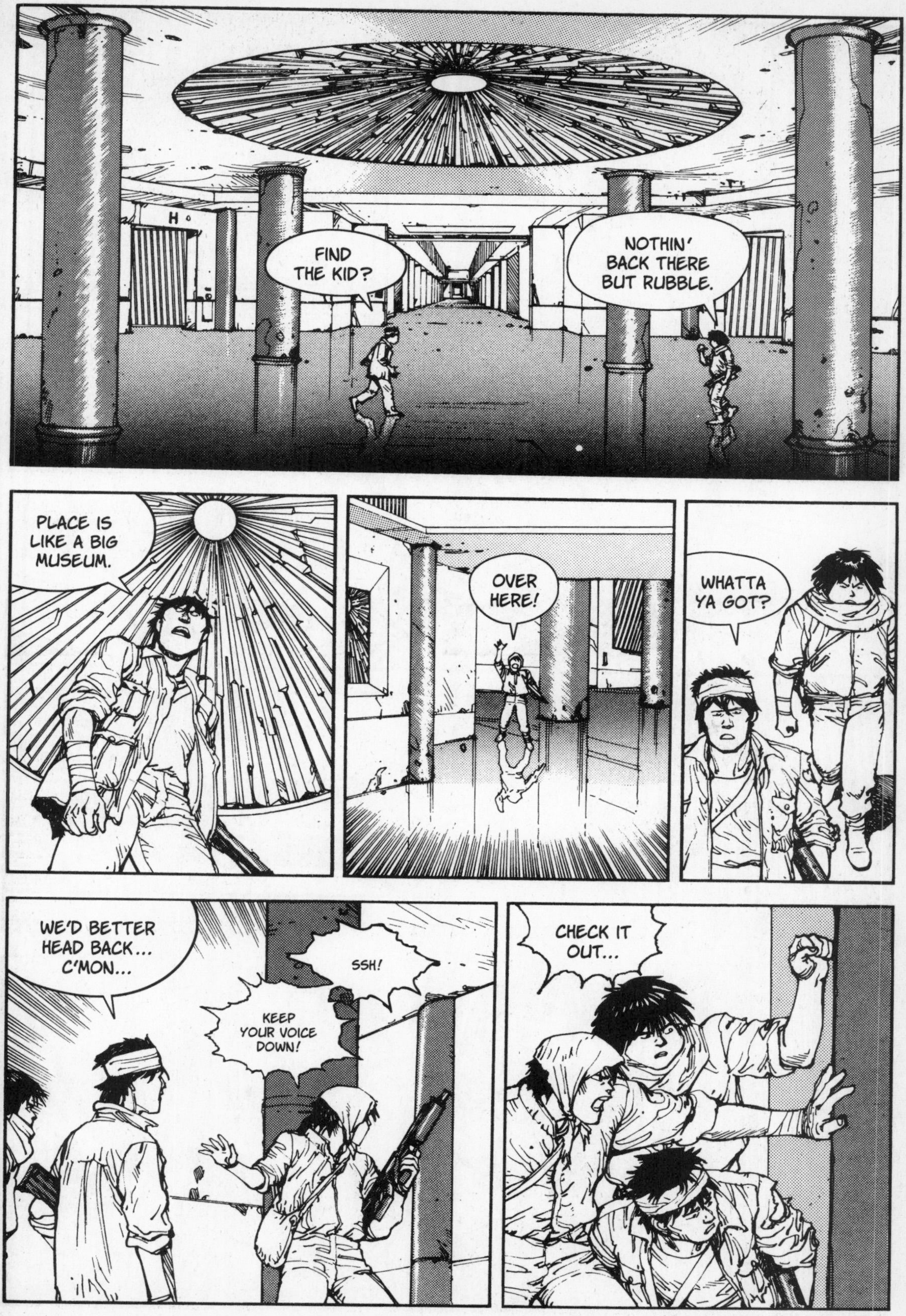
FIND THE KID?
NOTHIN' BACK THERE BUT RUBBLE.
PLACE IS LIKE A BIG MUSEUM.
OVER HERE!
WHATTA YA GOT?
WE'D BETTER HEAD BACK... C'MON...
SSH!
KEEP YOUR VOICE DOWN!
CHECK IT OUT...

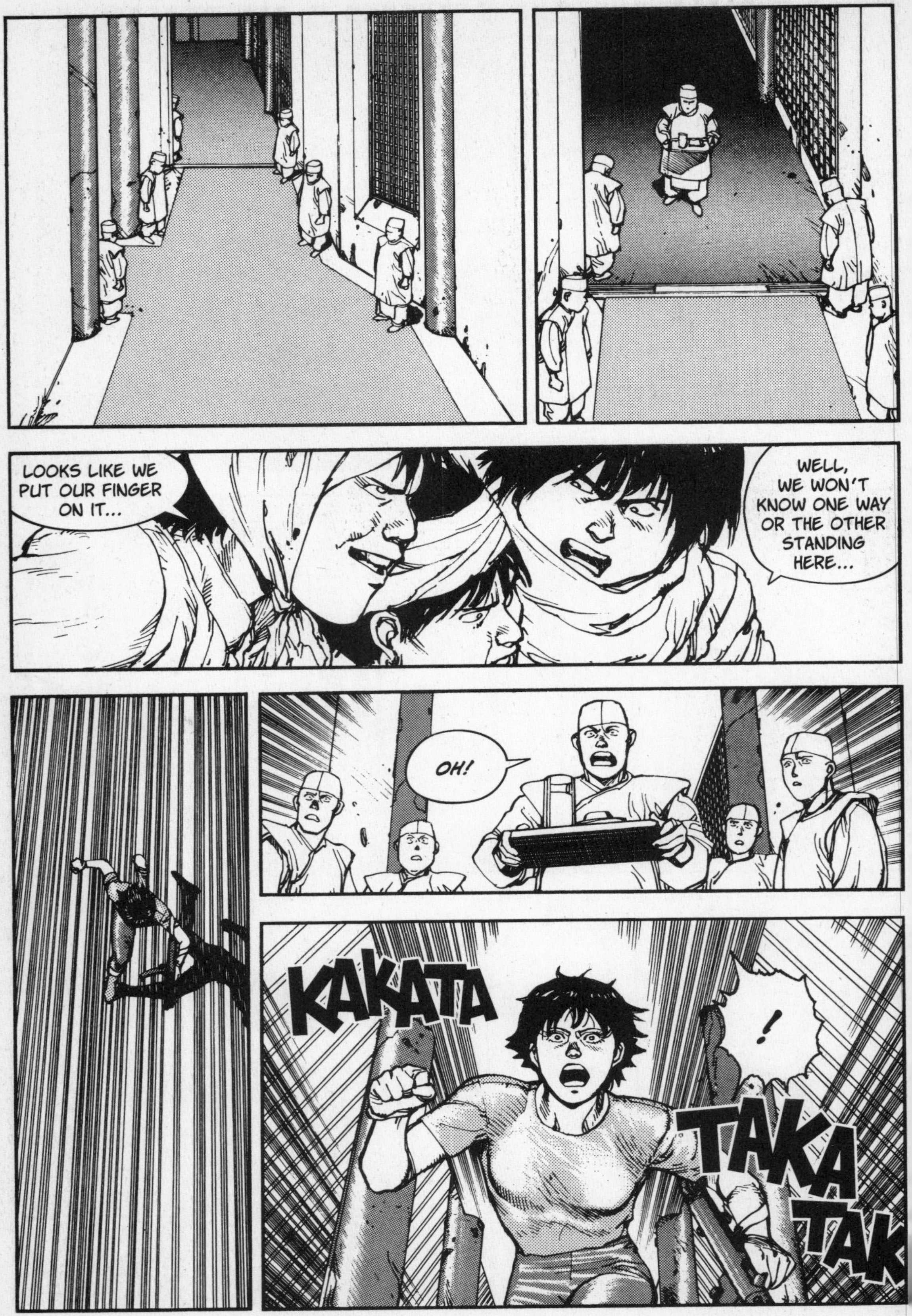
LOOKS LIKE WE PUT OUR FINGER ON IT...
WELL, WE WON'T KNOW ONE WAY OR THE OTHER STANDING HERE...
OH!
KAKATA
!
TAKA TAK

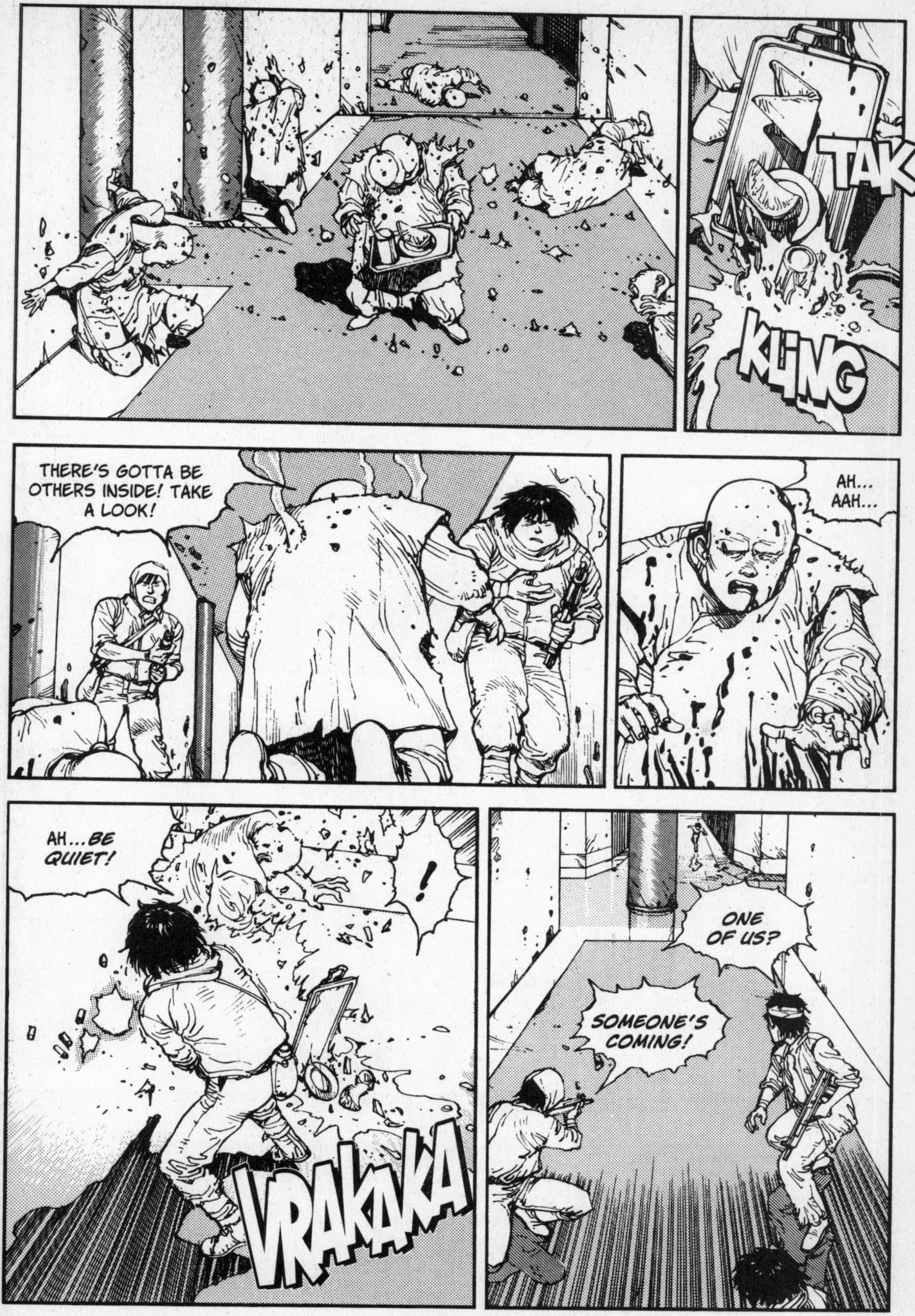

TAK
KLING
THERE'S GOTTA BE OTHERS INSIDE! TAKE A LOOK!
AH... AAH...
AH...BE QUIET!
!
VRAKAKA
ONE OF US?
SOMEONE'S COMING!

NO!

IT'S A GIRL...

A GIRL WITH A GUN!

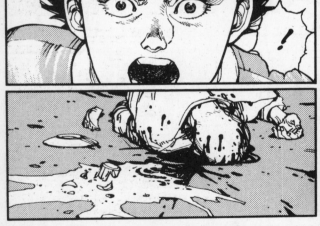

!

DON'T SHOOT HER!

ORDERS ARE TO TAKE HER ALIVE!

I DON'T CARE IF THERE *ARE* THREE OF YOU...

...YOU'RE ALL GOING DOWN!

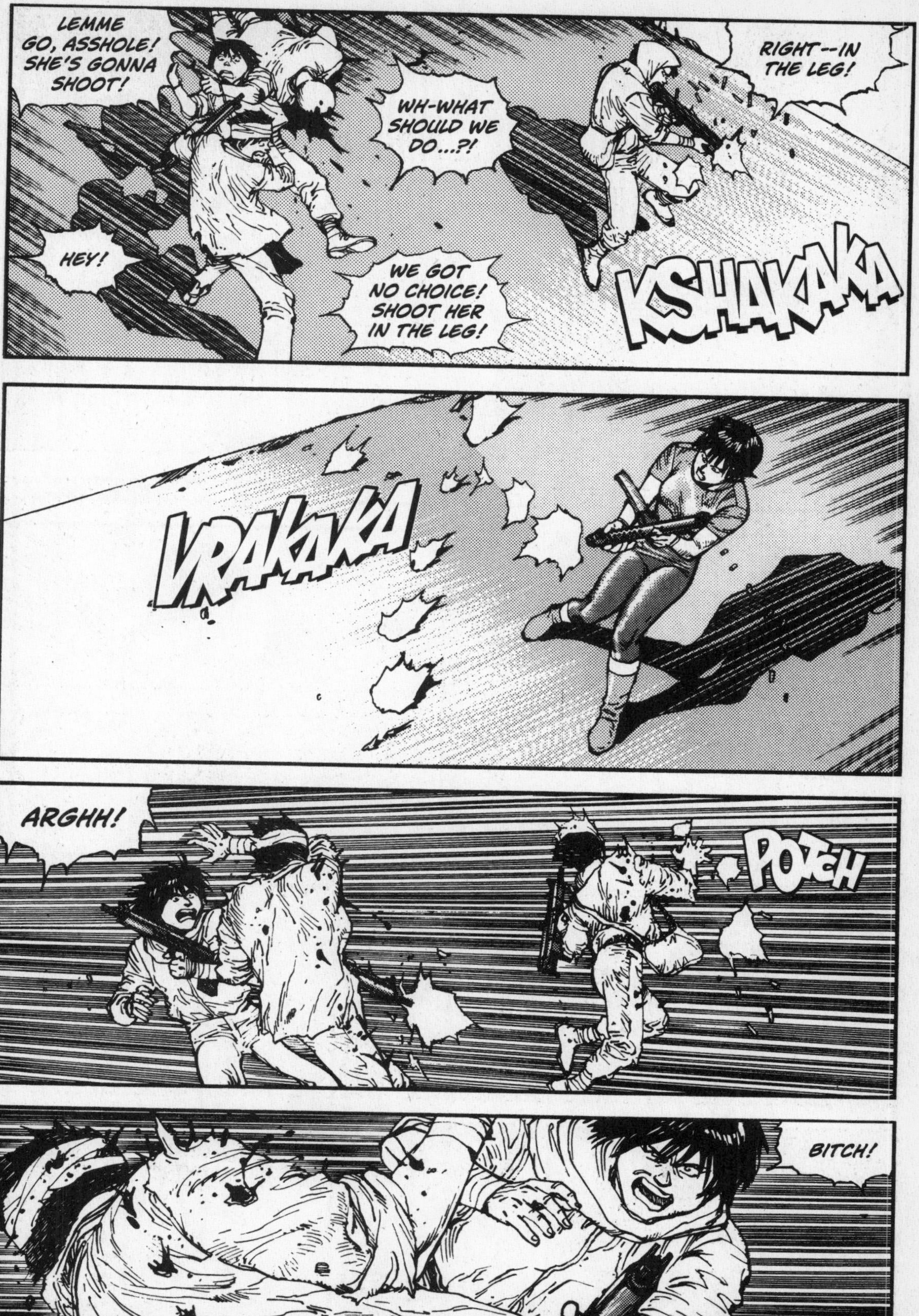
LEMME GO, ASSHOLE! SHE'S GONNA SHOOT!
WH-WHAT SHOULD WE DO...?!
HEY!
WE GOT NO CHOICE! SHOOT HER IN THE LEG!
RIGHT--IN THE LEG!
KSHAKAKA
VRAKAKA
ARGHH!
POTCH
BITCH!

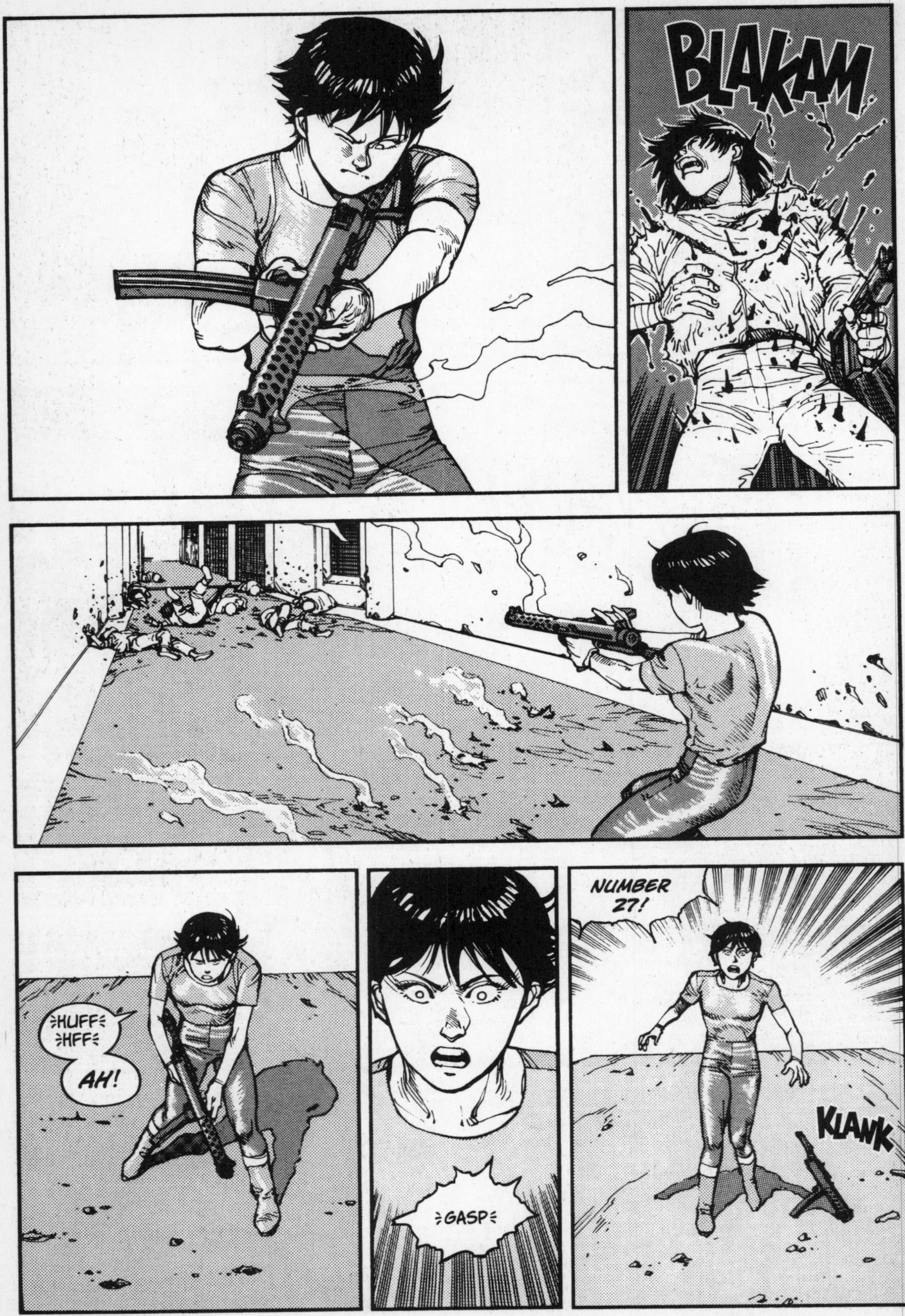

BLAKAM
HUFF
HFF
AH!
GASP
NUMBER 27!
KLANK

SLINK

SWAP

OH!

ARE YOU ALL RIGHT?

WHAT IS HAPPENING?

I TOOK CARE OF SOME TROUBLE...

HOW'S NUMBER 27?

STILL UNDER SEDATION.

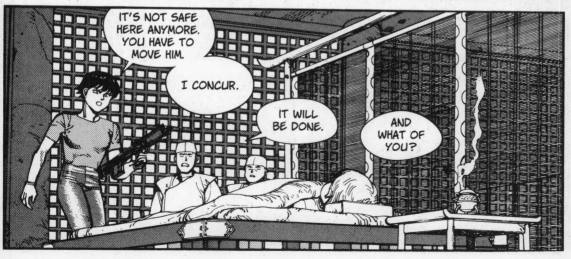

IT'S NOT SAFE HERE ANYMORE. YOU HAVE TO MOVE HIM.

I CONCUR.

IT WILL BE DONE.

AND WHAT OF YOU?

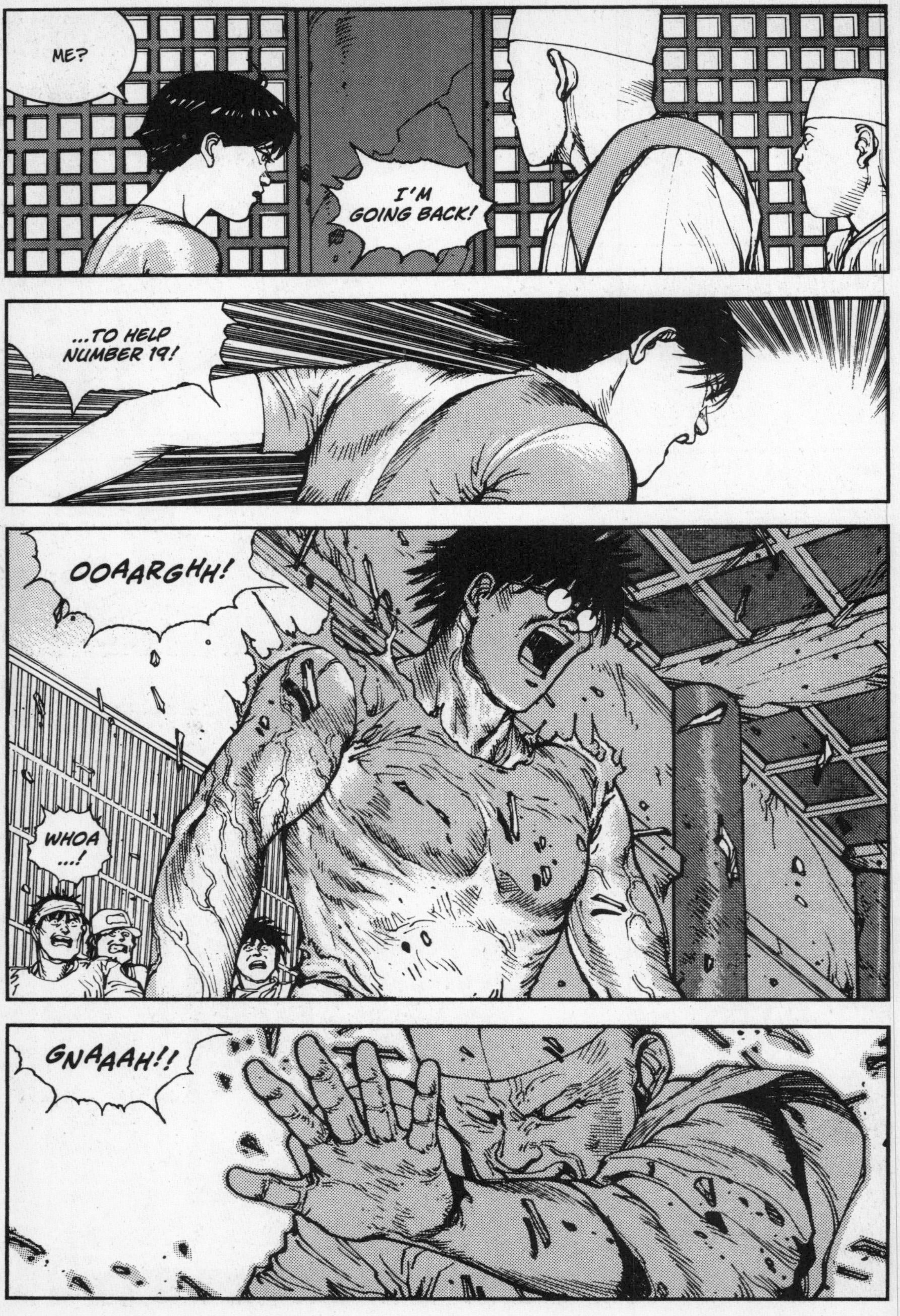

ME?
I'M GOING BACK!
...TO HELP NUMBER 19!
OOAARGHH!
WHOA ...!
GNAAAH!!

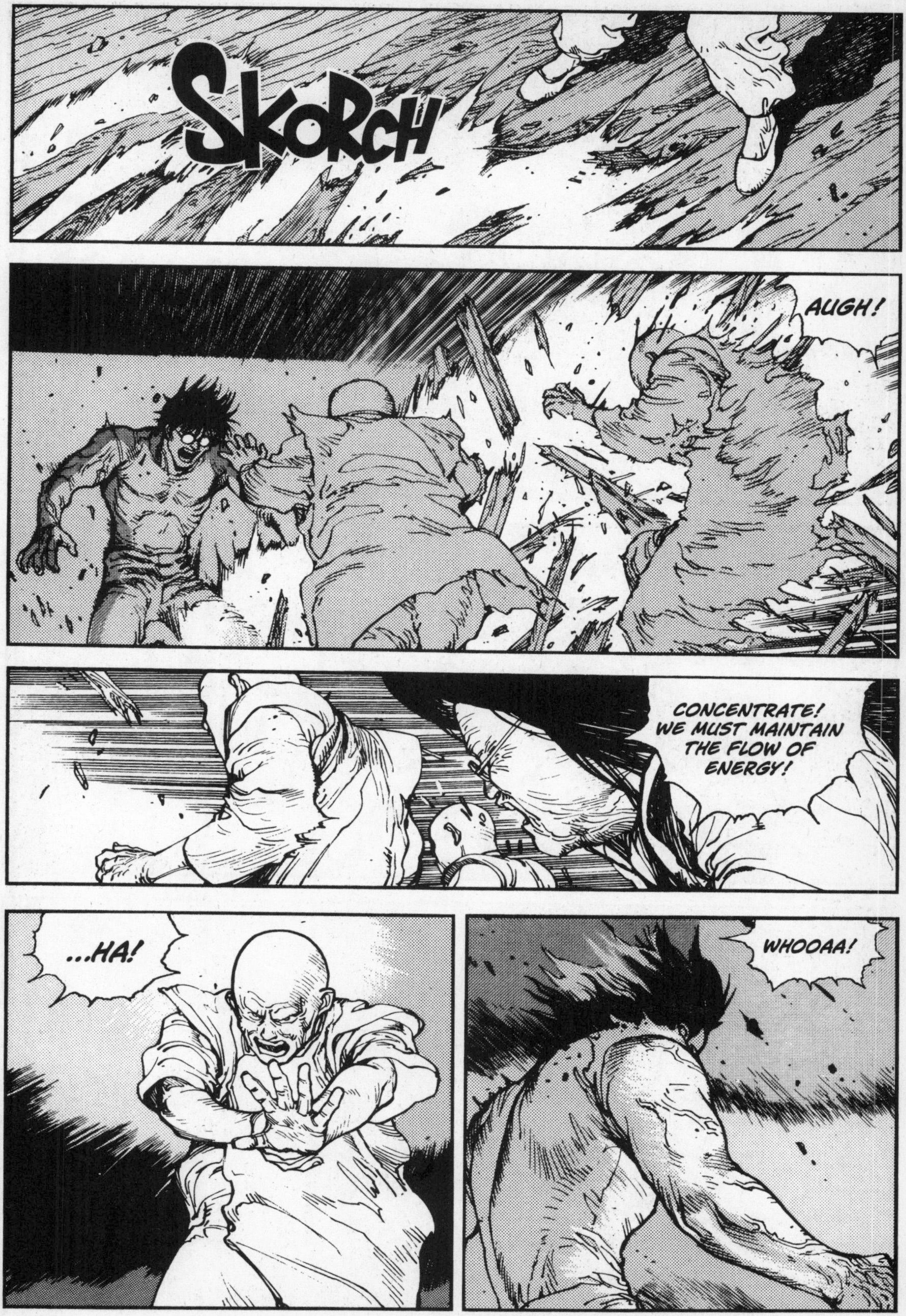
SKORCH
AUGH!
CONCENTRATE! WE MUST MAINTAIN THE FLOW OF ENERGY!
...HA!
WHOOAA!

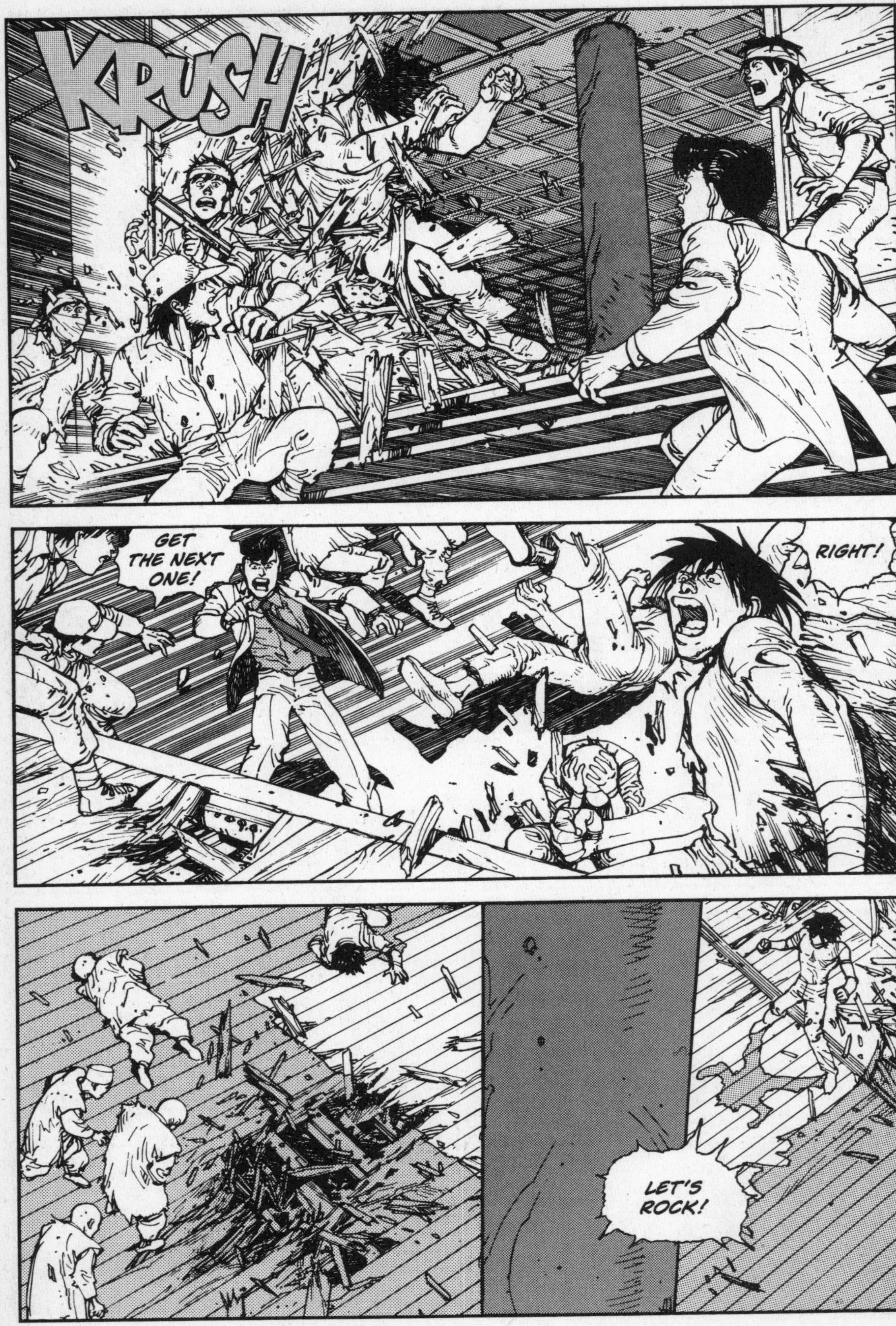
KRUSH
GET THE NEXT ONE!
RIGHT!
LET'S ROCK!

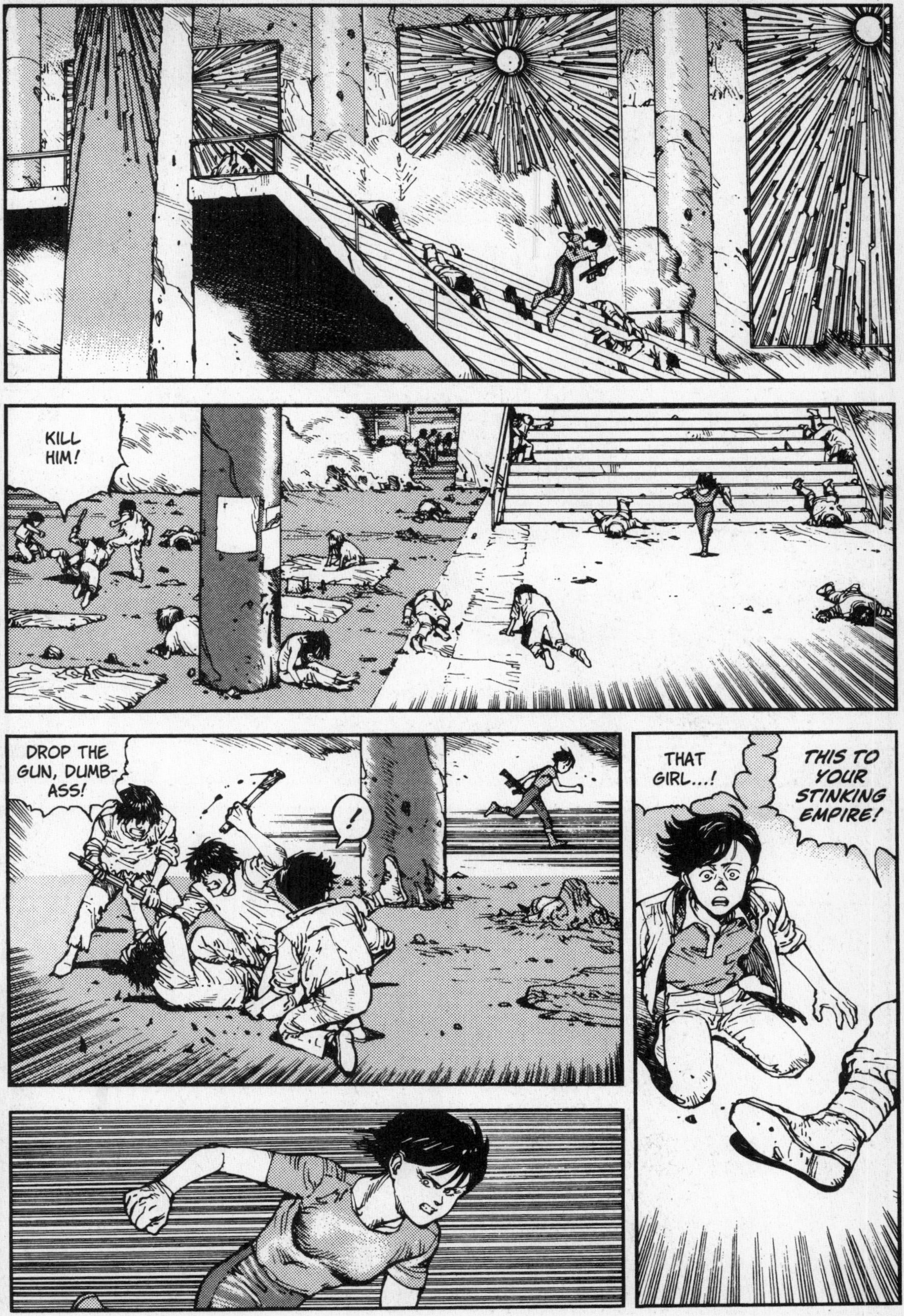
KILL HIM!
DROP THE GUN, DUMB-ASS!
!
THAT GIRL...!
THIS TO YOUR STINKING EMPIRE!

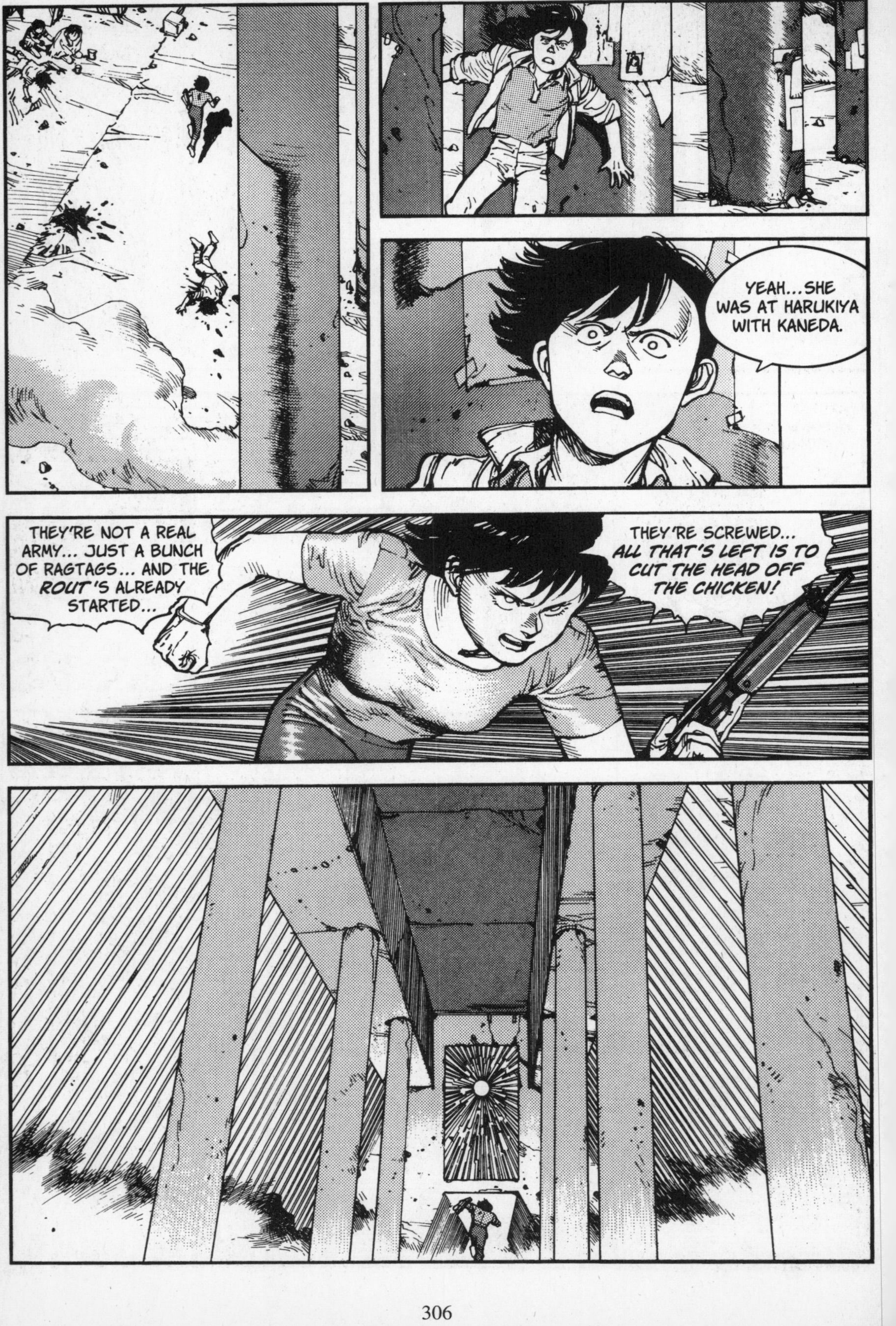
YEAH...SHE WAS AT HARUKIYA WITH KANEDA.
THEY'RE NOT A REAL ARMY... JUST A BUNCH OF RAGTAGS... AND THE *ROUT*'S ALREADY STARTED...
THEY'RE SCREWED... *ALL THAT'S LEFT IS TO CUT THE HEAD OFF THE CHICKEN!*

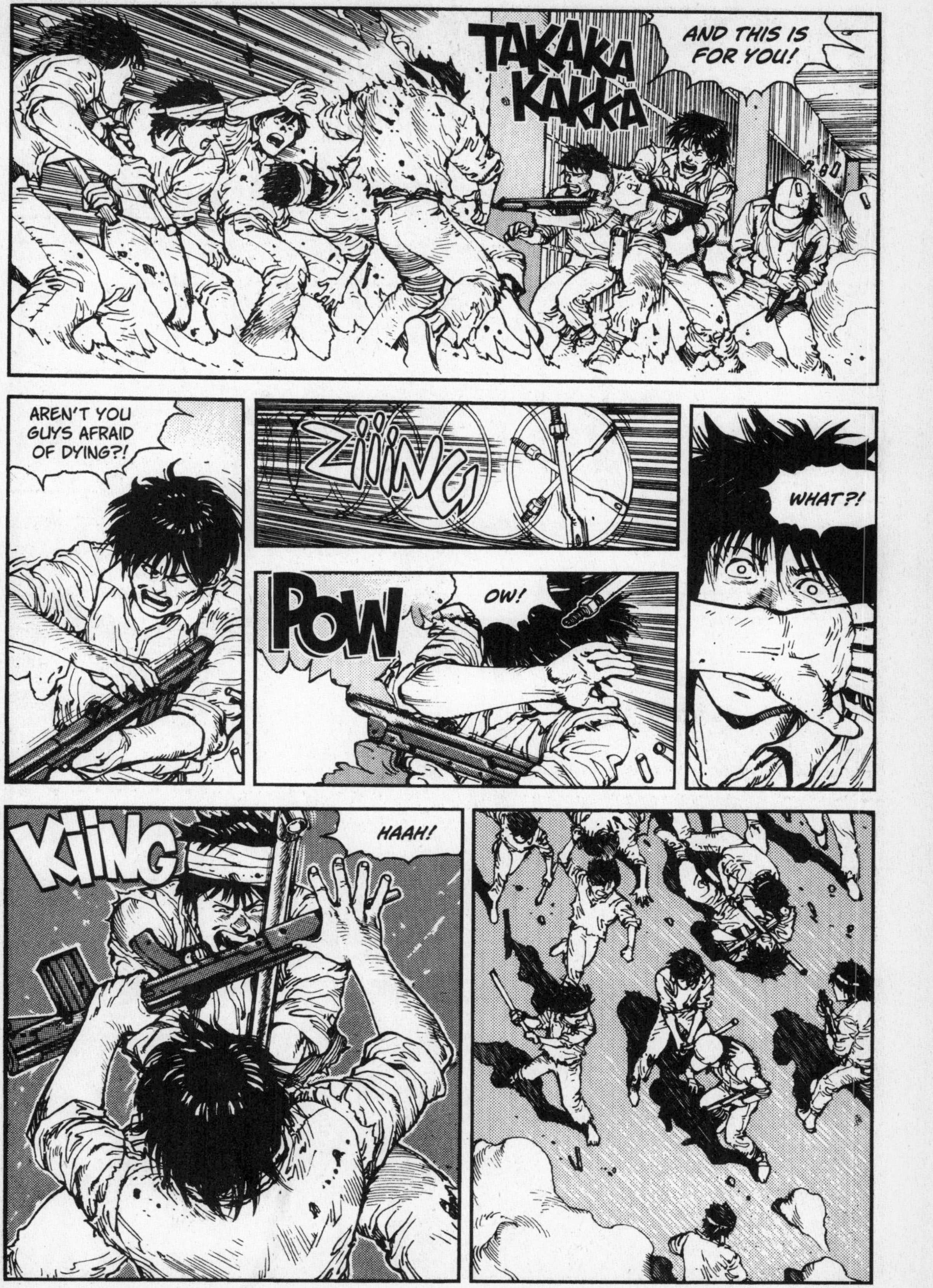
TAKAKA KAKKA
AND THIS IS FOR YOU!
AREN'T YOU GUYS AFRAID OF DYING?!
ZIIING
POW
OW!
WHAT?!
KIING
HAAH!

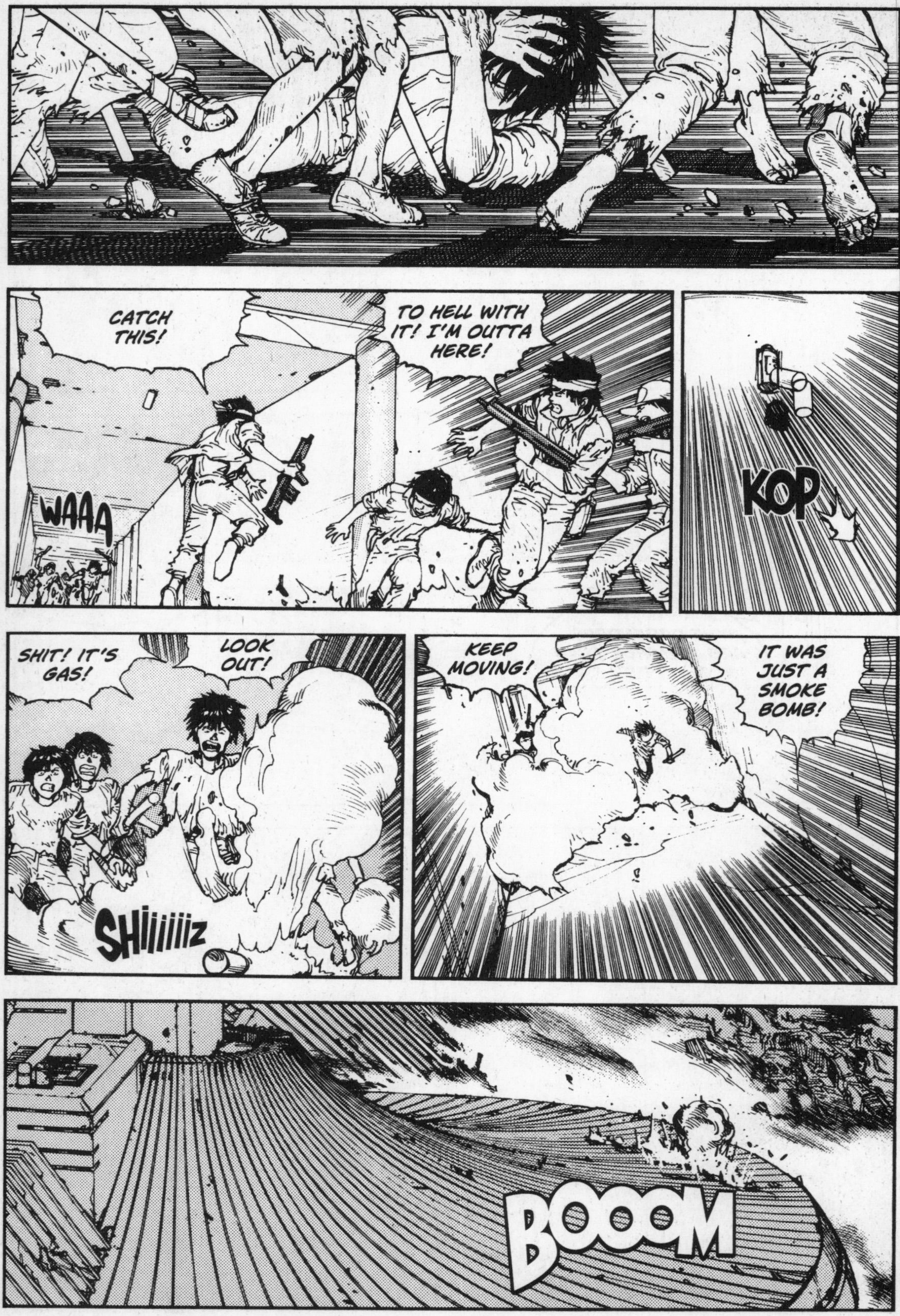
CATCH THIS!
WAAA
TO HELL WITH IT! I'M OUTTA HERE!
KOP
SHIT! IT'S GAS!
LOOK OUT!
SHIiiiiiz
KEEP MOVING!
IT WAS JUST A SMOKE BOMB!
BOOOM

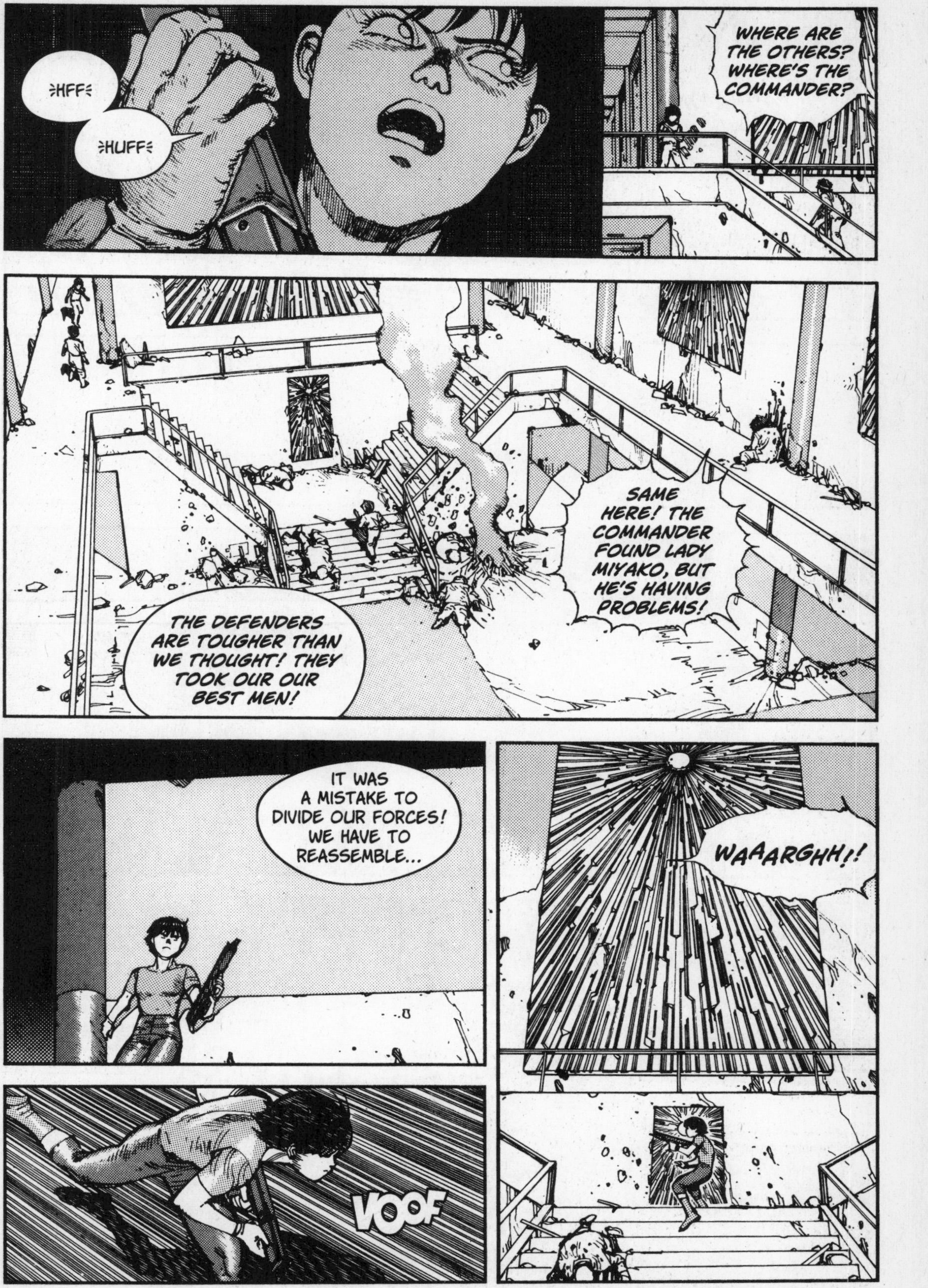
HFF
HUFF
WHERE ARE THE OTHERS? WHERE'S THE COMMANDER?
THE DEFENDERS ARE TOUGHER THAN WE THOUGHT! THEY TOOK OUR OUR BEST MEN!
SAME HERE! THE COMMANDER FOUND LADY MIYAKO, BUT HE'S HAVING PROBLEMS!
IT WAS A MISTAKE TO DIVIDE OUR FORCES! WE HAVE TO REASSEMBLE...
WAAARGHH!!
VOOF

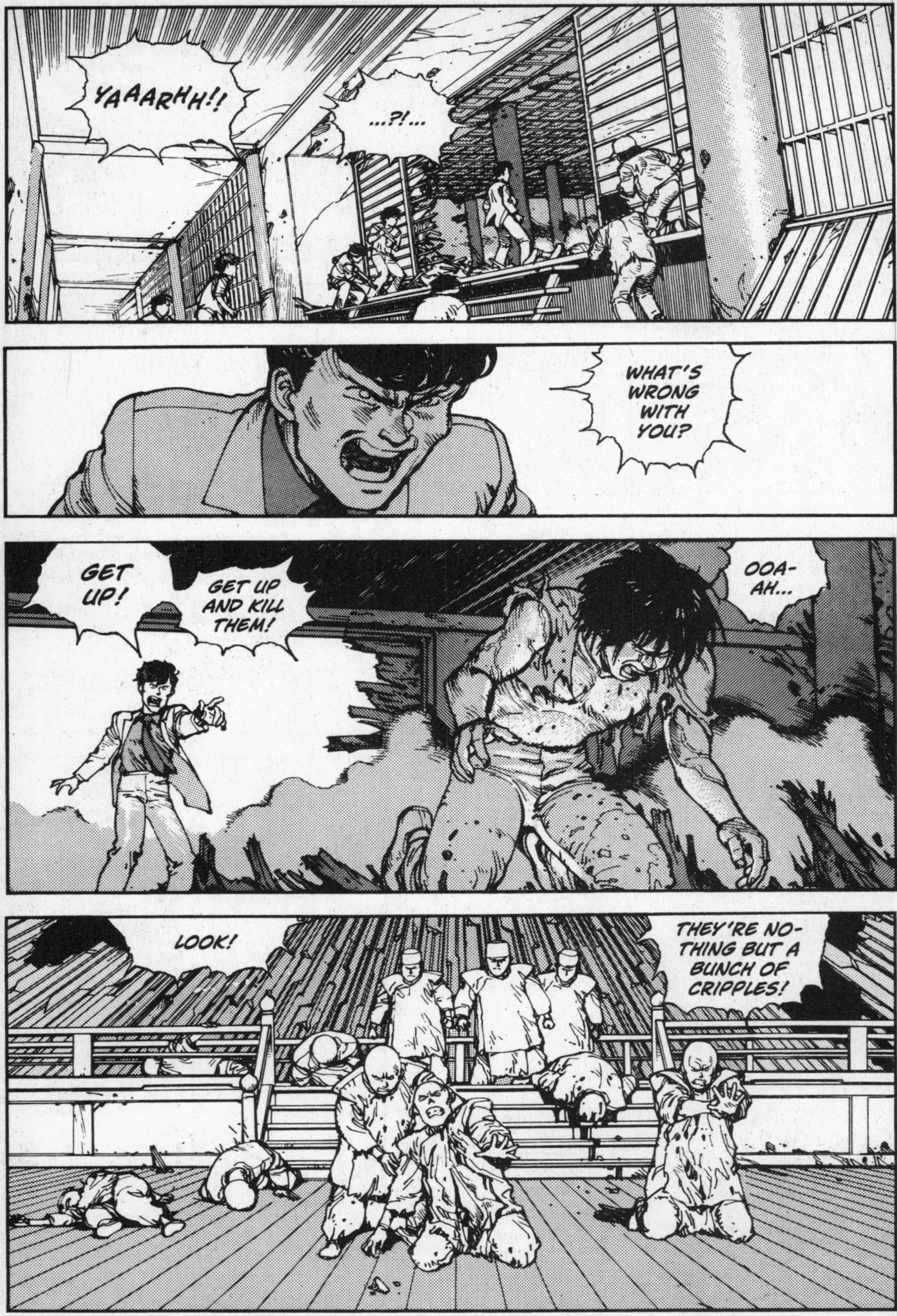
YAAARHH!!
...?!...
WHAT'S WRONG WITH YOU?
GET UP!
GET UP AND KILL THEM!
OOA-AH...
LOOK!
THEY'RE NO-THING BUT A BUNCH OF CRIPPLES!

O-OAA
...AH...

GOOD! THAT'S MORE LIKE IT!

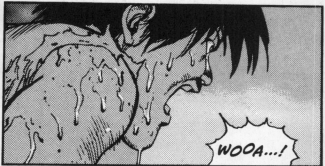

WOOA....!

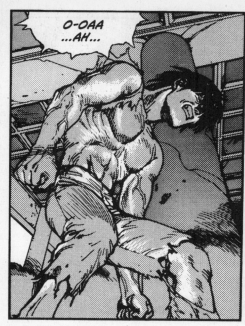

BAD NEWS, COMMAN-DER!

?!

THE MONKS AND THE REFUGEES ARE AFTER US!

≈HUFF≈

≈HUFF≈

WHAT ?!

WHAT'LL WE DO?!

SHUT UP!

WE'VE FAILED. WE HAVE TO LEAVE...

WHAT ?!

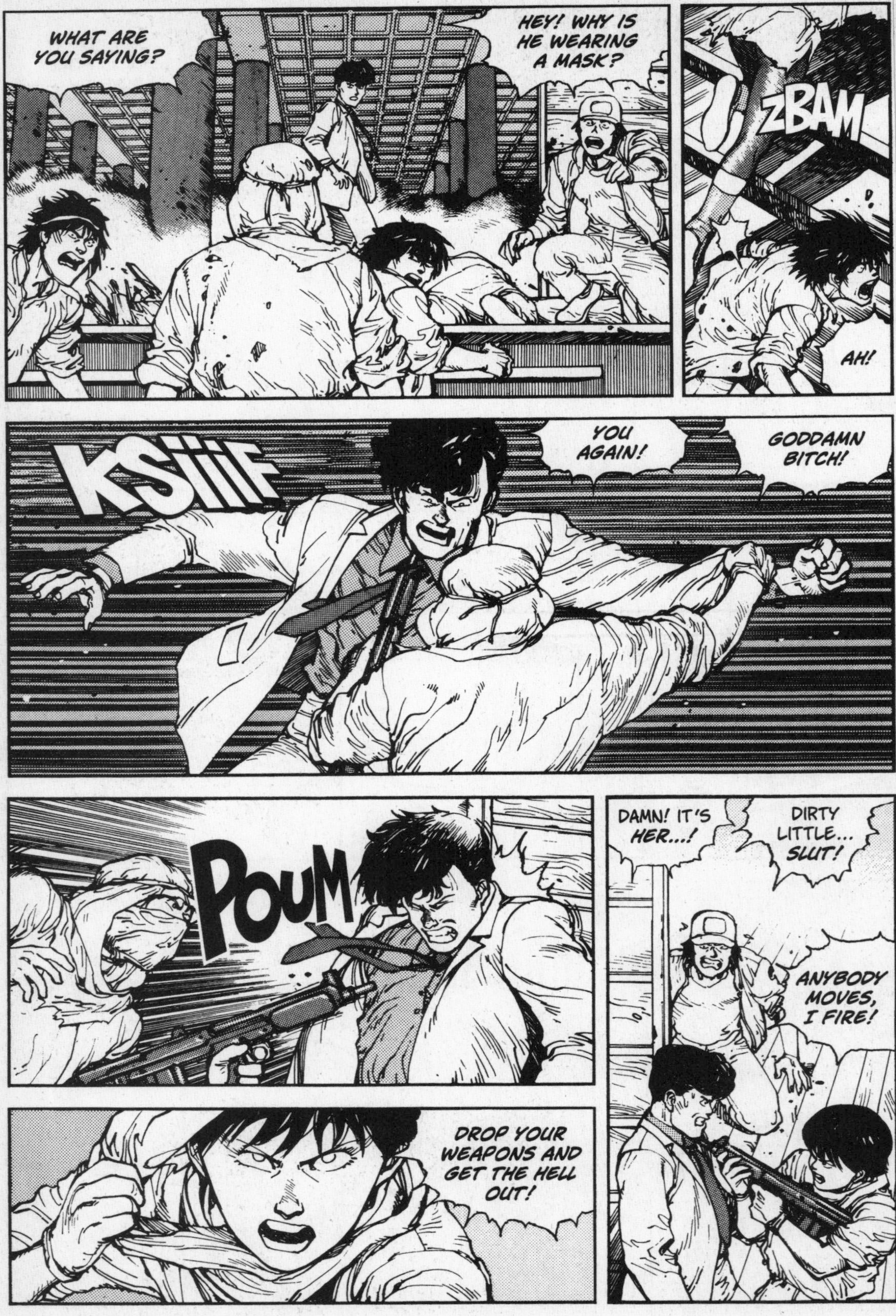
WHAT ARE YOU SAYING?
HEY! WHY IS HE WEARING A MASK?
ZBAM
AH!
KSIIIF
YOU AGAIN!
GODDAMN BITCH!
POUM
DAMN! IT'S HER...!
DIRTY LITTLE... SLUT!
ANYBODY MOVES, I FIRE!
DROP YOUR WEAPONS AND GET THE HELL OUT!

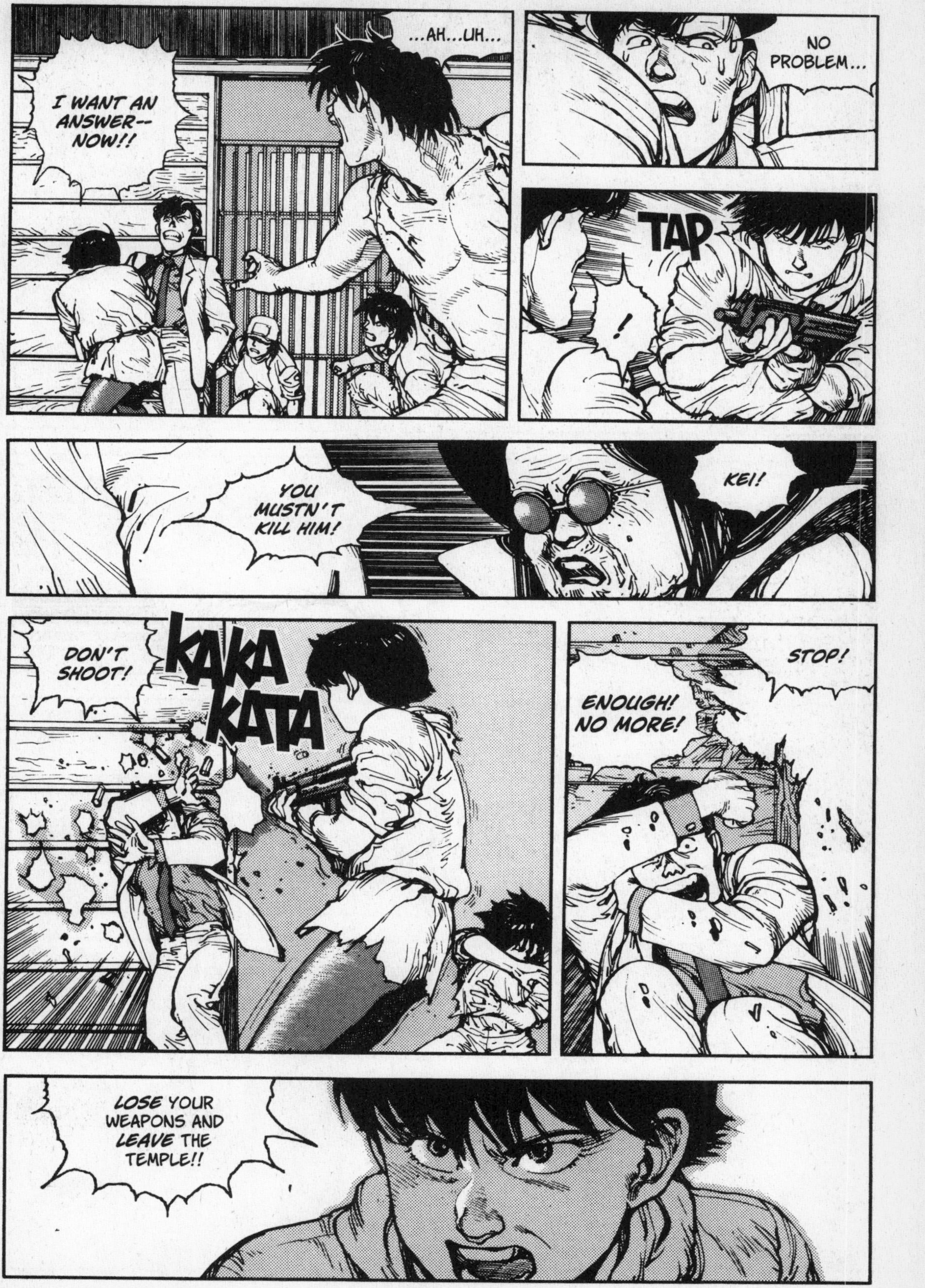
...AH...UH...
I WANT AN ANSWER--NOW!!
NO PROBLEM...
TAP
!
YOU MUSTN'T KILL HIM!
KEI!
DON'T SHOOT!
KAKA KATA
STOP!
ENOUGH! NO MORE!
LOSE YOUR WEAPONS AND LEAVE THE TEMPLE!!

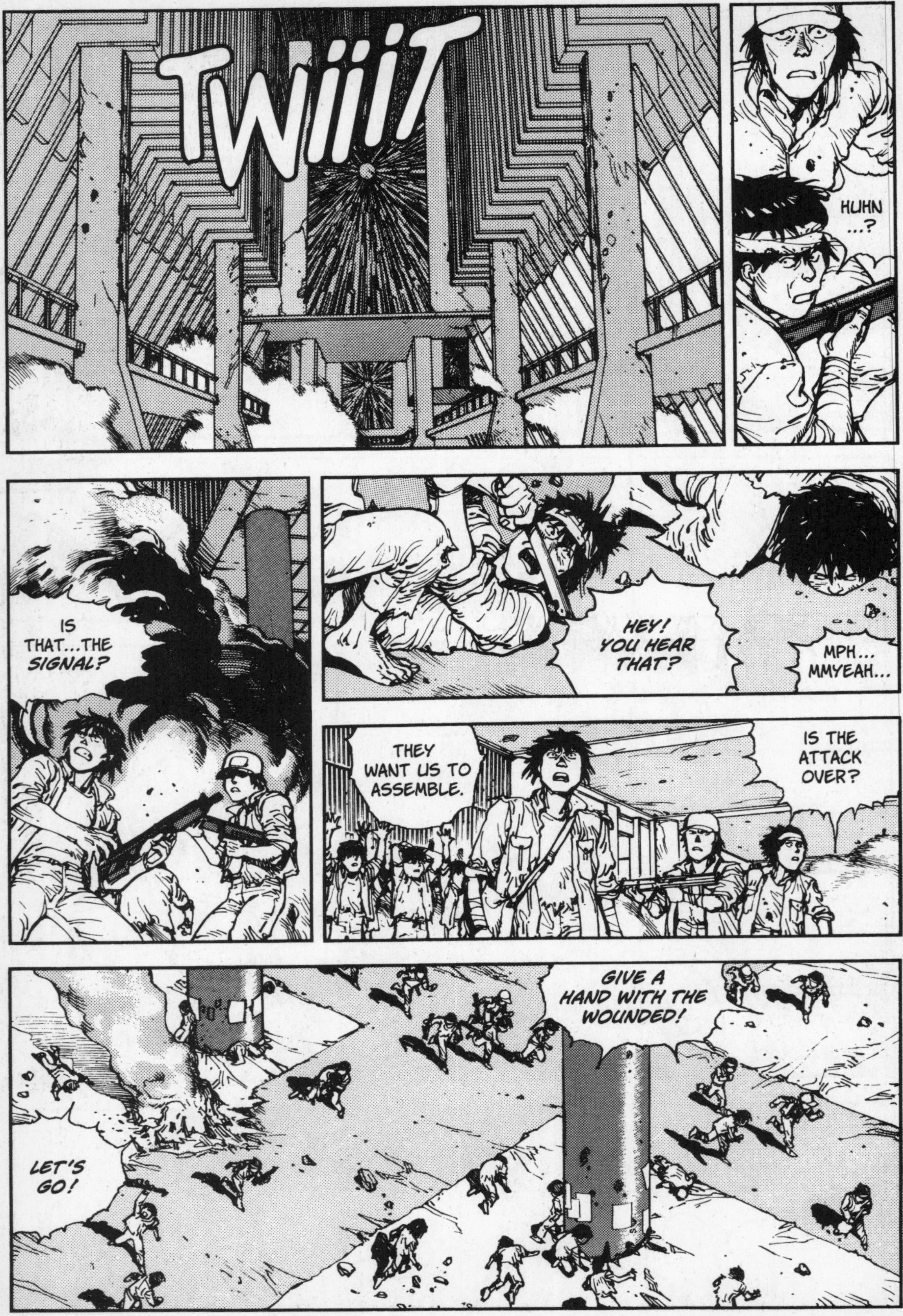
TWiiiT
HUHN ...?
IS THAT...THE *SIGNAL?*
*HEY! YOU HEAR THAT?*
MPH... MMYEAH...
THEY WANT US TO ASSEMBLE.
IS THE ATTACK OVER?
*GIVE A HAND WITH THE WOUNDED!*
*LET'S GO!*

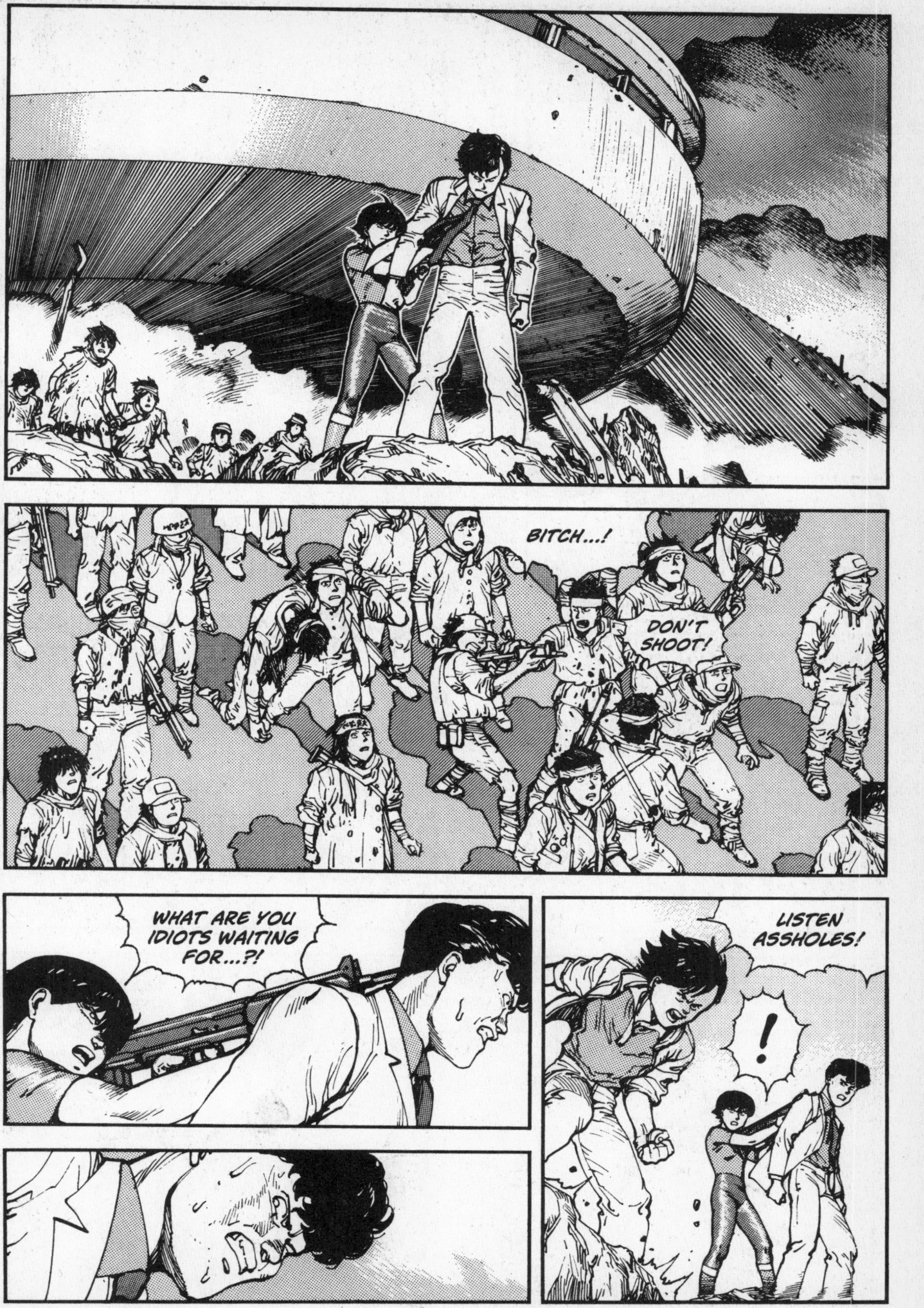

BITCH...!
DON'T SHOOT!
WHAT ARE YOU IDIOTS WAITING FOR...?!
LISTEN ASSHOLES!
!

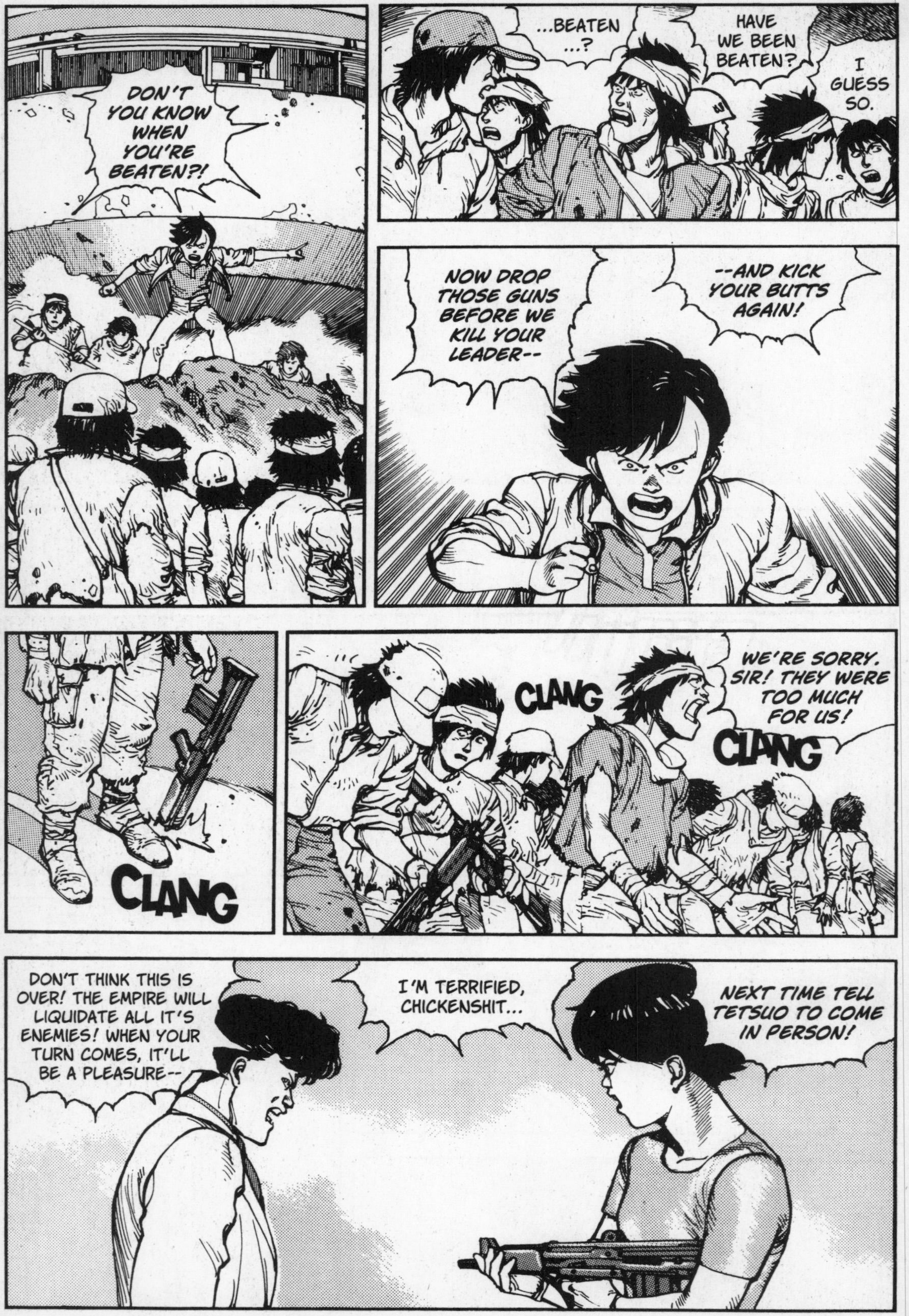
DON'T YOU KNOW WHEN YOU'RE BEATEN?!
...BEATEN ...?
HAVE WE BEEN BEATEN?
I GUESS SO.
NOW DROP THOSE GUNS BEFORE WE KILL YOUR LEADER--
--AND KICK YOUR BUTTS AGAIN!
CLANG
CLANG
WE'RE SORRY. SIR! THEY WERE TOO MUCH FOR US!
CLANG
DON'T THINK THIS IS OVER! THE EMPIRE WILL LIQUIDATE ALL IT'S ENEMIES! WHEN YOUR TURN COMES, IT'LL BE A PLEASURE--
I'M TERRIFIED, CHICKENSHIT...
NEXT TIME TELL TETSUO TO COME IN PERSON!

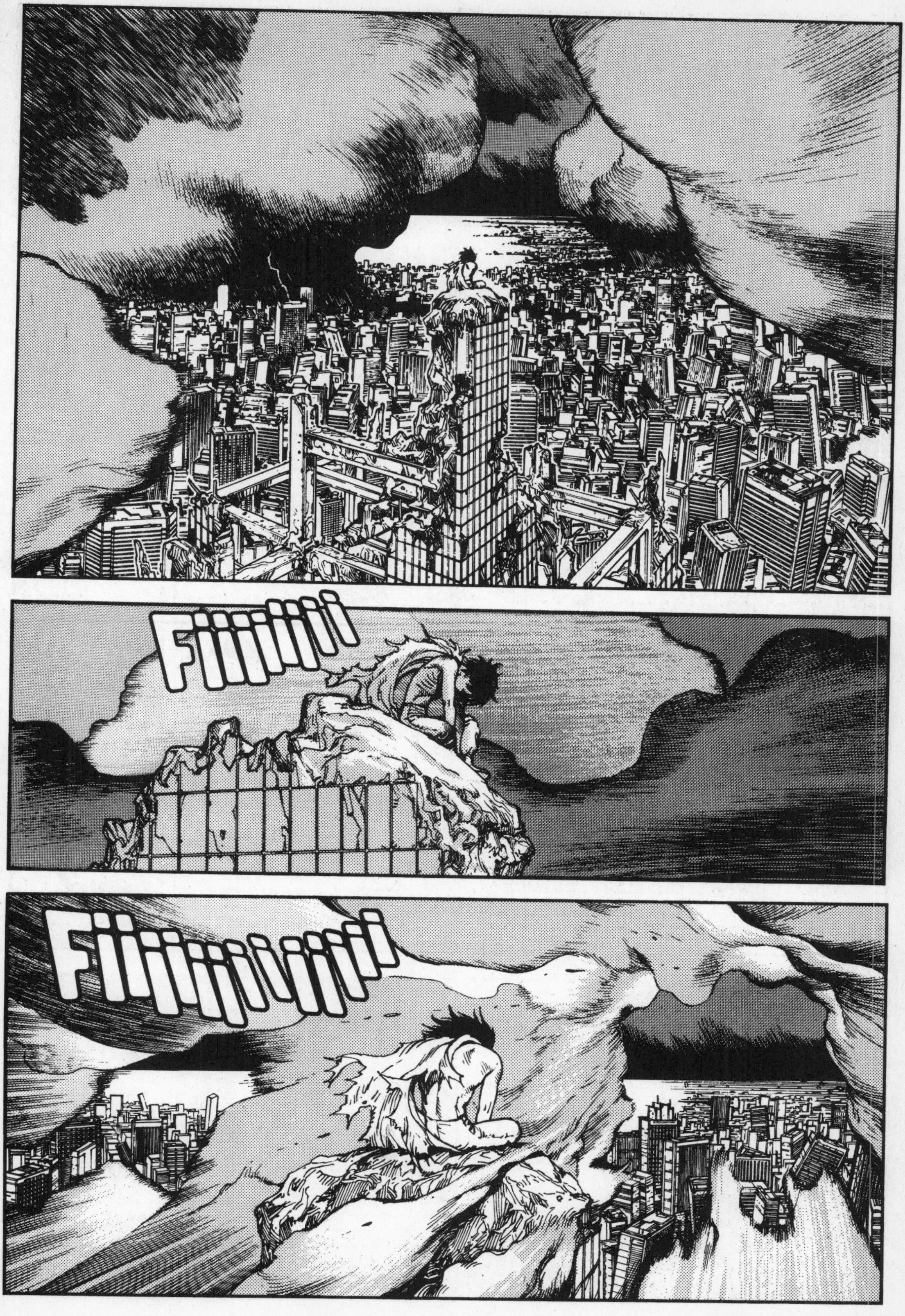
Fiiiiiii
Fiiiiiiiiiiiii

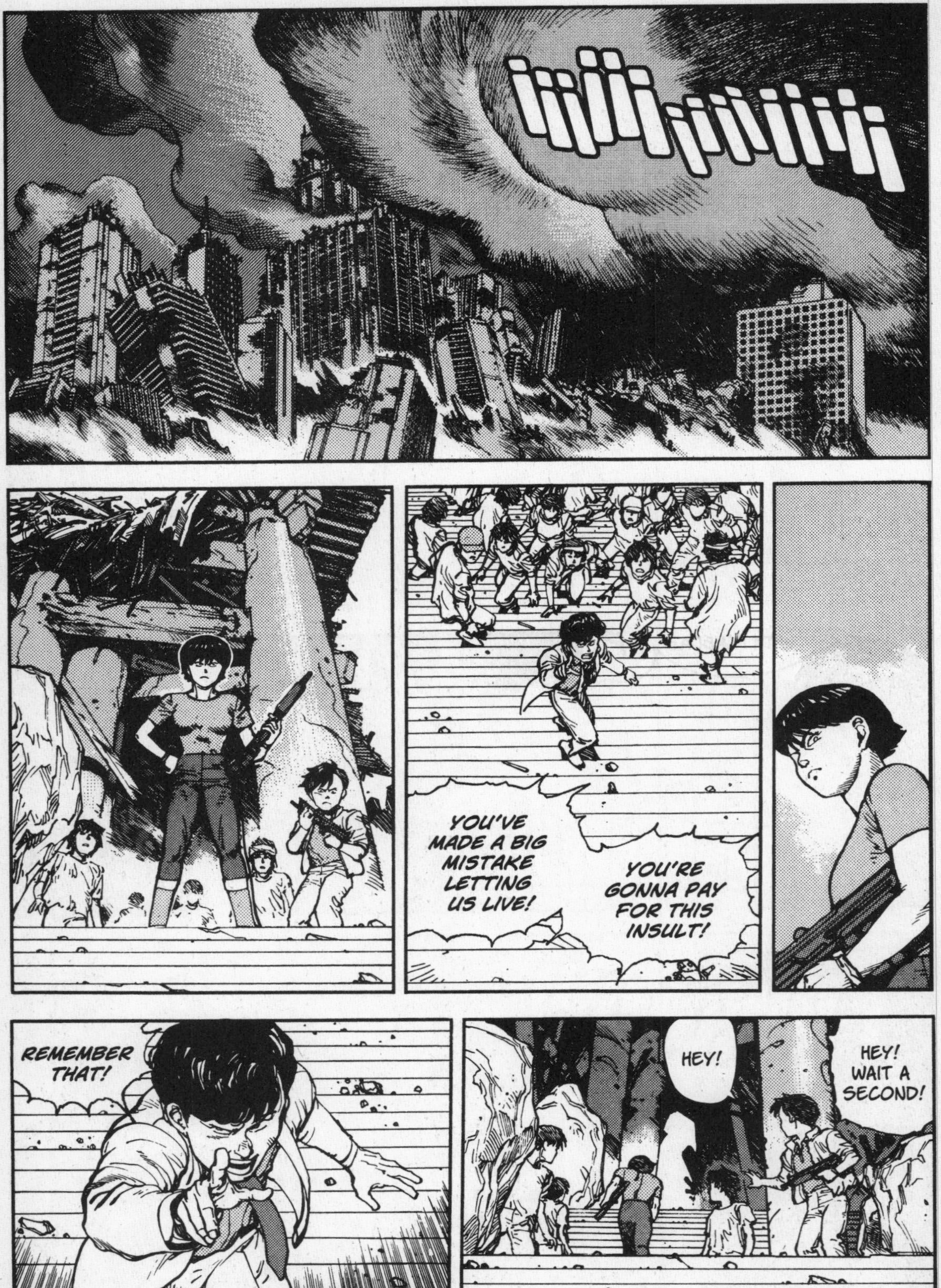
YOU'VE MADE A BIG MISTAKE LETTING US LIVE!
YOU'RE GONNA PAY FOR THIS INSULT!
REMEMBER THAT!
HEY!
HEY! WAIT A SECOND!

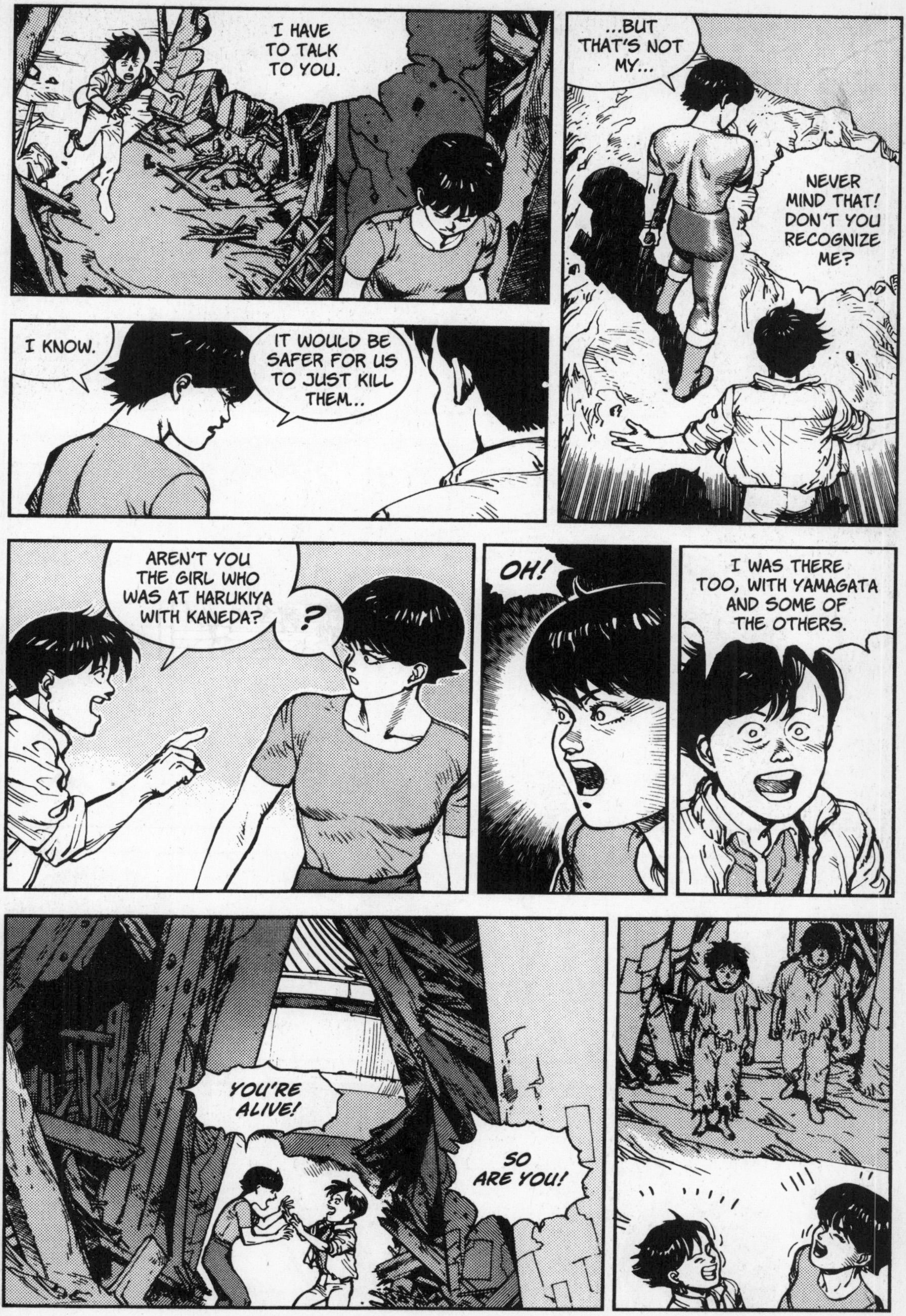
I HAVE TO TALK TO YOU.
I KNOW.
IT WOULD BE SAFER FOR US TO JUST KILL THEM...
...BUT THAT'S NOT MY...
NEVER MIND THAT! DON'T YOU RECOGNIZE ME?
AREN'T YOU THE GIRL WHO WAS AT HARUKIYA WITH KANEDA?
?
OH!
I WAS THERE TOO, WITH YAMAGATA AND SOME OF THE OTHERS.
YOU'RE ALIVE!
SO ARE YOU!

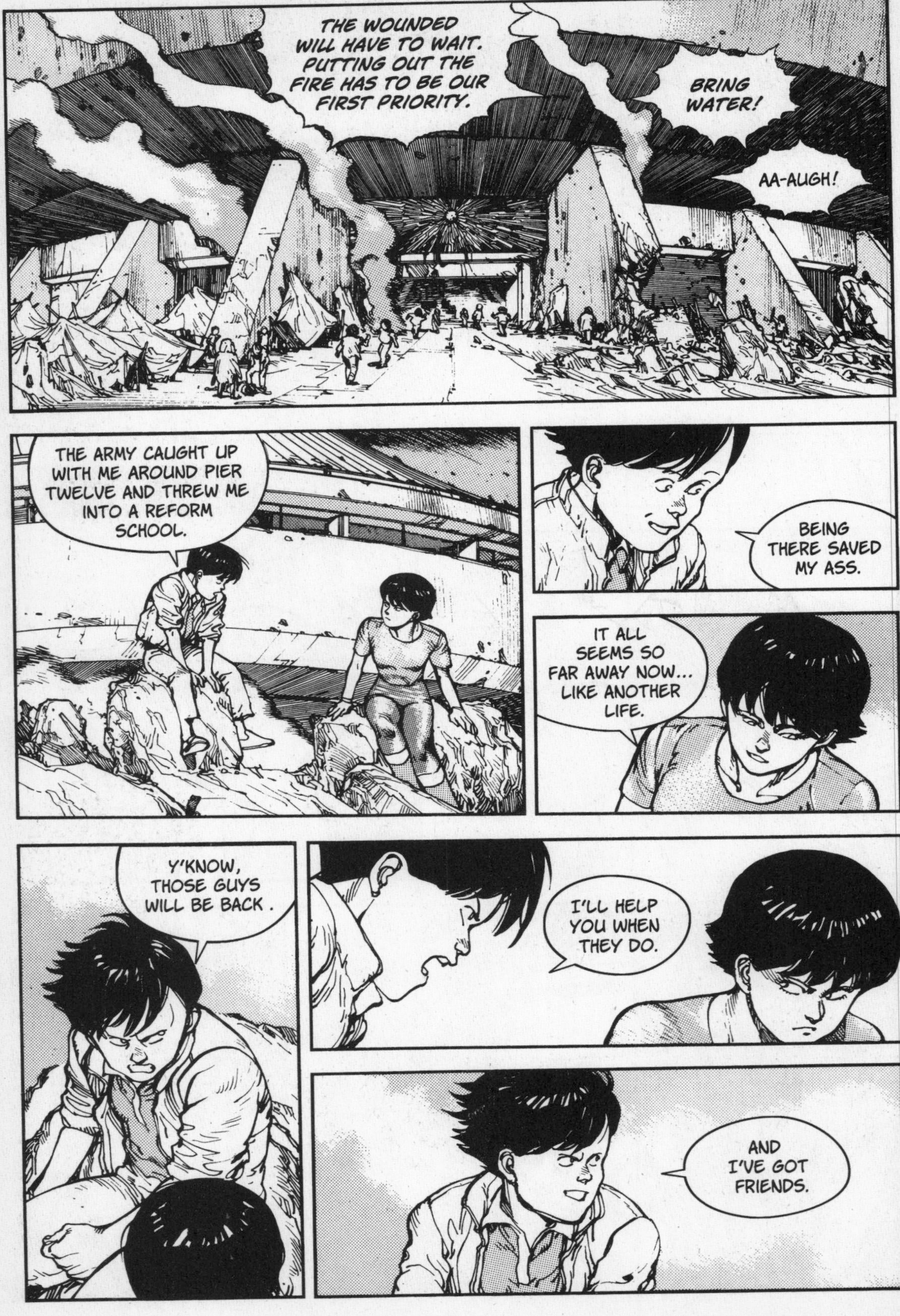
THE WOUNDED WILL HAVE TO WAIT. PUTTING OUT THE FIRE HAS TO BE OUR FIRST PRIORITY.
BRING WATER!
AA-AUGH!
THE ARMY CAUGHT UP WITH ME AROUND PIER TWELVE AND THREW ME INTO A REFORM SCHOOL.
BEING THERE SAVED MY ASS.
IT ALL SEEMS SO FAR AWAY NOW... LIKE ANOTHER LIFE.
Y'KNOW, THOSE GUYS WILL BE BACK.
I'LL HELP YOU WHEN THEY DO.
AND I'VE GOT FRIENDS.

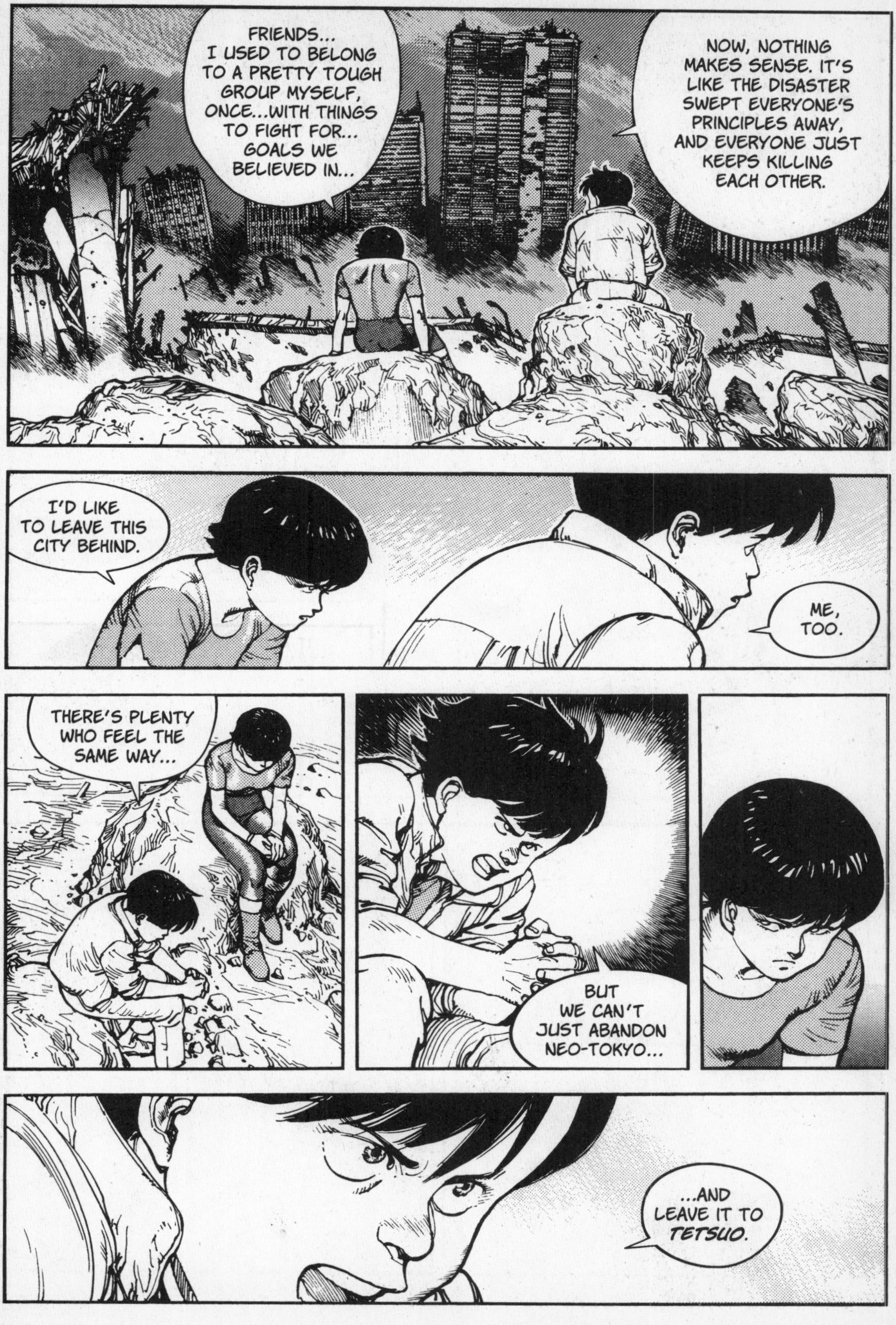
FRIENDS... I USED TO BELONG TO A PRETTY TOUGH GROUP MYSELF, ONCE...WITH THINGS TO FIGHT FOR... GOALS WE BELIEVED IN...
NOW, NOTHING MAKES SENSE. IT'S LIKE THE DISASTER SWEPT EVERYONE'S PRINCIPLES AWAY, AND EVERYONE JUST KEEPS KILLING EACH OTHER.
I'D LIKE TO LEAVE THIS CITY BEHIND.
ME, TOO.
THERE'S PLENTY WHO FEEL THE SAME WAY...
BUT WE CAN'T JUST ABANDON NEO-TOKYO...
...AND LEAVE IT TO *TETSUO*.

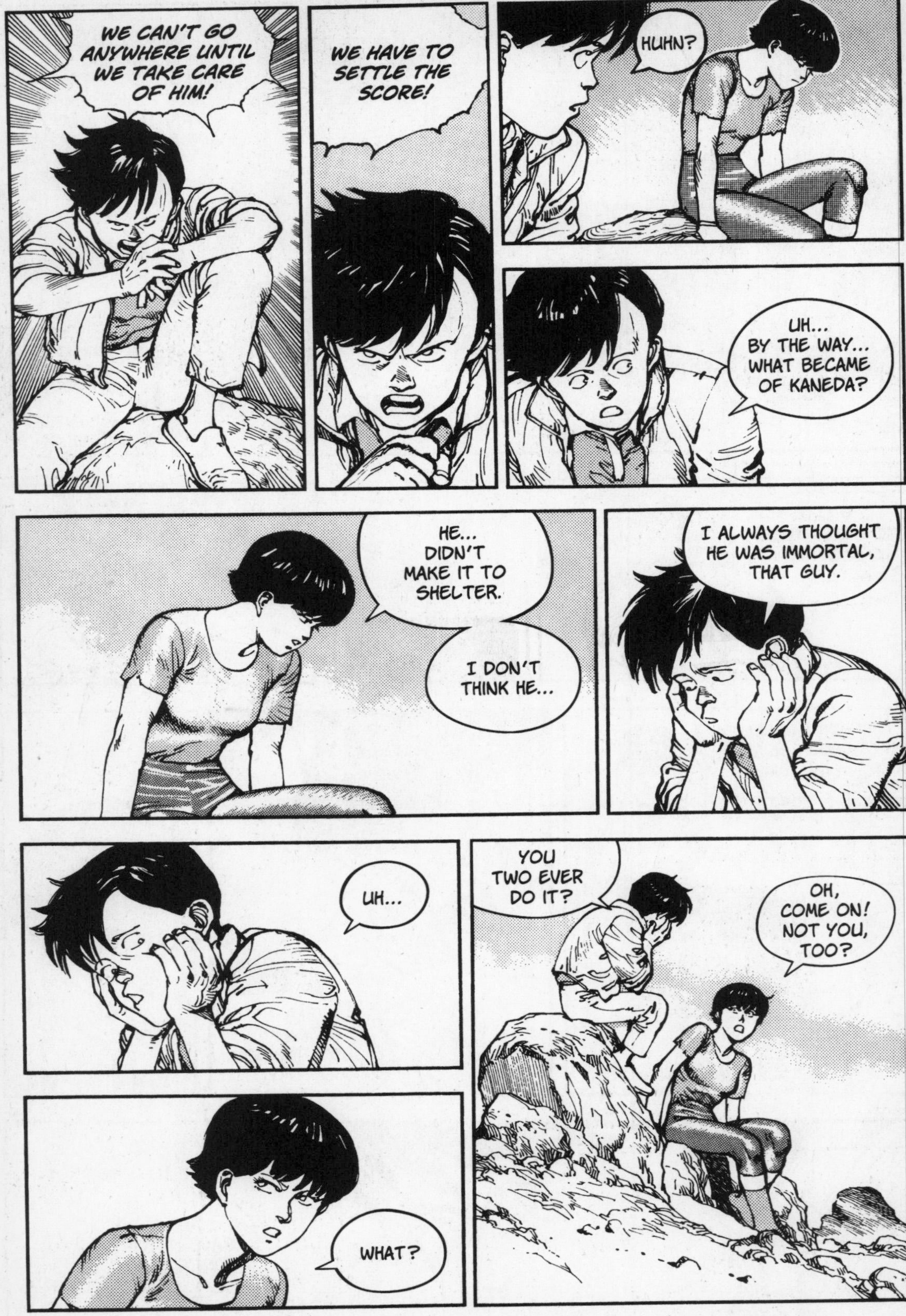
WE CAN'T GO ANYWHERE UNTIL WE TAKE CARE OF HIM!
WE HAVE TO SETTLE THE SCORE!
HUHN?
UH... BY THE WAY... WHAT BECAME OF KANEDA?
HE... DIDN'T MAKE IT TO SHELTER.
I DON'T THINK HE...
I ALWAYS THOUGHT HE WAS IMMORTAL, THAT GUY.
UH...
WHAT?
YOU TWO EVER DO IT?
OH, COME ON! NOT YOU, TOO?

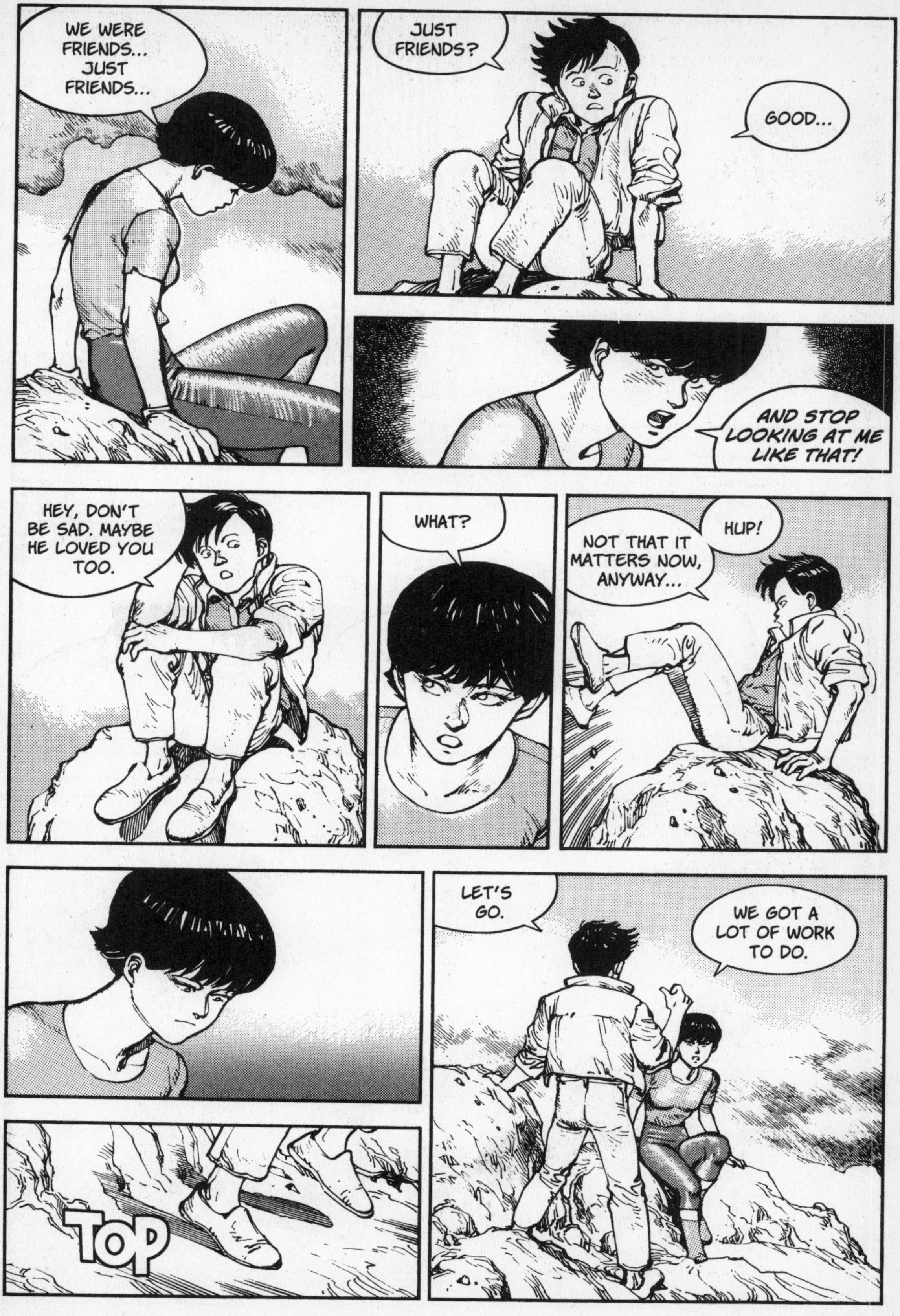
WE WERE FRIENDS... JUST FRIENDS...
JUST FRIENDS?
GOOD...
AND STOP LOOKING AT ME LIKE THAT!
HEY, DON'T BE SAD. MAYBE HE LOVED YOU TOO.
WHAT?
NOT THAT IT MATTERS NOW, ANYWAY...
HUP!
TOP
LET'S GO.
WE GOT A LOT OF WORK TO DO.

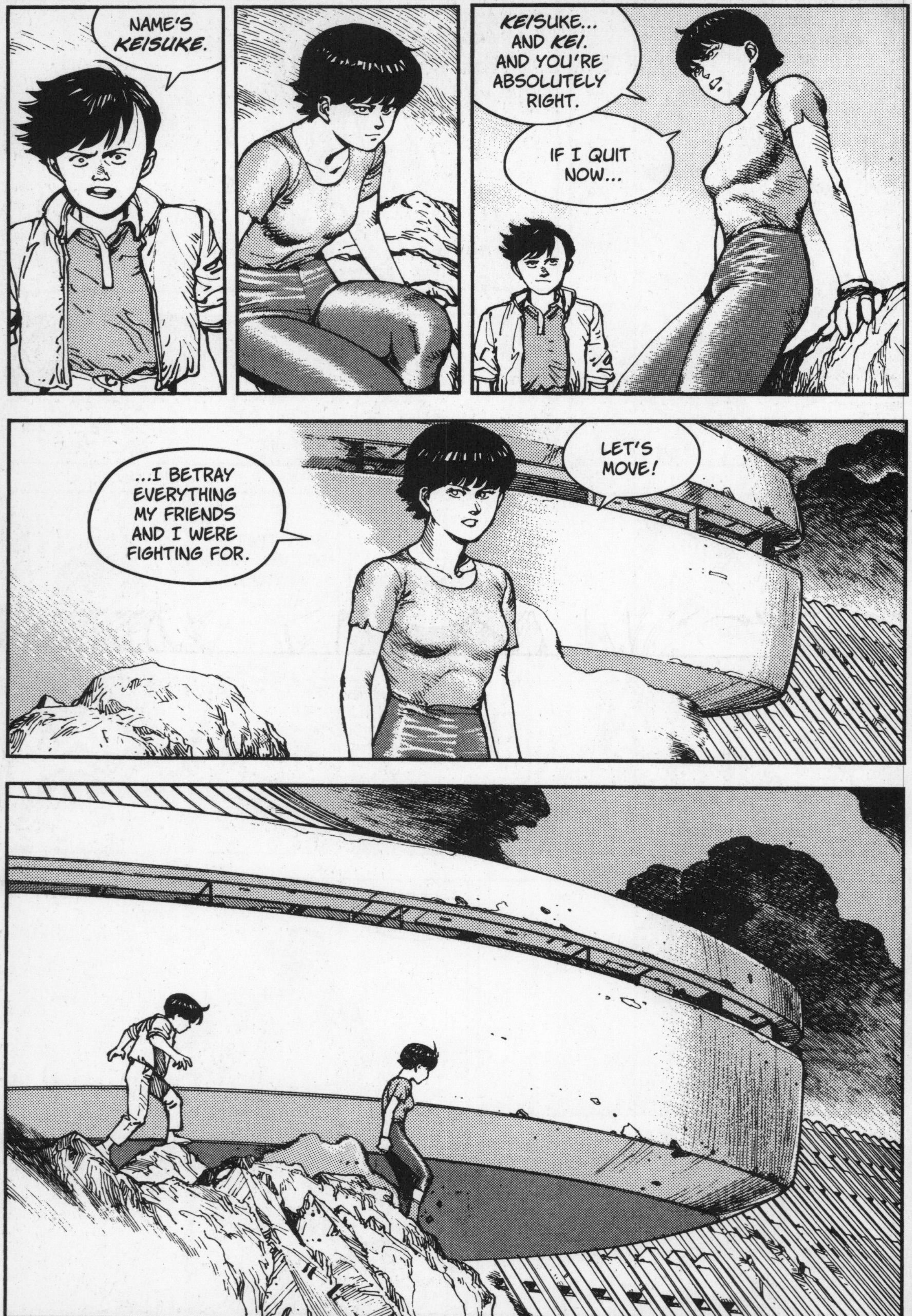
NAME'S KEISUKE.
KEISUKE... AND KEI. AND YOU'RE ABSOLUTELY RIGHT.
IF I QUIT NOW...
...I BETRAY EVERYTHING MY FRIENDS AND I WERE FIGHTING FOR.
LET'S MOVE!

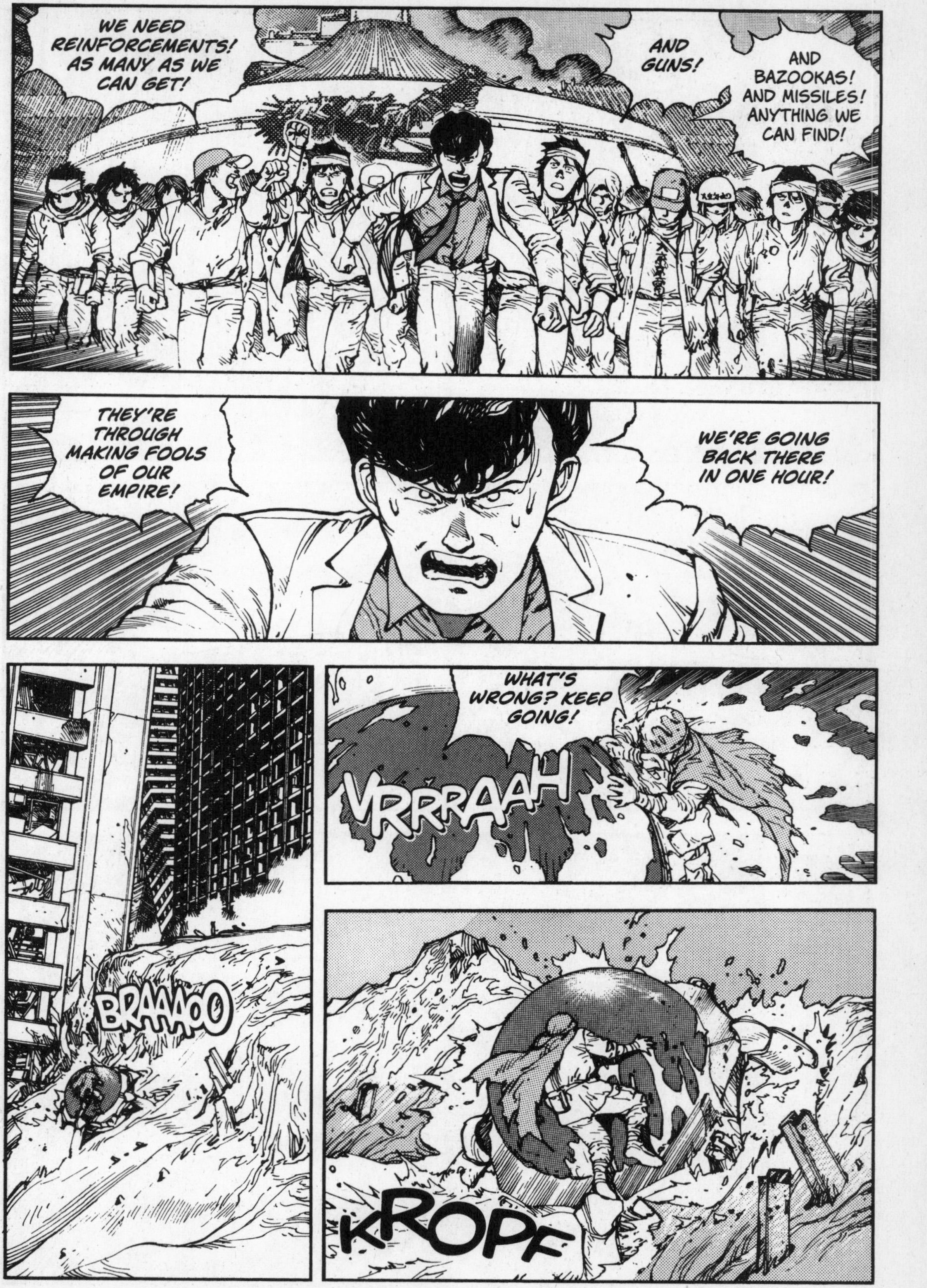
WE NEED REINFORCEMENTS! AS MANY AS WE CAN GET!
AND GUNS!
AND BAZOOKAS! AND MISSILES! ANYTHING WE CAN FIND!
THEY'RE THROUGH MAKING FOOLS OF OUR EMPIRE!
WE'RE GOING BACK THERE IN ONE HOUR!
BRAAAOO
WHAT'S WRONG? KEEP GOING!
VRRRAAH
KROPF

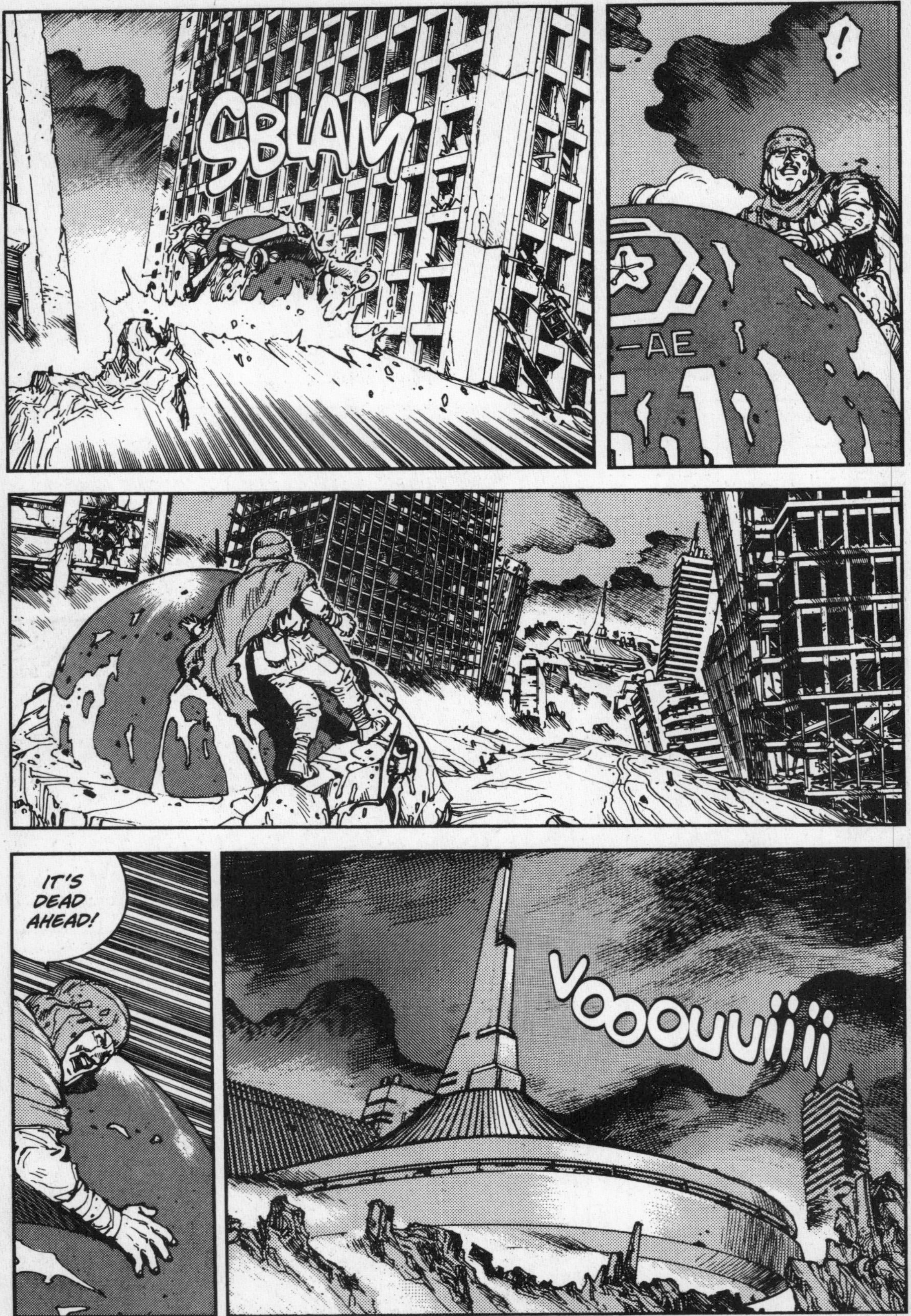
SBLAM
!
-AE
IT'S DEAD AHEAD!
VOOOUUIII

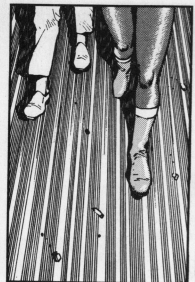

GET THE FIRE OUT!

WE NEED MORE WATER!

GET A STRETCHER OVER HERE!

OUT OF THE QUESTION!

MY PLACE IS HERE!

I REFUSE TO LEAVE THE TEMPLE!

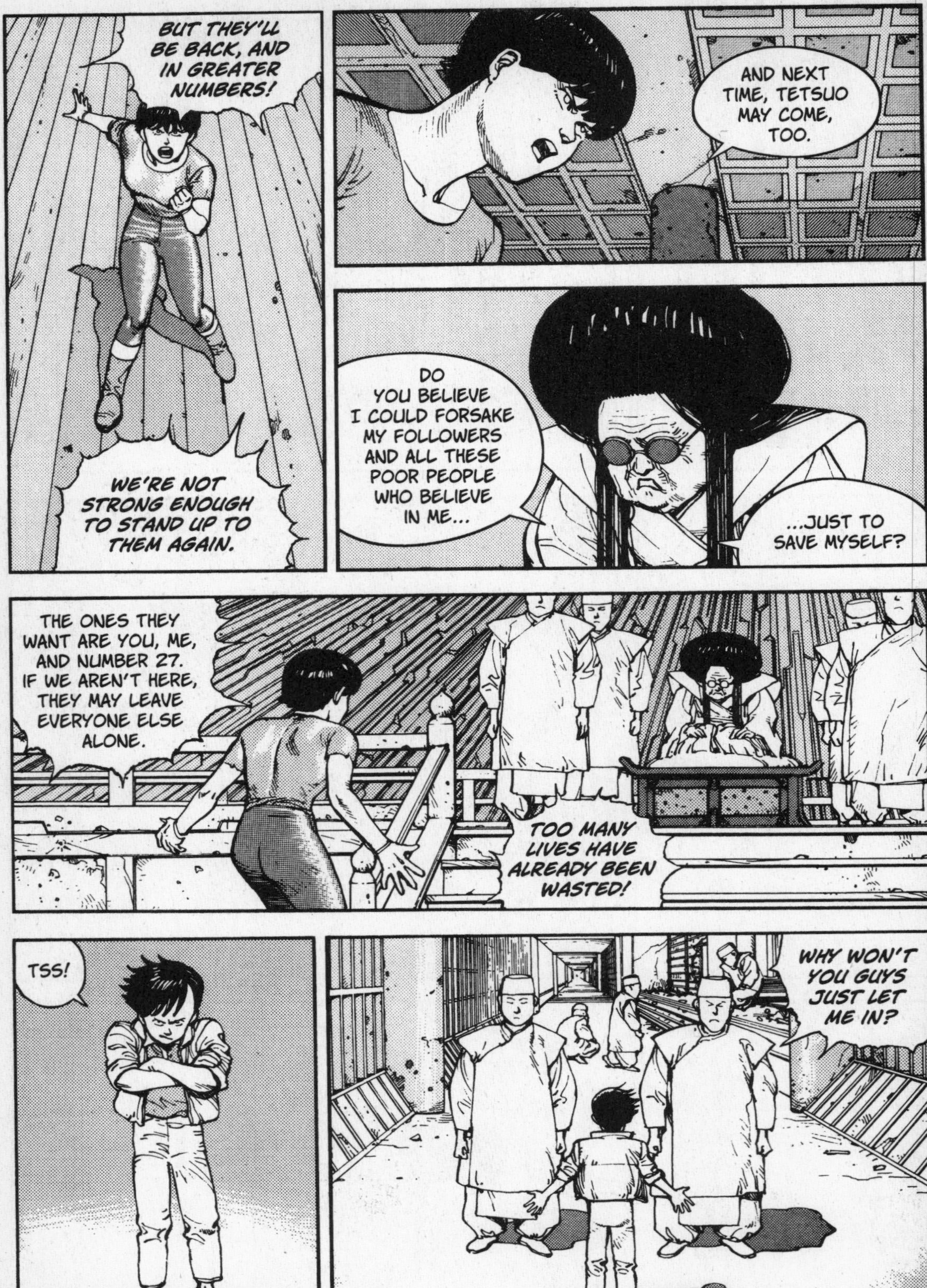
BUT THEY'LL BE BACK, AND IN GREATER NUMBERS!
WE'RE NOT STRONG ENOUGH TO STAND UP TO THEM AGAIN.
AND NEXT TIME, TETSUO MAY COME, TOO.
DO YOU BELIEVE I COULD FORSAKE MY FOLLOWERS AND ALL THESE POOR PEOPLE WHO BELIEVE IN ME...
...JUST TO SAVE MYSELF?
THE ONES THEY WANT ARE YOU, ME, AND NUMBER 27. IF WE AREN'T HERE, THEY MAY LEAVE EVERYONE ELSE ALONE.
TOO MANY LIVES HAVE ALREADY BEEN WASTED!
TSS!
WHY WON'T YOU GUYS JUST LET ME IN?

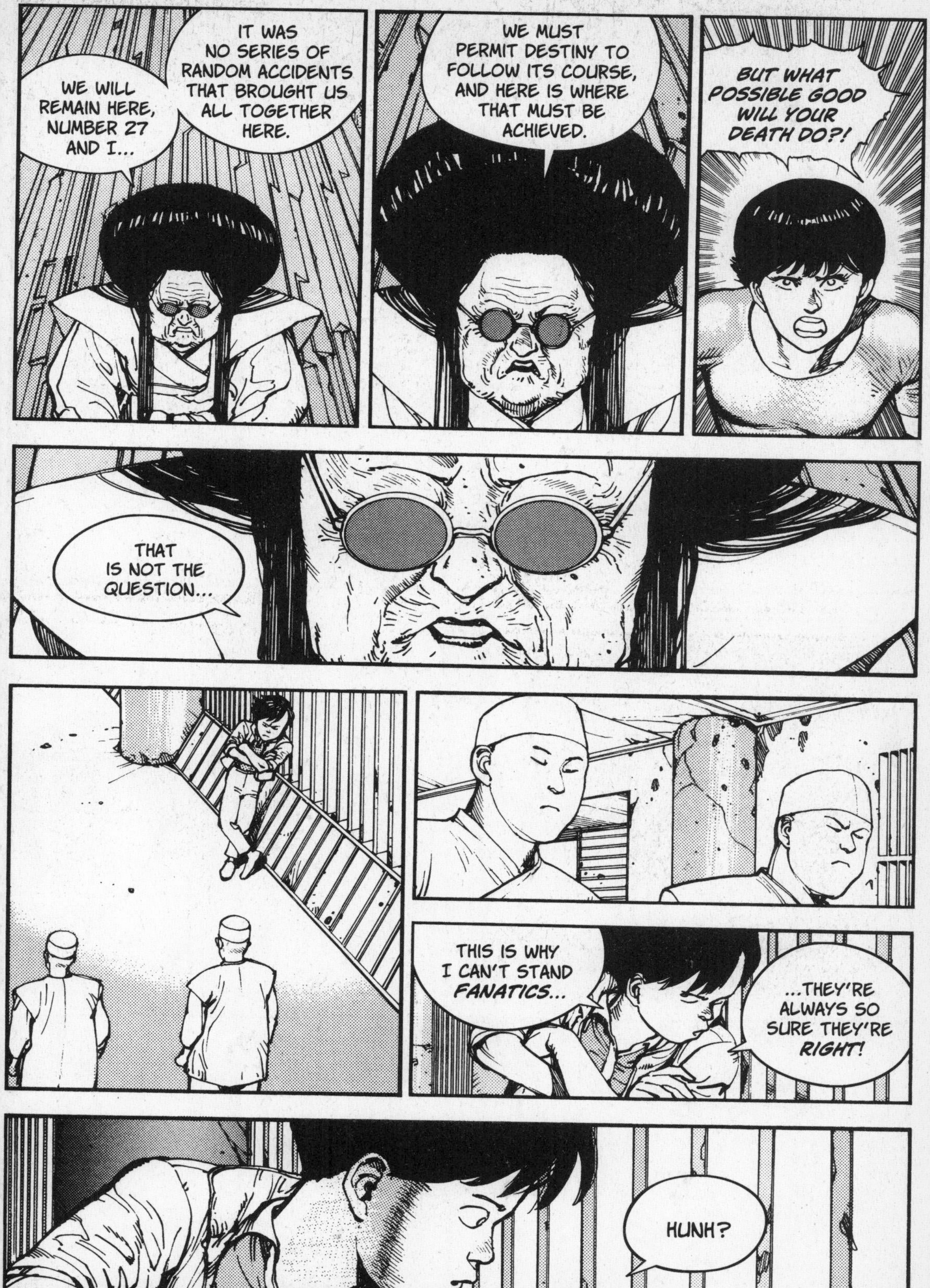
WE WILL REMAIN HERE, NUMBER 27 AND I...
IT WAS NO SERIES OF RANDOM ACCIDENTS THAT BROUGHT US ALL TOGETHER HERE.
WE MUST PERMIT DESTINY TO FOLLOW ITS COURSE, AND HERE IS WHERE THAT MUST BE ACHIEVED.
*BUT WHAT POSSIBLE GOOD WILL YOUR DEATH DO?!*
THAT IS NOT THE QUESTION...
THIS IS WHY I CAN'T STAND *FANATICS...*
...THEY'RE ALWAYS SO SURE THEY'RE *RIGHT!*
HUNH?

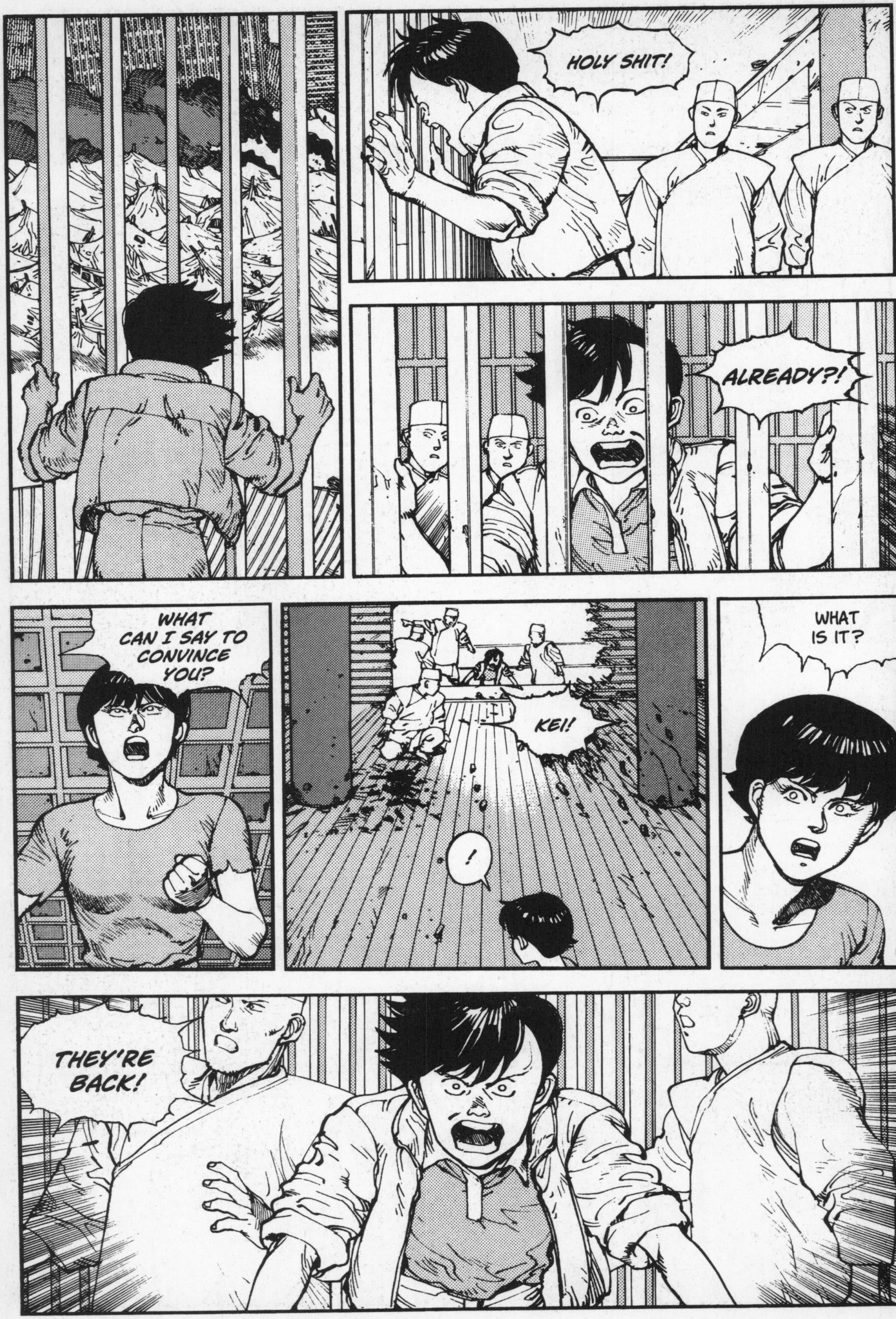
HOLY SHIT!
ALREADY?!
WHAT CAN I SAY TO CONVINCE YOU?
KEI!
!
WHAT IS IT?
THEY'RE BACK!

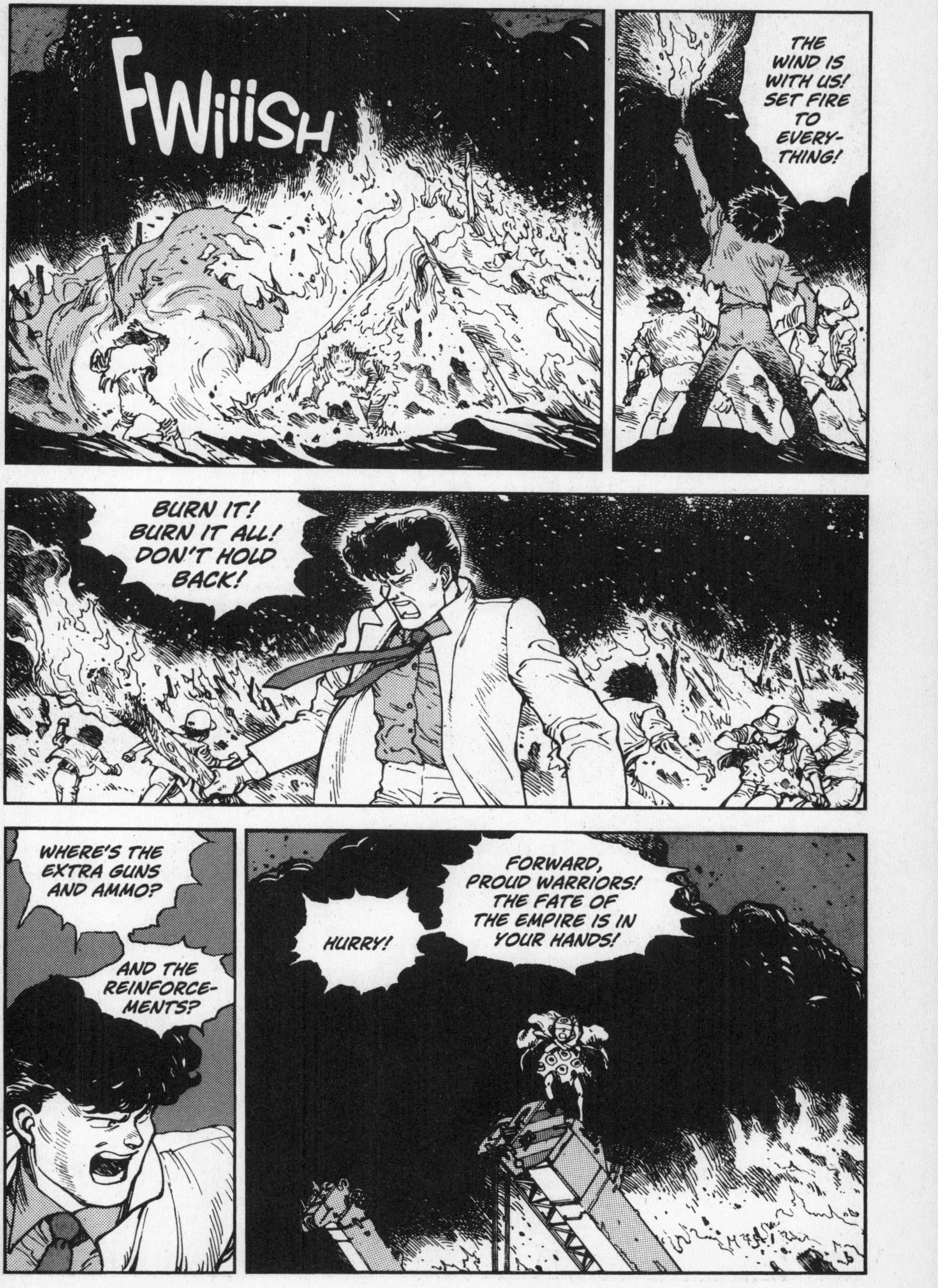
FWiiiSH
THE WIND IS WITH US! SET FIRE TO EVERY-THING!
BURN IT! BURN IT ALL! DON'T HOLD BACK!
WHERE'S THE EXTRA GUNS AND AMMO?
AND THE REINFORCE-MENTS?
HURRY!
FORWARD, PROUD WARRIORS! THE FATE OF THE EMPIRE IS IN YOUR HANDS!

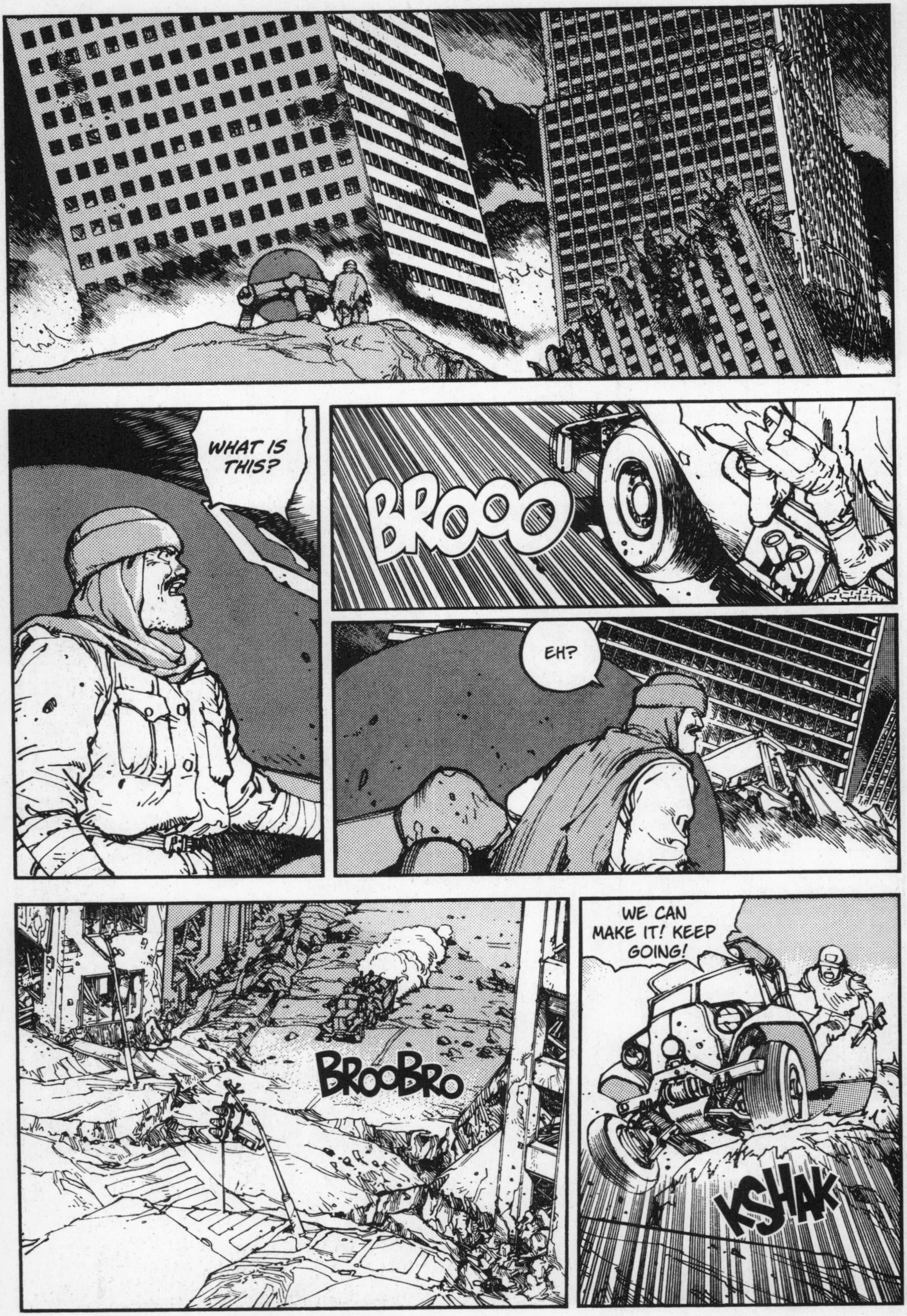
WHAT IS THIS?
BROOO
EH?
BROOBRO
WE CAN MAKE IT! KEEP GOING!
KSHAK

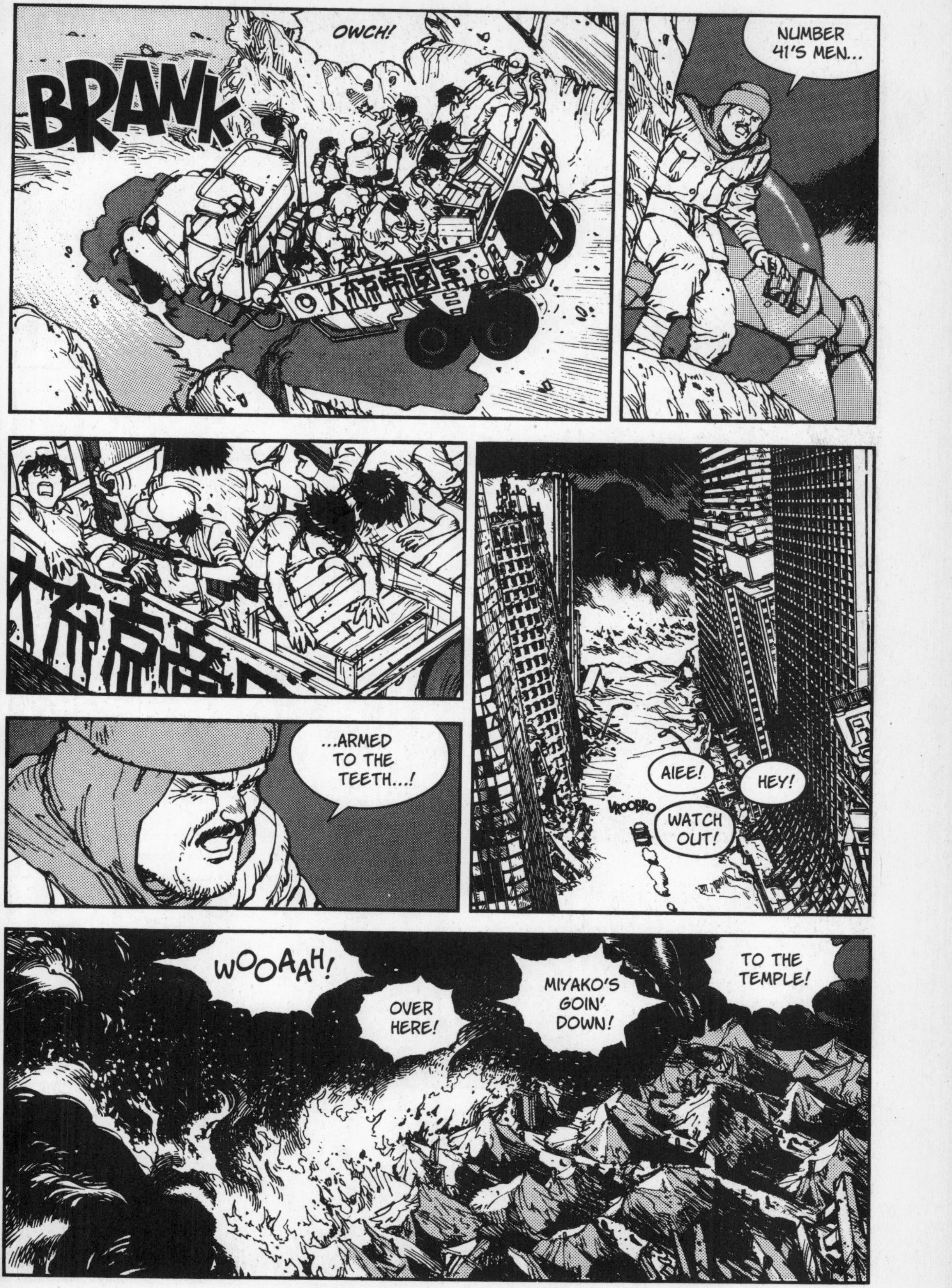
BRANK
OWCH!
NUMBER 41'S MEN...
...ARMED TO THE TEETH...!
VROOBRO
AIEE!
HEY!
WATCH OUT!
WOOAAH!
OVER HERE!
MIYAKO'S GOIN' DOWN!
TO THE TEMPLE!

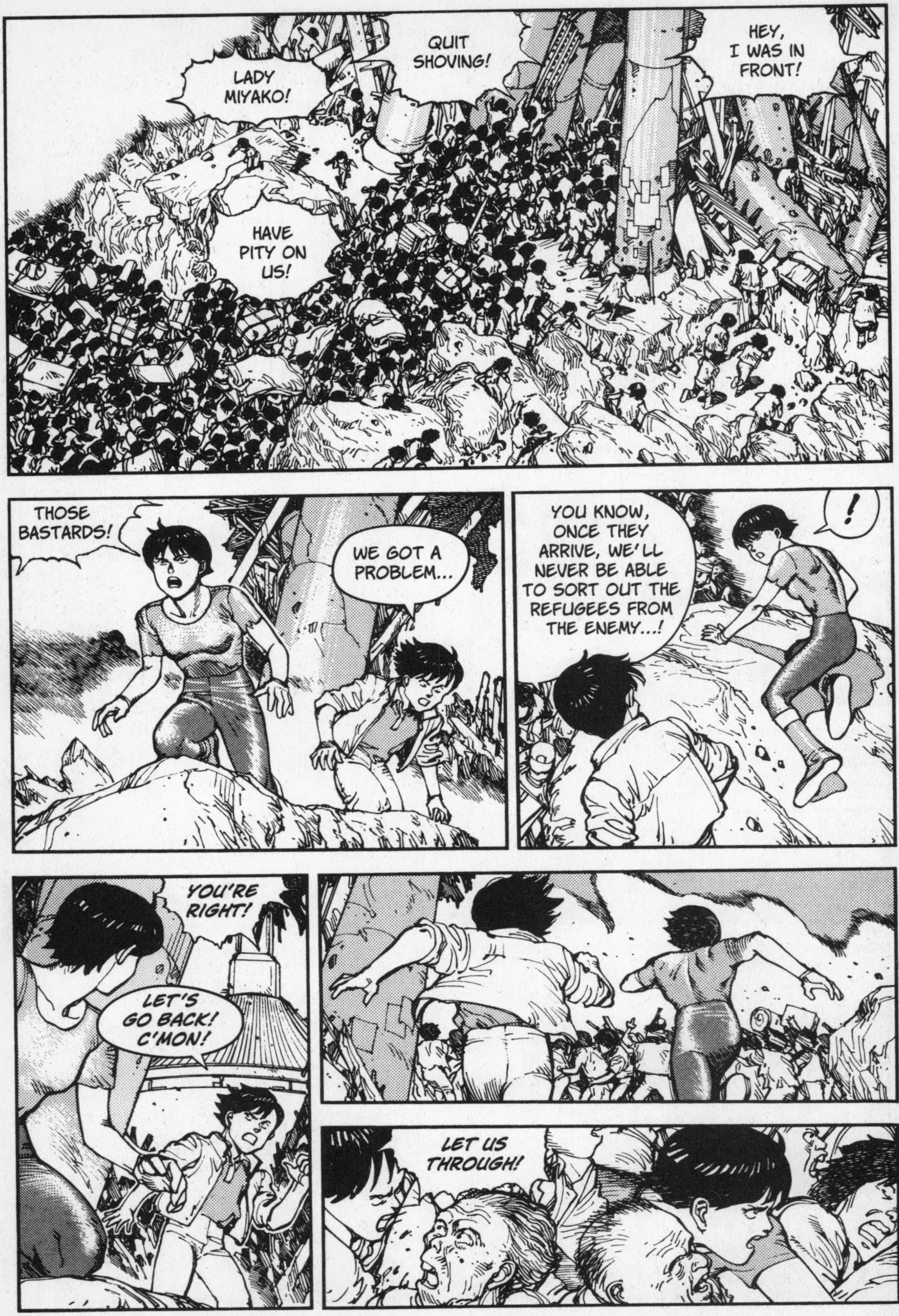
LADY MIYAKO!
QUIT SHOVING!
HEY, I WAS IN FRONT!
HAVE PITY ON US!
THOSE BASTARDS!
WE GOT A PROBLEM...
!
YOU KNOW, ONCE THEY ARRIVE, WE'LL NEVER BE ABLE TO SORT OUT THE REFUGEES FROM THE ENEMY...!
YOU'RE RIGHT!
LET'S GO BACK! C'MON!
LET US THROUGH!

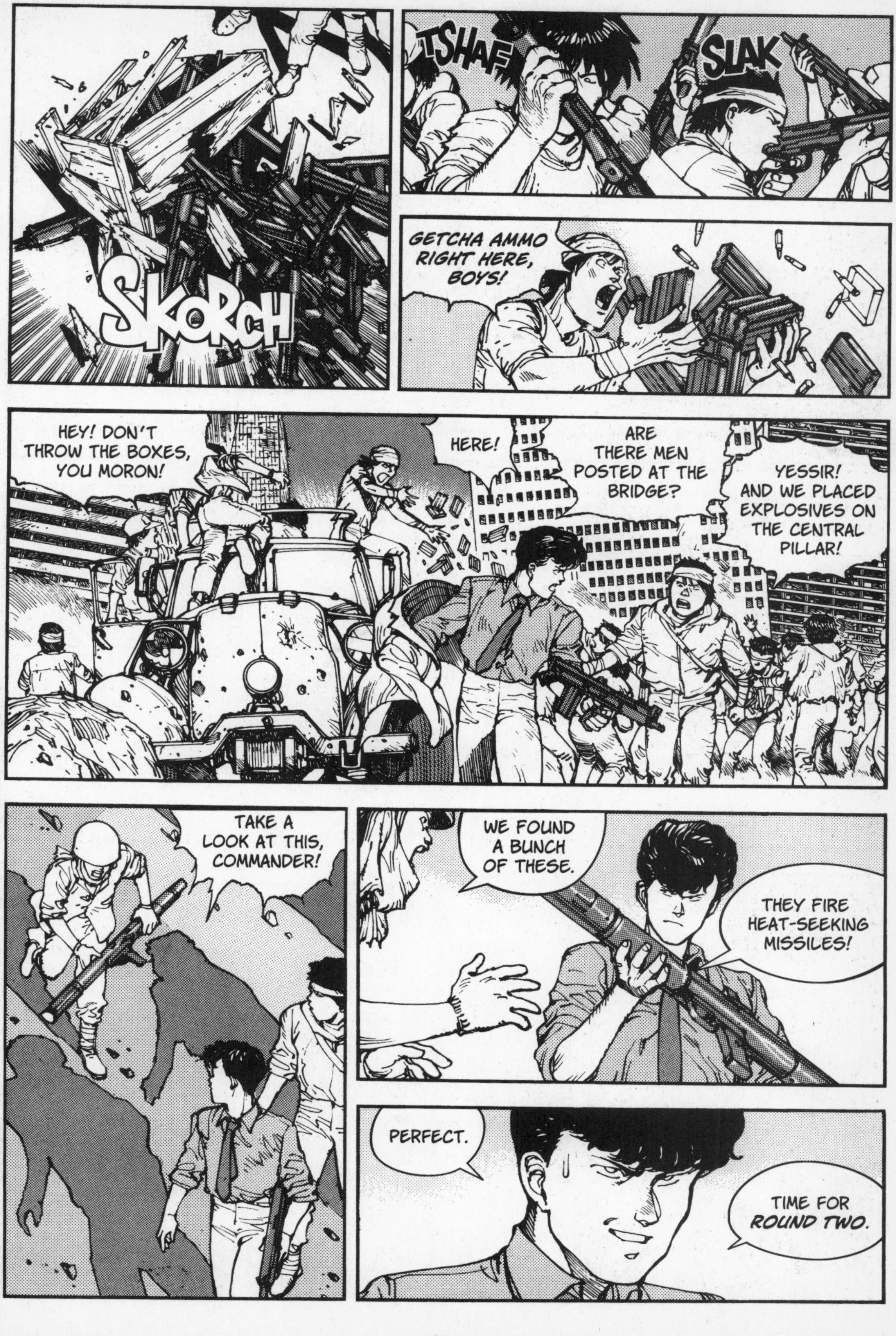
SKORCH
TSHAF
SLAK
GETCHA AMMO RIGHT HERE, BOYS!
HEY! DON'T THROW THE BOXES, YOU MORON!
HERE!
ARE THERE MEN POSTED AT THE BRIDGE?
YESSIR! AND WE PLACED EXPLOSIVES ON THE CENTRAL PILLAR!
TAKE A LOOK AT THIS, COMMANDER!
WE FOUND A BUNCH OF THESE.
THEY FIRE HEAT-SEEKING MISSILES!
PERFECT.
TIME FOR ROUND TWO.

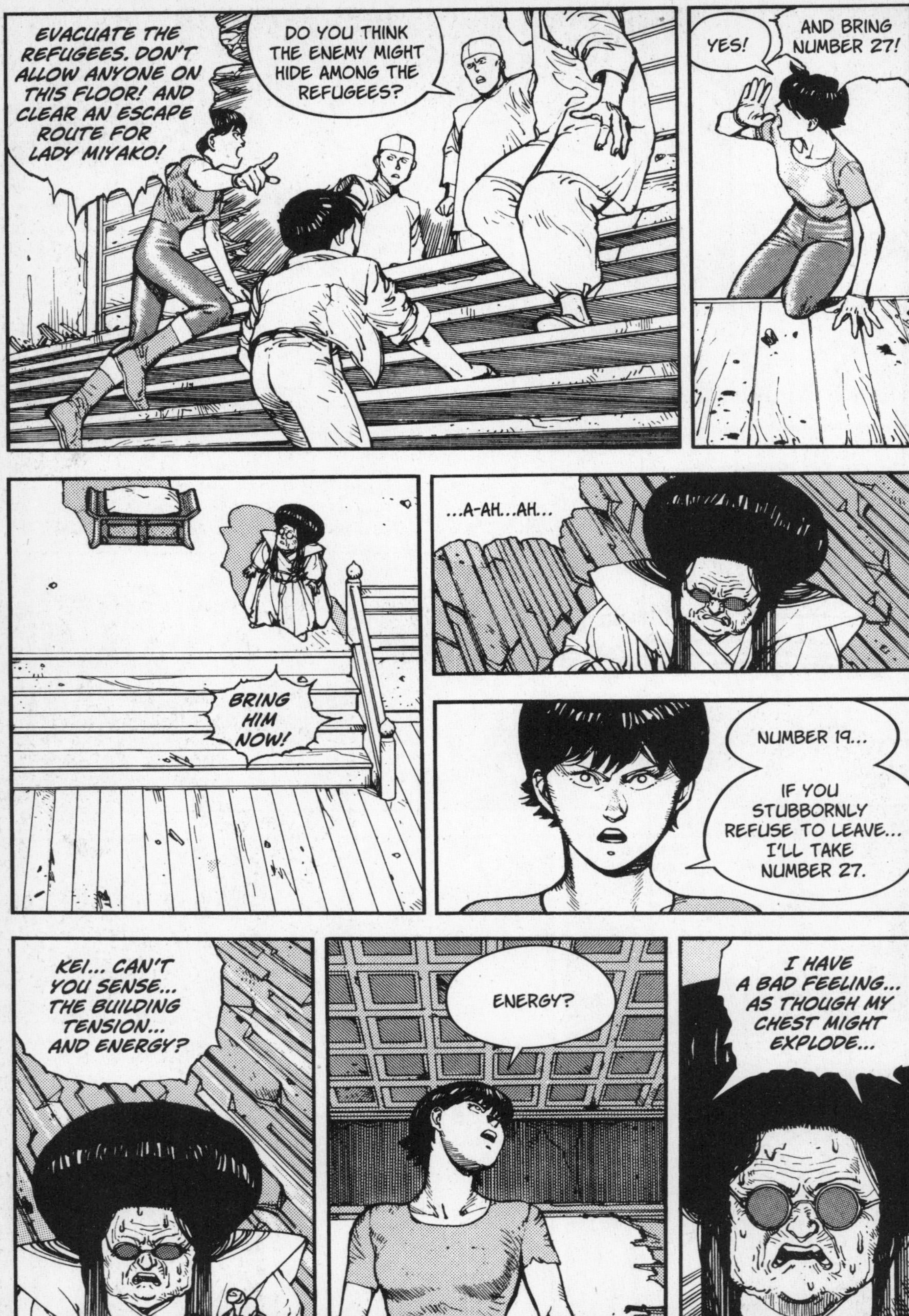
EVACUATE THE REFUGEES. DON'T ALLOW ANYONE ON THIS FLOOR! AND CLEAR AN ESCAPE ROUTE FOR LADY MIYAKO!
DO YOU THINK THE ENEMY MIGHT HIDE AMONG THE REFUGEES?
YES!
AND BRING NUMBER 27!
BRING HIM NOW!
...A-AH...AH...
NUMBER 19...
IF YOU STUBBORNLY REFUSE TO LEAVE... I'LL TAKE NUMBER 27.
KEI... CAN'T YOU SENSE... THE BUILDING TENSION... AND ENERGY?
ENERGY?
I HAVE A BAD FEELING... AS THOUGH MY CHEST MIGHT EXPLODE...

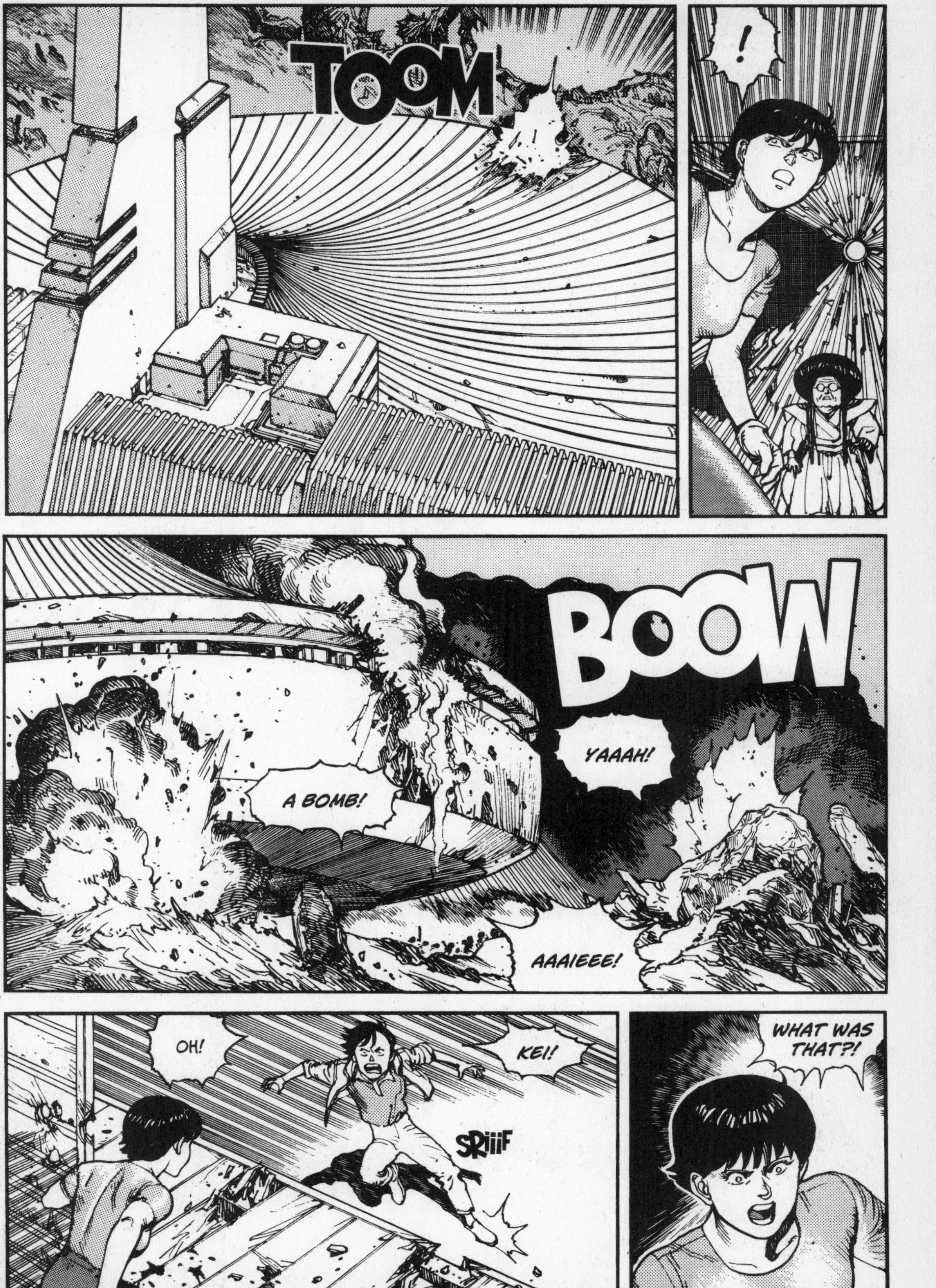
TOOM
!
BOOW
A BOMB!
YAAAH!
AAAIEEE!
OH!
KEI!
SRiiiF
WHAT WAS THAT?!

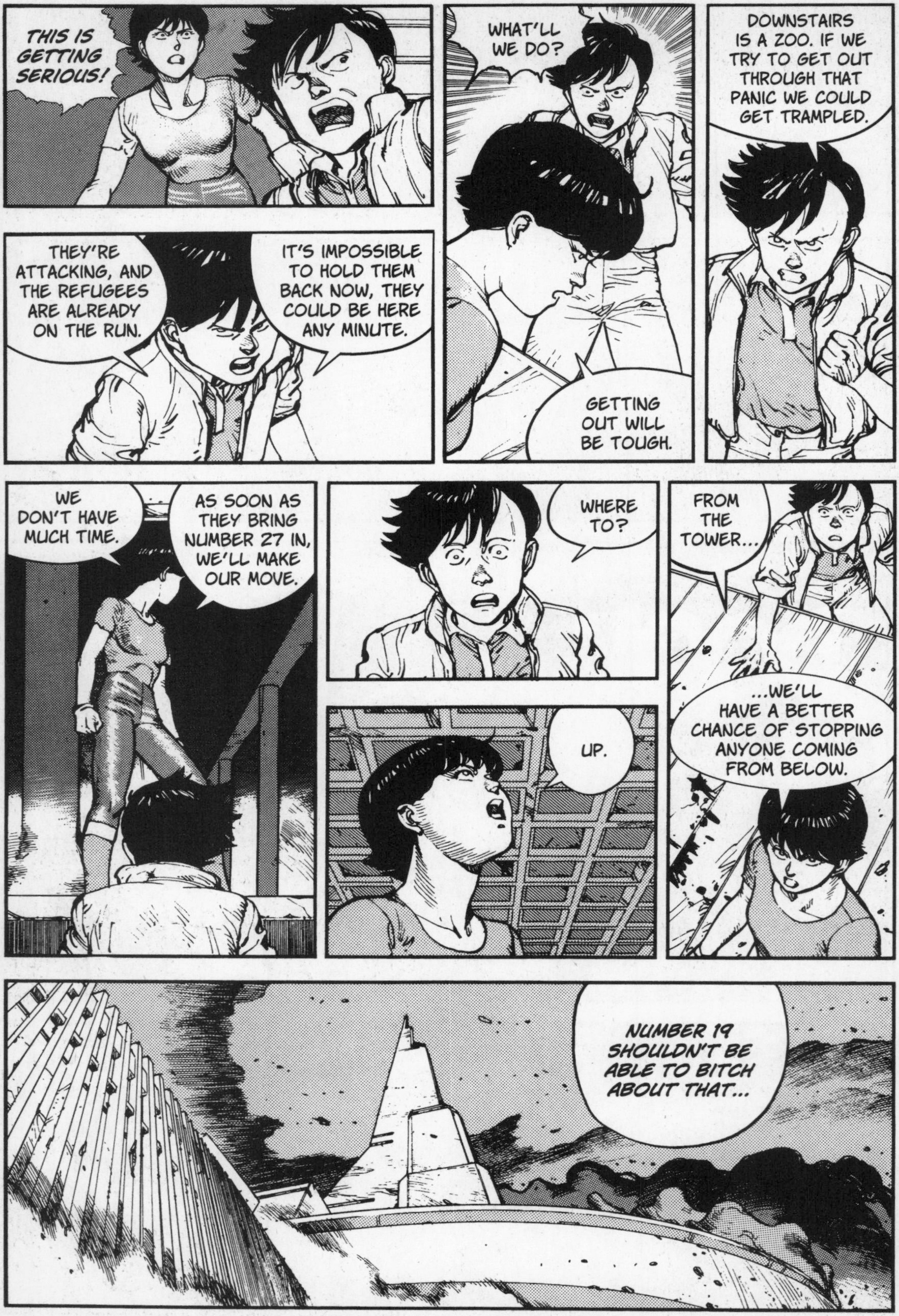
THIS IS GETTING SERIOUS!
WHAT'LL WE DO?
DOWNSTAIRS IS A ZOO. IF WE TRY TO GET OUT THROUGH THAT PANIC WE COULD GET TRAMPLED.
THEY'RE ATTACKING, AND THE REFUGEES ARE ALREADY ON THE RUN.
IT'S IMPOSSIBLE TO HOLD THEM BACK NOW, THEY COULD BE HERE ANY MINUTE.
GETTING OUT WILL BE TOUGH.
WE DON'T HAVE MUCH TIME.
AS SOON AS THEY BRING NUMBER 27 IN, WE'LL MAKE OUR MOVE.
WHERE TO?
UP.
FROM THE TOWER...
...WE'LL HAVE A BETTER CHANCE OF STOPPING ANYONE COMING FROM BELOW.
NUMBER 19 SHOULDN'T BE ABLE TO BITCH ABOUT THAT...

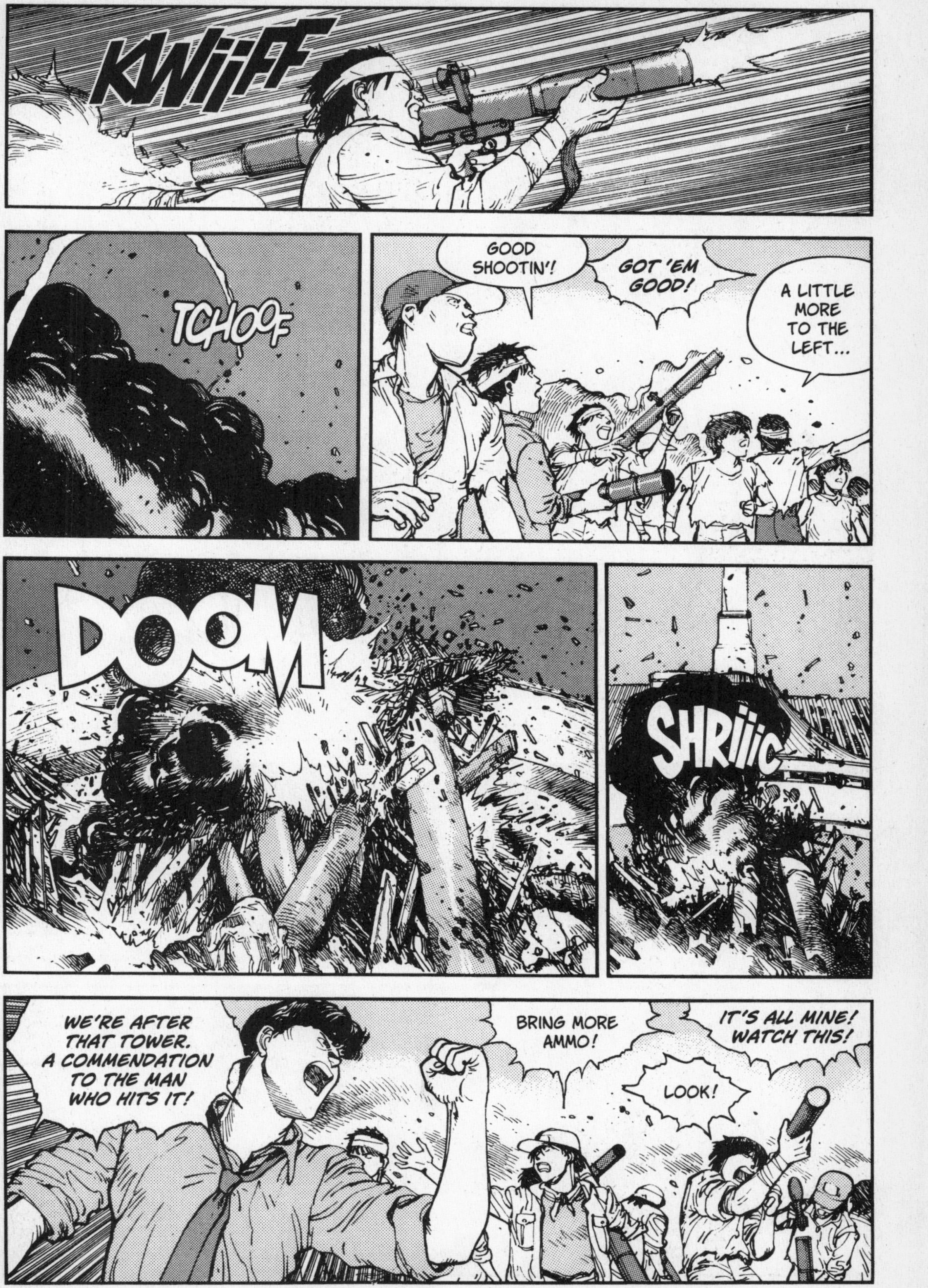
KWIIFF
TCHOOF
GOOD SHOOTIN'!
GOT 'EM GOOD!
A LITTLE MORE TO THE LEFT...
DOOM
SHRIIIC
WE'RE AFTER THAT TOWER. A COMMENDATION TO THE MAN WHO HITS IT!
BRING MORE AMMO!
IT'S ALL MINE! WATCH THIS!
LOOK!

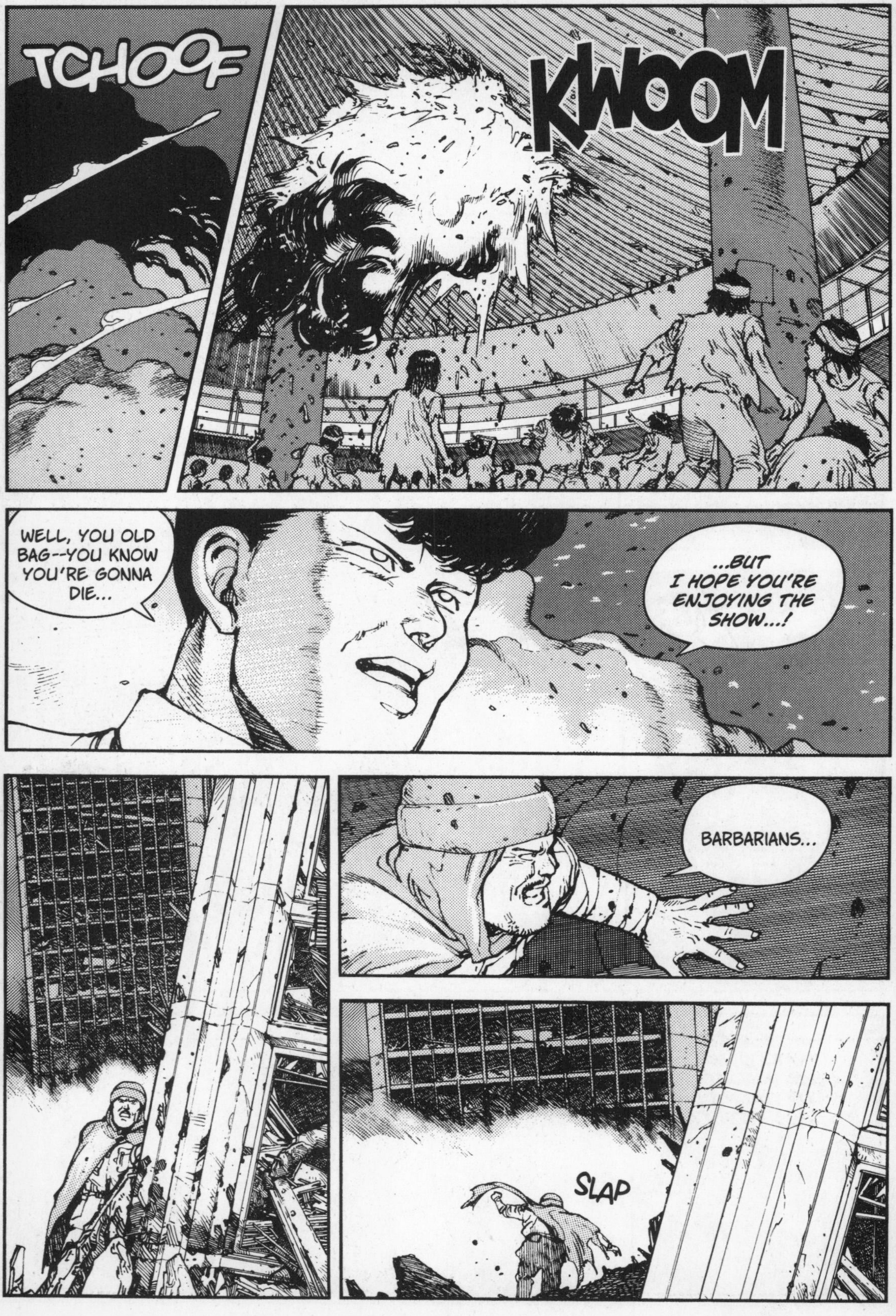
TCHOOF
KWOOM
WELL, YOU OLD BAG--YOU KNOW YOU'RE GONNA DIE...
...BUT I HOPE YOU'RE ENJOYING THE SHOW...!
BARBARIANS...
SLAP

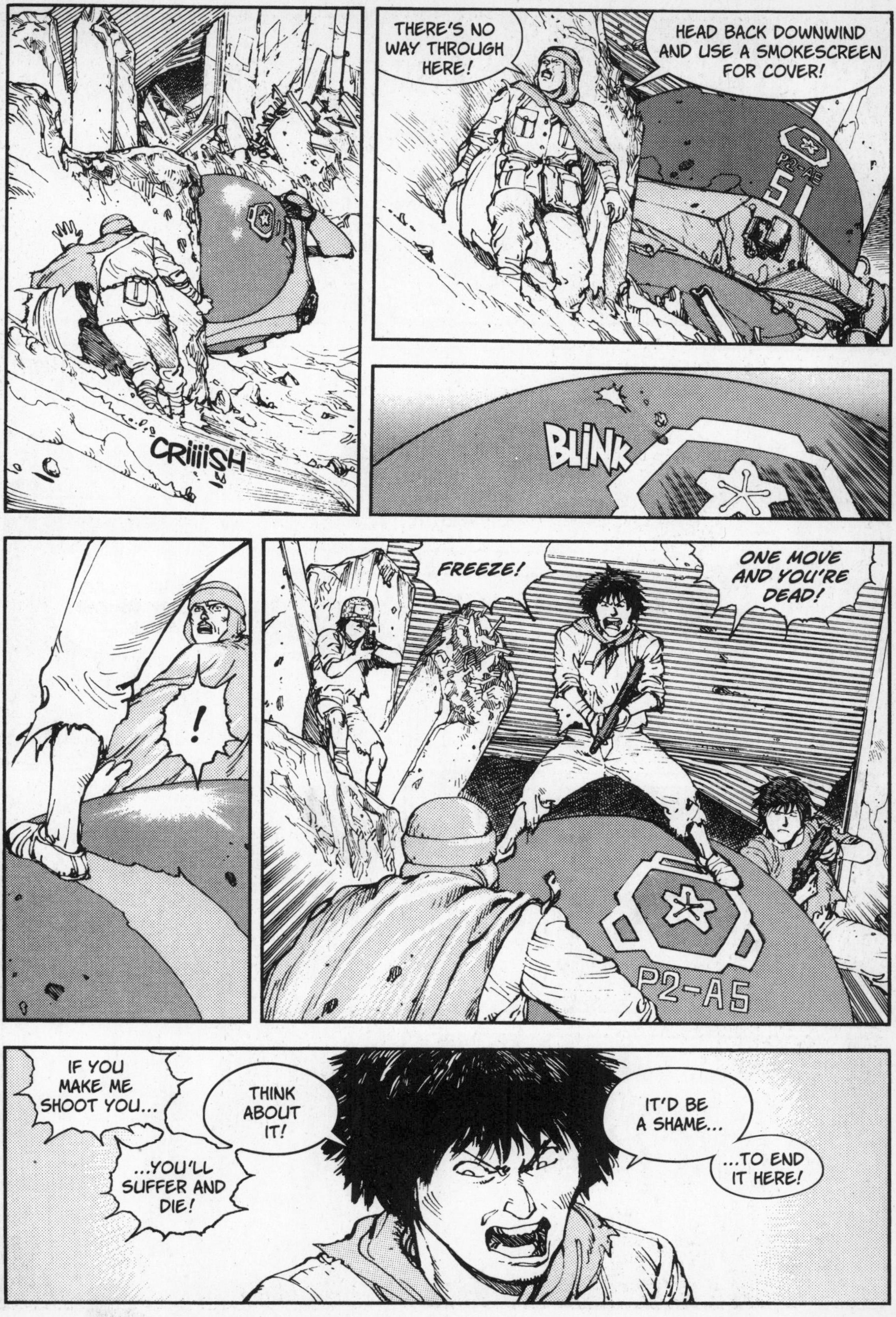
CRIIIISH
THERE'S NO WAY THROUGH HERE!
HEAD BACK DOWNWIND AND USE A SMOKESCREEN FOR COVER!
P2-A5
51
BLINK
!
FREEZE!
ONE MOVE AND YOU'RE DEAD!
P2-A5
IF YOU MAKE ME SHOOT YOU...
...YOU'LL SUFFER AND DIE!
THINK ABOUT IT!
IT'D BE A SHAME...
...TO END IT HERE!

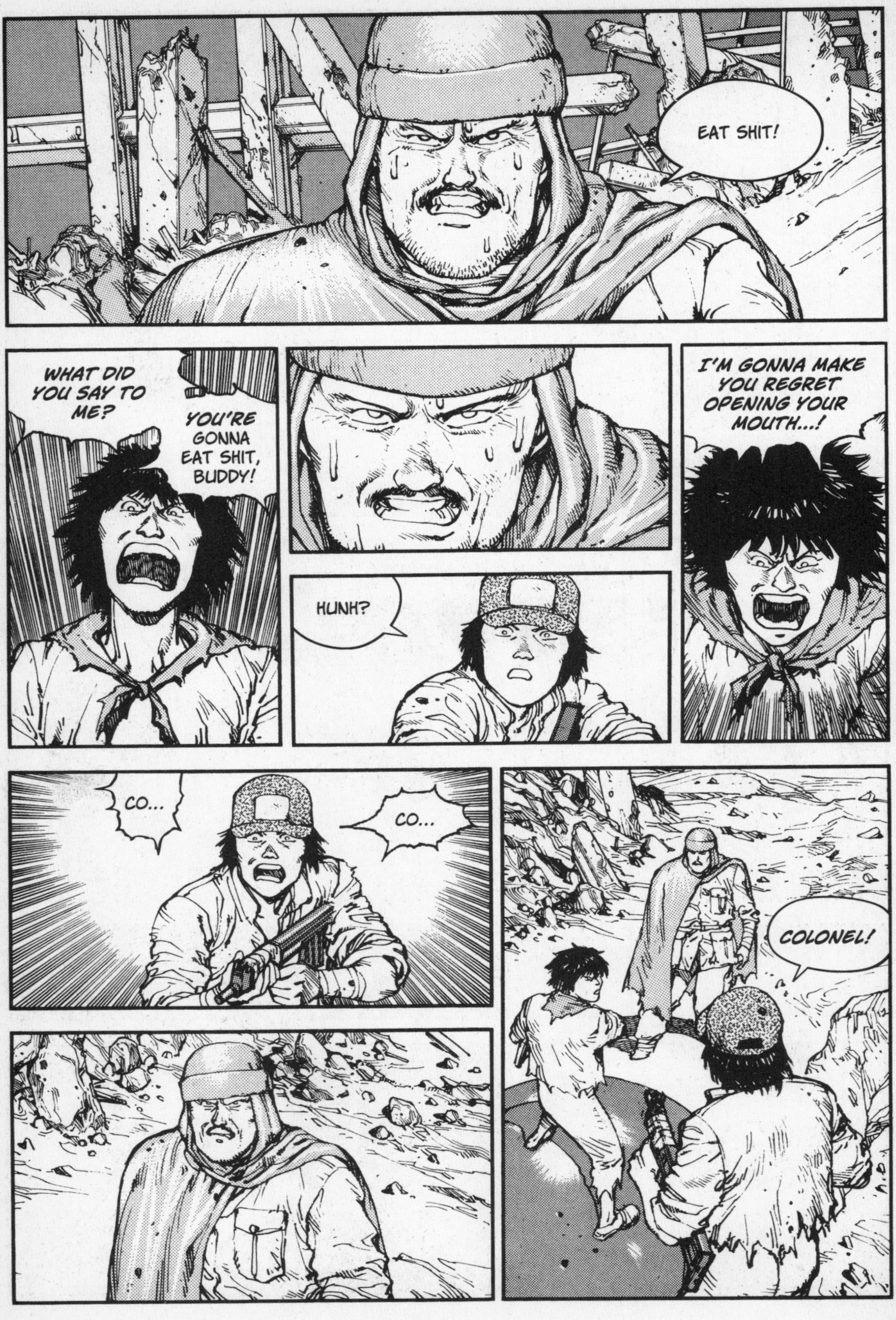
EAT SHIT!
WHAT DID YOU SAY TO ME?
YOU'RE GONNA EAT SHIT, BUDDY!
HUNH?
I'M GONNA MAKE YOU REGRET OPENING YOUR MOUTH...!
CO...
CO...
COLONEL!

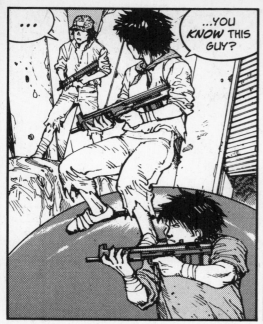

… …YOU *KNOW* THIS GUY?

… … UH… UHH…

I SEE… YOUR OLD BOSS… IS THAT IT?

YEAH…

THEN YOU SHOULD HAVE THE HONOR OF *KILLING* HIM.

BUT, I…

QUIT STALLING! BUST A CAP IN HIS ASS!

KILL 'IM!

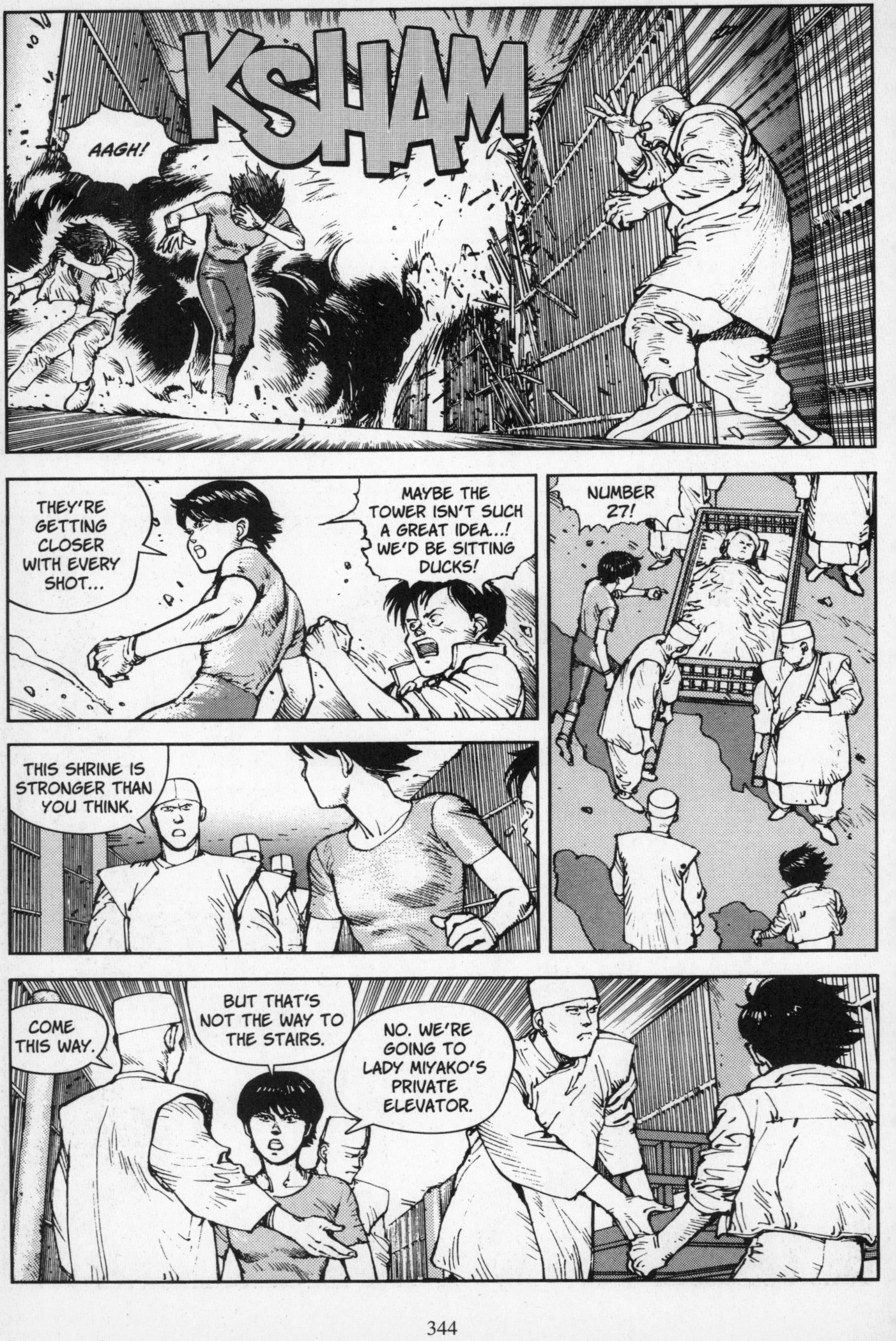
KSHAM
AAGH!
THEY'RE GETTING CLOSER WITH EVERY SHOT...
MAYBE THE TOWER ISN'T SUCH A GREAT IDEA...! WE'D BE SITTING DUCKS!
THIS SHRINE IS STRONGER THAN YOU THINK.
NUMBER 27!
COME THIS WAY.
BUT THAT'S NOT THE WAY TO THE STAIRS.
NO. WE'RE GOING TO LADY MIYAKO'S PRIVATE ELEVATOR.

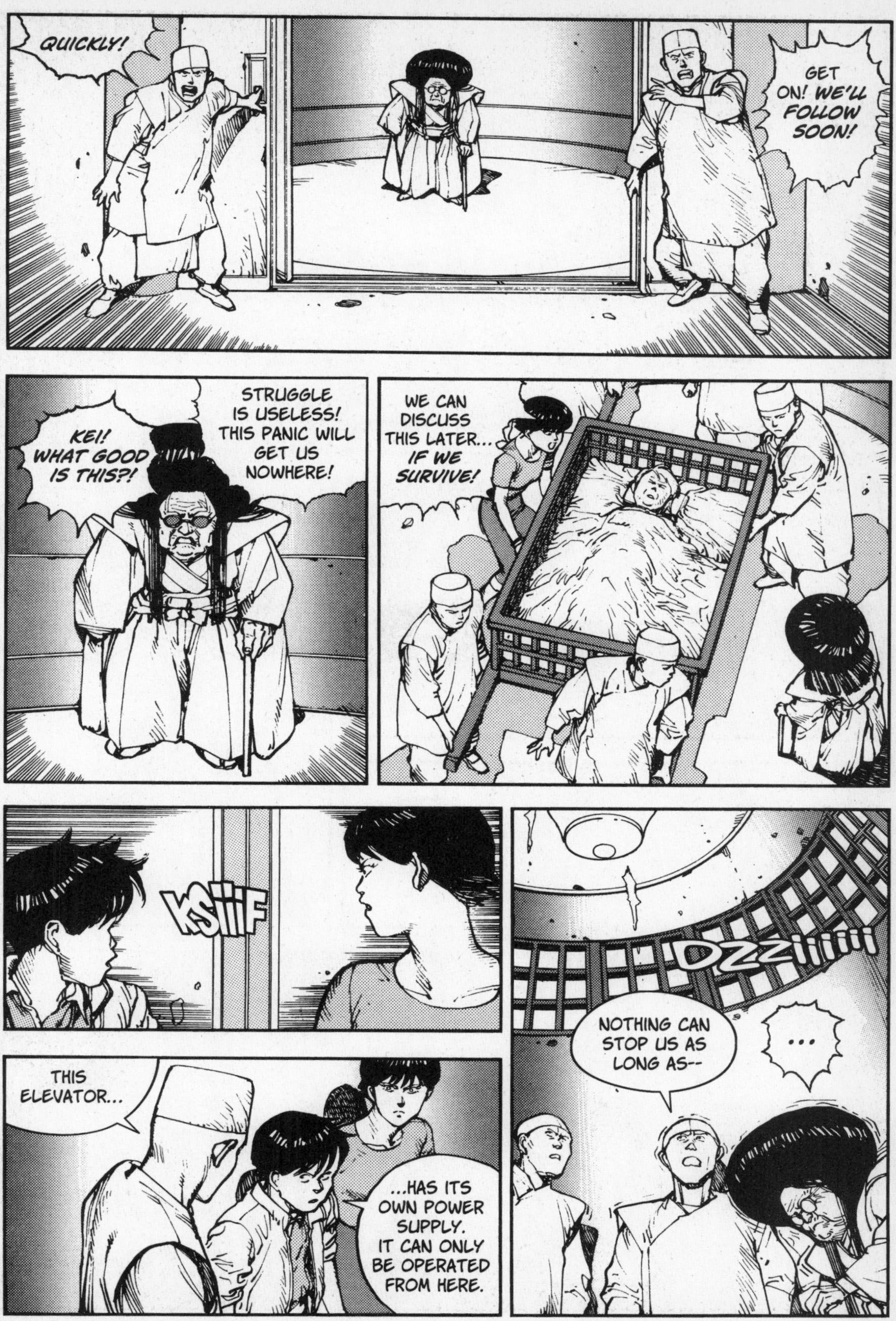
QUICKLY!
GET ON! WE'LL FOLLOW SOON!
KEI! WHAT GOOD IS THIS?!
STRUGGLE IS USELESS! THIS PANIC WILL GET US NOWHERE!
WE CAN DISCUSS THIS LATER... IF WE SURVIVE!
KSiiiF
THIS ELEVATOR...
...HAS ITS OWN POWER SUPPLY. IT CAN ONLY BE OPERATED FROM HERE.
DZZiiiiii
NOTHING CAN STOP US AS LONG AS--
...

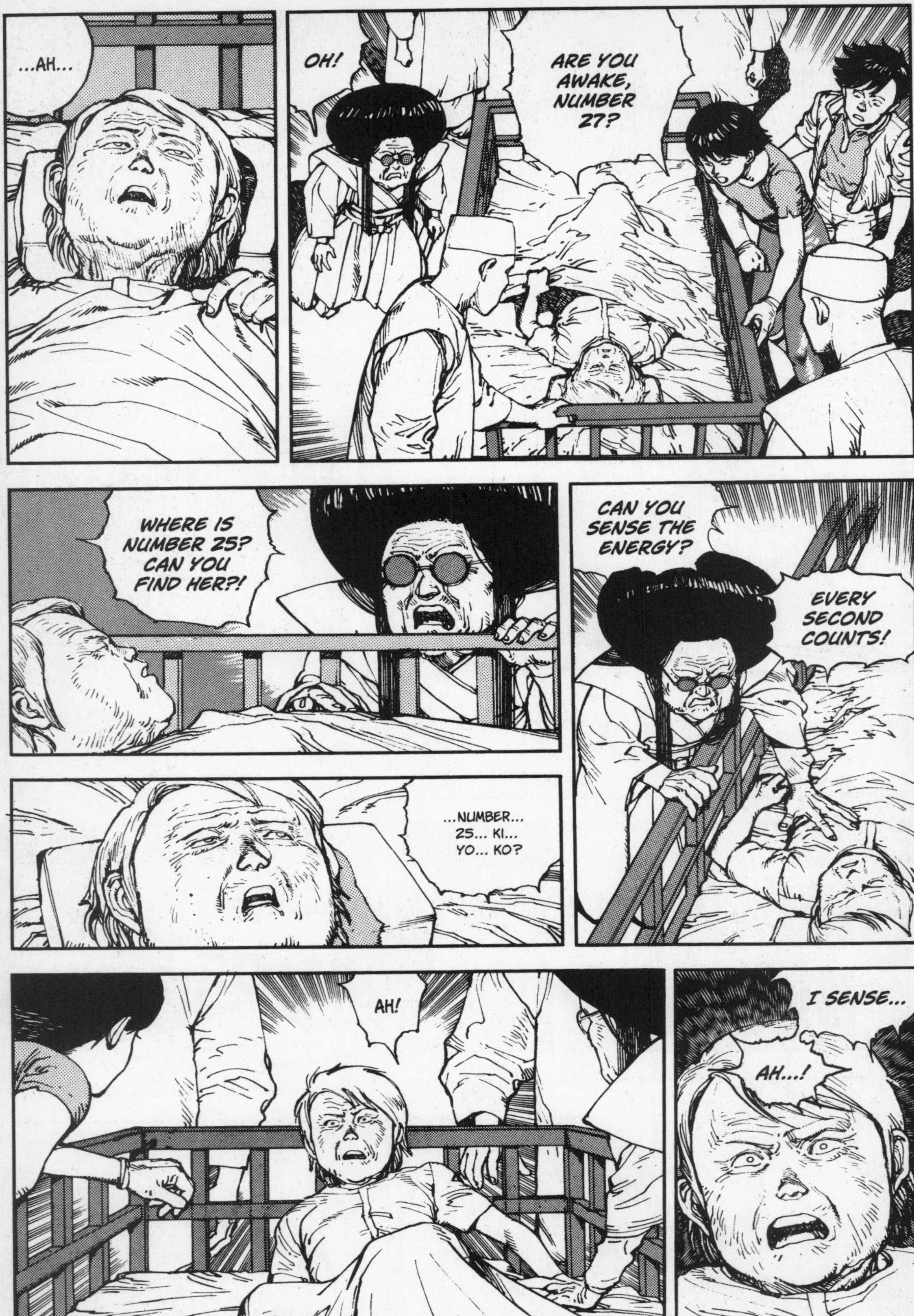
...AH...
OH!
ARE YOU AWAKE, NUMBER 27?
WHERE IS NUMBER 25? CAN YOU FIND HER?!
CAN YOU SENSE THE ENERGY?
EVERY SECOND COUNTS!
...NUMBER... 25... KI... YO... KO?
AH!
I SENSE...
AH...!

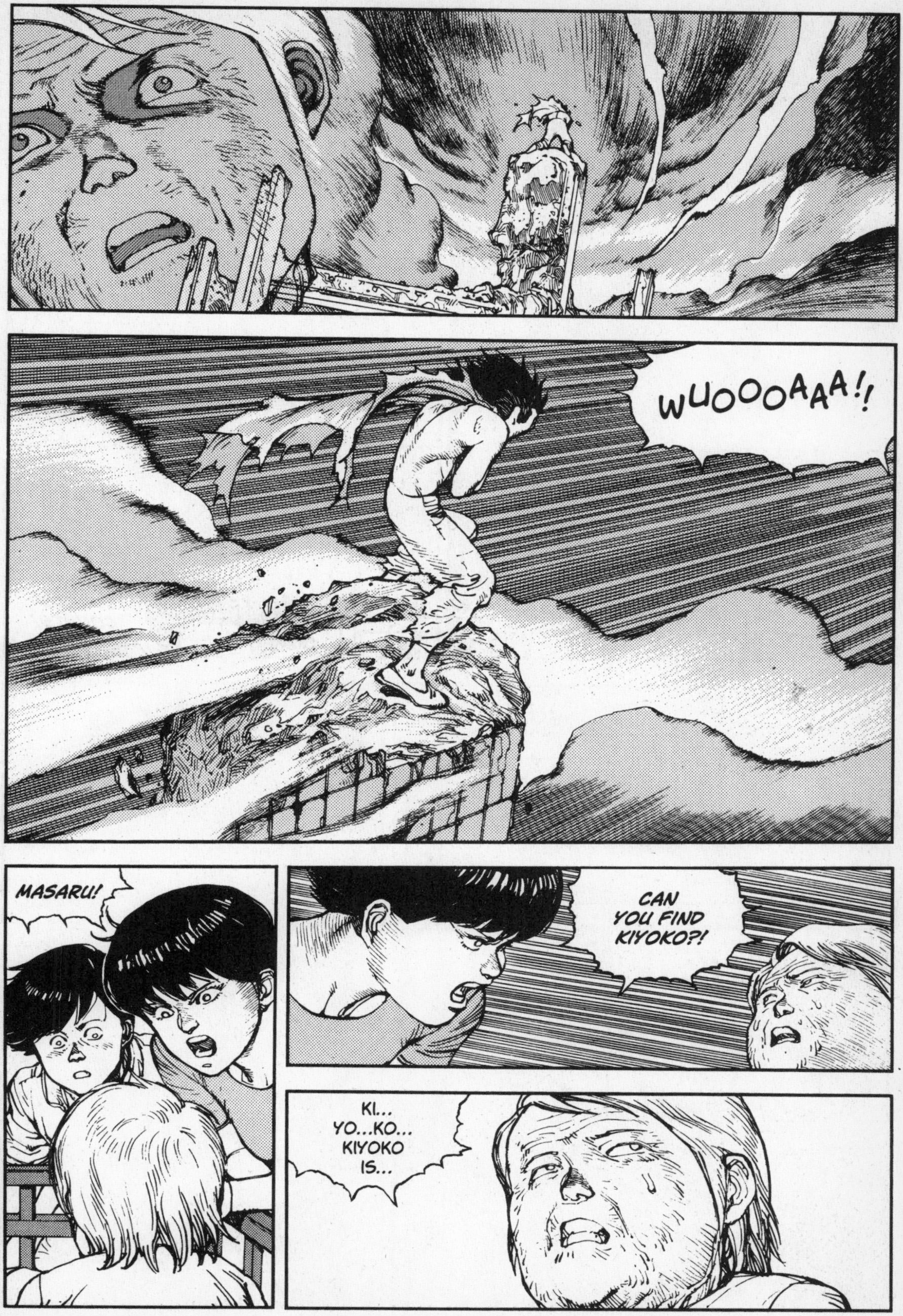
WUOOOAAA!!
MASARU!
CAN YOU FIND KIYOKO?!
KI... YO...KO... KIYOKO IS...

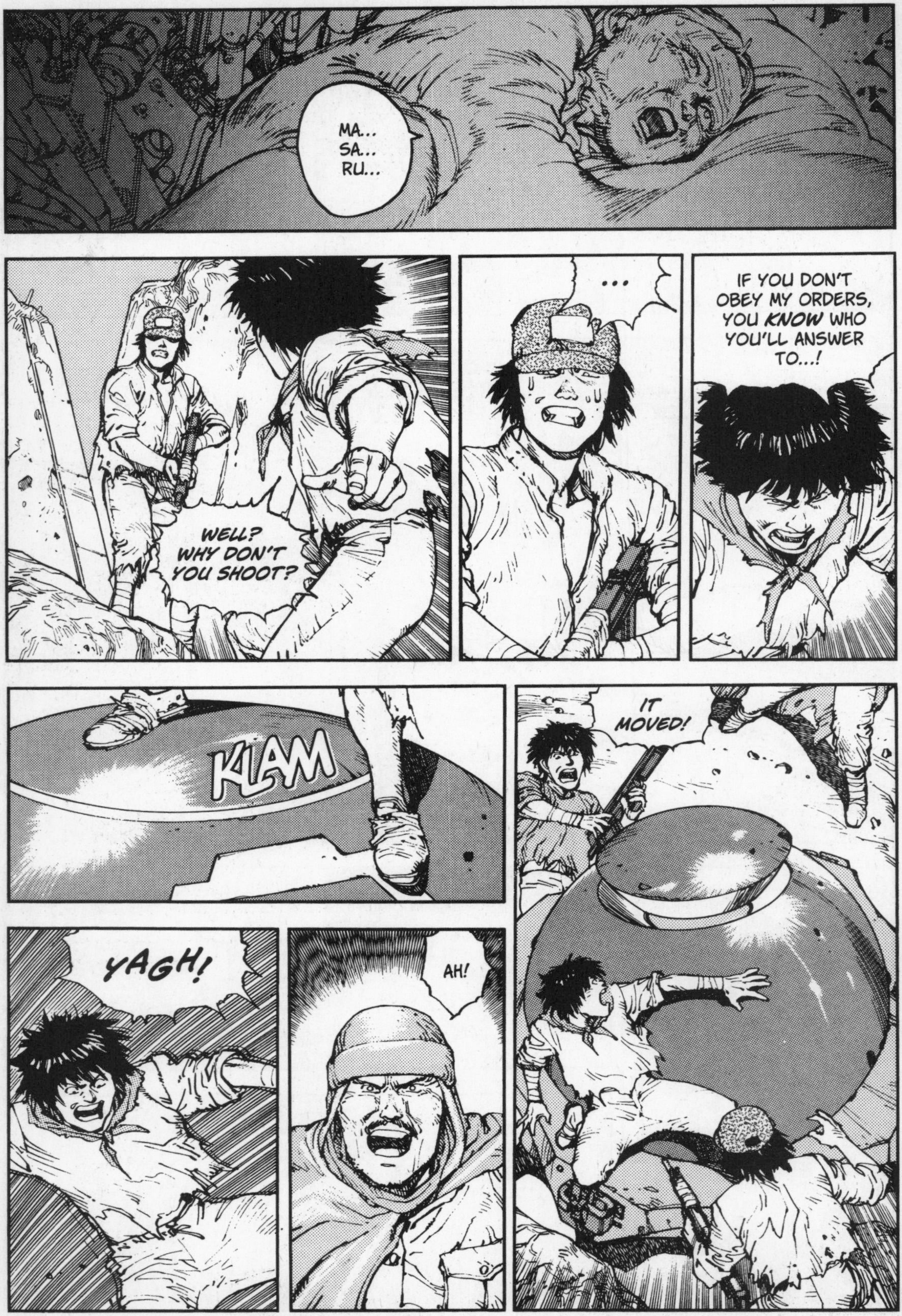
MA... SA... RU...
WELL? WHY DON'T YOU SHOOT?
...
IF YOU DON'T OBEY MY ORDERS, YOU *KNOW* WHO YOU'LL ANSWER TO...!
KLAM
IT MOVED!
YAGH!
AH!

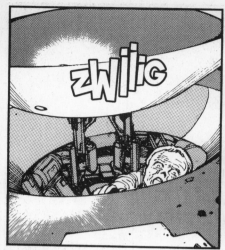

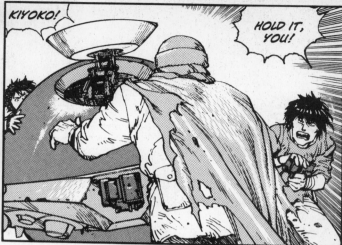

KIYOKO!

HOLD IT, YOU!

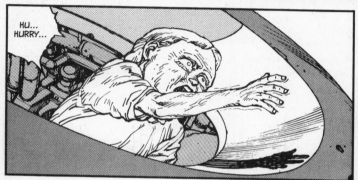

HU... HURRY...

LOOKS LIKE IT!

INFORM THE COMMANDER AT ONCE.

RIGHT!

HEY! THAT'S THE KID!

THE ONE FROM BEFORE?!

DOUBLE TIME!

HURRY... THE TOWER...

FIND... MASARU...

MASARU?!

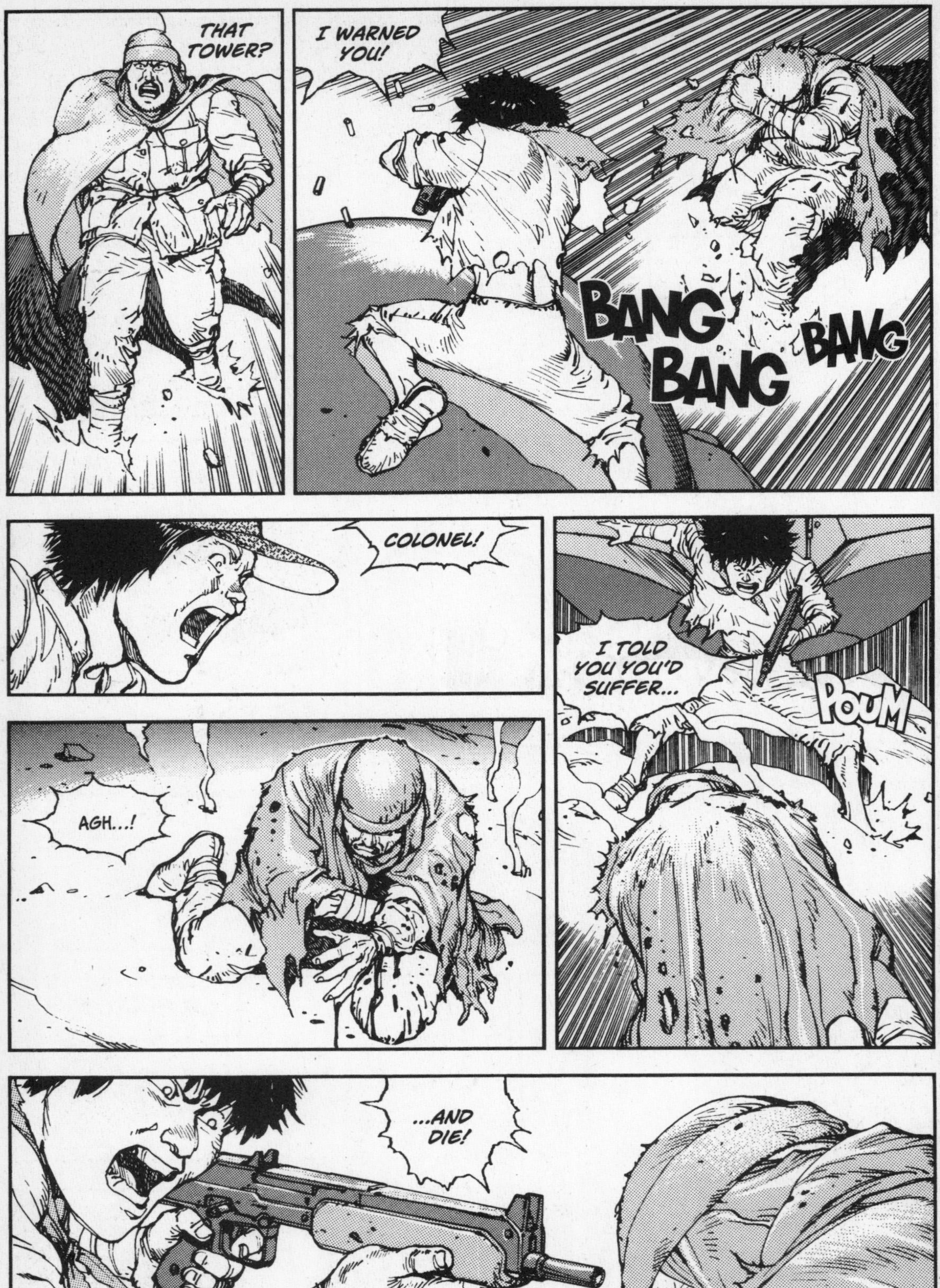
THAT TOWER?
I WARNED YOU!
BANG
BANG
BANG
COLONEL!
I TOLD YOU YOU'D SUFFER...
POUM
AGH...!
...AND DIE!

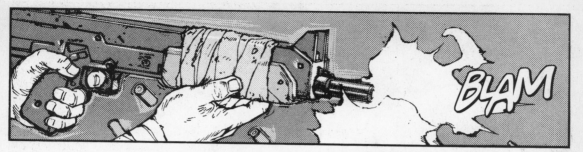

BLAM

...ARGH!

YOU... TRAITOR...

BAOF.

MY COLONEL!

HURRY...

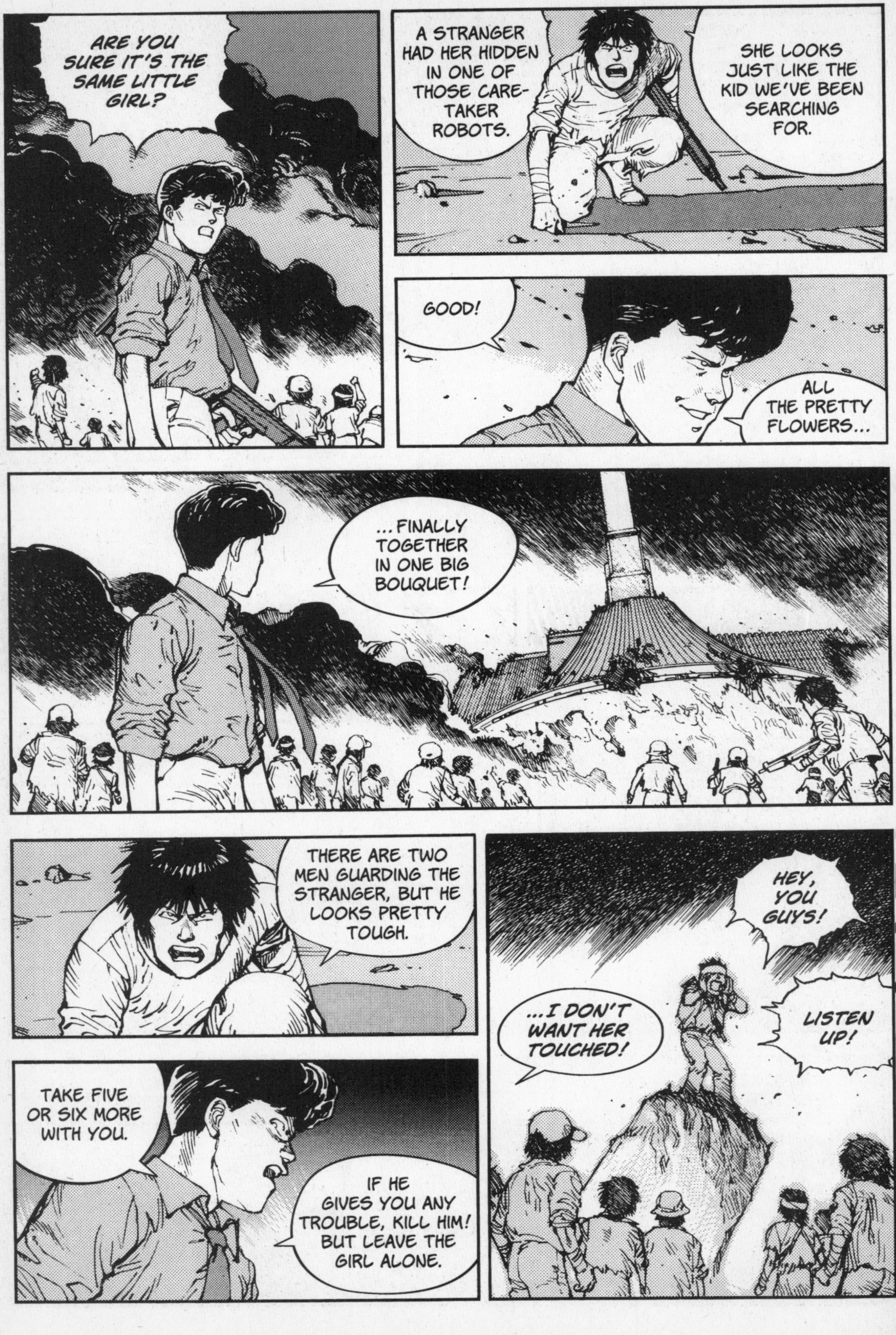
ARE YOU SURE IT'S THE SAME LITTLE GIRL?
A STRANGER HAD HER HIDDEN IN ONE OF THOSE CARE-TAKER ROBOTS.
SHE LOOKS JUST LIKE THE KID WE'VE BEEN SEARCHING FOR.
GOOD!
ALL THE PRETTY FLOWERS...
...FINALLY TOGETHER IN ONE BIG BOUQUET!
THERE ARE TWO MEN GUARDING THE STRANGER, BUT HE LOOKS PRETTY TOUGH.
TAKE FIVE OR SIX MORE WITH YOU.
IF HE GIVES YOU ANY TROUBLE, KILL HIM! BUT LEAVE THE GIRL ALONE.
HEY, YOU GUYS!
LISTEN UP!
...I DON'T WANT HER TOUCHED!

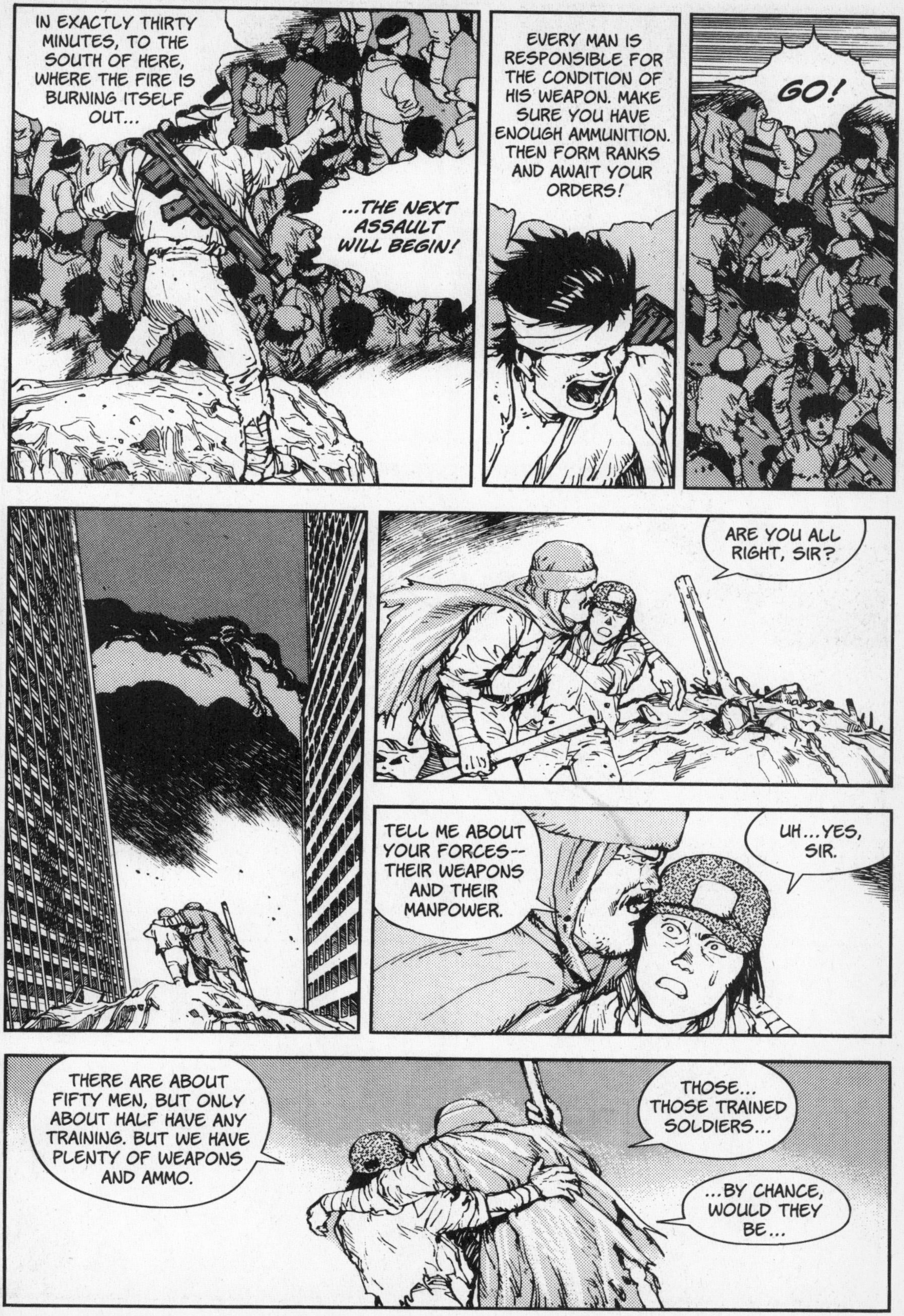
IN EXACTLY THIRTY MINUTES, TO THE SOUTH OF HERE, WHERE THE FIRE IS BURNING ITSELF OUT...
...THE NEXT ASSAULT WILL BEGIN!
EVERY MAN IS RESPONSIBLE FOR THE CONDITION OF HIS WEAPON. MAKE SURE YOU HAVE ENOUGH AMMUNITION. THEN FORM RANKS AND AWAIT YOUR ORDERS!
GO!
ARE YOU ALL RIGHT, SIR?
TELL ME ABOUT YOUR FORCES-- THEIR WEAPONS AND THEIR MANPOWER.
UH...YES, SIR.
THERE ARE ABOUT FIFTY MEN, BUT ONLY ABOUT HALF HAVE ANY TRAINING. BUT WE HAVE PLENTY OF WEAPONS AND AMMO.
THOSE... THOSE TRAINED SOLDIERS...
...BY CHANCE, WOULD THEY BE...

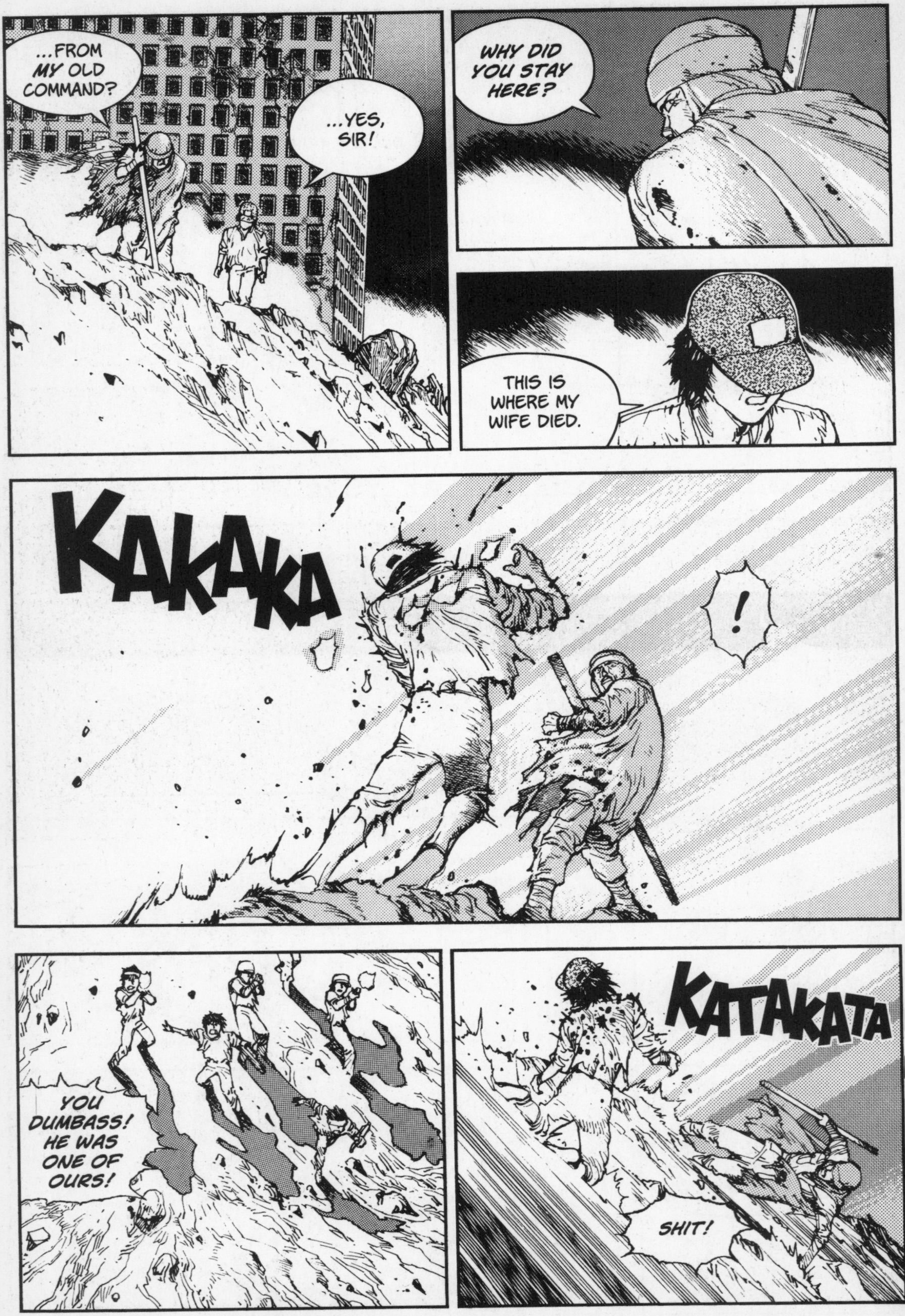
...FROM MY OLD COMMAND?
...YES, SIR!
WHY DID YOU STAY HERE?
THIS IS WHERE MY WIFE DIED.
KAKAKA
!
YOU DUMBASS! HE WAS ONE OF OURS!
KATAKATA
SHIT!

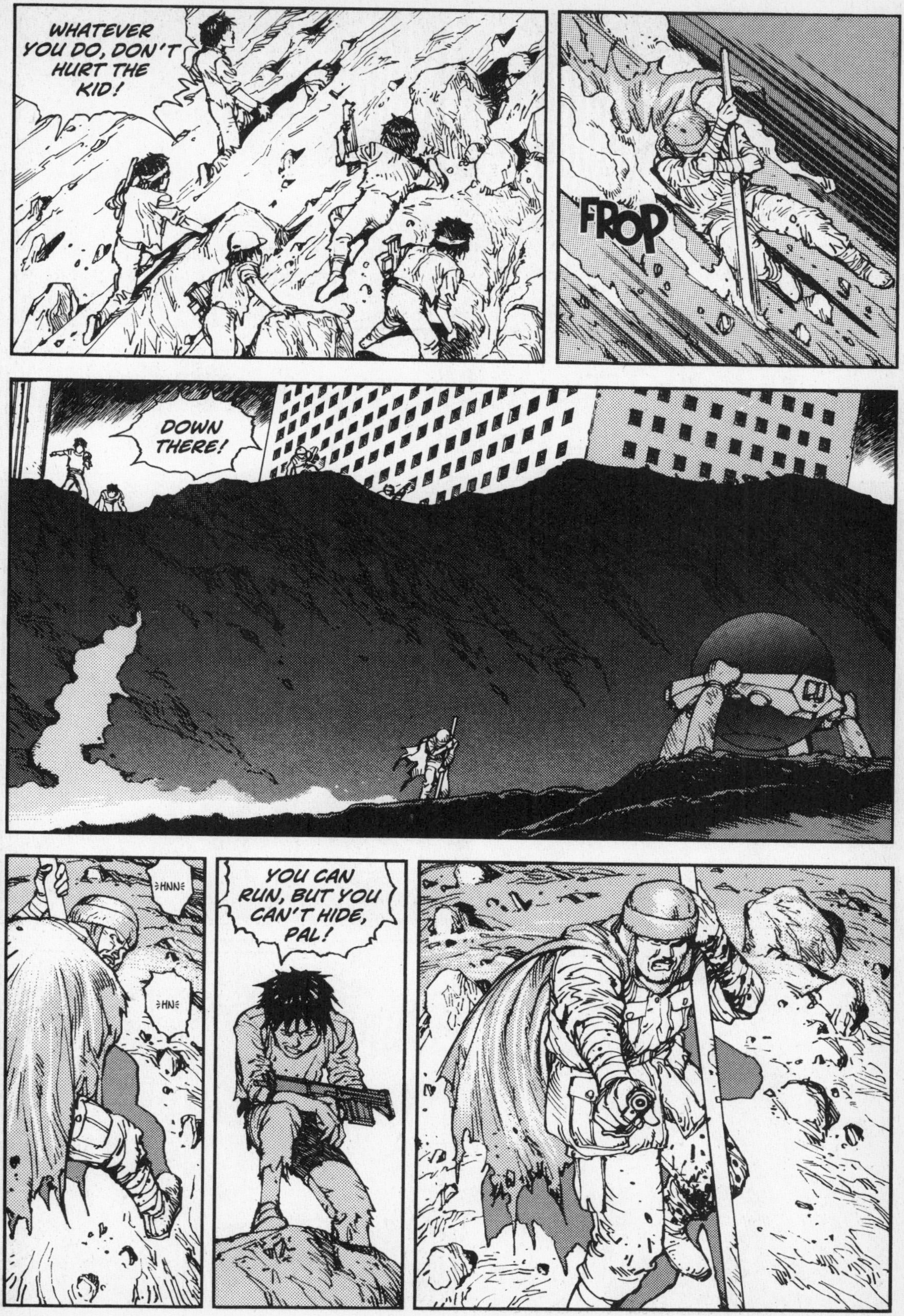
WHATEVER YOU DO, DON'T HURT THE KID!
FROP
DOWN THERE!
HNN
HN
YOU CAN RUN, BUT YOU CAN'T HIDE, PAL!

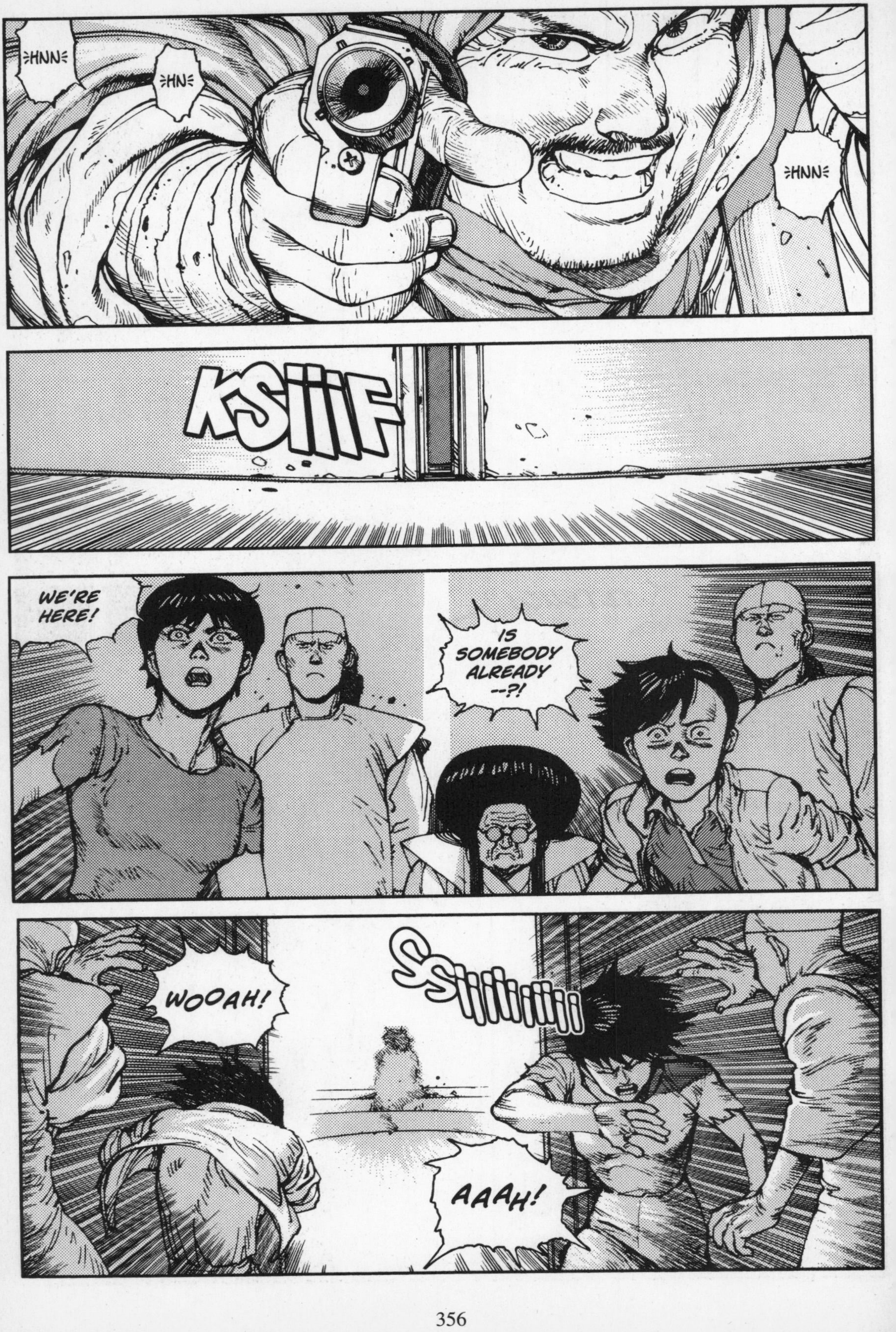

HNN
HN
HNN
KSIIIF
WE'RE HERE!
IS SOMEBODY ALREADY --?!
WOOAH!
SSIIIIIIIII
AAAH!

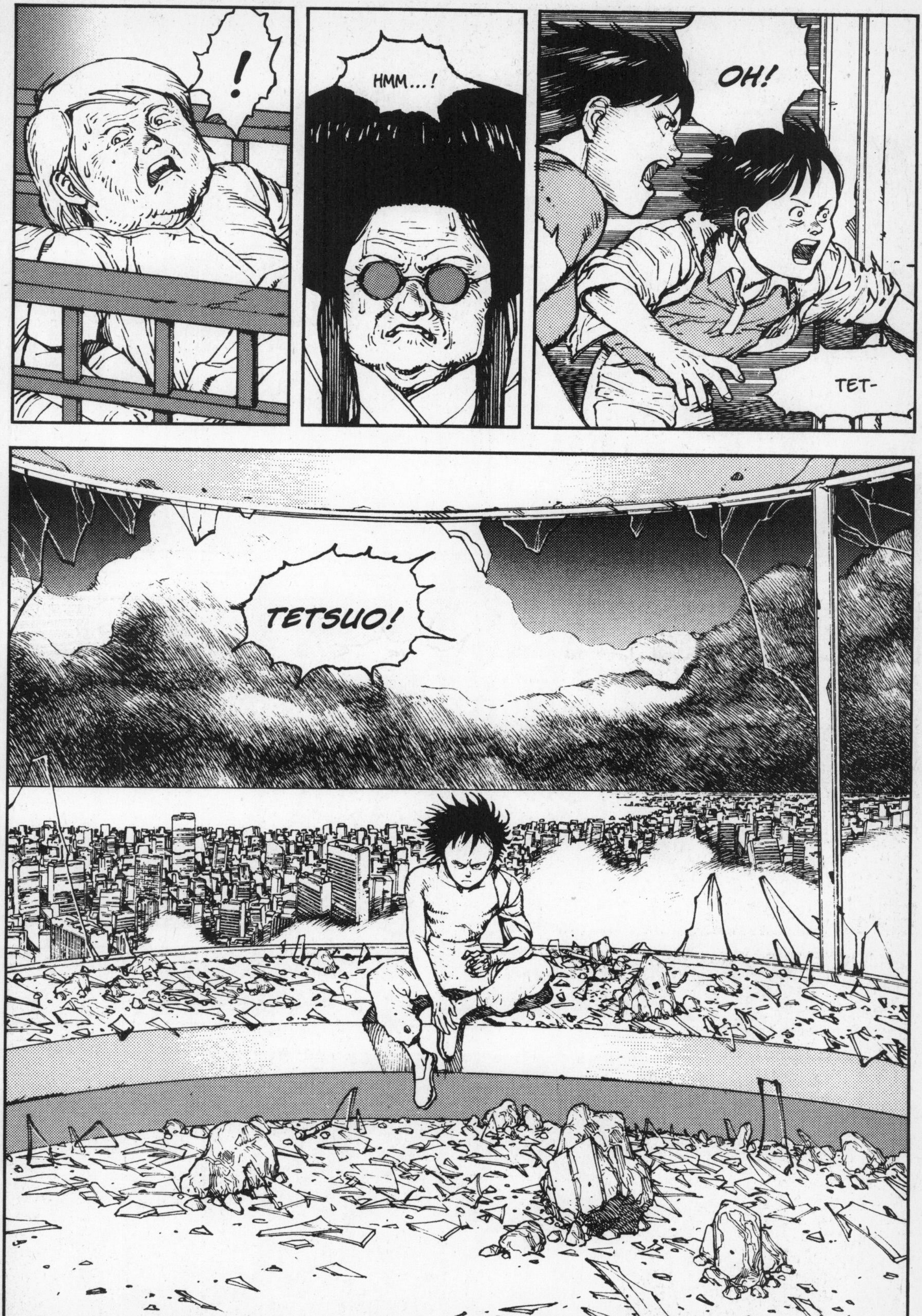
!
HMM...!
OH!
TET-
TETSUO!

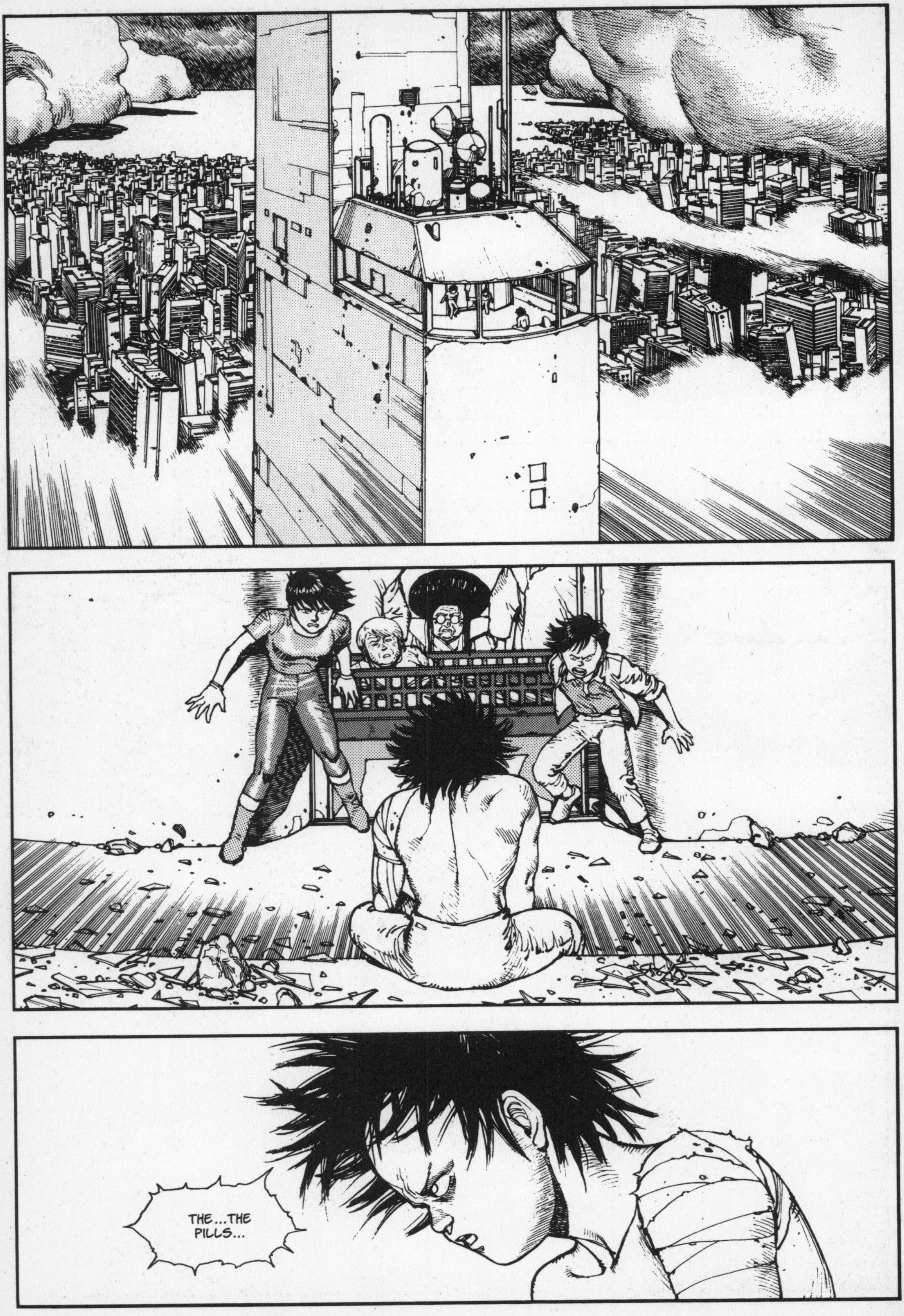
THE...THE
PILLS...

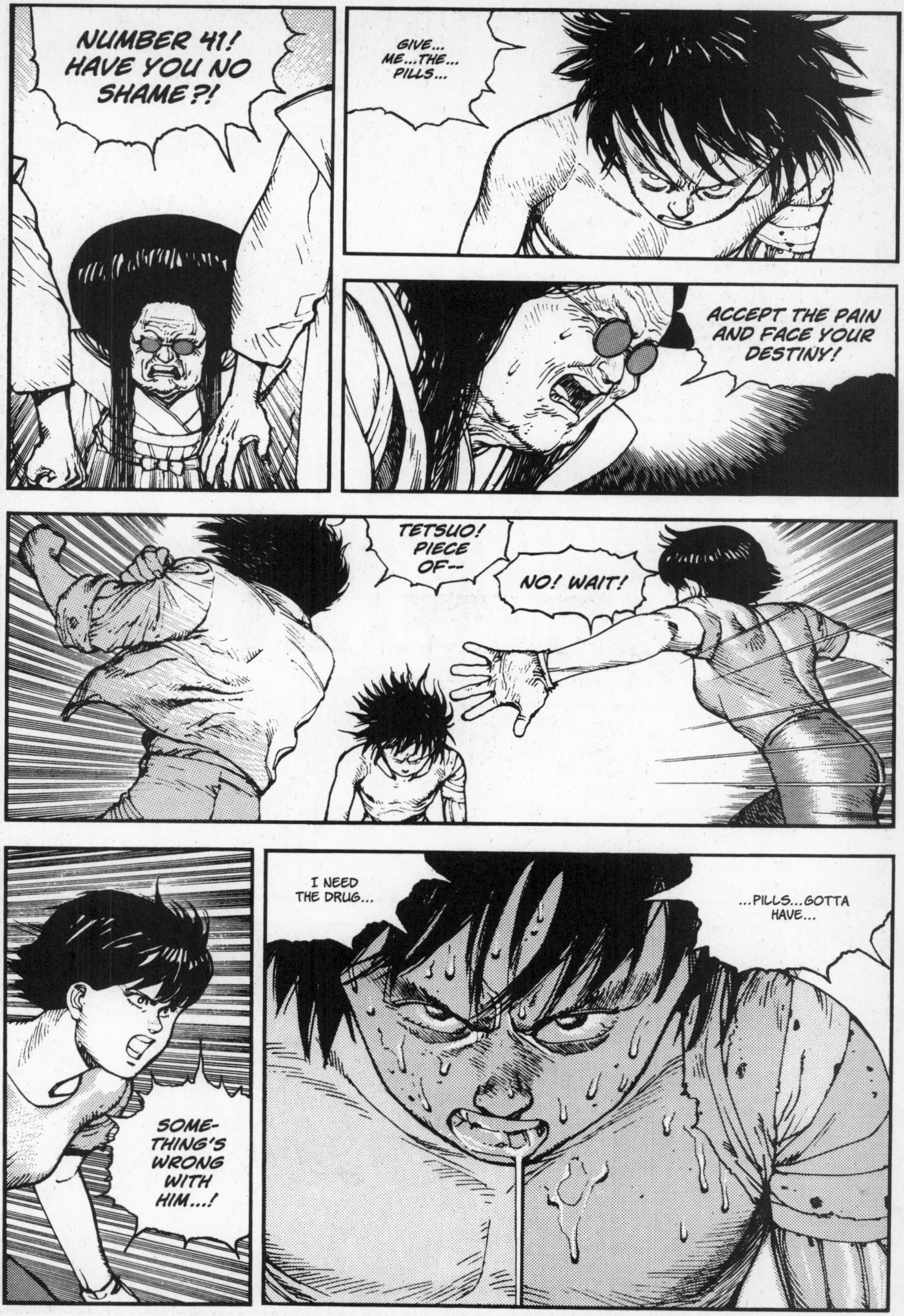
NUMBER 41! HAVE YOU NO SHAME?!
GIVE... ME...THE... PILLS...
ACCEPT THE PAIN AND FACE YOUR DESTINY!
TETSUO! PIECE OF--
NO! WAIT!
SOME-THING'S WRONG WITH HIM...!
I NEED THE DRUG...
...PILLS...GOTTA HAVE...

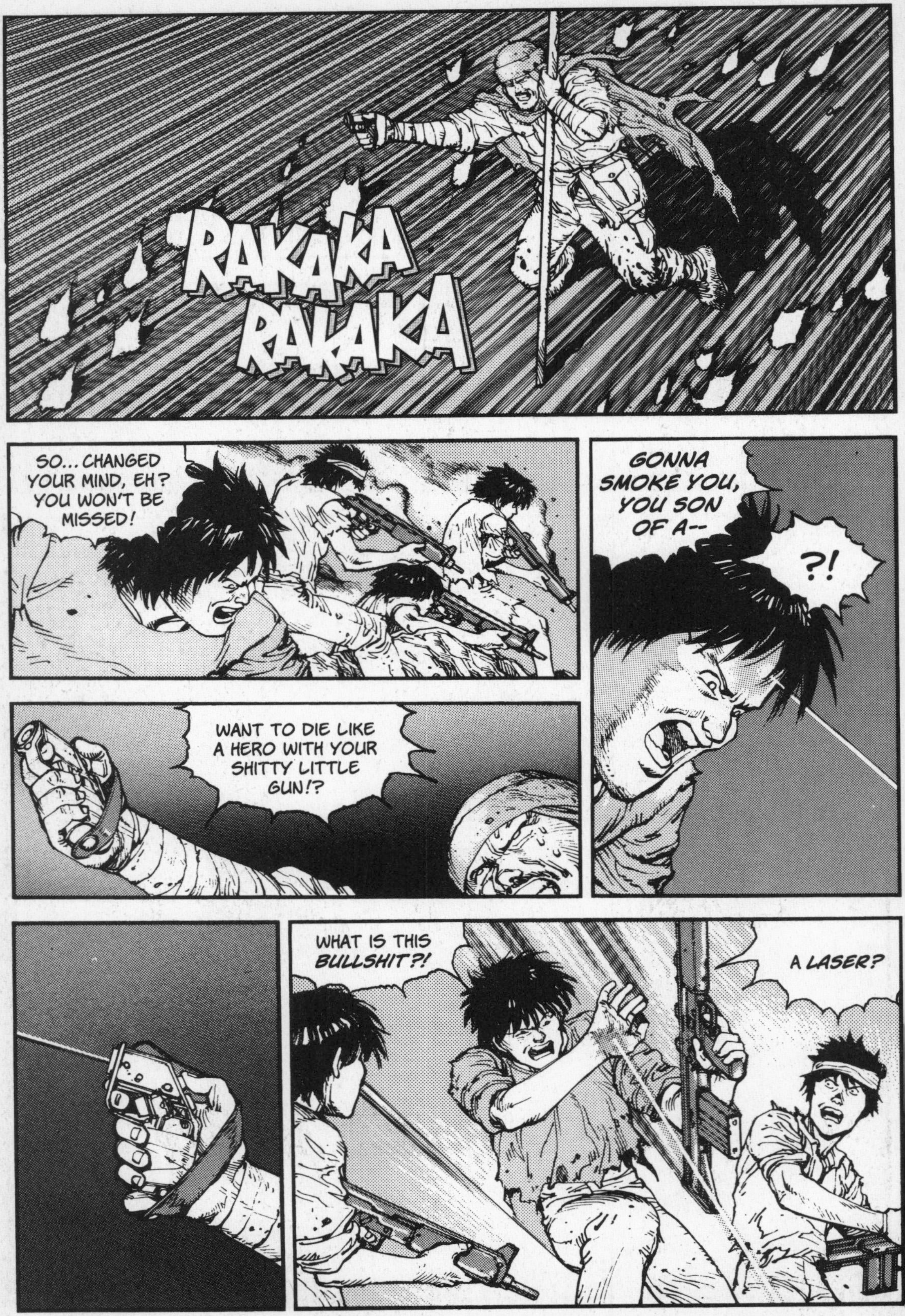
RAKAKA RAKAKA
SO... CHANGED YOUR MIND, EH? YOU WON'T BE MISSED!
GONNA SMOKE YOU, YOU SON OF A--
?!
WANT TO DIE LIKE A HERO WITH YOUR SHITTY LITTLE GUN!?
WHAT IS THIS BULLSHIT?!
A LASER?

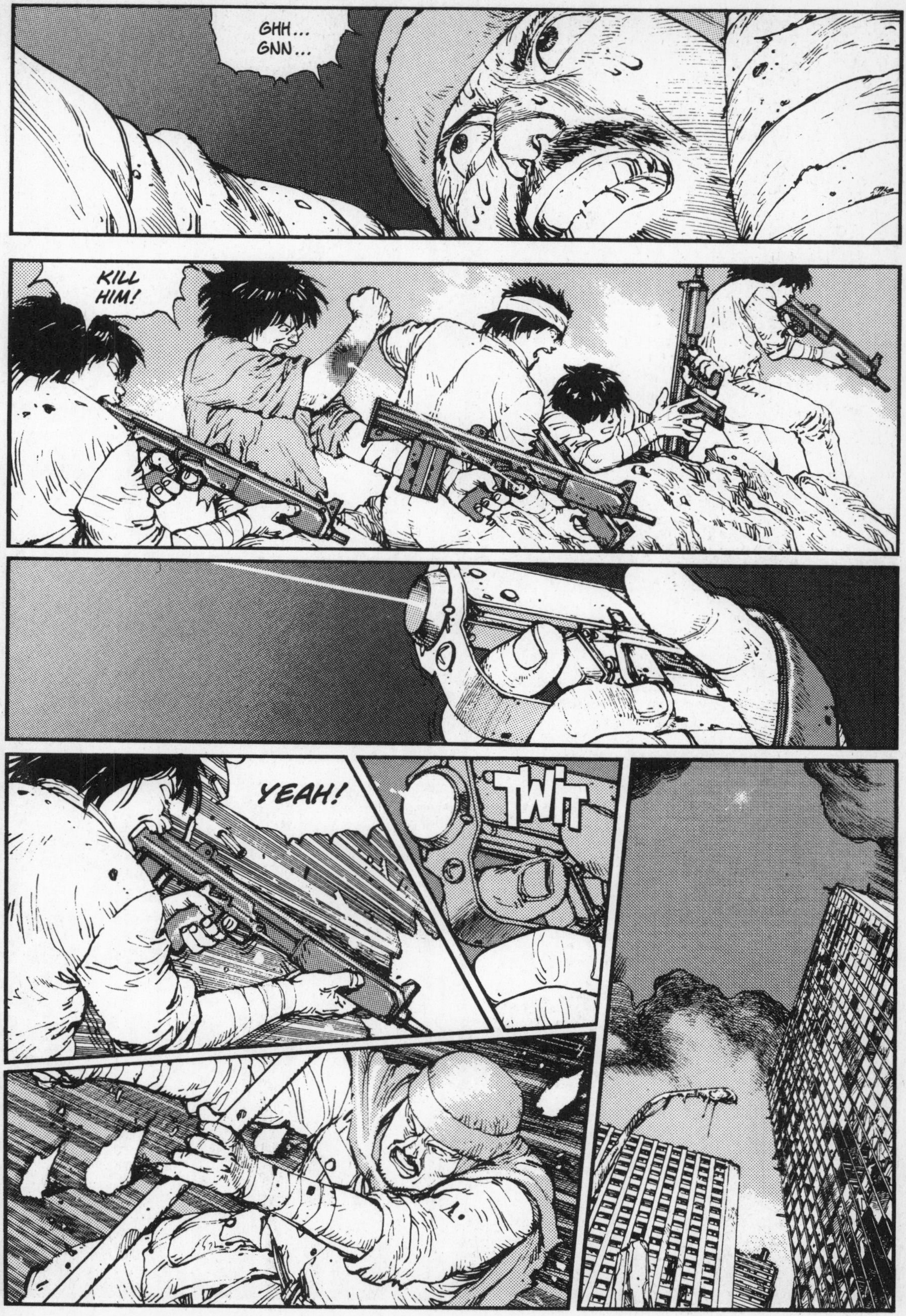
GHH... GNN...
KILL HIM!
YEAH!
TWIT

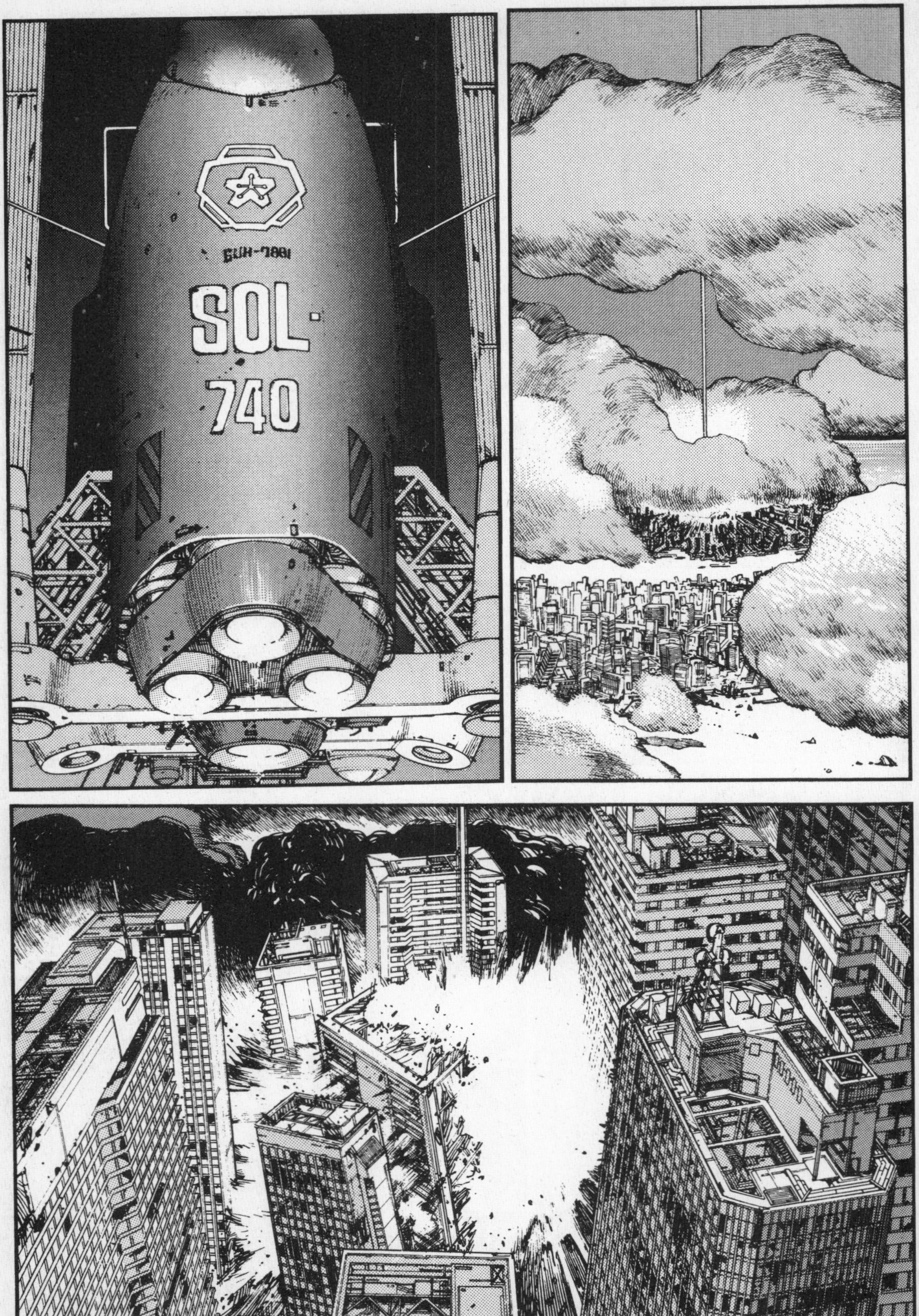
SOL-
740

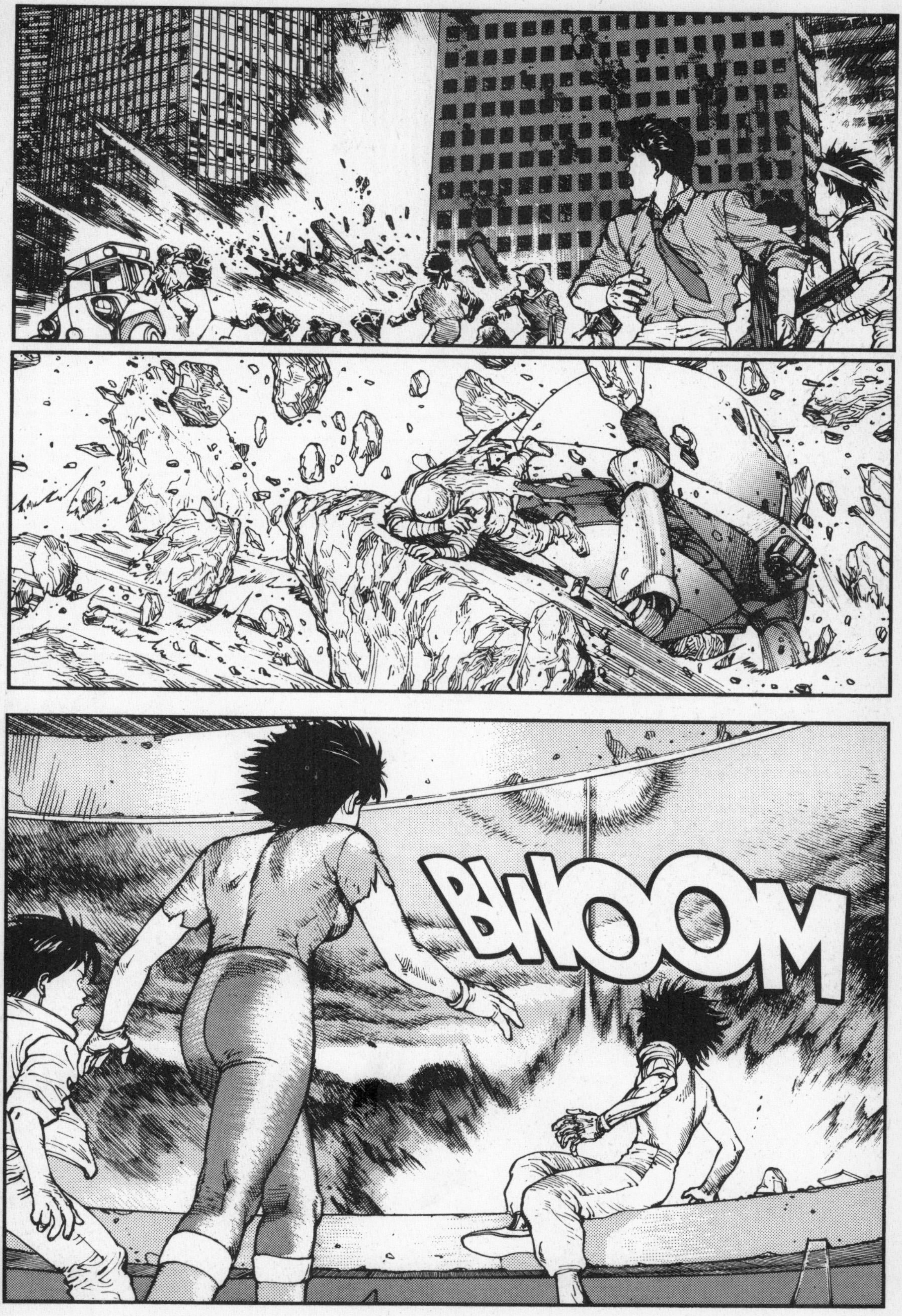
BWOOM

THAT
LIGHT...?!
WHAT--

...OH...

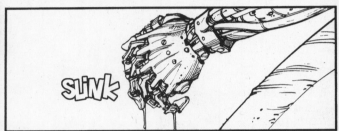

SLINK

OOOH...

...OOOOHHHH!

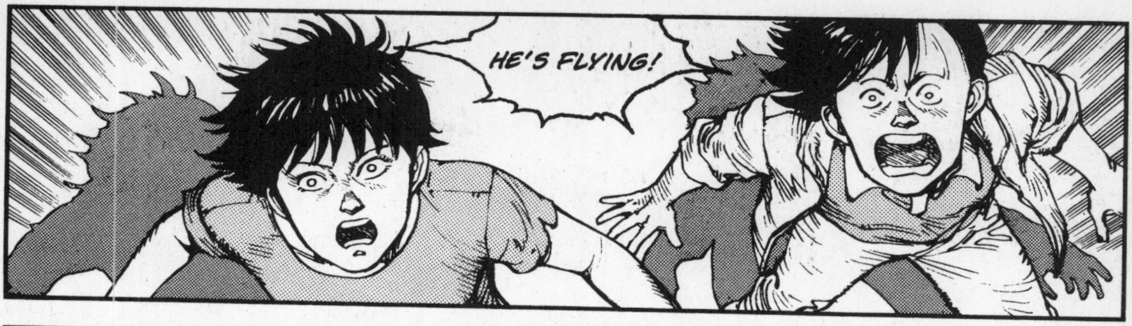
HE'S FLYING!
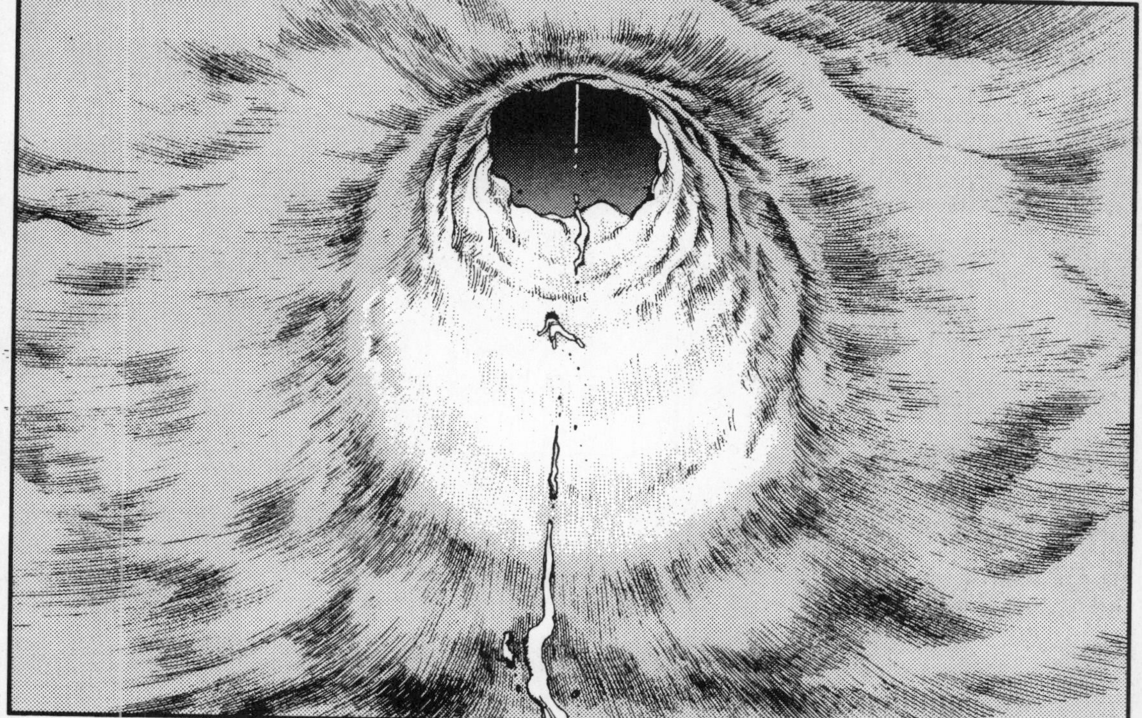
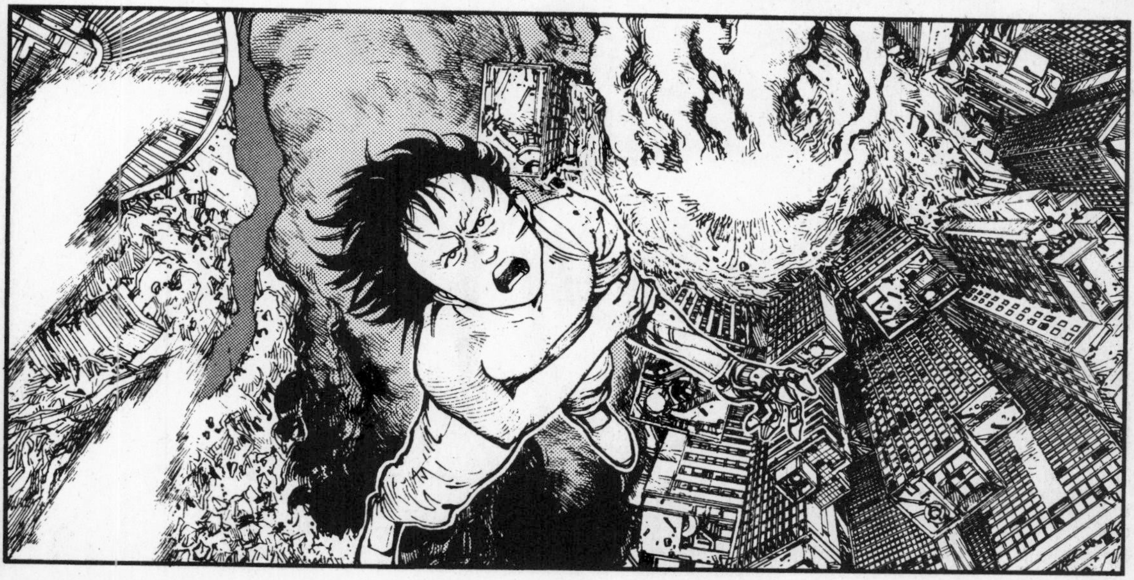

TLING

?

AKIRA... YOU'RE NOT EATING...

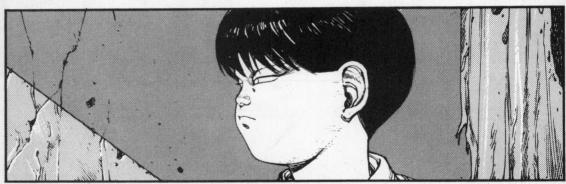

WOOOOAA!

OOOH!

LADY MIYAKO!

ANSWER ME, KIYOKO!

KIYOKO!

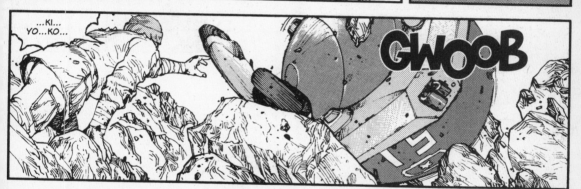

...KI... YO...KO...

GWOOB

UP THERE ...!

WHAT ...?

NO... IT'S NOT POSSIBLE...

DO YOU THINK...?

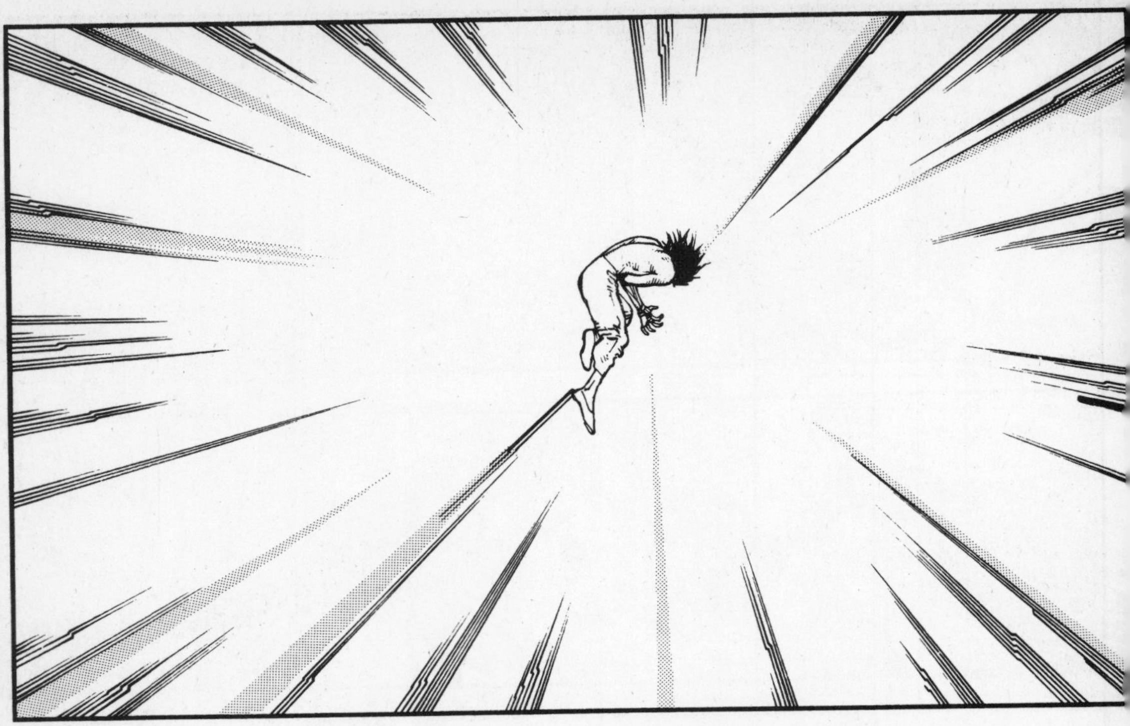

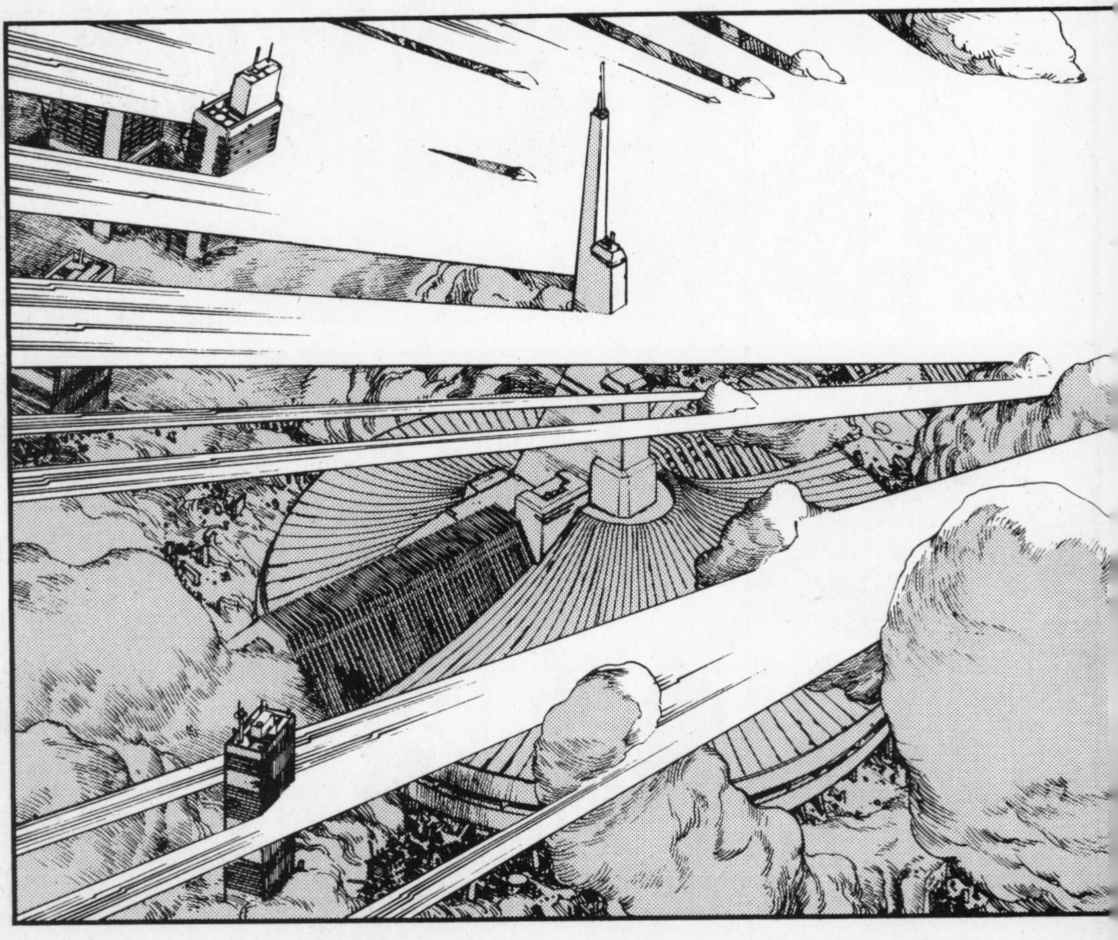

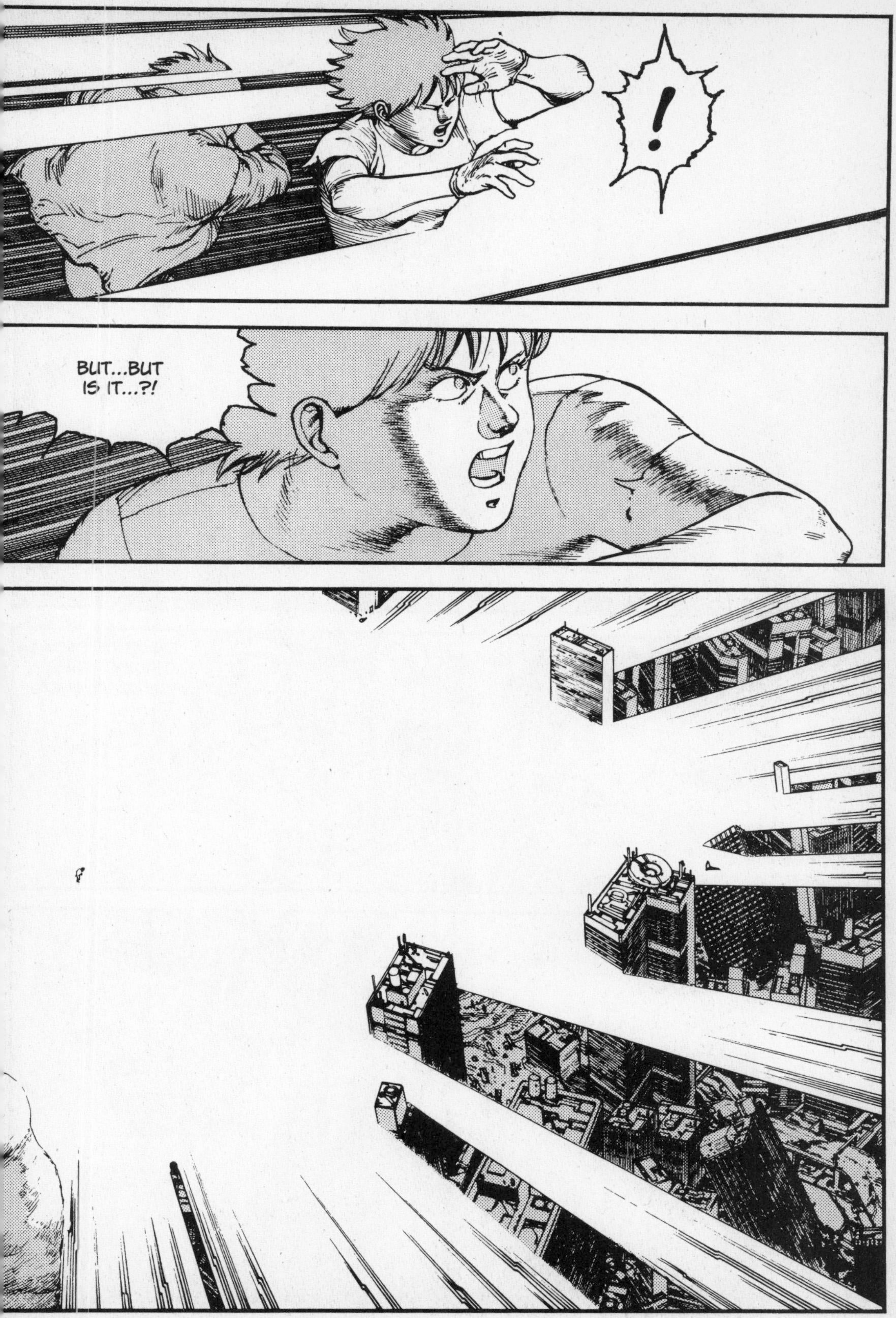
!
BUT...BUT IS IT...?!

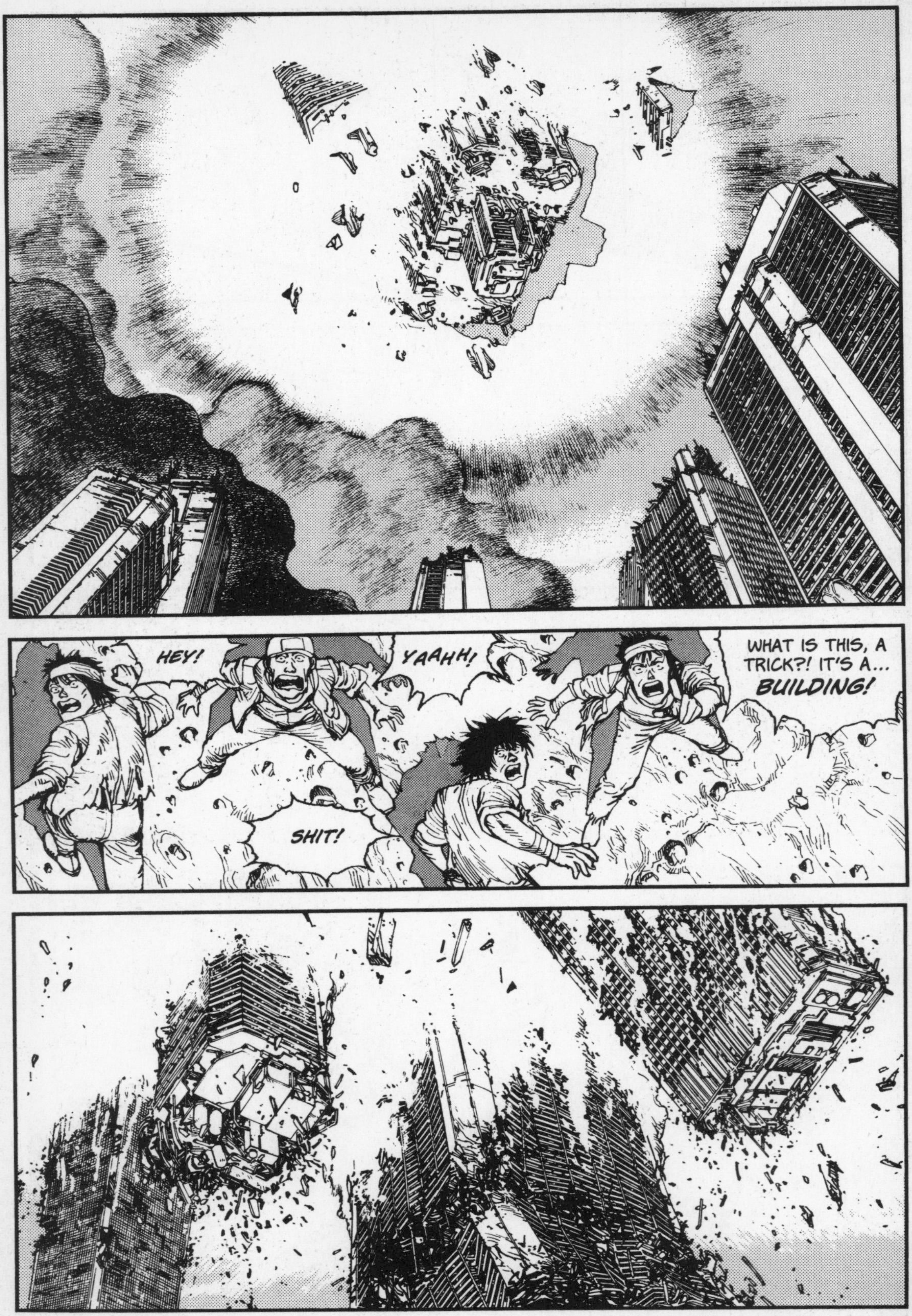
HEY!
YAAHH!
WHAT IS THIS, A TRICK?! IT'S A... BUILDING!
SHIT!

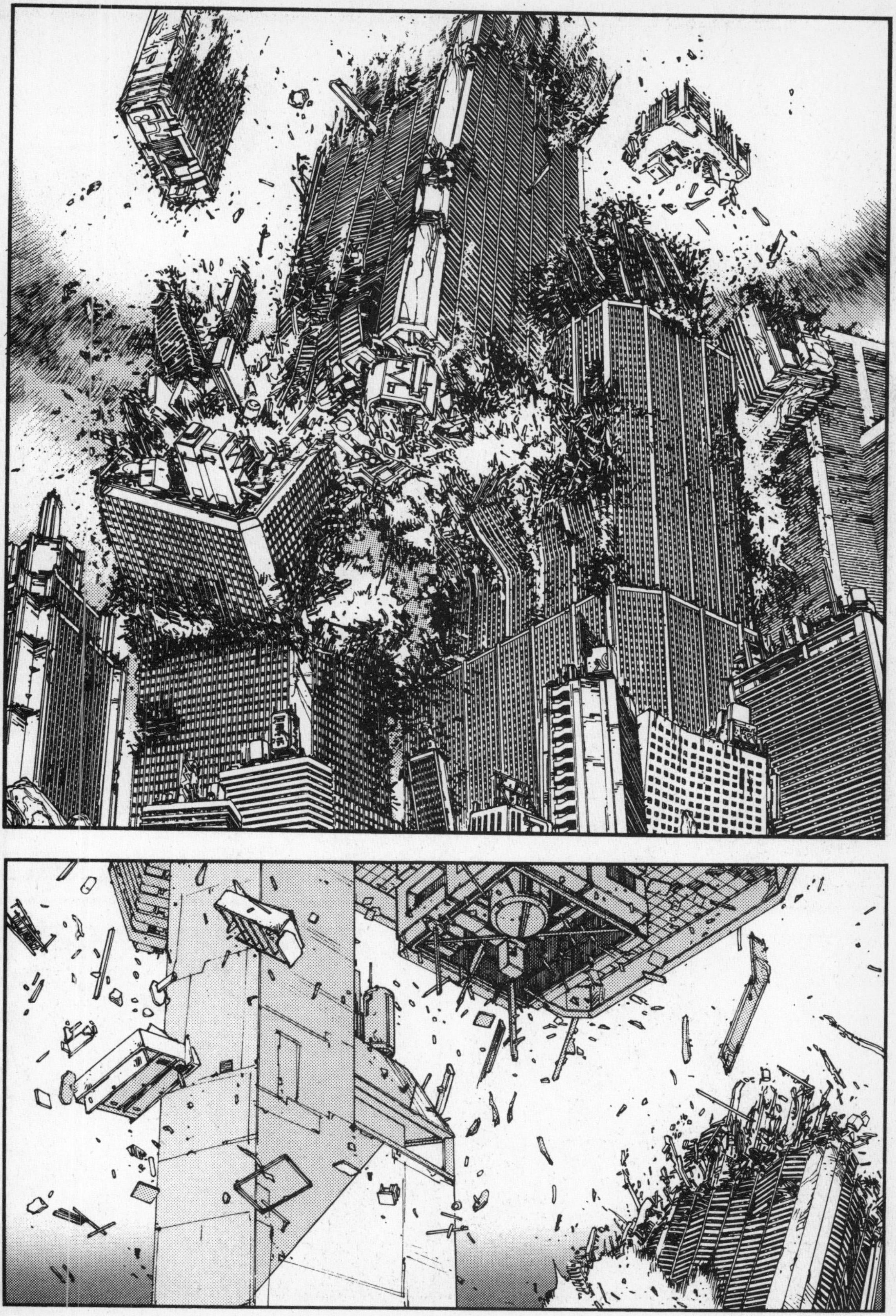

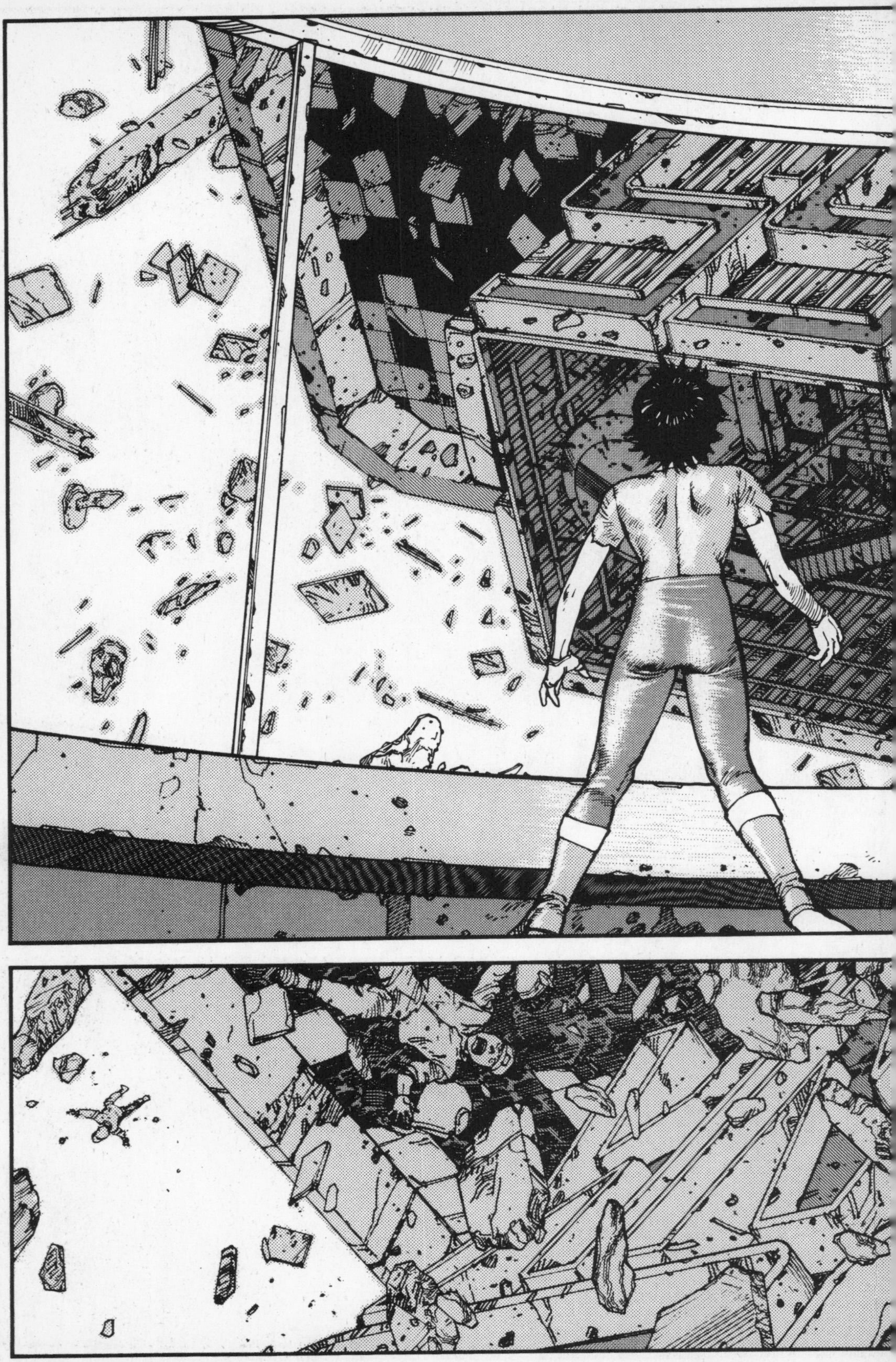

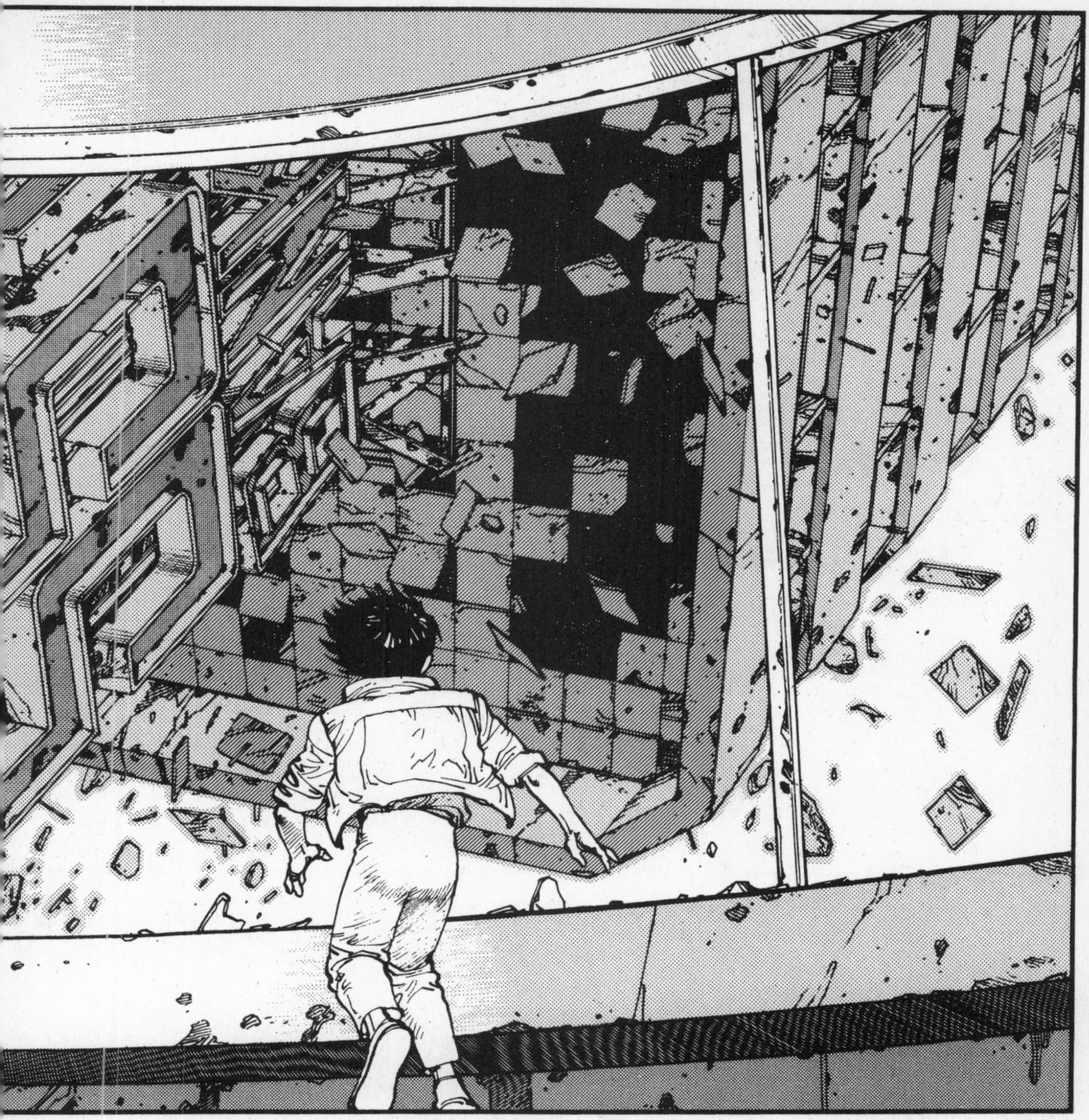
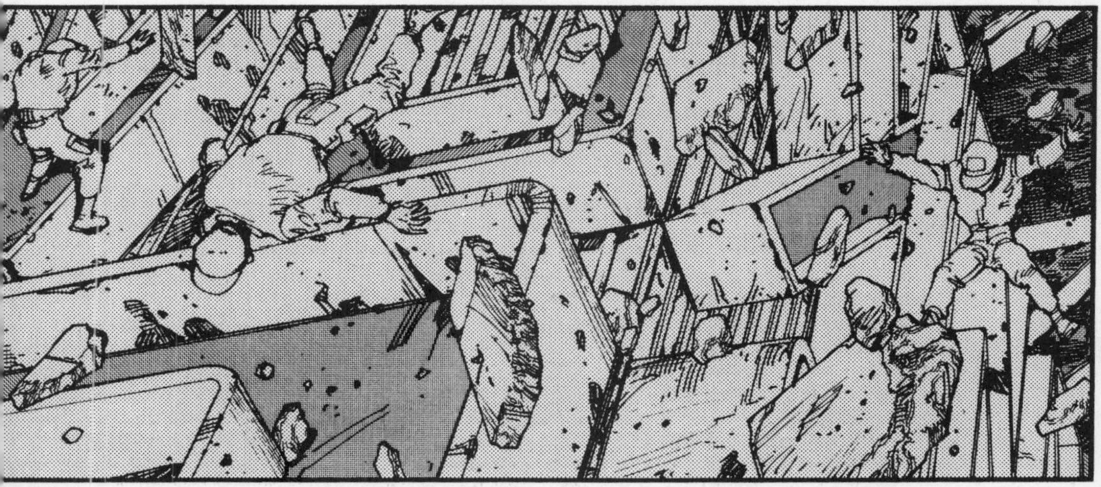

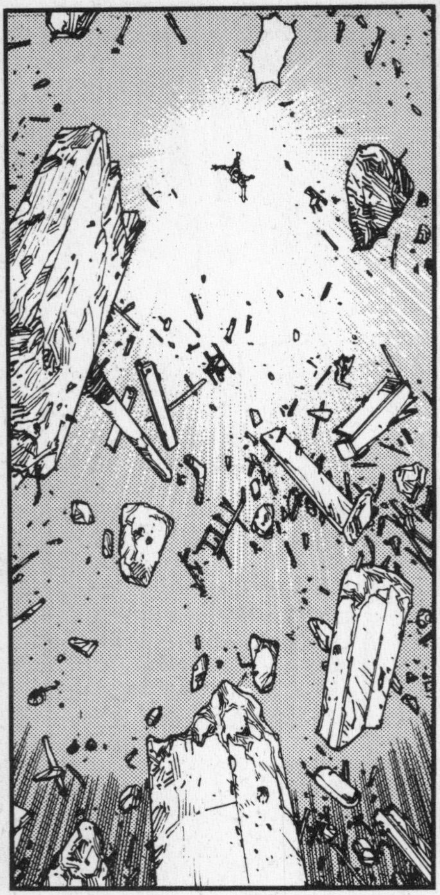

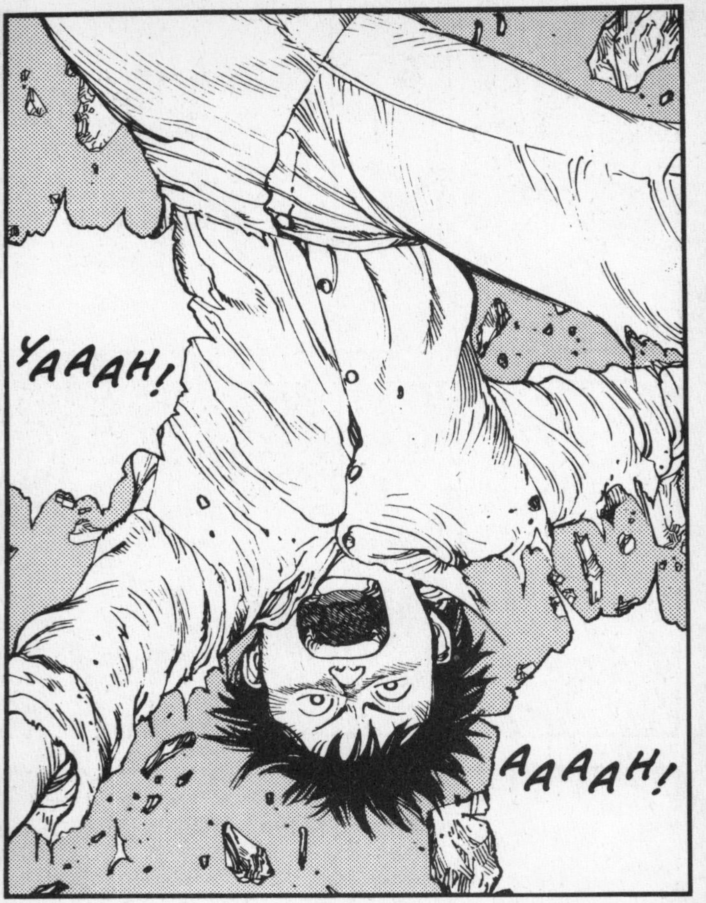
YAAAH!
AAAAH!

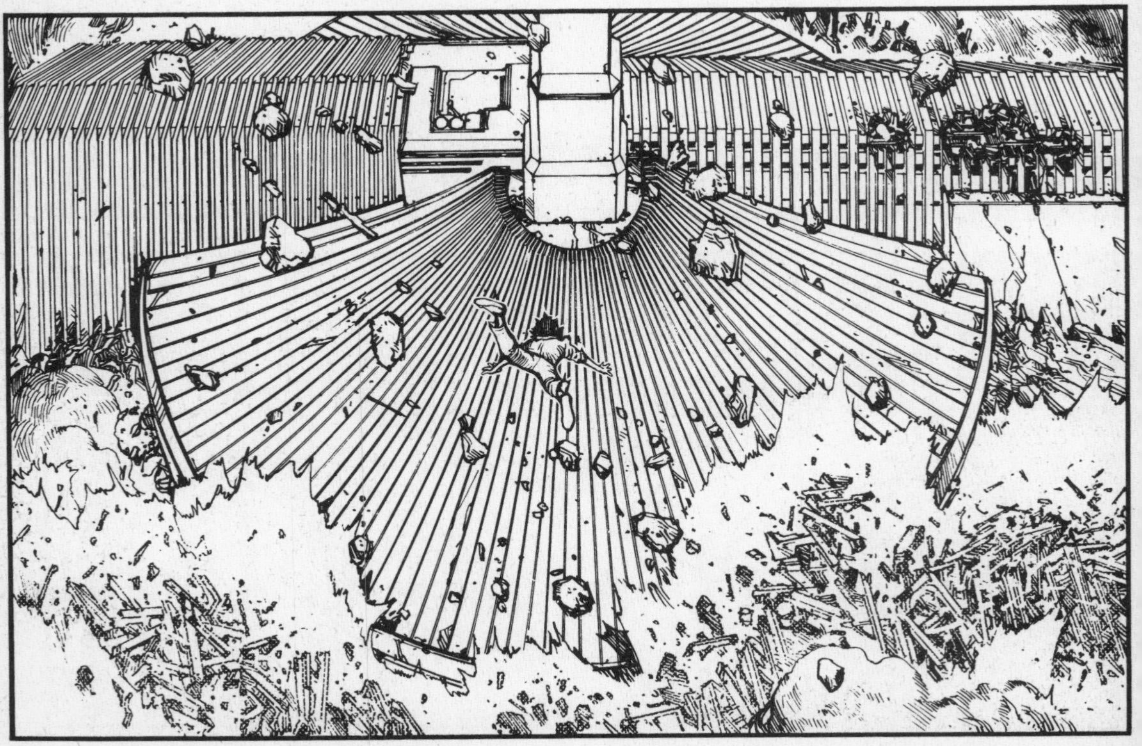

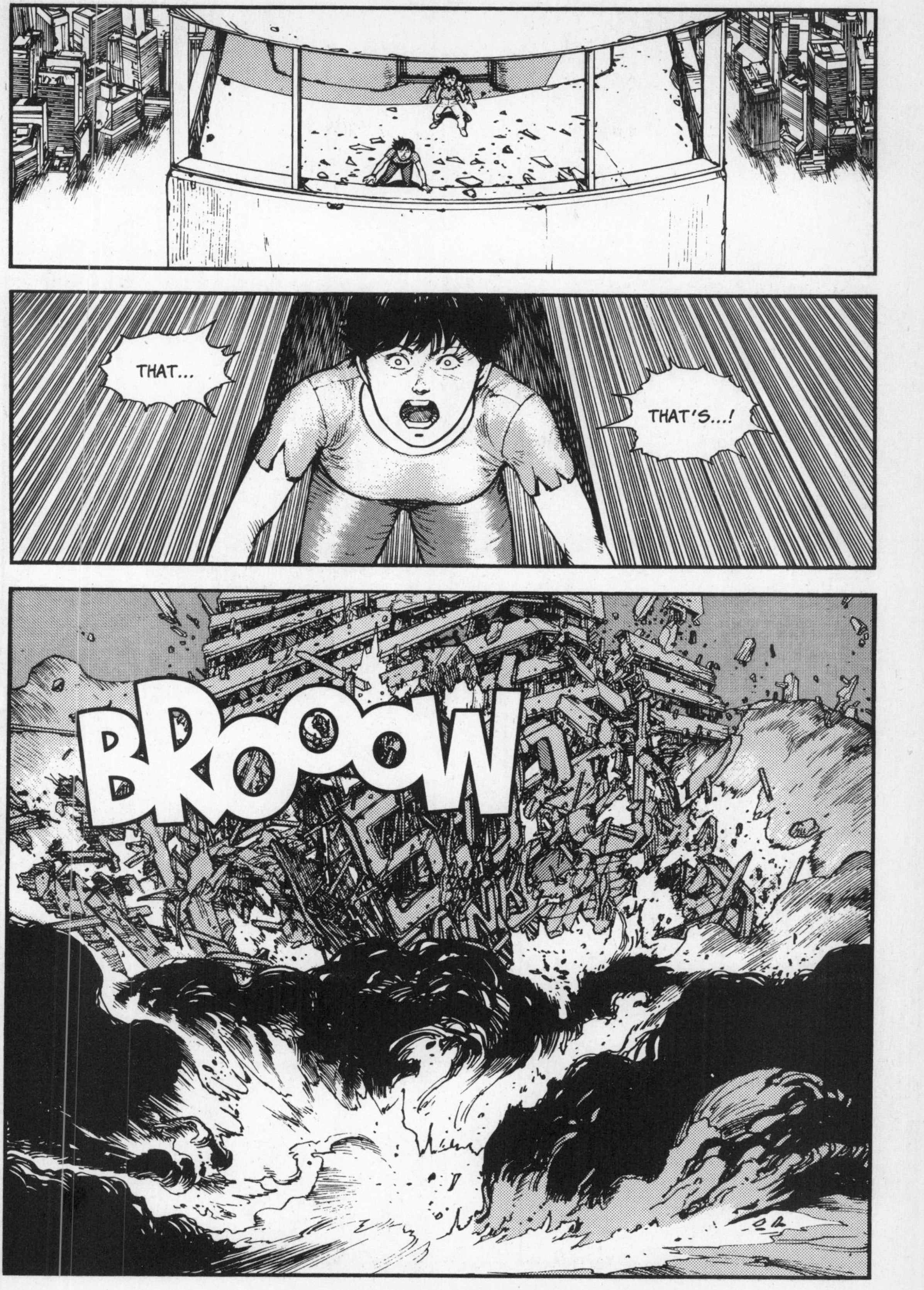
THAT...
THAT'S...!
BROOOW

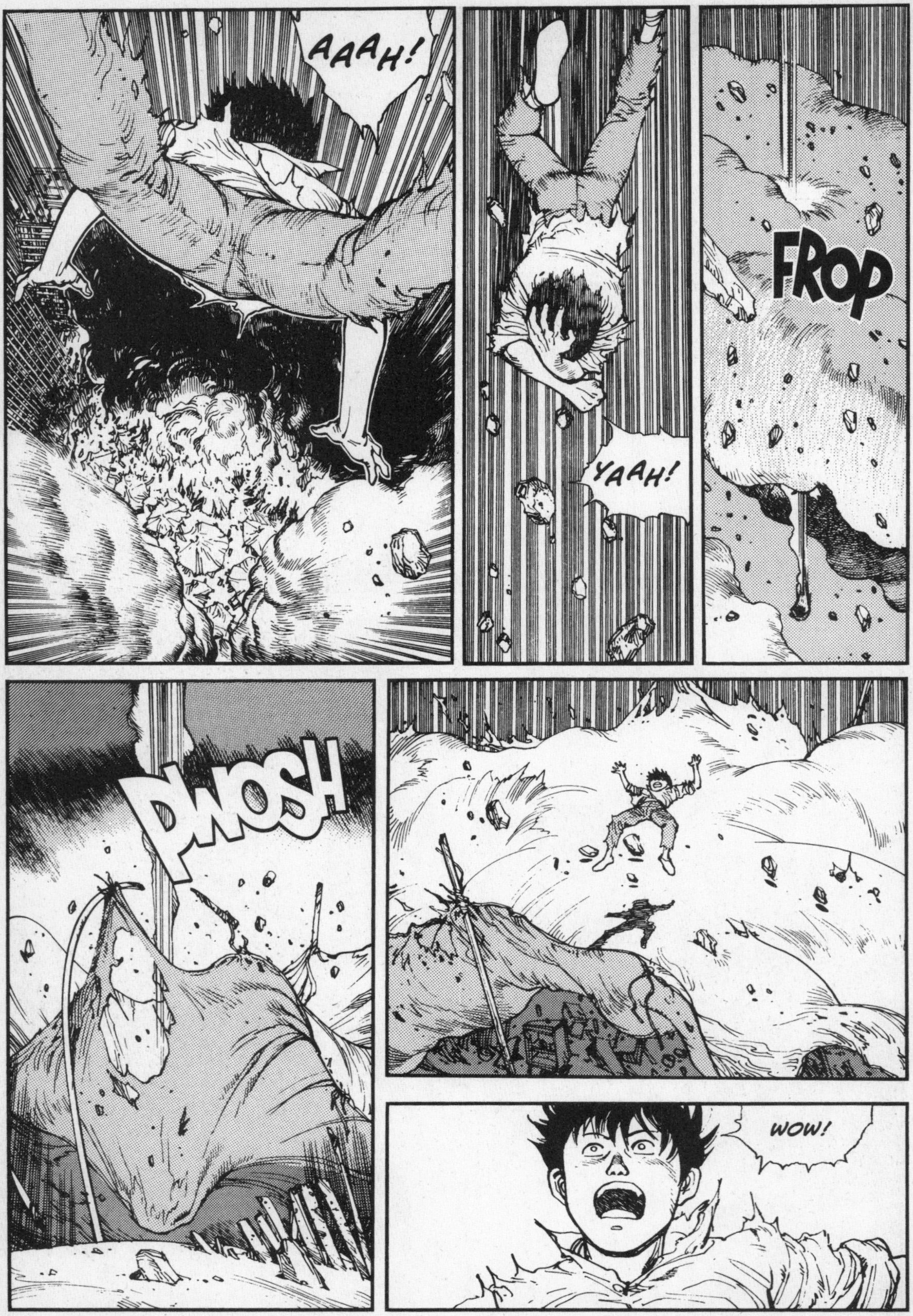
AAAH!
YAAH!
FROP
PWOSH
WOW!

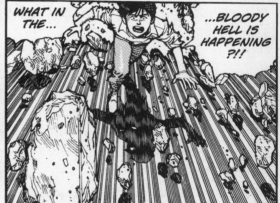

WHAT IN THE...

...BLOODY HELL IS HAPPENING?!!

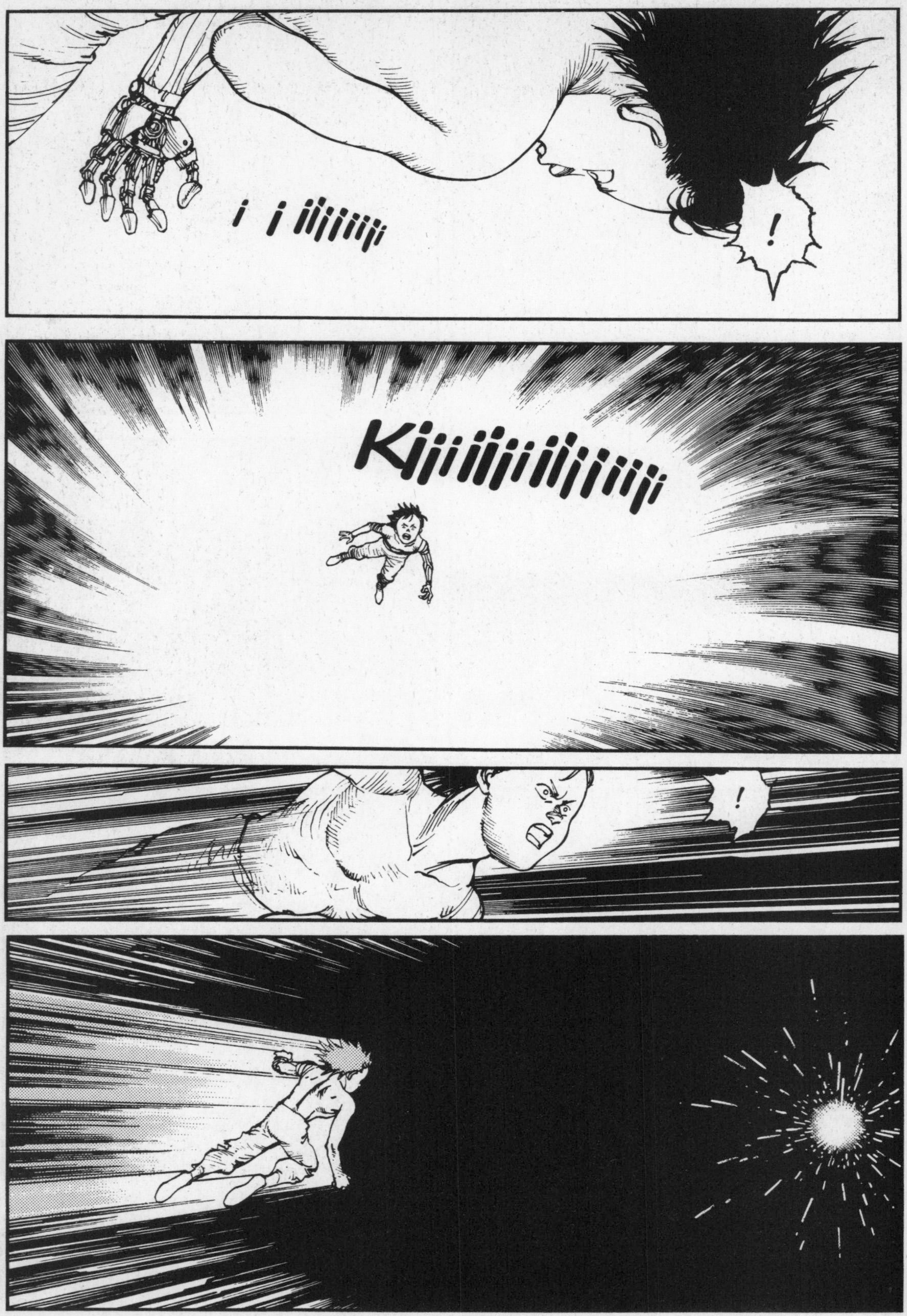
i i iiiiiiiii
!
Kiiiiiiiiiiiiiii
!

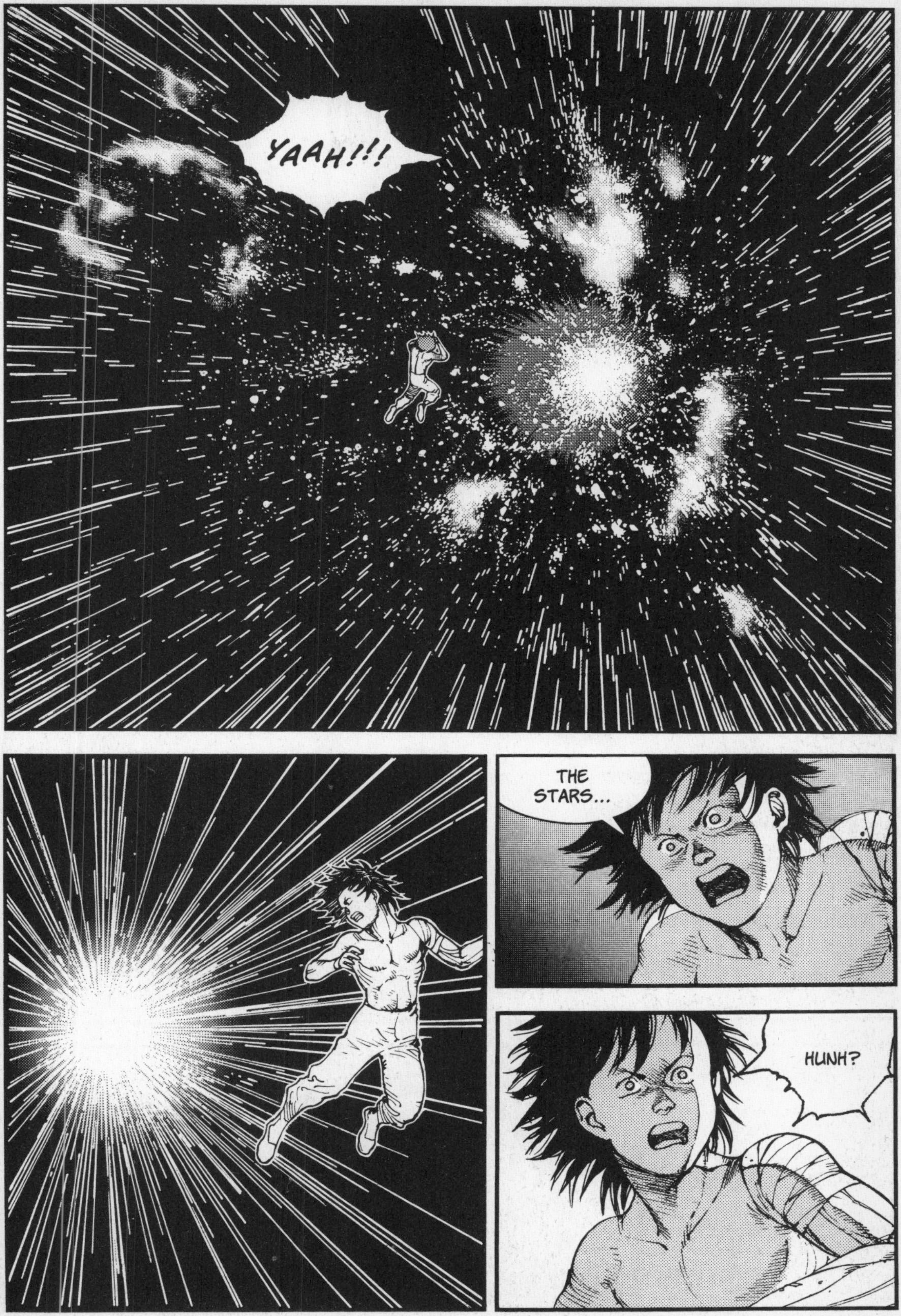
YAAH!!!
THE STARS...
HUNH?

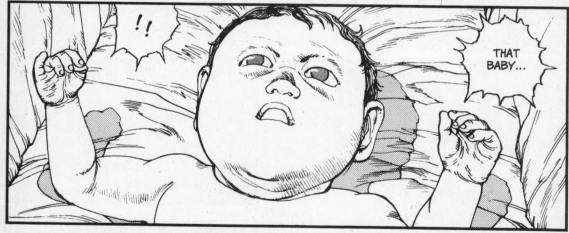

THAT BABY...

IT'S ME!

AND THERE...
ARE THOSE MY
...PARENTS?!

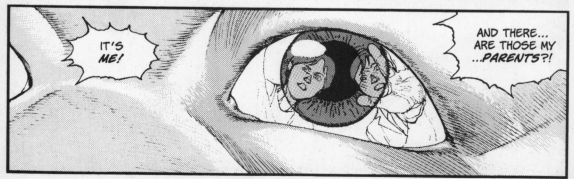

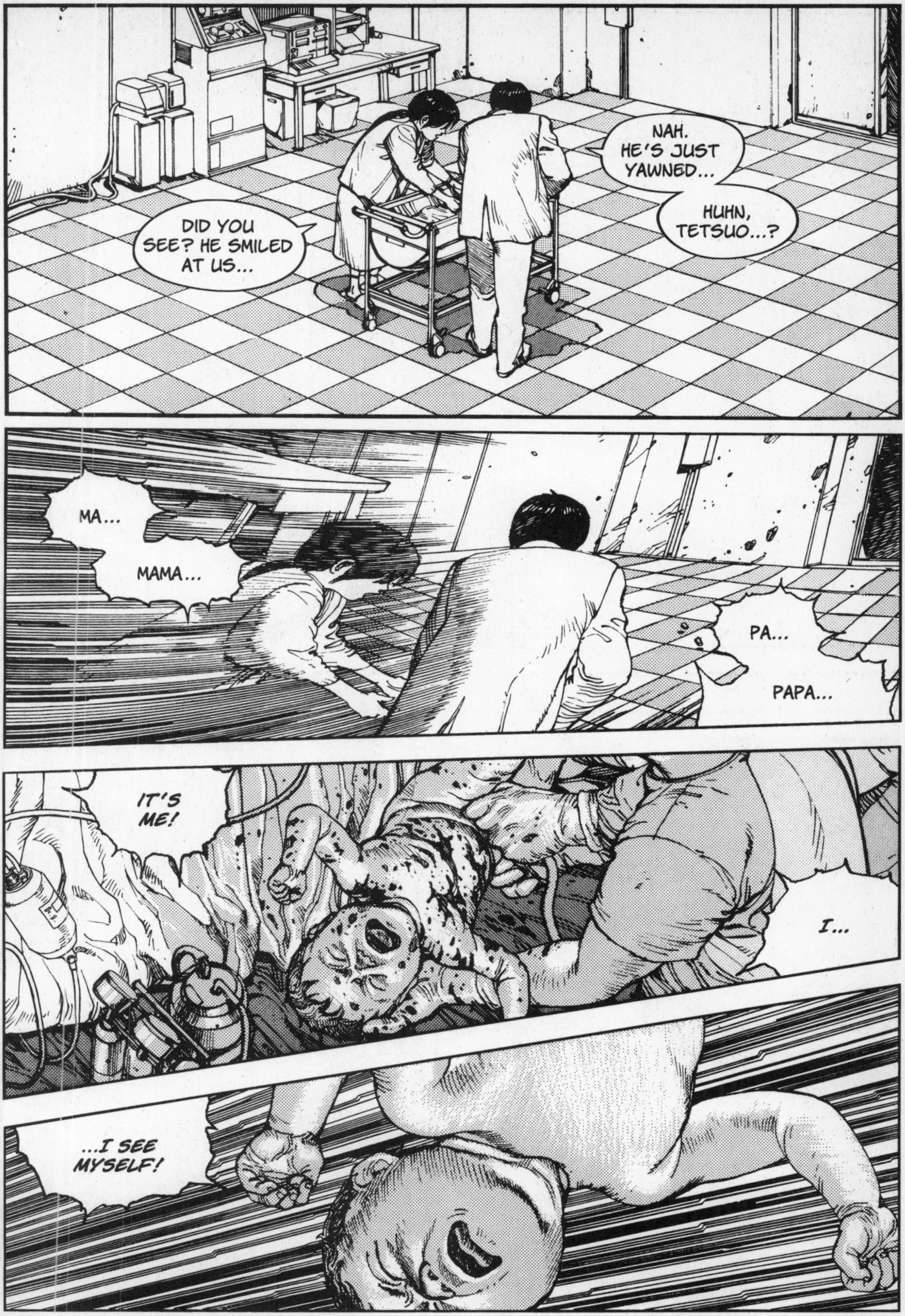
DID YOU SEE? HE SMILED AT US...
NAH. HE'S JUST YAWNED...
HUHN, TETSUO...?
MA...
MAMA...
PA...
PAPA...
IT'S ME!
I...
...I SEE MYSELF!

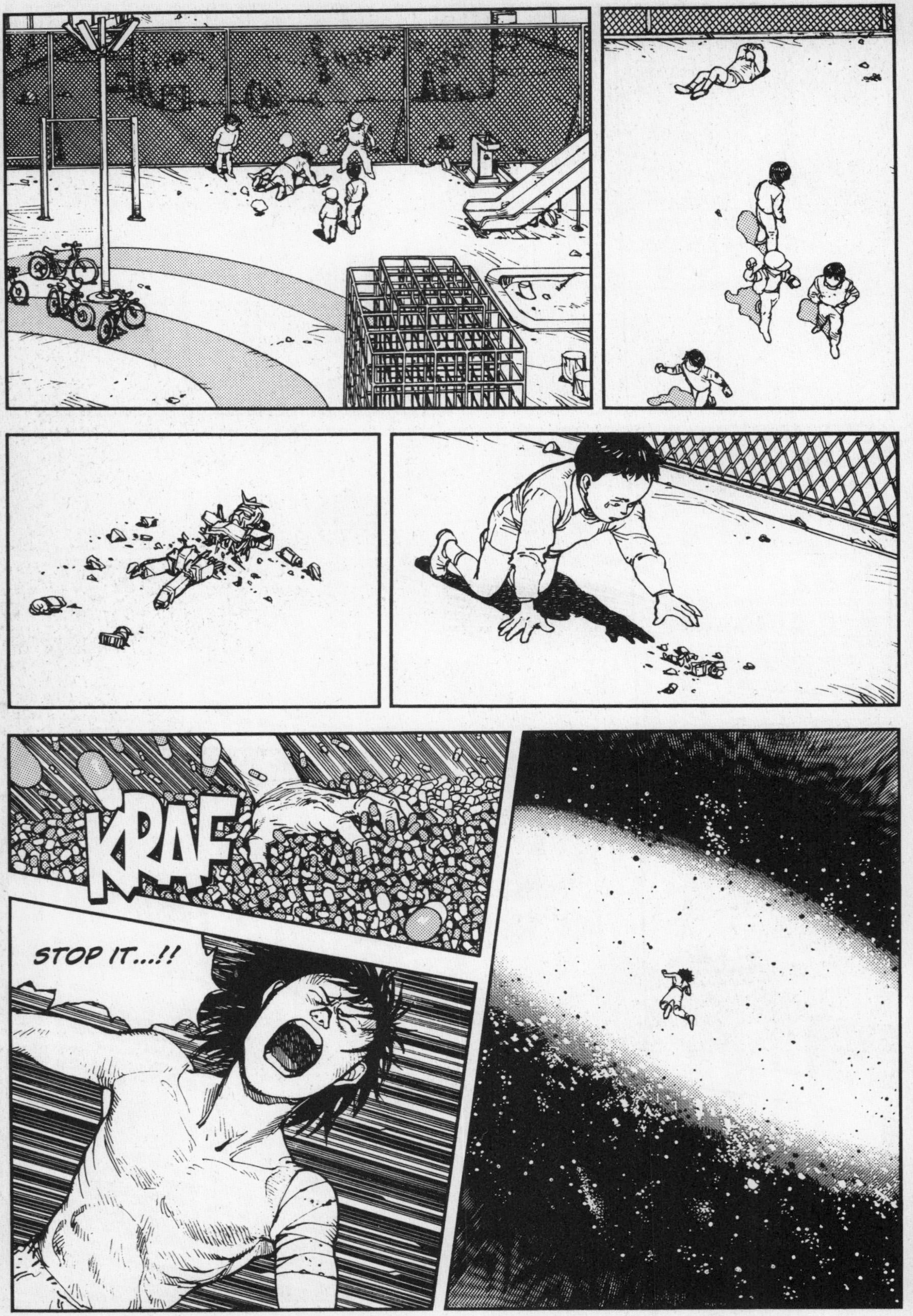
KRAF
STOP IT...!!

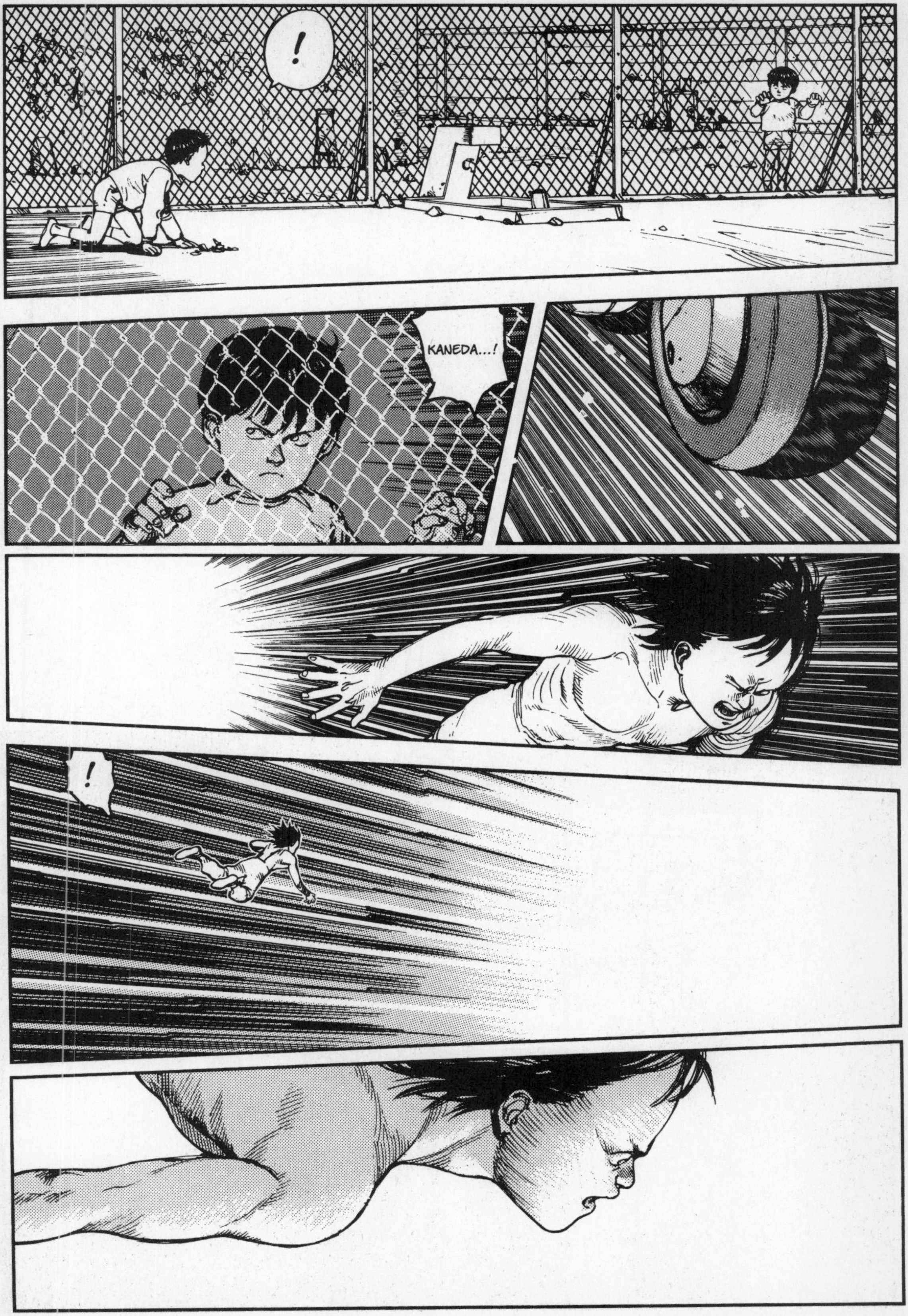
!
KANEDA...!
!

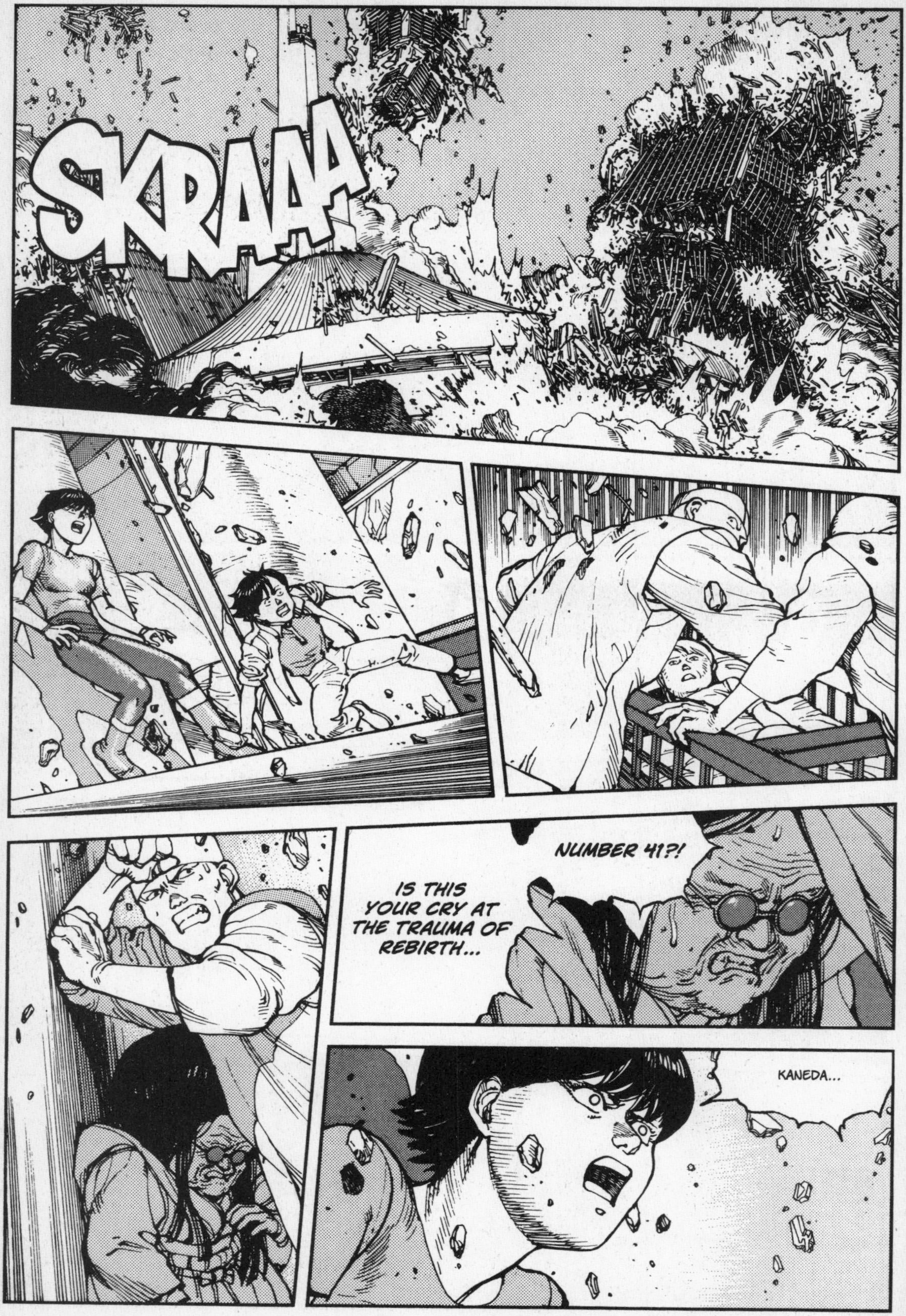
SKRAAA
NUMBER 41?!
IS THIS YOUR CRY AT THE TRAUMA OF REBIRTH...
KANEDA...

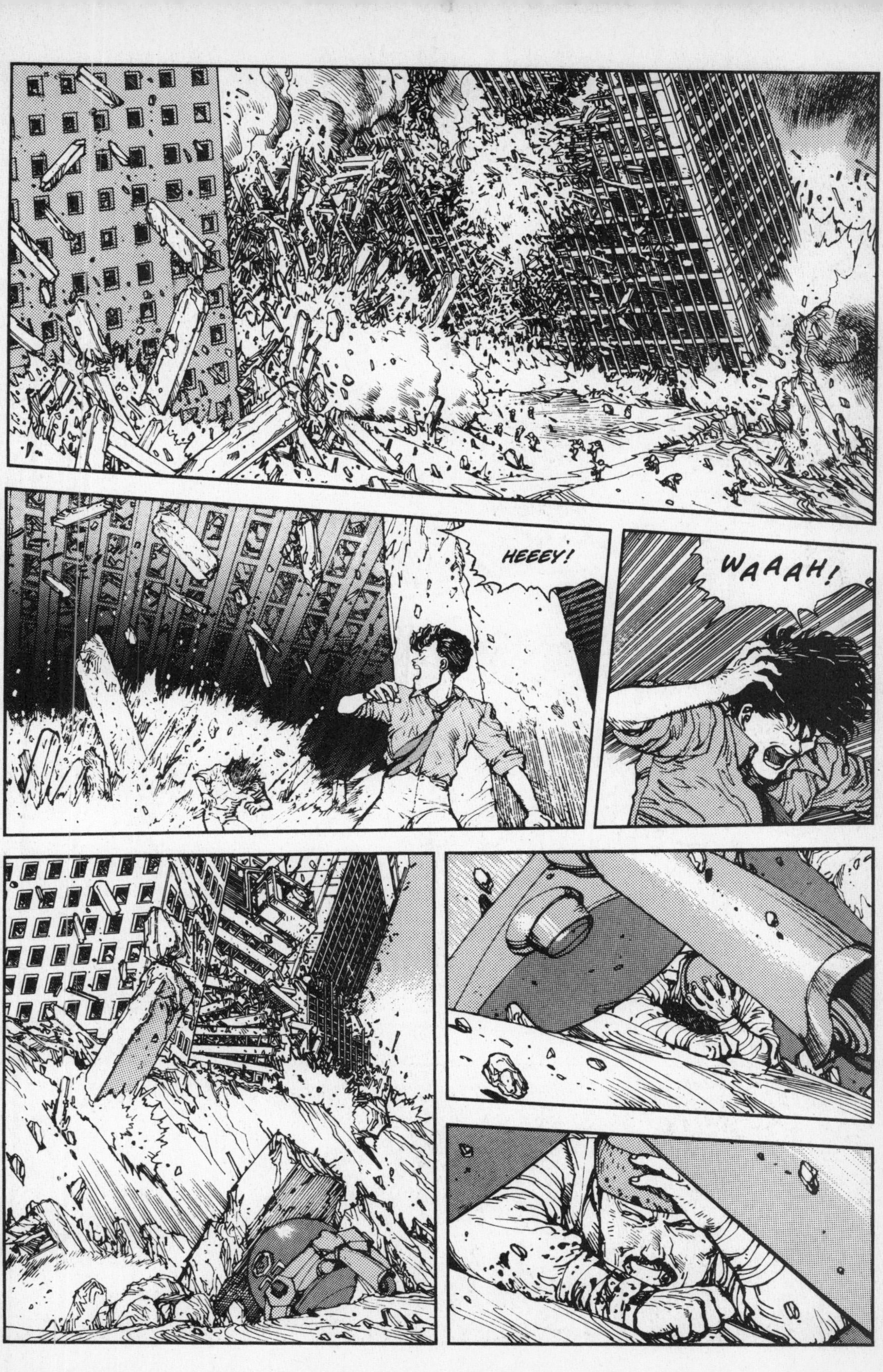
HEEEY!
WAAAAH!

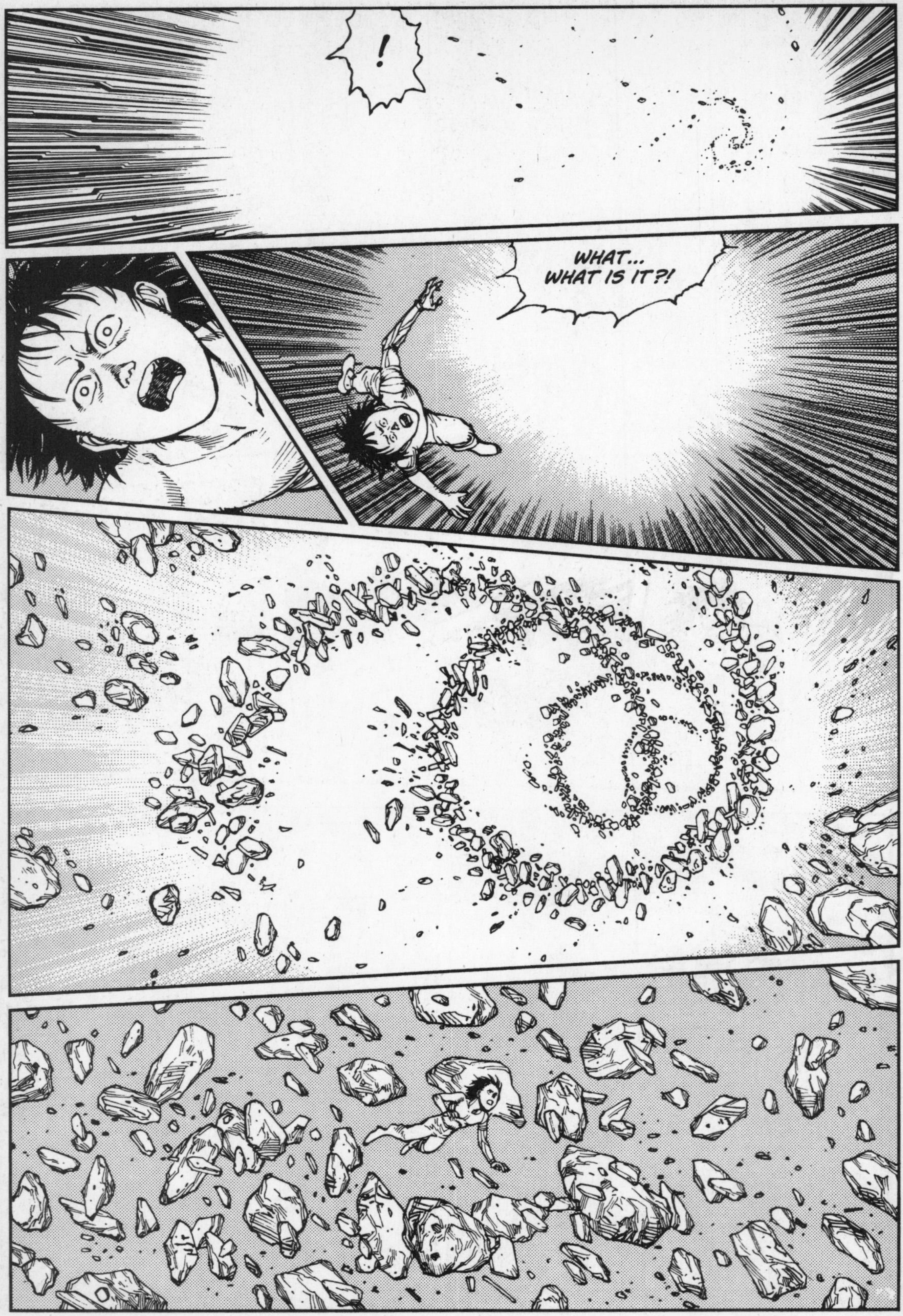
!
WHAT... WHAT IS IT?!

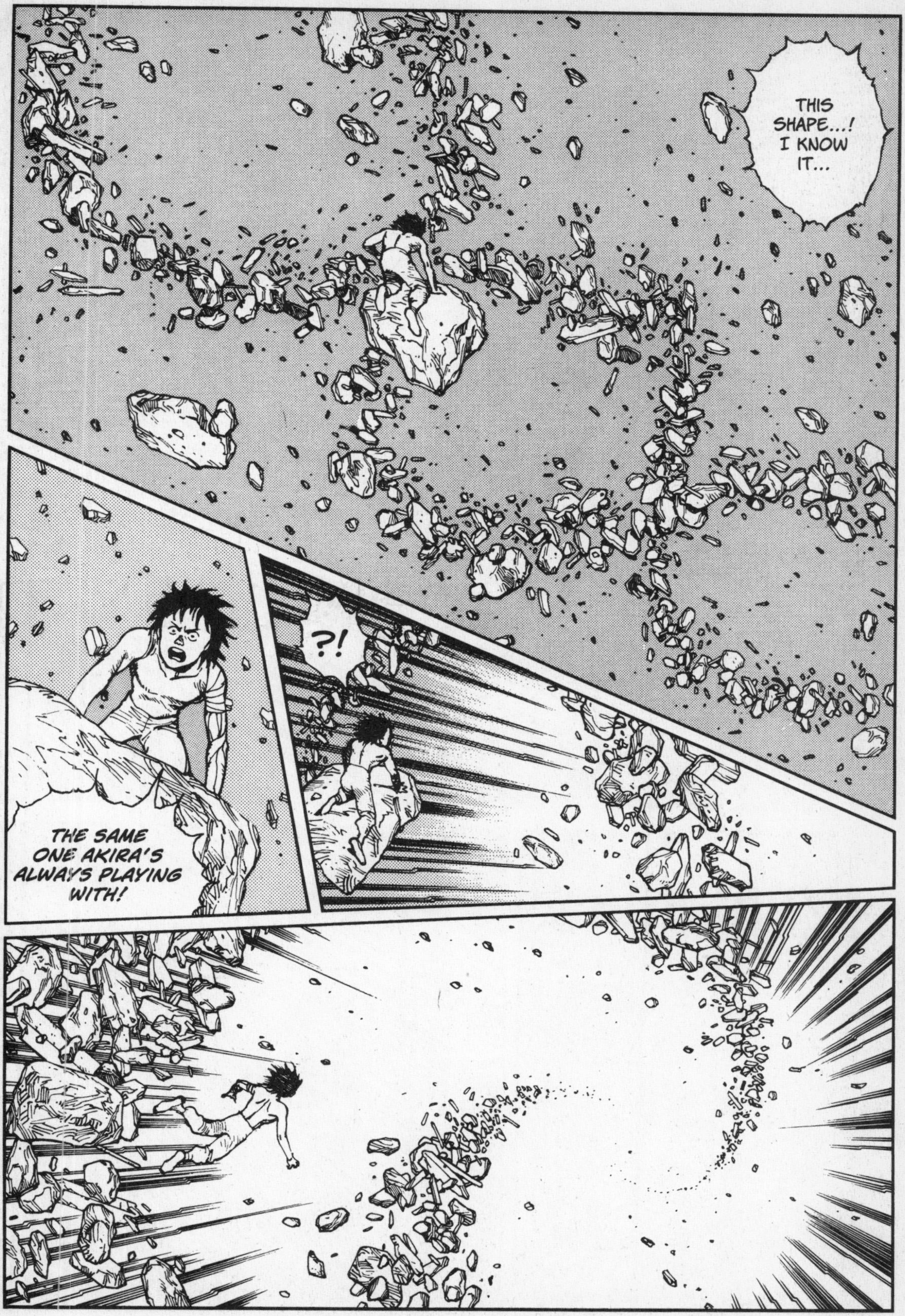
THIS SHAPE...! I KNOW IT...
THE SAME ONE AKIRA'S ALWAYS PLAYING WITH!
?!

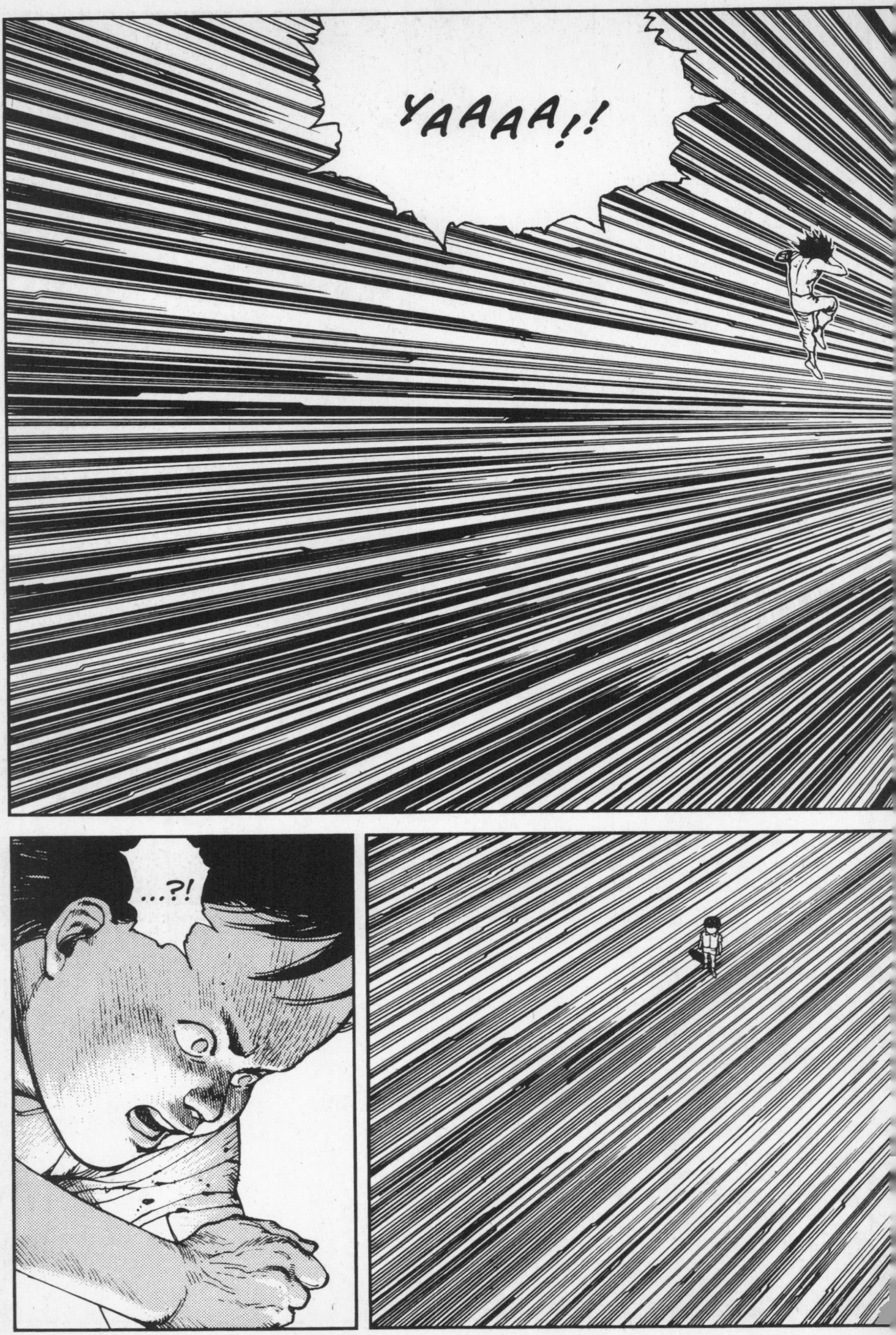
YAAAA!!
...?!

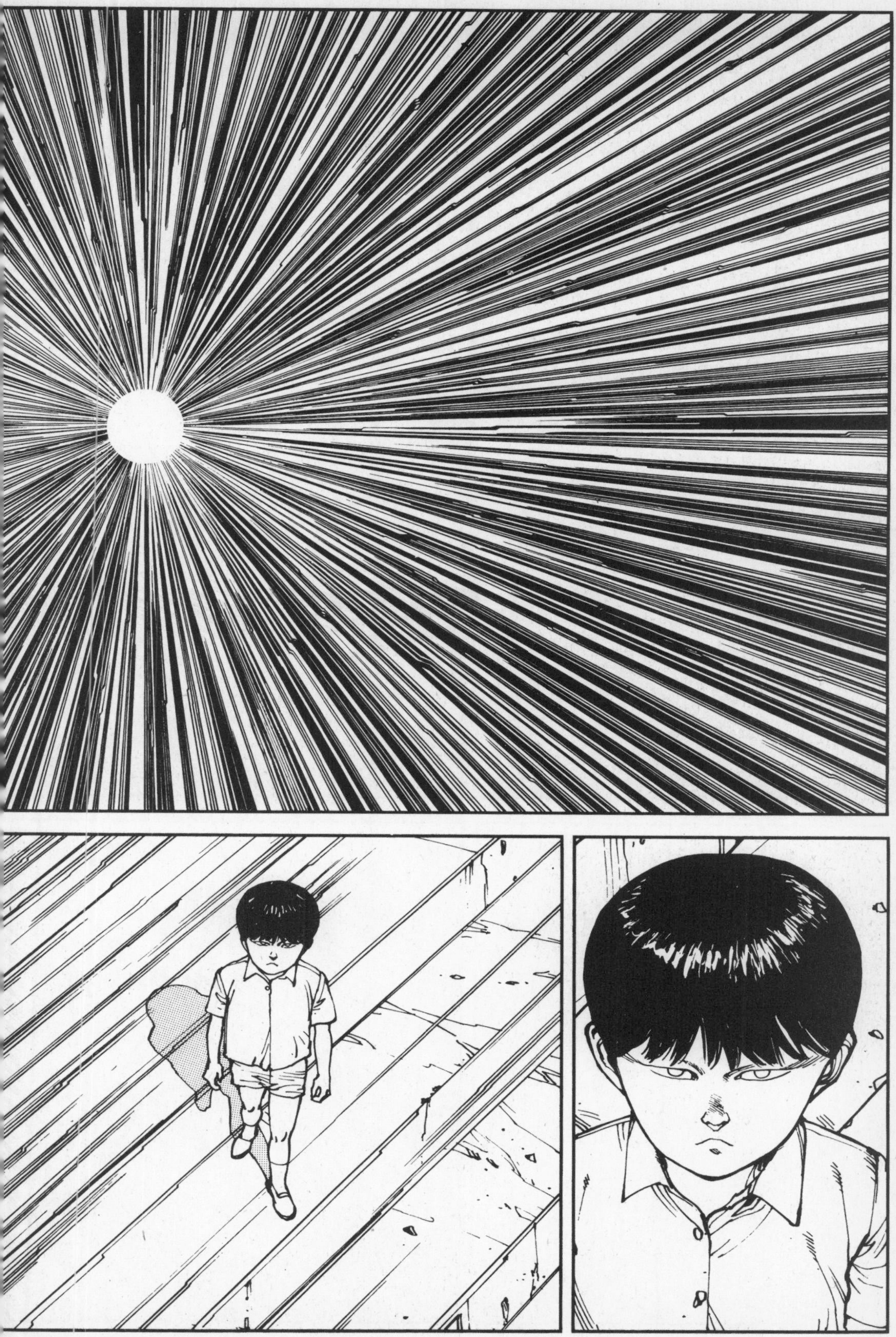

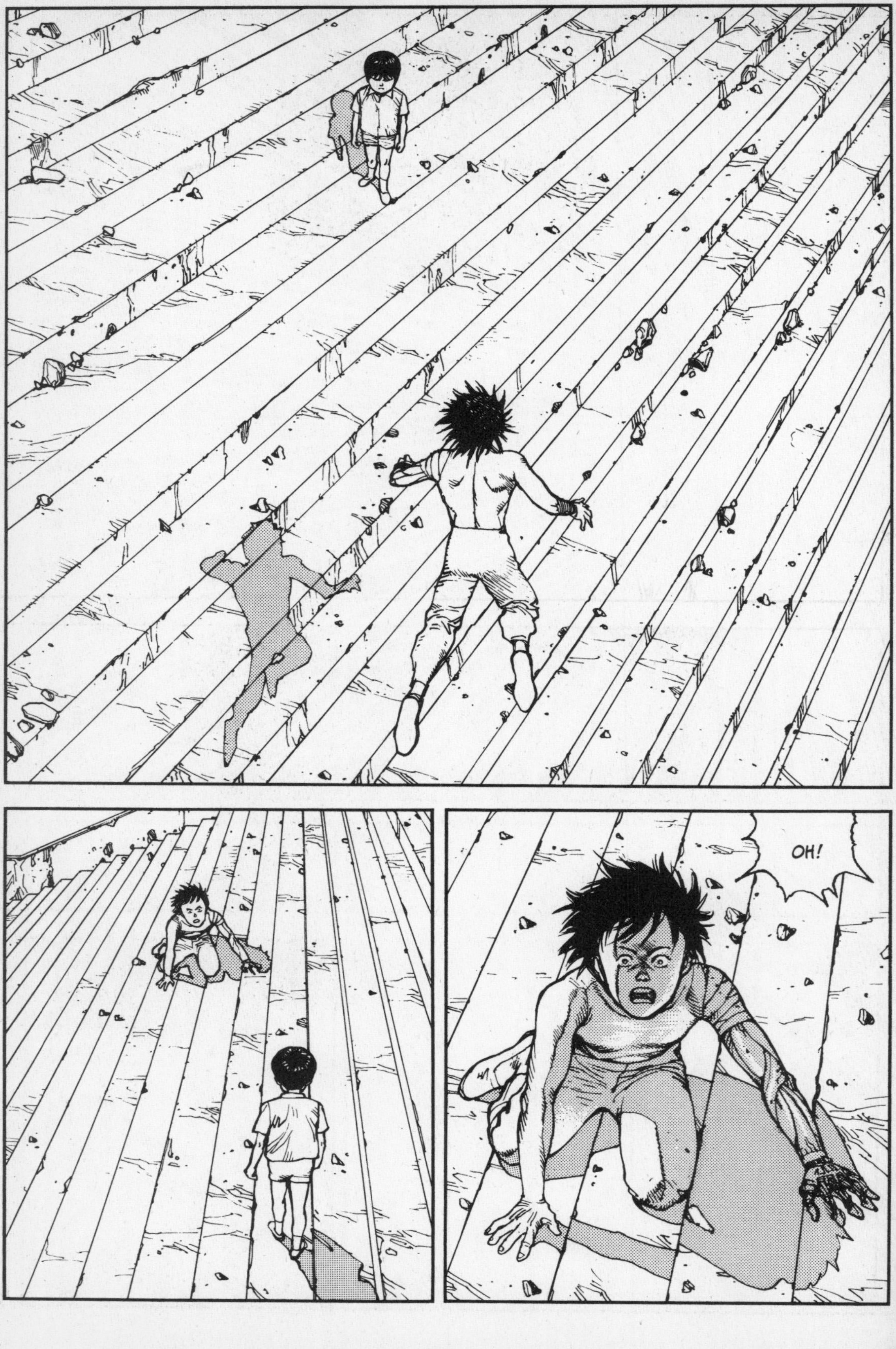
OH!

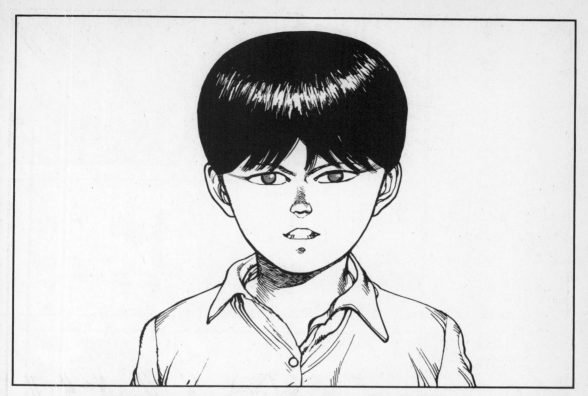

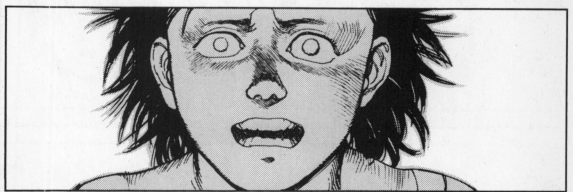

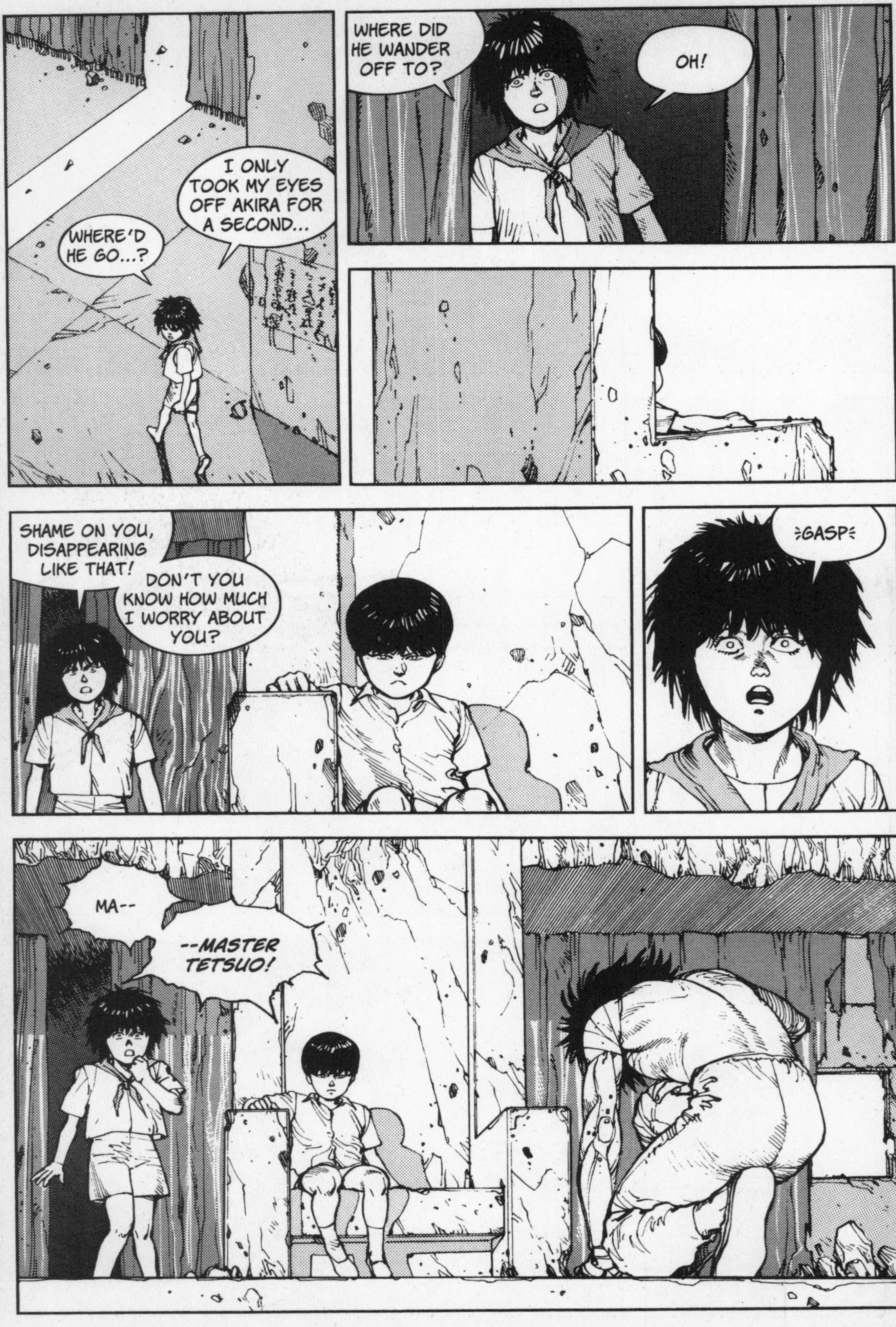
I ONLY TOOK MY EYES OFF AKIRA FOR A SECOND...
WHERE'D HE GO...?
WHERE DID HE WANDER OFF TO?
OH!
SHAME ON YOU, DISAPPEARING LIKE THAT!
DON'T YOU KNOW HOW MUCH I WORRY ABOUT YOU?
GASP
MA--
--MASTER TETSUO!

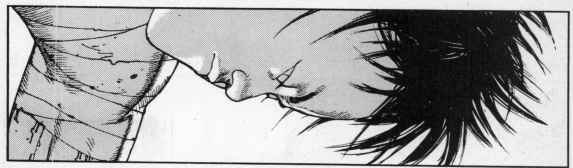

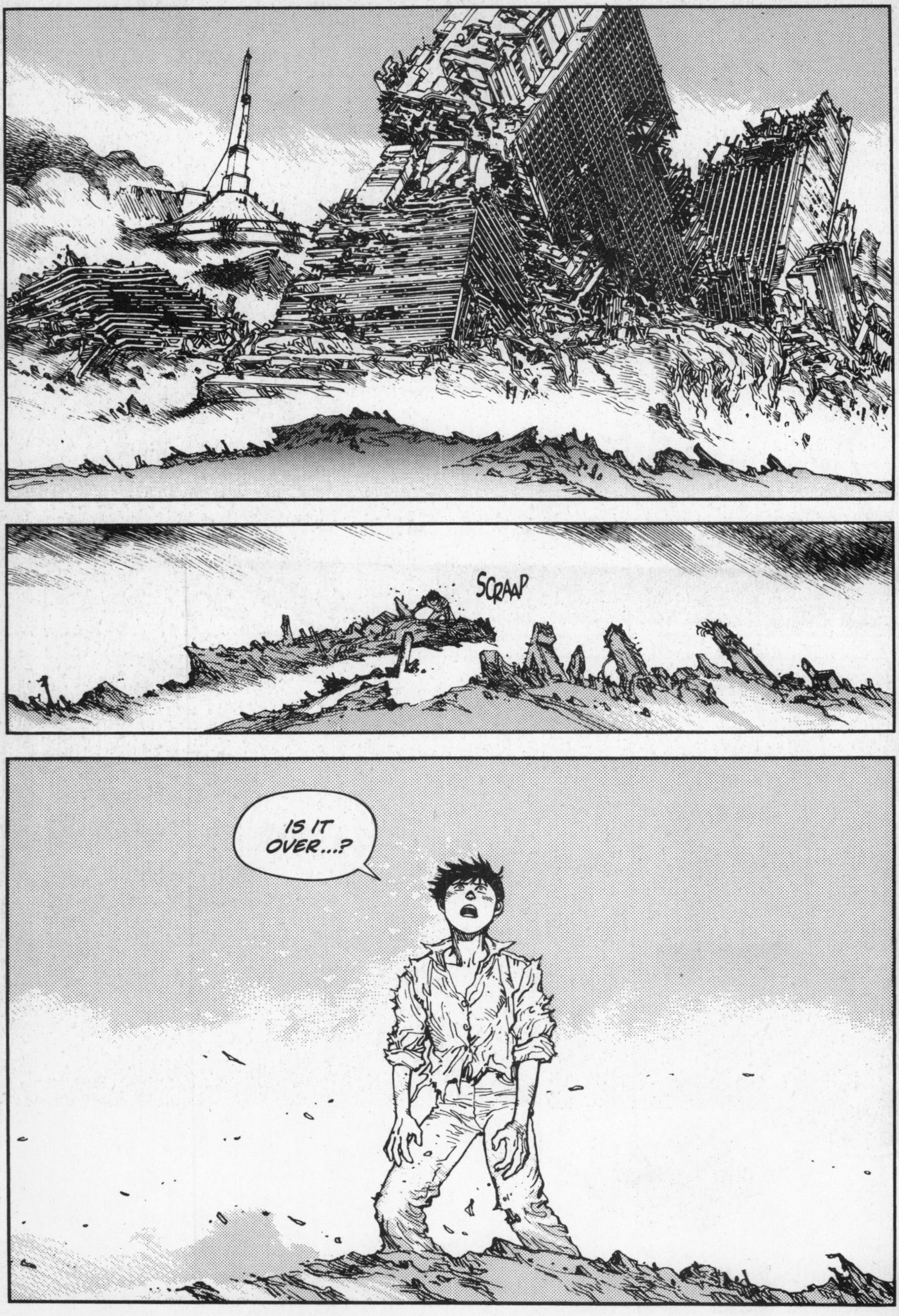
SCRAAP
IS IT OVER...?

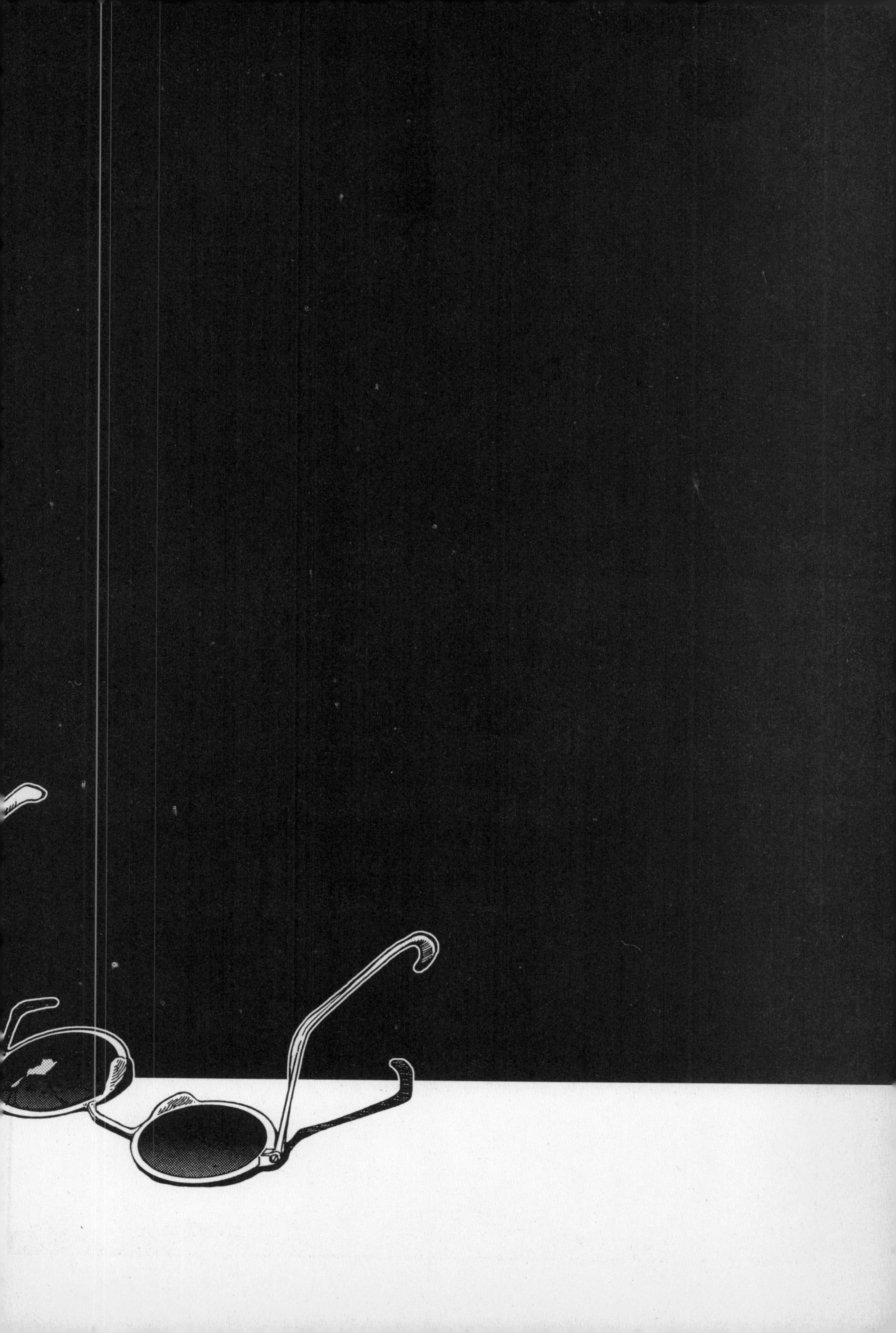

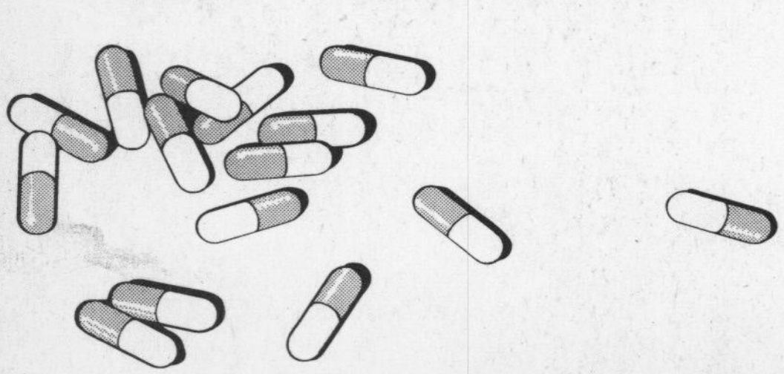

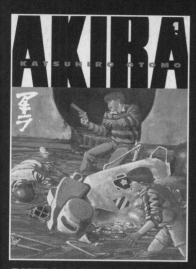
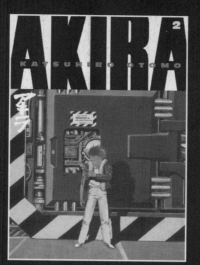
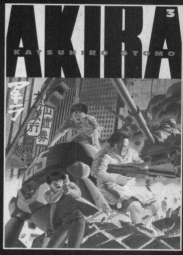

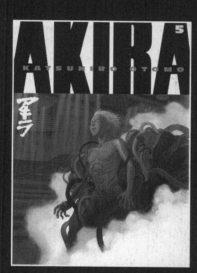
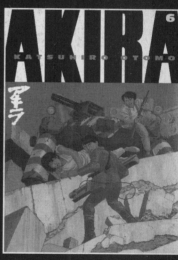

# 漫画 BACKLIST

## A SAMPLING OF 漫画 GRAPHIC NOVELS FROM DARK HORSE COMICS

**BOOK 1**
ISBN: 1-56971-498-3 $24.95

**BOOK 2**
ISBN: 1-56971-499-1 $24.95

**BOOK ONE**
ISBN: 1-56971-070-8 $16.95

**BOOK TWO**
ISBN: 1-56971-071-6 $16.95

**BOOK THREE**
ISBN: 1-56971-072-4 $17.95

**BOOK FOUR**
ISBN: 1-56971-074-0 $17.95

**BLOOD OF A THOUSAND**
ISBN: 1-56971-239-5 $14.95

**CRY OF THE WORM**
ISBN: 1-56971-300-6 $14.95

**DREAMSONG**
ISBN: 1-56971-357-X $14.95

**ON SILENT WINGS**
ISBN: 1-56971-412-6 $14.95

**ON SILENT WINGS II**
ISBN: 1-56971-444-4 $14.95

**DARK SHADOWS**
ISBN: 1-56971-469-X $14.95

**BLADE: HEART OF DARKNESS**
ISBN: 1-56971-531-9 $16.95

**GHOST IN THE SHELL**
ISBN: 1-56971-081-3 $24.95

**INTRON DEPOT**
ISBN: 1-56971-085-6 $39.95

**INTRON DEPOT 2: BLADES**
ISBN: 1-56971-382-0 $39.95